SCHOOL (PREVENTION AND INTERVENTION: THE PREP<u>a</u>RE MODEL

Second Edition

SCHOOL CRISIS PREVENTION AND INTERVENTION: THE PREPaRE MODEL

Second Edition

Stephen E. Brock
California State University, Sacramento

Amanda B. Nickerson
University at Buffalo, State University of New York

Melissa A. Louvar Reeves
Winthrop University (Rock Hill, SC)

Christina N. Conolly
Waukegan Public Schools District 60 (Waukegan, IL)

Shane R. Jimerson
University of California, Santa Barbara

Rosario C. Pesce
Loyola University Chicago (Chicago, IL)

Brian R. Lazzaro
Township High School District 211 (Palatine, IL)

NASP

NATIONAL ASSOCIATION OF
School Psychologists

From the NASP Publications Board Operations Manual

The content of this document reflects the ideas and positions of the authors. The responsibility lies solely with the authors and editors and does not necessarily reflect the position or ideas of the National Association of School Psychologists.

Published by the National Association of School Psychologists

Copyright © 2016 by the National Association of School Psychologists.

All rights reserved. No part of this publication may be reproduced or distributed in any form or by any means, electronic, mechanical, photocopying, recording, scanning, or otherwise, except as permitted under the United States Copyright Act of 1976, or stored in a database or retrieval system, without the prior written permission of the publisher, or authorization through payment of the appropriate per-copy fee to the Copyright Clearance Center, 222 Rosewood Drive, Danvers, MA 01923, 978-750-8400, fax 978-750-4474, www.copyright.com. Requests to the Publisher for permission should be addressed to Copyright Permissions, National Association of School Psychologists, 4340 East West Highway, Suite 402, Bethesda, MD 20814, 301-657-0270, fax 301-657-0275, e-mail publications@naspweb.org.

Photos on the covers are licensed stock photography being used for illustrative purposes only, and any person depicted is a model.

Copies may be ordered from:
NASP Publications
4340 East West Highway, Suite 402
Bethesda, MD 20814
301-657-0270
301-657-0275, fax
866-331-NASP, Toll Free
e-mail: publications@naspweb.org
www.nasponline.org

ISBN 978-0-932955-19-3

Printed in the United States of America

24   10 9 8 7 6

Dedication

This book is dedicated to the school-employed mental health professionals who engage in crisis prevention and response in support of the students they serve. Having been in your shoes, we want you to know how much we appreciate your efforts. It is our hope that this book contributes to your important efforts and helps to make this most difficult work more manageable.

For my father, Gerald F. Brock.

– Stephen E. Brock

For my parents, Arlene and Stanley Nickerson, the champions of preparedness!

– Amanda B. Nickerson

For my husband Shawn, my children Austin and Taylor, my parents Gary and Kathy Louvar, and Grandma Shirley.

– Melissa A. Louvar Reeves

For my daughter, Rachel, who gave me the love and the courage to keep writing.

– Christina N. Conolly

For my wife, Kathryn M. O'Brien, and children Gavin Jimerson and Taite Jimerson.

– Shane R. Jimerson

For my parents, Carmen and Mary Pesce.

– Rosario C. Pesce

For my mother and father, Mr. & Mrs. Charles Lazzaro.

– Brian R. Lazzaro

Table of Contents

Preface

This book has been written to complement and reinforce the PREP̲aRE School Crisis Prevention and Intervention Training Curriculum (Brock, 2011a; Reeves et al., 2011a). The PREP̲aRE curriculum was developed through the collaborative efforts of several workgroups sponsored by the National Association of School Psychologists (NASP). Specifically, the Crisis Prevention and Intervention Task Force, the PREP̲aRE Workgroup, and the School Safety and Crisis Response Committee have all had a role in the development of the curriculum. This endeavor further extends NASP's leadership in providing evidence-informed resources and consultation services related to school safety and crisis response. The PREP̲aRE curriculum is designed for educators and other school-employed mental health professionals committed to improving and strengthening their school's safety activities and crisis response procedures. Evaluations of the curriculum revealed that the PREP̲aRE workshops have a high degree of consumer satisfaction, positively affect participants' attitudes about their involvement on school safety and crisis response teams, and result in significant positive changes in their crisis prevention and intervention knowledge (Brock, 2006b; Brock, Nickerson, Reeves, Savage, & Woitaszewski, 2011; Nickerson, 2006; Nickerson, Serwacki, et al., 2014).

THE NEED TO BE PREP̲aRED

Today's schools are expected to play a critical role in crisis prevention and intervention (Brymer, Taylor, et al., 2012; Jaycox, Stein, & Wong, 2014; Kataoka et al., 2009; McDermott, Duffy, Percy, Fitzgerald, & Cole, 2013). This reality emphasizes the need for the PREP̲aRE curriculum. As demonstrated during recent school-associated crisis events, schools are integral to an overall community crisis response. When a crisis occurs, schools provide safe havens, disseminate information, identify individuals at risk, provide mental health services, link individuals with community services, help to track displaced families, support long-term recovery, and generally serve as models of control and normalcy in the face of trauma (Jaycox et al., 2007; Stuber et al., 2002). To serve these functions, schools must have comprehensive school safety and crisis response plans and teams in place. These plans and teams address all aspects of crisis preparedness—that is, prevention, protection, mitigation, response, and recovery (U.S. Department of Education, 2013).

The teams must be adequately trained to address a range of crisis events, understand the systems and procedures that must be in place for schools to respond to crises, and address the unique mental health needs generated by crisis exposure (Everly, Hamilton, Tyiska, & Ellers, 2008). School safety and crisis response plans and procedures must be fully integrated into community emergency response efforts, including law enforcement and fire and rescue providers and community-based mental health services. These procedures must also be clearly communicated to staff, parents, and community leaders.

When engaging in crisis prevention, protection, mitigation, response, and recovery, school safety and crisis response teams should emphasize (a) methods to promote the mental health, risk and resiliency factors, and coping capacity of the individuals affected by a crisis, particularly students; and (b) the unique opportunities and challenges schools face when preventing and responding to crises. Training for school safety and crisis response teams therefore must address a crisis as a mental health risk as well as a physical health and safety risk within the context of the school culture. Finally, an important goal of successful school crisis preparedness is to support academic functioning.

BASIC ASSUMPTIONS OF PREPaRE

PREPaRE provides school-employed mental health professionals and other educators with training on how best to fill their roles and responsibilities as members of school safety and crisis response teams. PREPaRE is the only comprehensive, internationally disseminated training curriculum developed by school-employed mental health professionals who have firsthand school crisis experience and have specific training. PREPaRE was conceived and developed based on three assumptions: (a) school-age youth have unique needs during times of crisis, (b) having school safety and crisis response teams that are multidisciplinary can best use the skills of school-employed mental health professionals, and (c) schools represent unique structures and have their own cultures. Using the guidance offered by this curriculum, schools can become better prepared to develop their own crisis prevention, protection, mitigation, response, and recovery resources, thereby enabling them to respond promptly and appropriately to the unique needs of the students they serve during and after a crisis.

School-Age Youth Have Unique Needs During Crises

The first and perhaps most fundamental assumption of the PREPaRE curriculum is that students, in particular younger children, have unique needs during and following a crisis. As emphasized by the National Commission on Children and Disasters (2010), children "are not simply small adults" (p. 20); they have unique vulnerabilities that must be addressed in crisis response activities and policies. Preparation for addressing the crisis-related needs and concerns of children is critical. Children represent an especially vulnerable population, and their crisis reactions or symptoms are often more significant than those observed among adults (Brymer et al., 2006). In addition, childhood trauma can affect adolescent development and have a longer term impact on physical and mental health (Barenbaum, Ruchkin, & Schwab-Stone, 2004; Gerson & Rappaport, 2013; Layne et al., 2014).

Again, according to the National Commission on Children and Disasters (2010): "Children may experience long-lasting effects such as academic failure, post-traumatic stress disorder, depression, anxiety, bereavement, and other behavioral problems such as delinquency and substance abuse" (p. 20). Evidence also has shown that traumatic stress can alter children's brain structure and function (Carrion & Wong, 2012). In other words, the stakes can be quite high, demonstrating the great need for a school safety and crisis intervention model addressing the needs of school-age youth, such as that offered by PREPaRE. Although progress has been made in addressing the unique needs of children (and we believe that the PREPaRE curriculum has been an important element of that progress), we would be naïve if we did not acknowledge how much needs to be done at the local, state, and federal levels to better serve children affected by crises (Save the Children, 2015).

Multidisciplinary Teams Are Essential

The second assumption of the PREPaRE curriculum is that the skill sets of school-employed mental health professionals are best utilized when they are embedded within a multidisciplinary team that engages in all aspects of crisis preparedness (i.e., crisis prevention, protection, mitigation, response, and recovery). Such school safety and crisis response teams allow school professionals to make optimal use of their unique professional skills and talents for preventing, preparing for, and responding to school crises. For example, by virtue of their professional training and job functions, school-employed mental health professionals are best prepared to address the psychological issues associated with school crises (and the presence of a multidisciplinary team allows them to focus on such).

Schools Have Unique Structures and Cultures

The final basic assumption of PREPaRE is that schools have their own unique structures and culture. Given this reality, without an understanding of how school systems function, even the most skilled professionals will be at a distinct disadvantage when providing crisis prevention, protection, mitigation, response, and recovery services in a school. Brown and Bobrow (2004) observe that when outside professionals enter a school specifically to provide mental health services, they need a clear understanding of the school's structure and culture. Thus, schools should have their own crisis response team models, such as those offered by PREPaRE, that take into account how their school functions.

ABOUT PREPaRE WORKSHOPS

The PREPaRE model emphasizes how school-employed mental health professionals, as members of school safety and crisis response teams, must be involved in a hierarchical and sequential set of activities (Figure P.1). The model also incorporates foundational knowledge provided by the U.S. Department of Education (2003, 2007b, 2013) and the U.S. Department of Homeland Security (2004, 2008). Specifically, PREPaRE describes school safety and crisis response team activities occurring across the five phases of crisis preparedness, that is, crisis prevention, protection, mitigation, response, and recovery.

Figure P.1. The PREPaRE Model Is a Sequential and Hierarchical Set of School Safety and Crisis Response Activities

P	**P**revent and prepare for psychological trauma
R	**R**eaffirm physical health and perceptions of security and safety
E	**E**valuate psychological trauma risk
P	**P**rovide interventions
a	**a**nd
R	**R**espond to psychological needs
E	**E**xamine the effectiveness of crisis prevention and intervention

Note. From *School Crisis Prevention and Intervention: The PREPaRE Model*, p. ix, by S. E. Brock et al., 2009, Bethesda, MD: NASP. Copyright 2009 by the National Association of School Psychologists. Reprinted with permission.

The PREPaRE curriculum includes two workshops: Workshop 1, Crisis Prevention and Preparedness: Comprehensive School Safety Planning (Reeves et al., 2011a); and Workshop 2, Crisis Intervention and Recovery: The Roles of School-Based Mental Health Professionals (Brock, 2011a). Workshop 1 gives educators and others involved in school safety and crisis planning efforts a basic understanding of crisis prevention and preparedness. Workshop 2 gives school-employed mental health professionals evidence-informed knowledge that helps them develop the skills they need to aid students and staff following a school-associated crisis event. The two workshops can be conducted sequentially or separately.

Workshop 1, Crisis Prevention and Preparedness: Comprehensive School Safety Planning (Reeves et al., 2011a) is a 1-day workshop designed for groups as large as 100. In one of its fundamental propositions, Workshop 1 asserts that schools must work to achieve a balance of both physical and psychological safety. The workshop emphasizes the system-level aspects of the prevention and preparedness element of PREPaRE. Furthermore, it makes a connection between ongoing school safety and crisis preparedness efforts, and the outcomes of those efforts, such as improved school climate, student behavior and academic functioning, student resilience, and staff crisis response capabilities. It also discusses the importance of (a) responding to crises within the structure of a comprehensive, multidisciplinary school crisis response team using the Incident Command System (U.S. Department of Homeland Security, 2004, 2008), and (b) integrating the roles of school personnel and community providers. Finally, the workshop presents approaches to developing, exercising, and evaluating schools' safety and crisis response plans, in addition to addressing media contacts, students with special needs, cultural considerations, the use of memorials, and the uses and challenges of technology. Activities and tabletop exercises are conducted within the workshop to reinforce workshop objectives.

Workshop 1 is appropriate for all school personnel who need to understand how the comprehensive school safety and crisis response team is organized and how it functions. Participants can include, but are not limited to, school-employed mental health professionals, administrators, teachers, school resource officers, front office staff, transportation directors, and coordinators of before- and after-school activities. The PREPaRE model builds on existing personnel, resources, and programs and can be adapted to individual school needs.

The Training of Trainers (ToT) sessions for Workshop 1, Crisis Prevention and Preparedness: Comprehensive School Safety Planning (Reeves et al., 2011b), provides the information and introductory practice needed to become a Workshop 1 trainer. A prerequisite for the ToT session is completion of Workshop 1. The ToT workshop reviews the logistics of workshop presentation and offers specific guidance on how to present the workshop (with special emphasis on a standardized delivery). Workshop participants are given the information they need to prepare to independently offer the workshop.

Workshop 2, Crisis Intervention and Recovery: The Roles of School-Based Mental Health Professionals (Brock, 2011a) is designed for 15 to 40 participants. The 2-day workshop reviews the elements of the PREPaRE model related to school-based mental health crisis intervention and recovery. Although specific mental health protocols for immediate intervention have not yet been validated (Stein et al., 2004; Vernberg et al., 2008), sufficient evidence supports the basic principles put forward by this workshop (Everly et al., 2008; Jaycox et al., 2014). Activities such as role-playing are embedded in the session to reinforce workshop objectives.

Workshop 2 is based on the assumption that, as members of a school safety and crisis response team, school-employed mental health professionals must be involved in the following hierarchical and sequential set of activities. First, they work to prevent avoidable events that can result in psychological traumas in schools and to prepare for those that are not prevented. Second, once an event has occurred, all school staff members, including mental health professionals, initially focus on helping to reaffirm physical health and students' perception that they are safe. Third, they evaluate the degree to which individuals have suffered psychological trauma. Fourth, using evaluation data and evidence-informed interventions, mental health professionals provide crisis interventions and respond to the psychological needs of the school community's members. Finally, they examine the effectiveness of the school crisis intervention and recovery efforts.

Workshop 2 is appropriate for any individual filling the specific Incident Command System's crisis intervention and student group. Participants could include school-employed mental health professionals (e.g., school psychologists, social workers, counselors, and nurses), administrators, classroom teachers, and other individuals identified by the team as appropriate providers of mental health crisis interventions. Moreover, this workshop can be helpful for community-based mental health professionals and school resource officers who may work with the school crisis response team or be brought into the school to assist in crisis response.

The ToT session for Workshop 2, Crisis Intervention and Recovery: The Roles of School-Based Mental Health Professionals (Brock, 2011b) is designed to provide the information and introductory practice needed to become a workshop trainer. A prerequisite for this session is completion of Workshop 2. This session includes a review of the logistics of workshop presentation and specific guidance on how to present the workshop (with special emphasis on a standardized delivery). Participants are given the information they need to prepare to independently offer the workshop.

All individuals who receive PREPaRE training through the two workshops gain a better understanding of the organization and function of a comprehensive school safety and crisis response team (i.e., crisis prevention and preparedness) and the knowledge and skills necessary to meet the mental health needs of students and staff in the aftermath of a crisis (i.e., crisis intervention and recovery). This understanding includes knowledge of crisis reactions, prevention of events that may result in psychological trauma, assessment of risk for psychological trauma, mental health crisis interventions, and evaluation of the effectiveness of school crisis preparedness.

THE PURPOSE AND PLAN OF THIS BOOK

This book provides a detailed examination of the rationale for and science of the PREPaRE model, and in so doing highlights best practices in school crisis preparedness. It is intended to supplement and make the contents of the PREPaRE workshops more accessible. It is also designed to specifically identify the empirical supports for the PREPaRE workshops. It is not a substitute for actual workshop participation or the workshops' many skill-building activities.

The structure of this book corresponds to the elements of the PREPaRE School Crisis Prevention and Intervention Training Curriculum. Section 1 discusses background information critical to preparing for crisis events. Section 2, with nine chapters, focuses on prevention and preparation. It begins with a discussion of the rationale, goals, and models underlying school crisis prevention and preparedness, and obstacles to preparation (Chapter 2). Chapters 3 and 4 explain the importance of ensuring physical safety and psychological safety, followed by discussions on establishing comprehensive school safety teams, plans, and training (Chapters 5 and 6). Chapter 7, on how to establish school crisis response teams, is followed by chapters addressing the basic emergency operations plan, and specific functional and threat/hazard annexes (Chapters 8 and 9). Chapter 10 discusses how to prevent psychological trauma by examining strategies designed to protect students from, or mitigate the harm associated with, a crisis event.

Section 3 reviews strategies designed to reaffirm physical health and safety (Chapter 11) and ensure perceptions of safety and security (Chapter 12). Section 4 reviews strategies for evaluating psychological trauma. It addresses the rationale and theoretical foundations for evaluating psychological injury (Chapter 13) and examines practical issues relevant to conducting psychological triage (Chapter 14).

Section 5 examines approaches to providing crisis interventions in response to individual psychological needs. Specifically, it considers the importance of reestablishing social support systems (Chapter 15), psychological education (Chapter 16), group crisis intervention (Chapter 17), individual crisis intervention (Chapter 18), and psychotherapeutic interventions (Chapter 19).

Section 6 reviews strategies designed to examine the effectiveness of both school safety and crisis preparedness efforts (Chapter 20) and crisis response and recovery efforts (Chapter 21). Finally, Section 7 offers discussions of caring for the caregiver (Chapter 22), PREPaRE research and applications (Chapter 23), and concluding comments (Chapter 24).

Contributors and Reviewers

The authors of this book wish to recognize the valuable assistance of the following individuals who contributed to this book:

Nicholas Alajakis (Waukegan Public Schools District 60; Waukegan, IL)
   for his assistance with the social media section

Franci Crepeau-Hobson (University of Colorado, Denver)
   for her editorial assistance and chapter reviews

Erin Cook (University at Buffalo, SUNY)
   for her contributions to the memorials section and assistance with the sections on EMDR and psychopharmacology, as well as the references

Ben Fernandez (Loudoun County Public Schools; Ashburn, VA)
   for his editorial assistance and chapter reviews

Toni Orrange-Torchia (University at Buffalo, SUNY)
   for her work on technology considerations

Kayse Reker (Loyola University Chicago)
   for her assistance with the chapter on examining school safety and crisis preparedness

Sheila Stein (California State University, Sacramento)
   for her contributions to the student psychoeducational groups discussion

Jilynn Werth (University at Buffalo, SUNY)
   for her assistance with the students with disabilities section

Scott Woitaszewski (University of Wisconsin–River Falls)
   for his editorial assistance and thoughtful reviews

Acknowledgments

FIRST EDITION ACKNOWLEDGMENTS

As with any project of this magnitude, development of the PREPaRE model was significantly influenced by a number of organizations and individuals. Specifically, the authors of this book would like to acknowledge the contributions of the California Association of School Psychologists' Crisis Specialty Group (whose members included past NASP president Lee Huff and the late Ross Zatlin, Sweetwater Union High School District, Chula Vista, CA); and the Colorado Society of School Psychologists' (CSSP) State-Wide Crisis Response Team, (whose members included past CSSP president Susan Compton, Susy Ruof, and Char Armstrong). We would also like to thank PREPaRE Workgroup members Christina Conolly-Wilson, Brian Lazzaro, Leslie Paige, and Melinda Susan for their ongoing commitment to this project and contributions to this book.

In addition, we acknowledge the following Crisis Prevention and Preparedness topic group members for their contributions: Loeb Aronin, Woodland Hills, CA; Carol Benroth, Grand Junction School District, CO, and Anchorage, AK; Alan Cohen, Community Stress Prevention Center of Tel Hai College, Kiryat Shmona, Israel; Cindy Dickinson, Fairfax County Public Schools, VA; Corrina Duvall, University at Albany, NY; Ken Greff, Bothell, WA; Leslie Paige, Fort Hays State University, KS; Susy Ruof, Johnstown, CO; Donna Smith, ARIN Intermediate Unit 28, Indiana, PA; Amber Warrell, University at Albany, NY; Sarah Wilke, Aurora Public Schools and Colorado Department of Education; and Elizabeth Zhe, University at Albany, NY.

The following Crisis Intervention topic group members are acknowledged for their contributions: Melissa Allen Heath, Brigham Young University, UT; Servio A. Carroll, Sheridan County School District #2, WY; Ray W. Christner, Philadelphia College of Osteopathic Medicine, PA; Alan Cohen, Tel Hai College, Kiryat Shmona, Israel; Sylvia Cohen, Scottsdale Unified School District, AZ; Rose DuMond, Campbell Union School District, CA; Lillie Haynes, Dallas Independent School District, TX; Ellen Krumm, Gallup-McKinley School District, Gallup, NM; Sharon Lewis, Lodi Unified School District, Lodi, CA; Michael Pines, Los Angeles County Office of Education, CA; Doug Siembieda, Long Beach Unified School District, CA; and Philip Saigh, Columbia University, NY.

Special topics group members are also acknowledged for their contributions. On the topic of threat assessment: Jill Sharkey (chair), University of California, Santa Barbara; Dewey Cornell, University of Virginia; Sally Dorman, Charles County Public Schools, MD; Gina Hurley, Barnstable

High School, MA; Linda Kanan, Cherry Creek School District, CO; Kathy Sievering, Jefferson County School District, CO; Melinda Susan, Sonoma County Office of Education, CA; Paul Webb, Clark County School District, NV; and Diana Browning Wright, California Department of Education Diagnostic Center, Southern California. On the topic of grief: Melissa Allen Heath (chair), Deon Leavy, and Kristy Money, Brigham Young University, UT; Rona Leitner, Anna Kirchgater Elementary School, Sacramento, CA; Rosario Pesce, J. Sterling Morton High School District, Cicero, IL; Joelene Goodover, Great Falls High School, MT; Dana Chmiel Doré, Hopewell Public Schools, VA; Nadine Larson Woodle, Naperville Community Unit School District, IL; and Christie Cremeens, Madison County Schools, KY. On the topic of bullying: Susan Swearer (chair), University of Nebraska, Lincoln; Preston Bodison, Baltimore School District, MD; Carly Cornelius, Madison County Schools, KY; Susan Eldred, Chapman University, CA; Marolyn Freedman, Santa Monica/Malibu Unified School District, CA; Lillie Haynes, Dallas Independent School District, TX; Ian MacLeod, Amos Alonzo Stagg High School, IL; Elizabeth Rivelli, Hingham Public Schools, MA; Bryony Rowe, University of Kentucky; Peter Sheras, University of Virginia; and Karen Sternat, Colonial Intermediate, PA. On the topic of terrorism: Cathy Kennedy Paine (chair), Springfield School District, OR; Craig Apperson, Washington State Office of Superintendent of Public Instruction; Jenny Wildy, Eastern Kentucky University; and Ralph E. "Gene" Cash, Nova Southeastern University, FL. On the topic of suicide: Richard Lieberman (cochair), Los Angeles Unified School District, CA, and David Miller (cochair), University at Albany, NY. On the topic of natural disasters: Judy Oehler-Stinnett (chair), Oklahoma State University; Carla Cruise, San Bernardino City Unified School District, CA; and Keith Marcantel, Woodland Park School District, CO.

Other Crisis Prevention and Preparedness topic group members who participated in this project include Jennifer Kitson, Safe Schools/Healthy Students and Education Development Center, Newton, MA; Linda Kanan and Cathy Lines, Cherry Creek School District, CO; and the following students from the University at Albany, NY: David Halta, Natasha Little, and Robin Roberts.

Other Crisis Intervention topic group members who participated in this project include Wendy Carria, Arlington Public Schools, VA; Deborah Crockett, Fayette County Board of Education, GA; Elliot Davis, Brandywine School District, DE; Michelle Demaray, Northern Illinois University; Kimberly Knesting, University of Northern Iowa; Stephanie Livesay, Montgomery County Public Schools, MD; Christine Malecki, Northern Illinois University; Joe Nail, Clayton County Public Schools, GA; Kris Rodriguez, San Joaquin County Office of Education, CA; Denise Snow, Woodinville High School, WA; and Rosemary Virtuoso, Clark County School District, NV.

Finally, we are indebted to Linda Morgan and Kathy Cowan at the National Association of School Psychologists, whose attention to detail, responsiveness, and dedication made the publication of this book a reality. We also thank our copyeditor, Kathy Kelly, for her careful work.

SECOND EDITION ACKNOWLEDGMENTS

This book builds upon the foundation established by its first edition. Thus, it is critical that we begin the second edition acknowledgements by recognizing the contributions of first edition authors Richard A. Lieberman and Theodore A. Feinberg. In addition to being first edition authors, Rich and Ted were founding members of the National Emergency Assistance Team, Crisis Prevention and Intervention Workgroup, and the PREPaRE Workgroup. Their early work in the area of school-based crisis prevention and response is very much appreciated by the authors of this book.

We would also like to recognize the contributions of our colleagues on NASP's PREPaRE Workgroup, National Emergency Assistance Team (NEAT), and School Safety and Crisis Response Committee who have contributed much to our thinking on the topic of school safety and crisis response: Franci Crepeau-Hobson, Cynthia Dickinson, Douglas DiRaddo, Benjamin Fernandez, Catherine Kennedy-Paine, Philip Lazarus, William Pfohl, Larisa Pikover Crookston, Shirley Pitts, and Scott Woitaszewski.

Finally, we are indebted to Linda Morgan, Brieann Kinsey, and Kathy Cowan at the National Association of School Psychologists, whose attention to detail, responsiveness, and dedication made the publication of this book a reality. We also thank our copyeditor, Kathy Kelly, for her careful work.

Section 1

INITIAL CONSIDERATIONS

The single chapter in this section provides background information that is the foundation of the PREPaRE model for school safety and crisis response. Although this discussion may be familiar ground for the seasoned school-employed mental health professional, for other educators and those new to this field, the information that follows is an essential starting point for promoting school safety and developing school crisis response plans and teams.

Chapter 1

BACKGROUND KNOWLEDGE

This chapter presents prerequisite background knowledge for schools planning crisis preparedness activities following the PREPaRE model. Specifically, it addresses the following questions:

1. What are the crisis *events* for which school safety and crisis response teams strive to prepare? What are the defining characteristics of these events, and how do these characteristics help to determine the appropriate level of school crisis response?
2. What are the crisis *reactions* seen among students, school staff members, parents, and other caregivers? What might be considered the personal consequences of crisis exposure and the focus of school mental health crisis intervention?
3. What are the school safety and crisis response team *activities* associated with school crisis preparedness, and how do these elements fit into the PREPaRE model?

The chapter concludes by giving a brief overview of the remainder of the book.

CRISIS EVENTS: THE CHARACTERISTICS OF CRISES

School safety and crisis response teams must be ready to respond to a variety of crisis situations, but what constitutes a crisis is often open to interpretation. Brock et al. (2009) suggests that a *crisis* is an event that is perceived to be (a) extremely negative, (b) uncontrollable, and (c) unpredictable.

The first and perhaps most fundamental characteristic of a crisis event is that it is viewed as being extremely negative (Brock, 2002a). Crises have the potential to objectively generate extreme physical and emotional pain, or to be subjectively viewed as having the potential to cause such pain. According to the American Psychiatric Association's (APA) *Diagnostic and Statistical Manual of Mental Disorders, Fifth Edition* (DSM-5; 2013), traumatic stress reactions (which may lead to posttraumatic stress disorder) can be the consequence of directly experiencing, witnessing, or being indirectly exposed to traumatic events. DSM-5 states:

> directly experienced traumatic events ... include but are not limited to, exposure to war as a combatant or civilian, threatened or actual physical assault (e.g., physical attack, robbery, mugging, childhood physical abuse), threatened or actual sexual violence (e.g., forced sexual penetration, alcohol/drug-facilitated sexual penetration, abusive sexual contact, noncontact sexual abuse, sexual trafficking), being kidnapped, being taken hostage, terrorist attack, torture, incarceration as a prisoner of war, natural or human-made disasters, and severe motor vehicle accidents. (p. 274)

DSM-5 also indicates that for children, developmentally inappropriate sexual experiences, even in the absence of physical violence or injury, can be considered sexual violence.

Examples of witnessed events judged capable of generating traumatic stress include "observing threatened or serious injury, unnatural death, physical or sexual abuse of another person due to violent assault, domestic violence, accident, war or disaster" (p. 274). Regarding indirect trauma exposure, DSM-5 specifies that learning about a crisis "is limited to experiences affecting close relatives or friends and experiences that are violent or accidental" (p. 274). These indirectly experienced crisis events include "violent personal assault, suicide, serious accident, and serious injury" (pp. 274–275). Indirect exposure to traumatic events does not include "exposure through electronic media, television, movies, or pictures unless this exposure is work related" (p. 271).

However, perhaps of more importance than the crisis event is how the individual views the event. As discussed in Chapters 13 and 14 of this book, the more negative the individual's perception of the event and its consequences, the more significant the personal crisis becomes (Bryant, Salmon, Sinclair, & Davidson, 2007; Hecker, Hermenau, Maedl, Schauer, & Elbert, 2013; Kelloway, Mullen, & Francis, 2012; Rubin, Bernsten, & Bohni, 2008; Shaw, 2003).

The second characteristic of a crisis event is that such events are relatively uncontrollable, and individuals who are exposed often feel they have lost control over their lives. The degree to which an event generates these feelings significantly affects how the event is perceived (Adams et al., 2014; Foa, Zinbarg, & Rothbaum, 1992). Some situations can be made to feel more controllable through preparedness training. For example, students who have not had earthquake preparedness training will likely judge an earthquake to be more uncontrollable, and thus more frightening, than students who have been given instructions on how to respond (Brock et al., 2009).

Finally, crisis events typically occur suddenly, unexpectedly, and without warning (Foa et al., 1992; Simmons et al., 2013). A key factor that makes the event traumatic is the lack of time an individual has to adapt to crisis-generated problems. Relatively gradual and predictable events, such as the death of a loved one following a long terminal illness, generate less traumatic stress than sudden and unpredictable events, such as random violence or accidental death. A crisis that is more predictable gives those involved more opportunity to prepare and to make cognitive and emotional adjustments (Saylor, Belter, & Stokes, 1997).

To clarify the types of events that school safety and crisis response teams address, Table 1.1 gives examples of specific events that have the crisis characteristics just described, and Table 1.2

Table 1.1. Events That May Require Crisis Intervention

Life-threatening illnesses	Disfigurement and dismemberment
Assaults	Road, train, and maritime accidents
Fires or arson	Suicide attempts
Explosions	Fatal accidents
Sudden fatal illnesses	Suicides
Homicides	Human aggression
Domestic violence	Kidnappings
Terrorist attacks	Invasions
Prisoners of war	Hostage taking
Hijackings	Torture
Hurricanes	Floods
Fires	Earthquakes
Tornadoes	Avalanches or landslides
Volcanic eruptions	Lightning strikes
Tsunamis	Airline crashes
Nuclear accidents	Dam failures
Exposure to noxious agents or toxic waste	Construction or plant accidents

Note. From *School Crisis Prevention and Intervention: The PREPaRE Model*, p. 2, by S. E. Brock et al., 2009, Bethesda, MD: NASP. Copyright 2009 by the National Association of School Psychologists.

Table 1.2. Crisis Event Classifications

1. Acts of war and/or terrorism
2. Violent and/or unexpected death
3. Threatened death and/or injury
4. Human-caused disasters
5. Natural disasters
6. Severe illness or injury

Note. From *Preparing for Crises in the Schools: A Manual for Building School Crisis Response Teams* (2nd ed.), p. 14, by S. E. Brock, J. Sandoval, & S. Lewis, 2001, New York: Wiley. Copyright 2001 by John Wiley & Sons. Adapted with permission.

gives more general crisis event classifications. Members of the school community who directly experience or witness one of these events, or learn about a significant other experiencing such an event, are *potential* psychological trauma victims and *may* require one or more of the PREPaRE interventions discussed in the chapters that follow (in particular those discussed in Section 5).

Crisis Event Variables

Some of the events in Tables 1.1 and 1.2 are more traumatic than others (Kumar & Fonagy, 2013). Supporting this observation, McLaughlin et al. (2013), using data provided by the National Comorbidity Survey, report risk of lifetime posttraumatic stress disorder (PTSD) for adolescents to range from 39.3% for the victims of rape to 6.5% for those exposed to a man-made or natural disaster, with the victims of interpersonal violence generally having higher rates than those who experienced an accident or witnessed a traumatic event. Brock (2002b) referred to the variables that make some crisis events more traumatic than others as *crisis event variables*. As illustrated in Figure 1.1, a crisis event's predictability, consequences, duration, and intensity interact with the event itself and make some events more traumatic than others. Knowledge of these factors is important for school safety and crisis response teams because it helps them determine the level of support needed to effectively respond to the crisis.

Generally, human-caused events, particularly those that involve personal assault by someone who is familiar to the victim, are more distressing than natural disasters (or "acts of god") and severe illnesses and injuries (Charuvastra & Cloitre, 2008; McLaughlin et al., 2013). According to DSM-5, traumatic stress "may be especially severe or long-lasting when the stressor is interpersonal and intentional (e.g., torture, sexual violence)" (APA, 2013, p. 275). For example, although only 5% to 10% of children and adolescents meet full PTSD criteria following exposure to natural disasters (La Greca & Prinstein, 2002), studies of children exposed to war-related stressors typically find PTSD rates above 30% (Feldman & Vengrober, 2011; Saigh, Yasik, Sack, & Koplewicz, 1999). Similarly, it can be concluded that events that are intentional are more distressing than events that are considered to be accidents (Charuvastra & Cloitre, 2008). Among a sample of eighth graders, lifetime prevalence estimates suggest that only 11.5% of females and 10.3% of males involved in a traffic or other serious accident had PTSD, whereas 37.5% of females and

Figure 1.1. How Crisis Event Variables Make Some Crisis Events More Traumatic Than Others

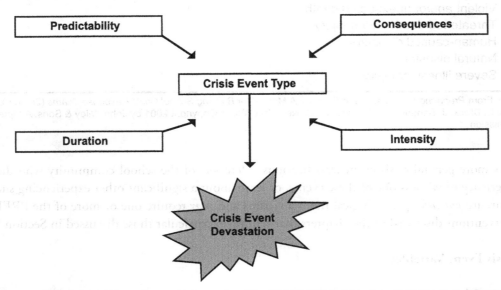

Note. From *School Crisis Prevention and Intervention: The PREPaRE Model*, p. 4, by S. E. Brock, A. B. Nickerson, M. A. Reeves, S. R. Jimerson, R. A. Lieberman, and T. A. Feinberg, 2009, Bethesda, MD: National Association of School Psychologists. Copyright 2009 by the National Association of School Psychologists. Reprinted with permission.

16.7% of males who had been physically abused had this trauma-related disorder (Elklit, 2002). However, natural disasters and accidents are also capable of generating severe traumatic stress.

As illustrated in Figure 1.1, natural disasters can be highly traumatic when they have one or more of the following characteristics: (a) they occurred suddenly, unexpectedly, and without warning (i.e., were not predictable); (b) they resulted in multiple fatalities and severe property destruction (i.e., had particularly devastating consequences); (c) they were associated with longer exposure to the crisis event (i.e., were of longer duration); and (d) they involved exposure to gruesome aspects of the crisis (i.e., resulted in exposures that were especially intense; Ayub et al., 2012).

The potential for natural disasters to be highly traumatic is illustrated by Hussain, Weisaeth, and Heir (2011), who studied psychiatric disorders among Norwegian tourists who escaped the 2004 tsunami in the Indian Ocean. Considered to be one of the deadliest natural disasters in recent history, this tsunami—a natural disaster that, given the lack of an early warning system in the Indian Ocean, was especially unpredictable—resulted in over 200,000 fatalities. This disaster also resulted in survivors being exposed to particularly gruesome aspects of the tsunami's aftermath. Despite the fact that these tourists were able to escape the longer term consequences associated with damaged infrastructure by having been able to return to undamaged homes in Norway, Hussain et al. (2011) documented that about two thirds (63.5%) of the survivors interviewed met the criteria for a psychiatric disturbance 2.5 years later. Most common were depression and PTSD, with 28.6% meeting criteria for major depressive disorder and 36.5% meeting PTSD criteria.

Although Hussain et al. (2011) focused on the long-term psychiatric morbidity observed among adult (18 years and older) tourists to the 2004 tsunami, Ghazali, Elklit, Yaman and Ahmad (2013) examined the rates of PTSD among adolescents living in villages directly affected by this natural disaster. In addition, the participants in this study did not have the advantage of being able to leave the disaster area and return to intact homes. For these adolescent survivors, the duration of disaster-related stressors was much longer, and not surprisingly the rates of PTSD were much higher than those found among Hussain et al.'s (2011) participants. Ghazali et al. (2013) found that 4 years after the tsunami, only 9.7% reported no significant PTSD symptoms, whereas 8.3% reported severe symptoms, 39.8% reported moderate symptoms, and 42.1% reported mild symptoms.

Further evidence of how a natural disaster can become highly traumatic is provided by Pynoos et al. (1993), who studied effects in youth following the 1988 Armenia earthquake. The earthquake—a type of natural disaster that is especially unpredictable—resulted in 55,000 fatalities. Its effects had a long duration, given that the associated damage to local infrastructure, particularly schools and hospitals, resulted in long-term survival challenges during the freezing winter months. This traumatic event also resulted in youth being exposed to particularly gruesome aspects of the earthquake's aftermath. At the time of the earthquake, most schools were inadequately designed, and as a result, two thirds of the total deaths were children and adolescents (Azarian & Skriptchenko-Gregorian, 1998a). Given the interaction of the crisis event variables of this natural disaster—unpredictability, duration, consequences, and intensity—it is not surprising to find that just over 90% of youth reported severe PTSD symptoms (Pynoos et al., 1993).

Finally, in the United States, Hurricane Katrina had similarly dramatic consequences. Although a hurricane is a relatively predictable event, the consequences of Katrina were profound. The storm and its aftermath resulted in more than 1,000 deaths, more than 500,000 people displaced, and over $100 billion in damage (Rosenbaum, 2006). Furthermore, the duration of crisis challenges and intensity of the crisis experiences were especially high for residents of New Orleans. Given these facts, the numbers are not surprising; almost half (49%) of a sample of adult residents of the New Orleans metropolitan area had a 30-day prevalence of an anxiety or mood disorder identified by DSM-IV-TR, and almost a third (30%) were estimated to have PTSD (Galea et al., 2007). Particularly relevant to educators is the fact that 3 years after Katrina, 28% of students ages 9 to 18 in St. Bernard Parish School District (in a county adjacent to New Orleans) reported significant symptoms of posttraumatic stress and depression. Study authors suggested that this result was not surprising given the long duration of crisis-generated challenges and their more intense trauma exposures (Kronenberg et al., 2010).

Levels of School Crisis Response

Figure 1.1 is an excellent tool for orienting crisis response team members during a time when rational thinking may be challenging, and different combinations of crisis event variables call for different levels of school crisis response. Accurately estimating the required level of crisis response is important because there are dangers associated with both over- and underreacting to a school associated crisis. Specifically, more extreme caregiver reactions to an event are associated with an increase in PTSD risk among children (Eksi et al., 2007). Overreacting to a crisis event (providing a more involved crisis response than is needed) may increase students' threat perceptions and the associated risk for traumatic stress. On the other hand, underreacting may result in students' needs not being met and valuable crisis response resources being wasted. The four levels of school crisis response, as recommended by the PREP_aRE model, are listed in Table 1.3 (Brock, Sandoval, & Lewis, 1996, 2001).

Table 1.3. Levels of School Crisis Response

1. *Minimal response*
   - Few school community members are affected by the event, and school staff members can manage the response without leaving traditional roles.

2. *Building-level response*
   - Many school community members are affected by the event. However, by temporarily suspending typical job duties, school staff members can independently manage the response.

3. *District-level response*
   - Many school community members are significantly affected by the event, and even after temporarily suspending typical job duties to conduct the crisis response, school staff members cannot independently manage the response. Additional district resources are required to manage the response.

4. *Regional-level response*
   - A large number of school community members are significantly affected by the event, and even with district resources the response cannot be managed independently. Additional regionally based staff members are required to manage the response.

Note. From *School Crisis Prevention and Intervention: The PREP_aRE Model*, p. 5, by S. E. Brock et al., 2009, Bethesda, MD: NASP. Copyright 2009 by the National Association of School Psychologists.

At the *minimal* level of school crisis response, the event is not highly traumatic for the vast majority of exposed individuals, and school crisis response team members can manage the crisis without leaving their traditional school roles (e.g., there is no need for school crisis response team members to clear their calendars). Any necessary crisis response activities or services can be fit into the normal daily schedule. As illustrated in Table 1.4, events that might require this level of response include nonfatal accidental injuries that are not considered to be human caused or intentionally inflicted. Events of this type are not likely to severely traumatize many school community members, so the need for mental health crisis intervention is minimal.

The second level of school crisis response, the *building* level, implies that although the crisis event is potentially traumatic, available school resources can manage the crisis. However, when responding to the event, crisis response team members are required to leave their traditional roles (e.g., to clear their calendars). Table 1.4 provides an example of an event that might be consistent with this level of response. Other crisis events that might require a building-level response include nonfatal accidental injuries that are human caused or natural disasters that are not associated with fatalities or long-term coping challenges.

The third and fourth levels of school crisis response are the *district* and *regional* levels. At these levels the crisis event has the potential to be highly traumatic, and not only are building-level personnel required to leave their traditional roles, but the number of school students and staff affected will likely overwhelm the building-level crisis response team resources. The affected school or district will need to call in crisis response teams who are not typically assigned to the schools affected by the crisis event.

In addition to the crisis event variables, whether a response is district or regional level also is determined by the availability of local resources. For example, a small school district with relatively few crisis response team members would need support from a regional response team much sooner than a larger school district would. Crisis events that might require this level of response typically include those that are caused by human aggression, have one or more fatalities or significant property destruction, occur with relatively little warning, present ongoing or long-term problems, or result in exposure to intense crisis images and actions. Again, Table 1.4 provides examples of events that might be consistent with these crisis response levels.

CRISIS REACTIONS: THE PERSONAL CONSEQUENCES OF CRISIS EVENT EXPOSURE

To identify appropriate mental health crisis intervention strategies, school safety and crisis response team members must be able to recognize crisis reactions. As with other models of crisis response (e.g., Brymer et al., 2006; Brymer, Taylor, et al., 2012), the PREPaRE model does not assume that all trauma-exposed students develop severe mental health challenges. Rather, the model is based on the assumption that students exposed to a crisis event display a range of reactions, some of which necessitate very little professional mental health support and others that require intense mental health crisis intervention. The following discussion of the crisis state is offered to facilitate understanding of the types of crisis reactions that require one or more of the PREPaRE mental health crisis interventions.

Table 1.4. Matching Level of Crisis Response With Crisis Event Variables

Crisis Event Example	Estimated Crisis Response Level[a]	Crisis Event Variable Examples				
		Type	Consequence	Predictability	Duration	Intensity
A student falls and breaks a leg while playing kickball.	Minimal	Accident (not human caused)	Nonfatal injury	Playground accidents are relatively common.	Minutes	Others see the student falling and crying.
A parent volunteer dies shortly after being diagnosed with cancer.	Building	Severe illness (not human caused)	One fatality	A terminal diagnosis had been given.	Month	Students were exposed only to the beginning stages of the illness.
A student commits suicide by hanging himself in a restroom.	District	Human caused (self-directed violence)	One fatal injury	Indirect suicide threats were not identified as suicide warning signs.	Minutes	Three students discover the body of the deceased, and many see the body being removed.
A gunman attacks on a crowded playground; students are in lockdown all day.	Community/ Regional	Human caused (violent assault)	Multiple fatalities	The event was sudden and unexpected.	Hours	Students are exposed to gruesome sights.

Note. Adapted from *School Crisis Prevention and Intervention: The PREPaRE Model*, p. 7, by S. E. Brock et al., 2009, Bethesda, MD: NASP. Copyright 2009 by the National Association of School Psychologists. Adapted with permission.

[a] The estimated crisis response levels are not prescriptive. Rather, they are intended to illustrate how crisis event variables may influence response levels. For example, relative to larger schools and school districts, smaller schools and school districts will require a greater level of response for the same crisis event than is required in larger schools.

The Crisis State

Figure 1.2 illustrates development of the crisis state and specifies that the primary focus of crisis intervention is to facilitate adaptive coping. Shaded in gray are aspects of the crisis state that mental health crisis intervention targets.

Prerequisite to the crisis state is exposure to a crisis event, and the perception of the event as extremely negative. Entry into the state of "crisis" is prompted by an inability to cope with crisis-generated problems. For example, when confronted with a common act of school-yard aggression, such as a fight with a peer, a student might choose from several previously developed coping options (e.g., fight back, ignore the peer, tell a teacher, or run away). Although possibly effective for these more common acts of school-yard aggression, these problem-solving strategies will not work for the individual confronted with a school-yard shooting. Thus, the problem (i.e., how to cope with being shot at while at school) would initially appear to be without a solution, and the student would consequently experience a loss of psychological homeostasis, a construct first defined by Stagner (1951).

The state of psychological equilibrium, or homeostasis, is achieved when a student is successfully coping with daily challenges. Disruption of this state generates distress and psychological disorganization (psychological disequilibrium), and it is often associated with impaired functioning. This disruption of homeostasis manifests itself as the symptoms recognized as crisis reactions. Chapter 13 examines specific ways that acute disruption can be manifested as warning signs of psychological trauma, but for now it is sufficient to acknowledge that they include emotional, cognitive, behavioral, and physical reactions (Brymer et al., 2006; Brymer et al., 2012).

The disequilibrium caused by the acute disruption of psychological homeostasis, and associated distress and disorganization, serves as a powerful motivator for the individual who is in crisis to

Figure 1.2. Relationships Among the Characteristics of the Crisis State

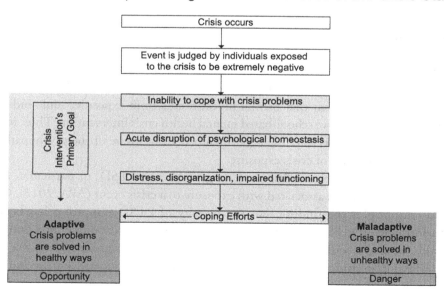

find a way to return to the steady state of homeostasis (Brent, 1978). In other words, it creates the impetus for the individual to find a way to cope with or solve crisis-generated problems. It is from the individual's drive to find a way to cope with crisis-generated problems that the final characteristic of the crisis state emerges: the potential for a radically positive or negative outcome. The potential for change is great in the wake of a crisis. Not only are individuals who adaptively cope with a crisis no longer distressed and disorganized, but they also have developed new problem-solving strategies as they return to precrisis levels of functioning. Developing these new strategies also can result in increased psychological resilience. For example, students may cope with a natural disaster by acknowledging that such events are relatively rare and by knowing that they can take actions to keep themselves safe (an adaptive, healthy, and radically positive outcome). Conversely, other students may cope with the same disaster by deciding not to leave their homes (a maladaptive, unhealthy, and radically negative outcome).

Finally, it is important to acknowledge that the crisis state differs from common stress in several ways. First, as a result of the need to restore psychological homeostasis, students in crisis are driven to find a way to cope with crisis-generated problems. Consequently, they have lowered defenses and are open to suggestion. In contrast, individuals who are simply stressed are often defensive. Second, a crisis has the potential for a radically positive or radically negative outcome. Change is mandated by the crisis experience. On the other hand, the typical outcome for the individual experiencing simple stress can be either adaptation and survival or a return to the status quo. Finally, although the crisis state is an acute problem, has a sudden onset, and is of fairly short duration, the stressed state usually builds up gradually and in many cases can become a chronic problem.

Although the symptoms of the crisis state may be similar to those of psychopathologies, they are not necessarily signs of mental illness. Given sufficient traumatic stress, anyone, regardless of how psychologically ill or healthy, can enter into a crisis state. Simply put, it is a common reaction to abnormal circumstances. Although the crisis state typically resolves itself within several weeks, longer-term coping difficulties can evolve into mental illness or psychopathology.

Psychopathology

In all but the most extreme crisis events, most individuals are expected to recover from the psychological trauma generated by event exposure (National Institute of Mental Health [NIMH], 2001). However, to the extent that mental illness results from exposure, some individuals need immediate and highly directive school-based mental health crisis intervention. Thus, it is important for all school safety and crisis response team members to be aware of the psychopathologies that are a potential consequence of crisis exposure.

Trauma- and stressor-related disorders, in general, and PTSD, in particular, are the most common psychopathologies associated with exposure to a crisis event (APA, 2013). Of particular interest to educators is the finding that the severity of PTSD symptoms has been linked to school performance (De Bellis, Woolley, & Hooper, 2013). For example, in a sample of 11- to 14-year-olds, students with severe to very severe PTSD had significantly lower grade point averages (GPAs) than students whose PTSD was described as moderate. Furthermore, following a group intervention designed to address traumatic stress consequences, reductions in PTSD symptoms were associated with improvements in students' GPAs (Saltzman, Pynoos, Layne, Steinberg, & Aisenberg, 2001). Additional research indicates that when adolescents with this disorder are compared to those without PTSD (including those who have been exposed to crisis events, but who do not have PTSD), they score significantly lower on measures of academic achievement (Saigh, Mroueh, & Bremner, 1997; also see Nickerson, Reeves, Brock, & Jimerson, 2009, for a review of literature and best practices regarding the identification, assessment, and treatment of students with PTSD at school). In addition to these academic concerns, PTSD also has negative physical health consequences (Pacella, Hruska, & Delahanty, 2013).

Despite the frequency and consequences of PTSD, it is not the only diagnosis linked with crisis exposure (APA, 2013; Berkowitz, 2003; Green, 1994; Hoven et al., 2004; Ritchie, 2003). Table 1.5 provides a list of other DSM-5 diagnoses that may afflict individuals following exposure to a crisis event.

Although psychopathological outcomes typically are found among a minority of those exposed to a crisis event, the exact percentage of the population who will have such outcomes will vary because some events are more traumatic than others. In addition, whether an individual will develop a psychopathology depends on the complex interaction between the nature of the crisis event, the crisis victim's unique crisis experiences, and his or her external environmental resources and internal personal vulnerabilities (Berkowitz, 2003; Brock, 2002c). Again, although exposure to a crisis event is necessary to trigger postcrisis psychopathology, it is not sufficient to explain its onset (Berkowitz, 2003; McFarlane, 1988; Saigh et al., 1999). This topic will be explored further in Chapter 13's discussion of psychological trauma assessment.

Consequences of Crises for the School

In addition to the effects already mentioned, other consequences of crisis events are unique to the school setting (see Table 1.6). Clearly, if these consequences are observed subsequent to a crisis event, a crisis response is warranted. Furthermore, assessment of these crisis consequences can be helpful in evaluating the effectiveness of a school crisis response (see Chapter 21).

Table 1.5. Possible Psychopathological Consequences Associated With Crisis Exposure

- Depressive disorders
- Anxiety disorders (e.g., specific phobia, social anxiety disorder, panic disorder)
- Trauma- and stressor-related disorders (i.e., disinhibited social engagement disorder, posttraumatic stress disorder, acute stress disorder, adjustment disorders)
- Dissociative disorders (e.g., dissociative identity disorder, dissociative amnesia, depersonalization/derealization disorder)
- Sleep–wake disorders (e.g., insomnia disorder, nightmare disorder)
- Substance-related and addictive disorders

Table 1.6. The Consequences of Crises on School Functioning

Consequence	Sources
School behavior problems, such as aggressive, delinquent, and criminal behavior	Azarian & Skriptchenko-Gregorian, 1998a; Carlson, 1997; Monahon, 1993; Nader & Muni, 2002
School absenteeism	Azarian & Skriptchenko-Gregorian, 1998a; Hurt, Malmud, Brodsky, & Giannetta, 2001; Silverman & La Greca, 2002
Academic decline[a]	Cook-Cottone, 2004; Goodman, Miller, & West-Olatunji, 2012; Nader & Muni, 2002; Silverman & La Greca, 2002; Thompson & Massat, 2005; Yule, 1998
Poorer school performance	Delaney-Black et al., 2002; Hurt et al., 2001; Saigh et al., 1997; Schwab-Stone et al., 1995
Decreased verbal IQ	Saigh, Yasik, Oberfield, Halamandaris, & Bremner, 2006
Exacerbation of preexisting educational problems	Vogel & Vernberg, 1993

Note. Adapted from *School Crisis Prevention and Intervention: The PREPaRE Model*, p. 11, by S. E. Brock et al., 2009, Bethesda, MD: NASP. Copyright 2009 by the National Association of School Psychologists. Adapted with permission.
[a] It is important to note that traumatic stress reactions, not simple crisis exposure, put students at risk for serious academic decline (Saigh et al., 1997).

Positive Outcomes Associated With Crises

As discussed earlier, school crises are not only times of danger, but also times of opportunity. Consistent with this observation, an emerging field of study has addressed the construct of *posttraumatic growth*, which has been defined as positive change resulting from the struggle with trauma (Kilmer, 2006). For example, meta-analytic research conducted by Shakespeare-Finch and Lurie-Beck (2014) has suggested that among traumatized individuals (with the exception of sexual assault victims), the potential exists for positive as well as negative outcomes. Shakespeare-Finch and Lurie-Beck concluded:

Research has moved past the idea that PTSD symptoms and perceptions of positive post-trauma changes are at opposite ends of a continuum and practitioners are advised to be mindful of the coexistence of positive and negative perceptions and manifestations of negotiating trauma. (p. 227)

Although much of the research investigating posttraumatic growth has been conducted with adults, there is at least preliminary support for this phenomenon occurring among children and youth (Meyerson, Grant, Carter, & Kilmer, 2011). There is even some evidence of the potential that such growth is greater among children (Shakespeare-Finch & Lurie-Beck, 2014).

Given these reports, school safety and crisis response teams should consider some of the positive outcomes their crisis response may achieve. Positive outcomes for individual students and staff members might include the following: (a) some survivors become better able to cope with future crises or other challenges, and (b) some change their lives in a positive direction (e.g., becoming helpers or advocates for others who later may be a victim or survivor). Evidence of such positive outcomes can help to document the success of a given school crisis response.

Similarly, at the school system level, positive outcomes may include (a) administrators and the public recognizing the need for crisis preparedness (i.e., crisis prevention, protection, mitigation, response, and recovery); (b) more school-employed mental health professionals and other staff members obtaining crisis preparedness training; (c) more assistance being available to schools in the form of grants, emergency aid, and other additional funds to increase crisis preparedness; and (d) more student support resources (e.g., school-employed mental health professionals) and programming becoming available.

SCHOOL SAFETY AND CRISIS RESPONSE TEAM ACTIVITIES

Finally, before school safety and crisis response team members consider specific crisis prevention, protection, mitigation, response, and recovery strategies, they must be knowledgeable about the range of activities that such teams provide and understand the primary goals of mental health crisis intervention.

The Range of Crisis Preparedness Activities and PREPaRE

Presidential Policy Directive 8 (PPD-8; Obama, 2011) and the U.S. Department of Education (2013) encourage all public and private entities, including school districts, to prepare for crises through the development of quality crisis plans that encompass five mission areas:

1. *Prevention.* Includes steps that schools take to prevent an incident or crisis from occurring. Examples include suicide and threat assessment programs, bullying prevention, and school mental health services.
2. *Protection.* Involves schools securing their networks, property, visitors, staff, and students against acts of violence and disasters (human caused or natural) and includes having exterior door locks, student supervision, firewalls on computers and the network, and visitor control systems.
3. *Mitigation.* Looks at the school's capabilities to eliminate or reduce the loss of life or property damage by lessening the impact of a crisis event. For example, when a school enacts a tornado emergency protocol and the tornado sirens sound, they are attempting to mitigate the crisis.
4. *Response.* Includes the school's capacity to stabilize emergency situations that are certain to happen or have already occurred. It also includes providing a safe and secure school environment, saving lives and property, and facilitating the transition to recovery. Examples include the school crisis response team's actions following the death of a school staff member or student, utility failure, or chemical spill.
5. *Recovery.* Includes the ability to restore the learning environment after a crisis event. Examples include providing multitiered mental health crisis interventions (a primary focus of the

PREPaRE model), providing temporary classrooms after a classroom is destroyed, and reestablishing payroll after a computer network crashes.

Consistent with these mission areas, the PREPaRE acronym refers to the range of crisis preparedness activities that school safety and crisis response teams work to provide. As illustrated in Figure 1.3, PREPaRE stands for five school safety and crisis response activities: prevent, reaffirm, evaluate, provide and respond, and examine.

Specifically, the PREPaRE model emphasizes that members of school safety and crisis response teams must be involved in the following hierarchical and sequential set of activities. First, team members work to prevent crises that can be avoided and to prepare for events that cannot be prevented. Such prevention activities involve not only avoiding or stopping crises before they occur, but also promoting student resiliency to enable them to better cope with crises that are not prevented. In the PREPaRE model, prevention also includes engaging in ongoing actions to develop the capabilities to protect students if a crisis is not prevented, and mitigating or lessening the impact of crises. Crisis mitigation can "also mean reducing the likelihood that threats and hazards will happen" (U.S. Department of Education, 2013, p. 2).

Second, once a crisis event has occurred, the PREPaRE model specifies that all crisis response team members initially focus on helping to ensure physical health and perceptions of security and safety. This immediate reaction to a crisis event is based on the assumption that for recovery to begin, school community members must have their basic needs met, and not only be safe but also believe that crisis-related danger has passed. Third, team members evaluate the degree to which individuals have suffered psychological trauma. This involves assessing individuals' crisis exposure and considering their internal and external resources and resulting threat perceptions. This activity also involves directly exploring the individual's stress reactions. Fourth, from assessment data, team members respond to the psychological needs of school community members, which primarily includes reestablishing and empowering naturally occurring social support systems. It may also include a range of psychoeducational and psychological interventions as indicated. Fifth and finally, the PREPaRE model calls for an examination of the effectiveness of crisis prevention and intervention efforts. This final activity includes both formative and summative evaluations of all school safety and crisis response team efforts.

Throughout its initial development and subsequent revisions, the PREPaRE model has tried to be consistent with guidance and direction offered by the U.S. Departments of Education (2003, 2007b, 2013) and Homeland Security (2004, 2008, 2011b), and the National Child Traumatic Stress Network (Brymer et al., 2006; Brymer, Taylor, et al., 2012). Most recently, referencing Presidential Policy Directive 8 (Obama, 2011), the U.S. Department of Education (2013) has defined crisis preparedness as being based on the five mission areas. Consistent with this guidance, the PREPaRE model directs school crisis response team members to be involved in a range of crisis preparedness activities. Specifically, school safety and crisis response teams are involved in activities designed to "avoid, deter or stop" crises (crisis prevention); "secure schools against acts of violence and manmade or natural disasters" (crisis protection); "eliminate or reduce the loss of life and property damage by lessening the impact of a crisis" (crisis mitigation); "stabilize an emergency" (crisis response); and "assist schools affected by an event . . . in restoring the learning environment" (crisis recovery; U.S. Department of Education, 2013, p. 2).

Figure 1.3. The relationship between (a) the phases of a crisis, (b) specific PREPaRE school crisis interventions, (c) the levels of crisis prevention/intervention, (d) crisis preparedness, and (e) psychological first aid.

	Preimpact — The period before crisis		Impact — When crisis occurs	Recoil — Immediately after crisis threats end	Postimpact — Days/weeks after the crisis	Recovery and reconstruction — Months to years after the crisis
	Preparation and planning	Threat and warning				
(a) Crisis Phase (Raphael & Newman, 2000; Valent, 2000)						
b) PREPaRE: School Crisis Prevention and Intervention Training Curriculum	**1. Prevent and prepare for psychological trauma risk** • Prevention of crises • Promotion of resiliency • Protection from crises that are not prevented • Mitigation of crises (also refers to reducing the likelihood of crises) o Keep students safe o Avoid crisis scenes and images			**2. Reaffirm physical health and security and perceptions of safety** • Meet basic physical needs (water, shelter, food, clothing) • Foster perceptions of safety	**3. Evaluate psychological trauma** • Assess crisis exposure, internal and external resources, threat perceptions, and crisis reactions **4. Provide interventions and Respond to psychological needs** • Reestablish social support systems • Provide psychoeducation: Empower survivors and caregivers	• Make psychotherapy treatment referrals • Provide psychological interventions o Group crisis intervention o Individual crisis intervention o Psychotherapy
	5. Examine the effectiveness of school safety, crisis prevention, and crisis response (spanning all phases)					
(c) Level of prevention (Caplan, 1964)	Primary		Primary	Primary and secondary	Secondary	Tertiary
(c) Level of preventive intervention (Gordon, 1983)	Universal		Universal	Universal and selected	Universal, selected, and indicated	Selected and indicated
(d) Crisis preparedness (U.S. Department of Education, 2013)	Prevention, Mitigation		Protection, Mitigation	Protection, Mitigation, Response	Recovery	
(e) Psychological First Aid (Brymer et al., 2006; Brymer, Taylor, et al., 2012)			1. Contact and engagement 2. Safety and comfort 3. Stabilization (if needed) 4. Information gathering: Needs and current concerns		5. Practical assistance 6. Connect with social supports 7. Information on coping 8. Links to services	

Note. Adapted from "Best Practices for School Psychologists as Members of Crisis Teams: The PREPaRE Model" (p. 1488), by S. E. Brock, A. B. Nickerson, M. A. Reeves, and S. R. Jimerson, in A. Thomas and J. Grimes (Eds.), *Best Practices in School Psychology V*, 2008, Bethesda, MD: National Association of School Psychologists. Copyright 2008 by the National Association of School Psychologists. Adapted with permission.

Though crisis events clearly have the potential to generate significant psychological injury, the PREPaRE model also acknowledges that—with the exception of the most extraordinary crisis circumstances and with the support of naturally occurring family, school, and community resources—the majority of school community members will recover from their crisis exposure. Given this reality, most of the school mental health crisis intervention services included in PREPaRE are considered to be indirect consultation services. Often when crisis response team members are implementing the elements of this model, they will be working behind the scenes as consultants to ensure that students, staff, and parents are well positioned to realize their natural potential to cope with a crisis. Of course these naturally occurring resources do have their limits, and this is where the assessment and response elements of PREPaRE become critical. Overall, PREPaRE aims at fostering natural recovery from psychologically traumatic events, while identifying the most severely distressed individuals and providing them with an appropriate mental health crisis intervention.

The Primary Goal of Mental Health Crisis Intervention

The National Disaster Recovery Framework (U.S. Department of Homeland Security, 2011a) instructs the following:

> A successful recovery process addresses the full range of psychological and emotional needs of the community as it recovers from the disaster through the provision of support, counseling, screening and treatment when needed. These needs range from helping individuals to handle the shock and stress associated with the disaster's impact and recovery challenges, to addressing the potential for and consequences of individuals harming themselves or others through substance, physical and emotional abuses. Successful recovery acknowledges the linkages between the recovery of individuals, families and communities. (p. 11)

To achieve the primary goal of crisis intervention, that is, to facilitate adaptive coping, school mental health crisis interventions, such as those delineated within the PREPaRE model, help restore crisis-exposed students' basic problem-solving abilities and in so doing return them to their precrisis levels of functioning (Sandoval & Brock, 2009). Given this perspective, crisis response team members should understand how children and adolescents typically cope with challenges. A useful framework for understanding such coping has been offered by Skinner and colleagues (Skinner, Edge, Altman, & Sherwood, 2003; Skinner & Zimmer-Gembeck, 2007; Zimmer-Gembeck & Skinner, 2011), who suggest that three general adaptive processes are associated with 12 specific families of coping. These three processes involve (a) the coordination of actions and contingencies in the environment (i.e., problem-solving, information seeking, helplessness, and escape); (b) the coordination of available social resources (i.e., self-reliance, support seeking, delegation, and social isolation); and (c) the coordination of preferences and available options (i.e., accommodation, negotiation, submission, and opposition). Although much is yet to be learned about how children cope with crisis events (Pfefferbaum, Noffsinger, & Wind, 2012), Tables 1.7 and 1.8 list the 12 families of coping and their associated functions, as well as identify the specific approaches to coping with challenges.

Table 1.7. Families of Coping That Crisis Intervention Typically Promotes

Coping Family	Coping Function
Problem solving (strategizing, instrumental action, planning)	Adjust actions to be effective
Information seeking (reading, observing, asking others)	Find additional contingencies
Self-reliance (emotion regulation, behavior regulation, emotional expression, emotional approach)	Protect available social resources
Support seeking (contact seeking, comfort seeking, instrumental aid, social referencing)	Use available resources
Accommodation (distraction, cognitive restructuring, minimization, acceptance)	Flexibly adjust preferences to options
Negotiation (bargaining, persuasion, priority setting)	Find new options

Note. Adapted from "The Development of Coping," by E. A. Skinner & M. J. Zimmer-Gembeck, 2007, in *Annual Review of Psychology, 58,* p. 126. Copyright 2007 by Annual Reviews. Adapted with permission.

Table 1.8. Families of Coping That Crisis Intervention Typically Tries to Prevent

Coping Family	Coping Function
Helplessness (confusion, cognitive interference, cognitive exhaustion)	Find limits of actions
Escape (behavioral avoidance, mental withdrawal, denial, wishful thinking)	Escape noncontingent environment
Delegation (maladaptive help-seeking, complaining, whining, self-pity)	Find limits of resources
Social isolation (social withdrawal, concealment, avoidance of others)	Withdraw from unsupportive context
Submission (rumination, rigid perseveration, intrusive thoughts)	Give up preferences
Opposition (other-blame, projection, aggression)	Remove constraints

Note. Adapted from "The Development of Coping," by E. A. Skinner & M. J. Zimmer-Gembeck, 2007, in *Annual Review of Psychology, 58,* p. 126. Copyright 2007 by Annual Reviews. Adapted with permission.

Section 2

PREVENT AND PREPARE

The first element of the PREPaRE model (the initial "P" in PREPaRE) stands for crisis prevention and preparedness. Consistent with guidance from the U.S. Department of Education's 2013 *Guide for Developing High-Quality School Emergency Operations Plans*, the PREPaRE model emphasizes that school safety and crisis response teams do more than simply respond to crisis events. These teams are active well before crises occur, as they simultaneously engage in school safety, crisis prevention, and crisis response preparedness activities. As illustrated in Figure 1.3, the majority of prevention and preparedness activities take place before a crisis occurs, during what Valent (2000) has identified as the preimpact phase, or what Raphael and Newman (2000) have identified as the planning and preparation and threat and warning phases. However, some prevention activities may take place during the impact and recoil phases (Raphael & Newman, 2000; Valent, 2000). During these phases (during or immediately following a school-associated crisis event) school crisis teams strive to keep students safe and to prevent exposure to potentially traumatizing crisis scenes and images.

The nine chapters in this section explore comprehensive school safety and crisis prevention, as well as the actions school crisis response teams take to ensure that they are ready to respond to school-associated crises. The section begins with an overview of school crisis prevention and preparedness and of comprehensive school safety and crisis response teams (Chapter 2). It then offers more specific recommendations for facilitating the two essential and complementary tasks of ensuring physical safety (Chapter 3) and psychological safety (Chapter 4). Chapters 5 and 6 then examine school safety teams and safety planning efforts. Chapters 7, 8, and 9 discuss crisis response teams and preparedness efforts, including the Incident Command System, general emergency operations plans, and specific threat protocols. Finally, the section concludes with a discussion about preventing and preparing for the psychological injuries that can be generated by exposure to a school-associated crisis event (Chapter 10).

Chapter 2

SCHOOL CRISIS PREVENTION AND PREPAREDNESS MODELS

Preventing and preparing for school crisis events are essential elements of the PREPaRE model. This chapter examines the rationale and goals of school crisis or emergency preparedness, provides information regarding legal requirements and legislative mandates, reviews current school-based preparedness models, and briefly discusses obstacles that interfere with safety and crisis planning.

REASONS FOR CRISIS PREVENTION AND PREPAREDNESS

Schools must prepare for various types of disasters, including expected and unexpected deaths, violence, domestic and global terrorism threats, health concerns, financial stresses, and bullying (Gainey, 2010; Gray & Lewis, 2015; Guha-Sapir, Hoyois, & Below, 2014; Jimerson et al., 2012; United Nations Office for Disaster Risk Reduction, 2014b). Although these threats are real and speak to the need for comprehensive school safety and crisis preparedness efforts, it is important that these efforts be placed in the proper perspective.

Schools are very safe places. During the 2013–2014 school year, 87.0% of U.S. public schools did not report any serious incidents of violence, and only 0.2% reported a school-associated violent death (Gray & Lewis, 2015). Although the number of active shooter incidents in colleges and universities increased from 2 incidents to 10 incidents between the periods 2000–2006 and 2007–2013, the number of such incidents in prekindergarten to 12th-grade schools stayed the same: 13 in the period 2000–2006 and 12 in the period 2007–2013 (Blair & Schweit, 2014; Kennedy-Paine & Crepeau-Hobson, 2015). In other words, serious violent crime is isolated to a very small number of schools, and contrary to public perceptions, large-scale incidences such as fatal school shootings are rare. In fact, schools are arguably the safest place for children (Brock, 2015a; Cornell, 2015; Nekvasil, Cornell, & Huang, 2015).

However, schools are not immune from crises. In a survey of 228 U.S. school psychologists, 93% reported that their schools had responded to a crisis (Adamson & Peacock, 2007). Because exposure to a crisis has the potential to negatively affect students' behavior, social–emotional adjustment, and education, crisis preparedness is essential. Schools are responsible for student safety, and even the best of prevention programs will not stop all crises from occurring (Brock et al., 2001; United Nations Disaster Assessment and Coordination, 2013). Such planning helps to ensure that all crisis response and recovery activities meet students' needs, and that available resources are effectively deployed to attend immediately to multiple demands that are outside of normal routines. Without plans in place, schools facing a crisis can neglect important tasks during and following a crisis event, which can lead to unnecessary chaos, trauma, and panic, and missed opportunities to build resilience.

The primary goals of school crisis prevention and preparedness efforts are to establish a safe school environment, mitigate potential threats, and, in the event of a crisis, provide quality intervention and recovery supports to restore learning. Schools that establish safety and crisis response teams and plans can then develop procedures and protocols that (a) help the school establish a safe climate to reduce the likelihood of crisis events occurring; (b) ensure response readiness for crises that are not, or cannot be, prevented; (c) provide direction immediately after a crisis event to minimize crisis impact and restore equilibrium; and (d) help repair crisis damage and return to at least precrisis (or baseline) operation and functioning (Reeves, Conolly-Wilson, Pesce, Lazzaro, & Brock, 2012). In other words, school safety and crisis response teams should engage in crisis prevention, protection, mitigation, response, and recovery activities (U.S. Department of Education, 2013) and provide critical leadership, guidance, and collaboration.

LEGAL, LEGISLATIVE, AND POLICY RATIONALES FOR CRISIS PREVENTION AND PREPAREDNESS

Schools and districts that invest in infrastructure for crisis prevention and preparedness in accordance with federal and individual state legislation can avoid potential legal actions and the costs incurred, both financial and to the school and district's reputation.

Legal Incentives

School systems' failure to establish crisis prevention and preparedness plans can result in litigation (Bailey, 2006). For example, federal antidiscrimination laws include protections against bullying and harassment (U.S. Department of Education, Office for Civil Rights, 2010). Consequently, if a school, district, or state does not take all necessary actions in good faith to create safe schools, especially if the risk was obvious (i.e., an incident was foreseeable; Taylor, 2001), the school or district could be vulnerable to a negligence lawsuit (U.S. Department of Education, 2007b). Courts will be asking four main questions in a civil liability (or tort) lawsuit (Pearrow & Jacob, 2012):

1. Did injury to a person's body, rights, reputation, or property occur?
2. Did the school owe a duty in law to protect the student?

3. Was there a breach of duty, or did the school fail to do what it should have done?
4. Is there a proximate causal relationship between the injury and the breach of duty?

In other words, was the risk foreseeable, and if so, did the school act in a proper way to do all it could to ensure safety? Or was the school negligent, and did the failure to act cause injury.[1]

The financial cost of defending lawsuits (Brickman, Jones, & Groom, 2004) and the potential for negative public relations can also be very damaging. Furthermore, crisis events can disrupt an entire organization, negatively affect services, jeopardize the school's and district's reputation, and inflict long-term damage on the organization and its relationships with the community and key stakeholders (Gainey, 2010). Schools that have preventive infrastructure—that is, safety and crisis response teams and plans in place—are in a much better position to help school communities mitigate and recover from the negative effects of crises. Schools that present themselves as having and following a crisis plan not only will help to protect themselves from litigation, but also will be better able to reduce the level of chaos that occurs during an emergency, to aid in the identification of individuals in need, and to help school communities return to learning more quickly.

Legislation and Policy Directives Supporting Crisis Prevention and Preparedness

International and national policy initiatives provide additional reasons for school districts to develop comprehensive school safety and crisis preparedness programs. For instance, on the international level, documents and policies pertain to the importance of disaster risk reduction and preparedness (UN Office for Disaster Risk Reduction, 2014b). Although primarily concerned with academic progress, the Elementary and Secondary Education Act (No Child Left Behind Act) of 2001 also required local school systems that received federal funding (under Title IV, Part A, Safe and Drug-Free Schools and Communities) to have a crisis plan. Furthermore, in July 2004, President George W. Bush signed Executive Order 13347 ("Individuals with Disabilities in Emergency Preparedness"), which requires public entities to include people with disabilities in their emergency preparedness efforts (U.S. Department of Education, 2006). In addition, President Obama issued a Presidential Policy Directive (PDD 8), "National Preparedness," to define the core capabilities necessary for government entities, including schools, to prepare for the specific types of incidents that pose the greatest national security risks and to achieve an integrated and layered national preparedness approach by optimizing available resources (Obama, 2011). Table 2.1 summarizes U.S. laws that pertain to crisis preparedness efforts.

---

1 While this book was being written, a challenge to this basic standard was in process. In May 2015, lawyers filed a first-of-its-kind class-action lawsuit against the Compton Unified School District (California) in federal court. The suit alleges that school district administrators failed to address the trauma stress, generated by events occurring off school grounds, which prevented students from being ready to learn. This lawsuit includes students who had experienced or witnessed violence, and who suffered grief and loss (Almeida, 2015; Guzman-Lopez, 2015). This case raises the possibility that the standard for negligence could be changed. It could mean that schools will be required to do more than just respond to the aftermath of a school-associated crisis event. Schools could be expected to provide interventions for those exposed to trauma outside of the school setting and even before they enrolled in the school district's school.

Table 2.1. A Summary of Laws in the United States Pertinent to School Crisis Preparedness

U.S. Constitution

Statutes and regulations enacted by federal and state government, including boards of education, are subject to the provisions of the Constitution (Russo, 2006).

1st Amendment	Although schoolchildren are not afforded the full range of freedoms guaranteed citizens under the Constitution, the courts have acknowledged the rights of students to free speech and assembly as long as the exercise of those rights does not significantly interfere with or disrupt schooling (*Tinker v. Des Moines Independent Community School District*, 1969).
4th Amendment	Students have a right to be free from unreasonable search and seizure in the schools. However, courts have allowed a more lenient standard of "reasonable suspicion" rather than "probable cause" for searches conducted by school personnel, and the search must not be "excessively intrusive" in light of the age of the pupil and the suspected violation of school rules (*New Jersey v. T.L.O*, 1985).
10th Amendment	State governments, rather than the federal government, have the authority to educate children and the duty to do so.
14th Amendment: Equal Protection Clause	Education is a state-created property right protected by the 14th amendment (*Goss v. Lopez*, 1975). The 14th Amendment Equal Protection Clause was the basis for federal civil rights (antidiscrimination) legislation. The Equal Protection Clause provides that no state shall "deny any person within its jurisdiction the equal protection of the laws."
14th Amendment: Substantive Due Process and Procedural Due Process	The mission of public schools is to educate children, maintain order, and ensure pupil safety (*Burnside v. Byars*, 1966). School rules restricting students' rights must be reasonably related to the purpose of schooling (*Tinker v. Des Moines Independent Community School District*, 1969). Procedural due process means that a state may not take away a liberty or property interest without some sort of procedural fairness to safeguard against wrongful infringement of a citizen's rights by state government. Schools may not suspend or expel students without due process. Due process also protects students from unwarranted stigmatization by the school that may interfere with the student's liberty or property interests. Schools may not assign a stigmatizing label to a student (e.g., emotionally disturbed) without notice, fair decision-making procedures, and the right to protest the classification.

Elementary and Secondary Education Act of 1965 (ESEA)

ESEA was the first major federal legislation to aid education. ESEA has been reauthorized and amended many times since 1965. Some of its progeny include the following.

Family Educational Rights and Privacy Act of 1974 (FERPA)	No federal funds will be available to schools unless they adhere to the student education record-keeping procedures outlined in the law. FERPA was passed to ensure parent access to the education records of their own children and to safeguard the confidentiality of student education records.
Protection of Pupil Privacy Act of 1978, amended in 1994 and 2001 (PPRA)	Schools that receive any federal funds must notify parents prior to distributing a survey that requests one of eight types of private information (including psychological problems) from students, and parents must be given the opportunity to have their child opt out of survey participation.
No Child Left Behind Act of 2001 (NCLB)	The act requires states receiving funds under ESEA to identify "persistently dangerous schools" and to allow students attending those schools to transfer to "safe" schools.
Gun Free Schools Act of 1994	The act requires schools that receive funds under ESEA to expel, for a period of not less than 1 year, any student who brings a weapon to school. However, the state must allow a chief school administrator to modify the expulsion on a case-by-case basis, and states may allow students expelled from their regular school to receive an education in an alternative setting. It also requires that incidents of students bringing weapons to school be reported to the juvenile justice system or criminal justice system.
Safe and Drug-Free Schools and Communities Act of 2001	Title IV, Part A, of No Child Left Behind develops proposed policies and makes federal funding available for school drug and violence prevention efforts. See http://www2.ed.gov/about/offices/list/osdfs/programs.html
Paul D. Coverdell Teacher Protection Act of 2001	As a condition for accepting ESEA monies, the act states that no punitive damages may be awarded against a school professional for harm caused by an act or omission if the school professional was acting on behalf of the school, within the scope of his or her authority, and in furtherance of efforts to maintain order in the school, and if the actions were carried out in conformity with federal, state, and local laws, unless clear and convincing evidence shows that the harm was proximately caused by willful or criminal misconduct on the part of the school professional or a conscious, flagrant indifference to the rights or safety of the individual harmed.

Table 2.1. Continued

U.S. Constitution	
Individuals with Disabilities Education Improvement Act of 2004 (IDEIA)	The 2004 IDEA Reauthorization allocates funds to states that offer a free appropriate individualized education program for all children with disabilities as defined by the law. IDEA outlines extensive procedural requirements that schools must follow when a disciplinary removal of a student with a disability from his or her educational placement is under consideration.
Federal Civil Rights (Antidiscrimination) Legislation	
Title VI of the Civil Rights Act of 1964, Title IX of the Education Amendments of 1972, Title II of the Americans with Disabilities Act of 1990	The legislation protects students from harassment based on race, color, national origin, sex, or disability. These laws make schools that receive any federal funds responsible for taking reasonable steps to remedy harassment when it is sufficiently severe, pervasive, or persistent so as to interfere with or limit the ability of an individual to participate in or benefit from the district's programs or activities.
Section 1983 of the Civil Rights Act of 1871	Under Section 1983 any person whose constitutional rights (or rights under federal law) have been violated by a government official may sue for damages in federal court, and the official may be held liable for the actual damages.

Note. The U.S. Department of Education website has links to statutes and regulations pertinent to education (www. ed.gov). Adapted from *Legal and Ethical Considerations in Crisis Prevention and Response in Schools* (pp. 361–363), by M. M. Pearrow & S. Jacob, 2012, Bethesda, MD: National Association of School Psychologists. Copyright 2012 by National Association of School Psychologists. Reprinted with permission.

Whereas NCLB sets the stage for the importance of schools being ready to address crises, the reauthorization of this Act, now called Every Student Succeeds Act (ESSA, 2015), continues this mandate with a focus on safety. The ESSA emphasizes that schools should improve school climate, safety, and access to high quality comprehensive learning supports. Districts must use at least 20% of Title IV Part A funds for at least one activity to improve student mental health and behavioral health, school climate or school safety and federal funds may be used to implement trauma informed practices and mental health first aid. Funding streams can also be used to implement positive behavioral interventions and supports or other activities to address skills such as social emotional learning, conflict resolution, effective problem solving, and appropriate relationship building. In addition, safety and crisis plans must comply with federal regulations as ESSA requires states to articulate how they will assist local education agency efforts to address bullying, harassment, and discipline. In addition, ESSA requires that states annually report school climate, bullying, and harassment data that, at a minimum, is contained in the Civil Rights Data Collection (K. Vaillancourt Strobach & K. Eklund, personal communication, December 17, 2015).

In addition to federal legislation in the United States, local and state laws and regulations will also guide a school district's prevention and preparedness efforts (National Education Association, 2007).

Following the high-profile school shootings during the 2012–2013 school year, numerous states passed laws requiring prevention programming, yearly crisis response training, regular practice of safety drills, and/or submission and practice of building- or district-level crisis plans. According to the School Health Policies and Practices Study (Centers for Disease Control and Prevention, 2013b), 96% of districts had a comprehensive plan to address crisis preparedness, response, and recovery, and 83% of states had used materials from the U.S. Department of Education (e.g., *Practical Information on Crisis Planning: A Guide for Schools and Communities*, 2007b) to develop policies related to crisis preparedness, response, and recovery. However, many federal and state laws lack specific guidelines or definitions, which results in great variability in how the laws are interpreted and subsequently implemented. During the 2 years before the study, more than 80% of states had developed, revised, or assisted in the development and distribution of model policies, policy guidance, or other materials for districts or schools on crisis preparedness, response, and recovery; electronic aggression or cyberbullying; and other bullying prevention. Over 80% of states also reported providing professional development funds for these initiatives (Centers for Disease Control and Prevention, 2013b). Although progress has been made, a continued focus on safety efforts is needed to ensure that schools are prepared for a variety of potential crisis situations.

Federal Education Rights and Privacy Act (FERPA) of 1974

FERPA is a federal law that protects the privacy of students' education records and applies to an educational agency or institution that receives funds from any U.S. Department of Education program (U.S. Department of Education, 2013). It has particular relevance to those crisis prevention activities that involve disclosing otherwise private information about a student who might be considered a danger to self or others. Table 2.2 shows what records are and are not considered educational records. Only school officials with "legitimate educational interest" may access FERPA-protected educational records. Teachers, counselors, school administrators, and other school staff are generally included in this definition. However, contractors, consultants, volunteers, and other parties may be included if they perform a service or function for which the agency or institution would otherwise use employees, if they are under direct control of the agency in regard to use and maintenance of educational records, and if they are using the educational records for the purpose of disclosure outlined under FERPA. For example, an employee who is not a school official, such as a school resource officer (SRO), security officer, or nurse, could be a member of the threat assessment team as long as he or she meets the guidelines outlined above. Also, if a teacher overhears a student making remarks that could potentially cause self-harm or harm others, that teacher can share the information with appropriate authorities, including the parents of the threatened students, because that information is not considered protected under FERPA.

In addition, FERPA allows schools to disclose otherwise confidential student records to "appropriate parties" (these typically include law enforcement officials, first responders, public health officials, trained medical personnel, and parents) without parental consent when there is an "actual, impending, or imminent emergency, such as articulable and significant threat. Information may be disclosed only to protect the health or safety of students or other individuals" (U.S. Department of Education, 2013, p. 42). Schools determine what constitutes a safety or health emergency and the

Table 2.2. FERPA Definition of Education Records

Education Records	Not Education Records
Transcripts	Records that are kept in the sole possession of the maker and used only as personal memory aids
Disciplinary records	Law enforcement unit records
Standardized test results	Grades on peer-graded papers before they are collected and recorded by teacher
Health (including mental health) and family history records	Records that are created or received by a school after an individual is no longer in attendance and that are not directly related to the individual's attendance at the school
Records on services provided to students under the Individuals with Disabilities Education Act (IDEA)	Employee records that relate exclusively to an individual in that individual's capacity as an employee
Records on services and accommodations provided to students under Section 504 of the Rehabilitation Act of 1973 and Title II of the ADA	Information obtained through a school official's personal knowledge or observation and not from the student's education records

Note. From *Guide for Developing High-Quality School Emergency Operations Plans* (p. 40), by U.S. Department of Education, 2013, Washington, DC: Author. This document is in the public domain. Retrieved from http://rems.ed.gov/EOPGuides

FERPA exception is "temporarily limited to the period of the emergency and does not allow for a blanket release of PII (Personally Identifiable Information)" (p. 42). When information is disclosed, the reason for the disclosure and to whom the information was released must be documented in the student's educational records. Additional guidelines, including those involving law enforcement records and frequently asked questions, can be found in the U.S. Department of Education's (2013) *Guide for Developing High-Quality School Emergency Operations Plans*.

HIPAA

In the United States, the Health Insurance Portability and Accountability Act, commonly known as the HIPAA Privacy Rule, protects individually identifiable health information (called protected health information). If a school provides healthcare to students in the normal course of business through a health clinic, then the school is considered a healthcare provider under HIPAA. However, even schools that are HIPAA-covered entities are not required to comply with the HIPAA Privacy Rule if the only health records maintained by the school are education records or treatment records of eligible students under FERPA. Thus, student health information maintained at a school is typically considered to be education records, and it falls under FERPA guidelines. More in-depth guidance regarding health records can be found in the document titled *Joint Guidance on the Application of the Family Educational Rights and Privacy Act (FERPA) and the Health Insurance Portability and Accountability Act of 1996 (HIPAA) to Student Health Records* (U.S. Department of Health and Human Services & U.S. Department of Education, 2008). As with FERPA, the HIPAA Privacy Rule permits a covered entity to disclose protected health information when there is "good faith belief that the disclosure: (1) is necessary to prevent or lessen a serious and imminent threat to the health or safety of the patient or others and (2) is to a person(s) reasonably able to prevent or lessen the threat" (U.S. Department of Health and Human Services & U.S. Department of Education, 2008. p. 9). For example, if an outbreak of a contagious illness occurred within a school, that information can be released in order to minimize further contagion.

SCHOOL MODELS

A broad range of school safety and crisis response models have been put forth over the years. However, current school crisis or emergency preparedness models that are particularly relevant for educators include the U.S. Department of Education's (2013) five mission areas, the M-PHAT model (Reeves, Kanan, & Plog, 2010), and the PREP_aRE model (Brock, 2011a; Brock et al., 2009; Reeves et al., 2011a).

U.S. Department of Education

In 2007, the U.S. Department of Education released a document titled *Practical Information on Crisis Planning: A Guide for Schools and Communities.* This document reviewed four phases of emergency management: prevention, preparedness, response, and recovery. In 2013, a new document was released titled *Guide for Developing High-Quality School Emergency Operations Plans* (U.S. Department of Education, 2013). Informed by Presidential Policy Directive/PPD-8, a shift occurred, and preparedness became the conceptual umbrella that now encompasses five missions: prevention, protection, mitigation, response, and recovery, which have been integrated into the PREP_aRE model (see Figure 2.1 and Table 2.3). Schools are also encouraged (in some locations required) to use the National Incident Management System's Incident Command System (U.S. Department of Homeland Security, 2013b), which provides a standardized approach to incident management (see Chapter 7).

M-PHAT Model

Developed by the lead author of PREP_aRE Workshop 1 (Crisis Prevention and Preparedness), the M-PHAT model (multiphase, multihazard, multiagency, and multitiered; Reeves et al., 2010) has also been an important guiding force for the PREP_aRE model. The M-PHAT model broadened school safety and crisis response planning to include a greater emphasis on comprehensive planning that balances both physical safety and psychological safety, rather than approaching them as separate priorities (Figure 2.2, Table 2.4).

Figure 2.1. Five Preparedness Mission Areas of Crisis Management

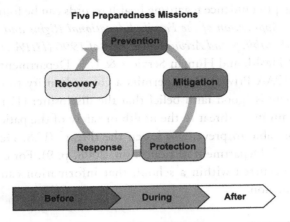

Note. From *Five Preparedness Missions,* by Colorado School Safety Resources Center, 2015, Denver, CO: Colorado Department of Public Safety. This document is in the public domain. Retrieved from https://www.colorado.gov/pacific/cssrc/5-preparedness-missions

Table 2.3. U.S. Department of Education's Five Emergency Management Mission Areas

Mission Area	Focus and Goal
Prevention	Prevention is the action schools take to prevent a threatened or actual incident from occurring; includes necessary actions to avoid, deter, or stop an imminent crime or threatened or actual mass casualty incident.
Protection	Protection focuses on ongoing actions that protect students, teachers, staff, visitors, networks, and property from a threat or hazard; includes actions to secure schools against acts of violence and human-caused or natural disasters.
Mitigation	Mitigation is reducing the likelihood that threats and hazards will happen; includes actions necessary to eliminate or reduce the loss of life and property damage by lessening the impact of an event or emergency.
Response	Response is the actions necessary to stabilize an emergency once it has already happened or is certain to happen in an unpreventable way; establish a safe and secure environment; save lives and property; and facilitate the transition to recovery.
Recovery	Recovery is the activities necessary to assist schools affected by an event or emergency in restoring the learning environment.

Note. Adapted from *Guide for Developing High-Quality School Emergency Operations Plans* (p. 2), by U.S. Department of Education, 2013, Washington, DC: Author. This document is in the public domain. Retrieved from http://rems.ed.gov/EOPGuides

Figure 2.2. The M-PHAT Approach to Comprehensive Planning for Safe Learning Environments

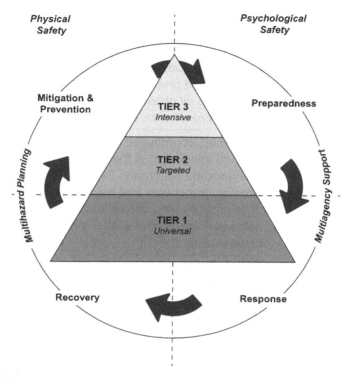

Note. From *Comprehensive Planning for Safe Learning Environments. A School Professional's Guide to Integrating Physical and Psychological Safety: Prevention Through Recovery*, p. 32, by M. Reeves, L. Kanan, & L. Plog, 2010, New York, NY: Routledge. Copyright 2010 by Routledge Publishing. Reprinted with permission

The PREPaRE Model

The PREPaRE model has been influenced by both the U.S. Department of Education's five preparedness missions and the M-PHAT model for comprehensive planning for crisis prevention and preparedness. However, PREPaRE specifically advocates additional goals, including that all school districts and schools have comprehensive safety and crisis response teams and plans that do the following:

- Focus on prevention efforts, initiatives, and programming.
- Incorporate all five mission areas of crisis preparedness.
- Take an "all hazards" approach to address likely events.
- Encompass both physical and psychological safety efforts.
- Are developed collaboratively with community-based partners.
- Are based on data and information.
- Are practiced on a regular basis.
- Are continually reviewed and updated.

Table 2.4. Comprehensive Planning for Safe Learning Environments: The M-PHAT Approach

	Focus and Goal
Multi-Phase	Includes all four phases of the U.S. Department of Education's original model (prevention/mitigation, preparedness, response, and recovery) and encompasses overall preparedness. Multiphase thinking ensures that the plan addresses all phases of a potential crisis. Each phase has established policies, procedures, and programming.
Multi-Hazard	Refers to the universal, coordinated approach to dealing with any and all emergencies and integration of the National Incident Management System's (NIMS) Incident Command System. The approach involves developing common procedures that respond to a variety of potential hazards, such as crisis events, natural disasters, and infectious diseases. Multihazard risk and vulnerability assessments are conducted first to assess for potential hazards.
Multi-Agency	Involves collaboration with first responders and community agencies that can help provide services. Collaboration with agencies such as police, fire, rescue, medical, local Federal Emergency Management Agency staff, social services and child protection and welfare, human services, and mental health agencies is critical, because they may serve as first responders or provide services in the recovery phase.
Multi-Tiered	Uses the premise of a multitiered service delivery system: that students have different strengths and needs and that interventions are provided on a continuum based on need. It provides for the educational and psychological needs of students (psychological safety) while balancing physical safety to support a safe and caring learning environment.

- Use the National Incident Management System's (NIMS) Incident Command System.
- Provide multitiered crisis interventions based on demonstrated need (not a one-size-fits-all approach to response).
- Are tailored to the needs of individual schools (Brock, 2011a; Brock et al., 2009; Reeves, Nickerson, & Jimerson, 2006a; Reeves et al., 2011a).

The PREPaRE model is shown in Figure P.1, and the elements are discussed in detail in this book.

OBSTACLES TO CRISIS PREPAREDNESS

Among the many potential obstacles to school crisis prevention and crisis preparedness are denial, a lack of resources, inadequate plans, territorial issues, insufficient use of school-employed mental health professionals' expertise, and misguided priorities. The belief that "it won't happen here" is still prevalent in many schools and, consequently, many schools wait until a crisis has occurred before they think about school safety and crisis preparedness planning (Brock et al., 2001).

Limited Resources

Limited resources, such as time for planning, training professionals, and securing funding, are ongoing challenges (Bischof, 2007; Gurdineer, 2013; Nickerson & Zhe, 2004). Financial constraints are prevalent in today's schools as federal and state funding for planning becomes less available. Furthermore, because of the recent focus on schools' academic achievement and associated consequences of not demonstrating academic growth (e.g., those generated by the No Child Left Behind Act and current emphasis on the Common Core State Standards), administrators have to make difficult monetary decisions. Often school safety initiatives and crisis preparedness efforts take a back seat to academic initiatives, even though safety initiatives are an essential element of quality academic programming and achievement. The amount of monetary resources devoted to school crisis prevention and preparedness is a significant predictor of a plan's quality (Gurdineer, 2013).

Inadequate Plans

Many plans are not (a) comprehensive; (b) practiced regularly; (c) coordinated with community-based emergency response agencies; (d) discussed with families, staff, and students; (e) attentive to the unique considerations of students with special needs; (f) based on factual data and circumstances; or (g) regularly updated and used (Burling & Hyle, 1997; Graham, Shirm, Liggin, Aitken, & Dick, 2006; Kano & Bourke, 2007; Phinney, 2004; Trump, 2000). Recent studies have demonstrated that many crisis plans still lack the elements necessary for achieving crisis prevention, intervention, and postvention objectives (Gurdineer, 2013). Themes for improvement identified by Tucker (2013) include the need to (a) prepare for more complete and effective communication, both during and following an emergency; (b) provide additional safety training; (c) have a plan to account for every child prior to releasing the child to an approved caregiver (i.e., a reunification plan); (d) consider plans that allow students to use cell phones; and (e) train and assemble a parent advisory team to help with emergency responses.

Territorial Issues

Territorial conflicts, or turf issues, include disagreement regarding who initiates and leads crisis prevention and preparedness efforts, who pays for needed training and supplies and long-term support services, and who is the incident commander when multiple agencies are involved. These considerations emphasize the importance of schools collaborating with key stakeholders, such as school boards, administrators, and other community-based emergency response agencies and personnel.

To make plans more collaborative and avoid competition, school boards and educational leaders need to take a leadership role in crisis planning through crisis recovery steps using school safety and crisis response teams. An example of such leadership is provided by the Virginia Department of Education, which advocates that school boards establish a policy and framework that convey the seriousness of school crisis prevention and preparedness (Black, 2004; Virginia Board of Education, 1999). Such guidance should reflect the various aspects of crisis prevention and preparedness, from designing, updating, and implementing school prevention efforts and preparedness plans, to rehearsing drills and integrating crisis roles and responsibilities into job descriptions.

Insufficient Use of School-Employed Mental Health Professionals' Expertise

School administrators and key decision makers need to better understand the expertise that school psychologists, counselors, social workers, and nurses can lend to comprehensive safety initiatives and crisis preparedness efforts. Optimal school safety planning and response should include school-employed mental health professionals serving on the multidisciplinary safety and crisis response teams, thus using their expertise for prevention and planning, not just response. School-employed mental health professionals should be prepared to work together to deliver universal prevention programs and mental health interventions that can prevent students from engaging in acts of aggression or violence. These professionals can take a leadership role at the school, district, state, and national levels to help develop policies and guidelines that advocate the implementation of comprehensive safety plans, with resource allocations dedicated to these efforts.

MISGUIDED PRIORITIES

In what appeared to have been a reaction to the tragedy at Sandy Hook Elementary School, one school district in Minnesota invested close to $25,000 in bulletproof white boards for students. This decision was criticized by many who argued these dollars would have been better spent on school resource officers, school-employed mental health professionals, prevention and intervention programs, radios, and cameras. Ken Trump, a school safety expert, encourages schools to "Focus on fundamentals and get back to the basics. There is a security product for every possible need that your budget will buy. The question is, is that the best use of limited resources?" (Holloran, 2013). This sentiment has been echoed by many school security experts who feel that schools have knee-jerk reactions when faced with savvy salespeople and don't think thoroughly about their decisions.

Before schools plan to invest in any school safety or crisis preparedness resource, PREPaRE recommends that they first conduct needs and vulnerability assessments for both physical and psychological safety. These data help direct a school safety committee to thoroughly discuss the investment of limited resources and help them avoid impulsive decision making. For example, even though experts know the odds of a K–12 student being killed at his or her school are 1 in 4.5 million (Brock, 2015a), some schools have engaged in elaborate drills to defend against active shooter incidents while ignoring other important school safety efforts, such as providing medical first aid training.

If school safety efforts are to have any long-term effects, they must be integrated with general school improvements and interventions that teach students skills that will help them cope with social issues that may arise in their lives (Morrison, Furlong, & Morrison, 1994). Schools also need to invest in prevention and intervention programming to meet the academic, social, and emotional needs of students (Osher, Dwyer, Jimerson, & Brown, 2012). These investments are more cost-effective than reactive physical security measures that run the risk of turning schools into fortresses and ignoring the mental health issues that may underlie violent acts.

CONCLUSION

Crisis preparedness efforts may at first appear overwhelming to school administrators and leaders when they consider all that is involved. To make these activities more manageable, schools can develop multidisciplinary school safety and crisis response teams and plans that (a) focus on overall school climate, (b) integrate safety initiatives with academic and social–emotional programming, and (c) prepare schools to respond in the event of a crisis to facilitate recovery. This work can feel overwhelming at first. Thus, a successful approach is for schools to use their needs assessment data to establish two or three short- and long-term goals for improving the school's and district's plan. Once those goals are met, teams can continue to identify additional goals. In other words, start small and take successive steps toward the goal of comprehensive school safety and crisis response readiness.

Chapter 3

SCHOOL CRISIS: ENSURING PHYSICAL SAFETY

School safety and crisis preparedness plans cannot use a one-size-fits-all approach. Consequently, no two school or district plans will look exactly alike. Each school should assess its unique needs and develop comprehensive and systematic approaches to crisis preparedness that address both physical safety and psychological safety, as described in the following excerpt from the National Association of School Psychologists (2013b):

> Effective school safety efforts should utilize evidence-based practices to ensure the well-being of all students as well as their physical safety. Reasonable building security measures, such as secure doors, lighted and monitored hallways, and check in–check out systems for visitors, are important. Although there have been calls to increase the presence of armed guards at schools, the research regarding schools that utilize armed security generally demonstrates nonsignificant impacts on reducing violence while at the same time resulting in students feeling less safe. Students' perception of safety is not a trivial consideration given that simply feeling unsafe impedes learning and the ability to develop a nurturing, supportive, and welcoming school environment. An overemphasis on extreme physical security measures alone, such as increasing armed security and/or arming school staff, will not improve school safety, and in fact may undermine the primary mission of schools to ensure learning while safeguarding our children. (p. 3)

This chapter begins by discussing the assessment of both physical safety and psychological safety. However, the chapter focuses foremost on ensuring the physical safety of children at school, consistent with the guidelines provided by the U.S. Department of Education (2013) and the United Nations International Strategy for Disaster Reduction (2014).

SAFETY ASSESSMENTS

Reeves et al. (2011a) developed one of the first vulnerability assessments that assessed both physical safety and psychological safety, which has been made part of PREPaRE Workshop 1. In addition, the U.S. Department of Homeland Security's (2013c, April) *K–12 School Security Checklist* is available in the public domain to help schools assess school safety. The U.S. Department of Education (2013) supports four main types of assessment to help secure physical and psychological safety: site assessment, culture and climate assessment, school threat assessment, and capacity assessment. Table 3.1 summarizes these four types of assessment.

When conducting these assessments, schools and districts should focus on mitigation, that is, on proactive measures taken to reduce or eliminate potential hazards and threats. For example, at the school level, a vulnerability assessment would examine the school building (e.g., window seals, HVAC systems, building structure) and security systems (e.g., locks, controlled access), assess the school's culture and climate (e.g., school climate and early detection of potentially dangerous behaviors), and evaluate its ability to conduct threat assessments (e.g., school personnel are trained to conduct threat assessments; Rhode Island Emergency Management Agency, 2013).

Effective planning relies on analysis of possible threats, hazards, and vulnerabilities (U.S. Department of Education, 2013). The U.S. Department of Homeland Security (2013d, September) refers to the following four-step process as THIRA (threat and hazard identification and risk assessment): (a) identify the threats and hazards of concern, (b) put the threats and hazards into context, (c) establish capability targets, and (d) apply the results. This process must include identification of both physical and psychological threats and hazards (Reeves et al., 2011a) by a team that includes both school and community agencies with expertise in conducting risk assessments. Community agencies to involve in the process might include emergency management offices, fire and police departments, American Red Cross, and emergency management teams at the local, state, and federal levels (U.S. Department of Education, 2013). School-employed and community-based mental health professionals should also be involved. Table 3.2 briefly summarizes the four-step THIRA process. More details on these important elements of school safety and crisis response preparedness are in the U.S. Department of Homeland Security's *Threat and Hazard Identification and Risk Assessment Guide* (2013d, September).

The plan should focus on threats that are of plausible concern (versus every possible crisis scenario) and would have a significant impact (U.S. Department of Homeland Security, 2013d, September). As discussed in Chapter 2, all possible crisis events are not probable events. Focusing on the more probable threats to school safety uses limited resources more efficiently. For example, the odds of a school-associated violent death are very low (Brock, 2015a), so devoting all resources to such a crisis event and ignoring other more common physical safety concerns, such as weather related emergencies, would be inappropriate.

Finally, for school-based professionals in developing countries, the United Nations Office for Disaster Risk Reduction (2014a) offers an assessment tool for local government agencies that includes the core indicators of the five action priorities of the Hyogo Framework for Action. Such assessments may be valuable for school psychologists and other leaders to obtain information regarding the infrastructure necessary to support disaster prevention and preparedness. The United

Table 3.1. Four Primary Types of Risk and Vulnerability Assessments

Type of Assessment	Description	Goals
Site assessment (see crime prevention through environmental design later in the chapter)	Examine safety, accessibility, and emergency preparedness of school buildings and grounds (e.g., access control, visibility, structural integrity, compliance with architectural standards for individuals with disabilities, emergency vehicle access).	• Identify and understand the impact of risk, threats, and hazards in school buildings and on school grounds. • Ensure that facilities are physically accessible to all, including those with disabilities and emergency response personnel.
Culture and climate assessment (see Chapter 4)	Examine student and staff perceptions of school safety and students' school connectedness.	• Obtain data regarding student and staff perceptions of safety and data on problem behaviors to address to improve school climate. • Increase likelihood that students will report concerns.
School threat assessment (see Chapter 4)	Analyze communication and behaviors to determine if a student, staff member, or other person poses a threat; develop a threat assessment team.	• Identify individuals that may pose a threat and, as appropriate, refer for supports and services.
Capacity assessment (see Table 3.2)	Identify available equipment, supplies, and personnel resources available. Examine capabilities and skill level of students, staff, and community partners to execute crisis response and recovery protocols.	• Increase knowledge of resources available. • Identify staff capabilities, and assign roles and responsibilities.

Note. Adapted from *Guide for Developing High-Quality School Emergency Operations Plans,* by the U.S. Department of Education, 2013, Washington, DC. This document is in the public domain.

Nations International Strategy for Disaster Reduction (UNISDR) also includes resources for schools to enhance their disaster prevention and preparedness (United Nations Disaster Assessment and Coordination, 2013). UNISDR emphasizes that schools can effectively reduce disaster risks by planning for mitigation and implementing these plans (UNISDR, 2014). Furthermore, UNISDR highlights that an important first step in planning is to complete appropriate assessments to identify needs and inform decision making.

Table 3.2. Four-Step Process for Completing a Threat and Hazard Identification and Risk Assessment (THIRA)

Step	Definition	Examples
Identify the threats and hazards of concern.	Identify a list of primary threats and hazards (consider *plausible* concerns that would have a significant impact).	*Natural hazards* include weather, pandemic. *Technological* threats include dam failure, hazardous materials or radiological release, power failure. *Human caused* threats include cyberattack; biological, chemical, or explosives attack; school violence.
Place the threats and hazards in context.	Describe the concerns and consider how they may affect the community.	*Time*: How would incident timing affect the ability to manage it? *Place:* How would location and population affect management? *Conditions:* How might atmospheric conditions (wind speed and direction) or multiple events at one time affect management?
Establish capability targets.	Assess each threat and hazard in context and define the crisis response elements and desired outcomes.	*Context description:* Describe how impact may affect the response, such as size of geographic region affected; number of people; possible fatalities, injuries, illnesses; disruption to critical infrastructure; economic impact; disruption to delivery of services. *Capability target:* Identify what actions or abilities are needed to mitigate and recover from the crisis.
Apply the results.	Estimate resources to achieve capability targets identified in step 3.	Consider school and district resources, community assets, and mutual aid; strategic, operational, and tactical plans; existing capacity. (Preparedness and mitigation activities are critical to this step to ensure readiness.)

Note. Adapted from *Threat and Hazard Identification and Risk Assessment Guide* (2nd ed.), by the U.S. Department of Homeland Security, 2013c, September, Washington, DC. This document is in the public domain.

PREVENTION ELEMENTS OF A CRISIS PLAN

Increasing evidence suggests that most behavior problems that result in suspension and expulsion can be prevented through proactive procedures (Metzler, Biglan, Rusby, & Sprague, 2001; Sprague et al., 2001). The Interdisciplinary Group on Preventing School and Community Violence (2013) has advocated comprehensive and coordinated efforts to prevent school crises (e.g., school violence). Such efforts should use a balanced approach that attends to physical safety; educational practices; and social, emotional, and behavioral well-being (i.e., psychological safety, discussed in Chapter 4).

Crime Prevention Through Environmental Design

Crime prevention through environmental design (CPTED) is an architectural design approach that looks at the physical environment of a building or school and evaluates what elements can be manipulated to produce behavioral effects that reduce incidents and fear of crime. The model has been used worldwide for controlling crime. CPTED originally included three principles important to the physical safety of a school: (a) natural surveillance, (b) natural access control, and (c) territoriality (Jeffery, 1971; Sprague & Walker, 2005). Recently, the U.S. Department of Education (2013) has begun to reference a fourth principle, identified as management and maintenance, to ensure that all school buildings are properly maintained and functioning as intended, and that the exterior of the building, including landscaping, is kept up.

Natural Surveillance

Natural surveillance refers to the arrangement of physical features to maximize visibility (U.S. Department of Education, 2013). Elements of natural surveillance are classified as organized (e.g., teachers monitoring the hallways during passing period), mechanical (e.g., cameras), and natural (e.g., glass windows; Crowe, 2000). Insufficient supervision is associated with violence and bullying (Meraviglia, Becker, Rosenbluth, Sanchez, & Robertson, 2003), and increasing adult supervision on playgrounds and in hallways reduces bullying (Boulton, 1994; DeVoe, Peter, Noonan, Snyder, & Baum, 2005). Other possibilities for increasing surveillance include using two-way communication between all staff members and the front office and employing school resource officers (Sprague & Walker, 2005). Encouraging statistics show that more than three fourths of school districts have adopted a policy requiring the use of communication devices (two-way radios, cell phones, walkie-talkies, intercoms) for security purposes, and two thirds of districts have adopted policies requiring adults to monitor halls between classes and also monitor school grounds (Centers for Disease Control and Prevention, 2013b).

Natural Access Control

Natural access control focuses on strategies to control who and what enters and exits the school. Natural access control strategies are classified as organized (e.g., security guards, hall monitors), mechanical (e.g., door locks), or natural (e.g., how the environment is built to deny access into and out of an area, such as barricades at certain parking lot exits during arrival and dismissal to direct traffic flow). Natural access control and natural surveillance work together and offer mutual supports (Crowe, 2000). Schools should guide visitors with clearly marked signs and entrances and should have one point of entry that is monitored by a person or is locked. All other doors to the building should be kept locked from the outside (while still allowing for unrestricted exits). Other strategies to control access include establishing a visitor screening policy and requiring employee and student identification badges. More than 80% of districts require identification badges for visitors (Centers for Disease Control and Prevention, 2013b), and approximately 50% require staff to wear identification badges (Gray & Lewis, 2015). Visitor screening procedures help schools monitor who is gaining access into the building and whether specific individuals should not have access to the building. Controlling roof access and installing surveillance cameras to deter intruders from entering the building can also promote physical safety. Limiting access to certain areas of the school (e.g., classrooms, teachers' rooms) by using real or symbolic barriers (e.g., flower beds, low decorative fences, signs) have also been suggested to promote safety (Sprague & Walker, 2005; U.S. Department of Education, 2013).

Although a potential element of natural access control, the use of metal detectors has been adopted by less than 10% of school districts (Centers for Disease Control and Prevention, 2013b). However, their effectiveness has not been shown (Bracy, 2011; Hankin, Hertz, & Simon, 2011; Kitsantas, Ware, & Martinez-Arias, 2004), and their use has been associated with increased student perceptions of fear (even after controlling for the level of school violence; Gastic, 2011). The National Association of School Psychologists (2013c) has cautioned against overemphasizing extreme natural access control measures (including the universal use of armed security in schools) because they "may undermine the learning environment while not necessarily safeguarding students" (p. 1).

Territoriality

Territoriality, or a reinforced sense of shared ownership and pride, helps students and staff members feel more empowered to challenge inappropriate school behavior when it occurs (Schneider, Walker, & Sprague, 2000). It also creates a welcoming environment. For example, groups of students could be assigned to different areas to paint, decorate, or clean up to help ensure a sense of ownership and pride in the school (Hill & Hill, 1994). Schools also could establish clear policies and an open climate so that students and others who identify a problem or potential threat feel comfortable sharing this information (Interdisciplinary Group on Preventing School and Community Violence, 2013; Schneider et al., 2000). A comprehensive study of school shootings indicated that most of the perpetrators had a specific plan for the attacks and that other people were aware of that plan (Vossekuil, Fein, Reddy, Borum, & Modzeleski, 2002). Despite these findings, only 48% of schools reported training their teachers and classroom aides how to recognize the early warning signs of student violence (Gray & Lewis, 2015).

Schools need to be deliberate about developing the capacity to identify potential threats. Having a confidential phone line, ability to send confidential text messages, or other options for anonymous reporting would allow students and parents to anonymously contact school personnel about bullying or safety concerns (Olweus, 1993). One school district has a prominent "Safety Concern" button on its seven high schools' websites to encourage the reporting of threats, bullying, potential fights, and all general safety concerns. The information is then sent directly to a dean or administrator. Students and teachers could also use incident reports to document threats, including those on smart phones and social media (Suckling & Temple, 2002). That information could be used to initiate a more formal threat assessment. Dr. Marissa Randazzo, a national expert on threat assessment and targeted violence, testified at length to the Sandy Hook Advisory Commission (2015) on the composition, workings, and goals of threat assessment teams, which gather information from multiple sources in response to indications that a student, colleague, or other person's behavior has raised alarms. The report states: "These teams should receive training in threat assessment that will enable them to review specific threats and help manage or support any person who issues a threat as well as warning the potential victims" (p. 195).

Collaboration With Community-Based Emergency Response Agencies

School, district, and community-level teams can work collaboratively if roles are clearly defined and teams are functionally organized (Crepeau-Hobson, Sievering, Armstrong, & Stonis, 2012). However, only 56% of U.S. school districts report engaging in collaborative crisis preparedness, response, and recovery efforts with community agencies, and even fewer school districts (35%) have made arrangements with mental health, social services, or other organizations to provide counseling in the aftermath of a crisis (Centers for Disease Control and Prevention 2013b).

Schools and emergency first responder agencies (e.g., police, fire, rescue) tend to have different approaches to decision making. Schools focus on a collaborative approach with an emphasis on the process of decision making, which often involves setting aside time to share ideas and weigh many options before reaching a consensus. Community police, fire, and rescue departments, by comparison, have to make very quick, often lifesaving decisions. This role necessitates a clear, hierarchical approach to decision making that focuses on the immediate outcome. For collaboration to succeed, these differences must be acknowledged, respected, and worked through before a crisis.

The *United Nations Disaster Assessment and Coordination Handbook* (UNDAC, 2013) describes the international infrastructure needed for coordinating prevention and preparedness plans and crisis response efforts. Similarly, agreements and infrastructure that are coordinated across schools, community agencies, and local, state, and federal government agencies are essential to optimize prevention, protection, mitigation, response, and recovery efforts. The International School Psychology Association (ISPA) is an emerging resource for international school crisis response. ISPA's Crisis Response Network is designed to

> organize an international crisis response network enabling school psychologists to obtain information and materials as they respond to violent and traumatic situations; to serve as a means of supporting colleagues who might need to discuss or share their experiences about working in such situations; to establish regional resource groups to communicate by phone or even to go to a specific location if this is feasible; to provide a forum as well as a means where children could share their experiences of having been in such situations with other adults and youngsters. (http://www.ispaweb.org/committees/international-crisis-response-network/)

Collaboration With Law Enforcement Agencies

Collaborating with law enforcement is critical for schools and districts, both in the prevention and crisis preparedness phases and in the aftermath of crisis events. In the event of police involvement, the school and district will receive accurate updates from the police incident commander that can be relayed to school staff and parents. Informing the parents and the community of new information and highlighting services available are critical to restoring safety and security and providing support services.

School resource officers (SROs) are police officers who provide services to the school well beyond those offered by a security guard. SROs, who often have special training, have become an integral part of many school crisis response teams and an important resource to help ensure both physical and psychological safety. In a majority of school shootings between 2000 and 2010, police force was used to end the event (Blair & Martaindale, 2013). The National Association of School Resource Officers (NASRO) advocates proper training of SROs that focuses on a collaborative model with school professionals and first responder agencies (James, 2013). The NASRO triad model of SRO responsibility focuses on three key roles: law enforcer, educator, and informal counselor (Canady, James, & Nease, 2012; James, Logan, & Davis, 2011). As law enforcers, SROs help to ensure a safe and secure campus. They are a deterrent to some crimes, provide additional supervision, investigate crimes, and are a liaison between the school and police community. SROs also educate students about law-related topics that support school rules and procedures. They serve as an educational resource for classrooms, district groups, parents, and the community. SROs also mentor students as informal counselors and serve as role models. NASRO's training includes topics regarding mental health, special education, and child and adolescent development. SROs can work closely with school-employed mental health professionals to support students and also help disseminate information on community services.

A recent survey conducted by NASRO (2010) found that 75% of respondents had taken weapons from students on school property; 27% reported an increase in gang involvement; over 50% described their schools' crisis plans as inadequate; and 55% reported that their schools only did tabletop exercises and full-scale drills for tornadoes, fires, and earthquakes. Over 55% of the SROs reported that school administration and teaching staff did not receive ongoing school safety training, and over 90% of the SROs felt that crimes were underreported to law enforcement. These statistics are especially concerning given the substantial attention given to school safety. They support schools having well-trained SROs that are a key information-sharing link between law enforcement and schools (Canady et al., 2012; Quinn, 2014).

SROs should be carefully screened. They must be interested in working with children and adolescents, have empathy for those with mental health and other special needs, and have excellent interpersonal skills that allow them to form relationships with students and work collaboratively on school teams (James et al., 2011). Canady et al. (2012) advocate that school districts and the law enforcement agency assigning SROs to the schools establish a memorandum of understanding (MOU) or interagency agreement that defines the role of the SRO and emphasizes collaboration between the school district and police agency. The MOU should be created within the context of federal and state laws, set boundaries to avoid liability by helping both the school and law enforcement agency clearly understand what duties can and cannot be done, and clarify the tasks performed by the SRO to help the school establish a safe and effective learning environment. The MOU between the school district and law enforcement agency should include the following (Canady et al., 2012):

- A clear delineation and description of the tasks that require the SRO to be fully engaged in the lawful execution of his or her legal duty as a law enforcement officer versus those situations that require the SRO to perform the duties of a school official.
- Discussion of when (if ever) the SRO should assist educators who are attempting to enforce school policy or rules.

- Clarification of circumstances when the SRO should (if ever) immediately intervene in campus disruptions without waiting for directions from school or police officials.
- Consideration of whether the SRO can work as a police officer or as a security guard for the school district when not in his or her SRO role (i.e., during his or her "off-time").

The absence of a carefully written MOU creates challenges for the school district and the law enforcement agency. For example, an MOU that states "the SRO is at the school as a law enforcement presence and is not responsible for discipline at school" can have legal implications (Canady et al., 2012, p. 48; *State of Tennessee v. R.D.S., A Juvenile*, 2009). This type of statement has been used to prevent the SRO from being considered a school official and assisting educators under the lower standards of reasonableness set forth under the Fourth Amendment (*R.D.S. v. State of Tennessee*, 2008). This limitation can potentially affect the SRO's ability to be involved in school safety activities, such as threat assessments, and their ability to access school records under the Family Educational Rights and Privacy Act (FERPA; see Chapter 2). Furthermore, if the SRO's role is limited to law enforcement, Fifth Amendment issues (which protect against self-incrimination) may come into play when the SRO is involved in student questioning. Typically, the Fifth Amendment does not apply to school officials, thus allowing them to question students freely for school discipline and safety purposes. Recent court cases have supported the expectation that an SRO is acting as a police officer and must ensure that the student understands that he or she is not under arrest and can leave without answering questions. In addition, statements made by students cannot be used against them unless they were read their Miranda Rights and knowingly made a voluntary statement (James, 2013).

Collaboration With Community Response Agencies

Agencies such as the American Red Cross and Federal Emergency Management Agency can be important partners, especially in the aftermath of a mass disaster that destroys property. However, a recent study by the Centers for Disease Control and Prevention (2013b) revealed that few districts collaborate with the local offices of such agencies in advance of a crisis. Specifically, only 30% of districts reported collaborating with health organizations (e.g., local Red Cross), 33% collaborate with hospitals, and 55% work with public safety agencies (e.g., police, fire, emergency services). Only 27% of districts reported collaborating in advance with faith-based organizations, 66% with mental health and social services staff, and 45% with mental health and social services agencies. School districts and community agencies must collaborate before a crisis event occurs to better understand each other's roles, responsibilities, resources, and crisis intervention and recovery services. In addition, one of the unique aspects of school crisis response is that school and district crisis teams are often personally affected; therefore, support from other qualified professionals and agencies can be essential.

Before a crisis event occurs, school safety and crisis response teams should initiate collaboration with community support resources (local, state, and federal) and discuss the logistics of how schools and agencies will work together. MOUs that outline the roles and responsibilities of each entity are important. Schools will want to consider (a) the qualifications of agency staff, and how they are screened and trained, to ensure they have the expertise to conduct crisis response work, especially with children and adolescents; (b) the agencies' limits to confidentiality; (c) understanding of who pays for the services being offered to students and families; and (d) the specific roles, responsibilities, and boundaries for each agency and the school.

CONCLUSION

Restoring physical safety, including the sense of safety and security, is critical to resuming normal activities and academic instruction. Thus, planning should begin with conducting vulnerability assessments that asses both physical safety and psychological safety and include a site assessment, culture and climate assessment, school threat assessment, and capability assessment. In addition, collaboration with police, first responder, and community response agencies is critical to establishing comprehensive school safety processes and meeting the physical and psychological safety and recovery needs of the school community. School resource officers and community mental health agencies can also provide important supports to schools, but a clear understanding of the roles, responsibilities, and duties to be performed is critical to successful collaboration and execution of response duties.

Chapter 4

SCHOOL CRISIS PREVENTION: ENSURING PSYCHOLOGICAL SAFETY

School safety and crisis prevention is more than just the absence of physical threat or harm, but also includes a proactive focus on psychological safety (National Association of School Psychologists, 2013a, 2013b). This balance of physical and psychological safety emphasizes both *school climate* and *risk assessment*. The approach reflects the shared vision and expertise of leading researchers and education associations, as articulated by the Interdisciplinary Group on Preventing School and Community Violence (2013) and in *A Framework for Safe and Successful Schools*, which was jointly developed by the American School Counselor Association, the National Association of School Psychologists, the School Social Work Association of America, National Association of School Resource Officers, the National Association of Elementary School Principals, and the National Association of Secondary School Principals (Cowan, Vaillancourt, Rossen, & Pollitt, 2013). This chapter explores these approaches to preventing and mitigating school crises.

SAFE SCHOOL CLIMATE

According to the National School Climate Center et al. (2008), *school climate* refers to the "quality and character of school life. It is based on patterns of school life experiences and reflects norms, goals, values, interpersonal relationships, teaching, learning and leadership practices, and organizational structure" (p. 5). School climate includes safety, connectedness, teaching and learning, and environmental and structural aspects of school life (Cohen, McCabe, Michelli, & Pickeral, 2009). A positive school climate can help prevent crises by reducing students' internalizing and externalizing behavior problems (Hill & Werner, 2006; Shochet, Dadds, Ham, & Montague, 2006) and bullying (Meyer-Adams & Conner, 2008; Nickerson, Singleton, Schnurr, & Collen, 2014; You et al., 2008). A positive school climate engages students in relationships with staff and peers, making students more likely to report potential threats to trusted adults (Eliot, Cornell, Gregory, & Fan, 2010; U.S. Department of Education, 2013).

Establishing and sustaining a safe school climate has been suggested to be a critical protective factor for schools and an effective crisis prevention strategy (Osher, Dwyer, & Jimerson, 2006; Osher, Dwyer, Jimerson, & Brown, 2012).

This section discusses school climate. It includes a brief review of evidence-based universal interventions, with a focus on positive behavioral interventions and supports (PBIS) and social–emotional learning (SEL). Considerations for selecting evidence-based prevention programs are also highlighted. That review is followed by a discussion of other approaches to promote both internal and external resilience of students.

School Climate Assessment

As part of a comprehensive needs assessment process (see Chapter 20), it is important to assess aspects of school climate such as school engagement, school safety, and the school environment (U.S. Department of Education, 2013). These assessments are conducted at the local level, by schools and school districts, as part of ongoing data-based decision making about policy and intervention (Astor, Van Acker, & Guerra, 2010; Greif & Furlong, 2006; U.S. Department of Education, 2013). Helpful reviews of school climate measures include the American Institute for Research's National Center on Safe Supportive Learning Environments, which presents a compendium of school climate measures (http://safesupportivelearning.ed.gov/topic-research/school-climate-measurement/school-climate-survey-compendium), and Voight and Hanson's (2012) review of school climate measures at the middle school level. Using these data, schools can make informed decisions about the types of evidence-based psychological safety measures to use to best meet their needs.

Positive Behavioral Interventions and Supports

PBIS is a systems-based approach that focuses on creating a safe and effective learning environment in schools by preventing disruptive and antisocial behavior and facilitating children's academic achievement and prosocial development (Sprague & Horner, 2006; Sugai & Horner, 2009). It emphasizes processes to define, teach, monitor, and acknowledge expectations for behavior and to correct problem behaviors through a consistently administered continuum of behavioral consequences, and it uses research-validated practices and active collection of data for decision making (Horner, Sugai, Todd, & Lewis-Palmer, 2005; Sprague & Horner, 2012). A key component of positive behavioral supports includes a clear code of behavior that outlines the rights and responsibilities of adults and students, describes expected positive behaviors as well as problem behaviors, and uses motivational systems. Research suggests that school-wide programs that emphasize positive behavioral supports likely contribute to students' safety and mental wellness (Pearrow & Jacob, 2012), decrease antisocial behavior and office discipline referrals (Irvin, Tobin, Sprague, Sugai, & Vincent, 2004; Metzler, Biglan, Rusby, & Sprague, 2001; Sprague et al., 2001), and increase protective factors, such as school engagement, academic achievement, and perceptions of safety (O'Donnell, Hawkins, Catalano, Abbott, & Day, 1998; Sprague & Horner, 2012). More information on these approaches is available at the Technical Assistance Center on Positive Behavioral Interventions and Supports (www.pbis.org).

Social–Emotional Learning

Social–emotional learning (SEL) is a multifaceted process that helps develop intrapersonal and interpersonal skills. The process is based on the premise that these social and emotional skills can be taught and learned, much like academic skills such as reading and math (Merrell & Gueldner, 2010). These skills may include (a) recognizing and managing emotions, (b) caring and showing concern for others, (c) developing positive relationships, (d) making responsible decisions, and (e) handling challenging situations constructively (Collaborative for Academic, Social, and Emotional Learning [CASEL], 2007; Elias et al., 1997). Well over a hundred studies conducted using experimental designs have documented the effects of SEL. The outcomes include improved academic functioning and social competence, better school attendance, less disruptive classroom behavior, and a reduced need for discipline and lower rates of suspensions (CASEL, 2012; Durlak, Weissberg, Dymnicki, Taylor, & Schellinger, 2011; Espelage, Low, Polanin, & Brown, 2013; Horner, Sugai, & Gresham, 2002). "These outcomes are achieved through SEL's impact on important mental health variables that improve children's social relationships, increase their attachment to school and motivation to learn, and reduce anti-social, violent, and drug-using behaviors" (CASEL, n.d.; ¶ 16). More information about SEL approaches and a guide to effective programs are available on their website (www.casel.org).

Prevention Programs

Mounting evidence shows that a variety of school-based prevention programs are successful in reducing a wide range of problems and in increasing positive outcomes (see e.g., Durlak et al., 2011; Wilson & Lipsey, 2007). Although a review of the many strategies and programs to prevent any specific type of crisis event is beyond the scope of this book, selecting a program should follow some basic principles. (Discussions of specific prevention programs are available in Brock and Jimerson, 2012, and Brock, Lazarus, and Jimerson, 2002.) First, the needs of the school and community should be identified through a needs assessment process (for more details, see Chapters 3 and 20). Using the results, the school can identify an area of focus from which to compile a list of empirically supported options. These may be broad approaches that involve systems change, such as PBIS; an overall approach to promoting social and emotional skills; or a more specific area, such as prevention of bullying, suicide, or gang involvement. Several resources have compiled information about prevention programs and their effectiveness, which facilitates the use of evidence-based programs (see Table 4.1).

Second, in addition to considering the evidence base of each program, schools need to consider the fit between their needs and the program. Therefore, selection of a program should be guided by several factors, including (a) the needs of the school and community, identified by a needs assessment; (b) the target population (e.g., students, teachers, or parents; age, race, and ethnicity); and (c) availability of school resources for implementing the program, such as financial resources and the staff's program knowledge and competencies (Elliott et al., 2002; Strein & Koehler, 2008). (Chapter 6 has a more thorough discussion of primary, secondary, and tertiary prevention interventions.)

Table 4.1. Resources for Best Practices in Prevention Programs and Practices

Source	Description
U.S. Department of Health and Human Services, Substance Abuse and Mental Health Service Administration (SAMHSA); *National Registry of Evidenced-Based Programs and Practices*, http://nrepp.samhsa.gov/	Provides a searchable online registry of more than 330 substance abuse and mental health interventions. NREPP was developed to help the public learn more about evidence-based interventions that are available for implementation.
U.S. Department of Education, Institute of Education Sciences, *What Works Clearinghouse*, http://ies.ed.gov/ncee/wwc/	Provides accessible databases and concise reports with reviews of the effectiveness of a variety of educational interventions (e.g., programs, products, practices, and policies related to academics, behavior, school safety, and other).
University of Colorado Boulder, Institute of Behavioral Science, Center for the Study and Prevention of Violence, *Blueprints for Healthy Youth Development* http://www.blueprintsprograms.com/	Allows users to select specific program criteria (topic, age, setting, etc.) and then will identify research-based programs that meet search criteria. Over 1,200 programs reviewed.
Center for the Study and Prevention of Violence, *Safe Communities – Safe Schools—Guide to Effective Program Selection: A Tool for Community Violence Prevention Efforts*, http://www.colorado.edu/cspv/publications/safeschools/SCSS-003.pdf	Provides information on model programs that have passed the most rigorous tests of program effectiveness, promising programs that have met some (but not all) criteria for model programs, and favorable programs that do not meet the stringent criteria (or may be for specific populations or very expensive to run) but may still be considered. The guide also provides information about effective program planning, as well as selecting, implementing, and evaluating programs.
Suicide Prevention Resource Center, *Best Practices Registry (BPR) for Suicide Prevention* http://www.sprc.org/featured_resources/bpr/index.asp or http://www.sprc.org/bpr	Identifies, reviews, and disseminates information about best practices in suicide prevention. Includes evidence-based programs that have demonstrated positive outcomes through rigorous evaluation, expert and consensus statements that provide recommendations to guide

Table 4.1. (Continued)

	program and policy development, and suicide prevention programs and practices (e.g., awareness materials, educational programs, and protocols) implemented in specific settings that adhere to standards. The BPR is organized into three sections. Section I: Evidence-Based Programs—Interventions that have undergone evaluation and demonstrated positive outcomes. Section II: Expert and Consensus Statements—Statements that summarize current knowledge and provide best practice recommendations to guide program and policy development. Section III: Adherence to Standards—Suicide prevention programs and practices whose content has been reviewed for accuracy, likelihood of meeting objectives, and adherence to program design standards.
U.S. Department of Health and Human Services, *Youth Violence: A Report of the Surgeon General,* http://www.surgeongeneral.gov/library/youthviolence/chapter5/sec1.html	Identifies model and promising programs as well as those that do not work for primary, secondary, and tertiary levels of prevention.
Collaborative for Academic, Social, and Emotional Learning (CASEL), *Effective Social and Emotional Learning Programs,* http://www.casel.org/guide/	Rates and identifies well-designed evidence-based SEL programs with potential for broad dissemination to schools across the United States using a systematic framework.
Alberti Center for Bullying Abuse Prevention, *Guide to School-wide Bullying Prevention Programs,* http://gse.buffalo.edu/gsefiles/documents/alberti/Bullying%20Prevention%20Program%20Guide%20-%20FINAL%203.16.12_0.pdf	Identifies school-wide (universal) bullying prevention programs for pre-K–12 students. Programs have been researched and evaluated in the United States, as evidenced by at least one peer-reviewed publication or comprehensive evaluation report.

Approaches to Fostering Student Resiliency

Whereas some students are more resilient and therefore less likely to be traumatized by a crisis event, others are more vulnerable. Resilience is broadly defined as "The capacity of a dynamic system to withstand or recover from significant challenges that threaten its stability, viability, or development" (Masten, 2011, p. 494). Resilience involves the mental and emotional processes that may account for individual differences in patterns of adaptation, function, or development that occur during or following threats or disturbances (Masten, 2011). Programs that promote youth resilience often focus on building skills to help avert downward spirals or on promoting upward spirals to increase the positive experiences and emotions of youth (Kranzler, Hoffman, Parks, & Gillham, 2014).

School safety teams can decrease the likelihood of students becoming psychological trauma victims by promoting both internal and external resilience. Internal resilience factors include positive coping skills, the ability to regulate emotions, self-confidence, self-esteem, a positive attitude, and an internal locus of control (Nelson, Schnorr, Powell, & Huebner, 2012). External resilience factors include a strong family and community support system, positive peer relationships and role models, involvement in activities, and a supportive learning environment (Smith Harvey, 2004). Fleming (2006), who conducted research on resiliency in severely abused children, found that personal relationships, a strong sense of independence, and self-reliance were among the factors that promoted resilience. These skills are among those emphasized within SEL, which is advocated as an approach to building resilience (Tran, Gueldner, & Smith, 2014). Social supports can affect both acute and long-term stress reactions (Pine & Cohen, 2002), and personal, familial, and social assets help to protect students.

Schools can actively promote health, competence, and internal resilience in their students in several ways. Programs that pay attention to positive youth development and strengths-based perspectives frame goals positively and further develop strengths and assets in children (e.g., Catalano, Berglund, Ryan, Lonczak, & Hawkins, 2004; Masten, Herbers, Cutuli, & Lafavor, 2008; Nickerson & Fishman, 2013; Search Institute, 2013). These models promote the skills that increase internal resilience, such as positive coping styles, self-regulation, problem solving, self-efficacy, stress management, and beliefs, faith, and hope (Masten et al., 2008; Smith Harvey, 2004). Building internal resilience is also an important part of school mental health programs, in which a basic assumption is that psychological wellness is a necessary condition for success in school (Nelson et al., 2012). Processes for promoting internal resilience may include active teaching of skills, modeling, framing challenging situations as learning opportunities, using praise, and providing thought-provoking questions that allow students to reflect on how behavior is guided by personal decisions and efforts (Smith Harvey, 2004). Creating a positive school climate in which students are encouraged to seek help and ask for support for themselves and their peers is also important.

Powerful protective relationships with families, friends, romantic partners, spiritual figures, and prosocial adults and institutions are central to the notion of external resilience (Masten et al., 2008). Schools can establish a foundation of collaboration and trust between home and school by forming positive parent–school partnerships in which parents feel welcome at school, are included in decision making, and can participate by providing suggestions (Smith Harvey, 2004). Parental involvement includes both home-based and school-based dimensions—that is, activities that take place between the parent and the child outside of school and child-focused activities that are typically accomplished at school (Walker, Wilkins, Dallaire, Sandler, & Hoover-Dempsey, 2005). The peer group provides another very important source of support, particularly as children enter later childhood and adolescence (Nickerson & Nagle, 2005). Schools can offer a wide variety of activities to increase students' sense of involvement by providing activities that engage students with their peers, such as clubs, sporting activities, leadership activities, and community service activities. Many of these activities also encourage volunteering and helping others (Smith Harvey, 2004. Providing access to community supports and positive adult role models through mentorship programs and other avenues also helps to increase external resilience. By promoting these factors in the lives of their students, schools may be able to lower the risk for psychological injury following exposure to a crisis event.

PSYCHOLOGICAL SAFETY THROUGH MITIGATION OF RISK

Despite the best prevention efforts, some youth will present a safety threat to themselves and others, and school-based mental health professionals must have the skills to assess and intervene appropriately to manage these risks. This section reviews general approaches schools use for conducting suicide risk assessments and other threat assessments of directed violence.

Suicide Risk Assessment

Within 12 months of completing the 2013 *Youth Risk Behavior Survey*, 17% of U.S. high school students had seriously considered attempting suicide, 13.6% had made a suicide plan, 8.0% had attempted suicide, and 2.7% had made a suicide attempt that required medical treatment (Kann et al., 2014).These statistics highlight the importance of schools being prepared to conduct risk assessments.

The use of suicide risk assessments in the school setting as a means of preventing youth suicide has some empirical support (Crepeau-Hobson, 2013). The following is a review of steps schools can take to address suicidal thoughts and behaviors and prevent student death by suicide. More comprehensive information about risk assessment and referral procedures and documentation are available in Brock, Sandoval, and Hart (2006); Eklund and Gueldner (2012); Erbacher, Singer, and Poland (2014); Lieberman, Poland, and Kornfeld (2014); and Miller (2011). The American Foundation for Suicide Prevention and the Suicide Prevention Resource Center's (2011) *After a Suicide: A Toolkit for Schools* and SAMHSA's (2012) *Preventing Suicide: A Toolkit for High Schools* provide particularly helpful information for schools.

All school community members should be aware of the risk factors and warning signs of youth suicide. Risk factors are variables that increase the odds of a person becoming suicidal. They include mental illness, social stressors, and personal vulnerabilities such as isolation (Klott, 2012). When present, they should direct attention toward the possible presence of suicide warning signs. Warning signs signal the possibility that the individual may be actively suicidal. Especially, when combined with risk factors, suicide warning signs signal the need for a suicide risk assessment.

In general, suicide warning signs include verbalizations and behaviors that reflect helplessness or fatalistic despair, hopelessness or severe devaluation, and self-hate. Verbal warning signs include direct (e.g., "I have a plan to kill myself") and indirect (e.g., "I wish I could just fall asleep and never wake up") threats. Behavioral warning signs include making final arrangements, giving away prized possessions, talking excessively about death, posting suicidal thoughts online, exhibiting social withdrawal and isolation, and taking risks (Brock & Lieberman, 2015; Klott, 2012; Miller, 2011; Miller & McConaughy, 2005; Poland & Lieberman, 2002). Sudden changes in behavior or habits, such as withdrawing from friends, shifting from agitation to peacefulness, suddenly being in a better mood after a period of depression, or sleeping more or having eating problems, are also warning signs (Brock, Sandoval, & Hart, 2006; Miller & McConaughy, 2005), as are symptoms of depression (Lieberman et al., 2014).

To determine whether a student's suicide warning signs are an indication of suicidal thinking (or ideation), all school community members need to be taught that direct inquiry about the presence of suicidal thinking is needed. For example, a teacher or other caregiver might ask the student who has risk factors (e.g., mental illness) and is displaying warning signs (e.g., has stated a desires to fall asleep and never wake up): "Sometimes when people have had your experiences and feelings they have thoughts of suicide. Is this something you are thinking about?" If the answer is yes, then a suicide risk assessment is indicated (Brock & Lieberman, 2015).

Although a single agreed-upon system for rating suicide risk does not exist, most systems conceptualize risk on a continuum from no risk to high and imminent risk (Berman, Jobes, & Silverman, 2006; Brock et al., 2006; Crepeau-Hobson, 2013). In schools these assessments are conducted by school-employed mental health professionals, who typically begin by determining whether the student has a suicide plan. The student should be asked questions such as "How would you die by suicide?"; "Do you have the means to complete your suicide plan?"; "When are you going to act on your plan?" The greater the detail in the student's plan, the greater the concern regarding suicidal actions. Other questions to ask consider psychological pain and how desperate the student is to ease that pain. The greater the pain and the more desperate the student is to ease it, the greater the concern. It is also important to make inquiries about the extent to which the student has anyone he or she views as a problem-solving resource. The more alone the student is, the greater the concern (Miller & McConaughy, 2005; Ramsey, Tanney, Lang, & Kinzel, 2004).

Suicide risk assessment also involves assessing (a) the presence of psychiatric symptoms associated with suicidality (e.g., aggression, impulsivity, hopelessness, or anxiety); (b) whether the student has prior suicidal behavior, especially a recent attempt; (c) current and past mental health treatment; (d) family history; (e) current stressors; and (f) strengths and protective factors (Miller, 2011). A previous suicide attempt, especially a recent attempt, is a powerful predictor of future suicidal behavior (Borges, Angst, Nock, Ruscio, & Kessler, 2008; Lewinsohn, Rohde, & Seeley, 1996).

During the risk assessment interview, the mental health professional should remain calm and be direct, empathetic, and respectful (Miller, 2011; Miller & McConaughy, 2005). The interviewer should avoid acting shocked, arguing against suicide, minimizing the problem, leaving the student alone, or promising confidentiality (Lieberman et al., 2014). This approach is especially critical when initially asking whether the individual is having suicidal thoughts (Brock & Lieberman, 2015). Figure 4.1 provides further guidance on conducting a suicide risk assessment. In addition, a

Figure 4.1. Worksheet for Conducting a Suicide Risk Assessment

Suicide Risk Assessment Summary Sheet

Instructions: When a student acknowledges having suicidal thoughts, use this checklist to assess suicide risk. Items are listed in order of importance to the risk assessment.

	Risk Present, but Lower	Medium Risk	Higher Risk
1. Current suicide plan			
A. Details	Vague	Some specifics	Well thought out
B. How prepared	Means not available	Has means close by	Has means in hand
C. How soon	No specific time	Within a few days or hours	Immediately
D. How (lethality of method)	Pills, slash wrists	Drugs/alcohol, car wreck	Gun, hanging, jumping
E. Chance of intervention	Others present most of the time	Others available if called upon	No one nearby, isolated
2. Pain	Pain is bearable; Wants pain to stop, but not desperate; Identifies ways to stop the pain	Pain is almost unbearable; Becoming desperate for relief; Limited ways to cope with pain	Pain is unbearable; Desperate for relief from pain; Will do anything to stop the pain
3. Resources	Help available; student acknowledges that significant others are concerned and available to help	Family and friends available, but are not perceived by the student to be willing to help	Family and friends are not available and/or are hostile, injurious, exhausted
4. Prior suicidal behavior of…			
A. Self	No prior suicidal behavior	One previous low-lethality attempt; history of threats	One attempt of high lethality, or multiple attempts of moderate lethality
B. Significant others	No significant others have engaged in suicidal behavior	Significant others have recently attempted suicidal behavior	Significant others have recently committed suicide
5. Mental health	History of mental illness, but not currently considered mentally ill	Mentally ill, but currently receiving treatment	Mentally ill and not currently receiving treatment
A. Coping behaviors	Daily activities continue as usual with little change	Some daily activities disrupted; disturbance in eating, sleeping, and schoolwork	Gross disturbances in daily functioning
B. Depression	Mild; feels slightly down	Moderate; some moodiness, sadness, irritability, loneliness, and decrease of energy	Overwhelmed with hopelessness, sadness, and feelings of helplessness
C. Medical status	No significant medical problems	Acute, but short-term or psychosomatic illness	Chronic debilitating, or acute catastrophic, illness
D. Other psychopathology	Stable relationships, personality, and school performance	Recent acting-out behavior and substance abuse; acute suicidal behavior in stable personality	Suicidal behavior in unstable personality; emotional disturbance; repeated difficulty with peers, family, and teacher
6. Stress	No significant stress	Moderate reaction to loss and environmental changes	Severe reaction to loss or environmental changes
Total Checks			

Note. Adapted from "Suicide Risk Assessment Summary Sheet," by D. N. Miller & S. E. Brock, 2010, *Identifying, Assessing, and Treating Self-Injury at School*, p. 45. Copyright 2010 by Springer. Originally based on a checklist developed by Ryan-Arredondo et al. (2001).

commonly used scale for assessing the severity of suicidal thinking, with established psychometric properties, is the *Columbia–Suicide Severity Rating Scale* (C-SSRS; Posner et al., 2011). In addition, interviews with teachers about warning signs may also be used for risk assessment and treatment planning (Miller, 2011).

Immediate preventive interventions, typically associated with the risk assessment, include the following:

- Breaking confidentiality and reporting suicidal thoughts or plans to parents, school administrators, police, a community-based mental health center, or the nearest hospital emergency department, depending on the circumstances. This response includes calling 911 where risk is extreme and the student requires immediate assistance.
- Notifying parents or legal guardians and asking them to come to the school immediately. The school should have plans in place in case the parent is uncooperative, unavailable, or appears to place the child at greater risk. This plan may include having school officials or other community-based social services escort the student to a mental health facility or hospital emergency department, notifying the police or child protective services, or contacting a mobile psychiatric response team.
- Contacting parents and/or police to ensure that weapons or lethal means to die by suicide are removed, if safe to do so.
- Teaching alternative methods of coping with acute feelings of distress, other than self-harm, and providing contact information for resources (e.g., therapist, psychiatrists, local hospitals, and suicide hotlines or text lines).
- Making appropriate referrals for other community-based services (Brock et al., 2006; Lieberman et al., 2014; Miller, 2011; Miller & McConaughy, 2005).

The results of the suicide assessment and immediate preventive interventions should be carefully documented (Miller, 2011; Miller & McConaughy, 2005; SAMHSA, 2012). In addition, the school-employed mental health professional should always consult with other mental health professionals about assessment results and possible actions. A sample suicide risk assessment and referral protocol, which incorporates many of the ideas expressed above, is presented in Table 4.2.

Violence Threat Assessment

Although students are safer at school than away from school, and school-associated incidents of violent crimes (e.g., assault with a deadly weapon, school-associated violent deaths) have decreased over the past two decades (Robers, Zhang, Morgan, & Musu-Gillette, 2015; Robers, Zhang, & Truman, 2012), even one act of violence in schools is cause for concern. In response to high-profile school shootings, the U.S. Secret Service, the U.S. Department of Education, and the Federal Bureau of Investigation and other organizations have advocated that schools use a standard approach to analyzing a variety of dangerous situations to determine the extent to which a student poses a serious threat to the safety of others (called *threat assessment*; Fein et al., 2002, 2004; O'Toole, 1999; Sandy Hook Advisory Commission, 2015). Threat assessment considers the

Table 4.2. Sample Suicide Risk Assessment and Referral Protocol

1. Discuss the reasons for referral with the person who referred the student (e.g., staff, parent, or self-referral).

2. Begin to establish rapport with the student suspected to be suicidal through a demonstration of empathy, respect, and warmth.

3. Ask questions to determine the student's risk of engaging in a suicidal behavior. The risk assessment should include the following:
   - Assess internalizing problems (affect, behaviors).
   - Have you been feeling sad or down today or recently?
   - Are you having trouble sleeping?
   - Have your appetite or eating habits changed recently?
   - Do you feel as if you have less energy than you used to?
   - Does life seem to be less fun (are you not as interested in things you used to enjoy doing?)
   - Identify suicidal ideation.
   - Identify suicidal intent through direct questioning (e.g., "With as tough as this has been for you, has it ever gotten so bad that you wished you were dead? Have you had thoughts of suicide?" Or with a younger student, "... have you wished you weren't alive anymore? Have you had thoughts of killing yourself?" And if yes, "have you thought about doing something to end your life?").
   - If there is suicidal ideation, assess suicide risk in the following areas.
     - Note: If no ideation is present, the rest of the questions will not be necessary and other helping models and interventions need to be employed.

Suicidal intent
- *Current suicide plan.* Inquire directly about the presence of a plan. The more detailed and specific the plan, the greater the risk).
  - Do you have a plan for how you might act on your thoughts of suicide?
  - How might you do it?
  - How soon are you planning on suicide?
  - Do you have access to weapons or the means to complete your plan?
- *Preparatory behaviors.* Address whether they engaged in any preparatory behaviors, such as writing good-bye letters or giving away possessions. If there have been preparatory behaviors, there is a greater risk.

Suicidal desire
- *Pain.* Ask directly about the degree to which the student is desperate to escape his or her pain (e.g., "Does your physical or emotional pain make you feel that you can't bear it anymore?"). The more unbearable the pain, the greater the risk.
- *Feelings.* Ask about feelings of hopelessness, helplessness, being a burden on others, being trapped, or being intolerably alone.

Buffers and connectedness
- *Resources.* Inquire about the individual's perceptions of being alone and internal and external supports and resources (e.g., "Do you have any reasons for living?"

"What has helped you when you have felt like this before?" "How would people in your life be affected if you died?"). Fewer resources and greater isolation increase the risk for suicide.

Suicidal capability
- *Prior suicidal behavior.* Ask about the individual's history of suicidal behavior (e.g., "Have you or anyone close to you ever attempted suicide before?"). The more recent and frequent the prior suicidal behavior the greater the risk.
- *History of mental illness.* Inquire about the individual's mental health history (e.g., "Have you ever had mental health care?"). Bipolar disorders, depression, schizophrenia, alcohol and substance abuse, trauma, conduct disorder, and borderline personality disorders are particular concerns.

4. Determine level of suicide risk.
   - If suicidal (a) intent, (b) desire, and (c) capability are all present, and (d) buffers or connectedness to others is absent, then student is at high risk.
   - If two to three of these suicide risk assessment variables are positive for suicide risk, then the student is at moderate to high risk.
   - If one to two of these variables are positive for suicide risk, then the student is at low to moderate risk.
   - If none of these variables are positive for suicide risk, then the student's risk is low. Suicidal thinking, absent the other risk assessment variables, is relatively common, and most people with these thought do not engage in suicidal behavior.

5. Consult with other school-employed mental health professionals regarding risk assessment results.

6. Consult with community mental health professionals. These are typically the individuals to whom the suicidal student would be referred.

7. Use risk assessment level and consultation guidance to develop an action plan. Action plan options are as follows.
   Note. If you are unsure of the risk classification, be conservative and move the classification to the next higher risk level.
   - *Extreme risk.* If the student has the means at hand to die by suicide and refuses to give them up, take immediate and directive action to reduce the likelihood of harm:
     a. Call local emergency services or mobile crisis services.
     b. Calm the student by talking and reassuring until the police or mobile crisis service providers arrive.
     c. Continue to request that the student give you the means of the threatened suicide and try to prevent the student from harming himself or herself. When doing so, make certain that such requests do not place anyone else (including the person conducting the risk assessment) in danger.
     d. Call the parents and inform them of the actions taken.

- *Moderate to high risk.* If the student's risk of harming himself or herself is judged to be moderate to high (i.e., there is a probability of the student acting on suicidal thoughts, but the threat is not immediate), follow these procedures:
  a. Determine if the student's distress is the result of parent or caregiver abuse, neglect, or exploitation. If so, contact child protective services instead of a parent or caregiver.
  b. Meet with the student's parents (or child protective services).
  c. Determine what to do if the parent or caregiver is unable or unwilling to assist with the suicidal crisis (e.g., call the police).
  d. Develop a plan to meet the student's needs for intervention (e.g., increased connectedness, substance abuse treatment, treatment of depression, empowerment) and make appropriate referrals.

- *Low risk.* If the student's risk of harming himself or herself is judged to be low (i.e., although the student has thoughts of suicide, the risk assessment suggests a very low probability of engaging in a suicidal behavior), follow these procedures:
  a. Determine if the student's distress is the result of parent or caregiver abuse, neglect, or exploitation. If so, contact child protective services instead of a parent or caregiver.
  b. Meet with the student's parents (or child protective services).
  c. Develop a plan to meet the student's needs for intervention (e.g., increased connectedness, substance abuse treatment, treatment of depression, empowerment) and make appropriate referrals.

8. When making referrals, protect the privacy of the student and family.

9. Follow up with the hospital or clinic to ensure that the student is receiving the appropriate care.

Note. Brems (2000); Brock et al. (2006); Miller (2011); National Suicide Prevention Lifeline (2007).

meaning and context of a student's threatening behavior and uses this information to address the underlying context of the presenting problem rather than relying on uniform discipline (Cornell & Allen, 2011). School discipline is a separate process that the school administration may implement after an initial threat assessment has been completed. For example, in one author's school district a student called in a bomb threat to delay final examinations. The threat assessment team convened and evaluated the threat as low risk. Therefore, it was determined that the student did not pose a threat. However, the school and legal consequences were intense, including a hearing for expulsion and potential felony charges.

According to Fein et al. (2004), assessing the level of threat posed by a student uses information from multiple sources and considers the facts and behaviors relevant to the student who made the threat, the situation, the setting, and the intended victim. The process is guided by six principles and 11 key questions concerning the student's motives, capability, and risk factors (Table 4.3). Threat assessment should be conducted by a multidisciplinary team that must include an administrator and school-employed mental health professional, and may also include school

Table 4.3. Threat Assessment: Principles and Key Questions

Principles

1. Targeted violence is the result of an understandable, and often discernible, process of thinking and behavior.
2. Targeted violence stems from an interaction among the person, the situation, the setting, and the target.
3. An investigative, skeptical, inquisitive mind-set is critical to successful threat assessment.
4. Effective threat assessment is based on facts rather than characteristics or "traits."
5. An "integrated systems approach" should guide threat assessment investigations.
6. The central question of a threat assessment is whether a student poses a threat, not whether the student made a threat.

Key Questions to Ask Regarding the Student Making the Threat

1. What are the student's motive(s) and goals?
2. Have there been any communications suggesting ideas or intent to attack?
3. Has the subject shown inappropriate interest in weapons (including recent acquisition of any relevant weapon) or incidents of mass violence (terrorism, workplace violence, mass murders)
4. Has the student engaged in attack-related behaviors?
5. Does the student have the capacity to carry out an act of targeted violence?
6. Is the student experiencing hopelessness, desperation, and/or despair?
7. Does the student have a trusting relationship with at least one responsible adult?
8. Does the student see violence as acceptable–or desirable–or as the only way to solve problems?
9. Is the student's conversation and "story" consistent with his or her actions?
10. Are other people concerned about the student's potential for violence?
11. What circumstances might support the likelihood of an attack?

Note. From *Threat Assessment in Schools: A Guide to Managing Threatening Situations and to Creating Safe School Climates*, pp. 30–32, 55–57, by R. A. Fein et al., 2004, Washington, DC: U.S. Secret Service and U.S. Department of Education. This document is in the public domain.

resource officers and other school staff members (e.g., deans of discipline, special education teacher/case manager, or general education teacher).

Figure 4.2 offers a decision tree representing the threat assessment process adapted from the empirically validated *Virginia Student Threat Assessment Guidelines* (Cornell & Nekvasil, 2012; Cornell & Sheras, 2006). The process is prompted by the observation or report of a threat, defined as an expression of intent to harm someone. The threat could take the form of spoken, written, or gestured direct or indirect communication (e.g., illustration of a gun pointed at someone's head and the caption saying "Once I get through with you, you are going to wish you had never been born"). Possessing a weapon is also presumed to be a threat unless it is clearly indicated otherwise (e.g., bringing a knife to slice food for lunch). All threats should be reported verbatim so that the team can accurately assess the severity of the threat.

Figure 4.2. Decision Tree for Student Threat Assessment

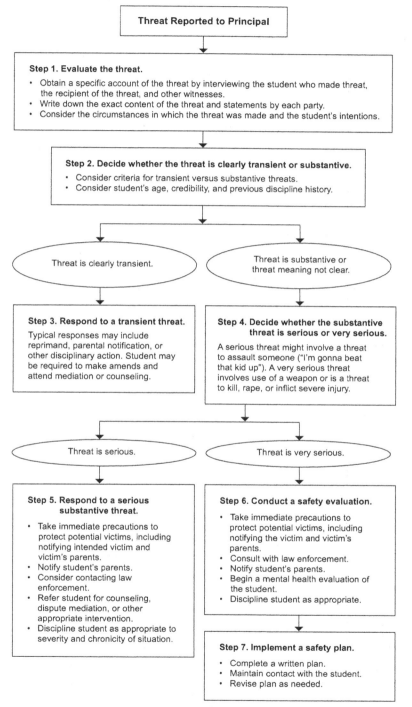

Threat Reported to Principal

Step 1. Evaluate the threat.
- Obtain a specific account of the threat by interviewing the student who made threat, the recipient of the threat, and other witnesses.
- Write down the exact content of the threat and statements by each party.
- Consider the circumstances in which the threat was made and the student's intentions.

Step 2. Decide whether the threat is clearly transient or substantive.
- Consider criteria for transient versus substantive threats.
- Consider student's age, credibility, and previous discipline history.

Threat is clearly transient.

Threat is substantive or threat meaning not clear.

Step 3. Respond to a transient threat.

Typical responses may include reprimand, parental notification, or other disciplinary action. Student may be required to make amends and attend mediation or counseling.

Step 4. Decide whether the substantive threat is serious or very serious.

A serious threat might involve a threat to assault someone ("I'm gonna beat that kid up"). A very serious threat involves use of a weapon or is a threat to kill, rape, or inflict severe injury.

Threat is serious.

Threat is very serious.

Step 5. Respond to a serious substantive threat.
- Take immediate precautions to protect potential victims, including notifying intended victim and victim's parents.
- Notify student's parents.
- Consider contacting law enforcement.
- Refer student for counseling, dispute mediation, or other appropriate intervention.
- Discipline student as appropriate to severity and chronicity of situation.

Step 6. Conduct a safety evaluation.
- Take immediate precautions to protect potential victims, including notifying the victim and victim's parents.
- Consult with law enforcement.
- Notify student's parents.
- Begin a mental health evaluation of the student.
- Discipline student as appropriate.

Step 7. Implement a safety plan.
- Complete a written plan.
- Maintain contact with the student.
- Revise plan as needed.

Note. From *Guidelines for Responding to Student Threats of Violence,* by D. Cornell & P. Sheras, 2006, p. 16, Longmont, CO: Sopris West. Copyright 2006 Cambium Learning Group–Sopris Learning (www.soprislearning.com). Reprinted with permission of the author.

After a threat is reported, the threat assessment team evaluates the threat by interviewing the student and any witnesses about the exact wording of the threat, the context surrounding it, and perceptions of the meaning of the threat. The determination is then made about the student's intention to carry out the threat by deciding whether the threat is transient or substantive. Transient threats are often rhetorical remarks or temporary expressions of anger or frustration that can usually be resolved through an apology or clarification on the scene or in the office (Cornell & Nekvasil, 2012; Cornell & Sheras, 2006). In some cases, this decision should be followed up by administering a consequence or providing interventions, as needed. In contrast, a substantive threat is one that poses at least some risk that the student will carry out the threat, evidenced by the expressed intent to injure someone beyond the immediate situation. Types of information to consider also include the age of the student, the credibility of the witnesses' stories, and the discipline history of the student. Some indicators of substantive threats include a specific plan (either verbal or written), a threat that has been repeated over time, or the recruitment of an accomplice or accomplices.

A substantive threat prompts the threat assessment team to conduct a safety evaluation. The school-employed mental health professional conducts the mental health assessment, which includes a student interview reviewing the threat and the student's relationship with the victims. The interview may include questions about stress and situational factors; mental health symptoms; access to the means to commit a violent act, including opportunity, ability, and desire; previous delinquent behavior; experiences of victimization; and coping and strengths. In addition, parents should be interviewed to ask about their knowledge of the threat, current stressors, recent behavior of the child, school functioning, peer relationships and experience of bullying, history of delinquent behavior, access to weapons, and willingness to assist in a safety plan.

In the case of substantive threats, the school must take precautions to protect the intended victim or victims by warning the students and their parents. Schools should consult with a law enforcement office regarding the best way to protect the victim and to respond to any legal considerations. It is also essential to determine the appropriate intervention for the student who made the threat, in the form of a carefully documented and monitored safety plan. This plan may include increasing supervision (e.g., not leaving the student alone or having designated daily check-ins with the student), removing access to any means of violence (e.g., requesting parents remove weapons from the home), developing a behavioral plan, and implementing problem-solving skills training or anger coping therapy (Halikias, 2005).

The effectiveness of the Virginia guidelines (see Cornell & Sheras, 2006) has been documented in several studies, demonstrating that it is a safe and effective procedure that relates to less bullying, greater student willingness to seek help for bullying and threats of violence, more positive perceptions of school climate, reduced use of long-term suspensions, and increased use of school counseling and parental involvement (Cornell, Allen, & Fan, 2012; Cornell, Gregory, & Fan, 2011; Cornell, Sheras, Gregory, & Fan, 2009; Cornell et al., 2004). This model was listed as an evidence-based program with the SAMHSA'S National Registry of Evidence-Based Programs (see http://www.nrepp.samhsa.gov/ViewIntervention.aspx?id=263). Figure 4.3 provides a worksheet based on the Virginia guidelines that can be used when conducting a threat assessment. However, as is the case with most of the crisis prevention and intervention practices discussed in this book,

Figure 4.3. Worksheet for Conducting a Threat Assessment

Violence/Harm Toward Others Screening Summary Worksheet

	Lower Risk	Medium Risk	Higher Risk
Plans			
A. Details B. How prepared C. Immediacy D. Lethality E. Chance for intervention	__ Vague __ Means not available; lacks realism __ No specific time __ Fists/fighting/kicking __ Others present most of the time	__ Some specifics __ Has means close by, or thoughts, to act __ Within a few days or hours; indication of time __ General statement about weapon availability __ Others available if called upon	__ Direct, plausible, specific, very detailed __ Means at hand; steps taken toward action __ Immediately __ Has lethal weapons or makes statement about acquiring such __ No one nearby; intended victim is isolated
Negative Emotions			
A. Tolerance B. Desperation C. Coping	__ Emotions are bearable __ Wants emotional pain to stop, but not desperate __ Identifies nonviolent ways to address emotional pain	__ Emotions are almost unbearable __ Becoming desperate for relief from emotional pain __ Has limited ways to cope with emotional pain	__ Emotions are unbearable __ Desperate for relief from emotional pain __ Few ways to cope with emotional pain
Resources			
A. Availability/quality B. Accomplices	__ Help available; acknowledges significant others are concerned and available __ No accomplices for plan	__ Family and friends are available, but are not perceived by the student as willing to help __ Indicates passive support from friends and/or family members	__ Family and friends are not available and/or are hostile, injurious, or exhausted __ Indicates active support from friends and/or family members
Prior Violent Behavior			
A. Self B. Significant others C. Bullying others	__ No prior violent behavior __ No significant others have engaged in violent behavior __ No prior bullying behavior	__ At least 1 violent incident in the past year, or a history of making threats/stalking __ Significant others have recently engaged in violent behaviors __ At least 1 bullying incident in the past year	__ History of multiple (2+) violent acts in the past year, and/or following through on a violent threat/stalking __ Significant others have a significant history of violent behaviors __ History of multiple (2+) bullying acts in the past year
Mental Health			
A. Coping behaviors B. Medical status C. Other psychopathology	__ Not currently considered mentally ill, but may have a history of such __ No significant medical problems __ Stable relationships, personality, and school performance	__ Mentally ill, but currently receiving treatment __ Acute, but short-term, illness (may be psychosomatic) __ Recent acting-out behavior and substance abuse; acute violent behavior in an otherwise stable personality	__ Mentally ill and not currently receiving treatment __ Chronic debilitating or acute catastrophic illness __ Violent behavior in unstable personality; emotional disturbance; repeated difficulty with peers, family, and teachers
Stress			
A. Current levels B. Bullying victim	__ No significant stress __ No prior incidents of being bullied	__ Moderate reaction to loss and environmental changes __ At least 1 incident of being bullied in the past year	__ Severe reaction to loss or environmental changes __ History of multiple (2+) incidents of being bullied in the past year
Total number of checks			

Violence/Harm Toward Others Screening Summary Worksheet Scoring

	Lower Risk	Medium Risk	Higher Risk
Total # of checks			
Multiplied by:	1	2	3
Weighted scores			
Total weighted scores			
Divided by:		3	
Final risk score			
Risk level	Transient threat (≤ 9)	Serious substantive threat (10 to 14)	Very serious substantive threat (≥ 15)

Scoring for Violence/Harm Toward Others Risk Assessment Worksheet:

1. Multiply total checks in the lower risk column by 1.
2. Multiple total checks in the medium risk column by 2.
3. Multiple total checks in the higher risk column by 3.
4. Add these three weighted scores.
5. Divide the total of the weighted scores by three.
6. Final risk assessment: Transient threat = score of ≤ 9; Serious substantive threat = score of 10 to 14; Very serious substantive threat = score ≥ 15

Note: The total score is not norm referenced but is to be used as a guide in consideration with other factors and data gathered.

Response to Transient Threat	Response to Serious Threat	Response to Very Serious Threat
Contact student's parents if necessary.	Mobilize crisis management team members as needed.	Mobilize crisis management team.
Notify intended victim's parents if necessary.	Notify student's parents and caution the student about the consequences of carrying out the threat.	Notify student's parents.
See that threat is resolved through explanation, apology, or making amends.	Protect and notify intended victim and parents or caregiver(s) of victim.	Protect and notify intended victim and parents/caregivers(s) of victim.
Consult with law enforcement, school resource officer, security personnel if necessary.	Provide direct supervision of student until parents assume control.	Provide direct supervision of student until parents assume control.
Refer for conflict mediation or counseling, to resolve problem, if appropriate.	Consult with law enforcement/security personnel.	Consult with law enforcement/security personnel.
Follow established discipline procedures.	Refer student for conflict resolution or counseling.	Follow established discipline procedures.
Develop Behavior Intervention Plan, as appropriate.	Follow established discipline procedures.	Refer for comprehensive mental health assessment.
Maintain threat screening documentation.	Develop/revise Behavior Intervention Plan.	Develop/revise Behavior Intervention Plan.
	Maintain threat screening documentation.	Maintain threat screening documentation.

Note: The above list of responses to threats is not exhaustive. The threat/risk assessment team determines appropriate action for each case.

Note. Cornell & Sheras (2006); Fairfax County Public Schools (n.d.); Ryan-Arredondo et al. (2001).

additional research regarding the efficacy of risk assessment protocols in the school setting is needed. While there is some empirical support for specific practices (e.g., the Virginia Student Threat Assessment Guidelines) the authors of this book recognize that different schools and students may need different approaches (in other words, one size may not fit all). Furthermore, given the need for additional research, in the years following this book's publication, the reader is encouraged to attend to the literature regarding the use of threat assessment protocols and to adjust local practice according to the results of such future study.

Although this chapter presents threat assessment procedures for suicide and violence separately, a close relationship exists between other-directed and self-directed violence (Evans, Marte, Betts, & Silliman, 2001; Nickerson & Slater, 2009; Swahn et al., 2008). Therefore, when a student presents as being at risk for either violence toward others or suicidal behavior, it is prudent for the practitioner to conduct both a violence threat assessment and a suicide risk assessment (Nickerson & Slater, 2009) to ensure that the needs of the student are met in a comprehensive manner.

School Safety and Technology

Although social media, smart phones, and e-mail are potentially helpful during times of crisis, they also are sometimes used to convey threats that may jeopardize school safety (Flitsch, Magnesi, & Brock, 2012). Cyberbullying, or deliberate and repeated acts of harm inflicted through computers, cell phones, and other electronic devices (Hinduja & Patchin, 2011), is a rapidly developing school safety concern, particularly among secondary school students (Ybarra & Mitchell, 2004). The legal standard applied consistently by courts is that schools can impose formal discipline of students even for off-campus cyberbullying if it creates, or threatens to create, a substantial disruption to the school's educational activities (Willard, 2007). Schools must therefore develop policies that prohibit the use of district networks or personal mobile communication devices to engage in offensive and harmful communication (Willard, n.d.).

Monitoring social media is a way that schools can identify potential problems, but it can impose time and financial burdens on the school. Some schools have used Web security systems and content filters (e.g., iBoss or Gaggle) to protect students, comply with regulations, and defend the school's network against threats and malware. These systems allow schools to identify the user name and GPS location of someone doing a search. For example, if a student is using his or her district-owned tablet at home to do a Web search on how to build a bomb, the content filter will flag the inappropriate content and send out an alert to an administrator. Schools would need to involve the district technology experts in procedures for threat identification. Schools also can establish procedures for students and community members to report suspicious posts seen on social media (Wendling, Radisch, & Jacobzone, 2013), but these tip sites must be regularly monitored. It would not be appropriate to wait until the next school day to read student-generated tips.

Some social media websites are becoming increasingly responsive to providing supports for their users who may be experiencing psychological distress. The National Suicide Prevention Lifeline (n.d.) provides specific instructions and contact information for safety teams at a number of social media sites (e.g., Facebook, Twitter, YouTube, and Tumblr). Facebook's Help Center allows users to report another Facebook user who has posted suicidal comments. If a user types "suicide" in the general search box in the Help Center, the link (https://www.facebook.com/help/594991777257121/) provides instructions that will help both the person who made the threat and the person that observed the threat. The instructions include directives to contact law enforcement or a suicide hotline for immediate help. It then gives additional instructions to report the suicidal threat to Facebook staff by providing a full name of the person, a link to the post in question, and instructions on how to upload a screenshot of the post. Facebook has contracted services with the National Suicide Prevention Lifeline program, and a trained counselor will contact the person who posted the suicidal threat. In addition, Facebook now has a Bullying Prevention Hub (see https://www.facebook.com/safety/bullying) that tells teens how they can connect with a trusted adult to get help, and also provides guidance for the parents, teachers, and even perpetrators on what they can do to address this problem.

Multidisciplinary Collaboration

Comprehensive safety planning, which includes risk assessment, is guided by the work of a multidisciplinary team that collaborates to create effective practices and systems of support. As articulated in *A Framework for Safe and Successful Schools* (Cowan et al., 2013), it is imperative that all levels of government work to strengthen and support schools' efforts to provide coordinated services to address mental health and school safety. Despite the fact that one in four adolescents have experienced mental disorders resulting in serious impairment, most do not receive mental health treatment (Merikangas et al., 2010; Merikangas et al., 2011). Although schools are ideal environments for the delivery of mental health services, these efforts are often uncoordinated and fragmented (Adelman & Taylor, 2008). Schools often lack enough school-employed mental health professionals (e.g., counselors, school psychologists, social workers, and school nurses).

CONCLUSION

Comprehensive crisis preparedness efforts can be overwhelming, and although promoting psychological safety is a focused task that is typically less expensive than physical safety measures, the magnitude of these efforts can still be immobilizing. Consequently, it is suggested that school safety teams begin by setting two or three goals for preventing, assessing, and mitigating school safety threats. Once these goals have been achieved, then teams can select another two to three goals. Ideally these goals are informed by a formal assessment of the school's psychological safety needs. The aim is to work steadily and deliberately toward a well-developed comprehensive school safety plan that addresses psychological safety and includes the development and maintenance of risk assessment protocols and procedures that monitor social media, and deliberate efforts to facilitate multidisciplinary collaboration.

Chapter 5

COMPREHENSIVE SCHOOL SAFETY TEAMS

Until recently, attention to school crisis planning has focused primarily on specific drill procedures and immediate physical safety; crisis prevention, overall preparedness, and mental health recovery have been relatively neglected. This approach suggested that once an event concluded, schools would simply resume normal functioning and the crisis could be considered over. However, as the field of school crisis preparedness has advanced, it has become apparent that this narrow approach to school safety has left schools vulnerable, and it has failed to proactively address the problems that often lead to crisis situations. Consequently, schools across the country have begun to embrace a multitiered intervention approach to help prevent and mitigate crisis events (Pearrow & Jacob, 2012; Sprague & Horner, 2012). School safety and crisis preparedness have become better aligned with other school-based interventions and with the day-to-day operations of the school; it is no longer seen as a discrete entity, attended to only in a crisis. To facilitate comprehensive safety planning, instruction related to school safety teams and safety plans was added to the second edition of the PREPaRE curriculum (Reeves, Kanan, & Plog, 2010; Reeves et al., 2011a). The second edition focuses on integrating into the curriculum a multitiered approach to safety and crisis response planning similar to that used in response-to-intervention, positive behavior supports, and other similar multitiered systems of support.

SAFETY TEAMS

School safety teams are responsible for comprehensive school safety efforts. They focus on the big picture of school climate and culture and help link safety initiatives to academic and social–emotional programming to promote safe, supportive, and effective schools (Dwyer & Jimerson, 2002; Osher, Dwyer, & Jimerson, 2006; Osher, Dwyer, Jimerson, & Brown, 2012). Safety teams include school and district leaders who help create a positive school climate by selecting appropriate prevention programs that build academic and social skills. The team also

---

obtains the support of other school staff members to implement the programs (Reeves et al., 2010; Reeves, Nickerson, & Brock, 2011). Safety teams focus on various types of prevention programming, including the following:

- School-based behavior management programs such as those that focus on discipline, alternative schools, and cooperative relationships with the police and legal system
- Educational and curriculum-based programs such as those that teach students behavior regulation and conflict resolution skills
- Environmental modification programs such as those that change student behavior by modifying physical and social environments (e.g., hiring security guards) and offering after-school programs (Rhode Island Emergency Management Agency, 2013)

Adelman and Taylor (2014) suggest that crisis response and intervention be woven into a unified, comprehensive, and equitable system of student and learning supports along with other content areas. These include regular classroom strategies to enable learning, supports for transitions, home and community involvement and engagement, and student and family assistance. The levels of intervention in this matrix range from efforts to promote healthy development and prevent problems, to a system for early intervention, and finally a coordinated system of care. The emphasis on comprehensive planning, prevention, risk reduction, crisis mitigation, intervention, and response are consistent with the contemporary recommendations of the United Nations Office for Disaster Risk Reduction (2014a, 2014b).

The district's and school's leadership team can often integrate these responsibilities into their other job and leadership duties. The optimal arrangement is to have safety teams at the district and school levels, with the district and school safety teams working collaboratively. These teams should include relevant school community stakeholders who help ensure a common language and a common vision, who improve the participation of staff members and the school community, and who delegate responsibilities for sustaining safety efforts over time (Reeves et al., 2010). Given that school staff members (especially administrators) change frequently, and that implementation of school safety programming can take years, responsibilities and duties must be shared to ensure continuity (Fixsen, Naoom, Blase, Friedman, & Wallace, 2005). Comprehensive school safety planning is not a one-time event; it requires sustained attention from one year to the next.

District Safety Teams

Functions of the district safety team include (a) providing district leadership; (b) providing individual schools with ongoing training and support; (c) making district-wide comprehensive safety and climate efforts sustainable; (d) helping schools conduct safety evaluations, vulnerability assessments, and audits; and (e) providing guidance on how to use behavioral and academic data for decision making (Reeves et al., 2010; Reeves, Nickerson, & Brock, 2011). Because multiple perspectives are critical to ensuring that needs are identified and support is provided, the team should have representatives of various departments and community agencies within the district (e.g., law enforcement, emergency, and community-based mental health services). Supporting this recommendation, Patton (2011) found that the involvement of law enforcement agencies was related to a reduced risk of violent incidents. The district team is primarily involved with prevention, protection, and mitigation mission areas, but select members may also be involved in crisis response if district support is needed. Other critical duties of the district team are to ensure (a) that both political and financial support are available to schools to sustain comprehensive safety efforts and (b) that those efforts remain a district priority. Establishing the initial comprehensive district safety plan requires substantial time and effort. These efforts should become less intense over time as the team is able to focus more on sustainability of existing initiatives (Reeves et al., 2010).

The district safety team is a valuable resource for school teams and can offer individual school sites the following assistance:

- A comprehensive school safety planning manual that provides guidance on how to establish safety teams and plans; components of a safe schools plan; types of data to collect, analyze, and report; key stakeholders to involve in safety planning; how to identify safety goals and staff development needs; how to perform a vulnerability assessment; among other elements.
- A crisis response and management guide that includes information on how to establish crisis response teams and plans, components of crisis response plans, templates to complete crisis planning, required district templates, and so on.
- An intranet safety folder that includes resources and safety-related information, and recommended templates for school teams.
- Quarterly updates to schools, that provide information on current safety topics, changes in district protocols, online resources, and more.
- Training videos that teach staff how to establish a positive school climate, identify early warning signs of self- and other-directed violence, report child abuse, and establish safety and crisis plans.
- A safe schools website for parents that includes links to safety-related topics.
- A crisis recovery manual that includes copy-ready handouts and other resources to help in times of crisis (Reeves et al., 2010).

Tables 5.1 and 5.2 summarize these team functions and members.

School Safety Teams

The school safety team has functions similar to the district safety team, including (a) providing comprehensive safety and overall school climate leadership at the school level, (b) providing school staff with needed support and training, (c) making ongoing school-wide comprehensive school safety and climate initiatives sustainable, (d) conducting evaluations and collecting data to make informed decisions on priorities and future directions to be taken, and (e) developing a comprehensive school safety plan.

In many schools, this team might already be established (e.g., a school leadership team), and the focus of that already established team may simply need to be broadened to include a focus on overall safety, climate, and other prevention efforts.

Table 5.1. District Safety Team Core Functions

1. **Provide leadership**
   - Facilitate data collection for multihazard and vulnerability assessment—district and school levels.
   - Develop district safety plans.
   - Support development of school-level safety plans and crisis response plans.
   - Solve problems.
   - Determine and provide staff development.
   - Evaluate effectiveness of prevention initiatives.
   - Make data-driven decisions.

2. **Provide schools with needed support**
   - Inform, train, and offer resources for prevention programming.
   - Help identify effective policies, procedures, interventions.
   - For prevention and mitigation, identify procedures and programs for schools to create a safe, respectful, inclusive, and positive school climate.
   - For intervention and response, support crisis response teams by providing consultation or direct response in an emergency.
   - Provide avenues of communication between schools and the district office.

3. **Support ongoing prevention and preparedness efforts to ensure sustainability**
   - Offer support, training, and coaching of district- and school-level staff.
   - Develop safety and crisis manuals, guides, updates, videos, and websites.
   - Secure financial resources needed to sustain climate and safety efforts.
   - Engage and collaborate with community partners.
   - Participate in crisis planning and practice of drills and exercises (for those who serve a specific Incident Command System role on a crisis response team).
   - Have high visibility and be open to hearing concerns regarding climate and safety concerns.
   - Offer outreach to parent and community groups.

4. **Evaluate planning, assessment, and preparedness**
   - Provide guidance and support to individual schools regarding data collection and analysis.
   - Provide descriptions of necessary data components to evaluate school climate and safety initiatives.
   - Monitor schools to ensure implementation fidelity of all climate, safety, and crisis prevention efforts.
   - Collect and analyze district data pertaining to safe schools and crisis planning initiatives.
   - Facilitate district-level physical and psychological safety needs and vulnerability assessments.
   - Perform district-level multihazard assessment.
   - Hold school staff members accountable for climate and safety initiatives.

Note. Adapted from *Comprehensive planning for safe learning environments: A school professional's guide to integrating physical and psychological safety – Prevention through recovery,* by M. A. Reeves, L. M. Kanan, and A. E. Plog, 2010, New York, NY: Routledge. Adapted with permission.

Table 5.2. District Safety Team Members

• Central office administration	• Additional representatives
• Section chiefs from district incident command team	▪ Information technology
▪ Planning	▪ Custodial and maintenance
▪ Logistics	▪ Transportation services
▪ Operations	▪ Nursing and medical staff
▪ Finance	▪ Parents
• District leaders	▪ Research and data personnel
▪ Public information officer	▪ Before- and after-school programs
▪ Safety officer	▪ Multilingual and multicultural department
▪ Liaison officer	▪ Legal services
▪ Mental health officer	▪ Union and association representation
• Mental health administrators	▪ Finance and budgets
• Prevention and intervention services	• Community agencies
• Curriculum administrators	▪ Police
• Special education administration	▪ Fire
• Safety and security personnel	▪ Health
▪ Risk management	▪ Hospital
Human resources	Local emergency management

Note. Adapted from *Comprehensive planning for safe learning environments: A school professional's guide to integrating physical and psychological safety – Prevention through recovery*, by M. A. Reeves, L. M. Kanan, and A. E. Plog, 2010, New York, NY: Routledge. Adapted with permission.

The school safety team is expected to meet regularly, complete the required safety assessments mandated by the district (e.g., vulnerability assessments) and coordinate with other school committees, such as the school crisis response team, student risk assessment teams, and academic support teams. These meetings should be held monthly and put on the calendar at the beginning of the school year (otherwise, finding common times in multiple schedules becomes impossible). This method relays the expectation that safety team meetings are a priority and that other meetings need to be scheduled around them.

The composition of the school safety teams will likely be different at the elementary, middle, and high school levels because of the size of the school and the number of departments to be represented on the team. As noted by Reeves et al. (2010), the team functions better with its own expertise in administration, discipline, academics, mental and physical health, prevention, data analysis, crisis response, and crisis recovery, with consultation sought from outside community agencies as needed. Some members may even serve on the school crisis response team. Tables 5.3 and 5.4 summarize these team functions and members.

Differences Between a Safety Team and a Crisis Response Team

As illustrated in Figure 5.1, although safety teams and crisis response teams differ, the two must collaborate and coordinate their efforts. Safety teams, sometimes with the support and assistance of an accountability committee that monitors safety goals, primarily focus on

Table 5.3. School Safety Team Core Functions

1. **Provide leadership**
   - Offer help with data collection for multihazard and vulnerability assessment at the school level.
   - Develop the school's comprehensive safety plan.
   - Develop school-level crisis response plans.
   - Solve problems.
   - Provide staff development regarding school climate and safety initiatives.
   - Evaluate effectiveness of prevention initiatives.
   - Make data-driven decisions.
   - Report individual concerns and safety priorities to the safety team.

2. **Provide school staff with needed support**
   - Inform, train, and offer resources for prevention programming.
   - Consult regarding behavior-related safety concerns.
   - For prevention and mitigation, implement procedures and programs to create a safe, respectful, inclusive, and positive school environment.
   - For intervention and response, execute regularly scheduled crisis drills and exercises.
   - Provide consultation and direct response to staff and students in an emergency.
   - Provide communication mechanisms between teachers, administration, parents, and students.

3. **Support ongoing prevention and preparedness efforts to ensure sustainability**
   - Support and coach school staff regarding prevention programs and safety initiatives.
   - Provide resources to the school crisis response team to develop and execute building crisis plans.
   - Secure financial resources to sustain school climate and safety efforts.
   - Engage and collaborate with the district safety team and community partners.
   - Participate in crisis planning and practice (for those who serve a specific incident command role on the crisis response team).
   - Have high visibility and be open to concerns regarding climate and safety concerns.

4. **Evaluate implementation and data collected**
   - Monitor implementation fidelity of all school climate and safety efforts.
   - Collect and analyze school data pertaining to climate and safety initiatives.
   - Perform multihazard and vulnerability assessments, including physical safety audits and psychological safety assessments.
   - Provide guidance and support to individual teachers for data collection and analysis.
   - Hold staff members accountable for prevention programs and school climate and safety initiatives.

Note. Reeves et al. (2010); Reeves et al. (2011a).

Table 5.4. School Safety Team Members

- School Incident Commander
- Section chiefs from school incident command team
  - Planning
  - Operations
  - Logistics
  - Finance
- School-employed mental health professionals
- Safety and security personnel, such as school resource officer
- Curriculum specialists

- Grade-level and subject area representatives
- Special education personnel
- Additional representatives
  - Teacher assistants and paraprofessionals
  - Cafeteria staff
  - Building and custodial staff
  - Before- and after-school program staff
- As needed
  - Student representatives
  - Parent representatives

Note. Reeves et al. (2010); Reeves et al. (2011a).

Figure 5.1. Integration of Safety and Crisis Response Team Roles

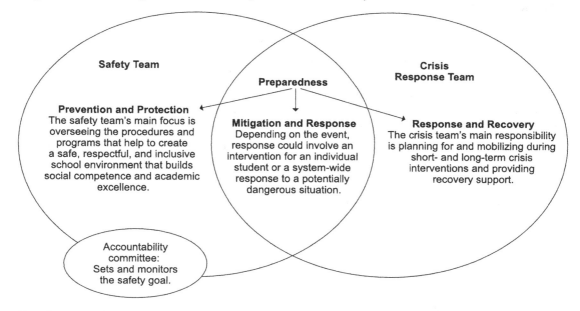

Note. Reeves et al. (2010).

prevention, protection, and mitigation, while providing guidance for response and recovery. Crisis response teams are specifically trained to be involved with mitigation efforts and to provide direct response and recovery interventions and supports. Crisis response teams help provide guidance to safety teams for prevention and protection initiatives that will have an impact on response and recovery efforts. In larger schools, the safety team and crisis response team may be two separate teams with a few members that serve on both teams. In smaller schools, the safety and crisis response teams may comprise the same individuals performing the duties of both teams.

Team Member Selection

The selection of school safety and crisis response team members should be based on expertise and personality factors that allow for effective collaboration with others. Members need to demonstrate positive leadership qualities and be influential, open-minded, and well-respected. Given the critical role these team members play in assessing and identifying the strengths and needs within the school, colleagues need to feel comfortable speaking the truth to them to ensure that school safety problems are not minimized, covered up, or used against teachers in their own performance evaluation. These team members also need to have the ability to remain calm, demonstrate good decision making, and be reliable in regard to showing up for meetings and following through with assigned tasks (Reeves et al., 2011a). Schools should avoid "passing the clipboard" and having individuals sign up without carefully screening for the characteristics mentioned above.

CONCLUSION

To promote safe schools, both individual school and overarching district safety teams should be established. Whereas school teams focus on the unique safety needs of specific schools, district-level teams provide overall leadership and supervision of school team efforts. Safety and crisis response teams address similar issues but have different functions. School safety teams focus primarily on crisis prevention and protection, and crisis response teams focus on crisis response and recovery. Especially in smaller schools and school districts, membership on these two teams may be identical. However, in some instances, safety and crisis response teams are made up of different groups of school staff members. In these instances communication between the two groups is essential. Finally, the members of safety teams and crisis response teams need to be carefully selected based on the specific individual skills and dispositions.

Chapter 6

SCHOOL SAFETY PLANNING AND TRAINING

The promotion of a safe school environment requires comprehensive planning and training that incorporates all of the concepts discussed in the preceding chapters. Building on the discussion of school and district safety teams in Chapter 5, the current chapter addresses how to establish comprehensive safety plans that include crisis prevention and intervention. The need for such planning is documented by the Centers for Disease Control and Prevention (2013b), which concluded that only 64% of school districts had health and safety objectives included in their improvement plans, and only 46% of districts required such objectives within their improvement plans. However, it is encouraging to note that 78% of districts report having addressed psychological and social environment, or school climate, and 88% address violence prevention as part of their planning for safe schools.

COMPREHENSIVE SCHOOL SAFETY PLANS

Effective safety planning links school climate, related safety issues, and prevention efforts to academic and social–emotional programming, and in so doing promotes safe, supportive, and effective schools (Dwyer & Jimerson, 2002; Osher, Dwyer, & Jimerson, 2006; Osher, Dwyer, Jimerson, & Brown, 2012). School safety plans should establish programs that foster safety and crisis prevention and preparedness, and facilitate the professional development schools need to make those programs work. Collaboration among educational and community safety professionals, with input from key stakeholders, is essential because it provides various perspectives and helps make programs sustainable (Reeves, Nickerson, & Brock, 2011).

A comprehensive school safety plan is multifaceted (Reeves, Kanan, & Plog, 2010; Reeves, Nickerson, Conolly-Wilson, et al., 2011a) and links all district and school safety initiatives. In addition, school safety programming must be driven by academic, behavioral, and safety data. Decisions regarding what data to collect, how assessments are carried out, and how the information is disseminated are made by the safety team and are outlined in the safety plan (Reeves et al., 2010).

These data help ensure that limited school resources are deployed responsibly and according to actual (not perceived) school safety needs. In other words, the school safety plan should be based on data, not opinions (Brock, 2015b).

In addition to ensuring the use of a common language regarding school safety efforts and a vision for how to make schools safer, school safety plans also address federal and state legal requirements. These plans distribute responsibility for the implementation and continuation of safety efforts among various professionals and identify safety goals that can be integrated into a school improvement plan. Figure 6.1 shows the overall components of a comprehensive safety plan, and Figure 6.2 provides a checklist for schools developing a safety plan. The checklist can be tailored to a school's specific needs, include components for overall school safety and climate, and address key elements of crisis preparedness. Chapter 8 contains more information on specific components to include in a crisis plan.

SAFETY AND CRISIS PLANNING ACROSS PREVENTION LEVELS

Consistent with Caplan's (1964) *Principles of Preventive Psychiatry*, the PREPₐRE model views school safety and crisis planning initiatives as taking place at the primary, secondary, and tertiary levels of prevention and intervention. Primary prevention includes interventions designed to prevent problems and promote wellness within the school community. For example, the primary prevention of school violence might include establishing school-wide positive behavioral supports and teaching all students problem-solving skills that may prevent violence and suicide.

Figure 6.1. Components of a Comprehensive Safe Schools Plan

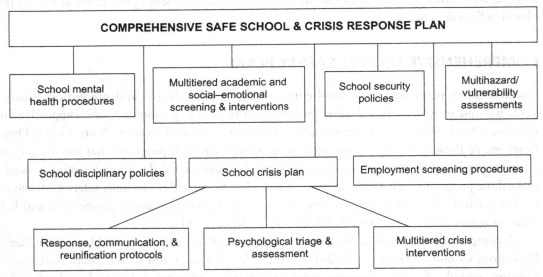

Note. From "Preparing for the Comprehensive School Crisis Response," by M. Reeves, C. N. Conolly-Wilson, J. Pesce, B. R. Lazzaro, & S. E. Brock, 2012, p. 249, in S. E. Brock & S. R. Jimerson (Eds.), *Best Practices in School Crisis Prevention and Intervention*, Bethesda, MD: National Association of School Psychologists. Copyright 2012 National Association of School Psychologists. Reprinted with permission.

Figure 6.2. Comprehensive School Safety Plan Checklist

COMPREHENSIVE SCHOOL SAFETY PLAN CHECKLIST
PREVENTION AND MITIGATION

School Safety and Climate:
- ☐ Develop safety team and assign duties.
- ☐ Assess school safety strengths and needs.
    - ☐ Conduct multihazard and vulnerability assessment.
    - ☐ Conduct physical safety assessment.
    - ☐ Conduct psychological safety and climate assessment.
    - ☐ Analyze physical safety and psychological safety/climate assessment data to identify areas of strength in regard to school safety and crisis planning.
    - ☐ Analyze physical safety and psychological safety/climate assessment data to identify areas of need and concerns in regard to school safety and crisis planning.
- ☐ Create a safe school climate.
    - ☐ Implement evidence-based prevention programs in areas identified in psychological safety assessment (e.g., violence prevention, bullying prevention).
    - ☐ Implement evidence-based prevention programs in areas identified in physical safety assessment (e.g., increased supervision, more lighting).
    - ☐ Implement evidence-based academic programs to meet a variety of educational needs and levels.
    - ☐ Implement measures to build supportive factors and promote positive youth development.
    - ☐ Enforce fair and consistent policies and procedures.
        - ☐ Develop school security and discipline policies.
    - ☐ Increase violence prevention awareness.
    - ☐ Provide anonymous reporting.
    - ☐ Develop school mental health procedures.
    - ☐ Provide comprehensive mental health and physical health services.
- ☐ Collaborate with key stakeholders, including parents.

Crisis Prevention and Mitigation:
- ☐ Collaborate with community response agencies and service providers.
- ☐ Conduct staff training to implement quality prevention and intervention programming with fidelity.
- ☐ Conduct staff training to ensure that crisis protocols are efficiently and effectively executed in a crisis event.
- ☐ Emphasize communication and reporting.

PROTECTION

School Safety and Climate:
- ☐ Identify staff development needs in regard to comprehensive school safety initiatives.
- ☐ Provide staff development in regard to school comprehensive safety initiatives and programs.
- ☐ Establish an ongoing data-based evaluation system for collecting and evaluating school climate and safety data.
- ☐ Assign data evaluation responsibilities regarding school safety initiatives and programs.

Crisis Protection:
- ☐ Identify staff development needs in regard to school crisis prevention through recovery.
- ☐ Provide staff development in regard to school crisis prevention through recovery.
- ☐ Develop crisis team and plans.
- ☐ Train safety and crisis team members in their roles and responsibilities.
- ☐ Hold regularly scheduled safety and crisis team meetings to assess ongoing school climate and safety.
- ☐ Conduct crisis drills and exercises.
- ☐ Develop standard response and recovery plans and procedures.
- ☐ Evaluate and modify crisis plans according to feedback from drills or exercises.
- ☐ Develop resource lists.
- ☐ Develop recording system to record expenditures and costs of future crisis response expenditures.

RESPONSE

School Safety and Climate:
☐ Respond to at-risk student needs: threat and suicide assessment.
☐ Provide interventions to meet identified needs and build skills: social skills groups, anger management groups, and so on).
☐ Continue to analyze safety data and program effectiveness data.
☐ Respond to safety concerns.

Crisis Response:
☐ Identify type of crisis and activate crisis team.
☐ Identify and implement appropriate level of emergency response needed.
☐ Verify facts and implement effective communication or notification plans.
☐ Begin initial psychological triage and assessment to identify crisis exposure.
☐ Provide immediate crisis interventions to ensure physical and psychological safety.
☐ Make contact to activate additional resources, if needed.
☐ Activate release and reunification plan, if needed.
☐ Debrief with staff and crisis team, plan for short-term needs.

RECOVERY

School Safety and Climate:
☐ Focus on reestablishing social support systems.
☐ Continue to monitor safe schools and climate data.
☐ Continue to monitor whole-school recovery—physical and psychological safety.
☐ Implement additional supports and prevention programming.

Crisis Recovery:
☐ Secure and restore physical structure and safety.
☐ Conduct ongoing psychological triage.
☐ Continue to provide crisis interventions.
☐ Rotate crisis interveners if needed due to fatigue.
☐ Communicate with staff, parents, and community regarding physical and psychological supports.
☐ Collaborate with stakeholders and community support agencies.
☐ Plan for memorial activities (establish guidelines and parameters if necessary).
☐ Send letter to parents reinforcing safety measures being implemented.
☐ Provide staff support.
☐ Return to structure and routine as soon as feasible.
☐ Plan for long-term needs.
☐ Conduct after-incident evaluation and modify plan if needed.
☐ Evaluate effectiveness of crisis plan.
☐ Track expenditures and submit reimbursement, if appropriate.

Note. Adapted from *Comprehensive Planning for Safe Learning Environments: A School Professional's Guide to Integrating Physical and Psychological Safety—Prevention through Recovery,* by M. A. Reeves, L. M. Kanan, & A. Plog, 2010, New York, NY: Routledge; *PREPaRE: Crisis Prevention and Preparedness (2nd ed.)—Comprehensive School Safety Planning,* by M. A. Reeves, A. Nickerson, C. Conolly-Wilson, M. Susan, B. Lazzaro, S. Jimerson, & R. Pesce, 2011, Bethesda, MD: National Association of School Psychologists. Adapted with permission.

Secondary prevention activities promptly address challenges of students who are struggling academically, emotionally, or behaviorally. They are targeted, building skills that help students be more successful and in so doing prevent emerging problems from becoming more substantial school safety threats. For example, for students who have just begun to display violent behavior, secondary prevention activities include interventions designed to promote those students' problem-solving and anger management skills. Similarly, for students who have just been exposed to a crisis event, secondary prevention activities include interventions that mitigate further damage or harm, such as teaching adaptive coping skills for crisis-generated problems (a topic discussed in greater detail in Section 5).

Tertiary prevention addresses the more debilitating and longer-term consequences of school-associated safety threats and crisis events. For example, for students who were the perpetrators or victims of school violence, tertiary preventive interventions might engage the resources and skills of community-based professionals such as community mental health or child protective services. All of the interventions offered in Chapter 19 are tertiary interventions.

Primary Preventive Interventions

Schools increasingly recognize the importance of universal, or primary, approaches to prevention that promote the physical and psychological safety of all school community members (Brock, 2011a; Gottfredson, 1997; Jimerson, Nickerson, Mayer, & Furlong, 2014; Reeves et al., 2010; Reeves, Nickerson, & Brock, 2011). Perhaps most fundamentally, primary prevention of threats to school safety involves providing effective instruction. The more a school's students are engaged in learning, the less likely they are to experience academic and behavioral difficulties (Sutherland & Wehby, 2001). In addition, having caring teachers and adults available to students, and creating a climate that accepts diversity, fosters a sense of connectedness and belonging, which in turn reduces potential harm to self or others (Larson, 2008; Miller & Eckert, 2009). Another critical aspect of primary prevention is the use of strategies to ensure that students *feel* safe, which can be independent of adults' evaluations of whether the student *is* safe. In universal prevention approaches, therefore, the student body's belief that their school environment is a safe place, where they are free from physical and psychological harm, is essential to learning (Ratner et al., 2006; Reeves et al., 2010; Rigby, 2007).

An essential element of all school safety plans is helping students understand the importance of breaking the "code of silence" and reporting safety concerns they have observed among their peers (Reeves et al., 2010). All students need to understand that they are not "narking" or "snitching"; they are getting help for a friend and helping to ensure that their school is safe. An example of how to promote this aspect of a school safety plan is Colorado's Safe2Tell tip line, which allows students and parents to anonymously report safety concerns (the program added a mobile app in 2015; http://safe2tell.org/what-can-you-do/safe2tell-mobile-app/). The success of the program is demonstrated by the 12,538 tip reports received—via calls, Web reports, or texts—between September 2004 and October 2014, from 163 Colorado cities and 59 counties. Of these reported incidents, 93% had positive intervention outcomes reported by school staff, parents, and school resource officers (Safe2Tell, 2014). Follow-up of the reported safety concern by the safety team or other school staff member is crucial to this process. When students do not perceive that their report has been addressed, they may become complacent and avoid future reporting.

Parental involvement in primary prevention efforts is critical. For example, parents can (a) partner with schools to help students learn nonviolent ways of responding to conflict and bullying, (b) enhance their own parenting skills, (c) help ensure that weapons are secured at home, (d) provide feedback to enhance safety and crisis planning, and (e) help plan and organize positive school activities to engage students (Reeves et al., 2010).

Given the numerous federal and state laws that pertain to school safety (see Chapter 2), primary prevention should also include written policies that protect students from harassment and bullying including cyberbullying and other electronic harassment (Pearrow & Jacob, 2012). These policies must include procedures for reporting threats and should be included in the district manual and school handbook, as well as be consistently disseminated to students, staff, and parents (Feinberg & Jacob, 2002). Establishing a tracking system to monitor disciplinary infractions and crimes and conducting school crisis preparedness activities are all part of primary prevention (Pearrow & Jacob, 2012).

Although many primary prevention strategies have been shown to be effective and to keep schools safe, zero tolerance policies are not among them. Policies that require suspension or expulsion following specific disciplinary infractions have not been found to be effective in reducing school violence (Kang-Brown, Trone, Fratello, & Daftary-Kapur, 2013).

Secondary Preventive Interventions

When students are not responding to universal prevention measures, secondary interventions should immediately be offered (Caplan, 1964). The goal of a secondary preventive intervention is to keep emerging problems from becoming debilitating and long-term behavioral or emotional health challenges, which sometimes are associated with the occurrence of a crisis event. Although typically only about 15% of students need secondary interventions (Burns & Gibbons, 2008), when indicated, school staff members need to be prepared to immediately deliver these secondary, or targeted interventions (Reeves, Nickerson, Conolly-Wilson, et al., 2011a). Thus, these resources are an essential element of a school safety plan.

As discussed in Chapter 4, suicide and threat assessment protocols are essential elements of secondary prevention (Pearrow & Jacob, 2012). However, other secondary preventive interventions should also be included in a school safety plan. These include the identification of resources that address students' specific skill deficits. Teaching students social skills and anger management techniques, for example, can help them to develop positive replacement behaviors and can decrease social–emotional challenges. These resources can also be used to address the student who has begun to exhibit behavior that threatens school safety (e.g., physically aggressive behavior). Secondary interventions also may include cognitive–behavioral counseling approaches to develop problem-solving, anxiety management, and anger coping skills. School mental health professionals can offer counseling within the school setting, and they should also become familiar with resources in the community that can provide these services.

Also important to the school safety plan's secondary preventive interventions is the school's response to students who have acute (one-time) or chronic (ongoing) trauma exposure. Given the well-documented effects of such exposure on academic functioning and students' social–emotional health (Nickerson, Reeves, Brock, & Jimerson, 2009; Reeves et al., 2010), safety plans must document the presence of school professionals trained to deliver secondary crisis interventions (such as those discussed in Section 5).

Finally, it is essential that all secondary preventive interventions involve parents and families. Clearly, the involvement of both home and school in addressing an emerging social–emotional or academic concern increases the chances that intervention will be effective. Thus, the school safety plan should include approaches like parent management training. Such training teaches parents to identify, define, and observe behaviors in new ways and to alter behaviors using effective behavioral management (e.g., reinforcement of appropriate behavior, mild punishment such as loss of privileges or time out, negotiation, or contingency contracting; Parent Management Training Institute, 2014). Parent management training has been shown to reduce aggressive behavior (Kazdin, 2003; Serketich & Dumas, 1996).

Tertiary Preventive Interventions

Tertiary interventions are used for the small percentage of students who may become a safety risk because they have chronic problems with aggression and antisocial behaviors. More than half of the total disciplinary referrals and nearly all of the serious offenses in schools are accounted for by only 6% to 9% of children (Sprague & Walker, 2000). Functional behavioral assessments and behavior intervention plans can be conducted at the secondary or targeted level of intervention, but are discussed in this section because they are often an element at the tertiary level and have proved to be effective (Steege & Watson, 2009). To determine why the student is behaving in a certain way, functional behavioral assessment gathers information about the antecedents (motivating operations and immediate triggers) of a student's behaviors, the behaviors themselves, and the consequences of those behaviors to determine the function of the challenging behavior (i.e., reinforcement, avoidance, or self-stimulation). Once the function or functions of the behavior is identified, a behavioral intervention plan is developed, which specifies the strategies to be used to modify or address the behavior. These plans set students up for success by manipulating environmental antecedents, then teach them that prosocial replacement behaviors are a more effective way of obtaining their behavioral goals (Zionts, Zionts, & Simpson, 2002).

It is important to acknowledge that some students with severe and chronic social, emotional, and behavioral problems have such extensive needs that the typical general education school environment will not have resources to accommodate those needs. Although the vast majority of students with mental health challenges never become a school safety threat, providing tertiary prevention resources when needed will increase the likelihood that none do. Therefore, having specialized therapeutic day schools, outpatient programs, day treatment classrooms, and even psychiatric hospitalization for youth with these challenges can be considered a part of the school safety plan (Quinn & McDougal, 1998).

Wraparound approaches are getting increased attention because multiple systems (e.g., family, peers, and schools) overlap to address the complex needs of at-risk students who perpetrate acts of school violence. The wraparound approach has been described as an evidence-based process that requires family members, providers, and key members of the family's social support network (e.g., teachers, coaches) to collaborate to build an intervention plan that responds to the particular needs of the child and family (Suter & Bruns, 2009). An array of services and supports is activated, with the entire team engaged in the plan's implementation. The team has regular meetings to monitor progress and make adjustments to the plan. When the student has achieved an identified level of progress, the team then reaches a consensus that a formal wraparound process is no longer needed. This process is in sharp contrast to more traditional forms of intervention, which have been criticized: they are often driven by professionals; tend to blame the child or family; focus on the child's deficits; and sometimes lack respect for the family's needs, beliefs, and values (Walker, Bruns, & Penn, 2008).

A recent study using a wraparound service delivery model for youth experiencing severe emotional disturbance showed favorable results, and a key factor in that success was the unique role played by the school district (Painter, 2012). The school district helped develop and fund the family resource centers that provided a gateway for youth and families to enter mental health and substance abuse treatment provided by community partners. In the study, colocated staff from community partners were able to provide services in neighborhood schools, which was a less stigmatizing location for students to receive services and allowed families to receive the help they needed in their neighborhoods. The district provides the buildings and licensed clinicians to manage the referrals, and the community partners provide the services. Consistent with Painter's (2012) findings, Juszczak, Melinkovich, and Kaplan (2003) reported that youth are 21 times more likely to visit a school-based health clinic for their mental health care than they are a community-based clinic.

Another tertiary intervention with demonstrated effectiveness is multisystemic therapy (MST). This approach works with the systems in a student's life, such as family and peer group, and empowers caregivers to serve as change agents for their children by identifying factors that interfere with their ability to provide the necessary nurturance, monitoring, and discipline. The MST team uses strengths (e.g., supportive extended family, caregivers' social skills) to address these factors and supports the implementation of planned interventions. MST is successful in the reduction of problem behaviors, residential placement, and recidivism rates for students with chronic and severe behavior problems (Henggeler, Schoenwald, Rowland, & Cunningham, 2002). It also increases family cohesion, adaptability, and interaction (Borduin et al., 1995). Families receiving family-based MST have shown significant reductions in negative behaviors within a short time, and early success was correlated with higher rates of successful completion of treatment goals. This finding supports the importance of therapists acknowledging a student's challenges and adjusting treatment strategies early to address factors that are impeding progress (Tiernan, Foster, Cunningham, Brennan, & Whitmore, 2015).

In the case of a student who poses a safety concern at the tertiary level—that is, presenting some risk of harm to self or others—district and school policies and handbooks should also include a statement that school mental health professionals can and may meet with a student, without parental consent, to conduct a risk assessment. In some districts, schools may in fact be required to conduct such a risk assessment and provide psychological assistance (Pearrow & Jacob, 2012). In addition, schools have a duty to warn and notify potential victims, and student information may be disclosed according to the guidelines established by the Family Educational Rights and Privacy Act and the Health Insurance Portability and Accountability Act of 1996 (see Chapter 2).

CONCLUSION

Comprehensive school safety plans and preventive interventions are essential to establishing safe schools. Schools that do this well build student resiliency, which serves as a protective factor in the event of a crisis and thus mitigates the negative effects of a traumatic event. Schools that have carefully considered how to better ensure student safety not only increase their chances of preventing crises in the first place, but they also are better positioned to recover from those crises they are not able to prevent.

Chapter 7

SCHOOL CRISIS RESPONSE TEAMS

Presidential Policy Directive 8 (PPD-8) on national disaster preparedness directs all public entities to develop capabilities to "protect property and the environment and meet basic needs after an incident has occurred" (Obama, 2011, p. 6). School districts comply with this directive by developing crisis response teams based on the Incident Command System (ICS). This chapter discusses how schools initiate the process of developing crisis response teams, then explores use of the ICS by districts, examines crisis response documentation and evaluation, and highlights the opportunities and challenges associated with technology and social media.

INITIATING SCHOOL CRISIS RESPONSE TEAMS

School crisis response teams typically are initiated by district-level administration. The individual responsible for team development is usually a school administrator. However, though top-down development is the norm, in some situations other school staff members, such as school psychologists, take a leadership development role (Brock, 2000).

The ICS provides a consistent structure for school crisis response teams and team member roles. However, schools exist within diverse contexts, and the size and infrastructure of a given school or district influence team composition and responsibilities. Given this reality, the following questions are offered to guide initiation of a crisis response team:

1. How large should the crisis response team be, and what organization and structure should be used?
2. How are team members selected, and what responsibilities will they be given? Will members share responsibilities so they can be given a break?
3. How are team members initially being trained, and how often are refresher trainings being offered?
4. How are community resources being used and integrated with school resources?

Initiation of a school crisis response team is challenging. For instance, teams might lack the necessary school and district policies, support, and commitment from school administration. They might lack the time and resources, or there may be disagreement with the concept that schools are responsible for meeting crisis recovery or mental health needs. Territorial issues (e.g., "Whose job is it?"), reactive positions (e.g., "Let's wait until there is a problem"), and the myth that taking action makes the crisis worse are also common obstacles (see discussions in Cornell & Sheras, 1998; Kline, Schonfeld, & Lichtenstein, 1995; McIntyre & Reid, 1989). The following sections explore how to meet these challenges.

Identifying or Establishing Policies

The first step in developing a crisis response team involves determining whether crisis management policies have been previously established. If such policies are already in place, they provide the basis for crisis response efforts. If no policies exist, they will need to be developed. Brock (2000) provides an example of how one school district went about establishing such a policy, as well as a sample school board crisis response policy statement.

Securing and Sustaining the Support of Administration and Colleagues

Having the support of both district-level administration and school principals is critical to establishing and sustaining crisis response teams. Unsupported district-level mandates typically yield superficial school crisis preparation (Brock, 2000). Ongoing communication with administrators is essential to remind them of the importance of the school crisis response team's activities in promoting students' physical and psychological safety and academic success. The following strategies provide guidance on securing the ongoing support of the school administration when initiating a crisis response team:

1. Provide a written proposal to the school board during a working meeting, including rationale, goals, and objectives for a school crisis response team (Brock, 2000). This information should be presented in a context where it can be thoughtfully considered and discussed, and where questions may be asked, rather than in a public forum with pressures that may prevent uninhibited discussion.
2. Use national, state, and local data to describe problems. Substantial information is available online. For instance, the *National Crime Victimization Survey* (Bureau of Justice Statistics, 2013), the *Youth Risk Behavior Survey* (Kann et al., 2014), the *Indicators of School Crime and Safety: 2014* (Robers, Zhang, Morgan, & Musu-Guillette, 2015), and the *School and Staffing Survey* (National Center for Education Statistics, 2015) are all useful resources.
3. Use effective persuasion strategies, such as crafting a clear and distinct position paper regarding the importance of school safety in student academic success. (See Cowan, Vaillancourt, Rossen, & Pollitt, 2013, for helpful guidance with this task.)
4. Define the types of situations that require a crisis response, highlighting salient local considerations that necessitate activities for crisis preparedness (e.g., use data obtained from vulnerability assessments).

5. Define the desired outcomes of crisis response and recovery so that it is clear to school board members, administrators, teachers, and parents that the focus is on facilitating the safety, health, well-being, and academic success of students.
6. Develop documents that delineate proposed staff responsibilities relative to crisis preparedness (e.g., incorporating crisis responsibilities into job descriptions).
7. Make humanitarian arguments (e.g., many crises are preventable, which could potentially lessen the effects of trauma or prevent the loss of life).
8. Point out that the school has a legal duty to intervene and that a good crisis response mitigates negative academic consequences.
9. State that high-quality interventions help to establish positive public relations for the district and its schools.
10. Encourage district administrators or board members to discuss crisis response approaches with their counterparts in other districts or with schools that have crisis response teams.

A written proposal that describes the school crisis response team should delineate the team's rationale, goals, objectives, and budget and should include any supporting documentation. National, state, and local statistics can be used to describe the problem or needs. For instance, the document might note that nationally, suicide is the second leading cause of death among youth ages 5 to 18 (Centers for Disease Control and Prevention, 2013a). Using local statistics often yields surprising results, as numbers can be higher than imagined and can thus be a catalyst for initiating a crisis response team.

Chapter 1's discussion of the unique school-associated consequences of crises can also be used to suggest the need for school crisis response teams. Specifically, the proposal could point out that school-associated crisis events are typically associated with school absenteeism; school behavior problems, such as aggressive, delinquent, and criminal behavior; academic decline; and exacerbation of preexisting educational problems. Stating the negative impact of conditions like posttraumatic stress disorder (PTSD) on academic functioning (Saigh, Mroueh, & Bremner, 1997) further strengthens arguments regarding the need for crisis response teams.

Maintaining School Crisis Response Team Coherence

Strategies to maintain communication and foster connections among crisis response team members include initiating precrisis collaboration and planning. This preparation helps to ensure that all team members are actively involved and contributing expertise related to their specialty. The team's structure also facilitates sharing and decision making, giving all team members multiple opportunities to contribute to discussions and decisions. A third strategy includes team-building activities and crisis response practice. For instance, professional development seminars, simulations, drills, and readiness exercises all provide opportunities for team members to develop skills and knowledge, and they also build professional relationships (a discussion of crisis response practice is in Chapter 8). Other approaches to maintaining team cohesion include accommodating diverse views and facilitating open discussions, maintaining a focus on common goals, and establishing a climate in which mistakes are viewed as learning opportunities.

NATIONAL INCIDENT MANAGEMENT SYSTEM

The September 11, 2001, terrorist attacks prompted the U.S. government to review how local, state, and federal agencies work together to respond to disaster. The establishment of the U.S. Department of Homeland Security (DHS) in 2002 combined 22 federal agencies, including the Federal Emergency Management Agency. In early 2003, President George W. Bush issued Homeland Security Presidential Directive 5 (*Management of Domestic Incidents*; Bush, 2003), which gave the secretary of homeland security the authority to develop and administer a National Incident Management System (NIMS). This system provides a common template for federal, state, tribal, and local governments; nongovernmental organizations; and private organizations to follow in the event of an emergency. NIMS helps organizations "work together to prevent, protect against, respond to, recover from, and mitigate the effects of incidents, regardless of cause, size, location, or complexity" (U.S. DHS, 2008, p. i). In addition, federal, state, tribal, and local governments are required to adopt NIMS within their local emergency response agencies (e.g., police, fire, rescue, and public health departments) as a condition for receiving federal support during an emergency. Many school districts across the country are also incorporating NIMS into their crisis response efforts (e.g., Illinois State Board of Education, n.d.; Rhode Island Emergency Management Agency, 2013). NIMS provides a structure for school crisis response teams and defines the roles and responsibilities of team members.

NIMS does not provide a standard one-size-fits-all crisis response plan. It provides a framework that includes key concepts for agencies and organizations to follow when responding to crises. Whereas traditional crisis plans provide guidance on responding to the first 5 to 15 minutes of an emergency, NIMS helps agencies and organizations determine how to respond to both short- and longer-term crisis needs. Its principles are based on the concept that although a crisis may start locally and then evolve to a large-scale event requiring external supports, it always concludes at the local level. NIMS asserts that crisis response needs to be scalable, depending on the type of crisis and the resources needed to respond to the event. NIMS also helps organizations better communicate with each other by ensuring that multiple agencies responding to an emergency use the same language, terms, and team structure. Doing so ensures that all responders understand their crisis response role (U.S. DHS, 2008). Table 7.1 summarizes key concepts, and Table 7.2 offers major elements of NIMS.

INCIDENT COMMAND SYSTEM

The Incident Command System (ICS) provides a common organizational structure for responding to emergencies. For example, the role and function of the Incident Commander (IC) is the same within any organization using the ICS. The IC is the person who is in charge regardless of the individual's organizational rank. Schools are encouraged to follow the ICS so that their crisis response teams are using the same system of response activities that local police and fire departments are using. The ICS directs the development of five functional areas or sections: Command, Operations, Planning, Logistics, and Finance/Administration, with command officers or section chiefs leading each functional area (U.S. DHS, 2008). Use of the ICS facilitates a more efficient crisis response (Crepeau-Hobson, Sievering, Armstrong, & Stonis, 2012).

Table 7.1. Key NIMS Concepts

A systematic approach to incident management, including multiagency, government, and organization response to an incident

- Is flexible and adaptable to any crisis situation.
- Offers standardization and common terminology for resource management.
- Provides guidance on crisis response team structure using the Incident Command System.
- Offers preparedness concepts and principles for all hazards.
- Is scalable (i.e., works in small- to large-scale emergencies).
- Is dynamic, with the crisis responses evolving and changing in response to crisis circumstances.

Note. Adapted from *National Incident Management System,* by U.S. Department of Homeland Security, 2008, Washington, DC: Author. This document is in the public domain. Available from http://www.fema.gov/pdf/emergency/nims/NIMS_core.pdf

Table 7.2. Elements of NIMS

1. *Preparedness.* Includes planning for emergencies; developing procedures and protocols for emergencies; conducting training and exercises; maintaining responders that have the proper qualifications, licensure, and certification; and properly maintained equipment.
2. *Communications and information management.* Includes maintaining a constant flow of information to the emergency responders to help guide the emergency response.
3. *Resource management.* Includes managing the resources needed to respond to an incident. Resources include people and materials that are needed during the response.
4. *Command and management.* Includes providing a framework to develop a response authority (i.e., who is in charge), obtaining resources, and managing all of the resources effectively to meet incident goals and objectives.
5. *Ongoing management and maintenance.* Includes the managing and maintaining of NIMS over time. The National Integration Center maintains this directive.

Note. Adapted from *National Incident Management System,* by U.S. Department of Homeland Security, 2008, Washington, DC: Author. This document is in the public domain. Available from http://www.fema.gov/pdf/emergency/nims/NIMS_core.pdf. See the ICS Resource Center for more information on the elements of NIMS, available from http://training.fema.gov/emiweb/is/icsresource/index.htm

ICS in School Settings

According to the U.S. Department of Education (2013), the mission areas (formerly called *phases*) of crisis preparedness—prevention, protection, mitigation, response, and recovery—are interconnected (see Figure 2.1). Consequently, developing district- and school-level crisis response teams requires partnerships between public health, mental health, law enforcement, public safety, and local government. Use of the ICS also helps promote the sustainability of crisis response teams by clearly delineating crisis response roles and responsibilities, and by identifying backup personnel in case the first assigned person is unavailable to fulfill assigned duties. The basic premise of ICS in schools is that when school staff respond to crises, they transition from their day-to-day jobs to perform similar functions within the crisis response team. For example, the school psychologist would transition from traditional counseling, consultation, and assessment to psychological trauma risk screening, crisis-related psychological education, and mental health crisis intervention.

Table 7.3 summarizes the five major ICS functions. (Additional ICS information and free independent study courses can be found online on the U.S. DHS Emergency Management Institute website at http://training.fema.gov/IS/NIMS.aspx.) Table 7.4 lists the school personnel who might fill ICS roles and serve on school and district crisis response teams, given their expertise and preservice training. It also identifies the individuals from community response agencies who might be part of these crisis response teams.

ICS Division of Labor and Span of Control

ICS functions apply whether a school crisis response team is addressing a small-scale crisis event or a district team is managing the response to a major disaster. Two ICS concepts relate to the crisis

Table 7.3. Five Major ICS Functions

Incident Command (*Managers*)	• Provides overall emergency policy and coordination. • Sets the incident objectives, strategies, and priorities and has overall responsibility for the incident. • Assisted by the incident command team comprised of public information officer, safety officer, liaison officer, and mental health officer.
Operations (*Doers*)	• Directs operational resources and implements response activities according to established emergency procedures, including care of students, first aid, mental health crisis intervention, search and rescue, site security, damage assessment, evacuation, and release and reunification.
Planning (*Intelligence* or *Thinkers*)	• Collects and analyzes information to measure the size, scope, and seriousness of the incident to direct the appropriate response; tracks resources; and maintains documentation.
Logistics (*Getters*)	• Secures and provides resources, personnel, equipment, and facilities; coordinates personnel; assembles and deploys volunteer teams; and facilitates communication among responders to resolve incident and conclude the response.
Finance/ Administration (*Payers*)	• Monitors and oversees all financial activities: purchases materials, tracks incident costs, arranges contracts for services, keeps timed chronology of events, submits documentation for reimbursement, and recovers school records.

Note. Adapted from *Rhode Island Model for School Emergency Planning, Mitigation/Prevention, Preparedness, Response, and Recovery,* pp. 42–43, by Rhode Island Emergency Management Agency, 2013, Providence, RI: Author. This document is in the public domain.

Table 7.4. School Personnel and Community Representatives Who Might Fill ICS Roles

• Principal	• Secretaries
• Assistant principals	• Cafeteria coordinator
• Dean of students	• Transportation coordinator
• School psychologist	• Community representatives, as team
• School counselor	members or consultants:
• School social worker	▪ Police
• Nurse	▪ Fire
• School resource officer or security	▪ Emergency medical services
• Special education teacher	▪ Emergency management
• Physical education teacher or coach	▪ Health and mental health
• General education teacher	professionals
• Head custodian	▪ Business professionals
	▪ Parent representatives

response to a variety of crises: division of labor and span of control. Division of labor applies because every crisis, no matter how large or small, requires that certain functions or tasks be fulfilled by the assignment of team members whose job assignments and expertise align most closely with the task. The second concept, span of control, specifies that no person should supervise more than seven other team members, with the optimum number being five (unless a large number are performing the same crisis response tasks, such as conducting mental health crisis interventions).

Incident Command

The IC is responsible for crisis management. For school crisis response teams, that person is most often a school principal, and for the district-level crisis response team that person is most often a district administrator. The IC delineates team objectives, assigns responsibilities, and coordinates the overall response. All crisis response responsibilities are assigned to the IC until he or she delegates them to other team members (see Figure 7.1). The IC is responsible for establishing immediate incident priorities, determining the incident objectives, approving the Incident Action Plan (IAP), and coordinating activities of the Command Staff and General Staff. This responsibility includes approving requests for resources and releases of information to the media, demobilizing the incident response, and making sure that After-Action Reports (AAR) are completed (the IAP and AARs are discussed later in this chapter). The IC is also responsible for maintaining a manageable span of control within the ICS team (U.S. DHS, 2008).

For example, in responding to a school library fire, an IC would convene the school crisis response team (or the district-level crisis response team, if school resources were judged insufficient) at a selected safe location, give team members the crisis facts, and set response priorities. The IC would have the Public Information Officer (PIO) develop a letter to parents about the fire and create a message to post to social media and on the school's website. The IC would also have the section chiefs of the Planning, Logistics, and Operations sections develop a plan for the school's

Figure 7.1. Flow Chart of the ICS Roles and Hierarchy

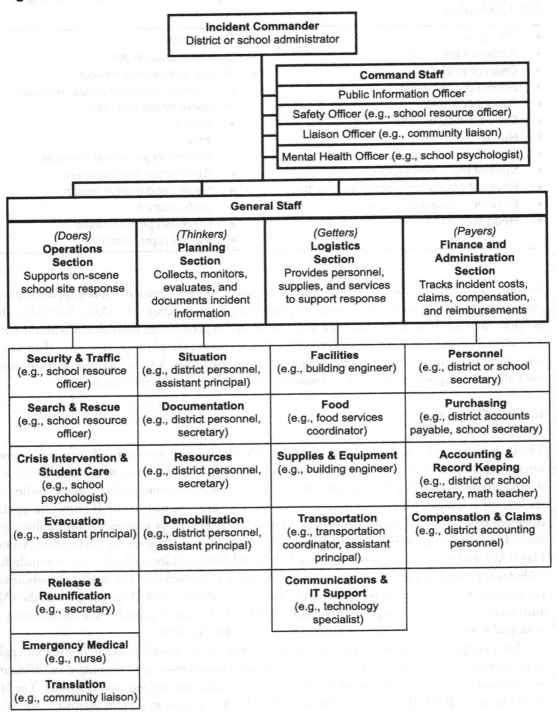

Note. From *School Crisis Prevention and Intervention: The PREPaRE Model*, p. 26, by S. E. Brock et al., 2009, Bethesda, MD: NASP. Copyright 2009 by the National Association of School Psychologists. Reprinted with permission.

response to the fire, such as relocating affected classes, taking pictures of the affected areas of the building for insurance purposes, and developing a perimeter around the affected areas to make off limits. When an incident such as the library fire is addressed by a school-based team, the school's IC would inform district-level administrators about the crisis response to the fire, and the district-level IC would in turn keep the superintendent, cabinet, and members of the school board informed. Depending on the level of impact, the IC may decide to complete all of the duties listed above, may delegate them to the members of the school crisis response team, or may request assistance form the district-level crisis response team.

Although a school principal is typically the IC for a school crisis response, the designation of the IC role can vary. The IC can be the first crisis response team member on the scene or the person who has the most crisis response experience. The IC is not necessarily the person with the highest rank or position. For example, during a district-level crisis team response, the superintendent may assign another administrator to fill the role of the IC. Under many circumstances the superintendent would be busy working with the school board, managing other aspects of the district, or working with local officials to get assistance for the district. In this case, the IC would report to the superintendent about the incident response, but the IC would oversee the crisis response team activities (Reeves, Nickerson, Conolly-Wilson, et al., 2011a).

When an immediate crisis response crosses multiple political boundaries or jurisdictions, with several local and state agencies having the authority and responsibility to deal with the incident (e.g., a community disaster such as a flood), the different ICS teams can form a unified command, which calls for a collective approach with one common set of crisis response objectives (U.S. DHS, 2008). The unified command is flexible and may look different in each situation, ranging from command by a committee to designation of a single IC who takes everyone's concerns into account (Green, 2002).

Command Staff

Typically the Command Staff includes three roles: the Public Information Officer (PIO), the Safety Officer, and the Liaison Officer (U.S. DHS, 2008). However, the National Association of School Psychologists also recommends that school districts add a mental health officer to the Command Staff (Brock et al., 2009; Reeves et al., 2011a). As illustrated in Figure 7.1, the Command Staff roles are typically filled by district-level personnel who in turn support the school crisis response teams. However, where districts have limited personnel resources, or in a small district, school-based staff members may fill Command Staff roles. Command Staff should be designated first and assigned tasks that are not considered functions of the general district staff. Because individuals are assigned to ICS roles in advance, it is possible that one or more of these crisis response team members will be unavailable. Thus, alternates should always be identified.

Public Information Officer
Districts generally assign a PIO to gather information about a crisis to be disseminated to the public, the media, and other agencies. With input from a school's Operations or Logistics Chief, who may draft a report on the incident facts, the district-level PIO will finalize the information about the cause of the crisis, its size, the current situation, and resources committed. Messages are

then approved by the IC and then delivered to the public, either by the PIO or a designated spokesperson (e.g., the school's principal, the district superintendent). For example, following the school library fire, the PIO would develop the message the principal delivers to the media, the letter to go to parents, messages for the website, content of calls and text messages to parents and staff, and social media messages.

Safety Officer

Some school districts may have multiple school-based Safety Officers. However, in most instances a district-level staff member fulfills the Safety Officer role and in turn supports individual school crisis response teams. The Safety Officer does the following:

- Establishes and maintains safety at the incident site and is responsible for the safety of response personnel, staff, and students
- Conducts ongoing assessments of hazardous environments
- Coordinates safety efforts among different agencies (e.g., police and fire departments)
- Implements measures to promote crisis responder safety (e.g., makes protective clothing or equipment available when environmental hazards are present)
- Advises the IC on all safety matters
- Contributes to the development of the IAP

During an emergency, the Safety Officer is typically given the authority to overrule the IC to stop or prevent unsafe activities during the crisis response (U.S. DHS, 2008).

The Safety Officer works closely with the Operations Section Chief to manage security during the crisis response. In the example of the school library fire, the Safety Officer would work with the fire marshal to make sure that school and community crisis responders could safely enter the building. In addition, the Safety Officer would write a safety message outlining actions the school crisis response team members should follow, for example, to ensure that anyone entering fire-damaged areas wears the appropriate protective equipment.

Liaison Officer

The Liaison Officer is typically a district-level employee who is the point of contact for representatives of other government agencies, nongovernmental organizations, and private entities that interact with the district-level or school crisis response teams. The Liaison Officer has the authority to speak on behalf of the school or district (U.S. DHS, 2008). For example, following the school library fire, the Liaison Officer would be responsible for communicating with the fire department that was assisting with the crisis response. The Liaison Officer also assists the IC in communicating with any additional agencies responding to the crisis (e.g., Red Cross, police) and works closely with the Operations Section Chief to ensure that physical and psychological safety needs are being met.

Mental Health Officer

The National Association of School Psychologists has recommended the designation of a Mental Health Officer who provides advice to the IC about the psychological effects of trauma exposure and monitors the mental health status of crisis responders (Brock et al., 2009; Reeves, Nickerson,

Conolly-Wilson, et al., 2011a). In larger K–12 school districts, this role is filled by the district-level administrator who oversees school-employed mental health professionals. In small school districts, a school-employed mental health professional occupies this role (e.g., school psychologist or counselor). The Mental Health Officer works closely with the Operations Section Chief to monitor and account for the mental health status of all crisis responders. In the example of the library fire, this officer may know that a member of the school crisis response team recently experienced a devastating house fire and might suggest that the IC not ask the individual to provide school crisis response services.

General Staff Roles

As illustrated in Figure 7.1, the general staff consists of section chiefs who are responsible for crisis response activities that fall under the four sections: Operations, Planning, Logistics, and Finance/Administration. Section chiefs designate appropriately trained individuals to occupy assigned roles within their section (U.S. DHS, 2008).

Operations Section Chief
The Operations Section Chief is responsible for conducting or overseeing all crisis response actions. In ICS terms, the Operations Section is responsible for all "tactical operations in response to an incident" (U.S. DHS, 2008, p. 97). The Operations Section Chief is often considered to be the second highest ranking decision maker on the team, after the IC. Whereas the IC provides the instructions for a response (based on the IAP prepared by the Planning Section Chief), the Operations Section Chief manages the resources needed to ensure that those instructions are followed and assigns tasks to team members to provide mental health services, security, and medical support to crisis victims. The Operations Section Chief also manages the staging area, where response personnel have gathered to direct the school crisis response, and works very closely with the other section chiefs to respond to the incident.

For example, following the school library fire, Operations Section responsibilities would likely exceed the resources of a school crisis response team, so a unified command would be formed that includes the school-, district-, and community-based operations section chiefs. Only one of those would be assigned primary decision-making responsibilities. Duties in this situation would include overseeing the process of relocating classes whose classrooms have been damaged, assigning security personnel to establish a safety perimeter around the library, ensuring that mental health interventions are provided, and offering medical first aid to any staff or students who do not need to be transported to the hospital.

Planning Section Chief
The Planning Section Chief is responsible for planning the overall crisis response. Individuals working with the Planning Section Chief gather information about the incident and the incident response, including reports provided by the Operations and Logistics Section Chiefs. It is from these data sources that the IAP is developed. This plan then goes to the IC for approval.

The Planning Section also provides incident status updates, plans the ongoing crisis response and coordination, and develops the IAP for the next day. In the example of the school library fire, while the Operations Section Chief is responding to the fire in the library, the Planning Section Chief would be documenting the response, making sure classes were relocated to appropriate locations, and observing whether the secured perimeter around the library caused congestion in the hallway during passing periods.

At the conclusion of a crisis response, the planning section is responsible for writing an AAR (U.S. DHS, 2008). That process not only enables the school crisis response team to improve its efforts but also gives feedback to the school safety team to identify strategies to prevent future crisis events, better protect students, and mitigate harm associated with future crises.

Logistics Section Chief

The Logistics Section Chief obtains crisis response resources and materials, including facilities, transportation, communications equipment, supplies, food and medical support for responders, and equipment maintenance. This section chief develops the communications, medical, and traffic plans specified by the IAP (U.S. DHS, 2008). In the example of a school library fire, the Logistics Section might obtain radios for the operations section to use, caution tape for the perimeter around the library, fans to blow smoke out of the hallways, "Do Not Enter" signs, and any other materials necessary to respond to the fire and its aftermath. In addition, the Logistics Section Chief makes sure that all receipts for these crisis response supplies are given to the Finance/Administration Section Chief.

Finance/Administration Section Chief

The Finance/Administration Section Chief is responsible for managing crisis response finances, including maintaining records of purchased items and services, managing personnel time records, providing financial and cost analysis information, and managing workers' compensation claims (U.S. DHS, 2008). In a school district, this person is someone who typically works closely with the business, insurance, and payroll departments. The Logistics Section Chief obtains items from a supplier and provides receipts, but it is the Finance/Administration Section Chief who authorizes the use of funds to make those purchases.

For example, following the school library fire, the Finance/Administration Section Chief may never set foot in the fire-damaged library, but this person makes sure that the bills incurred when responding to the crisis are paid. The Finance/Administration Section Chief may also work with the district's insurance agent to file claims. Documentation collected by this chief informs future budgetary allocations to purchase needed goods in advance of a crisis event (e.g., allocate monies in next year's budget to purchase additional walkie-talkies).

Although not all crisis responses call for deployment of this section, following larger disasters the Finance/Administration Section Chief has an especially important role. For example, following the shootings at Sandy Hook Elementary School in Newtown, Connecticut, the town received a grant for $1.5 million from the U.S. Department of Justice's Office for Victims of Crime, and the Newton Public School District received a grant for $3.2 million from the U.S. Department of Education's School Emergency Response to Violence (SERV) program ("Newtown receives," 2014) to help with crisis recovery.

School-Employed Mental Health Professionals
School-employed mental health professionals fill a variety of crisis response roles. Having a designated Mental Health Officer supporting these professionals is critical to ensuring that students' and teachers' mental health needs are met. The specific roles and duties of school-employed mental health professionals include

- Serving on school safety and crisis response teams to provide input on prevention activities; and on how to meet the psychological and educational needs of students before, during, and after crises
- Helping to develop various crisis response plan elements, or *functional annexes*, such as evacuation; lockdown; shelter-in-place; accounting for all persons; communication and warning; family reunification; continuity of operations (COOP); recovery; public health, medical, and mental health; and security
- Taking steps to ensure the physical *and* psychological safety of individuals when implementing emergency protocols
- Communicating with the Operations Section Chief and PIO (Crepeau-Hobson et al., 2012).
- Assisting in the evacuation and reunification process
- Helping to determine the need for additional mental health crisis intervention providers (from within and outside the district, if necessary)
- Determining how resources and responders are best used
- Determining when and where mental health crisis intervention services will be delivered
- Providing mental health crisis intervention both during and after a crisis event
- Conducting student, staff, and parent care activities as directed by the Operations Section Chief (Reeves, Kanan, & Plog, 2010; Reeves, Nickerson, Conolly-Wilson, et al., 2011a; Rhode Island Emergency Management Agency, 2013)
- Ensuring that students with special needs are attended to

Identification of the Incident Command Post

In all types of crisis events, an Incident Command Post (ICP) should be located in a safe area outside of the immediate crisis area (Green, 2002). This is the location from which all command staff members operate to ensure a coordinated response. The IC is required to remain in the command post during the crisis response so that team members can contact the IC at any time (U.S. DHS, 2008). The command post must have the resources needed to operate a response, such as phones, fax machines, computers and Internet access, and confidential meeting space.

If the school's administrative conference room is safe and not directly affected, it is usually a suitable location for a school command post. However, when determining the location of the ICP, the IC and the crisis response team must consider multiple factors, depending on the type, location, and needs of the crisis situation. For example, if the crisis affects multiple schools in one area of town, the ICP may be located close to the incident. If the crisis affects multiple schools in different areas around a district, the ICP may be centrally located in relation to the crisis response. If the crisis occurs in an area without good cell phone service, the ICP may need to be in the closest area where members of the crisis response team have a good cell phone signal to communicate. Table 7.5 reviews considerations when establishing an ICP.

Following disasters that affect multiple schools, school districts may also be required to set up an Emergency Operations Center (EOC). The EOC can be housed in a preestablished location where the district crisis response team, district-level officials, and local emergency responders can work together. The location may be a school district's central office, operations building, or similar location. A Joint Information Center and press conference area may also be housed at the EOC so that agencies working together during an incident can more easily provide an accurate, unified message to the public. The team at the EOC can analyze information from multiple ICPs to (a) assist in determining the next course of action for the individual school crisis response teams, (b) provide resources to school-level teams at multiple ICPs, and (c) allow district administrators to receive incident information from one source to reduce misinformation or rumors about the crisis and the crisis response.

DOCUMENTATION OF THE CRISIS RESPONSE

As introduced earlier in this chapter, Incident Action Plans (IAPs) and After-Action Reports (AARs) are the reports that the ICS team uses to document and evaluate crisis response actions. These two documents complement each other and assist the crisis response team when responding to crises.

Incident Action Plans

Whereas a district-level or school crisis response plan provides instructions on how to respond initially to crisis events, the IAP guides the response efforts for a particular incident. An IAP can be verbally communicated, but for more complex incidents it should be a written plan and be shared with all responders. The IC might delegate this activity to the Planning Section Chief, who coordinates with the Operations and Logistics Section Chiefs to develop the plan. General IAP templates could be developed in advance. For example, a template for utility failures helps a school respond to the crisis more quickly and consistently than if a response team develops a new plan each time a water main breaks. The IAP can be as simple or as complex as needed; Table 7.6 lists the primary elements of an IAP, and Figure 7.2 provides a sample IAP report.

Table 7.5. Incident Command Post Considerations

- Interior space needed for members of the ICS team
- Additional rooms so members of the ICS team can separate during individual planning time
- Supplies needed (e.g., tables, chairs, maps, dry erase boards, LCD projector, computers, printers, office supplies, extension cords)
- Communication supplies (e.g., phones, cell phones, Internet connection, cell phone service, bullhorn, speakers)
- Interior and exterior security and safety needs (such as staff monitoring the location, cameras)

Table 7.6. Incident Action Plan Components

- Name of incident
- Incident description
- Date of incident
- Time incident occurred
- Operations period of IAP (i.e., includes response and predicted recovery time frames)
- Weather report
- ICS assignments
- Incident response objectives
- Tactical objectives and resources needed

Note. Reeves et al. (2011a); U.S. Department of Homeland Security (2012).

After-Action Reports

Consistent with the PREPaRE model's call for examination of crisis prevention and response efforts, the IC should examine the effectiveness of crisis response actions by ensuring that the Planning Section Chief completes an AAR. Although primarily used by the crisis response team, the AAR can also help guide the school safety team in identifying ways to prevent, protect, and mitigate specific crisis events. The AAR identifies what resources or actions are needed to make the response more effective, considers the lessons learned, and helps plan for subsequent prevention or mitigation activities. The AAR is designed to examine what was done during the crisis response, and what can be done in the future to make the school safer and the crisis response more effective. The key components of an AAR include an overview of the incident, goals and objectives of the incident, analysis of the incident outcomes and the school's capacity to perform critical tasks during the incident, and a summary and recommendations for improvement (U.S. Department of Education, 2007a, 2007b). When the school district reviews and revises its school safety and crisis response plans, a comprehensive review of all AARs throughout the district should be a part of the revision process. Additional information on AARs is available from the Emergency Response and Crisis Management Technical Assistance Center (http://rems.ed.gov/docs/After_ActionReports.pdf).

THE ROLE OF TECHNOLOGY AND SOCIAL MEDIA

According to the Pew Research Center, of adults who use online services, 73% also use a social networking site, 42% use multiple social media sites, and 71% use Facebook (Duggan & Smith, 2013). The increasing popularity of social media (e.g., Facebook, Twitter, Instagram, or Pinterest) has changed the way schools respond to emergencies. In the recent past, before the widespread availability of smartphones and the use of social media, schools could often wait until the end of the school day to send a letter home informing parents of an emergency (what the PREPaRE curriculum refers to in Chapter 16 as "informational documents"). However, in today's schools students are using technology, such as smartphones, to send messages to their parents or caregivers

Figure 7.2 Sample Incident Action Plan

Incident Action Plan (IAP)

Name of Incident: Teacher's death at Main Street Elementary

Incident Description: Teacher Doe died as a result of a serious medical condition. Students became aware of the condition 2 weeks ago when the teacher unexpectedly went to the hospital.

Date of Incident: January 23, 2015.

Time of Incident: 1000 hours.

Operational Period of IAP: January 24, 2015, from 0600 hours to 1800 hours.

Weather Report: Cold, but sunny. High of 30 degrees.

ICS Assignments:

Incident Commander:	Assistant Principal Karen
Public Information Officer:	Teacher Sally
Liaison Officer:	Social Worker Katie
Safety Officer:	Gym Teacher Sharon
Mental Health Officer:	Counselor Rachel
Operations Chief:	Psychologist Kristen
Planning Chief:	Counselor Geoff
Logistics Chief:	Custodian Otis
Finance/Administration Chief:	Secretary Bill

Incident Objectives:
1. To ensure the safety and welfare of all students and staff.
2. To help students and staff begin to recover from this loss.

Tactical Objectives and Resources Needed:
1. Provide mental health crisis intervention support to Mr. Doe's classroom.
   a. The Mental Health Crisis Intervention Response Team A will provide PREPaRE classroom meetings and student psychoeducational group sessions to the students in Mr. Doe's classroom.
   b. As indicated, provide PREPaRE psychological interventions.
2. Provide mental health crisis intervention support to staff members.
   a. Mental Health Crisis Intervention Response Team B will provide PREPaRE psychoeducational and psychological intervention to affected staff members.
3. Make referrals to outside mental health agencies as needed.
   a. Liaison Officer will assist in finding available community-based mental health agencies.
4. As indicated, provide mental health support to students not in Mr. Doe's classroom.
   a. Mental Health Crisis Intervention Response Team C will provide psychoeducational interventions in other classrooms in the building and provide psychological interventions as needed.

Safety Message:
To all responders, if you are a staff member at Main Street Elementary, please remember that you may be emotionally affected as well. Also, do not let students remain unsupervised in the hallways or open areas.

Note. Reeves et al. (2011a).

about school-associated crisis events as the crisis is occurring. The reality of the 24/7 news cycle has also played a role in caregivers increasingly expecting real-time information regarding a crisis event. Thus, today's schools must post the information to social media sites or use other communication technology immediately to inform the community about a crisis situation (Porterfield & Carnes, 2012).

School districts without a social media presence should establish one and use it before a crisis occurs. Using social media before a crisis gives students, caregivers, and community members the opportunity to use and learn to trust the school's social media sites as accurate and timely sources of information. Absent other strategies for immediately receiving crisis information, caregivers go to other (potentially inaccurate) sources for information (Porterfield & Carnes, 2012). Without a way to quickly provide such information, the school loses what control it might have over how crisis facts are presented. From the available, albeit limited research on the use of technology and social media during a crisis, this section highlights some of the roles of technology and social media before, during, and after a crisis event and identifies a place for these activities within the ICS.

Technology, Social Media, and Crisis Preparedness

As schools develop their school safety and crisis preparedness plans, they should address the use of technology, especially as it involves the use of social media, by students, caregivers, schools, and districts. Following a review of school policies and procedures for sending information to the public, the school district's PIO can assist the IC with planning how the school uses technology, such as social media, during a response. Some have suggested that the ICS now include a Social Media Specialist (Brinkworth, Morris, Singh, & Lieberman, 2014).

Before beginning to develop procedures for using technology and social media, a school district should review existing school communication policies and procedures. For example, communicating via social media often uses quick, real-time informational updates. If the policies and procedures state that all external messaging must be approved by the superintendent or the school board, those policies may need to be revised to reflect the more rapid message cycle of social media posting during crises. Also, if the policy or procedures on the use of technology prohibit staff members from going onto social media sites while in a school building, or while using school computers and smartphones, an exemption must be made to allow the PIO to use social media in the event of a crisis. In addition, PREP$_a$RE curriculum authors also recommend that schools develop policies and procedures for how, and if, students will be allowed to use smartphones during a crisis (e.g., require that students copy a scripted message to text to caregivers).

Keeping in mind the span of control and the complexity of this task, the PIO might consider developing a technology team to assist in posting and reading social media messages. By making use of social media, school community members have the opportunity to place or post comments and questions, and should have the expectation that school officials will respond. Stakeholders might also share or retweet the information the district shares with the public, a process that increases the number of people with access to information provided via social media. All of these possible uses of social media increase the need for the PIO to have a technology team.

School districts may not have the resources to use and monitor multiple sites, so choosing one or two social media platforms should be sufficient. Schools could consider joining sites that can link messages, such as Facebook and Twitter. Some text messaging companies send group text messages and post the same information to the district's Facebook and Twitter accounts all at once. This system helps to ensure that messages are timely and consistent.

Technology, Social Media, and Crisis Response

An illustration of the power of technology in general, and social media in particular, during a crisis is found in the 2013 Boston Marathon bombings. After the explosions, race participants and spectators relied on Twitter to both post and acquire information. Individuals at the race tweeted pictures as well as their personal feelings. The social media response was significant, and the Boston Globe essentially turned their website into a blog to instantly offer reports from the Twitter accounts of public officials, news outlets, and other citizens (Gilgoff & Lee, 2013). Similarly, when a school crisis occurs, students and staff in the building can be expected to send out messages via smartphones using social media. Depending on the magnitude of the crisis event, social media may be the quickest way of sending information out and receiving information from stakeholders. For example, cell phone towers and local land lines may be overwhelmed with individuals wanting to speak with loved ones. Illustrative of this situation is the 2011 earthquake and tsunami in Japan, during which thousands of people went to Twitter and Facebook to send messages to people because the cell phone network was down (Blackburn, 2011).

During a crisis, school districts that post quickly and accurately to their website or social media sites assist in the crisis response by giving caregivers and members of the community specific information on how they can respond. The following example demonstrates how one school would have benefited from using social media to inform parents. During a lockdown drill, several students mistook the drill for an active shooter situation and sent text messages to their parents stating that an armed assailant was in the building. The parents in turn went to the district's social media and website. When they found no information about the drill, they immediately contacted local media. The resulting alarm and confusion could have been avoided by the prompt and timely use of technology and social media.

When using smartphones, text messaging, and social media during a crisis response, messages should be short and concise. Keeping messages below 120 characters ensures that the message goes out as one text message or tweet. If the message has to be translated, the message might have to be even shorter. Smartphone carriers (e.g., Verizon, AT&T, Sprint, Cricket, T-Mobile) can advise school districts on desired message length. Table 7.7 offers an example of a school's social media messages when police were responding to an emergency in the community.

Technology, like social media, can also be used by schools to assess the impact of a crisis event. For example, the PIO (and a "technology team") can monitor social media for personal crisis narratives that tell stories of how the event affected school community members. When using social media as an information source, the PIO must verify the accuracy of these postings. In addition, it is important to avoid plagiarizing messages. For example, if a school district wants to share information about a new Red Cross shelter, to avoid the district appearing to be the source of the information, the PIO should simply repost, share, or retweet the original message.

Table 7.7. Sample Social Media Messaging

Time	Script
2:32 p.m.	Jackson Elementary has gone into a hard (emergency) lockdown at the request of the police. More information to follow.
2:40 p.m.	Jackson Elementary is now on a soft (preventive; "secured perimeter") lockdown. Cause is a bank robbery in the area. No visitors are allowed in the building.
3:00 p.m.	Jackson Elementary dismissal will be delayed due to lockdown. More information to follow.
3:15 p.m.	Police have cleared the area near Jackson Elementary. All clear has been given. Dismissal delayed by 15 minutes.
3:15 p.m.	Jackson Elementary parents, please expect buses to arrive 15 minutes late.

Evaluation of the Use of Technology and Social Media in Crisis Response

As part of the AAR, the crisis response team evaluates the effectiveness of crisis communication. Evaluation questions used by the team to make recommendations on how to improve the use of technology and social media include the following: Which social media sites did the district use? Which social media sites did the majority of stakeholders use? How quickly was the crisis response message sent out to stakeholders? How many people viewed the messages on the social media site? What information was sent out to other individuals after it was received by the district (i.e., shared or retweeted)? How many people are following the district's social media account pages after the crisis event versus before the crisis event? For example, one such evaluation discovered that the school's voicemail system took almost an hour to send out a voicemail informing all parents of a crisis situation, while information sent out on Facebook and Twitter went out instantaneously.

CONCLUSION

District-level and school crisis response teams are an essential component of efforts to initiate and implement comprehensive plans to address all aspects of crisis preparedness. Crisis response teams must do more than simply react to immediate crisis circumstances. They must also (in collaboration with school safety teams) work to prevent and mitigate potential crises, prepare for those events that cannot be prevented, and develop protocols to address the immediate as well as long-term consequences of crises.

The vast array of responsibilities involved in crisis response requires that schools collaborate with professionals and agencies outside the school context to initiate, implement, and sustain crisis response teams. The ICS provides a standardized structure for teams and aids in efforts to collaboratively develop crisis response plans (U.S. Department of Education, 2013; U.S. DHS, 2014). School-employed mental health professionals are likely to be most effective when they fill a very specific ICS role and are surrounded by a multidisciplinary crisis response team whose members fill each of the other ICS roles.

Finally, schools must be able to effectively communicate with all stakeholders during and following a school crisis response. Schools not yet using technology and social media on a regular basis, or at least testing these modes of communication, should do so. Given increased expectations for immediate updates on crisis situations, schools should constantly work to deliver timely and accurate information to those affected by a school-associated crisis event.

Chapter 8

SCHOOL CRISIS RESPONSE PREPAREDNESS: THE BASIC EMERGENCY OPERATIONS PLAN

The U.S. Department of Education (2013) uses the term Emergency Operations Plan (EOP) to describe what the PREPaRE model refers to as the school crisis response plan. For consistency, the term *crisis response plan* will continue to be used in this chapter. The three main sections of this plan are the (a) basic plan, (b) functional annexes, and (c) threat and hazard annexes. Developing the crisis response plan, and acquiring the resources necessary to train staff and students to implement and follow that plan, takes time and diligent planning. This chapter describes how schools create the basic crisis response plan, while Chapter 9 describes how to develop the functional and threat- and hazard-specific annexes needed to effectively respond to and recover from crises. This chapter also gives special attention to three important aspects of planning: crisis response training exercises and evaluation, students with special needs, and cultural considerations.

The PREPaRE model identifies the following six steps in its crisis response planning process based on U.S. Department of Education (2013): (a) form a collaborative planning team; (b) understand the context or situation of the school; (c) determine goals and objectives; (d) develop the plan (or identify courses of action); (e) prepare, review, and approve the plan; and (f) implement and maintain the plan. Following these six steps results in a comprehensive school crisis response plan addressing a range of crises. Table 8.1 offers additional guidance and basic considerations in crisis response planning.

The district-level and school safety and crisis response teams need to work collaboratively, along with emergency management and community agencies to develop a crisis response plan. In addition to the discussion provided here, developing school crisis response teams will find a free downloadable app known as EOP ASSIST helpful in their planning efforts (http://rems.ed.gov/EOPASSIST.aspx).

Table 8.1. Guiding Principles and Basic Considerations of a Crisis Response Plan

1. *Secure leadership support.* School and district leadership are essential to the planning process and can help secure resources to successfully activate a crisis response.

2. *Build upon what's already in place.* Existing policies, plans, and procedures that are effective should be used as the foundation for new requirements.

3. *Carefully select crisis response planning and team leaders.* Identify school staff members who are able to provide planning leadership. These team members must be able to (a) estimate crisis risk and plan ahead; (b) make use of data; (c) organize planning efforts; (d) sustain the training process; (e) stay calm when responding to a crisis; and (f) be competent in facilitating the crisis response and recovery process. A school staff member's job title alone does not give a person these qualities, so careful selection is critical.

4. *Involve key stakeholders.* Various stakeholder groups to include in the development of the crisis response plan are administrators, regular and special education teachers, school-employed mental health professionals, school resource officers, first responder agencies, community-based mental health providers, parents, and students. Collaboration and various viewpoints are critical to developing an effective plan and can foster cooperative relationships among community partners by clearly identifying their roles and expectations.

5. *Have backup personnel ready to fulfill roles.* The plan should account for the possibility that team members will be unavailable. Each assigned role should have at least three people trained to fulfill a given role (primary person with two backup individuals).

6. *Use data to customize crisis response plans to the building level.* Effective plans use comprehensive, ongoing vulnerability assessments of the school building and immediate surrounding community. These assessments address both physical and psychological safety and take an all-hazards approach to include prevention, protection, mitigation, response, and recovery.

7. *Address all settings and times.* Schools must plan for crises that occur before, during, and after school hours and during the summer, and also include off-campus events.

8. *Make the plan user-friendly and free of jargon, with clearly defined roles and responsibilities.* Successful implementation occurs only if each member of the district and school crisis response teams understands the plan's comprehensive and interdependent requirements and is knowledgeable and prepared for his or her assigned role.

9. *Include comprehensive and condensed versions of the plan.* The comprehensive plan, which is used by the district and school crisis response teams, involves assigning specific roles, responsibilities, and procedures and integrating all areas of the Incident Command

System. The comprehensive plan includes details contained in a variety of threat- and hazard-specific annexes (e.g., lockdown, reverse evacuation, and fire) and specific functional annexes. A condensed version of this plan is also developed to provide school staff with guidance on the immediate execution of specific roles and responsibilities to ensure student safety and accountability during the crisis response. The condensed version is short, easy to follow, and placed in all classroom and common areas (Reeves et al., 2010).

10. *Incorporate the needs of special school populations.* Crisis response plans must address the needs of general and special education students, those with limited English, and other special student populations.

11. *Include training in risk assessment procedures.* Threat and suicide risk assessment procedures should be developed. All school staff members and students need to be taught the risk factors and warning signs of suicidal ideation and other threatening behaviors, and be empowered to report those signs. School-employed mental health professionals are the most appropriate staff members to conduct these assessments. More discussion of risk assessment is offered in Chapter 4.

12. *Provide professional development and practice.* A crisis response plan is only as good as the staff members who implement the plan. Staff training is necessary to advance knowledge and awareness related to the school crisis response plan and must include crisis drills and exercises. (See exercises and practice in this chapter; see Chapters 20 and 21 on examination of crisis response plan effectiveness.)

13. *Review and update plans periodically.* Changes in personnel, local conditions, and other factors require periodic reviews and updating of crisis response plans to ensure their applicability to current conditions and personnel. This updating is critical to long-term sustainability and effectiveness.

Note. Adams & Kritsonis (2006); Armstrong, Massey, & Boroughs (2006); Brock, Sandoval, & Lewis (2001); Brock et al. (2009); U.S. Department of Education (2013); University of the State of New York (2010).

THE BASIC PLAN

Guidance offered by the U.S. Department of Education (2013) outlines the basic plan. This is the first section of the crisis response plan, and it includes the basic plan elements that schools need to respond to crises.

Introduction

The introduction of the basic plan includes a cover page and a statement signed by the school district's authorizing official (e.g., superintendent) that recognizes and adopts the school crisis response plan. The introduction also has a page that (a) shows approval of the plan by the appropriate district leaders (i.e., signatures or statements of support), (b) states that the school crisis response plan supersedes all previous plans, and (c) identifies who has authority to modify the plan without the authorizing official's approval. The introduction also includes a page that tracks any changes that were made to the plan and who has received a copy of the plan (U.S. Department of Education, 2013).

Concept of Operations

The concept of operations section of the basic plan explains in general terms how the school or district administration intends to respond to crises. It states how schools protect students, staff, and visitors by identifying who has the authority to activate the plan. For example, these plans often specify that any school staff member can call for a lockdown or pull the fire alarm. It also describes how a school coordinates with local emergency response and other community agencies and with local heads of government with regard to the five mission areas of crisis response (i.e., prevention, protection, mitigation, response, and recovery). More specifically, this section outlines (a) a yearly schedule for plan review by the school safety and crisis response teams and local police and fire departments; (b) a schedule of fire drill observations by the local fire department; (c) cooperative efforts with police and fire departments that are required during an emergency to minimize the impact on life and property and to recover from the negative effects of the crisis; (d) how federal or state agencies assist the school team with the crisis response if needed, such as by establishing a unified command, opening up an Emergency Operations Center, or implementing a Joint Information Center; and (e) considerations for addressing individuals with special needs during crisis events (U.S. Department of Education, 2013).

Organization and Assignment of Responsibilities

This section of the basic plan delineates the responsibilities of all school staff members, caregivers, students, and community agencies during emergencies. The broad roles of community support (e.g., volunteers, American Red Cross) may also be included. This section includes agreements with the various agencies during an emergency, such as a memorandum of understanding with a church to use their facilities for family reunification (U.S. Department of Education, 2013).

Direction, Control, and Coordination

This section of the basic plan describes how the district's or school's Incident Command System (ICS) is used, how the crisis response plan would interface with other community crisis response plans (e.g., local police and fire departments), and who has control of the resources needed to support crisis response efforts. This element of the plan includes a chart of who is on the district-level or school crisis response team (including their two backups), with the specific responsibilities of each member delineated. This section also states who has the authority to purchase and move equipment, lend equipment to other schools in the district, or borrow equipment from others. In larger districts, such authority may be a function of the district-level crisis response team (e.g., district Incident Commander, Logistics Section Chief, or superintendent), whereas in smaller or more rural settings, the school crisis response team would assume these responsibilities (U.S. Department of Education, 2013).

Information Collection, Analysis, and Dissemination

This section of the basic plan describes the role that involves getting and receiving information during the emergency. Controlling information is critical, because misinformation, such as a rumor about someone in the building with a gun during a lockdown drill, can affect the actions of the crisis response team and local emergency responders.

The crisis response team also needs to determine how crisis information is analyzed and disseminated. The Public Information Officer (PIO) is responsible for receiving information from the media and the public, whereas the Liaison Officer receives the information from outside agencies assisting in the response. Both the PIO and the Liaison Officer should determine and verify the sources of their information, how they provide crisis information to those who need to know, and when and in what form the information should be shared (U.S. Department of Education, 2013; U.S. Department of Homeland Security [DHS], 2008).

The school safety team can help the crisis response team ensure that the plan includes information the team needs before, during, and after a crisis, such as lists of school- or district-approved volunteers, weather reports, law enforcement alerts, and news media alerts. Other lists can include contact information for mental health agencies, hotlines, and emergency management agencies (e.g., Federal Emergency Management Agency, American Red Cross); agencies that can assist with continuity of operations (discussed in Chapter 9; e.g., insurance company, companies that can provide equipment such as fencing or generators); and technology resources, along with technical support (e.g., satellite phones, Internet servers, computers, printers).

Administration, Finance, and Logistics

This section of the basic plan includes information on how schools or the district obtains and manages resources during emergencies. The plan covers policies and procedures for the Finance/Administration Section Chief, as well as procedures on managing the budget; purchasing equipment and other resources before, during, and after a crisis; and maintaining logs of events and key activities. This section also describes how to preserve vital records, which is also important to continuity of operations (U.S. Department of Education, 2013).

Plan Development And Maintenance

This section of the basic plan discusses the planning process, identifies the participants involved in developing and revising the plan, and includes a timeline for plan revision. Both the school safety and crisis response teams should check to see if their school district or state has guidelines on the recommended frequency for revising their plan. Table 8.2 provides a sample timeline (U.S. Department of Education, 2013).

Table 8.2. Potential Timeline for Biannual Review of the School Crisis Response Plan

Year One
- The Planning Section Chief writes After-Action Reports (AARs) after each crisis response and keeps a file of the reports for review.
- The Planning Section Chief makes recommendations to the school safety and crisis response teams for any areas of the school safety and crisis response plans that require immediate revisions.

Year Two
- September–October: The school safety and crisis response teams review the AARs from the previous school year. The teams look for information and patterns in the crisis response that might suggest the need to change the school safety and crisis response plans.
- November–January: Members of the school safety and crisis response teams start making recommendations for revising the school safety and crisis response plans.
- February: The teams provide recommendations for change to the local emergency management agencies for their review. Local emergency management agencies provide their feedback to the school safety and crisis response teams.
- March–May: The teams finalize their recommendations for changing the school safety and crisis response plans based on feedback. Recommendations are brought to the appropriate district-level representative for approval.
- June: The revised school safety and crisis response plans are signed and printed for mass distribution.
- July–August: District staff members are provided any necessary training on the revised school safety and crisis response plans. The school and district schedule discussion-based exercises and emergency drills so school staff and emergency responders can work together under the revised school crisis response plan.

Authorities and References

The final section of the basic plan provides a list of school board policies, laws, statutes, ordinances, regulations, and memoranda of understanding, along with any other formal agreements that are relevant to crises in schools and provide guidance in implementing the five mission areas (Obama, 2011; U.S. Department of Education, 2013). Chapter 2's discussion of the legal, legislative, and policy rationales for crisis prevention and preparedness may be helpful in developing this section.

TRAINING, EXERCISES, AND EVALUATION OF EFFORTS

The crisis response plan should include a schedule of monthly meetings to identify and address safety concerns and to ensure continual crisis response planning and preparation. Drills and exercises should be conducted throughout the year to allow the team, the rest of the school staff, and students to continue practicing and refining skills. Meetings, drills, and exercises should be scheduled before the school year begins, because trying to coordinate multiple schedules is very challenging after the school year has started.

Crisis response plans should also address vulnerability assessments. While these assessments are typically conducted by school safety teams, the information provided is important to the crisis response team as it develops a response plan. Assessments should be conducted annually to help determine what crisis events are most likely to occur in the school's setting and to schedule practice of the specific protocols to address the identified vulnerabilities. Preparation should start with simple, low-cost, discussion-based exercises, such as orientations, workshops, or tabletop exercises, and advance to more complex, and expensive, operations-based exercises, such as drills and full-scale exercises (Freeman & Taylor, 2010; National Association of School Psychologists [NASP], 2013a; U.S. Department of Education, Readiness and Emergency Management for Schools [REMS] Technical Assistance [TA] Center, 2006).

Discussion-Based Exercises

These exercises teach staff members what to do in crisis situations and provide opportunities for dialogue and discussion. They are less complicated than operations-based exercises; focus on strategic, policy-oriented issues; and do not involve deployment of resources. Specific types of discussion-based exercises include orientation seminars, workshops, and tabletop exercises. All are efficient ways to familiarize students and school staff members with crisis response plans, procedures, policies, agency agreements, and emergency procedures (Federal Emergency Management Agency [FEMA], 2014b; NASP, 2013a; U.S. Department of Education, REMS TA Center, 2006).

Orientation Seminars
Orientation seminars are relatively brief meetings that can be part of regularly scheduled school staff meetings, or at all school assemblies, and can include discussions facilitated by a safety or crisis response team. These seminars review the school's emergency response procedures and are often the first step to ensuring that the crisis response plan has been explained to all school staff, including cafeteria and other support staff, and to students and their caregivers as appropriate. Seminars allow school staff members to discuss crisis response coordination, roles, responsibilities, procedures, and the equipment that might be needed to respond to a school emergency. Presentations can use PowerPoint, handouts, or videos that illustrate the correct response in an emergency situation (Freeman & Taylor, 2010; NASP, 2013a).

Workshops
More involved than orientations, workshops typically last from a few hours to a few days. They use lectures, discussions, and breakout sessions to teach participants specific topics and skills, using interaction to solve problems, obtain consensus, and build teams. Workshops also include sharing information, obtaining different perspectives, and testing new ideas, policies, or procedures. They can also involve training groups to perform specific coordinated crisis response activities (NASP, 2013a; U.S. DHS, 2007).

Tabletop Exercises

These exercises, which typically last 1 to 4 hours, provide an in-depth, constructive problem-solving discussion about existing emergency response plans (Freeman & Taylor, 2011). Crisis response team participants must work together to resolve a crisis scenario that is presented verbally, in writing, or by video (Reeves, Conolly-Wilson, Pesce, Lazzaro, & Brock, 2012; U.S. Department of Education, 2006). A facilitator often designates a scribe and an observer. The scribe takes detailed notes of each action the team takes during specific steps of the drill. The observer watches the reactions of the team and provides feedback at the end of the drill, describing the strengths of the response and areas the team needs to improve.

Tabletop drills often inject unexpected events into the drill (e.g., in the middle of a lockdown students are texting their parents unverified reports that two students have died). Because crises typically do not unfold in a predictable manner, the use of tabletop drills helps the team learn how to adapt (NASP, 2013a). Tabletop drills should also include a discussion of psychological triage, in which the team evaluates and prioritizes individual mental health crisis intervention needs (covered in Section 4 of this book) and the ability to provide the specific mental health crisis interventions to be offered during the crisis response and recovery phases (Section 5).

Operations-Based Training

Operations-based training includes complex exercises, a variety of emergency drills, functional and full-scale exercises, and includes what is referred to as the armed assailant or "active shooter" drill. These training activities involve the deployment of resources and personnel and require execution of plans. Staff, students, first responders, and community agencies practice their assigned roles and then evaluate whether the response was efficient, effective, and consistent with the response plan. Lessons learned from training experiences help to clarify roles and responsibilities and improve individual and team performance (FEMA, 2014b; NASP, 2013a; U.S. Department of Education, 2006).

Emergency Drills

Operations-based exercises that involve the practice of specific school crisis response procedures are referred to as emergency drills (U.S. DHS, 2013a). Depending on the type of drill and its objectives, emergency drills can last from a few minutes to a few hours (Freeman & Taylor, 2010). Drills should be conducted in a variety of conditions and circumstances, such as during less convenient times of the day, before school or during lunch, and across the school year, not just during agreeable weather.

Zhe and Nickerson (2007) have evaluated the effectiveness of the traditional lockdown drill (not to be confused with what is referred to as the active shooter drill) and found that students' short-term knowledge and skill acquisition increased following a thoughtfully planned and executed training session followed by an intruder drill, all without increasing students' levels of anxiety. One of the long-term goals of emergency drills is to practice components of the crisis response plan to prepare teams, school staff members, and students for more extensive exercises in the future (Freeman & Taylor, 2011). Drills and exercises should start simple, build on each other, and be supported by adequate planning and resources so that schools do not rush into a full-scale exercise too quickly (Freeman & Taylor, 2011; U.S. DHS, 2013a). Table 8.3 provides a summary of common school crisis drills.

Functional Exercises

More involved than emergency drills, functional exercises involve activating the district-level and school crisis response teams to respond to realistic simulations of crises that increase the stressful feelings generated when responding to an actual event (U.S. Department of Education, 2013). Functional exercises typically test one or more of the functional or threat- and hazard specific annexes (discussed in Chapter 9) in response to a specified crisis that would require the school to implement its crisis response plan. These exercises last from 3 to 8 hours, but they do not involve the use of emergency response personnel and equipment.

Full-Scale Exercises

The most complex type of drill, the full-scale exercise, should be conducted only after discussion-based and functional exercises have been practiced. They involve multiple agencies and use the threat- and hazard-specific and functional annexes to test the effectiveness of the district-level and school crisis response plans (U.S. Department of Education, 2013). The full-scale exercise is a simulation of a specific emergency situation in real time, with all necessary resources deployed. The exercise allows school districts to evaluate the operational capabilities of their crisis response plan in a highly stressful environment that simulates actual conditions.

Before selecting a full-scale exercise scenario, a school district and all of its local schools should have first conducted vulnerability assessments (discussed in Chapter 3) that include a local hazard analysis (Reeves et al., 2011a). To design and conduct a full-scale exercise, districts must also collaborate with multiple agencies, including police, fire, and health departments; mental health agencies; transportation systems; local utilities; hospitals; and emergency management agencies. Full-scale exercises also may involve multiple municipalities and jurisdictions (Freeman & Taylor, 2010, 2011; U.S. DHS, 2007). A school district considering a full-scale exercise must ensure that the exercise does not cause harm, such as frightening participants. Caregivers must be informed about the exercise at least 1 month in advance, and the school should work with the media and the local government to inform all members of the surrounding community about the exercise. These exercises are elaborate, expensive, and time-consuming, lasting from a half-day to multiple days, and they often have a significant effect on instructional and professional work time (NASP, 2013a). Table 8.4 provides a list of essential considerations when conducting a full-scale exercise.

Armed Assailant (or Active Shooter) Drills

Since the tragic shootings at Sandy Hook Elementary School in Newtown, Connecticut, school districts have been under increasing pressure to practice active shooter drills. Contributing to this pressure, the U.S. Department of Education (2013) has recommended expanding the lockdown-only approach to an options-based "Run, Hide, Fight" model. This model empowers school staff

Table 8.3. Types of School Crisis Drills

Type of Drill	Description	Related Crisis Type
Lockdown	Participants remain in the school building when the environment outside the school is threatening or when movement within the school building is judged to be unsafe.	Dangerous intruder (which could include a dangerous animal) in school building, on school grounds, or in nearby community
	Participants sit quietly in locked rooms positioned away from windows and doors in an area that is out of sight of a potential intruder.	Act of violence (e.g., stabbing, shooting, or assault) occurring in school building
Evacuation	Participants leave an unsafe school building or facility and relocate at a predetermined setting safely away from the school.	Fire, bomb threat, gas leak
	Multiple evacuation sites should be designated to serve as backups.	
Reverse Evacuation	Participants move from the school grounds (e.g., playground) into the school building.	Unsafe intruder on school grounds or in community (e.g., bank robbery in community, rabid dog in the area)
	Reverse evacuation can lead to a lockdown or shelter-in-place procedure.	Unsafe weather conditions, such as a tornado or severe storm
Duck-Cover-Hold	Two procedures:	
	Participants take cover under a nearby desk or table, making sure as much of their body as possible is under cover. Participants then cover their eyes by leaning their face against their arm. Participants hold on to the legs of the desk or table until the event ceases.	Earthquake Tornado Acts of war or terrorist attack
	All participants move to the hallways of the first floor. Participants kneel on the ground then cover their face and head with both arms. Participants then drop their heads into their laps until the event ceases	

Shelter-in-Place	Participants relocate to predetermined rooms on the first level of a school building that has minimal or no windows and vents.	Severe weather (e.g., tornado) Chemical, radiological, or biological weapons
	Disaster kits are opened (these contain nonperishable food, bottled water, battery-powered radio, first aid supplies, batteries, duct tape, plastic sheeting, plastic garbage bags, etc.).	
	All windows and doors are sealed with duct tape and plastic sheeting (if necessary).	
	Mechanical systems are turned off (e.g., fans, heating or cooling systems)	

Note. Federal Emergency Management Agency (2003, March).

Table 8.4. Essential Considerations When Developing and Conducting Full-Scale Exercises

1. The exercise may require as long as 1 year to 18 months to develop.

2. It should be preceded by orientation sessions, emergency drills, and functional exercises. The school or district should have a long-term emergency exercise plan that begins with basic drills and culminates with the full-scale drill.

3. A full-scale exercises requires substantial financial planning, with significant staff and emergency personnel time. School districts should consider if money might be more effectively spent on prevention programming or on high likelihood hazards that were identified in the district's vulnerability assessment.

4. Collaboration with an outside expert or consultant can provide guidance in conducting a crisis exercise.

5. Efforts must be made to prevent an exercise from being mistaken for a real crisis event. The school district must inform the community about the drill, including school announcements and instructions, media reports about the drill, phone calls to parents, flyers around community businesses, and so on.

6. If the exercise exposes students and staff to potentially traumatic stimuli (e.g., guns firing blanks, fake blood), the school district must be prepared for the possibility that this exposure may lead to increased perceptions of threat, remind students of prior traumatic events, and generate distressing reactions.

Table 8.4. Continued

7. If students and staff are to be involved (e.g., play the role of a victim), they should be carefully screened for physical and emotional resilience. Participation should be voluntary.

8. Participating agencies should follow the National Incident Management System's Incident Command System and activate an Emergency Operations Center.

9. Participants should be required to sign in before the exercise begins, receive an initial briefing, and wear identification specifying their assigned roles.

10. A post-incident assessment must be conducted to identify what aspects of the response need correcting.

11. Establishing a no-fault, no-fail expectation emphasizes that mistakes or inconsistencies are learning opportunities that can be used to improve future crisis response.

12. A safe forum should be made available for all participants to discuss their experiences and process their emotions.

Note. Adapted from *Conducting Crisis Exercises and Drills: Guidelines for Schools*, p. 3, by NASP, 2013a, Bethesda, MD: Author. Copyright 2013 by the National Association of School Psychologists.

members to make independent decisions about how to protect their students, depending on evolving circumstances (e.g., evacuate the building rather than stay in a classroom if a teacher judged this to be the best way to keep his or her students safe).

At the time of this book's publication, the efficacy of active shooter drills has not been demonstrated. Moreover, school-associated violent deaths are extremely rare (Brock, 2015b; Cornell, 2015; Nekvasil, Cornell, & Huang, 2015; Robers, Zhang, Morgan, & Musu-Gillette, 2015). Thus, schools must consider the costs and benefits of practicing armed assailant or active shooter drills when allocating their limited crisis preparedness resources. For example, one of the authors observed a situation wherein a school district spent a substantial amount of money preparing for active shooter drills, but they chose not to invest in a suicide prevention program, despite having never experienced an active shooter situation and recently experiencing several student suicides.

Guidelines developed by NASP and National Association of School Resource Officers (2014) recommend that if a school chooses to conduct an armed assailant drill they must (a) always let participants know in advance when a drill will occur (never conduct unannounced armed assailant drills); (b) allow staff and students to opt out of such activities (to account for the possibility that personal histories may make the drill traumatic) and provide alternative instruction for those who opt out; and, perhaps most important, (c) continue to emphasize the use of traditional lockdown drills, particularly when the school has doors that can be locked from the inside. The basis for recommending a continued emphasis on lockdowns includes both expert opinion and review of past incidents. According to Mo Canady, executive director of the National School Resource Officers Association,

Typically, in the traditional active shooter scenario or situations that have occurred over the years, shooters have had a tendency to pass locked doors, to not go through a locked door. They're looking for easy, quick targets. (Cohen, 2013, ¶18)

In addition, the first recommendation of the Sandy Hook Advisory Commission's final report (2015) states:

> The [School Safety Infrastructure Council, 2014] Report includes a standard requiring classroom and other safe-haven areas to have doors that can be locked from the inside. The Commission cannot emphasize enough the importance of this recommendation. *The testimony and other evidence presented to the Commission reveals that there has never been an event in which an active shooter breached a locked classroom door.* Accordingly, the Commission reiterates its recommendation that all classrooms in K-12 schools should be equipped with locked doors that can be locked from the inside by the classroom teacher or substitute. (pp. 32–33)

Schools that are considering conducting an armed assailant drill should refer to the document *Best Practice Considerations for Schools in Active Shooter and Other Armed Assailant Drills* (NASP & NASRO, 2014; www.nasponline.org/BP-armed-assailant-drills). This document addresses factors that schools should take into account when considering and conducting these drills and describes how the drills might fit into a larger comprehensive approach to school safety and crisis response drills and exercises. The document includes a hierarchy of education and training options as well as a review of levels of developmentally appropriate safety awareness. The importance of careful planning is emphasized by the fact that lawsuits have been filed on behalf of employees against their employers seeking compensation for physical and psychological injuries incurred when these drills were conducted (Frosch, 2014).

STUDENTS WITH SPECIAL NEEDS

Three federal laws require the basic crisis response plan to attend to students with special needs: the Americans with Disabilities Act of 1990 (amended 2008), the Individuals with Disabilities Education Act of 1975 (amended 1997 and 2004), and Section 504 of the Rehabilitation Act of 1973 (amended 1978). In addition, President George W. Bush (2004) signed Executive Order 13347, *Individuals With Disabilities in Emergency Preparedness*, which requires public entities to include individuals with disabilities in their emergency preparedness efforts (U.S. Department of Education, 2006). Despite these requirements, most schools do not have crisis response plans and procedures to assist students with special needs (Graham et al., 2006; Kano & Bourque, 2007; Kano et al., 2007; Olympia, Wan, & Avner, 2005). The topic of assisting individuals with mental and physical disabilities is mentioned only briefly in approximately half of the planning materials provided by states to their local school districts (Annandale, Heath, Dean, Kemple, & Takino, 2011). Further, testimony by the U.S. Government Accountability Office (2007) revealed that less than one third of schools surveyed had procedures for students with special needs in their emergency or crisis response plans. Given that 8.8% of children ages 15 and under in the United States have a disability, a figure that increases to 10.4% when adolescents and young adults ages 15 to 24 are included, this lack of preparedness is troubling (Brault, 2008).

Inclusion of students with special needs into crisis response planning is limited by (a) vague and inconsistent definitions of special needs, (b) failure to distinguish between preparedness for everyday emergencies and disasters, and (c) minimal research on effective procedures for school crisis preparedness with regard to students with disabilities (Boon et al., 2011). How a school defines the term *special needs* may depend on the values, attitudes, and knowledge base of the school (Boon, Pagliano, Brown, & Tsey, 2012). One recommendation is to define the terms more broadly as "populations with varying needs" (Victoria Department of Education and Early Childhood Development, 2010, p. 16). Within federal emergency management systems, special needs are defined as additional needs in functional areas such as independence, communication, transportation, supervision, and medical care (Batten-Mickens & Spears, 2008). Under that definition, individuals with special needs include not only those with physical and psychological disabilities, but also those who live in institutionalized settings, ethnic minorities, limited or non-English speakers, individuals with special medical and dietary needs, children, the elderly, and the homeless (Batten-Mickens & Spears, 2008; Kailes & Enders, 2007).

Crisis Prevention, Protection, and Mitigation for Students With Special Needs

In terms of prevention, schools should plan their ongoing school-wide prevention activities to ensure that students with disabilities are receiving school safety information in ways that are appropriate for their needs and developmental level. For example, the high school student with an intellectual disability may require specially designed safety instructions. School-wide protection and mitigation strategies should include ensuring that special needs students are in classrooms that are easily accessible and from which evacuation can be readily accomplished. For example, classrooms for students with physical disabilities should be on the school's first floor, and in close proximity to exits and the school nurse.

Crisis response teams can also help mitigate the impact of crises by ensuring that school-wide procedures are in place for sharing students' medical or disability information with relevant personnel (e.g., transportation officials who might facilitate evacuations and emergency first responders), and develop strategies that build on existing accommodation plans and special services (Marin County Office of Education, 2010). Personal emergency kits should be a standard part of the safety materials developed for all students with severe handicaps. These kits should include written descriptions of their special needs and as well as any medications, copies of prescriptions, dosage information, vital contact information, and comfort items. To assist students with mobility challenges, school staff members should be trained to use proper lifting techniques when moving a student out of a wheelchair. These lifting techniques should be practiced during school drills so staff and students know what to expect when transporting students in wheelchairs. When schools engage in practices such as these and include the individuals with special needs, both staff members and students alike cope better in times of crisis (Martins, 2013).

Crisis Response and Recovery for Students With Special Needs

The crisis response plan should have procedures in place to appropriately alert all students with special needs about an emergency. For example, to alert students who are deaf or hearing impaired, or who speak a language other than English, the crisis response plan might direct school staff members to use prewritten instructions (e.g., placards in various languages) or sign language to inform the students about an emergency and to tell them what to do next. To account for the crisis response needs of deaf and hearing-impaired students, schools should have strobe lights installed in hallways and bathrooms to alert these students to a fire alarm.

School crisis response teams must also be aware that children with disabilities may find recovery from exposure to a crisis event more challenging than their typically developing peers (Boon et al., 2011). Therefore, the school's procedures for screening, monitoring, and intervening after a crisis need to be especially sensitive to the unique needs of students with disabilities (Council for Exceptional Children & Counsel for Children with Behavioral Disorders, 2013).

Individualized Emergency Plans

Clarke, Jones, and Yssel (2014) recommend a team approach when developing individualized emergency plans, and students, caregivers, general and special education teachers, school administrators, and first responders should all be involved. The U.S. Department of Education (2006) recommends including a disability specialist, such as special education teachers, on the crisis response team, not only to provide expertise on disability issues, policies, and legislation, but also to use that specialist's expertise with regard to crisis response needs and services for specific students with disabilities. Individualized emergency plans should be incorporated into a student's Individualized Education Program (IEP; Clarke et al., 2014) or Section 504 plan. An advantage of including individualized emergency plans within IEPs or 504 plans is that both outline the unique needs of students and both are subject to annual review. The school crisis response team should work with each student's teacher to determine multiple locations to store these plans so the plans are easily accessible in the event of an emergency (e.g., placed in administrator and teacher go-kits).

The U.S. Department of Education's (2013) *Guide for Developing High-Quality School Emergency Operations Plans* specifies that individualized emergency plans should include preparation, testing, notification and alerts, evacuation, transportation, sheltering, medical care, and services. Plans should include individuals (students and school staff members) with permanent or temporary (e.g., broken leg) disabilities (U.S. Department of Education, 2006) and include the provision of appropriate auxiliary aids and services (e.g., interpreters, captioning, accessible information technology) to ensure effective communication. In addition, plans should ensure that individuals with disabilities are not separated from their service animals, assistive devices, medication, and other needs. Table 8.5 lists, by disability type, the challenges these individualized emergency plans might address and specific strategies that might be employed to meet student needs. Table 8.6 provides plan example.

Table 8.5. Considerations for Students With Disabilities During an Emergency

Disability	Factors That Elevate the Individual's Risk in Emergencies	Strategies to Reduce Risk in Emergencies
Autism	• Works best in predictable routines (anxiety likely with change in routine) • Needs differentiation in tasks • Has difficulty with social responsiveness • May be nonverbal or have limited communication • Prone to wandering, hiding, or running away from a safe environment (to decrease stimulation) • May have little ability to recognize danger and stay safe • May have unique sensory needs or sensitivities	• Provide frequent practice with emergency procedures • Perform task analysis of responses (include least intrusive prompts and error correction) • Use the student's normal routine in emergency procedures (e.g., if the student uses a picture schedule, create one for emergency procedures; include a familiar toy, blanket, or other item in emergency kit) • Increase the number of staff members assigned to this group to help in drills and emergency situations • Provide special equipment to reduce stimulation (e.g., ear plugs or noise-reducing earmuffs)
Emotional disturbance	• May have limited ability to understand or comply with the demands of the environmental events, situations, or procedures • Exhibits externalizing (acting out, noncompliant) or internalizing behaviors (anxiety, depression, withdrawal) • May panic, shut down, withdraw, or not follow instructions the first time they are given	• Provide instruction and frequent practice with emergency procedures • Develop self-management skills needed to be safe during a crisis (following direction, managing panic) • Repeat instructions frequently to increase rates of compliance • Use incentives in individualized emergency plans if these are used in behavior contracts to comply with teacher requests
Hearing impairment	• Has complete or partial loss of hearing • May not respond to auditory cues, alarms, or announcements	• Train teachers to use sign language, hand signals, and specialized communication in an emergency (such as a flashlight) • Be prepared with prewritten instructions

	• May not be able to keep up with the fast talking of adults during a crisis	• Use interpreters, captioning, and accessible information technology • Use strobe lights, vibrating pagers, or phone alerts to supplement audible alarms
Intellectual disability	• Has difficulty acquiring new knowledge and skills, remembering information, or attending to features of a new task • Has limited adaptive behavior that may affect self-care and sense of danger	• Use explicit teaching and practice emergency procedures paired with active response opportunities across settings • Use the student's typical accommodations in emergency situations (e.g., augmentative communication device) • Be prepared to simplify instructions or repeat instructions multiple times to increase understanding
Multiple disabilities	• Has two or more impairments, the combination of which create unique needs	• Provide adaptive physical equipment, such as a cane, walker, or wheelchair • Be prepared to use an alternative evacuation route • Designate an assembly area[a] • Designate a fire evacuation safety area (FESA)[b] • Provide alternative protection procedures for students unable to perform traditional procedures (e.g., protect head, neck, and face with a pillow or arms if unable to duck under desk)
Students with special health concerns	• Has a disease or disorder such as cancer, sickle cell anemia, asthma, ADHD, or diabetes	• Continue medication management regime • Use incentives in individualized emergency plan if these are used in a behavior contract to comply with teacher requests
Speech or language impairment	• Has a disorder related to accurately producing or articulating the sounds of language to communicate	• Use sign language, hand signals, or specialized communication for response in an emergency

Table 8.5. Continued

Disability	Factors That Elevate the Individual's Risk in Emergencies	Strategies to Reduce Risk in Emergencies
Visual impairment	• Has partial or complete loss of vision • May or may not see colors, shapes, or movement	• Enlist guidance from a sighted person or service animal • Give opportunities to explore facility exits • Use Braille or audible directional signage • Prepare recorded directions on a CD • Use color-coded routes through the school
Orthopedic impairment	• Has a physical limitation that impairs complete motor activities, strength, vitality, or an alertness to environmental stimuli	• Use adaptive physical equipment (e.g., cane, walker, wheelchair, positioning device, brace) to move or maintain a safe position • Identify alternative, accessible evacuation routes or procedures (alternative lift) • Designate an assembly area[a] • Designate a fire evacuation staging area[b] • Devise an emergency transportation plan for students with specific needs • Provide alternative emergency procedures (move to specific shelter area in school)
Deaf-blindness	• Has significant loss of both hearing and sight	• Provide multiple opportunities to explore school • Practice moving to safe locations and positions • See recommendations under visual and hearing impairment

Note. This table is compiled from Adelman & Taylor, 2002; Boon et al., 2012; Clarke, Jones, & Yssel, 2014; Fairfax County Public Schools, 2013; Marin County Office of Education, 2010; Minnesota School Safety Center, 2011; National Autism Association, 2012; National Association of School Psychologists, 2002a. a. *Assembly area* is a designated area where staff and students have been trained to gather following directives to evacuate a building (Fairfax County Public Schools, 2013), b. *Fire evacuation staging area* (FESA) is a designated room on the upper floors of a building, where students with physical disabilities report if they are unable to evacuate the building without using the elevator when the fire alarm sounds. This is a transition area where students with disabilities wait for removal by the fire department (Fairfax County Public Schools, 2013).

Table 8.6. Sample Individualized Emergency Plan

Student Name: *Trevor*   Age: *10*
Grade: *4*
Teacher: *Mr. Dobson*   School: *Pinewood Elementary*

Student strengths (qualities that are helpful in a crisis): Trevor is comfortable with his teacher, other adults, and children at school. During emergency drills he has evacuated the building with different adults without difficulty.

Medical needs: Trevor is diagnosed with autism and epilepsy (with seizures, in which he stares into space about 3 times per day for about 30 seconds). His Diastat, which is kept in the nurse's office, is administered if the seizure lasts for more than 5 minutes or if another seizure begins shortly after the first.

Physical needs: Trevor is ambulatory and does not need assistance in relocating.

Communication needs: Trevor has minimal expressive language skills (3–5 words that are understandable). He uses an iPad to communicate and uses the Sounding Board app to request food and breaks (instruction for using that app can be found in the Notes app).

Sensory needs: Trevor seeks tactile stimulation through shoulder squeezes and hugs. He vocalizes loudly under stress, and the vocalization can be ceased if he is given a stress ball to squeeze or a chewable necklace or wearable sensory tool (e.g., Chewelry).

Other critical information (e.g., emotional or behavioral needs, triggers): Trevor becomes distressed at the sound of loud alarms and will hide or rock when an alarm (e.g., fire alarm) sounds. He has a picture book that signals what to do for the different procedures (e.g., lockdown, evacuation). In the case of an emergency, the aide or other designee for Trevor should show him the book and guide him through the procedure using gentle physical assistance (e.g., hand on back or under the arm), if needed.

Individualized emergency kit contents: Trevor's kit is located with Mr. Dobson's classroom go-kit. It includes a printed copy of this plan, emergency contact information, Diastat and instructions, a stress ball, Chewelry, and a picture book of emergency procedures.

Note. Adapted from "Supporting Students With Disabilities During School Crises: A Teacher's Guide," by L. S. Clarke, R. E. Jones, & N. Yssel, 2014, *Teaching Exceptional Children, 46,* p. 172. Copyright 2014 by the authors. Adapted with permission.

Crises that result in changes in the expectations, ecological setting, and support systems of students with special needs may put them at greater risk because of their physical, psychological, educational, or social vulnerability (Campbell, Gilyard, Sinclair, Sternberg, & Kailes, 2009; Peek & Stough, 2010). Therefore, many students may be unable to perform the activities that are expected during a school crisis response (Boon et al., 2011). For example, procedures that involve moving quickly; following directions; being part of a large crowd; communicating with emergency personnel; dealing with noise, sirens, or people shouting;

assuming unique positions to hide; and being silent during a lockdown could be difficult (Boon et al., 2011; Minnesota School Safety Center, 2011; Spooner, Knight, Browder, & Smith, 2012). Thus, identifying potential barriers includes compiling specific information about the nature and severity of the student's special needs; reviewing possible paths of travel through the school and potential obstacles, signage, and alarms; and considering how the school's safety planning can accommodate those needs (Marin County Office of Education, 2010; U.S. Department of Education, 2006). The plan might say that the student requires a particular type of access or other physical supports within the building but needs different supports when students must leave the building. The student also may need behavioral supports, modifications to school procedures, or accommodation for communication needs; for example, students who are nonverbal, are deaf, have communication disorders, or are non-English speakers may need additional devices and supports. The student's individualized emergency plan should therefore include a list of all devices and support resources the student relies on (e.g., mobility aids, communication devices, electronic equipment, service animals, and interpreters), with notes as to how a crisis might affect their access to or use of those aids (Marin County Office of Education, 2010).

The teams that generate these plans must consider a wide range of factors—intellectual, social, emotional, physical, and developmental—to ensure that the student is protected and not overwhelmed by the environmental exposure of the emergency response (Boon et al., 2012; Edwards, Mumford, Shillingford, & Serra-Roldan, 2007). Creating alternative emergency response procedures for students with special needs and providing explicit instruction and practice build students' capacity to adaptively respond during an emergency and help ensure that those skills are maintained and generalized across settings (Clarke et al., 2014; Zhe & Nickerson, 2007).

All school staff members who might work with special needs students during crises must be aware of individualized emergency plans, and these students should be listed on a confidential roster. The roster must be maintained and updated as students' needs change and when a new student with special needs enters school (Clarke et al., 2014). The roster should include the students' names; their teachers, classrooms, and daily schedules; and their individualized emergency plan. The roster should be kept in multiple locations (with the administration's emergency procedures and in any applicable classrooms) so it will be accessible to anyone who may work with the student, including administrators, teachers, support personnel (e.g., physical therapist, classroom aide, speech and language specialist, interpreter), and substitute teachers (Clarke et al., 2014; Martins, 2013). If the school intends to share and review individualized emergency plans and students' medical, physical, emotional, and sensory needs with local first responders during exercises or drills, consent from the parents is required before disclosure (Clarke et al., 2014). The plan should be reviewed annually by the student, the student's caregivers, and school staff members so they can become familiar with procedures (Marin County Office of Education, 2010). Schools also may encourage parents to provide an emergency response data form to local first responders, which can help ensure care for an individual's disability or medical needs during emergencies at home or within the community (Zymanek & Creamer, 2014).

CULTURAL CONSIDERATIONS IN CRISIS RESPONSE PLANNING

A comprehensive review conducted by the U.S. Government Accountability Office (2007) found that nearly three quarters of surveyed schools did not have communication procedures for students and their families with limited English proficiency. Similarly, research on the crisis response plans of a number of states found that only 10% reported including information on culture in their plans, and none appeared to recognize the utility of cultural competency training or the benefits of identifying the cultural composition of the community in school crisis response planning (Annandale et al., 2011).

When developing the basic crisis response plan, schools should consider the various individuals that the plan will support. Multiculturalism recognizes race, ethnicity, language, sexual orientation, gender, age, disability, socioeconomic status, education, religious or spiritual orientation, and other cultural dimensions (American Psychological Association, 2002). Schools should be aware of how these dimensions affect stakeholders in the school community, including students, staff, caregivers, visitors, and other community members who may use the school's resources.

Cultural Considerations of School and District Crisis Response Teams

The district-level and school crisis response teams should be aware of how cultural dimensions of their region affect their crisis response planning, and teams benefit from having members who understand and work on multicultural goals. Crisis response plans should consider the cultural characteristics and norms of students, school staff members, caregivers, community members, and other school stakeholders who are affected by a school's crisis response. And cultural factors should be considered across the five mission areas when preparing for a crisis event (Obama, 2011). School crisis response teams should learn certain crisis response phrases in other languages (and instruct school staff members to do so) so they can effectively communicate with all students when language barriers may affect safety.

Cultural Considerations of School Staff Members

School staff members should recognize not only how different cultural dimensions influence different groups within the school, but also how their own culture affects their crisis experience. Likewise, district-level and school crisis response team members' perceptions of the world affect how they respond to crises, and response team members should be aware of how their own culture affects their response to crises (Hays, 2008). For example, students or staff members who speak English in a school that speaks predominantly English may not realize that having a crisis response plan provided in their language is a privilege. Under these circumstances, schools might not consider asking what language their crisis response plan should be printed in. In another example, teachers whose culture expects strong verbal and physical grief reactions may perceive that silent students in the classroom are not grieving the death of a classmate, when they are grieving quietly according to their own cultural norms.

CONCLUSION

Effective models of school crisis response planning require schools to follow guiding principles and considerations to develop carefully thought out crisis response plans. Use of a collaborative approach that includes representatives within the school district and outside agencies (i.e., local fire and police departments) is needed to be sure all key elements are included in the basic crisis response plan. This approach should also include training staff and practicing crisis response protocols, attending to the crisis needs of those with special needs, ensuring that cultural considerations are addressed within the crisis response plan, and ensuring that these efforts are sustained over time through ongoing evaluation and review of efforts. Chapter 9 discusses more specifically how to develop the functional and threat- and hazard-specific annexes that direct crisis response activities during different types of emergencies.

Chapter 9

SCHOOL CRISIS RESPONSE PREPAREDNESS: FUNCTIONAL AND THREAT- AND HAZARD-SPECIFIC ANNEXES

As described in the U.S. Department of Education's (2013) *Guide for Developing High-Quality School Emergency Operations Plans*, school crisis response plans (described as Emergency Operations Plans) consist of three sections: (a) the basic plan, (b) functional annexes, and (c) threat- and hazard-specific annexes. Chapter 8 reviewed development of a basic plan, and this chapter describes how to develop the two classes of annexes. Functional annexes provide teams with directions for specific school crisis responses, such as school lockdown or evacuation, that are used in response to a number of different threats or hazards. Threat- and hazard-specific annexes describe procedures that school crisis response teams follow for specific incidents, such as a fire, chemical spill, or tornado.

THE FUNCTIONAL ANNEXES

According to the U.S. Department of Education (2013), the crisis response team identifies certain important functions or tasks that apply to more than one threat or hazard. For example, evacuating and accounting for all people are required in many different crisis responses and are the focus of two of the functional annexes. The U.S. Department of Education describes these annexes as follows:

> The Functional Annexes section details the goals, objectives, and courses of action of functions (e.g., evacuation, communications, recovery) that apply across multiple threats or hazards. Functional annexes set forth how the school manages a function before, during, and after an emergency. (p. 17)

The following discussion describes annexes considered most important by the U.S. Department of Education (2013). The discussion also adds to these descriptions specific key strategies that are part of the PREPaRE curriculum. Additional guidance on developing these annexes is available from the Readiness and Emergency Management for Schools (REMS) Technical Assistance Center (http://rems.ed.gov/K12FuncAnnex.aspx and http://rems.ed.gov/docs/REMS_K-12_Guide_508.pdf).

Evacuation Annex

Not only are evacuation procedures important to physical safety, but when done efficiently and effectively, they minimize students' perceptions of threats and thereby mitigate traumatic stress (Brock, 2011a; Brock et al., 2009; Reeves et al., 2011a). The Evacuation Annex should address how to safely move students, staff, and visitors from classrooms, outside areas, cafeterias, restrooms, and other school locations to predesignated assembly areas. Smaller school districts may have one common evacuation protocol. However, in most school districts, the district crisis response team helps each school team to develop its own school Evacuation Annex.

This annex should identify multiple shelters within walking distance of the school as well as those accessible by bus if transportation is available. It should also identify alternative evacuation routes to be employed when the primary route is unusable. Typical options for evacuation locations or shelters are neighboring schools, churches, or businesses. School safety and crisis response teams may work together to identify the best evacuation shelters in advance and develop memoranda of understanding (MOUs) with those sites. Development of protocols for this annex must involve transportation contractors and bus drivers.

As emphasized by the U.S. Department of Education (2013), selected evacuation sites also must accommodate students with disabilities (e.g., visual, hearing, mobility, cognitive, attention, and emotional challenges) and other functional challenges (e.g., language, transportation, and medical needs). The PREPaRE curriculum recommends that when developing this annex, school crisis response teams ensure that the location for assembly after evacuation (a) accommodates the number of affected individuals, (b) is sheltered from the media, and (c) has a number of rooms that would allow for privacy, which might become necessary should the crisis response team need to communicate difficult information, such as a death (Crepeau-Hobson, Sievering, Armstrong, & Stonis, 2012).

Exercises and drills (Chapter 8) must be conducted periodically to ensure that teachers and students have practiced evacuation protocols. Students should also be trained in how to respond during an evacuation if they are not with a teacher or staff member (e.g., they are in the restroom). Staff members must be trained to evacuate in a way that minimizes students' exposure to the scene of the crisis to reduce trauma exposure (Brock, 2011a).

The authors of PREPaRE suggest that a school evacuation can be assisted by the development of resources such as a "go-kit" or crisis response box that contains the essential supplies and information needed to conduct an orderly and rapid evacuation. A similar kit should be kept off-campus (e.g., at a local police or fire station) where it is accessible to district personnel in case the original go-kits inside the school cannot be retrieved. Classroom go-kits should have class rosters and safety equipment for each class. Tables 9.1 and 9.2 list the contents of these go-kits or boxes, which might also require a cart to transport the items. The crisis response team's go-kit and the kit being stored off-campus must contain the floor plans of all school buildings, which have been reviewed with emergency response personnel during crisis response planning. The floor plan should mark all windows, entrances, and exits; shut-off valves for water; and ventilation, electrical, and gas systems (Brickman, Jones, & Groom, 2004).

Table 9.1. Crisis Response Team or Administrator Emergency Response Go-Kit Contents

This list includes the specific materials that may be included in a crisis response team's or crisis administrator's response go-kit. This is not an exhaustive list, and teams should consider the special needs of their school.

- **Crisis response team phone numbers**
- **Crisis response team role descriptions**
- **Crisis response team identification vests with titles printed in large block letters on the back**
  - Incident Commander
  - Safety Officer
  - Public Information Officer
  - Liaison Officer
  - Mental Health Officer
  - Operations Section Chief
  - Logistics Section Chief
  - Planning Section Chief
  - Finance Section Chief
- **Aerial photos of the campus with the following clearly identified:**
  - Evacuation routes
- **Copy of building safety and crisis response team plans, including:**
  - Response protocols
  - Release and reunification plan
  - Traffic management plan
- **Campus map and floor plans (including details of individual buildings) with the following clearly identified:**
  - Emergency command and staging areas (including media) and alternate locations
  - Emergency Operations Center, with alternate location specified
  - Clearly marked evacuation routes
  - Individualized evacuation plans for students with special needs
  - Fire alarm deactivation switch
  - Sprinkler system deactivation switch
  - Heating and ventilation systems (HVAC) shutoff
  - Gas line shutoff valves
  - Cable television and satellite feed shutoff
  - Water shutoff valve
- **Copies of functional and threat-, and hazard-specific annexes**
  - Evacuation Annex
  - Accounting for All Persons Annex

Table 9.1. Continued

- ■ Reunification Annex
- ■ Communication Annex
- ■ Public Health, Medical, and Mental Health Annex
- ■ Security Annex
- ■ Recovery Annex
- ■ Memorial Annex
- ■ Continuity of Operations Plan (COOP)
- ■ Lockdown/Secured Perimeter Annex
- ■ Shelter-in-Place Annex
- **Reunification Go-Kit**[a]
- **Community resource list**
- **Rolling cart or rolling duffle bag (with itemized list of emergency items to be included)**
  - ■ First aid kit (at least 64 pieces)
  - ■ Building master keys
  - ■ Bullhorn or other external communication system
  - ■ Two-way radios with at least 10 different channels
  - ■ AM/FM battery-operated radio (with batteries)
  - ■ Battery-operated weather radio (with batteries)
  - ■ Emergency crank radio
  - ■ Battery-operated laptop (with access to the Internet)
  - ■ Site status report forms
  - ■ Damage documentation tools (e.g., cameras)
  - ■ Yellow caution tape
- **Reminder cards for specific PREPaRE mental health crisis interventions**[b]
  - ■ Evaluation of psychological trauma
  - ■ Classroom meeting
  - ■ Psychoeducational group
  - ■ Caregiver training
  - ■ Group crisis intervention
  - ■ Individual crisis intervention
- **Additional supplies**
  - ■ Mechanical #2 pencils
  - ■ Black ballpoint pens
  - ■ Black fine-point permanent marker
  - ■ Clipboards
  - ■ Writing pads (8.5″ × 11″ glue-top writing pad, legal ruled)
  - ■ 8.5″ × 11″ dry-erase whiteboard with markers and eraser
  - ■ Highlighters (yellow and pink)
  - ■ Flashlights (with extra batteries)
  - ■ Hand-cranked LED flashlight
  - ■ Cell phone and computer chargers
  - ■ Whistles attached to lanyards
  - ■ Stopwatch

- Solar calculator
- Bag of large rubber bands
- Light sticks (to last 12 hours)
- Adult rain ponchos
- Work or gardening gloves
- Latex-free medical gloves (large adult size)
- Gray duct tape (2 inches by 60 yards)
- Safety breathing masks
- Hand sanitizer
- Emergency thermal blankets
- Emergency energy food bars without nuts
- **Emergency resource budget information**
- **Emergency personnel sign-in/sign-out sheet**
- **Crisis response forms for internal (school) use**

a. See Table 9.7 for contents; b. These mental health crisis interventions are described in detail in Chapters 16, 17, and 18.

Table 9.2. Classroom Emergency Response Go-Kit Contents

This list includes the specific materials that may be included in a classroom response go-kit. The crisis response team is responsible for ensuring that each classroom has a go-kit and a large backpack to carry it.

- **School staff member crisis response procedures (e.g., condensed plan flip chart containing immediate response actions such as lockdown, secured perimeter, and evacuation annexes)**
- **School and campus map**
  - Staging areas indicated
  - Evacuation routes identified
  - Assembly location identified
- **Identification**
  - Safety vest or hat, with title imprinted in large block letters "Classroom Teacher"
  - Whistle attached to a lanyard
- **Keys for classroom**
- **Student information**
  - Descriptions of students with special needs (medical, prescription medicine, dietary)
  - Student roster
  - Student photos
  - Student emergency cards
  - Individualized evacuation plans
- **Student Release and Reunification Annex**
  - Caregiver sign-in/sign-out sheet
  - Clipboard
  - Black ballpoint pens, highlighters
  - Mechanical #2 pencils
  - Fine-point permanent marker

Table 9.2. Continued

- ■ Crayons
- ■ Writing pad
- **Hand-cranked LED flashlight**
- **Laptop computer and cell phone chargers**
- **First aid kit**
- **Light sticks (to last 12 hours)**
- **Rain poncho(s)**
- **Waterproof tarp**
- **Plastic sheeting (for shelter-in-place)**
- **Duct tape (2 inches by 60 yards)**
- **Emergency thermal blanket**
- **Paper cups**
- **Hand sanitizer**
- **Latex-free medical gloves**
- **Breathing masks**
- **Bottles of water**
- **Emergency food bars (without nuts)**
- **Age-appropriate student activities (books, cards, checkers, crayons, construction paper)**

Accounting for All Persons Annex

The *Guide for Developing High-Quality School Emergency Operations Plans* (U.S. Department of Education, 2013) recommends that schools have procedures for accounting for the whereabouts and well-being of all students, school staff members, and even visitors. In response to any crisis, and as soon as possible, the crisis response team should identify those who may be missing. This annex needs to attend specifically to the following: (a) how attendance in an evacuation assembly area is determined, (b) what happens when an individual cannot be located, (c) how information is reported to the principal (or the Incident Commander), (d) how and when students are released to their caregivers, and (e) where students in need of medical attention were sent for treatment. The PREPaRE curriculum recommends that the crisis response team designate a student accounting and release team leader and two assistants (i.e., a student accounting specialist and a student release specialist) that are trained to address these issues and execute the Reunification Annex. These individuals work under the Operations Section Chief and will find the PREPaRE curriculum's student accounting and release planning checklists useful (Tables 9.3 and 9.4).

A final observation relevant to the Accounting for All Persons Annex is that schools are increasingly moving toward electronic methods of taking student attendance and storing records. While these methods typically allow for easier remote access in a crisis, it could also mean that rosters are unavailable if the building has lost Internet or wireless access. Thus, teachers should have a backup method for taking and reporting attendance (e.g., using paper and pencil), and school crisis response teams should know how to access a wireless hotspot. Even in crisis situations, schools' electronic records systems must comply with federal privacy regulations. Crisis response

Table 9.3. Student Accounting and Release Planning Checklist

Steps for Crisis Response Planning and Preparedness:
- Identify student accounting and student release specialists to manage the Accounting for All Persons Annex. Ensure that they are available, they understand their roles, and they are willing and able to carry out or assign the duties described below.
- Establish student and staff accounting procedures. These procedures use current attendance rosters and include instructions on what to do if students and staff members are present or missing, safe and healthy, injured, or deceased.
- With the help of the crisis intervention and student care group, establish a protocol for informing caregivers that their children are missing, injured, or deceased. This protocol requires the identification of a secure, private notification area (i.e., a notification room).
- Establish a student release protocol that uses emergency cards and establishes areas for identity verification, caregiver waiting, and student–caregiver reunion. Caregiver waiting and reunion areas may be in the same location, but they should be separate from the areas that hold students prior to reunion (e.g., classrooms, evacuation sites). Caregivers of missing, injured, or deceased students must be given their own waiting areas (i.e., a notification room).
- In the student release protocol, recognize the importance of reuniting preschool and primary school children with their caregivers first.
- Working with the crisis intervention and student care group, identify strategies for working with caregivers in the waiting area to ensure that they understand the procedures (and the possible delays in reuniting with their children) as well as the importance of their reactions, upon reunification, in shaping children's traumatic stress reactions. Explain to the caregivers of older students why it will take longer for them to be reunited with their child (i.e., younger students have a greater need to be reunited with their primary caregivers).
- In periodic reviews of crisis preparedness, verify that the student accounting and release protocol has been disseminated to caregivers. Dissemination options include a letter to caregivers from the principal, articles in a school newsletter, placement in a student–parent handbook, and a link on the school website that can be easily activated if a crisis occurs. Such notifications should stress the importance of caregivers' reactions in shaping students' perceptions of the event.

Steps During Crisis Response:
- Identify the individuals designated to manage student accounting and release procedures and ensure that they are briefed by the Incident Commander (IC), the Operations Section Chief, and the Planning Section Chief on the situation, initial objectives, and priorities. Assemble the student accounting and release team and designate a student accounting specialist to help facilitate the process.
- Direct the student accounting specialist to obtain class rosters to determine the status (i.e., safe and healthy, injured, or deceased) and location of all students and school staff members.
- Direct the student accounting specialist to prepare an initial summary of student and staff information. Inform the IC of all deceased, injured, or missing students or staff members. Provide a copy of the information summary to the student accounting and release team leader.

Table 9.3. Continued

- Keeping in mind that the coroner is the only authority who can legally declare a person deceased, obtain the school IC's approval for caregiver notification. Work with the crisis intervention and student care group and the student release specialist to ensure that the caregivers of missing, injured, or deceased students are moved to a private location (i.e., notification room) that is separate from the caregiver waiting and reunion areas. Use school district or law enforcement personnel for face-to-face notification in cases of death, serious injury, or missing persons.
- Coordinate with the school security or search and rescue unit leader to search for missing students or staff members.
- After consulting with the student accounting and student release specialists, make a recommendation for releasing students to the IC. If students are released, ensure that a record is maintained showing the person to whom the student has been released, the time of departure, and other essential information.
- After consulting with the crisis intervention and student care group, recommend procedures for how the IC will inform caregivers about the status of students. Dissemination options include posting lists with the names of students who are accounted for and are safe and notifying caregivers individually if the students are missing, injured, or deceased.
- Direct the student release specialist to begin to release students to caregivers.
- Maintain a log noting information received and actions taken.

Note. Adapted from *School Crisis Prevention and Intervention: The PREPaRE Model* (pp. 62–63), by S. E. Brock et al., 2009, Bethesda, MD: NASP. Copyright 2009 by the National Association of School Psychologists.

Table 9.4. Annual Review of Student Release Procedures

- Identify the student accounting and release team leader, student accounting specialist, and student release specialist (and backup personnel).
- Identify reunification sites both on and off campus grounds, including alternate sites.
- Update current classroom rosters in crisis response team/administrator and classroom go-kits.
- Maintain an emergency card for each student and staff member (electronically, if possible) in the main office, in the crisis response team's or administrator's emergency response kit, and in each classroom's go-kit that lists family members or adults authorized to pick up a student.
- Know where to obtain tables, chairs, writing supplies, and yellow barrier tape for delineating areas for student release, waiting and reunion, and notification areas.

Note. Adapted from *School Crisis Prevention and Intervention: The PREPaRE Model* (pp. 63–65), by S. E. Brock et al., 2009, Bethesda, MD: NASP. Copyright 2009 by the National Association of School Psychologists.

teams must ensure that appropriate safeguards are in place. Jarmuz-Smith (2014) summarizes the importance of protecting data—using data encryption, protecting passwords, clarifying who owns the records when cloud-based data storage is used, and knowing who has access to necessary passwords.

Family Reunification Annex

The *Guide for Developing High-Quality School Emergency Operations Plans* (U.S. Department of Education, 2013) specifies that the Family Reunification Annex provides direction on how students are reunited with their families and caregivers. The Reunification Annex procedures must closely interface with the Accounting for All Persons Annex procedures since both of these annexes are often activated during a crisis response. Tasks this annex covers include, but are not limited to, (a) informing families and caregivers about reunification procedures; (b) verifying which adults are authorized take a student from school; (c) ensuring clear communication between school crisis response team members and caregivers at the check-in and student assembly and reunion areas; (d) ensuring that students do not leave on their own; (e) protecting students and caregivers from the media; and (f) addressing the language access barriers faced by students, staff, and caregivers. Additional considerations that must be decided when establishing a Family Reunification Annex include the following:

- Are students who are 18 years of age and older allowed to sign themselves out, or will a caregiver's signature still be required?
- What if a caregiver does not have a picture ID? Will verbal identification be accepted (e.g., the teacher confirms this is the student's caregiver)?
- How will the school have a sufficient number of staff members to provide the translation support required for families with limited English proficiency?
- How will the school care for students who are not picked up by a caregiver? Does a staff member drive the student home? Does the school contact child protective services or the local police department if a legal guardian cannot be located?

Because family reunification is one of the most frequently ignored or underdeveloped aspects of school emergency planning (Welko, 2013), the PREPaRE curriculum gives special attention to this annex. It has been observed that only 68% of school districts require family reunification procedures in their crisis response plans (Centers for Disease Control and Prevention [CDC], 2013a). This number is concerning given that well-executed reunification plans mitigate traumatic stress (especially at the early primary grade levels) and also decrease the potential for legal actions (National Commission on Children and Disasters, 2010). A poorly executed reunification plan is a source of chaos, resulting in caregivers panicking and making frantic phone calls to the school and traffic jams tying up main school access roads (Crepeau-Hobson et al., 2012; Trump, Burvikos, Bartlett, Greenberg, Stapleton, & Rosenstein, 2011).

Family Reunification Team
Consistent with guidance offered by FEMA (2011) and Trump et al. (2011), the PREPaRE curriculum recommends that this annex include a specially designated family reunification team to address all annex issues. Working within the ICS structure (Chapter 7) the "I Love U Guys" Foundation (Keyes, 2011), in collaboration with Adams 12 Five Star Schools in Colorado, has delineated the roles and functions of this team (Table 9.5) using the existing ICS structure schools should already have in place.

Table 9.5. Family Reunification Team Roles and Responsibilities

Role	Responsibilities
Incident Commander (IC)	Works closely with other command staff to oversee the reunification of students with their caregivers; works with other agency ICs in a unified command situation
Public Information Officer	Communicates with caregivers and press; coordinates use of mass calls, text messages, and/or social media posts
Social Media Coordinator	Posts information on social media sites (e.g., Facebook, Twitter, Instagram)
Safety Officer	Observes assembly and reunification areas and addresses any safety concerns
Liaison Officer	Communicates with fire, medical, law enforcement, community response agencies
Mental Health Officer	Coordinates the mental health support needed for students, staff, and caregivers; communicates with community mental health agencies
Operations Section Chief	Establishes and manages operational staff
Caregiver information representatives (e.g., greeters)	Help manage the caregiver waiting areas and informs caregivers about the reunification process; help verify the identity of caregivers who arrive without identification; locate caregivers whose children are injured and directs them to the notification room
Checkers	Verify identification and custody rights of caregivers, and direct them to student–family reunification location
Runners	Accompany students to family reunification area
Mental health crisis interveners	Work with caregivers in the notification room; support distressed students, staff, and caregivers
Teachers/staff	Help supervise students who are waiting for caregivers
Movie coordinator	Sets up a movie (for younger students to reduce stress and anxiety)
Traffic controller	Sets up parking area with directional cones and signs; maintains order in parking areas; reports to the Safety Officer any crowd control issues
Planning Section Chief	Thinks ahead to possible reunification needs
Documentation leader	Documents actions taken
Situation leader	Records strengths and areas in need of improvement

Logistics Section Chief	Thinks ahead and gathers the supplies needed for a reunification go-kit
Facilities leaders	Initially set up check-in area, place signs to direct caregivers to the appropriate areas, set up student staging area; may be assigned to operations when setup is completed
Finance/Administration Section Chief	Keeps track of expenses associated with the reunification process

Note. The information presented in this table is discussed in Standard Reunification Method: A Practical Method to Unite Students With Parents After an Evacuation or Crisis, by J. M. Keyes, 2011, Bailey, CO: "I Love U Guys" Foundation; Crisis Prevention and Preparedness: Comprehensive School Safety Planning (2nd ed.), by M. A Reeves et al., 2011a, Bethesda, MD: National Association of School Psychologists; and Rhode Island Model for School Emergency Planning, Mitigation/Prevention, Preparedness, Response, and Recovery, by Rhode Island Emergency Management Agency, 2013, Providence, RI: Author.

Selection and Setup of Family Reunification Sites

Schools need to prepare for family reunification both on school grounds and at off-site evacuation locations (National Education Association Health Information Network, 2007). When selecting off-site assembly and reunification areas, schools must consider accessibility for all students, parking, traffic flow, ability to quickly move students to designated points, communication needs (fax, phone, Internet), security, and a sufficient number of preferably separate entrances and exits to avoid congestion. Regardless of whether family reunification takes place on school grounds or at an off-site evacuation area, the Logistics Section needs to set up the reunification sites quickly, because caregivers can be expected to arrive at the reunification location almost immediately after learning of the location of their children. The movement and management of large numbers of people within the reunification areas need to be carefully planned to help reduce crowding and to facilitate traffic flow.

Family Reunification Process

Once a caregiver's identity is verified and matched with the information on student emergency contact documents, a runner (Trump et al., 2011) retrieves students from a student assembly area while the caregiver proceeds to the family reunification area (Philpott & Serluco, 2009; Washington State School Safety Center, 2008). The caregiver then signs a release and departs with his or her child. Keyes (2011), in collaboration with Adams 12 Five Star Schools, outlines a seven-step summary called the "Reunification Process in a Nutshell":

1. A caregiver check-in location is established.
2. Students are delivered to a student holding area (not visible to caregivers).
3. Greeters direct caregivers to a check-in location and help them understand the reunification process.
4. Caregivers complete reunification cards.
5. Runners retrieve students from a student holding area and reunite them with caregivers at the family reunification and student release area.

Table 9.6. Family Reunification Setup Elements

- Use clear, highly visible signs to establish a caregiver check-in area. Signs need to remind caregivers that they need photo identification.
- Set up check-in tables. Supply with paper, pens, pencils, clipboards, etc. Space tables at least 20 feet apart to reduce congestion.
- Place student emergency contact documents (or computers to access cards electronically) at each check-in table.
- Set up traffic signage directing caregivers into the appropriate parking lot and then from the parking lot to the caregiver check-in area within the building.
- Place alphabet signs (A–D, E–H, etc.) in readily visible locations (place on tall easels as signs taped to the table will be difficult to see when lines have formed).
- Identify a holding area where teachers take their students to wait for caregivers. Students should not be visible to caregivers who are in the check-in area.
- Identify the family reunification location or student release area.
- Establish traffic flow patterns.

Note. The information presented in this table is discussed in Standard Reunification Method: A Practical Method to Unite Students With Parents After an Evacuation or Crisis, by J. M. Keyes, 2011, Bailey, CO: "I Love U Guys" Foundation; and Rhode Island Model for School Emergency Planning, Mitigation/Prevention, Preparedness, Response, and Recovery, by Rhode Island Emergency Management Agency, 2013, Providence, RI: Author.

6. Controlled lines of sight allow communication and other issues to be handled with diminished drama or anxiety.
7. Medical or investigative support is anticipated and provided as needed.

The PREPaRE curriculum recommends that schools consider providing at least brief caregiver training at some point during this process. The training can update caregivers on the crisis facts, provide guidance on how to respond to their child's mental health needs, and provide informational bulletins or flyers that provide further guidance on helping children cope with crises (Chapter 16).

Accounting

Accounting for all students and school staff members is a critical element of this annex. Copies of student and staff rosters identifying students who are absent or who have left school early, staff members who are absent and their substitutes, and volunteers must be available to the family reunification team. Sign-out forms (available in the languages spoken in the school) are also critical (Keyes, 2011; Philpott & Serluco, 2009) to document the process, guide accounting procedures, and ensure that a caregiver signature is obtained before students are released from school. The go-kit for reunification is important to ensure the collection of supplies that facilitate the process of family reunification. Table 9.7 provides a list of items to include. In addition, reunification plans need to be practiced; successful family reunification is more likely to occur when teams have conducted drills (Keyes, 2011). At a minimum, tabletop drills should include the reunification process, and optimally, practice should involve school staff members, caregivers, and possibly students. Because reunification is a complex and often emotionally charged process, drills are an opportunity to learn which components of the plan work and which need to be refined.

Table 9.7. Family Reunification Go-Kit

- Teacher roster and classroom assignments
- School staff member phone tree and family contact information
- Student and staff emergency information (via paper or electronic)
- Current student, staff, substitute, and volunteer attendance roster
- Student and staff photos
- Student disposition and release forms
- List of students and staff with medical needs
- Floor plans with areas and traffic flow clearly marked (for both the school and off-site evacuation areas)
- Emergency contact documents and laptop computers (with extension cords to plug in computers)
- Reunification cards for caregivers' signatures, in multiple languages if needed
- Handouts of resources and referral information for caregivers
- Traffic signage
- Caregiver check-in and check-out area signs
- Bull horn (with extra batteries)
- File system to sort signed cards
- Folding tables
- Pens
- Flashlights
- Walkie-talkies
- Reunification team identification vests
- Community agency contact information
- Set of laminated sheets for sign-in tables: Alphabet sheets (A–D, E–G, etc.) or grade level (pre-K–12)
- Reunification cards (other languages)
- Water and food
- Directional signs
- Duct tape
- Clipboards
- TV and movies
- Sunscreen
- Internet hotspot or wi-fi access codes to the building

Communications and Warning Annex

The *Guide for Developing High-Quality School Emergency Operations Plans* (U.S. Department of Education, 2013) recommends that this annex include communication and coordination during crises, both within the school and with outside school community members (e.g., caregivers), and communication of crisis response protocols (e.g., family reunification procedures) before and after a crisis. Specific actions covered by this annex include (a) integrating the school's communications system with first responder communications networks; (b) ensuring that relevant school staff members are able to use communications equipment; (c) communicating with students, families, and the broader community before, during, and after an emergency; (d) accounting for the so-called digital divide and how some students, staff members, and caregivers have difficulty accessing or using technology; (e) accounting for student, staff member, and caregiver language differences; (f) working with the media; (g) accounting for individuals with communication difficulties (e.g., working with first responders to provide sign language interpreters during press conferences); and otherwise ensuring that all communications systems are accessible to all school community members. Mechanisms for communicating with school staff members, students, and their families are included in approximately 80% of school plans (CDC, 2013a). Because communication is a critical factor in any effective crisis response, the PREPaRE curriculum gives this annex special attention.

Crisis Identification and Notification

The Communications and Warning Annex must direct special attention to how school staff members and students are notified of a crisis and the need to implement specific functional annexes. All staff members should have permission to declare the existence of a crisis situation; thus, all staff members need to be trained in the various crisis notification methods. Staff members should be instructed in the protocol, which is that when declaring a crisis situation, they should state it simply and clearly. Unnecessary and graphic details should be avoided. For example, the school's secretary, in a calm, neutral voice, might announce over the intercom: "Staff, immediately go into lockdown. We have police reports of an armed bank robber in the area."

Schools can communicate about a crisis response in a variety of ways, each of which has its own strengths and challenges. The crisis situation dictates what form of communication is best, so this annex should plan for a variety of communication options: (a) within buildings; (b) between buildings; and (c) between the school administration, caregivers, and community resources and agencies. Table 9.8 summarizes several of the communication options. In addition, morning and end-of-day faculty meetings are effective ways to communicate information to school staff members. Substitute teachers also need to be provided information about the school's crisis response plan when they check in for their assignment (e.g., provide a summary sheet or a quick orientation) and where they can find written information about functional annexes.

Communication With Authorized Caregivers

In advance of a crisis, caregivers need to be informed of elements of the school's crisis response plan. This can be done via a newsletter or placed within the school handbook. Caregivers' first reaction to news of a school-associated crisis is often fear and anxiety. Schools must let them know that their child is safe as quickly as possible, as well as inform them how the crisis is being handled and where they can be reunited with their children. These communications should give facts about the event and dispel rumors, provide information on common reactions, provide guidance on coping strategies, and list available resources, including where caregivers can find updated information (Brock, 2011a). Clerical staff answering the phones need to be given a script for answering questions, and translation needs must be addressed.

Communication With Key Stakeholders

One of the first jobs of school crisis response teams, following crises, is to communicate the steps the district is taking to ensure the safety of students and school staff members. For example, following a gas leak in the school, a school administrator may want to say: "The local gas company has identified the faulty pipe, stopped the gas leak, and repaired the pipe that caused the problem. The chief of the fire department used gas meters to verify that the building is safe for people to return." Important messages such as this should be explicitly communicated to the public; sent to

Table 9.8. Emergency Communication Options Within and Beyond the School Campus

1. *Emergency channels and smartphone apps.* Many schools have an emergency channel reserved for school administration, police, and emergency personnel. Essential to using an emergency channel during crises is ensuring that crisis response team members are all on the same channel. In addition, smartphone apps are now available that allow school staff members to activate emergency protocols from their phones or tablets and communicate during a crisis (e.g., Punch Alert, http://punchalert.com).

2. *Land-line phones.* These are the most reliable communication method because they may also work when electrical power is off. Many schools have phones in every classroom so teachers are able to communicate with the main office. However, in the event of a crisis, lines can become overwhelmed by a large volume of calls, so backup communication methods need to be identified. In addition, schools should designate and advertise a recorded hot line for caregivers to call, which helps to ensure that other school lines are available to school and emergency personnel.

3. *Cell phones.* These are a powerful crisis response resource, but they also create challenges. Cell phone signals often become overwhelmed when there is a high volume of calls and may not work unless a portable cell phone tower is erected. In addition, many areas of school buildings may not receive a cell phone signal. Students often use them to send text messages and sometimes do so before the school has had a chance to activate its crisis response team. Conversely, in some crisis situations the school has directed students to text specific language to their caregivers, which has helped alleviate caregivers' anxiety by confirming that their child is safe.

4. *Reverse 911 calls.* These systems allow a recorded message (and text) to be disseminated to all phone numbers in a database. It can send a message to thousands of numbers within a few seconds. A caution regarding this option is that phone numbers change, and texts often get to the recipients faster than the phone call.

5. *Telephone trees.* This can be used to notify staff of a crisis when they are not at school. Given the ICS structure, the first call should be made by the IC to the section chiefs, and they in turn notify school staff members. The message should be a carefully crafted statement that is read only to another person on the calling tree. Details should never be left on answering machines, because the caller does not know who will have access to the message.

6. *Panic buttons.* Typically placed in a school's main office, these buttons are directly connected to the police and other emergency responders.

7. *E-mails.* If computers are accessible, e-mail can be a reliable and fast means of communicating between staff members and with the school community.

8. *Intercoms.* The intercom is another means of quickly communicating with students and school staff members. A caution regarding this option is that the sender has no control over who hears these messages. Thus, the intercom should not be used to share information on fatalities or other frightening details. Current practice promotes being direct and succinct when using the intercom to activate crisis response protocols. Instructions for using the intercom system need to be available in all classrooms.

Table 9.8. Continued

9. *Walkie-talkies or two-way radios.* These are one of the most reliable means of communication. Playground supervisors and school resource officers should always have a walkie-talkie that links them to the main office. Users need to be sure that they are on the same channel, and caution should be used when sharing sensitive information because they are not a secure means of communication.

10. *Bullhorns and megaphones.* A battery operated bullhorn or megaphone is helpful when assembling students and during reverse evacuations. Batteries should be checked frequently, and use of bullhorns or megaphones is not recommended for recess because students may learn to ignore them.

11. *Computers and tablets.* Wireless laptop computers and tablets are portable and can be used to send out messages. Evacuation, closure, and relocation information could be posted on the home page of the school or district using these devices. The ability to recharge laptops and tablets is critical.

12. *Fax machines.* These may be needed at the emergency operations site to fax medical information, forms, and authorizations to appropriate individuals or agencies. Smartphones can be used as fax machines via several different apps (e.g., iFax, Tiff Fax Viewer+, Breezy Print and Fax, JotNot Fax).

13. *Written memos.* For sharing specific details and facts, sending photocopied typewritten memos is the most reliable for consistency of information. The Communications and Warning Annex needs to address who is responsible for writing letters and for verifying the information through multiple sources (i.e., Public Information Officer, Social Media Coordinator).

14. *Social media.* Schools and the school district should have identified the social media used by the students and their families, and should have a system for communicating through at least two selected social media sites, such as Facebook, Twitter, or Instagram. Media messages should be updated at least as often as press releases are made available (Chapter 7). During and after the crisis, these sites should be monitored to identify and dispel rumors and also to disseminate psychoeducational material (Chapter 16).

Note. Adapted from *School Crisis Prevention and Intervention: The PREPaRE Model* (67–68), by S. E. Brock et al., 2009, Bethesda, MD: NASP. Copyright 2009 by the National Association of School Psychologists. This table was originally compiled using information from the Rhode Island Emergency Management Agency (2013).

the local media, caregivers, and staff members; and posted on the school website (see Chapters 4 and 7 for further discussion of the use of technology and social media during a school crisis response).

Individuals who have experienced a school-associated crisis may continue to feel the physical and emotional effects for weeks, months, and, in rare instances, even years. Anniversaries can be particularly poignant times during which crisis survivors may reexperience intense emotions. Therefore, ongoing communication with survivors and other identified individuals in the school community is important.

Lockdown Annex

The *Guide for Developing High-Quality School Emergency Operations Plans* (U.S. Department of Education, 2013) recommends that this annex focus on actions taken to secure schools during crises that occur in or around the school and present a threat of harm to students, visitors, and school staff members. The primary objective of this annex is to promptly ensure that all people on school grounds move inside school buildings (most typically classrooms) and away from safety threats. Specific actions included in this annex are (a) how to safely lock all exterior doors, (b) how the windows and doors of specific school buildings and classrooms effect lockdowns, (c) how to respond to situations where a safety threat originates inside the school, (d) when to employ different types of lockdowns (e.g., when to use a "soft lockdown," in which the perimeter of the school is secured, but students, visitors, and staff are allowed to move freely within the school building).

Each school district or school needs to work within local and state guidelines and collaborate with law enforcement agencies to determine the most effective way of conducting a lockdown. Table 9.9 gives examples of the two main types of lockdown procedures. School districts must have consistent procedures within their schools, and local emergency responders must be aware of the procedures, including the specific language or terminology used to describe them. As discussed in Chapter 8, having effective lockdown procedures is especially critical in armed assailant or active shooter situations.

Shelter-in-Place Annex

The *Guide for Developing High-Quality School Emergency Operations Plans* (U.S. Department of Education, 2013) recommends that this annex focus on actions taken when students, visitors, and school staff members are required to remain inside school buildings for extended periods of time because of environmental safety threats. Depending on the specific threat, individuals may be sheltered in rooms that either are windowless or can be sealed. Specific issues addressed in this annex are (a) what supplies are needed to seal a room; (b) what supplies are needed to provide for the general needs of students, visitors, and school staff members (e.g., water); (c) what supplies are needed to meet special needs of students and staff (e.g., medications and medical equipment); (d) how to move students, visitors, and staff to the shelters when the primary route to the shelter is unsafe; (e) how to find and move students and visitors who are not with a staff member to a shelter; and (f) the need for "safe rooms" that provide protection from extreme environmental threats, such as tornados, when an evacuation is not possible.

These activities differ from lockdowns in that students, visitors, and school staff members do not need to hide and lock the door in an area of the building. Sheltering in place to avoid exposure to a chemical spill or a biological incident outside the school may require staff members to place plastic sheeting around windows, heating and ventilation systems (HVAC), and electrical sockets that go to the outside of the room and to seal the room with duct tape. They may also need to turn off the HVAC system in the building and classrooms (Dorn et al., 2004). The annex should contain instructions on how to turn off the HVAC systems in the building and potentially within individual classrooms and offices. Shelter-in-place may be used over an extended period. In the event of a severe storm, for example, the school may shelter students and staff until they can safely leave the area.

Public Health, Medical, and Mental Health Annex

The *Guide for Developing High-Quality School Emergency Operations Plans* (U.S. Department of Education, 2013) recommends that this annex focus on the immediate actions taken to address emergency medical (e.g., heart attacks) and public health crises (e.g., pandemic illness, food contamination) and immediate mental health issues. The primary objective of this annex is to coordinate immediate emergency responses with community-based emergency medical, public health, mental health, and police and fire departments. Mental health needs that extend beyond the immediate crisis are addressed in the Recovery Annex. Specific issues this annex needs to address are (a) the role of school staff members in providing medical first aid and the identification of individuals with medical training (e.g., CPR, use of automated external defibrillators), (b) locations of all first aid supplies located, (c) who is responsible for maintaining these supplies, (d) procedures for reporting to health departments information about health-related crises (e.g., food poisoning, influenza, norovirus, meningitis), (e) how to support the school's threat assessment team, and (f) how to ensure that emergency or crisis intervention resources are available.

Table 9.9. Examples of, and Terms to Describe, the Types of Lockdown Procedures

Jane's Safe Schools Planning Guide for All Hazards (Dorn et al., 2004)	Preventive or Soft Lockdown	Lock doors and limit travel within the building. Classroom activities continue. Appropriate for when the threat is in the community near the school.
	Full or Hard Lockdown	Cease all classroom activities. Move students and staff away from windows. Lock all doors and move into an area where they cannot be seen.
Comprehensive Planning for Safe Learning Environments (Reeves, Kanan, & Plog, 2010)	Secured Perimeter	Secure staff and students inside building with locked outside doors. Move them to safe areas inside the buildings. Classroom activities continue as normal.
	Lockdown	Move away from windows and doors. Lock interior doors. Close blinds over windows. Sit quietly in room where not visible.
"I Love U Guys" Foundation (Keyes, 2011)	Lockout	Bring all students and staff into the building. Lock all exterior doors. Secure the perimeter of the building. Classroom activities continue as normal.
	Lockdown	Lock classroom doors. Turn off the lights and place students and staff out of sight. Remain quiet.

Security Annex

The *Guide for Developing High-Quality School Emergency Operations Plans* (U.S. Department of Education, 2013) recommends that this annex, in collaboration with local law enforcement, focus on establishing a secure environment, safe from both internal and external criminal threats. Specific activities this annex addresses are (a) documenting the daily role of law enforcement in and around the school, (b) employing Crime Prevention Through Environmental Design to make the school building more physically secure, (c) safely moving students to and from school, (d) responding to threats identified by threat assessment teams, and (e) sharing information with law enforcement, while keeping in mind the requirements and limitations of privacy laws (see Chapters 3 and 4 for detailed discussions of these activities).

Continuity of Operations (COOP) Annex

The *Guide for Developing High-Quality School Emergency Operations Plans* (U.S. Department of Education, 2013) recommends that this annex describe how a school district and its schools ensure that essential functions continue during and immediately after crises. The primary objective of this annex is to ensure that business services (payroll and purchasing), communications, computer and systems support, facilities maintenance, security and safety, and teaching and learning continue even in times of crisis. Specific issues addressed in this annex include (a) how to design the COOP Annex so it can be up and running at any time and be sustained for as long as 30 days, and (b) how to set priorities using the COOP Annex to reestablish essential functions of school operation (e.g., the learning environment).

Just as schools should foster the resilience of students to help them cope with crises, the school system should develop a COOP to increase the district's ability to cope with disaster (Federal Emergency Management Agency, 2013). For example, if a school is damaged or destroyed by a fire, the school staff members need to find a way to continue teaching students, and to the extent that the school staff and administrators have planned for continuity of operations, the school is better able to cope with this disaster. Similarly, if a tornado severely damages a school, along with its books, computers, and other learning tools, a COOP helps to ensure that students can access their classes, homework, teachers, and textbooks online. A COOP also requires the school district to keep a backup of its online learning tools, grades, textbooks, transcripts, and so forth on an off-site server so that this material can still be accessed using a backup server. School districts also must ask how they would continue to function if vital staff and student records were destroyed. Will the staff be able to order supplies and pay vendors? Will the human resources office be able to hire new staff? Will payroll and insurance claims continue to be processed? A COOP addresses all of these questions to make sure that the school district continues to function during and following disaster.

A COOP must cover 10 different areas to ensure that operations continue: (a) essential functions; (b) order of succession; (c) delegation of authority; (d) continuity facilities; (e) continuity communications; (f) essential records management; (g) human resources; (h) tests, training, and exercises; (i) devolution of control and direction; and (j) reconstruction. Obviously, when a school district considers its essential functions, the first consideration is the teaching of students.

To develop the COOP, a crisis response team (often assisted by the safety team) can gather information from various departments in the district to identify essential functions. In some school districts, many of these functions may be described within the district policies and procedures. The policies and procedures may also determine the order of succession (i.e., who takes charge when the building principal or superintendent is unavailable to perform his or her functions) and delegation of responsibilities (i.e., what authority individuals have when the principal or superintendent is unavailable). The COOP should contain a list of several individuals who may be designated as the second in command, as well as the responsibilities he or she has to complete. The order of succession and delegation of responsibilities may need school board or superintendent approval before the plan can be finalized (Federal Emergency Management Agency, 2014a).

A school district also needs to plan how it will continue to operate at a temporary location. This area of the plan includes (a) where temporary facilities are located; (b) how to communicate with students and their caregivers, and with staff when standard communication systems are not functioning; (c) how to get access to essential records that school staff members need for responding to the emergency (i.e., student records, business software for ordering supplies); (d) how to relocate offices and continue work at the temporary facility; and (e) how to delegate responsibilities to individuals or agencies that are assisting in the recovery efforts. Schools must also plan for reconstruction and the transition back to the school once the damage has been repaired (Federal Emergency Management Agency, 2014a).

Preparedness is the key to developing the COOP. The essential steps involved in activating a COOP are (a) readiness and preparedness; (b) activation of plans, procedures, and schedules to transfer activities, personnel, records, and equipment to alternate facilities; (c) full execution of essential operations at alternate operating facilities; and (d) transfer of operations from the alternate facility to resume normal operations (Federal Emergency Management Agency, 2009, 2014a). Many of the items listed above may require school districts to spend months planning, developing MOUs, and seeking approval from school officials at various levels.

Recovery Annex

The *Guide for Developing High-Quality School Emergency Operations Plans* (U.S. Department of Education, 2013) recommends that this annex address how schools facilitate recovery from crises. It specifies four recovery areas: academic, physical, fiscal, and psychological and emotional recovery.

Academic Recovery

Specific academic recovery issues include (a) when the school should be closed and reopened, (b) who has the authority to close and reopen the school, (c) what alternative building facilities can be used if the school does not immediately reopen, and (d) how to deliver educational services if students are unable to physically return to the school. Academic recovery involves helping students return to learning, and for optimal academic recovery to take place, students need to feel physically and psychologically safe in their learning environment (Reeves et al., 2010). Loss of instructional time, whether it is hours, days, or weeks, needs to be considered. Teachers or administrators should explain to students and their caregivers how and when lost instructional time or upcoming testing will be made up or rescheduled. However, returning students to learning too quickly without evaluating their emotional needs would delay academic recovery. In addition, the academic recovery period varies, depending on the amount of devastation, the availability of replacement books and computers, and the availability of an alternate classroom environment.

Physical Recovery

Specific physical recovery activities this annex addresses include (a) how to document school facility assets so as to be able to identify damage, (b) which school staff members have knowledge of school assets, (c) how and where records are stored that document school facility assets, and (d) how to work with utility and insurance companies before crises to better ensure a quick recovery. The school district's facilities personnel (e.g., maintenance and grounds staff, architects, engineers) conduct damage assessments to determine the physical recovery efforts needed following a crisis. These personnel often work with community agencies such as fire departments and public works departments. Depending on the amount of damage incurred, physical recovery may be one of the first recovery steps to implement.

Fiscal Recovery

Specific fiscal recovery topics addressed by this annex include (a) delineation of how district-level administrators (e.g., superintendent, business officer, risk manager) make fiscal decisions affecting crisis response and recovery, (b) how to provide information and notify school staff members about returning to work, and (c) identification of sources for schools seeking emergency relief funding. Fiscal recovery efforts are also part of the COOP.

Psychological and Emotional Recovery

Finally, specific psychological and emotional recovery issues addressed in this annex include (a) who leads the crisis intervention and student care group, (b) where such services are provided, (c) how all school staff members (especially teachers) create a calm and supportive school environment, (d) how all school community members are enabled to identify students and school staff members who need mental health crisis intervention, (e) how trained providers of mental health crisis interventions are identified, (f) how to address not only immediate but also long-term mental health counseling needs, and (g) how the Public Health, Medical, and Mental Health Annex helps guide the Recovery Annex. The Recovery Annex is a primary focus of the PREP_aRE model, and its activities are discussed in detail in Chapters 10 through 19. This annex also typically addresses issues associated with memorials. However, on the basis of the authors' experiences, the PREP_aRE model recommends that this be its own specialized annex.

Memorials Annex

Although the *Guide for Developing High-Quality School Emergency Operations Plans* (U.S. Department of Education, 2013) does not recommend a separate annex for memorials, it does recommend that school crisis response plans consider how to manage memorial activities or memorial markers and structures. Specifically, the guide specifies that school crisis response plans should consider when and how memorial sites will be closed and what will be done with notes and tributes placed at the site. Special consideration needs to be given to how any memorial activity strikes a balance among honoring loss; returning to normal school functioning, routines, and schedules; and facilitating a sense of hope and optimism.

The Function of Memorials

Memorials acknowledge a school's loss and may serve as a focal point, place of healing, and forum for the collective grief of the school community. Physical memorials are places for students, school staff members, and the community to express grief and to have feelings validated and normalized. Memorial events and activities can be healthy venues that promote a sense of hope and recovery for those who participate and can serve as common ground for people to share and engage in cultural rituals or traditions. Assisting survivors in reestablishing social support systems and decreasing feelings of loneliness and isolation are important steps in the healing process, and memorials help serve this purpose. Memorials can also serve a larger purpose by promoting positive action toward a cause (Paine, 2007). However, if not carried out appropriately, memorials can serve as traumatic reminders of the death or romanticize the death in a way that encourages suicide contagion (Underwood, Fell, & Spinazzola, 2010). Therefore, memorial policies and procedures can guide the school community in selecting appropriate memorial events and activities.

Memorial Planning and Policies

Memorial policies are best created with input from students and their caregivers, and faculty, then approved by the administration and school board. Establishing a shared policy helps schools handle school-related deaths uniformly and makes the school's response more timely (Underwood et al., 2010). It also provides guidance to administrators as to the do's and don'ts when planning and approving memorials. Designating a memorial committee and committee chairperson to help establish the policy and make decisions regarding memorials enables the committee to address requests of the grieving community (Kodluboy, 2010; Poland & Poland, 2004). For example, saying no to a memorial in the absence of an established memorial policy can be misinterpreted as a lack of support or insensitivity in the emotional days and weeks following a tragedy.

One of the most important considerations in a memorial policy is consistency; a policy that responds differently to a suicide and an accidental death could be perceived as discriminating or unfair, or result in reinforcing the stigma of suicide (American Foundation for Suicide Prevention and Suicide Prevention Resource Center, 2011). In addition, according to Underwood et al. (2010), without a consistent policy, the school is at risk for legal action. Memorial policies should address procedures for memorial requests, specify the types of memorials permissible (and their duration), and include protocols for how and when memorial policies should be updated (see Table 9.10).

Schools should have a uniform response for memorial requests; however, some specific considerations are recommended for memorials following a student's death by suicide (Substance Abuse and Mental Health Services Administration, 2012). Such memorials must not glorify, highlight, or accentuate an individual's death in any way, because relative to older adults, teenagers

Table 9.10. Guidance for Designing Memorials

Memorial planning

- Designate a committee to oversee current and future memorial activities.
- Create and refer to school policies that specifically address memorial plans and procedures.
- Provide a variety of memorial activities, at various developmental levels, so individuals can choose their own way to express grief.
- Demonstrate awareness and sensitivity toward culturally related expressions, practices, and activities.
- Avoid activities and memorials that set a difficult precedent for future deaths.
- Exclude subtle or obvious gang representation, such as symbols or colors.
- Promote memorials that benefit others (e.g., donations for a suicide prevention program) and activities that foster a sense of hope and recovery and encourage positive action.
- Collaborate with the family regarding funeral and memorial services.
- Encourage funerals and larger memorial events to be held outside of the school setting and after school hours by doing the following:
  - Community groups and churches can provide additional venues and activities.
  - Students should be allowed to leave school for memorial and funeral events with caregiver permission and adherence to regular school protocols. Closing or dismissing school for events is not recommended.
  - Do not allow school buses to be used to transport students to and from services.
- Locate memorial events and activities in places that are optional to visit.
- Educate students about memorial behavior and expectations in the following ways:
  - Consider the age of your students and what experience they might have with death and the grieving process.
  - Teach students about grieving and what to expect at memorial services, events, and activities.
  - Allow time for questions before and after events.

Memorial events

- Make attendance voluntary (suggest supervised alternative activities).
- Closely supervise to make sure the memorial is appropriate, safe, and does not cause harm (e.g., remove any inappropriate or angry notes about the deceased).
- Observe individuals and make sure they have access to mental health professionals, if needed (students indicating self-harm or violent intent need to be referred immediately).
- Disseminate facts and provide information about common grief and crisis reactions and adaptive and maladaptive coping responses.
- Provide students and staff with information on additional resources if they need help (e.g., counseling or support groups).

Note. Adapted from *After a Suicide: A Toolkit for Schools*, by American Foundation for Suicide Prevention and Suicide Prevention Resource Center, 2011, Newton, MA: Education Development Center; *Memorial Activities at School: A List of "Do's" and "Don'ts,"* by National Association of School Psychologists, 2002b, Bethesda, MD: Author; *Memorials After a Suicide: Guidelines for Schools and Families*, by M. Underwood, 2013, Freehold, NJ: Society for the Prevention of Teen Suicide; *Lifelines Postvention: Responding to Suicide and Other Traumatic Death*, by M. Underwood, F. T. Fell, & N. A. Spinazzola, 2010, Center City, MN: Hazelden.

and young adults appear to be prone to imitative behavior and are at greater risk for suicide contagion (Heath, Bingham, & Dean, 2008; Zenere, 2009). Choosing memorials that are temporary, nonrenewable, or in the form of positive actions that benefit the living, such as monetary donations to purchase a suicide prevention program for the school, are therefore preferable. These memorials have the potential to positively affect surviving students rather than glorify the students who died by suicide. Regardless of the circumstances of how the death by suicide occurred, imitation or contagion can occur; thus, suicide postvention should reflect sensitivity to this possibility (Underwood, 2013; Underwood et al., 2010). Table 9.11 provides suggestions for memorial activities and events.

Spontaneous memorials are likely to appear at the student's locker, desk, or parking space following the death of a student in the school community (Underwood et al., 2010). Assigned school staff members should monitor all spontaneous memorials for inappropriate messages or for signs that a student may be at risk (American Foundation for Suicide Prevention and Suicide Prevention Resource Center, 2011). Memorials should be physically safe (e.g., students should not gather on the side of a road to memorialize victims of a motor vehicle collision) and psychologically safe (e.g., school staff members should supervise to make sure the memorial is appropriate and respectful, and that necessary emotional support can be provided where needed). The school's policy on spontaneous memorials should designate an acceptable period that materials can be left (e.g., until the end of each school day, or until the day after the funeral) and what happens to the memorial items after that time (Underwood et al., 2010). Including students in the planning process or in a ceremony to disassemble the memorial can be beneficial. If spontaneous gatherings or candlelight vigils begin to form, administrators may consider enlisting local police support to monitor events and counselors to attend events to offer support, guidance, and supervision (American Foundation for Suicide Prevention and Suicide Prevention Resource Center, 2011).

The American Foundation for Suicide Prevention and Suicide Prevention Resource Center (2011) recommends that schools discourage the creation and distribution of T-shirts or buttons with photos of the deceased; if students come to school wearing these items without seeking permission, schools should allow this for only one day. School staff members can then explain to the students that wearing these items can be upsetting or disruptive to some students, and that they may glamorize the death or lead to contagion. Given the importance of social media to youth, students will likely use these methods to memorialize a death by suicide. The memorial policy can then be shared to provide students with guidance on selecting an approved memorial activity. The school has a responsibility to monitor these tributes, stay informed of students' reactions, plan for memorial events, and identify at-risk students (Underwood et al., 2010).

How to deal with the deceased student's desk is another issue that arises. One recommendation is that a school-employed mental health professional follow the student's schedule for 1 day to speak with each of the student's classes. Then, after an appropriate amount of time, and discussed in advance, the extra chair or desk may be removed and the classroom seats may be arranged in a new order. Teachers should explain to students that this allows the deceased student to be honored, but also allows students to return to the classroom curriculum after a period of time. Students can help plan how to respectfully remove the desk or rearrange the seats in the classroom (American Foundation for Suicide Prevention and Suicide Prevention Resource Center, 2011).

Table 9.11. Memorial Activities and Events

- Sponsoring mental health awareness programs or a mental health awareness day
- Performing fundraising activities
  - Activities, projects, or work with nonprofit organizations that will make a difference and prevent similar deaths in the future (i.e., suicide, violence, bullying, or substance abuse prevention organizations or programming, or cancer research institutes)
  - For the family
  - For a scholarship that highlights student resiliency
  - To purchase library books or other student resource materials that encourage resilience and development of healthy coping skills
- Sending sympathy cards and flowers to the family
- Encouraging community participation in an awareness or fundraising event (Relay for Life or Out of the Darkness Walks)
- Volunteering
  - At a community crisis hotline
  - Tutoring or mentoring to help younger students
- Organizing a community service day
- Creating a school-based community service program that focuses on prevention
- Making a book available in the guidance office for students to write messages to the family, share memories of the deceased, or offer condolences (before presenting the book to the family on behalf of the school community, assign a crisis response team member to screen the content)
- Working with the administration to develop and implement a curriculum focused on effective problem solving
- Opening online memorials: messages, poems, or pictures
- Allowing age-appropriate inspirational posters that reflect the character of the decreased

Note. Adapted from *After a Suicide: A Toolkit for Schools*, by American Foundation for Suicide Prevention and Suicide Prevention Resource Center, 2011, Newton, MA: Education Development Center; *Memorials After a Suicide: Guidelines for Schools and Families*, by M. Underwood, 2013, Freehold, NJ: Society for the Prevention of Teen Suicide; *Lifelines Postvention: Responding to Suicide and Other Traumatic Death*, by M. Underwood, F. T. Fell, & N. A. Spinazzola, 2010, Center City, MN: Hazelden.

The creation of permanent memorials, such as plaques, stone memorials, gardens, monuments, benches, trees, and walkways, are challenging and controversial projects that require a considerable amount of time, money, and consensus building among school stakeholders (Paine, 2007). The school should examine the long-term impact of these memorials, such as how the memorial will be perceived 10 years after the death, the message it sends, and whether the school can feasibly create permanent memorials for all students or other members of the school community who die. Caution is also warranted because permanent memorials can disrupt the school's goal of restoring learning (American Foundation for Suicide Prevention and Suicide Prevention Resource Center, 2011). Lasting reminders of the death may trigger trauma responses or symbolize premature death to the students (Underwood et al., 2010). Permanent memorials also pose challenges in terms of the resources required for long-term maintenance (Paine, 2007). Thus the creation of temporary memorials or memorials that benefit the living (e.g., donating money to a charity) are preferred.

If a graduation-related memorial is suggested, students should be reminded that the graduation ceremony is intended as a celebration of the accomplishments of living students. However, eliminating remembrance at graduation may be as detrimental as overemphasizing it. Balance and consistency in the approach is key. Schools can choose to announce the student's name at graduation, to have an empty chair at the ceremony, or to create a list in the program of students not present at graduation, regardless of the cause. In the yearbook, the student's picture could be included in alphabetical order without drawing undue attention to it (Underwood et al., 2010).

The school has an influential role in guiding the grieving community to an appropriate outlet by providing a variety of suggestions and ideas to commemorate the loss. Having an open, honest, and concise discussion of the concerns of contagion and the school's policies and procedures can guide students and families in selecting appropriate memorial activities (Underwood et al., 2010). Providing a number of choices of memorial activities also encourages participation and increases the likelihood that individual students can benefit while using their preferred mode of emotional expression.

THREAT- AND HAZARD-SPECIFIC ANNEXES

During planning, crisis response teams, often assisted by school safety teams, conduct vulnerability assessments to determine which types of threats and hazards their school or district is most likely to experience. From the data provided by these assessments, the teams then create specific annexes to address each of the threats. Four broad types of threats and hazards can occur: (a) natural hazards (e.g., earthquakes, tornadoes, hurricanes, severe storms, wildfires, severe winter weather, floods, tsunamis); (b) technological hazards (e.g., explosions, hazardous materials release, gas leak, dam failure, power failure, water supply failure); (c) biological hazards (e.g., infectious disease, contaminated food, illness or death); and (d) adversarial, incidental, and human-caused threats and hazards (e.g., fire, armed assailants, criminal threats or actions, bomb threats, gang violence, cyberattacks, school staff member or student arrest, suicide threat, suicide death; U.S. Department of Education, 2013). To avoid repetition when a functional annex is part of a crisis response, such as evacuation in the event of a fire, the threat-specific Fire Annex would indicate "see Evacuation Annex." Additional guidance on developing these annexes is available from the Readiness and Emergency Management for Schools (REMS) Technical Assistance Center (http://rems.ed.gov/K12ThreatAndHSAnnex.aspx).

CONCLUSION

Developing effective crisis response plans requires several components. Quality plans include a well-developed basic plan in addition to functional and threat- and hazard-specific annexes. Given the complexity of the guidelines discussed in this chapter, school crisis response planning can feel overwhelming, and it does, in fact, require a substantial commitment and resources from the school district. With this reality in mind, Table 9.12 provides advocacy tips that help schools begin the planning process (Conolly-Wilson & Reeves, 2013; Reeves et al., 2011a).

Table 9.12. Tips for Advocating Crisis Response Planning

1. *Develop good relationships with the district and school administration.* Having a good rapport with administrators increases your ability to present concerns you have about school safety.
2. *Attend trainings.* Professional development helps guide your efforts.
3. *Research legal requirements.* Find out the legal requirements for crisis response planning for your state and identify school board policies relevant to crisis response planning.
4. *Take advantage of opportunities.* Crises that have significant media attention help bring vulnerabilities to the attention of administration. Use these examples to advocate improvements to the crisis response plan.
5. *Request funding.* After a crisis event has occurred, request funding for crisis response planning activities. Make sure to request funding before the next school year's budget cycle starts.
6. *Follow the chain of command.* Address concerns with the appropriate school administrator in charge of crisis response planning first, so that the suggestions can be presented to the district-level administrator and others according to the organizational structure. Speaking at a school board meeting and describing how your school's crisis response planning does not comply with state law may not be productive.
7. *Conduct planning at the district level.* If the district crisis response plan is 5 years old or older, speak with your principal about contacting someone at the district office about revising the plan. If opportunities arise for your school's crisis response team representative to work with the district office during the revision process, ask your principal if you could represent the school.
8. *Use a team approach.* If you are asked to create or revise your school's crisis response plan, seek the help of others. One person cannot independently revise an entire crisis response plan.
9. *Use existing resources.* Remember that you do not have to reinvent the wheel. Many states have crisis response plan templates that they want schools to follow. In addition, the National Association of School Psychologists, the U.S. Department of Education, and the U.S. Department of Homeland Security have information about school crisis response planning.
10. *Be patient!* Changing the culture of a school can take at least 5 years.
11. *Be confident that you can effect change!* From a first-year school employee to a 20-year veteran, anyone can start the change process. If you have a desire to see improvement in crisis response planning in your school, be persistent and look for those opportunities that will help you achieve your goal.

Chapter 10

PREVENTING PSYCHOLOGICAL TRAUMA

The first eight chapters of this section discussed crisis preparedness at the school system level and supported the PREPaRE curriculum's *Workshop 1, Crisis Prevention and Preparedness*; this chapter focuses on the primary prevention of psychological trauma at the individual student level and supports the PREPaRE curriculum's *Workshop 2, Crisis Intervention and Recovery*. Consistent with the overlap in these two workshops, this chapter contains some information presented in earlier chapters of this book. As Figure 1.3 showed, some prevention activities take place before crises occur, such as the primary prevention of crisis events and actions to foster resilience, which helps students cope with events that are not prevented. However, other prevention activities take place immediately after crises and include developing and implementing protection and mitigation strategies to ensure that students are safe and to minimize exposure to frightening crisis-related scenes and images. These efforts have been referred to as *immediate prevention* (Brock & Jimerson, 2004) or *crisis protection and mitigation* (U.S. Department of Education, 2013).

All of the above interventions, whether implemented before or after an incident has occurred, aim to prevent psychological trauma and are considered forms of *primary prevention* (Caplan, 1964), or *universal preventive interventions* (Gordon, 1983), because they can benefit all students and are therefore directed toward the entire population. Other, more intensive, school crisis interventions need to be considered only to the extent that psychological trauma is not prevented. Clearly, if the school is able to prevent a crisis and the psychological effects of exposure to that crisis, school mental health interventions are not needed, and the magnitude of the school crisis response is minimized. As discussed in Chapter 1, providing a level of crisis intervention greater than what is needed may have the unintended effect of increasing students' exposure to and perception of threats. Especially when working with young children, it is critical for crisis interveners, educators, and other caregivers to be mindful that adult responses to crises are important and powerful determinants of threat perceptions and crisis reactions (Dyregrov & Yule, 2006).

CRISIS PREVENTION

As discussed in the other chapters of this section, comprehensive school safety and crisis response teams do more than just respond to critical incidents. They also aim to prevent them from occurring in the first place, thus preventing students' psychological trauma. Table 10.1 lists possible crisis prevention activities. As discussed in Chapters 3 and 4, when considering crisis prevention, the teams developing crisis response plans must address both physical safety and psychological safety (Reeves, Nickerson, Conolly-Wilson, et al., 2011a).

PROTECTION AND STUDENT RESILIENCY

As discussed in Chapter 4, some students are more vulnerable than others to becoming victims of psychological trauma. Conversely, other students are more resilient and less likely to become trauma victims (Bensimon, 2012; Bonanno & Mancini, 2008; Kronenberg et al., 2010; Masten & Obradović, 2008; Milan, Zona, Acker, & Turcios-Cotto, 2013; Pat-Horenczyk, Kenan, Achituv, & Bachar, 2014; Sagi-Schwartz, 2008; Zahradnik et al., 2010). For example, Zahradnik et al. (2010) found that, as measured by the Child and Youth Resilience Measure (Ungar et al., 2008), "resilience protects from the development of more severe [posttraumatic stress disorder, or] PTSD" (p. 416). More specifically, Kronenberg et al. (2010) reported that successful adaptation to traumatic events is associated with "self-efficacy, positive coping and problem-solving skills, self-regulation, and supportive social systems including family, peer group, and school" (p. 1254). Similarly, Masten and Obradović (2008) identify the following "adaptive systems" they consider fundamental to human resilience: (a) attachment; (b) agency,

Table 10.1. Recommended Crisis Prevention Activities

Ensure physical safety
- Secure the building
- Incorporate natural surveillance
- Incorporate natural access control
- Facilitate a sense of territoriality
- Conduct a multihazard needs assessment

Ensure psychological safety
- Provide school-wide positive behavioral supports
- Provide universal, targeted, and intensive academic and social–emotional interventions and supports
- Develop school safety and crisis response plans
- Provide safety education
- Identify and monitor potential hazards and dangers, including threats of self- and other-directed violence
- Provide student guidance and counseling services

Note. Adapted from *School Crisis Prevention and Intervention: The PREPaRE Model*, p. 104, by S. E. Brock et al., 2009, Bethesda, MD: NASP. Copyright 2009 by the National Association of School Psychologists. Adapted with permission.

self-efficacy, and mastery motivation; (c) intelligence or the capacity of the individual for problem solving and information processing; (d) regulation of arousal, affect, attention, and action; (e) microsystems, including family, peers, and classrooms; (f) community or collective efficacy; and (g) macrosystems, including culture, media, and national and international organizations. To the extent that promoting these resiliency factors is possible, school safety and crisis response teams can proactively decrease the likelihood of a student becoming a psychological trauma victim. An illustration of protective mechanisms that can be the source of such resiliency are offered in Figure 10.1. As illustrated by the figure, the school itself can be an important protective factor.

Fleming (2006), who conducted research on resilience in severely abused children, found that personal relationships, a strong sense of independence, and self-reliance were among the factors that promoted resilience. Social supports can affect both acute and long-term stress reactions (Pine & Cohen, 2002), and personal, familial, and social assets help to protect students. Similarly, O'Donnell, Roberts, and Schwab-Stone (2011) found that among Gambian youth, who experienced high levels of exposure to violence, a positive school climate (facilitated by community-based programs that brought together parents, school, and youth) appeared to play an important role in addressing the negative effects (e.g., PTSD) of such exposure.

Figure 10.1. Examples of Sources of Resilience Within Four Ecological Levels

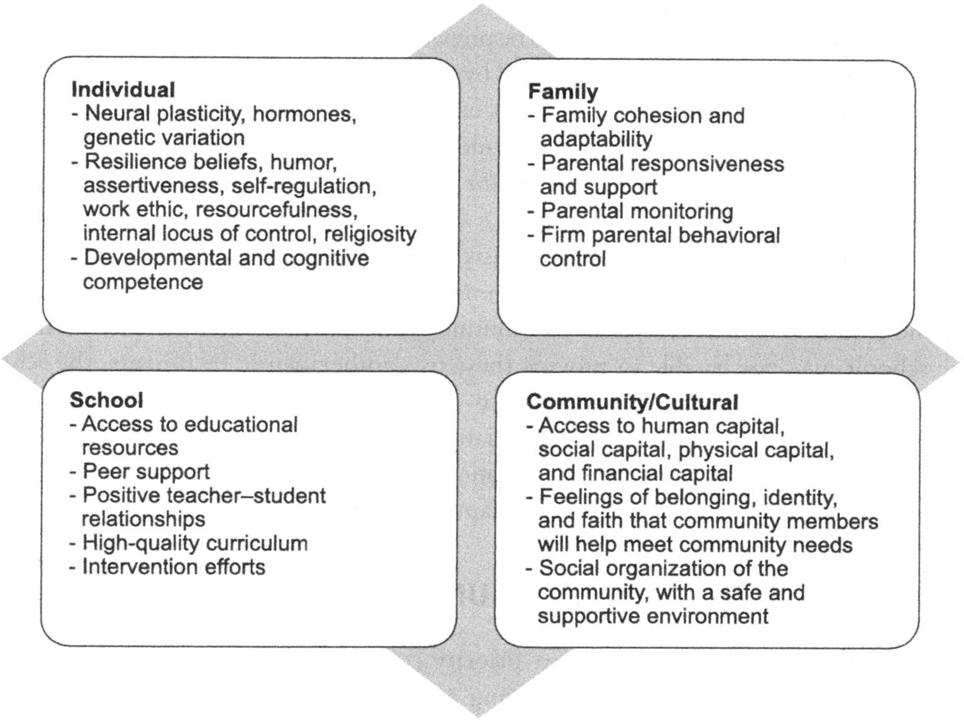

Individual
- Neural plasticity, hormones, genetic variation
- Resilience beliefs, humor, assertiveness, self-regulation, work ethic, resourcefulness, internal locus of control, religiosity
- Developmental and cognitive competence

Family
- Family cohesion and adaptability
- Parental responsiveness and support
- Parental monitoring
- Firm parental behavioral control

School
- Access to educational resources
- Peer support
- Positive teacher–student relationships
- High-quality curriculum
- Intervention efforts

Community/Cultural
- Access to human capital, social capital, physical capital, and financial capital
- Feelings of belonging, identity, and faith that community members will help meet community needs
- Social organization of the community, with a safe and supportive environment

Note. From "Adversity and Resilience: A Synthesis of International Research," by A. L. Noltemeyer and K. R. Bush, 2013, School Psychology International, 35, p. 482. Copyright 2013 by the authors. Reprinted with permission.

The Search Institute has surveyed over 4 million youth across the United States and Canada since 1989 to learn about the experiences, attitudes, behaviors, and number of "developmental assets" youth have. Their studies have consistently revealed a strong and consistent relationship between the number of assets present in young people's lives and the degree to which they develop in positive and healthful ways (www.search-institute.org).

Although the development of resilience among children is a complex subject and a dynamic process—according to Masten (2014), one that cannot ignore contextual factors such as culture—some general conclusions about how schools can foster resilience. For example, Table 10.2 lists specific examples of school-based activities that promote internal or individual resilience, and Table 10.3 lists activities that promote external resilience (e.g., family, school, and community factors). Again, to the extent educators are able to promote these factors in the lives of their students, they may be preventing psychological injury following exposure to a crisis event.

CRISIS PROTECTION AND MITIGATION

As discussed in earlier chapters, comprehensive school safety and crisis response planning cannot prevent all crises. Consequently, school crisis response teams need to be prepared to protect students from crisis-related dangers and to mitigate the effects of those dangers. Chapters 3, 4, 5, and 6 discussed specific protection and mitigation strategies. PREPaRE *Workshop 1, Crisis Prevention and Preparedness: Comprehensive School Safety Planning* (Reeves, Nickerson, Conolly-Wilson, et al., 2011a) is an example of a curriculum designed to help schools develop the skills needed to provide these services. However, schools also need to be prepared to provide mental health crisis interventions to address the psychological injuries generated by crisis exposure (Heath, Ryan, Dean, & Bingham, 2007). Sections 3, 4, and 5 of this book discuss the range of mental health crisis intervention services schools need to be prepared to provide. PREPaRE *Workshop 2, Crisis Intervention and Recovery: The Roles of School-Based Mental Health Professionals* (Brock, 2011a) helps schools develop the skills needed to provide these services.

Although the immediate mental health crisis interventions described in this book should prove sufficient for the majority of students, a minority of youth manifest more severe psychological injury and require longer-term (typically community-based) mental health interventions. Although public schools may not be able to provide these psychotherapeutic treatments, the school crisis response team's preparation for responding to crisis-related psychological trauma requires that schools identify and be able to make appropriate mental health referrals. Additional information on identifying psychotherapeutic treatment options and an examination of treatments for the most severely traumatized students are given in Chapters 13 and 19.

PROCEDURES TO MINIMIZE EXPOSURE

When a crisis occurs at school, the first priority is to keep students physically safe. Keeping students physically safe during and following a crisis event minimizes psychological trauma. Furthermore, how the immediate actions to protect students and mitigate effects are carried out can also be important in minimizing traumatic stress. For example, if medical triage is required,

Table 10.2. Fostering Internal Resilience at School

Promote active (or approach-oriented) coping styles. Positive coping skills can and should be taught directly by adults. Adult role modeling and guidance regarding appropriate coping strategies can lead to healthy student coping (as well as a positive school climate).

Promote student mental health. A balanced approach to meeting both the academic needs and the social and emotional needs of students is essential. Let students know that seeking help and asking for support are appropriate and promote healthy development.

Teach students how to better regulate their emotions. Many programs and frameworks directly teach skills on managing emotions. Teaching positive skills to replace negative coping strategies is most often done using interventions at selected and/or indicated levels but can also be done through student psychoeducational groups or other forms of classroom-based instruction.

Develop problem-solving skills. Direct instruction regarding problem solving can help students consider the pros and cons of various problem-solving strategies.

Promote self-confidence, self-esteem, and positive attitudes. Provide situations in which students experience success both academically and socially, and frame failure as a learning opportunity. Instruct students to reevaluate and adjust strategies that may not be working, while building upon their strengths.

Promote an internal locus of control. Individuals who have an internal locus of control believe that their behavior is guided by personal decisions and efforts. It is directly related to self-confidence, self-esteem, and the ability to regulate and control one's own emotions. Promote students' internal locus of control and personal responsibility by asking thought-provoking questions that allow for self-reflection about how behavior is guided by personal decisions and efforts, not just the result of external circumstances, chance, or fate.

Validate the importance of faith or belief systems. Faith or belief systems are important to many people and offer important supports that result in greater resiliency.

Nurture positive emotions. Demonstrate and give students the chance to practice positive emotions, such as optimism, respect, forgiveness, and empathy. Provide positive reinforcement and recognition for behaviors associated with such emotions. Train staff members to reinforce emotional intelligence, praise students for successes, and avoid judgmental or harsh criticism for failure. Administrators need to foster and reinforce positive attitudes among school staff members that help establish a positive climate for students.

Foster academic self-determination and feelings of competence. Provide consistent and clear expectations. Have students become involved in establishing school and classroom rules and expectations. Help students develop a menu of homework and study strategies. Encourage students to regularly attend school and complete homework, as well as to develop their talents in activities they enjoy. Teach them to set realistic goals and obtain necessary resources.

Note. Adapted from *School Crisis Prevention and Intervention: The PREPaRE Model*, pp. 106–107, by S. E. Brock et al., 2009, Bethesda, MD: NASP. Copyright 2009 by the National Association of School Psychologists. (Original based on Smith Harvey, 2004.) Adapted with permission.

Table 10.3. Fostering External Resilience at School

Support families. Forming positive parent–school partnerships in which parents feel welcome at school, are included in decision making, and can provide suggestions helps to establish a foundation of collaboration and trust between home and school. In addition, parent support services such as academic curriculum nights, parent education classes, and parenting skills classes help foster the conditions that support external resiliency.

Facilitate peer relationships. Provide activities that engage students with their peers, such as clubs, sporting activities, leadership activities, and community service activities.

Provide access to positive adult role models. Establish access to positive adult role models within the broader school community. Prior collaborative relationships with both school- and community-based organizations and agencies can be a valuable resource for role models.

Ensure connections with prosocial institutions. Help students connect with school activities or other associations that provide activities that engage students and foster a sense of belonging.

Provide a caring, supportive learning environment. Promote positive social connections between staff members and students, students and their peers, and home and school. Model acceptance and tolerance through school activities and behaviors. Establish a culture that includes the belief that getting help for a friend is the right thing to do (it is not "narking").

Encourage volunteerism. Social competence and resilience are developed through helping others at home, in school, and in the community. Create and promote a variety of opportunities for students to contribute to the well-being of others, both in school and in the broader community. Students will learn that helping others fosters a sense of control and minimizes feelings of despair and helplessness.

Teach peace-building skills. Students can learn how to be appropriately assertive without being aggressive and to have self-control. Teach conflict-resolution and peer-mediation skills, strategies for responding to bullies, and violence-prevention strategies.

Note. Adapted from *School Crisis Prevention and Intervention: The PREP_aRE Model*, p. 107, by S. E. Brock et al., 2009, Bethesda, MD: NASP. Copyright 2009 by the National Association of School Psychologists. (Original based on Smith Harvey, 2004.) Adapted with permission.

crisis response team members should shield students from viewing these medical interventions. Therefore, they should consider the traffic flow of emergency responders in relation to crisis response procedures, such as student evacuation routes, to minimize exposure. Obviously, minimizing student exposure to frightening crisis situations minimizes the degree of psychological traumatization (Udwin, Boyle, Yule, Bolton, & O'Ryan, 2000).

Psychological traumatization can also result from media exposure (Comer & Kendall, 2007; Hagan et al., 2005; Lengua, Long, Smith, & Meltzoff, 2005; Pfefferbaum et al., 2001; Pfefferbaum et al., 2003; Schuster et al., 2001). This effect may be especially true for individuals with a history of traumatic stress (Weems, Scott, Banks, & Graham, 2012). Thus, primary caregivers and school staff members should be provided with specific, developmentally appropriate guidance regarding the importance of limiting students' television viewing and social media/Internet exposure. Television and the Internet may have humanized mass violence and disasters, and put a face on the victims and bereaved (Bowis, 2007), increasing awareness of world events and atrocities and helping individuals understand their part in helping others. However, as will be further discussed in Chapter 13, repeated crisis exposures have a potentially negative impact.

CONCLUSION

Although school safety and crisis response teams strive to prevent crises before they occur, even the best of prevention efforts cannot prevent all crises from occurring. Therefore school safety and crisis response teams need to engage in a range of preparedness activities, including developing student resiliency to better ensure they have the internal and external resources needed to successfully cope with crises. Prevention activities also include the development of protection and mitigation strategies that keep students and staff safe in the event of a crisis. Finally, immediate and effective response to the crisis event is critical in preventing psychological trauma. When crisis protection and mitigation strategies are effective—that is, they keep students and staff physically safe and minimize exposure to traumatizing images—traumatic stress will be minimized and possibly even avoided.

Section 3

REAFFIRM

The second element of the PREPaRE model (the first "R" in PREPaRE) refers to reaffirming physical health and ensuring perceptions of safety. When a crisis occurs, PREPaRE directs schools to begin the crisis response by first reaffirming physical health and ensuring that all school community members (e.g., students, school staff, and other caregivers) perceive the school environment as secure and safe. As illustrated in Figure 1.3, these activities typically take place during and immediately after crisis threats end, during what Valent (2000) calls the impact or recoil phase and what Raphael and Newman (2000) called the immediate postdisaster phase. Before any other school crisis intervention can be implemented, the members of the school community not only must be objectively safe but also must have their basic physical needs met and believe that the threat of danger has passed. In the words of Everly (2003) "needs for food, water, shelter, alleviation of pain, reunification with family members, and the provision of a sense of safety and security should all precede the utilization of psychologically oriented crisis interventions" (p. 182). Figure 1.3 also illustrates that delivery of what has been referred to as psychological first aid would begin in this phase, in particular, the first three core actions of contact and engagement, safety and comfort, and, as indicated, stabilization (see Brymer et al., 2006; and Brymer, Taylor, et al., 2012, for detailed discussions of psychological first aid).

If these interventions take place after a crisis event has occurred, but before it has had a chance to psychologically traumatize school community members, they could be considered primary prevention. However, as they are also likely to be among the first actions taken to assist acutely distressed individuals, they may also be considered secondary prevention (Caplan, 1964). Furthermore, given that they are desirable for everyone, these interventions can be directed toward the entire population and are thus labeled universally preventive interventions (Gordon, 1983). Depending on the nature of the crisis event, the need for these crisis interventions can last days or weeks. Although they might occur simultaneously, mental health crisis interventions (i.e., evaluating psychological trauma and responding to individual psychological needs) are clearly secondary to ensuring physical health and perceptions of security and safety. Only after these basic needs are met do the school-based mental health professionals begin to use their unique skill sets (Brown & Bobrow, 2004).

The first chapter in this section (Chapter 11) reviews strategies designed to reaffirm objective physical health and safety. However, subjective perceptions of physical health and safety are at least as important as the objective situation. Thus, Chapter 12 reviews strategies designed to help ensure that students (as well as school community members) believe they are safe and that crisis related dangers have passed.

Chapter 11

REAFFIRM PHYSICAL HEALTH AND SAFETY

Following a school-associated crisis, the first priority is to keep students and staff members physically healthy and safe (Brymer, Taylor, et al., 2012; Haskett, Scott, Nears, & Grimmett, 2008; McNally, Bryant, & Ehlers, 2003; National Commission on Children and Disasters, 2010). In some instances, this response may involve implementing crisis response procedures such as evacuation or lockdown; in other cases, it may involve addressing basic physical needs (e.g., providing water, food, shelter, first aid, or medications); and in still other instances, a response may require reorganizing the school environment (e.g., providing instruction at another school site or a police presence on campus; Brymer et al., 2006; Haskett et al., 2008). Regardless of the cause, when such activities are needed, they are of primary importance, and mental health crisis intervention takes a back seat to ensuring physical health and safety (Everly, 2003; Joshi & Lewin, 2004; Ritchie, 2003; Ruzek et al., 2007; Watson, Brymer, & Bonanno, 2011). In the words of Brown and Bobrow (2004):

> The first step following a disaster is to ensure the safety, shelter, and sustenance of children and their caregivers. In our experience, mental health interventions are secondary. Once these basic needs are met, there is a role for mental health professionals. (p. 212)

Furthermore, before any psychological recovery and associated mental health crisis interventions can begin, crisis-related dangers must be eliminated and physical health challenges addressed (Levy, 2008). Barenbaum, Ruchkin, and Schwab-Stone (2004) noted: "Non-psychiatric interventions, such as provision of basic needs, food, shelter and clothing, help provide the stability required to ascertain the numbers of youth needing specialized psychiatric care" (p. 49). In fact, evidence shows that mental health crisis intervention is not effective if the crisis-related stressors are not first terminated (Thabet, Vostanis, & Karim, 2005).

This is not to say that mental health is not a concern immediately following a crisis event. Negative mental health outcomes such as posttraumatic stress disorder (PTSD), depression, and phobias clearly are more likely following crisis situations in which danger or threats are ongoing (Terr, 1991; Vásquez et al., 2012; Widom, 1999). Thus, when objective safety is quickly reaffirmed following a crisis, negative mental health outcomes can be minimized or even avoided (Dückers, 2013; Hobfoll et al., 2007). However, once objective physical health and safety are restored, individual perceptions of safety present another mental health challenge. Not only must students (and staff) actually be healthy and safe; they also must believe that crisis-related dangers have passed and that their health and welfare has been ensured.

This chapter focuses on reaffirming objective physical health and safety. It also recommends actions to be taken when a crisis event is ongoing and objective physical health and safety cannot be immediately reaffirmed. Though the recommendations that follow primarily address the needs of students, they also can be generalized to school staff members. To the extent that staff members' physical safety and security needs are not met, they may be unable to fill a caregiving role.

ENSURING PHYSICAL HEALTH AND SAFETY WITHIN THE GENERAL STUDENT POPULATION

The National Child Traumatic Stress Network and the National Center for PTSD (Brymer et al., 2006; Brymer, Taylor, et al., 2012) offer several practical suggestions for reaffirming physical health and safety among the general student population following crises. First, the school crisis response team should identify officials who can address, and ideally resolve, threats to physical safety that are beyond the control of team members. For example, law enforcement personnel would be brought in to address threats of assaultive violence, and weapons. Second, the team should ensure that objects that could cause harm are removed from the school environment as soon as possible, such as broken glass or broken furniture that could cause injury. Third, the team should ensure that students have a clean and safe environment in which to work and play, with adequate supervision provided at all times. For example, school crisis response teams might use law enforcement or physical barriers to prevent intrusions onto school grounds by unauthorized individuals. Finally, the team must be especially sensitive to individuals in particular subgroups who might be targets of crisis-related persecution because of their ethnic, religious, or other affiliations. For example, in the instance of an act of school violence that was perpetrated by an individual with a particular group affiliation, the team should make sure students from that group are provided with extra security and are able to get safely to and from school.

ENSURING PHYSICAL HEALTH AND SAFETY WITHIN SPECIAL NEEDS POPULATIONS

Among students in special education, with disabilities, or with chronic illnesses, special actions may be needed to ensure physical health and safety. Planning for these crisis response challenges was addressed in Chapter 9. Table 11.1 offers additional practical suggestions for reaffirming physical health and safety among these special populations during a school crisis response.

Table 11.1. Recommendations for Reaffirming Health and Safety Among Special Needs Populations

1. Ensure adequate lighting and implement protective measures to minimize slipping, tripping, and falling among those with physical challenges.
2. Ensure that students who lack mobility or may fall easily are placed in easily accessible areas. Avoid areas that require the use of stairs or are located in lower levels.
3. Ensure that students maintain access to mobility and sensory devices, such as wheelchairs, glasses, and hearing aids.
4. Be prepared for the possibility that student volunteers who normally help special needs students may not be available in an emergency. Plan to have other volunteers who help when the student cannot have that familiar and trusted individual to assist with transport if an evacuation is required.
5. For students in electric wheelchairs, confirm that provisions have been made for when the chair's battery runs out of power (e.g., extra batteries or the presence of individuals strong enough to push an electric wheelchair that has run out of power).
6. Ensure that all self-care needs continue to be met (e.g., assistance with eating, dressing, and toileting).
7. Plan to have an additional power source for students who have special health care needs, such as students who require suctioning.
8. Maintain a list of students who take medications, and ensure that a 72-hour supply of medications (e.g., insulin) is available.
9. Ensure that students with autism spectrum disorders avoid unfamiliar and overstimulating environments. Provide these students with social stories (or scripts) that describe crisis response procedures. Be mindful of the sounds, such as fire alarms, that may trigger strong emotional reactions from students with sensory issues.
10. Anticipate that some students may be unable to communicate their physical needs, which may increase their psychological vulnerability. For students with cognitive delays, who may not understand the threat presented by the crisis event, clearly communicating that they are physically safe will minimize psychological trauma.

Note. Brymer et al. (2006); Susan (2010).

RESPONDING TO ACUTE NEEDS

Reaffirming physical health and safety includes attending to the immediate medical and safety needs of both general and special education students (as well as school staff members). For example, if an individual displays signs of shock or has other medical needs, or appears to present a risk of harm to self or others, emergency medical assistance should be immediately obtained. Until help arrives, the school safety and crisis response team member should stay with the affected individual, remain calm, and do his or her best to ensure physical health and safety (Haskett et al., 2008; Ruzek et al., 2007).

Responding to acute needs also involves helping to calm and orient those individuals who present as emotionally overwhelmed and extremely disoriented (Brymer, Taylor, et al., 2012). Indications that an individual is overwhelmed are presented in Table 11.2, and some basic

Table 11.2. Signs of Emotionally Overwhelmed Staff and Students

Adults, adolescents, or school-age children
- Disoriented: engaging in aimless, disorganized behavior
- Disconnected: numb; startlingly unaffected by the event
- Confused: not able to understand what is happening around them; not making sense
- Panicked: extremely anxious; unable to settle; their eyes wide and darting
- Hysterical: sobbing uncontrollably; hyperventilating; rocking
- Excessively preoccupied: unable to think about anything else
- In denial: refusing to accept that the event took place
- In physical shock: not being able to move; frozen
- Glassy-eyed and staring vacantly; unable to find direction
- Unresponsive to verbal questions or commands
- Exhibiting frantic searching behavior
- Feeling incapacitated by worry
- Engaging in risky activities

Young children
- Staring blankly
- Unresponsive
- Displaying behaviors they had outgrown (e.g., urinating in inappropriate places, sucking a thumb)
- Screaming
- Crying or sobbing uncontrollably
- Hyperventilating
- Moving in an agitated way (thrashing, pushing away)
- Hiding (in a corner or under a table)
- Clinging excessively

Note. Adapted from Psychological First Aid for Schools: Field Operations Guide (2nd ed.), p. 36, by M. Brymer, M. Taylor et al., 2012, Los Angeles: NCTSN. Copyright 2012 by National Child Traumatic Stress Network and National Center for PTSD. Adapted with permission.

recommendations for taking care of individuals who are so affected by the crisis that they are unable to perform basic tasks (e.g., eating or making simple decisions) are presented in Table 11.3. More detailed discussions of how to orient and stabilize emotionally overwhelmed crisis survivors, including those who appear extremely distraught, are presented by Brymer et al. (2006, pp. 50–53); Brymer, Taylor, et al. (2012, pp. 35–40); and in Chapter 18 of this book.

ENSURING PHYSICAL COMFORT

Following crisis events, making the school environment more physically comfortable helps to ensure that basic needs are being met and can reduce students' anxiety (Brymer et al., 2006; Brymer, Taylor, et al., 2012; Haskett et al., 2008). If possible, school safety and crisis response team members should consider things like room temperature, lighting, and air quality. Brymer et al. (2006)

Table 11.3. The Initial Response to Emotionally Overwhelmed Students

For adults, adolescents, and school-age children

- Respect the person's privacy and give him or her a few minutes before you intervene. Say you will be available if the person needs you, or that you will check back in a few minutes to see how he/she is doing and whether there is anything you can do to help at that time.
- Remain calm, quiet, and present, rather than trying to talk the person directly, as your questioning may contribute to cognitive and/or emotional overload.
- Remain available, while giving the person a few minutes to calm down.
- Stand nearby as you talk to other individuals, do some paperwork, or do other tasks, watching to see if the person needs or asks for help.
- Offer support and help the individual focus on specific and manageable feelings, thoughts, and goals.
- Give information that orients the person to surroundings, such as how the setting is organized, what will be happening, and what steps he or she may consider.
- Clarify any misinformation or misunderstanding about what is taking place, while helping to curtail rumors.
- Attempt to determine what the student or adult is experiencing, so that you can address her or his immediate concern or difficulty.

For young children

- Remain calm, quiet, and reassuring. Sit with the child at eye level as you speak in a low tone and in a reassuring manner.
- Reassure and calm through physical contact, such as a protective arm across the shoulder, if it appears welcome. Some children may dislike or have a negative association with being touched. If you are unsure, ask them if you may touch them.
- Distract the child from the situation by asking questions about his/her favorite story, hobby, sport, or song. Keep the circumstances in mind so that you do not inadvertently trigger greater anxiety by asking about a topic that may be related to existing fears (such as asking, "What is your favorite bedtime story?" when the child is fearful for his or her caregiver's safety).
- Give age-appropriate information about what to expect, and always answer questions in an honest, developmentally appropriate way.
- Do not overwhelm children with too much information. Under stress, a child can only process so much information and will likely change the subject or move to a different activity when feeling overwhelmed. Watch for and be respectful of the cues the child gives.
- Reconnect children with their caregivers or staff who know them as soon as possible.

Note. Adapted from *Psychological First Aid for Schools: Field Operations Guide* (2nd ed.), pp. 37–38, by M. Brymer, M. Taylor et al., 2012, Los Angeles: NCTSN. Copyright 2012 by National Child Traumatic Stress Network and National Center for PTSD. Adapted with permission.

also suggested that giving younger children toys such as soft teddy bears not only can help to soothe and comfort, but also can be used to reinforce physical health care priorities. For example, the team member can tell students that on hot, humid days, their teddy bear needs to drink plenty of water.

RESPONDING TO ONGOING SAFETY THREATS

School safety and crisis response team members must avoid making promises they cannot keep (Brymer et al., 2006; Brymer, Taylor, et al., 2012). Specifically, they should not reassure students that they are safe and that crisis-related challenges have passed if they are not certain this is the case. However, crisis interveners should recognize that even in situations where health and safety threats are ongoing, individuals who are able to reestablish or maintain a relative sense of security have a significantly lower risk of negative mental health outcomes (Hobfoll et al., 2007; Watson et al., 2011). Therefore, crisis response teams should do everything possible to reaffirm physical health and safety, without giving false reassurances, while conveying to the school community that dangers are actively being addressed. During a situation involving an ongoing threat, crisis response teams should provide students and school community members with objective information about the steps being taken to ensure safety (Eagle & Kaminer, 2013). For example, during an extended school lockdown (with an armed criminal suspected of being in the area), students should be informed of the actions law enforcement are taking to find the criminal, and that the school's safety protocols make the chances of any student being harmed quite low.

Not giving false reassurances to students may also mean that crisis interveners do not promise to give students goods or services such as food, water, or blankets unless they are certain they are available (Brymer et al., 2006; Brymer, Taylor, et al., 2012). If a specific timeline for the availability of such items is known, the school safety and crisis response team can announce when these will be available.

Another approach to employ during a situation involving an ongoing threat is to provide students and the school community with strategies to cope with ongoing stressors. For example, in a situation involving aggression or violence, and with the perpetrator of the act still at large, the magnitude of law enforcement activity can be shared (e.g., police patrols around the area have been increased), and adaptive behaviors that help to ensure safety can be reinforced (e.g., have the class review stranger-danger rules). Among Israeli adolescents exposed to several years of ongoing terrorist attacks, emotion-focused coping, which Moos and Billings (1984) defined as affect regulation, emotional discharge, and resigned acceptance, was associated with posttraumatic stress and mental health problems. When combined with subjective exposure to the ongoing threat, individuals' coping style explained 26% to 37% of the variance of psychological problems experienced by the sample (Braun-Lewensohn et al., 2009). Therefore, schools that teach what Billings has referred to as appraisal-focused and problem-focused coping might see some benefits. Such an effort involves helping students to understand the crisis in a productive manner and to confront the reality of the problem. As discussed in Chapter 1 (see Table 1.7), these adaptive coping strategies include problem solving (and adjusting actions to be effective), information seeking (and finding additional contingencies), self-reliance (and protecting available social resources), support seeking (and making use of available resources), accommodation (and adjusting expectations or options to the current situation), and negotiation (for finding new options to address the coping challenge; Skinner & Zimmer-Gembeck, 2007).

Fortunately, the vast majority of U.S. schoolchildren live in environments where the threats posed by crisis events are situational, and no matter how threatening an event was when it occurred, schools and communities can, in a relatively short time frame (hours or days versus

Table. 11.4. Suggestions for Ensuring Student Safety

Following a school emergency, students and staff need to understand the broader context of the response activities that are occurring at the school and in the community. When even the most minimal of predictable schedules or activities is reestablished, individuals begin to feel more stable.

Provide information about:
- What to do next.
- The status of their classmates, teachers, other school staff, and relatives, if known and if they are safe.
- What is being done to assist them.
- What is currently known about the unfolding event.
- The support services available to them and their families.
- When and where school services will be resumed.
- The best way to get updated information about the situation in the hours or days ahead.

When providing information:
- Make sure school authorities have granted permission to share event-specific information, such as the circumstances of the current situation, the names of those directly affected by the event, and when school services will resume.
- Use your judgment as to whether and when to present specific information.
- Use clear and concise language while avoiding technical jargon.
- Position yourself, when feasible, at eye level with the individual.
- Use a calm, reassuring tone of voice and give the person time and space to talk.
- Provide accurate information, in easy-to-understand terms, to young students, about who will be supervising them and what to expect next. Consider using visual cues and materials to illustrate your information.
- Consider the following when talking to students:
  - Is it appropriate to share this information given the student's age?
  - Does the student appear able to comprehend what you are saying?
  - Is the student ready to hear the content of what you are saying?

Remember:
- To address immediate needs and concerns to reduce fears, answer pressing questions, and support adaptive coping.
- That students, staff, and family members may be getting information from many sources of technology (texting, Twitter, Facebook, TV, radio, phone, Internet). Ask about what they have heard or read and address any misinformation or distressing information.
- To *not* guess or invent information if you do not know it to provide reassurance. Instead, develop a plan, along with those you are helping, to get them the information.
- To *not* reassure people of the availability of goods or services (e.g., shelter, medicines, donations) unless you know that such goods and services will be available.
- When working with families, to include children when discussing and sharing information if it is appropriate. Do *not* just speak to the parent or caregiver. When children are left out of discussions, they may feel more insecure.

Note. Adapted from *Psychological First Aid for Schools: Field Operations Guide* (2nd ed.), pp. 26–28, by M. Brymer, M. Taylor et al., 2012, Los Angeles: NCTSN. Copyright 2012 by National Child Traumatic Stress Network and National Center for PTSD. Adapted with permission.

months or years), eliminate ongoing threats to physical security and safety. However, eliminating threats is not possible in some school environments (Pat-Horenczyk, 2006). For example, in the case of war, chronic threats of terrorism, or extreme community violence, teachers or other school officials cannot reaffirm for students that danger has passed. In these situations, recovery from crisis exposure is not possible because students are continuing to experience the crisis event (Shuster, Stein, & Jaycox, 2002). Educators can help by providing students with adaptive behaviors in which they can engage to minimize the threat of harm and maintain their physical health and safety. Not only does such instruction help keep students healthy and safe, but it may also result in the ongoing stress appearing more controllable, which in turn may lessen its traumatic impact. In these situations, school safety and crisis response team members must monitor students for the acute stress reactions presented in Table 11.2 and provide these students with the responses presented in Table 11.3. Finally, Table 11.4 presents Brymer, Taylor, et al.'s (2012) general suggestions of what to tell students during a school crisis response to ensure their physical and psychological safety.

CONCLUSION

Although restoring objective physical health and safety is essential, school safety and crisis response teams should be aware that the subjective perceptions of individuals involved in traumatic experiences can be as important as, if not more important than, objective physical security. Chapter 12 presents recommendations for effectively ensuring students' perceptions of safety and security.

Chapter 12

REAFFIRM PERCEPTIONS OF SAFETY AND SECURITY

It is not enough for school community members to actually be safe following a crisis. For psychological recovery to begin, individuals must *believe* they are safe (Charuvastra & Cloitre, 2008). Individuals who have had their psychological sense of safety reaffirmed have reduced risk for negative mental health outcomes. Conversely, individuals who believe that crisis-related dangers have not passed, or who exaggerate crisis-related risks, are at greater risk for negative mental health outcomes (Bryant, Salmon, Sinclair, & Davidson, 2007; Hobfoll et al., 2007). Believing that one is safe can affect both the biology and psychology of traumatic stress. For example, according to Ruzek et al. (2007), "Promotion of a psychological sense of safety can reduce biological aspects of post-traumatic stress reactions, and can positively affect cognitive processes that inhibit recovery, including a belief that 'the world is completely dangerous' and exaggeration of future risk" (p. 22).

This chapter begins with an examination of how students' psychological safety is affected by the way adults react to and behave in a crisis. It then presents steps to promote a subjective sense of safety, which may include minimizing exposure to crisis scenes and images, reuniting or locating students' caregivers, providing factual information about the crisis event, and returning to a school environment that makes school safety concrete and visible. Although this chapter primarily addresses the needs of students, many of the recommendations that follow can also be applied to school staff members. Obviously, to the extent that staff members' perceptions of psychological safety are not realized, they will find the caregiver role challenging.

THE EFFECT OF ADULT REACTIONS AND BEHAVIORS

Adult reactions are important in reaffirming not only objective physical health and safety, but also perceived safety and security, especially for young children (Dyregrov & Yule, 2006; Eksi et al., 2007; Li et al., 2010; Morris, Lee, & Delahanty, 2013). Young children often look to their adult caregivers for guidance regarding the level of threat presented by a given event. If adults behave as if an event is highly traumatic (regardless of its objective threat), younger children will more than likely respond accordingly (Masten & Gewirtz, 2006). For example, Kaufman-Shriqui et al. (2013) report on a study evaluating the posttraumatic stress observed among preschoolers exposed to war-related missile attacks:

> For young children, the caregiver is an "external regulator" relied upon to provide protection. Therefore, the child's ability to manage stress, such as exposure to traumatic events, is largely determined by the caregiver's response and his or her ability to help restore a sense of safety. Distressed mothers of young children are less available to respond to their children's emotional and physical needs and to assist their child in coping with their emotional reactions to traumatic events. (p. 429)

Kaufman-Shriqui further note that as children grow older they become better able to independently regulate their emotions, and associations between maternal and child distress decrease significantly. Similarly, a study by B. L. Green et al. (1991) reported that maternal posttraumatic stress disorder (PTSD) symptoms actually predicted child PTSD 2 years after a dam collapse and flood. Ostrowski, Christopher, and Delahanty (2007) also found caregivers' reactions to be predictive of PTSD among their children. Specifically, they found that boys' PTSD symptoms 6 weeks following a traumatic injury, and both boys' and girls' PTSD symptoms 7 months following the same type of injury, were predicted by maternal posttraumatic stress symptoms. Most recently, the results of two separate meta-analyses provided evidence that parental PTSD is associated with their children's posttraumatic stress symptoms, behavior problems, and distress (Lambert, Holzer, & Hasbun, 2014; Morris, Gabert-Quillen, & Delahanty, 2012).

Landolt, Vollrath, Timm, Gnehm, and Sennhauser (2005) found that the severity of the father's PTSD was an especially important predictor of the child's PTSD 12 months following a traffic accident. In interpreting this finding and addressing why fathers are important to the posttraumatic adjustment of their children, Landolt et al. (2005) stated: "One may speculate that children react more strongly to their fathers' symptoms because this is less common for them. In Western society, fathers are expected to be strong and to handle difficult situations without displaying excessive emotions" (p. 1281). These data can be interpreted as an indication that children look to adults to gauge the seriousness of a threatening situation. If they see what are judged to be excessive reactions among their caregivers, they are more likely to view the event as a traumatic stressor and in turn more likely to become psychological trauma victims.

The associations between adult and child traumatic stress represent correlational, not causal, connections. Furthermore, among biologically related parents and children, the similar levels of traumatic stress reactions may be related to genetically based biological factors, rather than psychological factors (Lambert et al., 2014). Nevertheless, a prudent recommendation is to carefully monitor the behavior of caregiving adults (especially those caring for young children). These data and their interpretations suggest that if school staff members are able to accurately assess the danger associated with a crisis and to implement emergency procedures in a calm and controlled manner, then students are likely to view the circumstances as more controllable and less threatening. Not only will students' needs be most effectively met, but they are more likely to react accordingly (i.e., behave as if they are safe). These points reinforce the discussion in Chapter 1, which offered that school crisis response teams must accurately assess the nature of a crisis event and the event's potential to generate traumatic stress. Failure to do so may result in the team overresponding to the crisis event and in doing so increasing the threat perceptions of student.

MINIMIZING CRISIS EXPOSURE

Consistent with the guidance offered in Chapter 11, minimizing exposure to the crisis event itself, its immediate aftermath (including the suffering of others), and subsequent media coverage may also foster a sense of psychological safety (Brymer et al., 2006; Ruzek et al., 2007). This effort may involve directing ambulatory students away from the crisis site and ensuring that they cannot view medical triage activities. Individuals who are shielded from potentially upsetting crisis-related scenes and images typically find reestablishing a sense of psychological safety easier compared with those who are directly exposed to such images.

Fostering a sense of psychological safety and security also includes minimizing the crisis exposure generated by media coverage of the event (Brymer et al., 2006; Lengua, Long, Smith, & Meltzoff, 2005; Propper, Stickgold, Keeley, & Christman, 2007). Consequently, parents are encouraged to (a) monitor their children's exposure to media and discuss their concerns or questions, (b) let their children know that they are monitoring the situation and will give them updates, (c) be careful about what is said around their children, (d) discuss and clarify potentially upsetting media reports, and (e) be mindful of children's developmental level and language abilities when providing access to media reports. A relatively new mechanism of crisis exposure that must be monitored is social media (Flitsch, Magnesi, & Brock, 2012). While not yet adequately studied, the available evidence suggests that use of this type of media to learn about a crisis event is associated with higher stress, when compared with individuals who use traditional media to learn about a crisis (Goodwin, Palgi, Hamama-Raz, & Ben-Ezra, 2013). Consequently, parents and educators must now also be prepared to monitor (and limit) this type of exposure.

Data that support these recommendations come from research conducted following the 1995 Oklahoma City bombing and the World Trade Center disaster in 2001. Pfefferbaum et al. (1999) reported that television exposure correlated significantly with posttraumatic symptoms at 7 weeks following the Oklahoma City bombing. In a later study, Pfefferbaum et al. (2001) reported that television exposure following a bombing disaster accounted for a slightly greater percentage of posttraumatic stress symptom variance (5.8%) than did physical or emotional exposure (3.2% and 5.3%, respectively). Among children surveyed who did not have physical or emotional exposure to the bombing (i.e., did not hear or feel the blast and did not know anyone injured or killed), self-reports of the amount of television exposure were significantly related to posttraumatic stress symptoms (accounting for 6.0% of the total posttraumatic stress symptom variance). Pfefferbaum et al. (2001) cautioned that the identified relationships were not necessarily indicative of direct causal effects. Higher levels of disaster-related television viewing may be a sign of distress (not a cause of such distress). Regardless of the nature of this relationship, the authors concluded that "disaster-related television viewing by children should be monitored," and children's caregivers "should be available to address their emotional reactions, to answer questions, and to correct misperceptions" (p. 209). Similar findings were reported by Gurwitch, Sitterle, Yound, and Pfefferbaum (2002), who found that, following the Oklahoma City bombing, children who were not physically or emotionally proximal to the bombing, but reported having extensive TV viewing of the event, also reported a higher number of traumatic stress symptoms than did children who reported lower amounts of such viewing. These findings suggest that being either directly exposed or simply a passive observer of a traumatic event, even by viewing it on TV, places students at risk for traumatic stress.

In research conducted following the World Trade Center disaster, Hoven et al. (2004) reported that, among children, media exposure was related to symptoms of separation anxiety disorder. Similarly, Saylor, Cowart, Lipovsky, Jackson, and Finch (2003) reported that among elementary school students, those who saw media images of death or injury and who saw reports on the Internet (versus TV or print media) had more PTSD symptoms. In addition, these researchers found that it did not matter if the images the children were exposed to were considered to be "positive" (e.g., a presidential address or heroic helping) or "negative" (e.g., distressed individuals, death or dying, or the attack itself). From their data, Saylor et al. (2003) reported: "It appears that greater amounts of exposure, both positive and negative, correspond with more PTSD symptoms" (p. 1636).

Blanchard et al. (2004) reported that among college students, hours of television watched following the World Trade Center attacks were in some cases a predictor of traumatic stress. Among adults, Ahern et al. (2002) reported that frequent viewing of people falling or jumping from the towers was strongly related to PTSD. This relationship was increased among respondents who were directly affected by the events of September 11 (a finding that had not been previously documented). The Ahern et al. (2002) study concluded that clinicians should recommend individuals directly affected by a disaster reduce their exposure to disaster coverage. In a more recent analysis, Ahern, Galea, Resnick, and Vlahov (2004) found that respondents had a higher prevalence of probable PTSD if they reported having viewed TV images of the attacks more frequently. Respondents who viewed the most TV had a 66% greater likelihood of having probable PTSD than those who viewed the least TV. Again, this association between TV viewing and traumatic stress represents correlational, not causal, connections. Researchers cannot be certain whether respondents who had more psychological symptoms watched more TV because of those symptoms or if their TV viewing contributed to the symptoms, However, as Quallich (2005) suggested, given that avoidance of trauma reminders is a core PTSD symptom, individuals with this disorder would be unlikely to watch a lot of television. Watching TV in response to trauma would be inconsistent with PTSD's known avoidance symptoms, which supports a causal connection between TV viewing and PTSD.

Even without definitive causal connections between TV viewing and traumatic stress, school crisis intervention teams should recommend monitoring the television viewing habits of children (especially younger children) following crises (Otto et al., 2007). The studies described above suggested that media viewing of crisis events may be sufficient to produce symptoms of traumatic stress among children and should be minimized.

REUNITING OR LOCATING PRIMARY CAREGIVERS AND SIGNIFICANT OTHERS

For younger students, separation from families can be particularly stressful during times of crisis (see Chapter 15). Studies have reported that, among preschool earthquake survivors, separation from parents and siblings during an evacuation was sufficient to generate symptoms of PTSD (Azarian &

Skriptchenko-Gregorian, 1998b). This finding is not surprising given that parents and other caregivers play an important role in promoting children's perceptions of safety and security. Failure to reunite students with primary caregivers increases the students' perceptions of the crisis situation as dangerous and threatening, which in turn increases the probability of traumatic stress reactions.

Given these observations, reconnecting students with their primary caregivers and significant others should be given a high priority following a crisis event (Brymer et al., 2006; Brymer, Taylor, et al., 2012; U.S. Department of Education, 2013), with special priority being given to reuniting the youngest students with parents (Brock, Sandoval, & Lewis, 2001). If reunification of students with caregivers is delayed, students should at least be informed about the location and status of their significant others and ideally be allowed to communicate with them in some way. However, school staff members should avoid making promises that cannot be kept.

If the status of primary caregivers or significant others is not clear, staff members should reassure children that they are physically safe and take them to a "child-friendly space" (Brymer et al., 2006, p. 31). Important elements of such an environment include (a) a quiet waiting room that is removed from crisis-related activities, (b) caregivers who are experienced in caring for children and who are able to constantly supervise them, and (c) developmentally appropriate games and activities that help them pass the time. Brymer et al. (2006) also suggests that an appropriate approach may be to ask older children and adolescents to mentor younger children, while giving these older children and adolescents developmentally appropriate opportunities to connect with their peers.

Finally, before students are reunited with their primary caregivers, the staff should remind these caregivers how important their initial reactions are in shaping their child's perceptions of the threat. They need to be told "to be careful about what they say in front of their children, and to clarify things that might be upsetting for them" (Brymer et al., 2006, p. 32). Additional information on reunification planning is in Chapter 9, and Chapter 16 has guidance on providing caregivers with information about how to help their child cope with the crisis event.

PROVIDING CRISIS FACTS AND ADAPTIVE INTERPRETATIONS

Psychological education and intervention activities are also helpful in fostering perceptions of safety and security (see Chapters 16, 17, and 18). Specifically, students feel safer if they are helped to understand the reality of the danger. For example, following one school shooting, a rumor persisted that only one of two gunmen had been found. In reality, the lone gunman had committed suicide. Announcements that dispelled this rumor were important in helping students understand that the danger had passed and that they were in fact safe (Brock et al., 2001). Given that students (in particular younger students) can be confused by a crisis and have incorrect beliefs about it (Allen, Dlugokinski, Cohen, & Walker, 1999), providing factual information is especially critical. Children's beliefs about a stressor can be more frightening than reality (Armstrong, 1990; Blom, Etkind, & Carr, 1991), and excessively negative appraisals about a crisis are significant contributors to traumatic stress (Hobfoll et al., 2007).

Bryant et al. (2007) concluded that "[t]he current data suggest that early interventions that aim to enhance adaptive interpretations, particularly addressing perceptions of ongoing threat or vulnerability, may be effective in reducing subsequent PTSD reactions in children" (p. 2506).

School staff can foster perceptions of safety and security by informing students about (a) the current status of the crisis and what is being done by the school and community to address the situation, (b) how they can ensure their own personal safety, and (c) services available to students and their families that address crisis-related challenges (Ruzek et al., 2007). Brymer et al. (2006) suggested that the following take place:

Ask [students] if they have any questions about what is going to happen, and give simple accurate information about what they can expect. ... Be sure to ask about concerns regarding current danger and safety. ... Try to connect [students] with information that addresses these concerns. If you do not have specific information, do not guess or invent information in order to provide reassurance. Instead, develop a plan with the [student] for ways you and he/she can gather the needed information. (p. 29)

As discussed in Chapter 11, the crisis intervention team must not reassure students that they are safe unless they have factual information that this is the case. In such an instance, the team members should focus on providing students with the knowledge and skills needed to address ongoing threats, such as reviewing lockdown procedures in situations that present an ongoing threat of violence. Giving students such information helps them perceive the threat as more controllable and therefore less traumatic. Furthermore, before proceeding with these activities, the team should ensure that the students are emotionally stabilized and are able to process crisis facts and make adaptive interpretations (see Tables 11.2 and 11.3). For example, Table 12.1 offers helpful crisis facts and interpretations that might be provided to students during and following a lockdown situation prompted by an armed criminal being in the area of the school.

RETURNING STUDENTS TO A SAFE SCHOOL ENVIRONMENT

Returning students and staff to their school environment—especially when the steps taken to ensure safety are not only effective, but also concrete and visible—helps foster perceptions of security and safety. Doing so helps extinguish any associations between dangerous, crisis-related stimuli and harmless school-related images, people, and things (Ruzek et al., 2007). For example, having a strong police presence on campus following acts of violence might be helpful for students who have learned to view law enforcement officers as sources of security and safety. In addition, the routines and presence of friends, teachers, and other professionals at school offer natural supports that help with healthy adjustment (see Chapter 15). At the same time, although a return to normal school routines can be reassuring, postponing high-stakes testing or the introduction of new curriculum and concepts for a short time is appropriate.

PROVIDING OPPORTUNITIES TO TAKE ACTION

Finally, feelings of helplessness or dependency are defining features of traumatic stress. Schools can reduce these feelings by encouraging school community members to participate in getting supplies needed for comfort. For example, assuming the environment is safe and students are able, teachers might send them to the cafeteria or to the office to get needed supplies, rather than asking an adult

Table 12.1. Information to Ensure Students' Perceptions of Security and Safety

- Tell students what they can do to ensure their physical safety.
  - "By following the lockdown rules we have previously practiced, you help make sure that you and your classmates are safe."
- Inform them about what others are doing to ensure the students' safety.
  - "The adults at school will make sure that no one comes on our school's grounds without permission. Also, the police are looking very carefully for the criminal and will be here to help us if we need them."
- Report on the current status of the crisis event (e.g., whether the danger has passed or is still present).
  - "The criminal robbed a bank two miles away from our school. When he was last seen he was running in a direction opposite where we are now. We don't think he will come to our school. But to be safe the principal has asked us to stay in our classrooms."
- Provide resources that can better ensure safety (e.g., have a police officer on school grounds).
  - "If you have any questions about your safety, feel free to ask."

Note. Adapted from *School Crisis Prevention and Intervention: The PREPaRE Model*, p. 122, by S. E. Brock et al., 2009, Bethesda, MD: NASP. Copyright 2009 by the National Association of School Psychologists. Adapted with permission.

to bring supplies to the classroom. A student psychoeducational group (discussed in Chapter 16) may help by talking to students about ways they can care for themselves and others. For example, at a school district in Illinois, during group lessons, the group's leaders ask students to help monitor how their peers are coping (including their social media posts) and to be on the lookout for students who may need adult assistance. The student psychoeducational group teaches students about crisis reactions and the importance of supporting each other—at school, outside of school, and online. The school district has found that in the days following such group meetings, students are more likely to share with staff if any of their peers need additional assistance. The district has further observed that such training helps students feel that they are taking action (thereby making crisis events or consequences appear more controllable). Literature supporting this approach suggests that, following traumatic events, experiences of having received help and having helped others are associated with the development of altruism and posttraumatic growth (Staub & Vollhardt, 2008). Similarly, to the extent that the school is able to promote a sense of self-efficacy through its postcrisis mental health intervention, students can be expected to have less pain, fatigue, or disability (Luszczynska, Benight, & Cieslak, 2009).

CONCLUSION

In response to crisis events, schools provide primary, or universal, interventions that reaffirm physical health and ensure students' perceptions of safety and security. Crisis responses that help to ensure perceptions of safety and security include (a) ensuring that adult behavior does not unnecessarily frighten students and exaggerate their threat perceptions, (b) minimizing exposure to crisis scenes and images, (c) reuniting or locating students' caregivers, (d) providing factual information about the crisis event, and (e) returning to a school environment that makes the perception of school safety concrete and visible.

As crisis-related dangers are terminated and the school environment begins to stabilize, other school crisis responses, including the mental health crisis interventions described in Chapters 15 through 19, begin. However, before any school-based mental health interventions are initiated, assessment of individual psychological trauma risk must take place. Section 3 (Chapters 13 and 14) examines this important element of crisis intervention.

Section 4

EVALUATE

The third element of the PREP<u>a</u>RE model (the first "E" in the PREP<u>a</u>RE acronym) refers to evaluating the psychological impact of a crisis event. After physical health and safety have been reaffirmed, PREP<u>a</u>RE directs schools to evaluate the degree to which students (and their caregivers) have been psychologically traumatized. The term commonly used for the evaluation of psychological trauma following crises, psychological triage, is defined by the National Institute of Mental Health (NIMH, 2001) as follows:

> The process of evaluating and sorting victims by immediacy of treatment needed and directing them to immediate or delayed treatment. The goal of triage is to do the greatest good for the greatest number of victims. (p. 27)

Although secondary to ensuring actual and perceived physical health and safety, depending upon available resources, and as illustrated in Figure 1.2, these interventions may actually begin as soon as the immediate threat of a crisis ends, during the recoil phase (Valent, 2000) or the immediate postdisaster phase (Raphael & Newman, 2000). However, some evaluation activities may take place months or even years after the crisis event, that is, during the recovery and reconstruction phases (Raphael & Newman, 2000; Valent, 2000). For example, although it is rare, crisis reactions can have a delayed onset. In addition, crisis anniversaries (e.g., the 1-year anniversary of the crisis event) and other similar crisis events often renew crisis reactions and may require assessment of the need for crisis intervention.

Also illustrated in Figure 1.2 are a variety of different terms that can be associated with the evaluation of psychological trauma. Specifically, because these interventions aim at identifying psychological trauma victims as soon as possible, they are considered a form of secondary prevention (Caplan, 1964). Evaluation of psychological trauma is initially directed toward the entire population, as school crisis interveners attempt to identify subgroups of students who have an above-average risk for being psychologically traumatized, so such interventions are also labeled universally preventive interventions. As these individuals are identified, interveners can then direct their attention toward those who display warning signs of psychological trauma or have a predisposition for traumatization, so the interventions can also be considered selected and indicated preventive interventions (Gordon, 1983). Finally, all of the above actions involve information gathering, which is a core activity of psychological first aid (Brymer et al., 2006; Brymer, Taylor, et al., 2012).

The first chapter in this section (Chapter 13) reviews the rationale for, and conceptual foundations of, psychological triage. This chapter includes a review of risk factors that increase the odds of an individual becoming a psychological trauma victim, as well as the warning signs of traumatic stress. The second chapter in this section (Chapter 14) examines practical issues critical to the evaluation of psychological trauma.

Evaluation is not a discrete intervention or event; rather, it is a process. This process begins with crisis interveners identifying psychological trauma risk among the students they serve and directing mental health crisis intervention accordingly. Next, as they begin providing crisis intervention services and make contact with students and their caregivers, the crisis interveners observe and receive reports of traumatic stress warning signs. From this additional information, they are able to refine their crisis intervention decisions. Finally, as the crisis event enters the postimpact and recovery and reconstruction phases, data gathered as a part of mental health crisis interventions are used to make decisions regarding students who need longer-term psychotherapeutic mental health interventions, most commonly some form of cognitive behavioral therapy, and appropriate referrals are made.

Chapter 13

EVALUATING PSYCHOLOGICAL TRAUMA

This chapter provides guidance important to the identification and subsequent support of psychological trauma victims. It examines why the evaluation of psychological trauma is prerequisite to mental health crisis intervention, and then discusses the empirical basis for the risk factors and warning signs of psychological trauma. Knowledge of these variables is essential to the practice of psychological triage (Chapter 14), and is also valuable when providing psychological education to caregivers (Chapter 16).

RATIONALE FOR ASSESSING PSYCHOLOGICAL TRAUMA

Psychological triage is an essential component of crisis intervention (North & Pfefferbaum, 2013; Pfefferbaum & Shaw, 2013). Making the evaluation of psychological trauma a primary crisis intervention is important for several reasons, including that the consequences of crisis exposure are idiosyncratic, and that some crisis interventions have the potential to cause harm.

Idiosyncratic Consequences of Crisis Exposure

The evaluation of psychological trauma is made necessary by the fact that not all individuals are equally affected by crisis exposure (Brymer et al., 2006; Gerson & Rappaport, 2013; Hornor, 2013; McNally, Bryant, & Ehlers, 2003). For example, although a majority of adolescents (ages 13–17) in the United States have had lifetime exposure to a potentially traumatic event (61.8%), the lifetime prevalence of PTSD is estimated to be only 4.7% (McLaughlin et al., 2013). Consequently, different individuals require different interventions (Berkowitz, 2003; Kiliç, Özgüven, & Sayil, 2003; Lonigan, Phillips, & Richey, 2003; Watson, Brymer, & Bonanno, 2011). Though a few crisis survivors need intensive and highly directive crisis intervention, others need very little, if any, assistance (Cohen et al., 2010; Vijayakumar, Kannan, Ganesh Kumar, & Devarajan, 2006). Furthermore, it is clear that in crisis intervention, "one size does not fit all" (National Institute of Mental Health [NIMH], 2001; Ritchie, 2003, p. 46). At this time, no evidence has demonstrated that any one global crisis intervention prevents subsequent psychopathology (Litz, Gray, Bryant, & Adler, 2002). Therefore, from the evaluation of psychological trauma, school mental health crisis interventions need to be tailored to address individual needs.

Although anyone with sufficient trauma exposure will display some initial crisis reactions, according to the National Institute of Mental Health (2001):

> [A] sensible working principle in the immediate post incident phase is to expect normal recovery. The presumption of clinically significant disorders in the early post-incident phase is inappropriate, except for individuals with preexisting conditions. (p. 6)

Given that recovery is the norm, assistance in the form of mental health crisis intervention should be offered only in response to a demonstrated need (Everly, 1999). Therefore, school crisis interveners should take their lead from students, school staff, and other caregivers, providing assistance according to need rather than universally providing all students with the same intervention. In the words of McNally et al. (2003): "Not everyone exposed to trauma either needs or wants professional help" (p. 73).

Idiosyncratic Consequences of Crisis Intervention

The need to identify and assist individuals who require immediate mental health crisis intervention support is readily apparent; however, less obvious is the need to identify those who may *not* require assistance. This approach is important, because providing highly directive crisis interventions to students who do not need them can cause harm. For example, intervention that takes place in a group setting has the potential for contamination effects. Students, and especially staff members, who are visibly distressed can actually increase the crisis exposure of otherwise unaffected students (Berkowitz, 2003; Everly, 1999; Wei, Szumilas, & Kutcher, 2010).

Furthermore, providing crisis intervention assistance to individuals who do not need it may unintentionally and inaccurately communicate that they are not capable of independently coping with the crisis. As a consequence, they may fail to recognize the sources of internal and external resilience present in their lives; moreover, individuals' perceived ability to cope and to control the recovery process are an important factor in successfully adjusting to traumatic circumstances (Frazier, Tashiro, Berman, Steger, & Long, 2004; Norris, Byrne, Diaz, & Kaniasty, 2002). Finally, providing highly directive crisis intervention when it is not needed may generate self-fulfilling prophecies and stigmatize individuals.

ASSESSMENT VARIABLES

As discussed in Chapter 1, the evaluation of psychological trauma begins by examining crisis event variables, as not all crises are equally traumatic. An event's relative predictability, consequences, duration, and intensity interact with crisis type and increase the likelihood that some events are more devastating than others. However, whereas such knowledge generates a basic estimate of *how many* students or staff members are psychological trauma victims, it does not inform crisis response teams about *which* of those individuals are most likely to be traumatized by a crisis. Determining what crisis interventions individuals need requires the evaluation of psychological trauma risk factors and warning signs.

As illustrated in Figure 13.1, crisis event variables interact with psychological trauma risk factors and in turn generate the warning signs of psychological traumatization—that is, the initial and durable crisis reactions. Although many initial crisis reactions should not be pathologized (and can be considered common), if these reactions persist over time, they may in fact be symptoms of mental illness, such as PTSD. In addition, some initial reactions are so severe that they require immediate referrals for mental health treatment and are predictive of subsequent psychopathology. The rest of this chapter explores the empirical basis for (a) the risk factors and (b) the warning signs that serve as the basis for making decisions about what school crisis interventions individuals should receive.

Figure 13.1. Factors That Should Be Considered When Evaluating Psychological Trauma

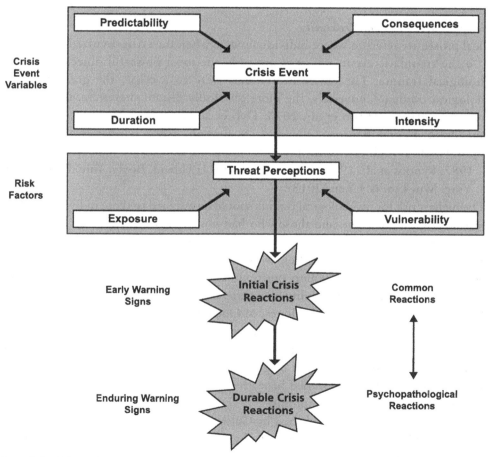

Note. From *School Crisis Prevention and Intervention: The PREPaRE Model*, p. 130, by S. E. Brock et al., 2009, Bethesda, MD: NASP. Copyright 2009 by the National Association of School Psychologists. Reprinted with permission.

Psychological Trauma Risk Factors

As illustrated by Figure 13.1, crisis event variables interact with psychological trauma risk factors and result in psychological trauma warning signs (or the initial and durable crisis reactions that are concrete manifestations of traumatic stress). The primary determinant of psychological trauma is the individual's subjective appraisal of the crisis event (i.e., threat perceptions) and his or her reactions to that event (Trickey, Siddaway, Meiser-Stedman, Serpell, & Field, 2012). Although these event perceptions are themselves difficult to immediately identify, identifying the risk factors that determine these perceptions, that is, crisis exposure and personal vulnerabilities, is relatively straightforward. Consequently, the discussion that follows begins by examining (a) crisis exposure, which is divided into physical proximity and emotional proximity and has been suggested to be the most important risk factor (Ozer, Best, Lipsey, & Weiss, 2003; Trickey et al., 2012); and (b) personal vulnerability factors, which are divided into internal and external factors. This section then explores the role of threat perceptions in generating psychological trauma.

Crisis Exposure: Physical Proximity

Physical proximity refers to where individuals were when the crisis occurred, or how close they were to the traumatic event, and it is arguably the most powerful objective risk factor for psychological trauma. The closer individuals were to a crisis, the greater their risk for psychological trauma. Conversely, the more physically distant they were, the lower their risk (Bradburn, 1991; Dell'Osso et al., 2013; Dyb et al., 2014; Gil & Caspi, 2006; Groome & Soureti, 2004; Keppel-Benson, Ollendick, & Benson, 2002; Lawyer et al., 2006; Lonigan, Shannon, Finch, Daughtery, & Taylor, 1991; Ma et al., 2011; McDermott et al., 2013; Pynoos et al., 1987; Pynoos et al., 1993; Scrimin et al., 2011; Udwin, Boyle, Yule, Bolton, & O'Ryan, 2000; Ying, Wu, Lin, & Chen, 2013).

The highest risk for psychological trauma should be assigned to those individuals who required medical or surgical attention, and those who had crisis exposures that were particularly intense and of long duration (NIMH, 2001). For example, Kolaitis et al. (2003) reported that, following the 1999 Athens earthquake, children who sustained injuries and those whose homes were damaged were most likely to have more posttraumatic stress. Not surprisingly, more severe injuries are associated with a greater probability of experiencing significant traumatic stress among young adults and children (Haden, Scarpa, Jones, & Ollendick, 2007). Similarly, following the World Trade Center attacks, Hoven et al. (2004) reported that direct exposure was related to symptoms of separation anxiety disorder among children. Finally, Ma et al. (2011) reported that among adolescents (ages 12–18) exposed to a magnitude 8.0 earthquake in China, having been injured and having witnessed someone buried beneath rubble, wounded, or dying were associated with severity of posttraumatic stress symptoms.

Results of a phone survey conducted by Galea et al. (2002) 5 to 7 weeks following the 9/11 attacks further illustrate the importance of physical proximity in determining traumatic stress. Specifically, those adults who lived closest to ground zero (i.e., residents who lived south of Canal Street) were more likely to report PTSD symptoms than those who were more distant from the

World Trade Center (i.e., residents who lived between 110th Street and Canal Street). Although only 6.8% of the latter group reported having PTSD, 20% of those who lived near ground zero reported these symptoms. Furthermore, regardless of residence, directly witnessing the attacks on the World Trade Center also had a significant effect. Among those who were not eyewitnesses, only 5.5% reported PTSD symptoms. In contrast, among those who had witnessed the attacks, 10.4% had these symptoms.

Another earlier study by Pynoos et al. (1987) also demonstrated the dominant influence of exposure to a crisis event in predicting the development of posttraumatic stress reactions among schoolchildren. This study assessed self-reports of children's (ages 5–13) stress reactions following a sniper attack on a school playground that killed one student and one passerby, and wounded 13 others. As illustrated in Figure 13.2, a strong relationship between physical proximity and PTSD symptoms was demonstrated using the PTSD Reaction Index.

These studies suggest that school crisis response teams should consider physical proximity when making all initial crisis intervention treatment decisions. More specifically, all individuals directly involved in or exposed to a crisis event should be given a high priority for mental health crisis intervention. Conversely, those who were more physically distant from a crisis should typically be given a lower priority. However, physical proximity is not the only crisis exposure factor that needs to be considered (Marshall et al., 2007). For example, Pynoos et al. (1987) reported that a significant number of students (18%) who were physically removed from the crisis event (i.e., they were on vacation, or "off track," from school at the time of the shooting)

Figure 13.2. Relationship Between Physical Proximity to a Crisis Event and Traumatic Stress Reactions

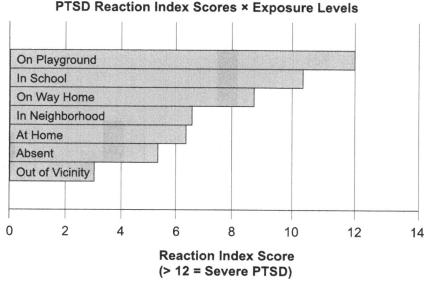

Note. From "Life Threat and Posttraumatic Stress in School-Age Children," by R. S. Pynoos et al., 1987, *Archives of General Psychiatry, 44,* p. 1059. Copyright 1987 by the American Medical Association. Reprinted with permission.

were significantly affected by the shooting, that is, they demonstrated moderate to severe PTSD symptoms (see Figure 13.3). Among the other variables that might explain such traumatization is emotional proximity or the relationships students may have had with crisis victims.

Crisis Exposure: Emotional Proximity

After physical proximity, emotional proximity is the next most powerful objective predictor of crisis reactions. Knowing someone who was a crisis victim, who was directly exposed to the event, or who feared for the safety of someone close is associated with negative mental health outcomes (Adams et al., 2014; Ma et al., 2011; Ying et al., 2013). In particular, individuals who are bereaved are an especially high-risk group (Dawson et al., 2014; Eksi et al., 2007; NIMH, 2001). For example, 17.8% of Manhattan Island residents who had a friend or relative killed on September 11, 2001, reported symptoms of depression 5 to 8 weeks after the attack, versus 8.7% who did not suffer such a loss (Galea et al., 2002). Similarly, following the 1999 Athens earthquake, youth who demonstrated more significant traumatic stress included those whose relatives were injured (Kolaitis et al., 2003).

Figure 13.4, which provides data from a report on the effects of 9/11 on New York City Public School students, reveals the power of emotional proximity (Applied Research and Consulting et al., 2002). As illustrated in the figure, the closer students' relationships were with 9/11 victims, the more likely they were to demonstrate PTSD. Furthermore, a dramatic increase in PTSD was noted

Figure 13.3. Relationship Between Crisis Event Exposure Categories and Severity of Traumatic Stress Reactions

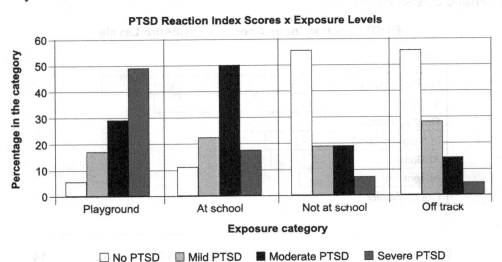

Note. According to Pynoos et al. (1987), "Using PTSD Reaction Index categories (< 7 = no PTSD; 7 to 9 = mild; 10 to 12 = moderate; > 12 = severe), ... a $\chi 2$ analysis indicated significant differences in the proportion in these categories across the four exposure levels ($\chi 2 = 61.5$, df = 9, $p = <.001$)" (p. 1059). From "Life Threat and Posttraumatic Stress in School-Age Children," by R. S. Pynoos et al., 1987, *Archives of General Psychiatry, 44,* p. 1059. Copyright 1987 by the American Medical Association. Reprinted with permission.

Figure 13.4. Relationship Between Traumatic Stress and Relationships With Crisis Victims

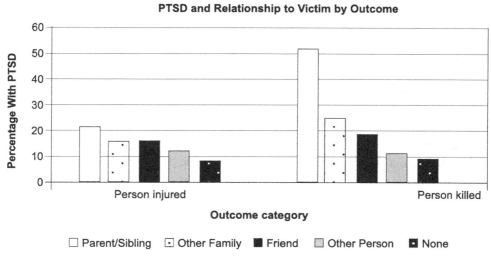

PTSD and Relationship to Victim by Outcome

☐ Parent/Sibling ⊡ Other Family ■ Friend ▨ Other Person ▣ None

Note. From Effects of the World Trade Center Attack on NYC Public School Students: Initial Report to the New York City Board of Education (p. 34), by Applied Research and Consulting, Columbia University Mailman School of Public Health, & New York Psychiatric Institute, 2002. Copyright 2002 by the New York City Board of Education. Reprinted with permission.

among those who had a parent or sibling killed in the attacks. These findings emphasize that the bereaved, especially children who have lost a parent or sibling, should be given a high priority for mental health crisis interventions (Eksi et al., 2007).

Emotional proximity extends to knowing someone who knew crisis victims and those who were exposed to media coverage. For example, a study of sixth graders who lived within 100 miles of Oklahoma City at the time of the 1995 bombing found that media exposure and having a friend who knew someone killed or injured were both predictors of traumatic stress, even for those who had no direct physical exposure and did not personally know any victims (Pfefferbaum et al., 2000). Similarly, Busso, McLaughlin, and Sheridan (2014) found that among Boston area residents, media exposure to the Boston Marathon bombings in 2013 was positively correlated with more posttraumatic stress symptoms. Finally, Silver et al. (2013), from their study of adults exposed to media images of the 9/11 terrorist attacks and the Iraq war, suggested that both the frequency and content of media exposure had powerful effects.

Vulnerability Factors

Whereas physical proximity addresses where students were at the time of a crisis, and emotional proximity reflects whether students knew someone involved in a crisis, personal vulnerabilities address *who the student is* at the time of the crisis. Though not considered to be as important to the development of traumatic stress as crisis exposure (Trickey et al., 2012), internal and external vulnerability factors have been suggested to increase the probability of psychological trauma. For example, from a systematic literature review, DiGangi et al. (2013) state:

[T]he conclusions of these 54 studies suggest that not all negative aspects of trauma are outcomes of it; rather these studies suggest that certain factors predispose individuals to PTSD. The major conclusion of this review is that many factors, historically thought to be consequences of trauma, are most likely risk factors for PTSD. More specifically, some studies suggest that the very symptoms of PTSD are, in fact, not symptoms of an index trauma, but may play a causal role in its etiology. (p. 742)

Although crisis exposure variables are specific to the crisis situation, personal vulnerabilities are general risk factors that are applicable to all situations, not just the crisis event. This discussion separates personal vulnerability into two general risk classes: internal and external.

Internal vulnerability factors. As shown in Table 13.1, a number of internal vulnerability factors can increase a student's psychological trauma risk. The first factor has its origins in the children's coping literature, which makes distinctions between active (or approach) and avoidance coping strategies (Ayers, Sandler, West, & Roosa, 1996; Ebata & Moos, 1994). Active coping strategies are direct and deliberate actions aimed at solving crisis-generated problems. Avoidance coping, on the other hand, involves thoughts and actions that attempt to focus away from a stressful situation, that is, to stop thinking about or dealing with the stressor (Sandler, Wolchik, MacKinnon, Ayers, & Roosa, 1997). This latter type of coping behavior is consistently associated with a greater incidence of mental illness.

However, in extremely high-stress situations, some initial avoidance coping responses are adaptive. For example, in the instance of an individual who is held up at gunpoint in the parking lot of a local shopping center, the victim, after giving his wallet to the robber, calmly gets into his car and drives home. However, the moment he walks in the door, he breaks down, cries, and begins to feel distressed. In this instance, avoidance coping can be seen as having bought the individual time to get to a place where he was physically and emotionally safe and could confront a frightening reality. Nevertheless, it is clear that individuals who continue to employ avoidance coping as a longer-term problem-solving strategy are more likely to have a poorer mental health outcome (Dawson et al., 2014; Deković, Koning, Stams, & Buist, 2008; DiGangi et al., 2013; Gil & Caspi, 2006; Krause, Kaltman, Goodman, & Dutton, 2008). Consistent with this observation, a meta-analysis conducted by Trickey et al. (2012) suggests avoidance coping as being a powerful

Table 13.1. Internal Vulnerability Factors

1. Avoidance coping
2. Preexisting mental and physical illness
3. Social withdrawal
4. Trauma history
5. Low developmental or cognitive levels of functioning
6. Poor self-efficacy
7. High psychophysiological arousal
8. Pessimism

vulnerability factor for children and adolescents. Specifically, thought suppression, the blaming of others for something bad happening, and distractions were among the coping styles with the largest effect sizes for predicting traumatic stress.

Silver, Holman, McIntosh, Poulin, and Gil-Rivas (2002), in their nationwide longitudinal study of psychological responses to 9/11, made the point that several coping strategies, particularly those involving denial or disengagement from coping, related to higher levels of distress 6 months after the event. In contrast, active coping strategies, such as accepting the event, were associated with less long-term stress. Similarly, Stallard and Smith (2007) found that children's cognitive coping style was a significant predictor of posttraumatic stress 8 months following a traffic accident.

Finally, two other types of avoidance coping—state (i.e., situation-specific) and trait (i.e., typical)—are associated with an increased risk for PTSD (Dempsey, Overstreet, & Moely, 2000; Gil & Caspi, 2006) and indicate a greater need for crisis intervention support (Gil, 2005). Regarding how such coping may affect traumatic stress, Dempsey et al. (2000) speculated that the use of avoidance coping strategies impedes children's ability to understand and integrate crises or prevent the habituation to recurrent trauma-related thoughts.

The second internal vulnerability factor is the individual's baseline physical and mental health (Deković et al., 2008; McDermott et al., 2013; Ozer et al., 2003; Perrin et al., 2014). Mentally healthy individuals are better able to cope with crises than those with preexisting mental illness (Busso et al., 2014). Both Trickey et al.'s (2012) meta-analysis and DiGangi et al.'s (2013) systematic review of the literature identify pretrauma psychopathology (including anxiety, conduct problems, and depression) as being associated with an increased risk of traumatic stress. Not surprisingly, a prior diagnosis of PTSD was one of the strongest predictors of current symptoms (Trickey et al., 2012). Similarly, Gil-Rivas, Holman, and Silver (2004) reported that a history of mental health disorders was associated with increased reports of high levels of 9/11-related acute trauma symptomatology. Furthermore, these acute symptoms signaled greater risk for higher levels of longer-term symptomatology.

In addition to poor mental health, emerging evidence suggests that poor physical health may also be associated with the development of traumatic stress. Specifically, in a retrospective cohort study of adults who were physically proximal to the March 2011 Great East Japan Earthquake, Momma et al. (2014) report that measures of predisaster lifestyle (drinking) and physical functioning (hypertension and lower leg extension power) were associated with self-reported symptoms of traumatic stress.

The third internal vulnerability factor is a tendency toward social withdrawal. As will be discussed in Chapter 15, provision of social supports is arguably the most powerful of the mental health crisis interventions. Consequently, it is not surprising that withdrawal from this helpful resource is a predictor of traumatic stress (Trickey et al., 2012).

The fourth factor is having a history of prior traumatization (Bremner, Southwick, Johnson, Yehuda, & Charney, 1993; Breslau, 1998; Brewin, Andrews, & Valentine, 2000; Hoven et al., 2004; Imanaka, Morinobu, Toki, & Yamawaki, 2006; Möhlen, Parzer, Resch, & Brunner, 2005; Nader, Pynoos, Fairbanks, & Frederick, 1990; Nemeroff, 2004; Nemeroff et al., 2006; Olff, Langeland, & Gersons, 2005; Ozer et al., 2003; Trickey et al., 2012; Ying et al., 2013). Particularly when combined with pretrauma anxiety and depression, prior exposure to violence is predictive of traumatic stress (Busso et al., 2014). According to Yehuda and Hyman (2005), "it may be that the real consequence of terrorism in children is to create a basis for risk for psychopathology in response to subsequent trauma exposure" (p. 1777).

As discussed in Chapter 1 (see Positive Consequences of Crises), some literature suggests that individuals who have adaptively coped with stressful events, such as natural disasters, might be better able to cope with future traumas (Adams et al., 2014; Kilmer, 2006; Meyerson, Grant, Carter, & Kilmer, 2011). However, this result may not be the case for all crises, especially when an individual has had a high level of exposure to an extreme stressor, such as sexual assault (Lecic-Tosevski, Gavrlovic, Knezevic, & Priebe, 2003; Shakespeare-Finch & Lurie-Beck, 2014).

Children who have experienced repeated traumatic stressors, especially child abuse and neglect, are more likely to have traumatic stress reactions, disassociate, and display mood swings than single-incident trauma survivors (Terr, 1991; Vásquez et al., 2012; Widom, 1999). In explaining how trauma history serves as a risk factor for traumatic stress, Olff et al. (2005) suggested that these experiences can adversely affect the development of coping skills and that they promote a heightened automatic response to stress.

Research conducted by Galea et al. (2002) highlights the importance of assessing trauma history. For example, a phone survey of Manhattan Island residents, conducted several weeks after the World Trade Center attacks, found that among individuals who had no prior trauma history, only 4.2% reported symptoms of traumatic stress. By contrast, among individuals with two or more significantly stressful events in their personal histories, 18.5% reported PTSD symptoms. In addition, among those with no trauma history, only 5.6% reported symptoms of depression, whereas 24.1% of those with two or more stressful events reported such symptoms. It is especially important to identify individuals who have experienced prior crises that are similar to the current crisis event. Supporting this observation, Nader et al. (1990) reported that a school shooting was more traumatic for youth who had previously been the victims of violent acts such as child abuse.

The fifth internal vulnerability factor is having low developmental or cognitive levels of functioning. Once an event is judged to be threatening, with all other factors held constant, low developmental level predicts psychological trauma (Applied Research and Consulting et al., 2002; Banks & Weems, 2014; Hoven et al., 2004; King, King, Foy, & Gudanowski, 1996; Schwarz & Kowalski, 1991; Silva et al., 2000; Singer, Flannery, Guo, Miller, & Leibbrandt, 2004). This greater vulnerability of younger children and developmentally delayed youth is likely due to several factors, including (a) a relative lack of coping experience and skills (Boymyea, Risbrough, & Lang, 2012); (b) perception, understanding, and memory of the event; (c) susceptibility to parental distress (Caffo & Belaise, 2003); (d) a smaller social support network; and (e) less well developed emotional regulation (Lonigan et al., 2003). In addition to chronological age, relative cognitive ability is related to risk for PTSD among trauma-exposed individuals. For example, Silva et al. (2000) reported that higher IQ was associated with lower severity of PTSD symptoms following exposure to traumatic stressors (i.e., experiencing war, witnessing violence, or being sexually abused). Conversely, small but significant associations between low IQ and greater risk for traumatic stress has been identified (DiGangi et al., 2013; Trickey et al., 2012). Poor executive functioning has also been suggested to be a risk factor for traumatic stress (Boymyea et al., 2012).

Although lower developmental level is generally a risk factor for psychological trauma, there is an exception to this rule. As Stallard and Salter (2003) have observed, children under the age of 11 years "may not, however, have the necessary knowledge or level of cognitive development to understand the degree of threat or potential implications posed by the trauma" (p. 451). Groome and Soureti (2004) further reported that, following the 1999 Athens earthquake in the district closest to the earthquake, younger children had higher scores on measures of PTSD and anxiety. However, in the district farthest away from the earthquake, older children had the highest scores on these measures. In interpreting these results, Groome and Soureti suggested that although the younger children who were closer to the earthquake had more symptoms because of fewer coping strategies (among other factors), older children who were more distant from the earthquake had more symptoms because of a greater understanding of the event.

The sixth internal vulnerability factor is a poor sense of self-efficacy (Trickey et al., 2012). Specifically, Boymyea et al. (2012) report that beliefs about oneself, including feelings of limited worth and ability to cope with the crisis are associated with greater PTSD symptoms. Related to the construct of self-efficacy is locus of control, as children with high self-efficacy are likely to believe that they have control over the outcome of a given situation. In a study of adolescents (12–20 years) several months after a magnitude 8.0 earthquake in China, Zhang, Jiang, Ho, and Wu (2011) found that an external locus of control (e.g., believing that the outcome of a situation is related to chance or powerful others) predicted the severity of traumatic stress symptoms. This finding is not surprising given that the perception of an event as a crisis is associated with the degree to which the event is viewed as uncontrollable (Foa, Zinbarg, & Rothbaum, 1992). The more uncontrollable a crisis event is perceived to be, the greater the event's potential to generate traumatic stress.

The seventh internal vulnerability factor is high baseline psychophysiological arousal (e.g., startle reactivity). DiGangi et al.'s (2013) literature review identified 10 studies related to arousal, and 8 of those suggested that this factor predicted symptoms of traumatic stress. Behaviorally, arousal differences may manifest as differences in temperament, and it has been suggested that individuals with easy temperaments are less prone to emotional reactions subsequent to crisis exposure. Conversely, individuals who are known to have a negative temperament, become easily upset, and have difficulty calming down appear to be more vulnerable to psychological trauma and thus should be given a higher priority for crisis intervention treatment (McNally et al., 2003).

Recently a study of Boston area adolescents conducted by Busso et al. (2014) used pretrauma measures of sympathetic reactivity (the part of the central nervous system responsible for the fight or flight response) to evaluate the role of arousal in traumatic stress. These researchers found that high levels of pretrauma sympathetic reactivity, as measured by electrocardiogram recordings in response to a laboratory stressor (the Trier Social Stress Test, which included asking participants to give a speech that was critically evaluated), were associated with elevated posttraumatic stress symptoms after participants' naturally occurring media exposure to the 2013 Boston Marathon bombings.

The eighth internal vulnerability factor is broadly defined as the tendency to be pessimistic (DiGangi et al., 2013). Specifically, Boymyea et al. (2012) reported the following tendencies to be associated with traumatic stress reactions: dwelling on negative emotions and events; attributing events to internal, stable, and global causes; and tending to pervasively predict environmental threats combined with feeling that such threats are quickly increasing.

External vulnerability factors. For the purposes of this discussion, this section discusses two general classes of external vulnerability: (a) lack of family support and resources, and (b) lack of extrafamilial social resources (see Table 13.2; Lai, Kelley, Harrison, Thompson, & Self-Brown, 2014). The one word that best summarizes most of these risk factors is *aloneness*, and it is consistent with research suggesting that among children, low levels of social support are associated with traumatic stress (Murphy, Shevlin, Armour, Elklit, & Christoffersen, 2014). In other words, these are variables that, when present, at the very least result in trauma-exposed individuals viewing themselves as being alone when coping with the stressor. Results of three meta-analyses have documented that the absence of such external support systems is a predictor of traumatic stress (Ozer et al., 2003; Trickey et al., 2012). Given these findings, a primary goal of crisis intervention is to reestablish naturally occurring social support systems (see Chapter 15).

The first external vulnerability factor is the physical absence of family support and resources. Most fundamentally this includes the physical absence of familial support. When such support systems are absent or depleted, trauma-exposed youth are at greater risk for traumatic stress reactions (Yorbik, Akbiyik, Kirmizigul, & Söhmen, 2004). For example, among Cambodian refugee children, not being able to reunite and live with a nuclear family member after being forced to leave their country (following the massive trauma inflicted by the Pol Pot regime) was predictive of maladaptive adjustment (Kinzie, Sack, Angell, Manson, & Rath, 1986). The researchers concluded that "having reestablished some contact with family members in this setting [the United States] mitigated some of the symptoms of the severe trauma, while being alone or in a foster family exacerbated the disorder" (p. 375).

While necessary, for some individuals the presence of a family is not sufficient to prevent aloneness and foster recovery from exposure to a traumatic event. In some circumstances, family resources may be physically present but practically (or psychologically) unavailable to provide support. When families are functioning poorly, and this essential support system is practically absent, youth are more alone and thus at greater risk for traumatic stress and maladaptive coping (Barenbaum, Ruchkin, & Schwab-Stone, 2004; DiGangi et al., 2013; Trickey et al., 2012). When a family is dysfunctional, trauma-exposed youth may have increased difficulty adapting to stressors and may look to other less prosocial resources, such as substance abuse, to cope

Table 13.2. External Vulnerability Factors

1. Lack of family support and resources
   a. Physical absence of family resources
   b. Poor family functioning
   c. Parental traumatic stress and family history of PTSD
   d. Parental psychological problems
   e. Poverty or low socioeconomic status
2. Lack of extrafamilial social resources
   a. Social isolation or low social support
   b. Perceived lack of social support

(Hilarski, 2004). For example, it has been established that the nature and quality of the parent–child relationship is an important source of resilience. Specific parenting characteristics that have been associated with resilience include warmth, structure, and high expectations (Doll & Lyon, 1998). Furthermore, the degree of family support predicts children's long-term emotional response to stressful events (Shaw, 2003). According to Qouta, Punamäki, and El Sarraj (2005), "It is well accepted that supportive and wise parents enhance children's mental health and favorable cognitive-emotional development, in general . . . , and in traumatized families in particular" (p. 150).

Unique factors related to family functioning are also sources of vulnerability. From their study of families who had been exposed to a petrochemical plant explosion that killed 30, wounded 3,000, and destroyed 30,000 homes, Birmes et al. (2009) suggested that factors typically identified as negatively affecting family functioning were associated with lower levels of traumatic stress. Specifically, they suggested that children's perceptions of enmeshed family cohesion (i.e., extremely strong family bonds, emotional ties, and limited autonomy within the family system) and rigid family adaptability (i.e., an extremely low capacity to alter family rules regarding discipline and relationships with authority) served as protective factors. Children from both types of families had significantly lower rates of traumatic stress. Within the context of a crisis that affected all family members, the feeling of belonging to an extremely close-knit family was helpful. Children in families characterized by rigid adaptability may feel more secure because they are in environments where the rules are especially firm, clear, and predictable and parenting is consistent.

Parents' traumatic stress (e.g., PTSD) has been linked to more severe symptoms of distress and PTSD among their children (Kadak, Nasiroğlu, Boysan, & Aydin, 2013; Lambert, Holzer, & Hasbun, 2014; Morris, Gabert-Quillen, & Delahanty, 2012; Salloum, Stover, Swaidan, & Storch, 2014). However, that increased prevalence in children may be associated with a family's history of PTSD and the child's genetic, rather than environmental, vulnerability to PTSD (Boymyea et al., 2012). Parental traumatic stress may also make family support resources practically unavailable to traumatized youth and thus increase both actual and perceived aloneness. For example, when a family's caregivers are significantly distressed, they are less likely to recognize their children's need for mental health support and intervention (Brown & Bobrow, 2004). However, parental traumatic stress does more than simply render family resources unavailable to youth. As discussed in Chapter 12, adults' reactions to traumatic events may be a cause of traumatic stress. When a primary caregiver suffers from traumatic stress, not only does it deprive the child of an important coping resource, but it also increases the child's perceptions of the event as threatening, because children (especially younger children) often look to adult reactions to gauge the danger presented by an event. If parents and other caregivers behave as if an event is very dangerous, then children are likely to respond accordingly (Kadak et al., 2013; Qouta et al., 2005; Shaw, 2003).

Parents' psychological problems may also result in a lack of familial support and have been identified as an external vulnerability risk factor (Kadak et al., 2013; Ozer et al., 2003; Trickey et al., 2012). Parental mental health is an important determinant of how well children cope with traumatic events (Kiliç et al., 2003; Qouta et al., 2005).

Poverty or economic status is another external vulnerability factor that, when lacking, can increase the risk of psychological trauma (Brymer et al., 2006). Students who come from impoverished backgrounds are more likely to have experienced prior traumatic events and trauma-related psychopathology, such as PTSD (Buka, Stichick, Birdthistle, & Earls, 2001; Seedat, Nyamai, Njenga, Vythilingum, & Stein, 2004). These families often have less access to resources needed to mitigate crisis-generated problems (Brymer et al., 2006).

The second general class of external personal vulnerability factors is a lack of extrafamilial social resources. In addition to the absence of family resources, the actual or perceived absence of extrafamilial social relationships is another important factor associated with vulnerability to traumatic stress (Trickey et al., 2012) and a causal factor in the development of children's posttraumatic stress (McDermott, Berry, & Cobham, 2014). Individuals who must face a crisis without supportive and nurturing friends or relatives have been found to suffer more from PTSD than those with such resources (McNally et al., 2003). Close peer friendships, access to positive adult models outside of the family, and strong connections to prosocial organizations or institutions are protective, as are positive academic or nonacademic school experiences.

Threat Perceptions

The final risk factor considered when assessing trauma risk is the individuals' threat perceptions (Ozer et al., 2003). According to some researchers, these subjective impressions are the most important risk factor (Ma et al., 2011; Weaver & Clum, 1995) and an important predictor of psychological trauma (Ehlers & Clark, 2000; Ellis, Nixon, & Williamson, 2009; Giannopoulou et al., 2006; Gil & Caspi, 2006; Kiliç, Kiliç, & Aydin, 2011; King, King, Fairbank, Keane, & Adams, 1998; Kutz & Dekel, 2006; Lai et al., 2014; Laubmeier & Sakowski, 2004; Shaw, 2003; Tatum, Vollmer, & Shore, 1986; Trickey et al., 2012; Warda & Bryant, 1998). Individuals viewing a crisis as highly threatening and having catastrophic thoughts about themselves immediately after being exposed to a crisis predicted traumatic stress (Ehlers, Mayou, & Bryant, 1998). For example, Groome and Soureti (2004) reported that among children exposed to an earthquake, subjective reports of believing that their lives were in danger were associated with greater amounts of anxiety.

Adult reactions also are important influences on children's threat perceptions (Morris, Lee, & Delahanty, 2013), especially among younger children. For example, in the instance of a child who has fallen from a swing, if the child looks at the parent's face and sees a look of panic, he or she may respond to the parent's distress by crying. Conversely, the parent who responds to the child's fall in a calm and controlled manner is less likely to generate additional distress within the child. This is a common example of children looking to adults to gauge the degree to which a given situation is threatening. As discussed in Chapter 12 and earlier in this chapter, parents' traumatic stress reactions increase a child's vulnerability to traumatic stress. Events that were not initially perceived as threatening may become more threatening to children if they observe adults behaving in a way that suggests the event was dangerous or traumatic (Shaw, 2003). B. L. Green et al. (1991) found that following a dam failure, traumatic stress symptoms among children 2–7 years were more influenced by parental reactions (i.e., severity of parental PTSD) than by children's direct disaster exposure.

Psychological Trauma Warning Signs

The final evaluation variable considered when evaluating traumatic stress is warning signs, which are the emotional, cognitive, physical, and interpersonal or behavioral reactions to crises. As illustrated in Figure 13.1, warning signs are consequences of the individual's perceptions of the threat presented by the crisis (which are influenced primarily by the objective factors of crisis exposure and, to a lesser extent, of personal vulnerabilities). These reactions and their consequences are among the specific targets of crisis intervention efforts.

While the risk factors discussed earlier in this chapter increase the odds of psychological trauma, warning signs (or crisis reactions) are variables that indicate the presence of psychological trauma. As such, they are important indicators of crisis intervention treatment priorities. Especially when combined with risk factors, the presence and durability of warning signs indicate that an individual has become a psychological trauma victim and requires directive mental health intervention.

As illustrated in Figure 13.1, early warning signs are the initial crisis reactions displayed during the impact and recoil phases of a crisis event. They are not necessarily indicative of psychopathology. On the other hand, enduring warning signs are the more durable crisis reactions that are displayed during the postimpact and recovery and reconstruction phases, and they are more likely to reflect an underlying psychopathology.

Chapter 1 defined the crisis state and suggested that responding to associated crisis reactions was a primary reason for mental health crisis intervention. This chapter provides greater detail regarding the crisis reactions that are the result of that crisis state. This discussion examines the distinction between common crisis reactions (early warning signs) and potentially psychopathological crisis reactions (enduring warning signs). Although some reactions are expected following crisis exposure, there are not any common, normal, or expected crisis reactions. Different individuals have different reactions to the same event. Thus, this section also examines factors that contribute to individual differences in crisis reactions, including developmental level and culture.

Early Warning Signs

Especially in the immediate aftermath of exposure to a traumatic event, some crisis reactions are expected. In fact, some anxiety is normal and part of the healthy response to situations that require increased vigilance (Hobfoll et al., 2007). Thus, at least initially, crisis responders should avoid classifying crisis reactions as mental illness (see Table 13.3; Brymer et al., 2006; NIMH, 2001; Ruzek et al., 2007). In most cases, these are common reactions to uncommon circumstances, and they subside within a few days to weeks. The classification of crisis reactions as being possible indicators of psychopathology should not begin until a week or more after objective crisis threats have terminated (McNally et al., 2003). However, when these common crisis reactions are especially acute or are combined with certain specific risk factors, they should be carefully monitored. For example, if the crisis resulted in physical injury to the student or the death of a family member, if the individual had preexisting psychopathology, or if exposure to the crisis event was particularly intense or of long duration, the individual may require more immediate mental health crisis intervention (NIMH, 2001).

Table 13.3. Common Initial Crisis Reactions

Emotional		Cognitive	
Shock	Depression or	Impaired	Decreased
Anger	sadness	concentration	self-esteem
Despair	Grief	Impaired decision-	Decreased
Emotional numbing	Irritability	making ability	self-efficacy
Terror or fear	Hypersensitivity	Memory impairment	Self-blame
Guilt	Helplessness	Disbelief	Intrusive thoughts or
Phobias	Hopelessness	Confusion	memories[b]
	Loss of pleasure	Distortion	Worry
	from activities		Nightmares
	Dissociation[a]		

Physical		Interpersonal/Behavioral	
Fatigue	Impaired immune	Alienation	Avoidance of
Insomnia	response	Social withdrawal or	reminders
Sleep disturbance	Headaches	isolation	Crying easily
Hyperarousal	Gastrointestinal	Increased	Change in eating
Somatic complaints	problems	relationship	patterns
	Decreased appetite	conflict	Tantrums
	Decreased libido	Vocational	Regression in
	Startle response	impairment	behavior
		Refusal to go to	Risk taking
		school	Aggression
		School impairment	

Note. From *School Crisis Prevention and Intervention: The PREPaRE Model*, p. 140, by S. E. Brock et al., 2009, Bethesda, MD: NASP. Copyright 2009 by the National Association of School Psychologists. Reprinted with permission. The table was originally compiled from *Psychosocial Issues for Children and Adolescents in Disasters*, by A. H. Speier, 2000; and *Disaster Mental Health Services*, by B. H. Young, J. D. Ford, J. I. Ruzek, M. Friedman, and F. D. Gusman, 1998.
a. Examples include perceptual experiences reported as dreamlike, tunnel vision, spacey, or on automatic pilot.
b. Reenactment play among children.

Although crisis response teams should avoid pathologizing initial crisis reactions, they also should be aware that some students, typically a minority of those exposed to a crisis event, demonstrate more severe reactions that signal the need for referral to a mental health professional. Those reactions include behaviors that interfere with necessary activities such as sleeping, eating, drinking, decision making, and other essential life tasks. Not only do these functional impairments threaten physical health and welfare, but they also predict trauma- and stressor-related disorders (Hobfoll et al., 2007).

Additional research has also shown that individuals who were acutely distressed during a crisis event—for example, they had extremely negative emotional reactions or demonstrated acute panic and dissociative states—were more likely to develop PTSD than those who remained calm and in control of their emotions (Bernat, Ronfeldt, Calhoun, & Arias, 1998; Lawyer et al., 2006; Martin

& Marchand, 2003; McFarlane & Yehuda, 1996; Ozer et al., 2003; Vásquez et al; 2012). Similarly, Vaiva et al. (2003) reported that among individuals hospitalized after a motor vehicle accident, those who had "fright" reactions ("having, at least momentarily, a complete absence of affect, or lack of thought, or loss of words, or being spaced out, or all of these symptoms") had a 17 times greater risk of meeting PTSD diagnostic criteria (p. 397). In addition, Frommberger et al. (1998), who also studied motor vehicle accident victims, reported that individuals who developed PTSD demonstrated more symptoms of depression, anxiety, and PTSD a few days after the accident than individuals who did not develop such mental illness.

Among individuals who were hospitalized for blunt force or penetrating trauma and were considered victims of community violence, the severity of acute traumatic stress symptoms, measured 5 days after the traumatic event, was the most powerful predictor of PTSD a year later (Denson, Marshall, Schell, & Jaycox, 2007). Similarly, in a prospective study of adults hospitalized following a medically serious injury, Whitman, North, Downs, and Spitznagel (2013) found PTSD symptoms of avoidance and numbing present one week after the injury predicted who would develop PTSD (sensitivity of 94%). These findings suggest that crisis response team members responsible for evaluating psychological trauma should identify those students who were observed or reported to be acutely distressed during and immediately following the crisis event.

Another group of initial crisis reactions that has been suggested to be predictive of persistent traumatic stress includes increased arousal (e.g., exaggerated startle responses, hypervigilance, irritability, and sleep disturbance). These reactions have been found to differentiate individuals who developed PTSD from those who did not develop this disorder. In contrast, persistent reexperiencing (e.g., having distressing and intrusive memories) was suggested to be less worrisome in the days after a crisis event and was considered to be part of normal reappraisal (McFarlane & Yehuda, 1996).

In addition to crisis reactions, maladaptive coping strategies—that is, counterproductive behaviors used by the individual to manage or cope with crisis experiences and reactions—that present a risk of harm to self or others sometimes emerge as a consequence of exposure to crisis events (American Red Cross, 1991; Azarian & Skriptchenko-Gregorian, 1998b; Berman, Kurtines, Silverman, & Serafini, 1996; de Wilde & Kienhorst, 1998; McNally et al., 2003). The presence of the following maladaptive behaviors would signal the need for an immediate mental health referral: (a) extreme substance abuse or self-medication, (b) suicidal or homicidal thinking, (c) extreme inappropriate anger toward and abuse of others, and (d) the taking of excessive precautions (e.g., only sleeping with a weapon nearby). Table 13.4 lists the initial crisis reactions that may signal the need for referral to a mental health professional. These reactions may reach the point at which they meet the criteria for one or more diagnoses under the *Diagnostic and Statistical Manual of Mental Disorders* (DSM-5; American Psychiatric Association [APA], 2013).

Enduring Warning Signs
Even for less worrisome initial crisis reactions such as persistent reexperiencing, if reactions do not remit or they worsen after a week or more, they may be developing into a psychopathology. Although initial crisis reactions are common and might be adaptive or protective, prolonged states of emotional distress lead to a variety of mental health challenges (Harvey & Bryant, 1998; Shalev & Freedman, 2005).

Table 13.4. Warning Signs of Psychopathology and Indicators of the Need for Immediate Mental Health Crisis Intervention

Peritraumatic dissociation[a]
- Derealization (e.g., feeling as if in a dream world)
- Depersonalization (e.g., feeling as if your body is not really yours)
- Reduced awareness of surroundings (e.g., being in a daze)
- Emotional numbness or detachment (e.g., feeling emotionally detached or estranged; lacking typical range of emotional reactions; having reduced interest in previously important or enjoyed activities; feeling as if there is no future career, marriage, children, or normal lifespan)
- Amnesia (i.e., failure to remember significant crisis event experiences)

Intense peritraumatic emotional reactions[b]
- Fear (e.g., of dying)
- Helplessness
- Horror

Intense peritraumatic hyperarousal[c]
- Panic attacks
- Hypervigilance and exaggerated startle reactions (e.g., unusually alert and easily startled)
- Difficulty falling or staying asleep (sometimes a result of the reexperiencing symptom of disturbing dreams)

Significant depression[d]
- Feelings of hopelessness and worthlessness
- Loss of interest in most activities
- Early awakening
- Persistent fatigue
- Virtually complete lack of motivation

Psychotic symptoms[e]
- Delusions
- Hallucinations
- Bizarre thoughts or images
- Catatonia

Maladaptive coping[f]
- Extreme substance abuse or self-medication
- Suicidal or homicidal thinking, extreme inappropriate anger toward or abuse of others, or the taking of excessive precautions (e.g., only sleeping with a light on or with a weapon nearby)

Note. From *School Crisis Prevention and Intervention: The PREPaRE Model*, p. 143, by S. E. Brock et al., 2009, Bethesda, MD: NASP. Copyright 2009 by the National Association of School Psychologists. Reprinted with permission. a. Bernat et al., 1998; Ehlers et al., 1998; Grieger, Fullerton, & Ursano, 2003; Koopman, Catherine, & David, 1994; Lawyer et al., 2006; Tichenor, Marmar, Weiss, Metzler, & Ronfeldt, 1996; Weiss, Marmar, Metzler, & Ronfeldt, 1995; Whitman et al., 2013. b. Bernat et al., 1998; Brewin, Andrews, & Rose, 2000; Lawyer et al., 2006; Simeon, Greenberg, Knutelska, Schmeidler, & Hollander, 2003; Vaiva et al., 2003. c. Galea et al., 2002; Galea et al., 2003; Lawyer et al., 2006; McFarlane & Yehuda, 1996; Tucker, Pfefferbaum, Nixon, & Dickson, 2000. d. Frommberger et al., 1998. e. Gracie et al., 2007; Kaštelan et al., 2007. f. Azarian & Skriptchenko-Gregorian, 1998b; Berman et al., 1996; de Wilde & Kienhorst, 1998; Matsakis, 1994; McNally et al., 2003.

Acute stress disorder and PTSD are the two most common diagnoses associated with exposure to a traumatic event (see Table 13.5 for PTSD diagnostic criteria). Although treating students and school staff members who develop these serious and potentially debilitating psychopathologies may not be a part of the school-employed professional's mental health crisis response, school psychologists and counselors should, at the very least, be able to recognize them and make appropriate referrals.

Developmental Variations

Crisis reactions depend on the child's level of development to a significant extent (Joshi & Lewin, 2004), a fact recognized by the recent revision of the *Diagnostic and Statistical Manual of Mental Disorders* (DSM-5; APA, 2013). The importance of recognizing the effects of developmental status on crisis reactions was emphasized by the results of several studies of PTSD symptoms among children (Carrion, Weems, Ray, & Reiss, 2002; Scheeringa, Wright, Hunt, & Zeanah, 2006; Yorbik et al., 2004). Collectively these studies suggested that developmental differences in children's expression of symptoms, and difficulty verbalizing how a crisis event is affecting them, underestimated the number of preschool youth who met DSM-IV criteria for PTSD (APA, 1994, 2000). For example, Carrion et al. (2002) concluded that DSM-IV PTSD diagnostic criteria were not appropriate for younger children and that, among children, the failure to meet all of the PTSD diagnostic criteria did "not indicate a lack of posttraumatic stress problems, but may be due to developmental differences in symptom expression" (p. 172). A similar conclusion was reached by Yorbik et al. (2004), who studied a sample of children ages 2 to 16 years who had presented with symptoms of PTSD following an earthquake. They also concluded that DSM-IV diagnostic criteria were not sufficient for PTSD diagnosis among preschool children.

It was from such findings that APA (2013) modified its PTSD criteria. In addition to continuing to include several notes regarding how children over age 6 may demonstrate PTSD's symptoms of intrusion, DSM-5 also added new criteria for the disorder's symptoms among children 6 years and younger (see Table 13.5). Regarding intrusion symptoms associated with a traumatic event, DSM-5 specifies that among children these symptoms may occur in play (wherein these or aspects of the trauma are expressed) or in dreams (wherein the content of the dreams may be frightening, but without recognizable content), and that dissociative reactions (e.g., flashbacks) may manifest as trauma-specific reenactment play.

Regarding new PTSD criteria for children 6 years and younger, DSM-5 specified in Criterion A that witnessing or learning about a traumatic event is especially challenging when it involves a parent or other primary caregiver. Criterion B continues to offer the qualifiers regarding intrusion symptoms mentioned above. Criteria C and D are combined (into what is Criterion C for preschoolers) and do not require the young child to report symptoms associated with memories or remembering; thoughts or cognitions; or feelings, negative beliefs, or expectations. Symptoms associated with feelings of detachment are replaced with "social withdrawal," and the criterion has no reckless or self-destructive behavior symptom (APA, 2013; see Table 13.5).

Given these observations, a critical component of crisis intervention is understanding how students' developmental level influences their crisis reactions (and directs specific crisis interventions; Feeny, Foa, Treadwell, & March, 2004). The following are some of the unique

Table 13.5. DSM-5 Diagnostic Criteria for Posttraumatic Stress Disorder (309.81 [F43.10])

Posttraumatic Stress Disorder

Note: The following criteria apply to adults, adolescents, and children older than 6 years. For children 6 years and younger, see corresponding criteria below.

A. Exposure to actual or threatened death, serious injury, or sexual violence in one (or more) of the following ways:
  1. Directly experiencing the traumatic event(s).
  2. Witnessing, in person, the event(s) as it occurred to others.
  3. Learning that the traumatic event(s) occurred to a close family member or close friend. In cases of actual or threatened death of a family member or friend, the event(s) must have been violent or accidental.
  4. Experiencing repeated or extreme exposure to aversive details of the traumatic event(s) (e.g., first responders collecting human remains; police officers repeatedly exposed to details of child abuse).
  Note: Criterion A4 does not apply to exposure through electronic media, television, movies, or pictures, unless this exposure is work related.

B. Presence of one (or more) of the following intrusion symptoms associated with the traumatic event(s), beginning after the traumatic event(s) occurred:
  1. Recurrent, involuntary, and intrusive distressing memories of the traumatic event(s).
  Note: In children older than 6 years, repetitive play may occur in which themes or aspects of the traumatic event(s) are expressed.
  2. Recurrent distressing dreams in which the content and/or affect of the dream are related to the traumatic event(s).
  Note: In children, there may be frightening dreams without recognizable content.
  3. Dissociative reactions (e.g., flashbacks) in which the individual feels or acts as if the traumatic event(s) were recurring. (Such reactions may occur on a continuum, with the most extreme expression being a complete loss of awareness of present surroundings.)
  Note: In children, trauma-specific reenactment may occur in play.
  4. Intense or prolonged psychological distress at exposure to internal or external cues that symbolize or resemble an aspect of the traumatic event(s).
  5. Marked physiological reactions to internal or external cues that symbolize or resemble an aspect of the traumatic event(s).

C. Persistent avoidance of stimuli associated with the traumatic event(s), beginning after the traumatic event(s) occurred, as evidenced by one or both of the following:
  1. Avoidance of or efforts to avoid distressing memories, thoughts, or feelings about or closely associated with the traumatic event(s).
  2. Avoidance of or efforts to avoid external reminders (people, places, conversations, activities, objects, situations) that arouse distressing memories, thoughts, or feelings about or closely associated with the traumatic event(s).

D. Negative alterations in cognitions and mood associated with the traumatic event(s), beginning or worsening after the traumatic event(s) occurred, as evidenced by two (or more) of the following:
    1. Inability to remember an important aspect of the traumatic event(s) (typically due to dissociative amnesia and not to other factors such as head injury, alcohol, or drugs).
    2. Persistent and exaggerated negative beliefs or expectations about oneself, others, or the world (e.g., "I am bad," "No one can be trusted," "The world is completely dangerous," "My whole nervous system is permanently ruined").
    3. Persistent, distorted cognitions about the cause or consequences of the traumatic event(s) that lead the individual to blame himself/herself or others.
    4. Persistent negative emotional state (e.g., fear, horror, anger, guilt, or shame).
    5. Markedly diminished interest or participation in significant activities.
    6. Feelings of detachment or estrangement from others.
    7. Persistent inability to experience positive emotions (e.g., inability to experience happiness, satisfaction, or loving feelings).

E. Marked alterations in arousal and reactivity associated with the traumatic event(s), beginning or worsening after the traumatic event(s) occurred, as evidenced by two (or more) of the following:
    1. Irritable behavior and angry outbursts (with little or no provocation) typically expressed as verbal or physical aggression toward people or objects.
    2. Reckless or self-destructive behavior.
    3. Hypervigilance.
    4. Exaggerated startle response.
    5. Problems with concentration.
    6. Sleep disturbance (e.g., difficulty falling or staying asleep or restless sleep).

F. Duration of the disturbance (Criteria B, C, D, and E) is more than 1 month.

G. The disturbance causes clinically significant distress or impairment in social, occupational, or other important areas of functioning.

H. The disturbance is not attributable to the physiological effects of a substance (e.g., medication, alcohol) or another medical condition.

Specify whether:

With dissociative symptoms: The individual's symptoms meet the criteria for posttraumatic stress disorder, and in addition, in response to the stressor, the individual experiences persistent or recurrent symptoms of either of the following:
    1. **Depersonalization:** Persistent or recurrent experiences of feeling detached from, and as if one were an outside observer of, one's mental processes or body (e.g., feeling as though one were in a dream; feeling a sense of unreality of self or body or of time moving slowly).
    2. **Derealization:** Persistent or recurrent experiences of unreality of surroundings (e.g., the world around the individual is experienced as unreal, dreamlike, distant, or distorted).

Note: To use this subtype, the dissociative symptoms must not be attributable to the physiological effects of a substance (e.g., blackouts, behavior during alcohol intoxication) or another medical condition (e.g., complex partial seizures).

Table 13.5. Continued

Specify if:

With delayed expression: If the full diagnostic criteria are not met until at least 6 months after the event (although the onset and expression of some symptoms may be immediate).

Posttraumatic Stress Disorder for Children 6 Years and Younger

A. In children 6 years and younger, exposure to actual or threatened death, serious injury, or sexual violence in one (or more) of the following ways:

1. Directly experiencing the traumatic event(s).
2. Witnessing, in person, the event(s) as it occurred to others, especially primary caregivers.

Note: Witnessing does not include events that are witnessed only in electronic media, television, movies, or pictures.

3. Learning that the traumatic events(s) occurred to a parent or caregiving figure.

B. Presence of one (or more) of the following intrusion symptoms associated with the traumatic event(s), beginning after the traumatic event(s) occurred:

1. Recurrent, involuntary, and intrusive distressing memories of the traumatic event(s).

Note: Spontaneous and intrusive memories may not necessarily appear distressing and may be expressed as play reenactment.

2. Recurrent distressing dreams in which the content and/or affect of the dream are related to the traumatic event(s).

Note: It may not be possible to ascertain that the frightening content is related to the traumatic event.

3. Dissociative reactions (e.g., flashbacks) in which the child feels or acts as if the traumatic event(s) were recurring. (Such reactions may occur on a continuum, with the most extreme expression being a complete loss of awareness of present surroundings.) Such trauma-specific reenactment may occur in play.
4. Intense or prolonged psychological distress at exposure to internal or external cues that symbolize or resemble an aspect of the traumatic event(s).
5. Marked physiological reactions to reminders of the traumatic events(s).

C. One (or more) of the following symptoms, representing either persistent avoidance of stimuli associated with the traumatic event(s) or negative alterations in cognitions and mood associated with the traumatic event(s), must be present, beginning after the event(s) or worsening after the event(s).

Persistent Avoidance of Stimuli

1. Avoidance of or efforts to avoid activities, places, or physical reminders that arouse recollections of the traumatic event(s).
2. Avoidance of or efforts to avoid people, conversations, or interpersonal situations that arouse recollections of the traumatic event(s).

Negative Alterations in Cognitions

3. Substantially increased frequency of negative emotional states (e.g., fear, guilt, sadness, shame, confusion).

4. Markedly diminished interest or participation in significant activities, including constriction of play.

5. Socially withdrawn behavior.

6. Persistent reduction in expression of positive emotions.

D. Alterations in arousal and reactivity associated with the traumatic event(s), beginning or worsening after the traumatic event(s) occurred, as evidenced by two (or more) of the following:

1. Irritable behavior and angry outbursts (with little or no provocation) typically expressed as verbal or physical aggression toward people or objects (including extreme temper tantrums).

2. Hypervigilance.

3. Exaggerated startle response.

4. Problems with concentration.

5. Sleep disturbance (e.g., difficulty falling or staying asleep or restless sleep).

E. The duration of the disturbance is more than 1 month.

F. The disturbance causes clinically significant distress or impairment in relationships with parents, siblings, peers, or other caregivers or with school behavior.

G. The disturbance is not attributable to the physiological effects of a substance (e.g., medication or alcohol) or another medical condition.

Specify whether:

With dissociative symptoms: The individual's symptoms meet the criteria for posttraumatic stress disorder, and the individual experiences persistent or recurrent symptoms of either of the following:

1. **Depersonalization:** Persistent or recurrent experiences of feeling detached from, and as if one were an outside observer of, one's mental processes or body (e.g., feeling as though one were in a dream; feeling a sense of unreality of self or body or of time moving slowly).

2. **Derealization:** Persistent or recurrent experiences of unreality of surroundings (e.g., the world around the individual is experienced as unreal, dreamlike, distant, or distorted).

Note: To use this subtype, the dissociative symptoms must not be attributable to the physiological effects of a substance (e.g., blackouts) or another medical condition (e.g., complex partial seizures).

Specify if:

With delayed expression: If the full diagnostic criteria are not met until at least 6 months after the event (although the onset and expression of some symptoms may be immediate).

Note. Reprinted from the *Diagnostic and Statistical Manual of Mental Disorders*, Fifth Edition, (pp. 271–274). Copyright 2013 by the American Psychiatric Association. All rights reserved. Reprinted with permission.

features of crisis reactions at different developmental levels, based on several sources (APA, 2013; Berkowitz, 2003; Cook-Cottone, 2004; Dulmus, 2003; Joshi & Lewin, 2004; NIMH, 2001; Yorbik et al., 2004).

In general, the crisis reactions of preschool youth are not as clearly connected to the crisis event as is typically observed among older children. For example, in this age group, reexperiencing the trauma might be expressed as generalized nightmares. Crisis reactions also tend to be expressed nonverbally and may include clinginess, tantrums, crying and screaming more readily and often, trembling, and having frightened facial expressions. The temporary loss of recently achieved developmental milestones might be observed (e.g., loss of bowel or bladder control, bed-wetting, thumb sucking, fear of the dark, or fear of parental separation). Finally, the preschool child may reexperience the crisis event through trauma-related play (that does not relieve accompanying anxiety), which may be compulsive and repetitive.

Reactions among students in the primary grades tend to be more directly connected to the crisis event, and event-specific fears may be displayed. However, to a significant degree, the crisis reactions of young school-age children continue to be expressed behaviorally (e.g., behavioral regression, clinging and anxious attachment behaviors, refusal to go to school, irritability, or anxiety). Diminished emotional regulation (e.g., irrational fears) and increased behavior problems (e.g., outbursts of anger and fighting with peers) may be observed. In addition, feelings associated with traumatic stress reactions are often expressed in terms of concrete physical symptoms (e.g., stomachaches and headaches). Older intermediate-grade students may continue to reexperience the trauma through play, but such play is more complex and elaborate (when compared with that of preschoolers) and often includes writing, drawing, and pretending. Repetitive verbal descriptions of the event (without appropriate affect) may also be observed. Given these reactions, it is not surprising that problems paying attention and poor schoolwork may also be noted.

As adolescents begin to develop abstract reasoning abilities, crisis reactions become more and more like those manifested by adults. A sense of a foreshortened future may be reported. This age group is more prone to using oppositional and aggressive behaviors as coping strategies as they strive to regain a sense of control. Other maladaptive coping behaviors reported in this age group include school avoidance, self-injurious behaviors, suicidal ideation, revenge fantasies, and substance abuse. Again, given these reactions, it is not surprising that older school-age youth and adolescents may have particular difficulty concentrating or be moodier, which may cause learning problems.

Cultural Variations

Other important determinants of crisis reactions in general, and grief in particular, are family and cultural and religious beliefs (Seirmarco et al., 2012). Jones (2005, 2008) argues that when responding to children in crisis, school crisis response teams must give greater attention to the child's perspective, including attending to the child's "individuality and the cultural, social and political context in which they live" (p. 291). According to Tearfund (2006), "Every culture provides its members with recognizable languages of distress with which to communicate their suffering. If we are able to understand this language, which may be verbal or non-verbal, physical or psychological, our humanitarian interventions may be better informed" (pp. 32–33). For example, in the dominant African American culture, coping is often viewed as an act of will that is controlled by the individual, and failure to cope is associated with weakness. In the dominant Asian American culture, feelings and problems are often not expressed to avoid losing respect. In both instances, crises can cause feelings of shame, which can affect crisis reactions (Sullivan,

Harris, Collado, & Chen, 2006). Culture also influences the types of events that appear to be threatening in the first place, and it affects how individuals assign meaning to a threat, how individuals or communities express traumatic reactions, and how the traumatized individuals or communities view and judge their own responses (Jones, 2008; Tramonte, 1999; van Rooyen & Nqweni, 2012; Zheng-gen, Yu-qing, Yin, Ning, & Kan-kan, 2011).

Klingman (1986) highlighted the importance of cultural awareness. In describing the interventions conducted by crisis workers as they notified parents of their child's death in a school bus accident, he stated that cultural awareness among crisis interveners

> proved valuable in that they were prepared for various culturally based manifestations of traumatic grief reactions, and thus refrained from requesting the use of sedatives in cases in which the parents' reactions to a death notification on the surface seemed extreme but were in line with their cultural norms. (p. 55)

All providers of crisis intervention should inform themselves about cultural norms with the assistance of community cultural leaders who best understand local customs. Marsella (2010) states: "Although perfect cultural competence is never attainable, especially when crossing cultural boundaries, competence may be assessed by reference to knowledge of a different culture's important features" (p. 20). (Further discussions of this topic are found in Sandoval and Lewis, 2002, and Ortiz and Voutsinas, 2012.)

CONCLUSION

The development of psychological trauma is the result of a complex interaction between the nature of the crisis event (some events are more frightening than others) and the affected individuals' perceptions of the event. Although initial threat perceptions are difficult to identify, the survivor's crisis exposure (physical and emotional proximity) and preexisting vulnerabilities can be used to predict these perceptions. From the interaction between the crisis and the individual's perceptions of the event, crisis reactions emerge. In other words, psychological trauma is a consequence of what happened (the nature of the crisis event), where crisis victims were and who they knew at the time of the crisis (crisis exposure), who they were and the environment that supported them at the time of the crisis (personal vulnerabilities), how the event was viewed (threat perceptions), and how they reacted to the crisis (crisis reactions). Though these factors can provide guidance regarding who is in need of crisis intervention, the interactions among these variables are complex and not completely understood. Thus, crisis interveners need to be attentive to the literature for future guidance regarding the variables (and variable combinations) that best predict traumatic stress reactions.

Chapter 14

CONDUCTING PSYCHOLOGICAL TRIAGE

Psychological triage necessarily involves multiple methods and sources and is a dynamic process, not an event (North & Pfefferbaum, 2013; Saltzman, Pynoos, Layne, Steinberg, & Aisenberg, 2001). The PREPaRE model of triage reviewed in this chapter describes the evaluation of psychological trauma as occurring at three different overlapping levels—primary, secondary, and tertiary. These levels are summarized in Table 14.1.

Primary assessment of psychological trauma establishes priorities for initial crisis intervention and makes initial decisions about what form of intervention (if any) school community members need. Primary assessment is based on known crisis facts, such as which students were physically proximal to the crisis, and previously identified precrisis personal vulnerabilities. In addition, when available, the initial crisis reactions of individuals may inform the primary evaluation of psychological trauma.

Secondary assessment of psychological trauma takes place during the delivery of mental health crisis interventions. This level goes beyond the known crisis facts, previously identified personal vulnerabilities (or risk factors), and initial crisis reactions (or early warning signs). It also examines individual threat perceptions and documents durable crisis reactions (or enduring warning signs). Enduring warning signs of psychological trauma are identified through direct observation by crisis interveners, self-reports, or caregiver reports. This level of triage reevaluates and refines the crisis intervention decisions made during primary assessment. As the magnitude of individual crisis reactions is recognized, this level of triage begins to identify which individuals may require long-term psychotherapeutic treatment, as well as which ones are coping well with the crisis and likely do not need additional mental health assistance.

Finally, the *tertiary assessment* of psychological trauma takes place during the concluding stages of the mental health crisis intervention. This level continues to evaluate known crisis facts, precrisis personal vulnerabilities, and threat perceptions (or risk factors), and continues to monitor crisis reactions (or enduring warning signs). Tertiary assessment identifies those individuals for whom school-based crisis intervention by itself may be insufficient. Its goals are to (a) identify individuals who require long-term psychotherapeutic treatment and (b) make appropriate referrals.

Table 14.1. Levels of Psychological Triage

Triage Level	Timing	Variables Considered	Goals
Primary	Before crisis interventions are provided	Selected psychological trauma risk factors (crisis exposure, vulnerabilities) and warning signs (initial crisis reactions)	1. Establish initial crisis intervention priorities 2. Make initial decisions about individual crisis interventions
Secondary	During the delivery of crisis interventions	Psychological trauma risk factors and warning signs	1. Refine crisis intervention priorities 2. Match crisis intervention to individual needs 3. Begin to consider psychotherapeutic treatment referrals
Tertiary	As the crisis intervention concludes	Psychological trauma risk factors and warning signs	1. Identify individuals who require ongoing psychotherapeutic treatment

Note. Adapted from *School Crisis Prevention and Intervention: The PREPaRE Model*, p. 150, by S. E. Brock et al., 2009, Bethesda, MD: NASP. Copyright 2009 by the National Association of School Psychologists. Adapted with permission.

Before presenting the different levels of psychological triage, several qualifications about the triage process need to be made. First, little empirical guidance regarding the effectiveness of any specific approach to psychological triage is currently available (Litz, 2008). Though clearly based on an understanding of the available literature (summarized in Chapter 13), the practical model presented in this chapter would benefit from empirical validation. Dependent measures of particular interest would be low rates of false negatives with regard to the identification of psychological trauma victims. An empirically supported triage process would result in very few crisis-exposed individuals "slipping through the cracks." In addition to making sure that the individuals who need mental health crisis intervention receive that support, an empirically validated triage model would also ensure that individuals who do not need assistance are allowed to cope with a stressful event on their own or with the assistance of their social support systems.

Second, conducting psychological triage is not nearly as objective as conducting medical triage. Unlike physical injuries, the negative mental health outcomes of crisis exposure may not be readily apparent (North & Pfefferbaum, 2013). This process directs the crisis interveners to collect information that allows them to make a best guess as to who is (and who is not) affected by a crisis. It is not a substitute for the use of clinical judgment in determining who needs mental health support and what specific types of crisis intervention individuals might need.

A third preface to this discussion notes that the assessment of psychological trauma takes place within the broader context of a multidisciplinary school crisis response team. For example, in a crisis response that involves the Incident Command System, although it is the Operations section's Crisis Intervention and Student Care Group that actually conducts psychological triage, the Planning section is important in gathering the crisis facts important to the triage process, and the Logistics section uses that information when determining the resources needed to support crisis survivors. These resources may include, but are not limited to, school-employed and community-based mental health professionals, private conference or meeting rooms, food, and personal comfort items (e.g., tissues, teddy bears, paper, and crayons).

Fourth, as with all other aspects of the school crisis response, the practice of psychological triage requires preparation. Before conducting any triage of psychological trauma victims, the crisis intervention and student care group must have previously identified the resources that crisis intervention requires. Inservice staff development training (such as participation in a PREP_aRE workshop) might be one way to develop school resources; additional community resources might include community mental health centers, university counseling or psychology training programs, and private mental health practitioners. To help with this process, Brock, Sandoval, and Lewis (2001) recommended using the Private Practitioner Referral Questionnaire to identify the community mental health resources that severely traumatized students require (see Figure 14.1). The questionnaire is used to identify community-based mental health resources and to survey local professionals regarding a variety of psychotherapy issues. A benefit of identifying these resources before a crisis event is that it gives the school system time to first review the credentials of community mental health care providers and to ensure that they are appropriately trained and screened to provide support to students. In addition to identifying mental health resources, the Crisis Intervention and Student Care Group should identify other resources for community-based support that might be required to address crisis problems. Examples of these resources include American Red Cross chapters, victim advocate programs, the Federal Emergency Management Agency (FEMA), local public health departments, local emergency management agencies, and state offices of emergency services.

Finally, other important preparedness activities for evaluating psychological trauma, which are discussed in detail later in this chapter, include obtaining and developing psychological trauma screening tools and developing crisis intervention referral forms.

PRIMARY EVALUATION OF PSYCHOLOGICAL TRAUMA

Given that the first priority of all school crisis response team members is to reaffirm physical health and perceptions of safety and security, the initial evaluation of psychological trauma may take place during a crisis or immediately after a crisis event has ended. For example, as a school-employed mental health professional helps to ensure that students are physically and psychologically safe (as discussed in Chapters 11 and 12), he or she can be making note of students who are demonstrating acute distress. However, regardless of exactly when the formal psychological triage process begins, for the reasons discussed in Chapter 13 (i.e., not all

Figure 14.1. Private Practitioner Referral Questionnaire

Private Practitioner Referral Questionnaire

Thank you for providing us with information that will help us to make more appropriate referrals to you and your colleagues. Please complete as much of the questionnaire as possible and return it in the attached, self-addressed envelope.

Name_____ Title _____

Office Location_____ License(s)_____

Phone Number(s) _____ License Number(s)_____

Training and Experience
1. What degrees do you hold?_____
2. What schools did you attend? _____
3. How long have you been in practice? _____
4. What other types of special training do you have? _____

Financial Questions
5. What type of insurance do you accept?_____
6. What payment options do you offer? _____
7. Would you consider a therapeutic fee adjustment?   YES / NO
8. Do you offer a sliding fee schedule?   YES / NO
9. What are your current fees? (Attach fee schedule if available)_____

Logistics
10. Are you currently taking new referrals?   YES / NO
    If no, when will you do so? _____
11. What are your work hours?_____
12. Do you work evenings?   YES / NO
13. Do you work Saturdays?   YES / NO
14. Do you have a waiting list?   YES / NO
    If yes, how long is the typical wait before the first session? _____

Therapeutic Issues
15. With which of the following populations do you feel you are best trained to work? (Circle all that apply to you.)

    Children   Adults   Adolescents   Families

16. Which of the following issues and/or areas do you consider to be your specialty(ies)? (Circle all that apply.)

substance abuse	*child abuse*	*grief processing*
eating disorders	*crisis therapy*	*attention deficit disorders*
anger issues	*suicide prevention*	*suicidal ideation*
empowerment issues	*codependency*	*crisis intervention*
creative divorce	*divorce mediation*	*transitional issues*
decision making	*family communication*	*self-esteem/self-concept*
depression	*behavior analysis*	*conduct disorders*

Others? (please list)_____

17. Which of the following therapeutic techniques do you employ? (Circle all that apply.)

behavior modification	*bio-feedback*	*hypnosis*
EMDR	*client-centered*	*cognitive–behavioral*
RET	*relaxation*	*sand tray*
play therapy	*stress inoculation training*	*cognitive therapy*
creative therapies	*psychoanalysis*	*supportive group therapy*

Others? (please list) _____

18. What special programs or services do you offer? _____
19. Do you conduct group therapy?   YES / NO
20. Are you bilingual?   YES / NO
    If yes, what language(s) do you speak? _____
21. Are the services of an interpreter available to you?   YES / NO
    If yes, what language(s) do your interpreters speak? _____
22. Do you have expertise working with specific ethnic/cultural groups? YES / NO
    If yes, specify the group(s). _____
23. When making a referral to you, what information would you find most helpful? _____
    _____
24. What type of arrangements do you make with your clients for assistance when they are experiencing
    a crisis during your non-work hours? _____
    _____
25. On average, how many times per month will you see the typical client? _____
26. How long are your sessions? _____
27. Please list any other information that may help us make more appropriate referrals to you. _____
    _____
    _____
    _____
    _____
    _____
    _____
    _____
    _____
    _____
    _____
    _____
    _____

Note. Adapted from *Preparing for Crises in the Schools* (pp. 131–132), by S. E. Brock, J. Sandoval, & S. Lewis, 2001, New York, NY: Wiley. Copyright 2001 by John Wiley & Sons. Adapted with permission.

individuals are equally affected by the crisis event, and some crisis interventions have the potential to cause harm), the evaluation should be conducted before individuals are offered school mental health crisis intervention.

According to Litz, Gray, Bryant, and Adler (2002), these initial evaluations are "not intended for diagnostic purposes, but rather to flag those individuals who may require special attention because they are statistically more likely to develop problems as time progresses" (p. 129). Consistent with this observation, primary evaluation is designed to identify individuals who are at risk for psychological trauma and therefore are most likely to need crisis intervention. Identification of individuals is based on the crisis intervener's knowledge of the crisis facts (i.e., physical and emotional proximity to the crisis event) and familiarity with the population affected by the crisis event (i.e., the individuals' personal vulnerabilities). When available, information regarding the initial crisis reactions displayed by individuals during the crisis event are also part of the primary evaluation.

An example of primary triage is shown in the situation of a teacher's death in a car accident that occurred while he was driving home from work. The school crisis response to such an event would typically begin with the school principal receiving the death notification. As the Incident Commander (in the Incident Command System described in Chapter 7), the school principal would first call the Operations Section Chief and the Public Information Officer to inform them of the accident. They would then collaboratively develop the Incident Action Plan (IAP) to direct the Crisis Intervention and Student Care Group on how to respond to school students and staff members on the next school day and after. Important to the primary triage process, at this stage the crisis response team's Planning Section would spearhead efforts to gather facts about the crisis, including who may have been physically exposed to the accident scene, which students and staff members had especially close personal relationships with the deceased, and who may have preexisting vulnerabilities that make coping with this tragic loss more difficult (e.g., someone who recently lost a friend or family member). To gather this information, the Planning Section could use the Crisis Fact Sheet provided in Figure 14.2. Just as a triage nurse in a hospital emergency room asks questions to get preliminary information on the medical status of a patient before a doctor arrives, the school Crisis Intervention and Student Care Group must ask the appropriate questions before responding to the crisis event. The answers to these questions provide details that are important to preparing the IAP.

In the example of a teacher's death in a car accident, the Crisis Fact Sheet gives the Crisis Intervention and Student Care Group important details about the deceased, such as what teachers he was very close to and the fact that he supervised students in the ROTC club and was married to an assistant principal at another school in the district. The school crisis response team's Planning Section also should monitor the local media (including social media) for information that might be relevant to primary triage. For example, in the case of the teacher's fatal car accident, a fact sheet could document that the accident was on the evening news and that video of the accident is on the websites of local news organizations, thereby increasing students' and school staff members' emotional proximity to the event. Social media should also be monitored, and in the current example, the Planning Section should not be surprised to find news videos being posted to student and staff Facebook pages and memorial pages created on Facebook and Instagram, further increasing crisis exposure. Information such as this is important to the crisis response team as it determines crisis response priorities and develops the IAP. In the current example, the plan might include providing mental health crisis intervention for the deceased teacher's department colleagues and students in the ROTC club. Furthermore, social media comments and posts will identify additional individuals who need support. Using all of these data sources, the crisis intervention and student care group learns the number of students and school staff members in need of assistance, determines the level of mental health crisis intervention, and selects specific interventions.

Complementing the Crisis Fact Sheet, an additional triage tool is the Primary Risk Screening form. Adapted from a document developed by Brock et al. (2001), this form (provided in Figure 14.3) is designed to facilitate this level of triage. Considering the risk factors for psychological trauma discussed in Chapter 13, this form quantifies risk of

Figure 14.2. Questions to Ask During Primary Triage

Crisis Fact Sheet

	Sources
Basic Information 1. What happened?_____ 2. When did the event occur? _____ 3. Where did the event occur? _____ 4. Is law enforcement involved (did a criminal activity take place)? _____ 5. Who was involved (i.e., who are the crisis victims)?_____ 6. What is the prognosis for those involved? _____ 7. Was anyone injured or killed? YES NO a. If YES, who was killed? _____	
Physical Proximity 1. Who witnessed the event? _____ 2. Who was exposed to the aftermath of the event (e.g., saw victims being medically treated)? _____	
Emotional Proximity 1. Who knew the crisis victim(s)? _____ 2. Who are considered close friends of the crisis victim(s)? _____ 3. What classroom(s) were the crisis victim(s) a part of? _____ 4. What activities (e.g., clubs, athletics, organizations) did the crisis victim(s) participate in? _____	
Personal Vulnerability 1. Have there been other crisis events that have affected students/staff this past year? _____ 2. Have any of the staff or students been affected by an event similar to the current crisis? _____ 3. Has anyone experienced a sudden loss of a loved one over the past year? ___ 4. Are there staff or students that have any mental health concerns that may affect their ability to cope with the crisis? _____ 5. Have staff and/or students already learned of the event? YES NO a. If YES, how were staff and students informed (e.g., media, social media, pictures, videos)? _____	

Note. Adapted from *Preparing for Crises in the Schools* (p. 98), by S. E. Brock, J. Sandoval, & S. Lewis, 2001, New York, NY: Wiley. Copyright 2009. Adapted with permission. With Conolly-Wilson (2009).

Figure 14.3. Primary Risk Screening Form

Primary Risk Screening

Student _____ M___ F___ Date _____

Referred by _____ Teacher/Counselor _____

Dominant Language _____ Screener _____

A. Crisis Exposure

Physical Proximity

10	8	6	4	2	0
Crisis victim; physically injured	Crisis victim; physically threatened	Crisis witness	In the vicinity of the crisis	Absent by chance from the site of the crisis event	Out of the vicinity of the crisis event

Describe crisis event exposure: _____

_____

Duration of Exposure

5	4	3	2	1	0
Weeks	Days	Hours	Minutes	Seconds	None

Emotional Proximity

5	4	3	2	1	0
Parent(s) or sibling(s)	Other family member(s)	Best and/or only friend(s)	Good friends	Friend(s) or acquaintance(s)	Did not know victim(s)

Elaborate on relationship(s) with crisis victim(s): _____

_____

B. Personal Vulnerability(ies)

	Yes	No	Elaborate
Avoidance coping style			
Known/suspected mental illness			
Social withdrawal			
Previous trauma or loss			
Lack of family resources			
Lack of social resources			
Total Yes √s (0 to 6)			

C. Immediate Crisis Reactions

5	3	1	0
Acutely distressed	Moderately distressed	Mildy distressed	Remained calm

Primary Risk Screening Rating

Primary Risk Screening Category	Rating
Physical proximity to the crisis event (0 to 10)	
Duration of exposure to the crisis event (0 to 5)	
Emotional proximity or relationship(s) with crisis victims(s) (0 to 5)	
Preexisting personal vulnerability(ies) (0 to 6)	
Immediate crisis reactions (0 to 5)	
Total (0 to 31)	

Note. To be completed for all individuals from the population judged to be at risk for psychological trauma. Adapted from *Preparing for Crises in the Schools* (pp. 138–139), by S. E. Brock, J. Sandoval, and S. Lewis, 2001, New York, NY: Wiley. Copyright 2001 by John Wiley & Sons. Adapted with permission.

psychological traumatization using variables known to be correlated with psychological trauma. A Total Primary Risk Screening Rating score can be used to rank individuals in terms of their crisis intervention treatment priority, with higher scores suggesting greater treatment needs. A caution is needed here: although this tool is considered to be empirically informed (i.e., it quantifies variables known to be correlated with traumatic stress), it is not norm referenced; thus, clinical judgment should guide its use.

During crisis intervention, a Crisis Intervention and Student Care Group member who is directly observing a student, or consulting with a teacher about the student, would complete the form. That group member would then ensure that the Operations Section Chief is given a copy of the form to track individuals and assign priorities for crisis intervention. Use of the form would assist in assigning the highest intervention priorities to individuals who (a) were most intimately involved in the crisis, (b) had or have the closest relationships with crisis victims, (c) have the most personal vulnerabilities, and (d) displayed acute stress reactions during the crisis event. Conversely, those who were relatively removed from the crisis, who had or have no relationship with the crisis victims, have no personal vulnerabilities, and remained calm during the crisis event would be the lowest intervention priorities. The individuals with the highest priority would receive mental health crisis intervention immediately or as soon as possible, whereas individuals in the latter group could be delayed until after the needs of the highest treatment priorities have been addressed (or not provided at all if they continue to show no demonstrated need).

Along with determining crisis intervention priorities, the primary evaluation of psychological trauma guides the initial selection and provision of specific types of crisis interventions. (These crisis interventions are discussed in greater detail in Section 5 of this book.) In the primary evaluation process, evaluation data can be used to qualitatively classify individuals as being at low, moderate, or high risk for psychological trauma. As shown in Figure 14.4, the Psychological Trauma Risk Checklist can be used to begin estimating these risk levels (as well as used later as part of the secondary evaluation of psychological trauma). In addition to reaffirming physical health and perceptions of safety and security, the other universal interventions described in Chapters 15 and 16 may be appropriate for the individual in the low-risk category. The selected interventions described in Chapters 16, 17, and 18, may be appropriate for the individual in the moderate to high-risk categories. Finally, the indicated interventions described in Chapter 19, would be considered only for the individual in the high-risk category.

SECONDARY EVALUATION OF PSYCHOLOGICAL TRAUMA

In the days following a crisis event, initial crisis interventions are provided based on the primary evaluation of psychological trauma. As these initial interventions are offered, secondary evaluation of psychological trauma begins. This secondary level of triage involves ongoing careful monitoring of individual crisis reactions and adjustment. It is designed to identify those who are demonstrating not only early warning signs, but also enduring warning signs (i.e., more durable crisis reactions) of psychological trauma.

When considering the crisis reactions demonstrated immediately following a crisis event, the Crisis Intervention and Student Care Group must be aware that initial distress and impairment are not necessarily signs of pathology (Litz, 2008), and that the classification of these reactions as

Figure 14.4. Psychological Trauma Risk Checklist

Psychological Trauma Risk Checklist

Low Risk	Moderate Risk	High Risk
Physical distance from trauma ☐ Out of vicinity of crisis site	☐ Present on crisis site	*Physical closeness to trauma* ☐ Crisis victim or eyewitness
Emotional distance from trauma ☐ Did not know victim(s)	☐ Friend of victim(s) ☐ Acquaintance of victim(s)	*Emotional closeness to trauma* ☐ Child or sibling of victim(s) ☐ Relative of victim(s) ☐ Best friend of victim(s)
Internal resilience ☐ Active coping style ☐ Mentally healthy ☐ Socially connected ☐ No trauma history ☐ High developmental level ☐ Good sense of self-efficacy ☐ Low psychophysiological arousal level ☐ Optimistic outlook on life	*Internal vulnerability* ☐ No clear coping style ☐ Questions exist about precrisis mental health ☐ Some difficulties with social connectedness ☐ Trauma history ☐ At times appears immature ☐ Marginal sense of self-efficacy ☐ Moderate psychophysiological arousal level ☐ Ambivalent outlook on life	*Internal vulnerability* ☐ Avoidance coping style ☐ Precrisis psychopathology ☐ Socially withdrawn ☐ Significant trauma history ☐ Low developmental level ☐ Poor sense of self-efficacy ☐ High psychophysiological arousal level ☐ Pessimistic outlook on life
External resilience ☐ Living with nuclear family members ☐ Good family functioning ☐ No parental traumatic stress ☐ No family trauma history ☐ Parent(s) mentally healthy ☐ Good social resources/relations ☐ Acknowledges multiple social resources	*External resilience* ☐ Living with some nuclear family members ☐ Family functioning at times challenged ☐ Some parental traumatic stress ☐ Some history of family trauma ☐ Possible parental psychopathology ☐ Social resources/relations at times challenged ☐ Acknowledges few social resources	*External vulnerability* ☐ Not living with any nuclear family members ☐ Poor family functioning ☐ Significant parental traumatic stress ☐ Family history of PTSD ☐ Parental psychopathology ☐ Poor or absent social resources/relations ☐ Perceived lack of social support
Immediate reactions during the crisis ☐ Remained calm during the crisis event	*Immediate reactions during the crisis* ☐ Displayed mild to moderate distress during the crisis event	*Immediate reactions during the crisis* ☐ Displayed acute distress (e.g., fright, panic, dissociation) during the crisis event
Current/ongoing reactions and coping ☐ Only a few common crisis reactions displayed ☐ Coping is adaptive (i.e., it allows daily functioning at precrisis levels)	*Current/ongoing reactions and coping* ☐ Many common crisis reactions displayed ☐ Coping is tentative (e.g., the individual is unsure about how to cope with the crisis)	*Current/ongoing reactions and coping* ☐ Mental health referral indicators displayed (e.g., acute dissociation, hyperarousal, depression, psychosis) ☐ Coping is absent or maladaptive (e.g., suicidal/homicidal ideation, substance abuse)
Total:	Total:	Total:

Note. The checklist is used to classify psychological trauma risk factors and warning signs into low, moderate, and high risk categories. From "Best Practices for School Psychologists as Members of Crisis Teams: The PREPaRE Model" (p. 785), by S. E. Brock and J. Davis. In A. Thomas and J. Grimes (Eds.), *Best Practices in School Psychology V*, 2008, Bethesda, MD: National Association of School Psychologists. Copyright 2008 by the National Association of School Psychologists. Reprinted with permission.

suggesting mental illness does not typically begin until a week or more after the crisis event has ended (Litz et al., 2002). Thus, the secondary evaluation of psychological trauma initially avoids labeling common crisis reactions as symptoms of psychopathology. However, the crisis interveners should be vigilant for the more extreme and more durable crisis reactions and coping behaviors (typically displayed by only a minority of crisis survivors). These warning signs *may* be psychopathological and signal the need for more involved mental health crisis intervention. When initial reactions are extreme or present a danger to self or others, and they do not lessen over time, psychotherapeutic treatment (as discussed in Chapter 19) is indicated.

Two primary methods of evaluating psychological trauma are recommended for use by the crisis intervention and student care group as they begin to provide crisis interventions. The first is to obtain and use crisis intervention referral procedures and forms. The second is to obtain and use crisis reaction screening tools.

Crisis Intervention Referral Procedures and Forms

Primary evaluation of psychological trauma is likely unable to identify all psychological trauma victims; therefore, the use of a crisis intervention referral mechanism is essential. One possible mechanism for making referrals involves developing a school crisis intervention referral form (Figure 14.5). The essential elements of such forms, which help to further document the presence of both psychological trauma risk factors and warning signs, include the individual's identifying information, plus questions about crisis exposure (physical and emotional proximity), personal vulnerabilities, initial and durable crisis reactions, and the presence of maladaptive or dangerous coping behaviors (especially those that involve any degree of lethality).

Psychological Trauma Screening Tools

As crisis interveners begin to have contact with students (and their teachers and other caregivers), they have the opportunity to further assess psychological trauma. One approach to such assessment is to conduct traumatic stress screenings (Ohan, Myers, & Collett, 2002; Strand, Sarmiento, & Pasquale, 2005). The importance of including such direct assessment in psychological triage is emphasized by Stover, Hahn, Im, and Berkowitz (2010), who found that adult caregivers greatly underestimate their child's exposure to certain types of trauma and to report a much lower impact of such events. They state: "An outstanding conclusion from this study is that parent–child agreement on the numbers and types of potentially traumatic experiences and their subsequent impact is poor beginning in the acute peritraumatic period. In general, parent–child communication about youth experience of upsetting events and its accompanying distress appears to be lacking" (p. 165).

According to Brewin et al. (2002), a good screening instrument would have adequate psychometric properties, and also be concise, cost-effective, and easy to administer and understand. The measures presented in Table 14.2 appear to meet these criteria. For a more exhaustive listing of measures of trauma for children and adolescents, the reader is referred to Strand, Pasquale, and Sarmiento (n.d.), and Crandal and Conradi (2013).

Figure 14.5. School Crisis Intervention Referral Form

School Crisis Intervention Referral Form

Date: _____   Parent: _____

Student: _____   Address: _____

Birth Date: _____   Phone: H _____

Teacher: _____   W _____

Grade: _____   Primary Language:

                                                                              Student _____

                                                                              Parent(s) _____

REASON FOR REFERRAL TO THE CRISIS INTERVENTION TEAM

_____

_____

_____

_____

_____

_____

1. Physical closeness to the crisis _____

_____

2. Duration of crisis exposure _____

_____

3. Relationship(s) with crisis victims _____

_____

4. Immediate reactions to the crisis _____

_____

5. Did the youth view the crisis as threatening?   YES   NO
    (Elaborate)_____

    _____

6. Has the youth experienced a similar event in the past?   YES   NO
    (If YES, elaborate)_____

7. Has the youth experienced any other traumas within the past year?   YES   NO
    (If YES, elaborate) _____

8. Does the youth have an emotional disturbance (e.g., depression)?   YES   NO
    (If YES, elaborate) _____

9. Is the youth developmentally immature   YES   NO
    (If YES, elaborate) _____

10. Crisis Reaction Checklist[1]
    (Check all that you believe apply to the student you are referring for crisis intervention.)

SPECIFIC FEELINGS AND BEHAVIORS GENERATED BY THE CRISIS

*a. Reactions suggesting **reexperiencing** of the crisis*

___Reports constant, automatic, spontaneous, and intrusive distressing memories of the event *(among children, such memories may be expressed in repetitive play; among preschoolers, such memories may not appear to be distressing)*
___Reports having distressing dreams about, or related to, the event *(among preschoolers and children, they may have nightmares not clearly related to the event and without recognizable content)*
___Reports feeling as if the event is reoccurring
___Behaves as if the event were reoccurring *(among children this may occur in play)*
___Exhibits repetitive play that may be symbolic of the event *(among preschoolers, such play may simply have frightening themes and may not necessarily be symbolic of the event)*
___Displays intense emotional distress when exposed to crisis reminders

*b. Reactions suggesting a **negative mood** following the crisis*

___Reduced expression of positive emotions (e.g., happiness, satisfaction, or love)
___Increased expression of negative emotions (e.g., fear, guilt, sadness, or shame)
___Reduced interest or engagement in significant activities (e.g., play)
___Appears more socially withdrawn
___Appears to be depressed

*c. Reactions suggesting an **avoidance** of crisis reminders*

___Reports trying to avoid memories, thoughts, or feelings about/associated with the event
___Avoids places, activities, and/or objects associated with the event
___Avoids people, conversations, and/or interpersonal situations associated with the event

*d. Reactions suggesting increased physical **arousal** following the crisis*

___Displays increased irritability (with little or no provocation)
___Displays increased verbal or physical aggressiveness (with little or no provocation)
___Appears to be hypervigilant
___Appears to have difficulty concentrating
___Displays an exaggerated startle response
___Has difficulty falling or staying asleep, or has restless sleep
___Has difficulty completing tasks
___Reports physical problems such as stomachaches and headaches

*e. Reactions suggesting increased **detachment** following the crisis*

___Reports feeling in a daze
___Does not remember important elements of the event
___Reports feeling separated, detached, or estranged from others
___Reports feeling separated or detached from own body

---

[1] Adapted from the *Diagnostic Criteria for Acute Stress and Posttraumatic Stress Disorders* (American Psychiatric Association, 2013, pp. 271–274, 280–281), and from Schäfer et al. (2004) and Young et al. (1998).

Note. Adapted from *Preparing for Crises in the Schools* (pp. 152–154), by S. E. Brock, J. Sandoval, and S. Lewis, 2001, New York, NY: Wiley. Copyright 2001 by John Wiley & Sons. Adapted with permission.

The use of these measures should not take the place of clinical skills and judgment. These measures are not sufficient to make a mental health diagnosis. However, they are helpful in identifying individuals who require more direct and intensive crisis interventions and who need to be evaluated for psychotherapeutic treatment. The following discussion reviews the measures listed in Table 14.2.

The *Child PTSD Symptoms Scale* (CPSS; Foa, 2002; Foa, Johnson, Feeny, & Treadwell, 2001) is a criterion-referenced, 26-item self-report measure designed to assess PTSD and general distress. Developed for youth ages 8–18 years, it assesses the frequency of PTSD symptoms within the past month as well as functional impairment. It can be administered individually or in a group setting such as a classroom. Scores can be calculated for each of the DSM-IV-TR symptom clusters (American Psychiatric Association, 2000). Administration time is approximately 10 minutes. The completed protocol takes approximately 5 minutes to score. Strand et al. (2005) reported that "preliminary studies reveal strong psychometric properties" (p. 65), and in a subsequent study, Gillihan, Aderka, Conklin, Capaldi, and Foa (2013) report findings that "confirm the strong psychometric properties of the CPSS for assessing PTSD severity and related functional impairment

Table 14.2. Traumatic Stress Screening Tools

Measure	Author	Age Group	Admin. Time	Availability
Child PTSD Symptoms Scale	Foa et al. (2001)	8–18 yrs	10 min	foa@mail.med.upenn.edu
Child's Reactions to Traumatic Events Scale–Revised	Jones et al. (2002)	8–12 yrs	5 min	www.psyc.vt.edu/sites/default/files/inline_files/Page84/crtes.pdf
Children's PTSD Inventory	Saigh et al. (2000)	6–18 yrs	5–20 min	www.pearsonclinical.com/psychology.html
Children's Revised Impact of Event Scale	Children and War Foundation (1998)	8 yrs & older	5–10 min	www.childrenandwar.org/measures/
Pediatric Emotional Distress Scale	Saylor (2002)	2–10 yrs	5–10 min	conway.saylor@citadel.edu
Trauma Symptom Checklist for Children	Briere (1996)	7–16 yrs	15–20 min	www4.parinc.com
UCLA PTSD Reaction Index: DSM-5 Version	Pynoos et al. (1998)	6 yrs–adult	20 min	hfinley@mednet.ucla.edu

in female survivors of childhood sexual assault" (p. 28). Its psychometric properties have recently been updated and suggested to be generally good to very good, with a score of 16 or above suggested as a revised cutoff (Nixon et al., 2013).

The *Child's Reactions to Traumatic Events Scale–Revised* (CRTES-R; Jones, Fletcher, & Ribbe, 2002) is a criterion-referenced, 23-item self-report questionnaire designed to assess psychological responses to stressful events. Developed for youth ages 8–12 years, this measure can be administered through an interview or with paper and pencil. Administration time is 10 minutes, and a completed protocol takes approximately 5 minutes to score. Napper et al. (2014) have suggested this measure to be reliable and valid.

The *Children's PTSD Inventory* (CPTSD-I; Saigh, 2004; Saigh et al., 2000) is a norm-referenced, commercially available, 50-item structured interview designed to establish the presence of PTSD symptoms. Unlike most of the other measures discussed in this section, it cannot be administered in a group setting. Thus, it is best reserved for use with those individual students for whom concern regarding psychological trauma is great. Developed for youth ages 6–18 years, this measure assesses PTSD symptoms, trauma history, and current functioning. Its five sections correspond to the DSM-IV-TR symptom clusters (i.e., crisis event exposure and reactions; reexperiencing, avoidance, and emotional numbing; increased arousal symptoms; and acute distress or impairment). Administration time depends on trauma history. Youth without a history of traumatic event exposure can be assessed in 5 minutes; among those with such a history, the interview requires 15–20 minutes. The completed protocol takes approximately 10 minutes to score. Strand et al. (2005) reported this measure to have "strong psychometric results" (p. 58), and Christopher (2007) reported that the CPTSD-I "can be a practical assessment instrument if used by skillful, knowledgeable, and experienced clinicians" (¶ 10). Finally, Doll and Osborn (2007) reported "the inventory's reliability and validity are promising. … Early indications are that the Children's PTSD Inventory will be a very strong diagnostic tool" (¶ 8). It is available in Spanish.

The *Children's Revised Impact of Event Scale* (CRIES; Children and War Foundation, 1998) is a screening tool for symptoms of traumatic stress among children 8 years of age and older (a parent version of this same measure has been validated for use as a screening tool; Verlinden et al., 2014). Originally developed by Horowitz, Wilner, and Alvarez (1979), it has been used in a variety of international settings and has versions in 18 different languages. Eight-item (CRIES-8) and 13-item (CRIES-13) versions have been developed, with the CRIES-8 consisting of four items measuring intrusion symptoms and four items measuring avoidance; the CRIES-13 adds five items to measure arousal symptoms. From an evaluation of its validity, Perrin, Meiser-Stedman, and Smith (2005) suggest that cutoff scores of 30 and 17 maximized both sensitivity and specificity on the CRIES-13 and CRIES-8, respectively. They further suggest that the CRIES-8 worked as well as the CRIES-13 in correctly classifying children with and without PTSD. This finding is consistent with the Children and War Foundation's (1998) recommendation that the CRIES-8 be used as a screening tool.

The *Pediatric Emotional Distress Scale* (PEDS; Saylor, 2002; Saylor, Swenson, Reynolds, & Taylor, 1999) is a 21-item paper-and-pencil parent-report scale designed to detect elevated levels of symptoms and behavior following traumatic event exposure. Developed for children ages 2–10 years, it includes behaviors suggested to be associated with traumatic event exposure. Average administration time is 7 minutes, and the completed protocol takes 4 minutes to score. Regarding its psychometric properties, Strand et al. (2005) reported that "it is among the most robust of the one-page symptom checklists" (p. 69). Spilsbury et al. (2005) have also documented the measure's psychometric properties.

The *Trauma Symptom Checklist for Children* (TSCC; Briere, 1996) is a norm-referenced, commercially available, 54-item self-report measure designed to assess both PTSD and trauma-related psychological symptomatology (a 44-item version is also available that does not include items related to possible sexual abuse). Developed for youth ages 8–16 years, it is a paper-and-pencil questionnaire that can be administered individually or in a group setting such as a classroom. A 90-item version to be completed by a caregiver and appropriate for children as young as age 3 is available (Trauma Symptom Checklist for Young Children; Briere, 2005) and has been suggested to have adequate psychometric properties (Mackler, 2007; Stinnett, 2007). Administration time is approximately 15–20 minutes. Strand et al. (2005) reported that this measure is "exceptionally well-evaluated" (p. 65). Boyle (2003) reported that "the TSCC is a very useful, if somewhat limited, measure for the psychometric assessment of traumatic symptoms in children and adolescents" (¶ 10). Viswesvaran (2003) reported that "the TSCC is a short and useful instrument to assess trauma symptoms in children" (¶ 12). Most recently, Wherry, Corson, and Hunsaker (2013) found that a 32-item version of the Trauma Symptom Checklist for Young Children had adequate psychometric properties.

The *UCLA PTSD Reaction Index: DSM-5 Version* (Pynoos, Rodrigues, Steinberg, Stuber, & Frederick, 1998; Steinberg & Beyerlein, n.d.) is a self-report instrument (there is also a caregiver-report version) designed to screen for trauma exposure and assess symptoms of PTSD among children over 6 years of age. Part I of this measure is a clinician-administered trauma exposure screener. Part II is a 15-item self-report screener for trauma exposure history. Finally, this measure includes a 27-item PTSD symptoms scale, with four additional items to assess for the dissociative PTSD subtype. A particular strength of this measure is that training regarding its use is available on the Internet at http://mediasite.nctsn.org/NCTSN/Viewer/?peid=8481a2b1c094456e 9844ba431edf3459. Although the psychometric properties of this measure are still under study, its predecessors (upon which this measure is based) have strong psychometric properties (Contractor et al., 2013; Elhai et al., 2013; Steinberg et al., 2013; Strand et al., 2005).

Finally, the Psychological Trauma Risk Checklist (a primary evaluation tool shown in Figure 14.4) is an additional informal screening tool that parallels the risk factors and warning signs of psychological trauma discussed in Chapter 13. In addition, Figure 14.6 presents an informal, semistructured interview form (*Secondary Screening of Risk Interview*) for use during individual crisis interventions. The tool helps in collecting data important to the secondary evaluation of psychological trauma.

By using these secondary evaluation techniques, the crisis intervention and student care group gains a better understanding of how a given crisis event has affected their student body. For example, following the previously described crisis of a teacher's death in a car accident, secondary triage might further identify specific groups of students and staff who, for various reasons (e.g., having recently had other similar losses, having had important upcoming events with the deceased), are having particular coping difficulties. With this information, the school crisis response team can adapt the IAP and begin to estimate how long it will take before the school can return to normal operations.

Figure 14.6. Secondary Screening of Risk Interview

Secondary Screening of Risk Interview[1]

Student Name _____ Teacher _____

Crisis Intervener _____ Date _____

What were the student's crisis exposure, perceptions, and reactions?

1. What do you remember about the crisis? *[Note aspects of the crisis the youth does not remember.]*

_____
_____
_____
_____

2. How close were you to the crisis? *[Note physical proximity to the crisis.]*

_____
_____

3. How long were you exposed to the crisis? *[Note duration of the crisis exposure.]*

_____
_____

4. How threatening was the crisis for you? Did you feel as if you could have been killed or injured? *[Note any aspect(s) of the event that was perceived as involving actual or threatened death or serious injury, or a threat to physical integrity of self.]* _____

_____
_____

5. How well do(did) you know the crisis victim(s)? *[Note if the victim was a crisis fatality, how important the victim(s) was to the interviewee, and if the victim was a parent or sibling.]* _____

_____
_____

6. How did you react when the crisis occurred? *[Note any reports of acute distress (e.g., panic and/or dissociation).]* _____

_____
_____

Does the student report intrusive thoughts about the crisis?

7. Do you constantly think (or find yourself frequently playing) about the crisis? *[Note recurrent/intrusive memories (e.g., images, thoughts, smells) that the interviewee finds distressing and wishes could be stopped.]* _____

_____
_____

8. Do you have bad dreams?   YES   NO

    8a If YES, ask for description of dreams *[Note if there are frightening dreams without recognizable content].* _____

    _____

    8b. If YES, ask how frequently they occur. _____

    _____

9. Do you ever feel as if the event were happening again? *[Note reports of illusions, hallucinations, and flashbacks, and keep in mind that in children this may include play reenactments.]* _____

_____
_____

---

[1] Adapted from the Los Angeles Unified School District (1994), APA (2013), and Brock et al. (2001).

---

10. What does it feel like when [What do you think it would feel like if] you return to the scene of the crisis? *[Note reports of intense psychological distress.]* _____

_____

11. What does it feel like when someone or something reminds you of the crisis? *[Note reports of psychological distress.]* _____

_____

12. How do you physically respond when someone or something reminds you of the crisis? *[Note reports of physiological reactivity.]*_____

_____

Does the student avoid people, situations, and/or things that are considered crisis reminders?
13. Do you find yourself trying to avoid thinking, feeling, and/or talking about the crisis?_____

_____

14. Do you try to avoid activities, places, people, or situations that remind you of the crisis? _____

_____

Does the student report negative alterations in thoughts and feelings since the crisis?
15. Do you have difficulty remembering aspects of the crisis? _____

_____

16. Do you feel really bad about yourself, others, or the world since the crisis? *[Note exaggerated negative beliefs or expectations about self, others, or the world including, but not limited to, feeling they are "bad" or "can't be trusted," or that the world is very "dangerous."]*_____

_____

17. What do you think caused the crisis? *[Note any distorted beliefs regarding the cause or consequence of the crisis. Do they blame themselves or others?]* _____

_____

18. Do you feel guilty about what happened? _____

_____

19. Do you think you could have done something to prevent the crisis? _____

_____

20. Do you want to "get even" or seek revenge?_____

_____

21. How are you feeling in general since the crisis? *[Note the presence of a negative emotional states such as persistent fear, horror, anger, guilt, or shame.]*_____

_____

22. Are there activities that were important to you before the crisis that are no longer of interest? _____
_____
_____

23. Since the crisis, have you found yourself feeling different or separated/apart from other people, your friends, or your family? *[Note feelings of detachment and/or estrangement.]* _____
_____
_____

24. Are you finding it difficult to feel happy? _____
_____
_____

25. What emotions have you been able to feel since the crisis? *[Note a restricted range of affect. Note feelings of numbing, detachment, or a lack of an emotional response.]* _____
_____
_____

Does the student report an increased level of arousal and reactivity since the crisis?
26. Since the crisis, have you found that you have had difficulty controlling your temper? *[Note any reports of irritability or angry outbursts.]* _____
_____
_____

27. Do you feel that you are/have been constantly tense and on guard since the crisis and, as a result, very aware of your surroundings? *[Note if they are constantly on the lookout for threats.]* _____
_____
_____

28. Have you found yourself to be easily startled since the crisis? _____
_____
_____

29. Have you had difficulty listening to your teacher and/or concentrating on your schoolwork? _____
_____
_____

30. Are you having sleeping difficulties? *[Note difficulties falling or staying asleep.]* _____
_____
_____

31. Since the crisis, have you found yourself doing dangerous things that could hurt you?_____
_____
_____

32. Do you find yourself acting impulsively since the crisis? _____
_____
_____

33. Have you engaged in any behaviors that might harm yourself or others since the crisis? _____
_____
_____

Does the student report any self-destructive thoughts and/or dangerous impulsive behaviors?

34. Either prior to or since the crisis, have you had thoughts of suicide/homicide? YES NO
    *[If YES, continue with question 35; if NO, skip to question 36. If YES, make an **immediate** crisis intervention referral.]*

35. How often have you had these suicidal/homicidal thoughts? _____

    35a. Do you have a plan? YES NO
          [IF YES, continue with question 35a-i; if NO, skip to question 35b.]

          35a-i. How would you commit suicide/homicide? _____
          _____
          _____

          35a-ii. Do you have the means to carry out your plan? _____
          _____
          _____

          35a-iii. When would you commit suicide/homicide? _____
          _____

    35b. Have you ever previously attempted suicide/homicide?_____
          _____
          _____

    35c. How desperate are you to stop the pain you are experiencing?_____
          _____
          _____

    35d. Is there anyone or anything that could keep you from killing yourself/others? _____
          _____
          _____

Does the student report more physical illnesses, aches, and/or pains since the crisis?

36. Have you felt sick since the crisis? *[Note any reports of headaches, stomachaches, bowel or bladder problems, etc.]* _____
    _____
    _____

Does the student report crisis reactions to have an effect on their daily functioning?

37. Have you had difficulty completing your schoolwork since the crisis? _____
    _____
    _____

38. What will you do when you leave school today? _____
    _____
    _____

39. Will you be in school tomorrow? _____
    _____

40. Have you had difficulty taking care of yourself since the event? _____
    _____
    _____

41. Have you had difficulty playing with your friends since the crisis?_____
_____
_____

Does the student acknowledge the presence of any resources that could help him or her cope with the crisis?

42. How do you think the crisis will affect your family and friends? _____
_____
_____

43. Is there anyone in your family that you can talk to about the crisis?_____
_____
_____

44. Is there anyone outside of your family that you can talk to about the crisis? _____
_____
_____

45. Would you like to talk again, or perhaps join a group of students to discuss the crisis?_____
_____
_____

46. What type of coping strategies have you used in the past? Which ones have worked well and which ones did not help you as much? _____
_____
_____

47. Are you currently involved in any activities that you enjoy? _____
_____
_____

48. When you have free time, what do you enjoy doing? _____
_____
_____

49. What strategies do you think you will use or can use to help you cope with this crisis?_____
_____
_____

50. Do you think you have learned anything from the crisis that will help to make you a stronger person?
_____
_____

Summary *[Is response in proportion to degree of exposure? Is the student over- or underreacting to the crisis?]* _____
_____
_____
_____
_____
_____
_____
_____
_____
_____
_____

Note. From *School Crisis Prevention and Intervention: The PREPaRE Model*, pp. 164–167, by S. E. Brock et al., 2009, Bethesda, MD: NASP. Copyright 2009 by the National Association of School Psychologists. Based on APA (2013), Brock et al. (2001), and the Los Angeles Unified School District (1994).

TERTIARY ASSESSMENT OF PSYCHOLOGICAL TRAUMA

The tertiary assessment of psychological trauma takes place during the concluding stages of the school's mental health crisis intervention response (in some cases weeks after crisis event stressors have ended). This assessment level continues to evaluate known crisis facts and individual characteristics (or risk factors) and to monitor individual crisis reactions (or warning signs), and it is designed to identify the minority of individuals for whom the school's immediate mental health crisis intervention response was insufficient. This level has as its primary goals (a) the identification of those students who appear to require psychotherapeutic treatment and (b) the making of appropriate referrals. Important to this level of triage is knowing who were identified as needing, and who were provided, one or more of the more immediate mental health crisis interventions (discussed in Chapters 15 to 18).

Especially following major disasters, the crisis intervention and student care group requires a tool for tracking the large numbers of school community members who are potential psychological trauma victims. Figure 14.7 provides a Psychological Triage Summary Sheet (developed by Brock et al., 2001), which helps document students who were brought to the attention of crisis interveners following a crisis event. In addition to listing crisis intervention treatment priorities, this form also allows crisis interveners to quickly view the general psychological trauma risk factors, identify crisis intervention group members who have been responsible for providing mental health crisis intervention services, and document each individual's current intervention status. Finally, it also documents any parental contacts that have been made.

Generally speaking, this level of triage is focused on individuals with severe or potentially dangerous crisis reactions and those whose reactions do not lessen with the passage of time. Sometimes students' crisis intervention needs are beyond what the school can provide, and community-based mental health resources are required. This level of triage also can rule out intervention for trauma-exposed individuals who do not manifest symptoms after approximately 2 months. According to the National Institute of Mental Health (2001), these individuals "generally do not require follow-up" (p. 9). Consistent with this conclusion, a review of the literature found that delayed onset PTSD, in the absence of any previous symptoms, is rare (Andrews, Brewin, Philpott, & Stewart, 2007).

Returning one last time to the example of a teacher's death in a car accident, the psychological triage summary sheet can be used to help identify and monitor students and school staff members who are having significant difficulty coping with this loss. To the extent that these challenges continue unabated for over a week, concern about the need for psychotherapeutic assistance increases. The tertiary assessment activities in this example may take place weeks, months, and in rare circumstances even a year or more after this teacher's death.

CONCLUSION

Before moving on to the specific school-based mental health crisis interventions discussed in Chapters 15 through 19, this chapter describes the evaluation of psychological trauma that is prerequisite to the provision of these interventions. Figure 14.8 illustrates the relationship between the crisis event, the evaluation of psychological trauma, assessed trauma risk levels, and specific

Figure 14.7. Psychological Triage Summary Sheet

Psychological Triage Summary Sheet
(Confidential, for School Crisis Team use only)

Date	Name	Teacher	Risk Rating[1]	Risk Category[2]	Crisis Intervener	Parental Contact[3]	Status[4]
1.							
2.							
3.							
4.							
5.							
6.							
7.							
8.							
9.							
10.							
11.							
12.							
13.							
14.							
15.							
16.							
17.							
18.							
19.							
20.							

[1] Record initial risk screening rating from the Primary Risk Screening Form.
[2] Record the risk category(ies) that is likely to have caused psychological trauma. Category Codes: V = victim; I = directly involved; W = witness; F = familiarity with victim(s); MI = preexisting mental illness; DIm = developmental immaturity; TH = trauma history; R = lack of resources; Em = severe emotional reactions; PT = perceived threat.
[3] Record information regarding parental contact. Parental Contact Codes: SM = attended school meeting; HV = home visit; Ph = phone contact.
[4] Record information regarding the current need for crisis intervention services and support. Status Codes: A = active (currently being seen); W/C = watch and consult (not currently being seen); Ft = needs follow-up; I/A = inactive (not being seen and no follow-up is judged to be needed); PT = community-based psychotherapeutic treatment referral (immediate crisis intervention not sufficient).

Note. This form is used to assist in the documentation of psychological triage decisions; also for use in conjunction with the Primary Risk Screening Form in Figure 14.3. From *Preparing for Crises in the Schools* (p. 140), by S. E. Brock, J. Sandoval, and S. Lewis, 2001, New York, NY: Wiley. Copyright 2001 by John Wiley & Sons. Adapted with permission.

school-based mental health crisis interventions. As the figure illustrates, after a crisis event occurs, the first steps are to (1) reaffirm physical health (i.e., make sure school community members actually are safe) and (2) ensure perceptions of safety and security (i.e., make sure school community members believe they are safe). As soon as possible, and necessarily before providing mental health crisis intervention, the next step is to (3) evaluate psychological trauma risk. Using primary risk assessments, the crisis intervention and student care group (4) makes initial decisions regarding crisis interventions. As initial interventions are provided, the degree of psychological injury is reevaluated (5) and more informed crisis intervention decisions are made.

Figure 14.8. Relationship Between the Evaluation of Psychological Trauma and the Specific Crisis Interventions Suggested by Obtained Data

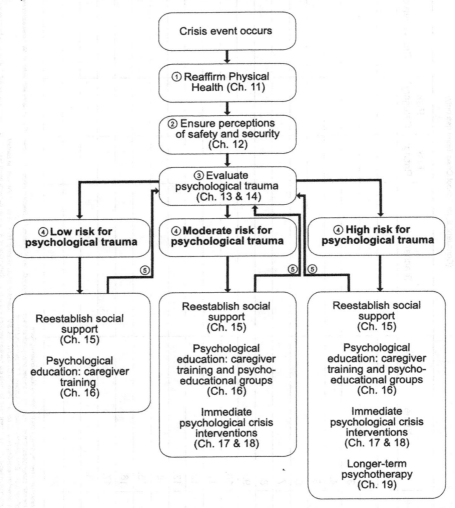

Note. Adapted from *School Crisis Prevention and Intervention: The PREPaRE Model* (p. 169), by S. E. Brock et al., 2009, Bethesda, MD: NASP. Copyright 2009 by the National Association of School Psychologists. Adapted with permission.

Section 5

PROVIDE INTERVENTIONS AND RESPOND

The fourth element of the PREPaRE model (the "PaR" in the PREPaRE acronym) refers to providing interventions and responding to psychological needs. After physical health and safety have been reaffirmed, schools use data provided by the evaluation of psychological trauma risk to provide affected students (and their caregivers) with specific interventions. The PREPaRE model offers three general classes of mental health crisis intervention: (a) social support, (b) psychological education, and (c) psychological intervention. As illustrated in Figure 1.3, these interventions may begin as soon as the immediate threat of a crisis ends, during the recoil phase. Most occur during the postimpact phase. However, some interventions may take place months or years after a crisis, that is, during the recovery and reconstruction phase (Raphael & Newman, 2000; Valent, 2000). In rare instances, severe crisis reactions can have a delayed onset. In addition, crisis anniversaries (e.g., the 1-year anniversary of the crisis event or the birthday of a crisis victim) often renew individuals' crisis reactions, potentially requiring mental health crisis intervention assistance.

The interventions described in this section are delivered as soon as possible to individuals who have been affected by a crisis, and as such are consistent with what Caplan (1964) has identified as secondary prevention. These interventions are directed toward individuals within the school community who are judged to have at least some risk for being psychological trauma victims, and they include the approaches designed to respond to individuals who have signs or symptoms of psychological trauma or who are judged to have a predisposition for being traumatized (high level of risk). As illustrated in Figure S5.1, PREPaRE conceptualizes school mental health crisis interventions as employing a multitiered system of support consistent with Gordon's (1983) three levels of intervention: universal, selected, and indicated. Universal interventions (or Tier 1) are provided to all individuals who have a risk of psychological trauma (e.g., from physical or emotional proximity to a crisis event). Selected interventions (or Tier 2) are provided to individuals who are judged to be moderately to severely traumatized. Indicated interventions (Tier 3) are provided to individuals who are judged to be severely traumatized.

Figure S5.1. Levels of School-Based Crisis Interventions, From Least (Tier 1) to Most (Tier 3) Restrictive

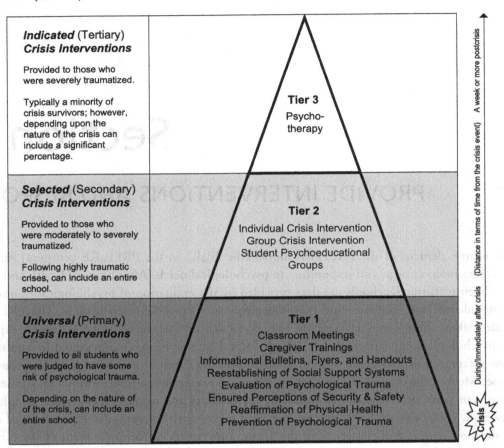

Note. Adapted from "Best Practices for School Psychologists as Members of Crisis Teams: The PREPaRE Model" (p. 1495), by S. E. Brock, A. B. Nickerson, M. A. Reeves, and S. R. Jimerson. In A. Thomas and J. Grimes (Eds.), *Best Practices in School Psychology V*, 2008, Bethesda, MD: NASP. Copyright 2008 by the National Association of School Psychologists. Adapted with permission.

School-employed mental health crisis interveners should first use the least restrictive level of crisis intervention (Tier 1) to avoid interfering with natural recovery mechanisms (such as naturally occurring social support systems).

The elements of PREPaRE that have been discussed so far—prevention of psychological trauma (Chapter 10), reaffirmation of physical health, (Chapter 11), ensuring of perceptions of safety and security (Chapter 12), and evaluation of psychological trauma risk (Chapters 13 and 14)—all fall into the category of universal intervention. Assuming that the school-employed mental health professionals have reason to believe that all the school's students and staff members have been exposed to a given crisis event, these interventions would be provided on a universal, or school-wide, basis.

This section adds four interventions to the category of universal intervention: reestablishing support systems (Chapter 15) and, from the four psychoeducational interventions in Chapter 16, disseminating information, providing caregiver training, and leading classroom meetings. The chapters in this section also examine three mental health crisis interventions that might be considered Tier 2, or selected interventions: student psychoeducational groups (Chapter 16) and group and individual crisis intervention (Chapters 17 and 18, respectively). Finally, this section concludes with a review of some Tier 3, or indicated, crisis interventions that are offered to individuals who have been severely traumatized and require longer-term professional mental health assistance (Chapter 19).

The reestablishment of naturally occurring social support systems (Chapter 15) is a primary, or universal, mental health crisis intervention that is consistent with the psychological first aid approach's core action of connecting with social supports (Brymer et al., 2006; Brymer, Taylor, et al., 2012). For many (and in some cases most) students exposed to a school-associated crisis event, these resources, which include parents, other caregivers such as teachers, and peers, are sufficient in promoting adaptive coping. However, for others, simply reconnecting them with their support systems may be insufficient. Thus, Chapter 16 discusses psychological education, which is consistent with the psychological first aid core action of providing information on coping (Brymer et al., 2006). Chapters 17, 18, and 19 offer discussions of PREPaRE's psychological interventions. Chapters 17 and 18 discuss the group and individual approaches to mental health crisis intervention that a school-employed mental health professional might use when directly intervening with traumatized students. These interventions would typically employ all of the core actions of psychological first aid (i.e., making contact and engaging the individual, verifying their safety and comfort, stabilizing as needed, gathering information about needs and current concerns, providing practical assistance, facilitating connections with social supports, providing information on coping, and if necessary, linking the individual to other services; Brymer et al., 2006; Brymer, Taylor, et al., 2012). Finally, Chapter 19 reviews the psychotherapeutic treatment options that highly traumatized students will require. Typically offered to a minority of individuals exposed to a school-associated crisis event, the mental health interventions discussed in Chapter 19 may not be offered in the school setting and may require community-based mental health resources.

Chapter 15

REESTABLISH SOCIAL SUPPORT SYSTEMS

Long before school mental health crisis interventions became part of the professional literature, teachers, students, and their families found ways to cope with adversity, and this typically involved using naturally occurring social support systems. Reestablishing students' social support systems is one of the oldest and arguably the most powerful mental health crisis intervention. Numerous studies have documented that the presence of social support reduces the risk for traumatic stress and other negative mental health outcomes following school crises (e.g., Banks & Weems, 2014; Charuvastra & Cloitre, 2008; Dyb et al., 2014; Haden, Scarpa, Jones, & Ollendick, 2007; Hahn, Hays, Kahn, Litwin, & Ganz, 2014; Ma et al., 2011; Trickey, Siddaway, Meiser-Stedman, Serpell, & Field, 2012; Zhang, Jiang, Ho, & Wu, 2011). This chapter defines social support and reviews relevant theory and research about its importance in fostering recovery following potentially traumatic events. It also presents practical suggestions for reestablishing social support after crises and reviews the limitations of, or barriers to, establishing social support. All of the strategies for reestablishing social support are considered Tier 1 (primary) or universal mental health crisis interventions (see Figure S5.1). Finally, the chapter examines cultural considerations important to reestablishing these support systems.

SOCIAL SUPPORTS: DEFINITION AND IMPORTANCE

Caplan (1974) defined social support as important interpersonal relationships that affect an individual's psychological and social functioning and lead to greater resiliency in the face of adversity. Similarly, Cobb (1976) described social support as information from others indicating that one is loved, cared for, valued, and belongs. More recently, social support has been defined as "an individual's perception that he or she is loved or cared for, esteemed, and valued by people in his or her social network, which enhances personal functioning, assists in coping adequately with stressors, and may buffer him or her from adverse outcomes" (Demaray, Malecki, Davidson, Hodgson, & Rebus, 2005, p. 691; Kerres Malecki & Kilpatrick Demaray, 2002). In exploring the concept of social support, mental health professionals have made distinctions between (a) social embeddedness, which refers to the structural components of support (size of network, level of activity, and closeness); (b) received support; and (c) perceived support (or one's sense of belonging and belief that support is available; Norris, Friedman, et al., 2002).

Despite differences in definitions, social support is accepted as being important to positive adjustment. According to Pfefferbaum and Shaw (2013), "Social support . . . is essential throughout all phases of a disaster. Providers [of crisis intervention assistance] should help families to access social supports and use community resources" (p. 1230). More specifically, they recommend, "children should be encouraged to talk to parents, teachers, and other caretakers" (p. 1230).

Two primary theoretical frameworks attempt to explain how social support influences adjustment: the main effect hypothesis and the stress-buffering model. The *main effect hypothesis* asserts that all people, regardless of the amount of stress they experience, benefit from social support (Cohen, Gottlieb, & Underwood, 2001; Cohen & Wills, 1985). According to this hypothesis, accessible social support provides individuals with ongoing opportunities to experience positive, stable, and socially rewarding interactions with others in their community (Cohen & Wills, 1985; Joseph, 1999). Indeed, research reveals that social support has a positive impact on an individual's mental health (Cohen et al., 2001; Galand & Hospel, 2013). For example, higher quantities of, and fewer disruptions to, social support in early childhood are associated with fewer internalizing and externalizing behaviors over time (Appleyard, Egeland, & Sroufe, 2007). Further, among seventh and eighth graders, perceived social support from parents, teachers, or peers had positive effects on depression, self-efficacy, and school disaffection (Galand & Hospel, 2013).

The other theoretical framework is the *stress-buffering model*, which asserts that social support may serve as a buffer that protects individuals in stressful situations (Cohen & Wills, 1985; Demaray, Malecki, & DeLong, 2006). According to this model, social support may influence psychological and adjustment outcomes by (a) preventing an individual from responding in a way that would exacerbate a typically stressful event, or (b) reducing the number of physiological responses experienced during the situation, thereby preventing the onset of maladjusted outcomes (Cohen & Wills, 1985; Frey & Röthlisberger, 1996; House, 1981). Although some support for this model is found in the literature, most studies tend to support the main effect model (Galand & Hospel, 2013).

Social support comes from multiple sources. Cauce, Felner, and Primavera (1982) identified three major sources of potential support for children: family; formal support (e.g., teachers, therapists); and informal support (e.g., friends, other adults). In House's (1981) description (used by Malecki and Demaray, 2003), sources of social support include parents, teachers, classmates, and close friends. Not only does a child's developmental level affect how he or she will react to crisis events, but it also influences who are the most important social support providers. Specifically, younger children tend to primarily rely on family members such as parents and grandparents for social support (Frey & Röthlisberger, 1996; Furman & Buhrmester, 1992), whereas adolescents have begun to rely more on peers, extended family members, and romantic partners for support (Furman & Buhrmester, 1992; Levitt, Guacci-Franco, & Levitt, 1993; Levitt et al., 2005; Nickerson & Nagle, 2005). In a study of Spanish adolescents (ages 12–18 years), Hombrados-Mendieta, Gomez-Jacinto, Dominguez-Fuentes, Garcia-Leiva, and Castro-Travé (2012) reported that for youth age 15 and older, the support of classmates became equal to or greater than that provided by parents. However, for Spanish youth age 14 years and younger, the mother was viewed as the main provider of social support.

Hombrados-Mendieta et al. (2012) also examined the different types of support that might be offered by parents, classmates, and teachers. Specifically, they collected data on who provided emotional support to the adolescents they studied (i.e., giving affect and listening when the adolescent wants to talk and express feelings); instrumental support (i.e., is willing to do specific things for the adolescent, such as helping with homework or other activities); and informational support (i.e., providing the adolescent with helpful tips and information to address problems and tasks). Among students ages 12 to 18, parents were viewed as providing mostly emotional and instrumental support, peers as providing informational and emotional support, and teachers as primarily providing informational support. Of these different types of support, informational support was most frequently provided and appreciated by the adolescents studied.

Teacher support has been reported to decline as a child grows older. In secondary school, students' ability to connect with several teachers might not be as realistic, compared with the elementary school environment, when children typically have one teacher (Furman & Buhrmester, 1992). However, contemporary initiatives to develop small learning communities in middle schools and high schools are an example of efforts to build social support within the secondary school context, and positive outcomes have resulted among students and teachers (Cotton, 2001; Oxley, 2001, 2004; Raywid, 1996). So although teachers potentially are not as powerful a social support system for students at the secondary school level, middle and high school teachers should not be overlooked as providers of such assistance.

Evidence supporting the importance of the secondary teacher as a provider of social support is offered by Joyce and Early (2014). Using data from the National Longitudinal Study of Adolescent Health (from a sample that included 11,852 adolescents from 132 different schools), their study found that school connectedness and feeling cared about by teachers had protective effects against symptoms of depression. Regarding school connectedness, students agreed (or disagreed) with the following statements: "I feel close to people at this school," "I feel like I am part of this school," "Students at your school are prejudiced," "I am happy to be at this school," and "I feel safe in my school." Feeling cared about by teachers was measured by the following questions: "Since school started this year, how often have you had trouble getting along with your teachers?" and "How much do you feel that your teachers care about you?" This protective effect against depression was especially important for youth from ethnic minority backgrounds.

In light of the potent influence of social support, it is not surprising that an individual's recovery from trauma is aided by the availability of those supports (Galek, Flannelly, Greene, & Kudler, 2011; Kaniasty, 2012; Litz, Gray, Bryant, & Adler, 2002). Low levels of social support following crises have been found to be strong predictors of posttraumatic stress disorder (PTSD), whereas higher levels are associated with a lower likelihood of developing this mental illness (Hahn et al., 2014; Ozer, Best, Lipsey, & Weiss, 2003). Furthermore, lower levels of support are related to more severe traumatic stress symptoms in children exposed to chronic violence (Jones, 2007), and social support serves as a strong moderator for acute and long-term mental health problems in children exposed to trauma (Caffo & Belaise, 2003). In one study, the importance of encouraging students to use their social support systems was demonstrated following a natural disaster. Specifically, the levels of depression among third, fourth, and fifth graders were lower among those students who had sought out social support relative to those who did not seek such assistance (Jeney-Gammon, Daugherty, Finch, Belter, & Foster, 1993).

In addition to actual social support, perceptions of such support from friends and family have been found to mediate the relationship between child maltreatment and the development of a variety of positive outcomes, such as trust, autonomy, and intimacy (Pepin & Banyard, 2006). The perception of social support has also been linked to positive outcomes for children facing many different life circumstances, such as those classified as at risk or disadvantaged (Cauce et al., 1982; VanTassel-Baska, Olszewski-Kubilius, & Kulieke, 1994) and those with a history of sexual abuse (Asberg & Renk, 2014; Tremblay, Hébert, & Piché, 1999). Perception of support also is linked to a resiliency factor that is protective against suicide (Kleiman, Riskind, & Schaefer, 2014; Kleiman, Riskind, Schaefer, & Weingarden, 2012). Conversely, the lack of perceived support from adults and peers is a risk factor for victimization (Brock, Nickerson, O'Malley, & Chang, 2006; Duncan, 2004; Hazler & Carney, 2000). For example, victims of bullying and school violence report lower levels of perceived support from teachers and peers than do nonvictims (Furlong, Chung, Bates, & Morrison, 1995; Rigby, 2000). In addition, bullies, victims, and bully-victims with moderate peer support report the lowest levels of anxiety and depression (Holt & Espelage, 2007), although other research has found that peer and parent support are insufficient to mitigate the strong negative effects of bullying (Rothon, Head, Klineberg, & Stansfeld, 2011). Lower perceived social support has also been associated with suicidal ideation (Endo et al., 2014; Miller, Esposito-Smythers, & Leichtweis, 2015; Rigby & Slee, 1999).

REESTABLISHMENT OF SOCIAL SUPPORT AFTER A CRISIS

Given expectations for recovery following exposure to a crisis event (National Institute of Mental Health [NIMH], 2001), reestablishing and empowering naturally occurring social support systems should be a primary crisis intervention (Berliner, Gongóra, & Espaillat, 2011; Brock & Jimerson, 2004; Litz et al., 2002; Norris, Byrne, Diaz, & Kaniasty, 2002; Shalev, Tuval-Mashiach, & Hadar, 2004). Both children and parents are likely to identify family members as the greatest source of support in times of crisis (Horowitz, McKay, & Marshall, 2005), and often just allowing this support to happen is the only intervention required (Barenbaum, Ruchkin, & Schwab-Stone, 2004). Generally, with appropriate support from these resources, the vast majority of children demonstrate positive adjustment over time (Gist & Lubin, 1999). Consequently, all other school crisis interventions should complement the assets of naturally occurring social support systems and be prepared to pick up where they leave off. As noted by Berkowitz (2003) and addressed in Chapter 13, providing highly directive crisis intervention assistance when it is not required may unintentionally and inaccurately communicate to families and other support systems that they are inadequate in aiding students' adaptive coping.

A variety of specific techniques might reestablish naturally occurring social support systems (see Table 15.1). These techniques include reuniting students with their caregivers, friends, teachers, and classmates, and returning students to familiar school environments and routines.

Table 15.1. Activities That Schools May Consider to Help Foster Social Support

- Reunite students with their caregivers and close friends.
- Reunite students with their teachers and classmates.
- Return students to familiar school environments and routines.
- Empower caregivers with crisis recovery information.
- Make get well or condolence cards for the victims and victims' families.
- Provide Caregiver Training (see Chapter 16).
- Structure classroom discussions to focus on tolerance and caring for each other.
- Support communications between students and families, and with community agencies and organizations, to help them get access to resources and aid.
- Encourage and teach the appropriate use of social media to gain social support.
- Monitor the levels and consistency of available social supports in the weeks following a crisis.

Note. Adapted from *School Crisis Prevention and Intervention: The PREPaRE Model*, p. 178, by S. E. Brock et al., 2009, Bethesda, MD: NASP. Copyright 2009 by the National Association of School Psychologists. Adapted with permission.

Schools also can help connect families with individuals, agencies, and other community-based organizations. Finally, specific techniques for reestablishing natural social support systems should include giving caregivers information on crisis recovery that empowers them and maximizes their caregiving potential.

Reuniting Students With Primary Caregivers

Following school-associated crises, children should be reunited with their primary caregivers and families as soon as practically possible. This reunification is especially important for younger preschool and primary-grade students (Brock & Jimerson, 2004). Children's separation from primary caregivers during crises can have long-term emotional effects (McFarlane, 1987; Wilson, Raphael, Meldrum, Bedosky, & Sigman, 2000), and fewer symptoms of PTSD have been observed among children living with their families compared with those separated from their families (Yorbik, Akbiyik, Kirmizigul, & Söhmen, 2004).

As noted in Chapter 9's discussion of the Reunification Annex, to reunite children and families efficiently, schools must have plans and policies in place so that these practices can be implemented during crises (Joshi & Lewin, 2004). Schools must keep accurate and updated emergency cards to know how to contact primary caregivers in the event of an emergency. These records should also include a list of names of other caregivers authorized to pick up a student if primary caregivers (e.g., parents) cannot be reached.

For example, the Montgomery County Public Schools (n.d.) crisis response plan emphasizes informing caregivers not to go to the school during crises, which allows the school to assess the situation and activate the appropriate crisis response procedures. This provision is important because the process and sites for reunification may vary depending on the nature of the crisis. In the case of a hazardous chemical release, the students would be evacuated, and parents coming to the school would be placed in danger and unable to reunite with their children. Schools should have several means of notifying parents of emergencies, such as an automated emergency communication system (e.g., *Connect*-ED or Blackboard Connect, [http://www.blackboardconnect.com/default.asp?z=20080603135825]), e-mail, the school Internet site, local media, reverse 911, and phone trees. Social media may also prove to be a helpful tool for such communication (Flitsch, Magnesi, & Brock, 2012).

When an event affects the community outside the school, the school's plan also must cover reunifying staff and teachers with their own children and family members after their crisis response duties are completed. Teachers and other school personnel are often torn between wanting to help their students and ensuring the safety and security of their own loved ones. This situation becomes especially challenging if the crisis response requires them to stay beyond normal contract hours. Staff members' emergency cards should have contact information for their own children's school, in case a staff member is unable to pick up his or her own child.

As presented in Chapter 9, implementing an orderly and efficient process for reunifying students and caregivers is important. This process includes posting signs to direct parents through the process and having crisis response team members available to receive and direct parents arriving at the reunification area, verify that an individual is authorized to pick up a student, and escort students to meet their parents (Montgomery County Public Schools, n.d.). When reuniting students with their caregivers, schools must have someone present who is familiar with families' language and culture to ensure effective communication (Barenbaum et al., 2004). Having close working relationships between schools and cultural and religious leaders in the community can be very helpful in this regard, so that when a crisis occurs, these leaders can help facilitate communication and provide support.

In some crisis situations (e.g., natural disasters), children may be separated from their primary caregivers by conditions beyond the school's control, which places them at greater risk of injury. For example, during and after Hurricanes Katrina and Rita, more than 5,000 children were separated from their families. As the community tried to quickly get people to safety, many families were separated and ended up in different locations as they moved from their homes to the evacuation centers and elsewhere. These situations called for large-scale planning and coordination. After Hurricane Katrina, the National Center for Missing and Exploited Children activated the Katrina Missing Persons Hotline and handled 32,716 calls (Broughton, Allen, Hannemann, & Petrikin, 2006).

Reuniting Students With Peers and Teachers

Peers and teachers are also important providers of social support. With the onset of early adolescence, peers become an even greater source of support (J. P. Allen & Land, 1999; Hombrados-Mendieta et al., 2012). For instance, although fourth graders were much more likely to report turning to a parent rather than a peer when feeling upset, eighth graders were twice as likely to report turning to a peer rather than a parent (Nickerson & Nagle, 2005). Similarly, from a sample of 243 children (ages 8–17 years; $M = 11.3$, $SD = 2.5$) who had traffic-related injuries, Marsac, Donlon, Hildenbrand, Winston, and Kassam-Adams (2014) found that students reported almost universally (97%) that their peers helped them cope with their injuries by encouraging a return to normal activities.

Furthermore, study participants reported that their friends had helped by providing distractions (79%) or by helping them emotionally process the events (60%). From these findings, Marsac et al. (2014) suggest that caregivers consider integrating important peers into the child's recovery.

Morley and Kohrt (2013) conducted another study documenting the importance of peers to children's recovery from traumatic stress. Their study of child soldiers in a postwar civilian environment found that peer support was associated with higher levels of hope, lower levels of functional impairment, and lower levels of traumatic stress. Conversely, problematic peer relations were associated with less hope and greater symptoms of traumatic stress. From these findings, Morley and Kohrt (2013) suggested that maximizing peer support should be made a priority when addressing the consequences of experiences such as having been a child soldier.

Together, these findings highlight the importance of positive peer relationships and specific ways that friends may provide support, such as providing distractions and helping youth to emotionally process the event. Opportunities for peer interaction should be structured and well supervised (e.g., through recreational activities, focused art activities) to promote supportive peer relationships (Swick, Dechant, & Jellinek, 2002). This method may be important given findings that middle school girls in an urban area reported that they did not trust peers, and boys said they relied on membership in gangs for support (Horowitz et al., 2005). Adults can take an active role in ensuring that the support offered by peers will be helpful and productive, as opposed to compounding the problem.

Teachers can also be important providers of social support for many students (Hombrados-Mendieta et al., 2012; Joyce & Early, 2014; Klingman, 2001; Vernberg, La Greca, Silverman, & Prinstein, 1996). Supportive relationships with teachers are important predictors of the psychological well-being of students who have been traumatized (Barenbaum et al., 2004). Therefore, in the hours, days, and weeks following a crisis, making provisions for students to access these supports is important. For instance, after a crisis, some schools open their doors for staff and students to congregate during nonschool hours to give them opportunities to provide support to each other. Designing activities that focus students' attention away from the negative emotions caused by a trauma may also be helpful (Prinstein, La Greca, Vernberg, & Silverman, 1996). However, teachers should remember to maintain appropriate professional boundaries with students, such as not inviting students to gather at the teacher's home.

When physically reconnecting students with their teachers and peers at school is not possible, an alternative is to consider using social media to provide social support (Flitsch et al., 2012). Longman, O'Connor, and Obst (2009) reported that social support can be derived from online sources. More recently, Indian and Grieve (2014) suggested that Facebook may be a preferred means of obtaining social support (relative to face-to-face interactions) for individuals who are socially anxious.

Returning Students to Familiar Environments and Routines

Restoring structured education by returning students to familiar environments and routines following crises helps establish stability and continuity (Barenbaum et al., 2004; Moscardino, Axia, Scrimin, & Capello, 2007). The school setting provides predictable routines, as well as consistent rules for behavior, which help promote a sense of safety and predictability (Barenbaum et al., 2004;

Cole et al., 2005; Demaree, 1994). The tasks and responsibilities assigned to students within the school environment can also be designed to help them cope and avoid isolation (Barenbaum et al., 2004). Therefore, getting the school ready to be occupied after a crisis (e.g., natural disaster) and identifying alternate locations for schooling, such as a neighboring school or community center, should be a top priority of schools and school districts.

A return to community routines and familiar environments is important to recovery, as evidenced by the association of reduced community disruption with less stress following traumatic events (Brymer et al., 2006). Ungar (2011) asserted that aspects of the community's social and physical ecology are more important to resilience than the individual qualities of its members. Thus, nurturing individual and community resilience requires a complex set of interrelated processes—physical, natural, financial, human, and social—for helping community members to navigate the resources they need to care for others after a crisis.

Crisis situations are less traumatic when disruptions to family life are minimized (Kolaitis et al., 2003), as the highest risk of psychopathology comes when families are displaced or disrupted (Caffo & Belaise, 2003). In addition to physically returning children to their homes, schools, and communities, reconnecting children with the traditions, culture, and spiritual practices that were part of their lives prior to the crisis is helpful in reaffirming hope for the future (Barenbaum et al., 2004). Parents often want to minimize the expectations placed on children after they have been through a traumatic event; however, routine, structure, and familiarity are essential in helping children know that they will recover and life will go on.

Having a sense of community, characterized by cohesion, participation, and safety, is helpful in building resilience (Joshi & Lewin, 2004). For example, survivors of the Columbine High School shooting reported that they were helped by the feeling that a large network of community support was available to them. Concrete indicators of this support included people wearing ribbons to represent the school and memorials in the form of posters, cards, and flowers (Hawkins, McIntosh, Silver, & Holman, 2004). Even though survivors grieve in different ways and may not all agree on outward expression of grief, community solidarity can greatly support the grieving process.

Tangible forms of support from extended family and community members can also be very helpful for parents who need to focus on being physically and emotionally available for their children (Swick et al., 2002). After a school shooting, parents reported that child care, prepared meals, and necessary supplies were helpful in relieving normal household responsibilities (Hawkins et al., 2004). In some situations, having a member of the extended family move in or move closer can provide additional support (Swick et al., 2002). The conclusion to be drawn from all this evidence is that mobilizing powerful, inclusive, and long-lasting community support within indigenous networks should be a primary objective of school crisis response and intervention (Norris, Byrne, et al., 2002).

Empowering Caregivers With Knowledge

The goal of reestablishing natural social supports presumes that caregivers are willing and able to provide the support needed for children to recover from their crisis exposure. Because of the importance of social support in aiding recovery from psychological trauma, caregivers must be given the knowledge they need to realize the potential of that support. Doing so is important because primary caregivers often underestimate the traumatic stress being experienced by their children (Pfefferbaum & Shaw, 2013). As discussed further in Chapter 16, psychoeducation with caregivers focuses on anticipated reactions to traumatic events, signs of potential problems that deserve further attention, and ways parents can respond appropriately to their children.

Mental health practitioners and educators generally agree that caregivers should respond by listening and understanding when children and adolescents express their fear, anger, and distress about what has happened (Barenbaum et al., 2004; Grosse, 2001; Heath & Sheen, 2005). In addition, in the weeks following a crisis, caregivers should spend more time with their children and try to be a calming influence. Maintaining clear, consistent, and developmentally appropriate limits for behavior is also important in promoting a sense of safety and predictability (Cole et al., 2005; Swick et al., 2002). In terms of specific behaviors that are helpful, adolescent survivors from the Columbine High School shooting reported that spending time talking with and being hugged by others was helpful (Hawkins et al., 2004).

LIMITATIONS OR BARRIERS TO SOCIAL SUPPORT

Although naturally occurring social support systems are very powerful, they do have their limitations (Rothon et al., 2011). The most obvious and devastating challenge is when the crisis results in the death or loss of the child's source of social support (Eksi et al., 2007; Norris, Friedman, et al., 2002). As discussed in Chapter 13, children who have a family member or close friend die are at especially high risk for posttraumatic stress disorder (PTSD; NIMH, 2001). For children, the death of a parent is especially traumatic. Following 9/11, of the students in the New York City public schools who lost a parent, 52% had PTSD (Applied Research and Consulting et al., 2002).

Another important consideration is that more significant trauma exposure reduces the ability of social supports to protect children or adolescents from traumatic stress. Banks and Weems (2014) studied over 1,000 school-age youth (ages 7–18 years) who attended schools in New Orleans neighborhoods that were significantly damaged and almost totally flooded following Hurricane Katrina. Results suggested that high hurricane exposure (e.g., those responding yes to questions such as "Did you get hurt during the hurricane?" or "Was your home badly damaged or destroyed by the hurricane?") appeared to lower the positive effects of peer support in preventing the development of symptoms of traumatic stress (relative to study participants who had lower levels of hurricane exposure). In other words, these data support the assumption that interventions that reconnect students with their peers following a crisis are more effective for students with less exposure to the crisis than for those with greater crisis exposure. Banks and Weems (2014) therefore concluded that "the effect of high hurricane exposure may overwhelm the benefit of peer social support against the development of PTSD symptoms for some youth" (p. 350).

Another challenge is faced by caregivers who may need financial, emotional, and other assistance (Swick et al., 2002), which underscores the importance of schools developing collaborative relationships with community support agencies. Caregivers who survive a crisis may have been traumatized, which limits their own capacity to provide the support needed for their child (Norris, Friedman, et al., 2002). For example, exposure to life-threatening conditions or chronic exposure to a crisis may result in psychological distress or psychopathology that inhibits a caregiver's capacity to share experiences with their child or be sensitive and encouraging (Qouta, Punamäki, & El Sarraj, 2005; Yap & Devilly, 2004). In such cases, to help the child, the caregiver must be helped first.

The ability to reestablish social support is sometimes limited when that offered support is not perceived by the recipient as helpful. Pepin and Banyard (2006) found that although *perceived* social support from friends and family was highly related to positive developmental outcomes, the same relationship was not found for *received* support. Therefore caregivers should avoid providing support that is judged as unhelpful. For example, in a qualitative study of survivors of a school shooting, adolescent survivors reported that the following types of support were not helpful: (a) requests from parents to talk about things, with parents then quickly becoming angry; (b) parents' attempts to overprotect or smother (e.g., screening calls, offering unwelcome gestures); and (c) efforts to get students to talk about the incident, particularly in structured counseling settings (Hawkins et al., 2004).

Naturally occurring social support systems may also be insufficient to meet the needs of children and adolescents with preexisting mental health challenges. Such supports are not irrelevant for these high-risk students; in fact, social supports may be especially important for individuals with such challenges, but in the context of more targeted crisis interventions. For example, in a national study of adolescents following 9/11, Gil-Rivas, Holman, and Silver (2004) found that adolescents with a history of mental health difficulties needed greater parental support to help them use adaptive coping strategies and to regulate their emotional responses. However, these children and adolescents may have also needed additional supports, such as psychotherapeutic treatments, as discussed in Chapter 19.

Although social support received in a community context can lead to a greater sense of cohesion, trust in the goodness of others, and mutual helping, experience has established that such support often deteriorates beyond the immediate aftermath of a disaster. Survivors may begin to feel bitter and disappointed that they are not receiving the help they need, a situation that may arise when those providing support are also affected and cannot keep up with others' need for help. Competition for resources also can exacerbate preexisting social inequities. This potential strain points to the need for response and recovery efforts that, if they are to contribute to a sense of social cohesion and trust, not only *are* efficient and generous but also *appear* to the survivors to be equitable, transparent, and helpful (Kaniasty, 2012).

CULTURAL CONSIDERATIONS

Several cultural considerations are relevant to reestablishing social support after a crisis. For instance, racial and ethnic differences have been found in students' perceptions of the need for and importance of social support (Cauce et al., 1982; Demaray & Malecki, 2002). The different cultural groups of which students' families may be a part have different values, beliefs, and preferences for accessing social support, and those differences should be acknowledged and respected by schools seeking to support students and families after a crisis. For example, although African Americans have faced ongoing challenges with political, economic, and cultural oppression in the United States, Black adolescents have reported perceiving a greater degree of total social support available to them than their White or Hispanic peers report (Cauce et al., 1982).

The source of social support also may differ for different cultural groups. For example, African American children and parents living in urban areas also indicated a clear preference for turning to family members for social support, as opposed to relying on professionals, who are often viewed with distrust (Horowitz et al., 2005). Jones (2007) found that formal kinship support, spirituality, and an Afrocentric perspective were protective factors for African American children exposed to chronic violence. The church and religious community are also important sources of social support for many African Americans (Kim & McKenry, 1998). In addition, use of collaborative religious coping, which views the self and God as working together to solve problems, is related to resilience among African Americans (Molock, Puri, Matlin, & Barksdale, 2006). Altogether, this research suggests that school-employed mental health professionals seeking to help African American students cope with crises should be particularly aware of the formal kinship support—which may embody values of harmony, interconnectedness, authenticity, and balance—and of the importance of the Black church.

Evidence suggests that the social supports needed by many Asian Americans also differ from the dominant culture. Asian American children and adults have reported perceiving less social support than White children (Demaray & Malecki, 2002; Liang & Bogat, 1994; Wellisch et al., 1999). Within many traditional Asian American families, members have highly interdependent roles within a cohesive patriarchal structure (Harrison, Wilson, Pine, Chan, & Buriel, 1990), and they often believe that needs should be met within the family (Herrick & Brown, 1998; Wellisch et al., 1999). In addition, Asian culture tends to value self-discipline, which may lend itself to self-directed coping (e.g., try harder, control thoughts; Liang & Bogat, 1994), as opposed to eliciting support from friends, which may lead to feelings of vulnerability, indebtedness, or obligation (Wellisch et al., 1999). A comparative study of Anglo American and Chinese college students found that although social support played a stress-buffering role for Anglo Americans, it did not play a role for Chinese students. In some cases social support had negative stress-buffering effects, such as for Chinese students who had an external locus of control (Liang & Bogat, 1994). When planning interventions, school-employed mental health professionals working with Asian Americans should be aware of the value the culture places on self-discipline and the meeting of needs within the family and on the patriarchal structure present in many Asian American families.

The Hispanic culture is characterized by a strong sense of family, such as family obligations, frequent contact, and family support (Harrison et al., 1990; Zayas, Lester, Cabassa, & Fortuna, 2005). Hispanic families generally provide high levels of emotional support; however, instrumental or informational support may be lacking if parents do not have such resources available (Valle & Bensussen, 1985). Research has also found that despite Hispanic students' reported attempts to receive support from parents and teachers (Morrison, Laughlin, San Miguel, Smith, & Widaman, 1997; Wintre, Hicks, McVey, & Fox, 1988), they reported receiving less social support from teachers than did White students (Demaray & Malecki, 2003). Clearly, Hispanic and Latino students will seek support from families; however, students who are acculturated may also seek support from close friends.

Native Americans reported less frequent total social support and social support from a variety of sources (e.g., parents, teachers, classmates, and close friends), compared with children and adolescents from other ethnic groups. Native American students rated overall total social support or social support provided by a particular source as less important compared with students of other ethnic groups (Demaray & Malecki, 2003). Many Native Americans are at risk for a variety of negative outcomes; however, extensive outreach through formal environments (e.g., health clinics and social welfare programs) and less formal or unconventional environments (e.g., outdoor places where youth congregate, community events, and neighborhood volunteers) has been found helpful in reducing these risks (May, Serna, Hurt, & DeBruyn, 2005).

The preceding discussion of cultural responses to social support interventions includes generalizations and does not apply to all individuals within a given group. However, it is important to offer this discussion to better sensitize readers to the influence culture can have on the provision of social support and crisis intervention. In addition, *culture* can be defined in many different ways. For example, there is a Deaf culture, an LGBTQ culture, and so on. This book's space limitations do not allow an exhaustive treatment of the subject of culture. Nevertheless, it is hoped that this section helps school crisis intervention and student care group members to begin to consider the special issues that culture generates when it comes to the provision of social support.

CONCLUSION

Social support systems have been shown to have a variety of positive outcomes when used as part of schools' crisis interventions following psychological trauma. Therefore, reestablishing and empowering social support systems should be a primary (universal) intervention for schools and their surrounding communities following crises. Reuniting students with their parents or caregivers, peers, and teachers as well as returning students to familiar environments and routines are essential activities following crisis exposure. However, as discussed, cultural differences may make certain social support interventions less effective for some individuals within the school. Therefore interventions aimed at reestablishing social supports should be sensitive to and guided by these important cultural considerations.

Chapter 16

PSYCHOLOGICAL EDUCATION

School mental health crisis interventions that are aimed at providing a student with social support without fostering a sense of empowerment may actually impede the natural recovery process, in part by inadvertently defeating the student's sense of self-efficacy (Howard & Goelitz, 2004). In some instances, mental health crisis intervention may need to do more than simply link students to their family, teachers, and friends; it may need to explicitly teach students and their caregivers what they can do to take care of themselves and others (Phipps & Byrne, 2003). Consistent with this observation, the PREPaRE model includes psychological education (or psychoeducation) as another set of mental health crisis interventions. Most of the interventions offered in this chapter are considered Tier 1, or universal (primary) mental health crisis interventions. However, it is within this group of interventions that the PREPaRE model offers what it considers to be the first of its Tier 2, or selected (secondary) crisis interventions (see Figure S5.1).

PSYCHOEDUCATION: DEFINITION AND IMPORTANCE

Within the context of school mental health crisis intervention, psychological education has been defined by Brock (2011a) as

> The provision of direct instruction and/or the dissemination of information that helps crisis survivors and their caregivers in understanding, preparing for, and responding to the crisis event, and the problems and reactions it generates (both in themselves and among others). (slide 98)

In other words, during the recoil and postimpact phases of a crisis (see Figure 1.3), the primary goal of psychological education is to provide students, and their parents, teachers, and other caregivers, with knowledge that assists them in understanding, preparing for, and responding to the crisis situation, along with the resulting crisis-generated problems and initial crisis reactions. During the recovery and reconstruction phase, these activities also can help predict and prepare the school community for anniversary reactions.

Evidence shows that the parents of children experiencing mental health challenges support psychoeducational interventions (Riebschleger, Onaga, Tableman, & Bybee, 2014). Evidence also shows that for people with mental disorders, enhancing the individual's knowledge using psychological education mitigates depression and anxiety (Shah, Klainin-Yobas, Torres, & Kannusamy, 2014). In addition, meta-analytic research conducted by Van Daele, Hermans, Van Audenhove, and Van den Bergh (2012) concluded that within the general population: "Learning about stress and extending techniques to cope with it seems to contribute positively to mental health" (p. 479). Further, they state that psychological education appears to be effective for a range of developmental levels and personal backgrounds.

Psychological education gives crisis survivors increased control over their recovery process, promotes social support, and teaches coping strategies that let them take a direct, action-oriented approach to addressing their crisis challenges (Hobfoll et al., 2007; Phoenix, 2007; Ruzek et al., 2007; Shah et al., 2014). These strategies are related to a reduced risk of posttraumatic stress (Charuvastra & Cloitre, 2008; Frazier, Steward, & Mortensen, 2004; Stallard & Smith, 2007). They may reduce the stigma associated with mental health interventions, capitalize on personal strengths, and increase individuals' sense of self-worth. Psychological education can also be beneficial by providing early connections to mental health resources (Howard & Goelitz, 2004; Lukens & McFarlane, 2004). An advantage of using psychoeducational approaches following a crisis is that they present individuals with a range of mental health crisis interventions.

Research conducted by Allen, Dlugokinski, Cohen, and Walker (1999) confirms the need for psychological education following crisis exposure. They studied more than 6,000 elementary school children in Oklahoma City following the 1995 bombing of the Murrah Federal Building. These researchers found that younger children needed to be given clear facts about the crisis, because they were the least likely to understand what was going on, were the most likely to be confused, and had the highest number of facts wrong. In addition, this same study highlighted the need to provide students (particularly younger children) with adaptive coping strategies, as this group was most likely to use avoidance as a coping mechanism, which as a long-term coping strategy is associated with negative mental health outcomes (Stallard & Smith, 2007).

Additional reports support the use of psychological education as a mental health crisis intervention strategy (Lukens & McFarlane, 2004; Phoenix, 2007; Sahin, Yilmaz, & Batigun, 2011). According to Brown and Bobrow (2004), "Emerging studies of school-based psycho-educational programs for children exposed to trauma have found improvements in participants' knowledge of trauma and attitudes to risk-taking behavior" (p. 212). Furthermore, the clinical observations of Howard and Goelitz (2004), when they provided psychological education to individuals proximal to and affected by the 2001 World Trade Center disaster, suggest that this intervention has merit. Specifically, they observed that recipients of psychological education were clearly relieved when they learned that their reactions to the crisis event were typical responses to unusual circumstances. In addition, Howard and Goelitz (2004) suggested that "psychoeducation allows the natural recovery process to unfold without over helping the approximately 75% of the population that does not require formalized mental health care" (p. 8).

This chapter offers four examples of psychological education: (a) dissemination of information, such as fact sheets and brochures, (b) Caregiver Training, (c) Classroom Meetings, and (d) Student Psychoeducational Groups. Informational documents and Caregiver Training are primarily designed to help school staff and family members achieve their caregiving potential. Using these interventions, school crisis interveners teach caregivers how best to foster their child's or students' adaptive coping. As described in this chapter, Caregiver Training can be conducted in approximately 45 minutes, although more time should be set aside if a significant number of questions are anticipated. The Classroom Meeting is a relatively recent addition to the PREPaRE model and is from the work of Reeves, Kanan, and Plog (2010). Their firsthand experiences with school crisis intervention emphasize the need to have a universal crisis intervention available that can quickly deliver crisis facts to many different classrooms and thus answer students' questions and dispel rumors.

Of all the psychoeducational options, the Student Psychoeducational Group is the most direct mental health crisis intervention. As illustrated in Figure S5.1, this is the only psychoeducational strategy that is considered a Tier 2, or selected (secondary), mental health crisis intervention. Although this direct instruction approach does not specifically address students' crisis experiences or reactions, it is designed to teach coping techniques and to help identify coping resources (e.g., caregivers, mental health crisis interveners). Schools should devote approximately 60 minutes, or a class period at the secondary school level, to Student Psychoeducational Groups. These groups are typically provided shortly after a crisis event (within a day or two after the event). For example, if a student dies in an accident after school, these groups may take place the morning after the accident. Because psychological education is considered to be instructional, and direct instruction is a routine practice in a school setting, parental consent is typically not required, although informing parents that such lessons will be provided is a good idea.

INFORMATIONAL DOCUMENTS

The first psychological education strategy involves development and dissemination of informational documents to students, caregivers, and others. Typically, these materials are designed to give students and their caregivers facts about the crisis event; advise them about potential crisis effects and how to cope with the event; and identify school, community, and online resources available to help them manage crisis-generated problems (Litz, Gray, Bryant, & Adler, 2002). One example is the initial crisis fact sheet, which may be prepared by the school or district crisis response team and used in Caregiver Training, Classroom Meetings, or Student Psychoeducational Groups.

In the school setting (especially at the elementary school level), these informational documents are primarily aimed at giving caregivers the information they need to help children under their care cope with a crisis. However, at the secondary school level, providing these documents to the students themselves may also be appropriate. The school can make the documents available as printouts sent home with students, on websites, or through e-mail or social media. Print and electronic journalists may also be willing to help disseminate these resources. In schools using the Incident Command System structure, the school's Public Information Officer (Chapter 7) should review and approve the documents before they are distributed to students, families, and the community.

Schools also need to translate all of the materials for families that speak languages other than English. When done well, translation can be time-consuming, so to the extent possible, the documents should be written and translated during planning and preparation for school crisis responses. Brock, Navarro, and Terán (2008) report on their use of a procedure similar to Brislin's (1970) back-translation method. The process began by having a native Spanish speaker translate the original English document (i.e., Jimerson, Brock, & Cowan, 2003) into Spanish. A second native Spanish speaker who did not know the wording of the original English version then translated the document back into English. Next, one of the original English-version authors reviewed the retranslated English version and (using the track changes function) indicated where wording had changed from the original document. Finally, the native Spanish speakers collaborated to make the indicated changes to the Spanish translation and produced a final translation of the handout (i.e., Jimerson, Brock, & Cowan, 2007). A range of informational documents in many different languages and relevant to psychological education following crisis events is available at the National Association of School Psychologists website (www.nasponline.org).

Although distribution of psychoeducational documents may be sufficient to address the needs of individuals with limited trauma exposure or those who are considered to have low risk for psychological trauma, this mental health crisis intervention has its limitations. Specifically, among acute trauma victims (i.e., those treated in a hospital emergency room following a traumatic injury), self-help informational booklets that address psychological trauma have been found insufficient by themselves. More sophisticated interventions, with direct crisis intervener contact, are required for those with more direct or severe trauma exposure and psychological injury (Scholes, Turpin, & Mason, 2007).

CAREGIVER TRAINING

In some instances, school mental health crisis interveners need to provide parents, teachers, and other caregivers with more active and direct training on how to care for others. The importance of Caregiver Training is highlighted by Berkowitz (2003), who states: "Parental attention and support are among the factors that may be most amenable to early intervention efforts as well as most salient in prevention of poor outcomes for children" (p. 297). Caregiver training may be used after many types of crises, and training sessions can be held in a variety of settings and at different times (e.g., during emergency staff meetings, after-hours parent meetings, or family reunification following a crisis).

PREPaRE Caregiver Training is similar to the Student Psychoeducational Group to be discussed later in this chapter. Whereas Caregiver Training is oriented toward taking care of others (versus taking care of oneself) and teaches adults how they can help their children or students, the Student Psychoeducational Group is concerned primarily with teaching students about self-care, and secondarily with teaching them to care for others. In addition, the direct contact with crisis interveners provided by Caregiver Training gives interveners an opportunity to identify those parents, teachers, or other caregivers who may not be able to provide emotional support to the children in their care (Howard & Goelitz, 2004).

Caregiver Training Goals

PREPaRE Caregiver Training has four goals (see Table 16.1). The first is to ensure that caregivers know crisis facts. With this knowledge they are better able to help the children in their care understand the crisis. With the facts, adults can also dispel frightening crisis rumors (Howard & Goelitz, 2004).

The second goal of Caregiver Training is to ensure that caregivers learn about common crisis reactions, that these reactions are normalized, and that they are prepared for reactions they might see in their own children (as well as those they might experience themselves). Caregivers also should be informed that recovery is the norm (Brown & Bobrow, 2004; Howard & Goelitz, 2004). Because crisis survivors often fear they are "going crazy," caregivers should be advised to dispel these beliefs in children and help them recognize that most initial crisis reactions are common responses to abnormal situations (Howard & Goelitz, 2004). The discussion of crisis reactions in Chapter 13, including Tables 13.3 and 13.4, provides guidance to help crisis interveners achieve the goals of Caregiver Training.

Although the training should stress the normality of crisis reactions and the likelihood of recovery following crisis exposure, the school mental health crisis intervener also must inform caregivers that more severe psychological injury is possible. Thus, the third goal of Caregiver Training is to ensure that caregivers can recognize psychopathological crisis reactions and dangerous coping strategies, and that they know how to request a referral for mental health crisis intervention (Berkowitz, 2003). Briefly, the following behaviors and symptoms signal the need for an immediate mental health crisis intervention referral: dissociation, intense emotional reactions, and significant panic or arousal (Lawyer et al., 2006), as well as any dangerous immediate coping behaviors, such as suicidal or homicidal ideation (see Chapter 13). Reactions that have not begun to dissipate after a week or more also suggest the likelihood of significant psychological trauma (American Psychiatric Association, 2013).

The fourth goal of Caregiver Training is to teach caregivers specific strategies for managing crisis reactions. Caregiver training can help promote healthy forms of coping by identifying a range of available helping resources (Brown & Bobrow, 2004; Howard & Goelitz, 2004) and by teaching

Table 16.1. Caregiver Training Goals and Subgoals

Following Caregiver Training, caregivers
2. Gain knowledge of crisis facts.
3. Are able to recognize common crisis reactions and appreciate that they are normal reactions to an abnormal situation.
4. Are able to recognize psychopathological crisis reactions and coping behaviors.
   - Caregivers know how to make mental health crisis intervention referrals.
   - Caregivers who are having difficulty coping are identified and offered assistance.
5. Have been taught strategies for responding to and managing crisis reactions. In particular, they understand that their crisis reactions influence children's reactions.

Note. From *School Crisis Prevention and Intervention: The PREPaRE Model* (p. 190), by S. E. Brock et al., 2009, Bethesda, MD: NASP. Copyright 2009 by the National Association of School Psychologists. Reprinted with permission.

active or approach-oriented coping strategies (Litz et al., 2002). Related to this goal is the need for the school mental health crisis intervener to describe how some caregiver reactions to children's traumatic stress, such as being calm and controlled and being empathetic, are more helpful than others. Caregivers also often need to be specifically instructed on how best to respond to their children's reactions. For example, they should be taught how their own crisis reactions can shape their children's perceptions of the crisis event (Brymer et al., 2006; Morris, Lee, & Delahanty, 2013) and the importance of limiting exposure to traumatizing images (e.g., media and social media exposure). As discussed in Chapter 13, parental reactions to crises are a predictor of a young child's traumatic stress reactions (Scheeringa & Zeanah, 2001).

Caregiver Training Elements

PREPaRE Caregiver Training sessions typically last less than an hour and consist of four specific elements or steps (see Table 16.2). Ideally initiated by at least one school mental health crisis intervener who is familiar to the group, the first step is the introduction, which lasts about 5 minutes and includes orienting caregivers so they understand the goals, process, and elements of the training. If the leaders of the training session are not familiar to the group, then a school staff member who is known to the group (e.g., the school principal) should introduce them to participants.

The second step in a Caregiver Training lasts about 10 minutes and ensures that caregivers have the crisis facts that allow them to help children understand the crisis. If the event was particularly complicated or if caregivers are likely to have a significant number of questions about the event, then additional time should be allocated to this step. The trainer can begin by reading a crisis fact sheet developed by the crisis response team's Planning Section. When providing these facts, the trainer should tell caregivers that the way children learn about a crisis can possibly lead to PTSD (Baranowsky, Young, Johnson-Douglas, Williams-Keeler, & McCarrey, 1998; Kassai & Motta, 2006; Klarić, Kvesić, Mandić, Petrov, & Frančišković, 2013). Also, trainers should suggest that caregivers let their child's questions guide the information they provide and advise them to be careful about giving potentially frightening details about the crisis that have not been requested. In particular, they should avoid giving young children information that they would not likely learn about on their own and that would unnecessarily frighten them.

The third step lasts about 15 minutes and prepares caregivers by giving them information about the common initial crisis reactions seen among both children and caregivers, which also alerts caregivers to psychopathological crisis reactions. In addition to giving adults direction on how to

Table 16.2. Steps in a PREPaRE Caregiver Training

1. *Introduce* caregivers to the training (5 minutes).
2. *Provide* crisis facts (10 minutes).
3. *Prepare* caregivers for the reactions that may follow crisis exposure (15 minutes).
4. *Review* techniques for responding to children's crisis reactions (15 minutes).

Note. Adapted from *School Crisis Prevention and Intervention: The PREPaRE Model* (p. 191), by S. E. Brock et al., 2009, Bethesda, MD: NASP. Copyright 2009 by the National Association of School Psychologists. Adapted with permission.

care for children, Caregiver Training sessions also give adult caregivers guidance on recognizing their own reactions and caring for themselves. In fact, the authors have observed that, following some crisis events, the adult caregivers have been more affected by the crisis than their children. Thus, Caregiver Training can give adults valuable direction on how to address their own crisis reactions, including direction on how to obtain additional mental health assistance for themselves. The discussion of crisis reactions in Chapter 13, including Tables 13.3 and 13.4, provides guidance to help the school mental health crisis intervener perform this step of the training.

In the fourth and final step, which lasts about 15 minutes, the session reviews techniques for responding to children's crisis reactions. Specific strategies might include (a) direct instruction regarding stress management and relaxation techniques; (b) bibliotherapy (using stories and books that would help children think about and understand the crisis event); (c) identification of existing supports (e.g., parents, friends, teachers, and school psychologists and counselors); and (d) identification of adaptive coping strategies and redirection away from maladaptive strategies (e.g., exercise instead of alcohol abuse). It is also important to provide caregivers with information regarding how to make referrals for individuals who may require further school and community-based mental health assistance. Informational documents that may prove useful during this final step are available at www.nasponline.org. In addition, "Information on Coping," in the *Psychological First Aid for Schools Field Operations Guide* (Brymer, Taylor, et al., 2012, pp. 57–69), may be especially helpful in training caregivers.

When instructing caregivers about responding to children's crisis reactions, crisis interveners need to be aware of the ways in which youth from diverse cultural groups may attribute meaning to the crisis. They should suggest caregiver responses that are sensitive to and respectful of individual beliefs and customs. For example, many individuals from diverse cultures rely on extended family or on spiritual support systems to help them cope, and caregivers should be encouraged to think about those unique sources of support.

CLASSROOM MEETING

From their firsthand experiences as school crisis interveners, Reeves et al. (2010) suggested that brief Classroom Meetings immediately following some crises can quickly disseminate facts about an event, and mitigate the traumatic stress generated by crisis rumors. The PREP_aRE Classroom Meeting is typically led by a classroom teacher who has been provided with a crisis fact sheet or a script developed by the school crisis response team's Planning Section. Use of these meetings has the potential to free school-employed mental health professionals so they can focus more on the individuals who need more assistance. From the authors' experiences, in many instances a significant number of students only need to be told what happened. For example, in an elementary school, a young staff member of a Before and After School program died suddenly during the night from an undiagnosed heart condition. He had worked at the school for 5 years and knew many students, some in the current program and others from past years. He was a positive male role model to many, and the school mental health crisis interveners were not sure how to assess student impacts beyond the students currently in the program. The school had 32 classrooms, and rumors were spreading, so the crisis response team judged that the facts needed to be disseminated before recess.

The Classroom Meetings allowed the quick dissemination of facts and helped teachers determine which students had been in the program at some point and might be affected by the news. The meeting format also helped the crisis response team identify how many other professionals were needed to help provide school mental health crisis interventions.

Classroom Meeting Goals

The PREPaRE Classroom Meeting has three goals (see Table 16.3): (a) helping the student to begin to understand the crisis event, (b) allowing the teacher to identify what information (both accurate and inaccurate) students already have about the crisis, and (c) giving the teacher the opportunity to begin assessing how his or her students are coping with the crisis.

Table 16.3. Classroom Meeting Goals

Following a Classroom Meeting, students
1. Gain knowledge of basic crisis facts.
2. Have crisis-related rumors replaced by crisis facts.

Following a Classroom Meeting, teachers
1. Begin to identify students in need of additional mental health crisis intervention.

Classroom Meeting Elements

PREPaRE Classroom Meetings can typically be completed in about 15 minutes, and they consist of four specific elements (see Table 16.4). Ideally, the classroom teacher leads the meeting. However, some teachers may not be able to participate because of their physical or emotional proximity to the event, their personal vulnerabilities, or collective bargaining contractual limitations. Thus, all teachers should be given permission to ask mental health crisis interveners for assistance with such meetings. Also, in instances where crisis response team members feel a teacher may lose emotional control, he or she should be excused from participating in a Classroom Meeting, and a crisis intervener should lead the session. Further, as is the case with any crisis group session, students identified as having significant physical or emotional proximity to the event should not be required to participate. Their needs should be addressed individually. Table 16.5 provides an example of a script and outline that could be given to a classroom teacher prior to a Classroom Meeting.

Table 16.4. Steps in a PREPaRE Classroom Meeting

1. *Introduce* students to the meeting (5 minutes).
2. *Provide* crisis facts (5 minutes).
3. *Answer* student questions (5 minutes).
4. *Refer* students who appear to have coping challenges.

Table 16.5 Sample Classroom Meeting Script and Outline

NOTE: *If you feel you are unable to read this script to your class please let us know and we will have a school mental health professional come to your room and facilitate this meeting. Know you are not required to read this message to your students.*

READ TO STUDENTS THE FOLLOWING: I have some very sad news to share with you. John Collins, a third-grade student here at ABC Elementary School, died in a car accident Saturday afternoon. The family is planning the funeral and it will probably be on Thursday afternoon of this week. We will let you and your parents know when we have more information about this.

When something like this happens, people sometimes have questions, and I would like to answer any questions you may have. I will answer by telling you the facts, or by saying "I don't know," or I will tell you to ask your parents or wait for me to get back to you with more information. I also want to let you know that different people react to this type of event in different ways, and that is OK. Some people cry, others have trouble eating or sleeping, some people find it hard to do work, and others don't have much of a reaction at all. If you want to talk to someone about your feelings or reactions regarding John's death, tell me, and I can make sure you get to talk to someone. Does anyone have any questions?

WHEN ANSWERING QUESTIONS, PLEASE REMEMBER THE FOLLOWING:
1. Provide ONLY verified facts.
    a. Tell the truth (don't ignore or minimize facts).
    b. Use brief and simple explanations for younger children. When discussing the death, avoid euphemisms ("went to sleep and did not wake up," "went away," or "lost"), which may be taken literally and cause fear or misunderstanding.
    c. Expect to repeat facts.
    d. Do not give details that students do not ask for, especially those that you think might frighten children (e.g., that car accidents are very common).
    e. Avoid sensationalizing or speculating.

2. Allow students to ask questions and use the following options when responding to what students ask and say.
    a. Explicitly identify what information is rumor, not fact, and dispel crisis rumors.
    b. Let students' questions guide what information you share.
    c. Three general responses are
        i. "This is what we know," when sharing verified crisis facts.
        ii. "I don't know," when addressing crisis circumstances that have yet to be verified.
        iii. "Talk to your parents," when addressing crisis circumstances that are not appropriate for classroom discussions (e.g., why did God let this happen?).

3. Balance the information with reassurance about what is being done to keep them safe. Remember the referral procedures in case a student needs more support.

4. Let your students know that they can go to the _____ office if they would like to discuss this event or feel they would like some help coping with this loss.

Note. Also see "Talking to Children About Death," Hospice, http://www.hospicenet.org/html/talking.html; and Reeves et al. (2010, pp. 265–266, and Table 9.3 on p. 267).

The first step of the Classroom Meeting is to introduce the leader (if not known to the class) and outline the meeting goals. In the second step, the meeting leader reads a fact sheet prepared by the school crisis response team's Planning Section. The information on the fact sheet should avoid giving students potentially upsetting details that they are unlikely to learn about on their own. One goal of sharing the information is to provide students with a developmentally appropriate understanding of the crisis, especially at the elementary school level. Therefore, the Planning Section Chief, in consultation with the Crisis Intervention and Student Care Group, may need to develop more than one statement (e.g., one for preschool, kindergarten, and special education classes; one for primary-grade classes; and one for intermediate-grade classes).

The third step is to give students a brief opportunity to ask questions about the crisis. This is also an appropriate time to dispel rumors. Written guidelines help teachers respond to anticipated questions; however, students' questions may guide any discussion that goes beyond the provided script. If students ask questions that are not related to the crisis facts, they should be redirected with a statement such as, "I understand there are a lot of emotions around this event, and in the near future we can explore those further, but right now we are just sharing the basic facts." Teachers can make a note of students who want to talk more about the event to help identify those who may need additional support. This last element of the Classroom Meeting involves having the teacher or meeting leader observe how students reacted to crisis facts and potentially recommending that a student be referred for additional assistance.

The Classroom Meeting differs from the Student Psychoeducation Group discussed next: the Classroom Meeting *does not* provide an opportunity for students to discuss common crisis reactions or coping strategies. Rather, the meeting focuses on clarifying the facts, although incidentally it also serve as a primary triage tool for teachers to assess which students might be most affected and need additional support.

STUDENT PSYCHOEDUCATIONAL GROUPS

For some groups of students or in some crisis situations, simply training caregivers and providing students with factually oriented Classroom Meetings is not sufficient. Consequently, school mental health crisis interveners must be prepared to provide more direct interventions. The Student Psychoeducational Group is a Tier 2 crisis intervention for selected students during the postimpact phase of a crisis. As was mentioned earlier, these sessions are similar to Caregiver Trainings, with the primary difference being that the Student Psychoeducational Group is oriented toward taking care of oneself (versus taking care of others). The sessions are concerned primarily with helping students learn to take care of themselves, and secondarily with teaching them how best to care for their peers. Students receiving this intervention may be in classes, in preexisting groups (e.g., the debate team), or with other individuals who have been selected based on psychological triage data. Crisis interveners are also encouraged to consider students' developmental levels, language proficiency, and chronological age when selecting and implementing a Student Psychoeducational Group.

Stein, Chiolan, Campisi, and Brock (2015) recently developed sample PREPaRE curricula for use by PREPaRE-trained leaders of Student Psychoeducational Groups, including teachers, school psychologists, and counselors. Targeting students who are moderately traumatized by a crisis, four curricula are generally identified for primary (grades K–3), upper elementary (grades 4–6), middle school (grades 7–8), and high school (grades 9–12). Regardless of their age or ability, participants in a Student Psychoeducational Group develop skills to reengage their basic problem-solving abilities and manage their self-care. These goals are met through direct instruction in a scripted classroom-based intervention that considers the generic conventions of modern lesson planning, thus making the curricula structurally familiar to teachers, including objectives, materials, and procedures.

All of the Stein et al. (2015) sample lesson plans incorporate the goals and elements discussed in the following sections, yet each adjusts the activities for those with different learning needs. Elementary-grade lesson plans are characterized by increased visual stimuli and decreased linguistic demand, a more prescriptive and teacher-directed facilitation style, greater parental involvement, and learning products commensurate with young students' typical developmental level. Middle school and high school lesson plans place greater emphasis on student self-reliance and internal faculties by using a more descriptive approach. Students in these grades generate more of their own self-care plan and identify resources for support. These alterations are examples of differentiation through which students' developmental characteristics are recognized. All four lesson plans incorporate principles of cognitive behavioral therapy and instruct students in a small exercise in progressive muscle relaxation. Each lesson offers different levels of complexity and scaffolding to address characteristic needs of learners.

Stein et al. (2015) argue that for any teaching to be effective, two elements are essential: student understanding and student engagement (Tomlinson, 1999). For students to understand the lesson, group leaders need to select or create curricular material within students' zone of proximal development (Vygotsky, 1978). Teachers of group participants should always be involved in this lesson because they are intimately aware of their students' current levels of performance. A teacher or leader of a Student Psychoeducational Group that comprises students who perform significantly below grade level or have limited language proficiency may determine that materials designed with decreased linguistic demand will be more appropriate.

The Stein et al. (2015) curricular materials offer one concrete approach to leading Student Psychoeducational Groups; however, many classes are heterogeneous and may require differentiation within the group. Thus, true differentiation of a lesson plan would strive to engage all learners by attempting to match individual needs with the content being taught. This aim is often achieved by creating separate student groups based on "a student's readiness level, interests, and preferred mode of learning" (Tomlinson, 2004, p. 188). Provided the school has adequate staffing levels of trained leaders, differentiation using the sample materials could occur within an intact classroom of diverse learners. (Copies of the differentiated Student Psychoeducational Group materials developed by Stein et al., 2015, are available at https://apps.nasponline.org/professional-development/convention/session-handouts.aspx.) The following discussion offers a more general discussion of how to lead a Student Psychoeducational Group.

Student Psychoeducational Group Goals

PREP₌RE Student Psychoeducational Groups have four goals (see Table 16.6). The first goal of these groups is to ensure that students are in possession of crisis facts and that crisis-related rumors are dispelled (Brock, Sandoval, & Lewis, 2001). Achieving this goal helps to ensure that students have a reality-based understanding of the crisis (Howard & Goelitz, 2004).

Table 16.6. Student Psychoeducational Group Goals and Subgoals

Following Student Psychoeducational Groups, students have knowledge of
1. Crisis facts (rumors are dispelled)
2. Common crisis reactions
3. Psychopathological crisis reactions and coping strategies, and how to obtain mental health crisis intervention
4. Strategies for managing stress reactions

Note. Adapted from *School Crisis Prevention and Intervention: The PREPaRE Model*, p. 193, by S. E. Brock et al., 2009, Bethesda, MD: NASP. Copyright 2009 by the National Association of School Psychologists. Adapted with permission.

The second goal of Student Psychoeducational Groups is to identify and normalize common crisis reactions. Achieving this goal prepares students for reactions that they might see in themselves as well as those that their peers might experience. As is the case during Caregiver Training, when school mental health crisis interveners are discussing these common reactions, they should inform students that recovery from their crisis reactions is the norm (Brown & Bobrow, 2004; Howard & Goelitz, 2004). Because crisis survivors often fear they are "going crazy," crisis interveners should help dispel these beliefs and help students recognize that most initial crisis reactions are common reactions to abnormal situations (Howard & Goelitz, 2004). The importance of normalizing crisis reactions is emphasized by McNally, Bryant, and Ehlers (2003), who cite studies suggesting that individuals who believe they are going crazy, rather than experiencing a temporary and expected response to a traumatic event, may increase their risk for PTSD. Specifically, the authors state:

> For example, appraisal of intrusive thoughts as meaning that one is about to lose one's mind ... may foster attempts to suppress intrusive thoughts, which in turn may lead to a paradoxical increase in their frequency. ... [E]xcessively negative appraisals of the trauma and its consequences motivate trauma survivors to engage in behaviors that maintain the problems. (p. 53)

As in Caregiver Training, the leader of the psychoeducational group should stress the normality of crisis reactions and reinforce that recovery is the norm; however, it should also help students identify the signs of more severe psychological trauma. Thus, the third goal of a Student Psychoeducational Group is to ensure that students are able to recognize psychopathological crisis reactions and coping strategies, and that they know how to refer themselves for school- and community-based mental health crisis intervention. The importance of providing referral information is emphasized by reports that two-thirds of New York City public school students with PTSD subsequent to 9/11 did not seek any treatment (Applied Research and Consulting et al., 2002). In addition, this form of mental health crisis intervention provides direct contact with students, which gives school crisis interveners the opportunity to identify students who may need more intensive interventions (Howard & Goelitz, 2004).

The fourth and final goal of a Student Psychoeducational Group is to ensure that specific strategies for managing crisis reactions are described or explicitly taught. Achieving this goal provides students with tools they can use to adaptively respond to their own crisis reactions and crisis-generated problems. Specifically, Student Psychoeducational Groups are designed to help promote healthy forms of coping and include the identification of a range of support resources (Brown & Bobrow, 2004; Howard & Goelitz, 2004). When successful, students emerge having developed their own plan for coping with crisis reactions.

Student Psychoeducational Group Elements

Student psychoeducational groups typically last about 1 hour (or one class period at the secondary level) and consist of five specific elements or steps (see Table 16.7). Ideally initiated by a trained teacher or school mental health crisis intervener who is familiar to the students, the first step in the Student Psychoeducational Group lasts about 5 minutes and involves orienting students to the group. This introduction involves ensuring that students understand the goals, process, and elements of the session. If the group leader is not familiar to the students, then a school staff member who is known to the students (e.g., a classroom teacher) should introduce the leader to the students. Group rules can either be identified or, as is the case in many classrooms that already have established group discussion procedures, reinforced. Table 16.8 provides an example of a generic lesson plan that could be used by a crisis intervener when leading a Student Psychoeducational Group.

The second step lasts about 20 minutes and involves answering questions students have about the crisis. The recommended strategy is a question-and-answer format. Because these details can be overwhelming, the group leader or leaders should anticipate that students might have difficulty understanding a given fact the first time it is presented. Thus, they need to be prepared to repeat crisis facts (Brock et al., 2001). When completing this step, leaders should keep in mind that young children may have particular difficulty understanding the crisis and therefore be much more susceptible to distortions. For example, following a schoolyard shooting that involved a lone gunman attacking a primary school playground and then killing himself, there was a persistent rumor that two gunmen were involved (a rumor fueled by the fact that the gunman had shot at the playground from two separate locations; Brock et al., 2001). In this instance, giving the children crisis facts resulted in the event becoming less threatening.

However, this observation does not mean that the group leader should give students all the crisis facts. The possibility that learning about a crisis can generate traumatic stress must be kept in mind. In some cases, even though an individual was not personally exposed to a crisis or did not witness the event, being told about an event that constituted a direct threat to the life or

Table 16.7. Steps in a PREPaRE Student Psychoeducational Group

1. *Introduce* the lesson (5 minutes).
2. *Answer* questions and dispel rumors (20 minutes).
3. *Prepare* students for the reactions that may follow crisis exposure (15 minutes).
4. *Teach* students how to manage crisis reactions (15 minutes).
5. *Close* by ensuring that students have a plan to manage crisis reactions (5 minutes).

Note. Adapted from *School Crisis Prevention and Intervention: The PREPaRE Model*, p. 195, by S. E. Brock et al., 2009, Bethesda, MD: NASP. Copyright 2009 by the National Association of School Psychologists. Adapted with permission.

Table 16.8. Generic Student Psychoeducational Group Lesson Plan

1. **Introduction**
   a. Introduce yourself to the adult caregiver (typically the teacher) who is responsible for group supervision and explain why you are there.
   b. Have the group's adult caregiver introduce you to the students who are a part of the group (e.g., the teacher should identify you by name, position, where you typically work).
   c. Explain to students that you are on the crisis intervention team and why you are there.
   d. Briefly share your understanding of the crisis event. If possible, have a script prepared by the crisis response team's Planning Section.
   e. Explain group rules. Say that if the students have questions, they need to raise their hand and wait their turn. Depending on the nature of the event and the characteristics of the group, it may also be appropriate to tell students that some questions may need to be addressed individually after the group has ended.
   f. Explain that participation in the group is voluntary and that they will be allowed to leave if they do not want to participate. Identify for students a safe, nonthreatening area on school grounds that they will be brought to if they choose not to participate.
   g. To document attendance, use a sign-in sheet for secondary classrooms or take role using the teacher's attendance sheet in primary classrooms.

2. **Answer Questions About the Crisis and Dispel Rumors**
   a. When judged to be developmentally appropriate and helpful, use carefully screened newspaper or video accounts of the crisis. Ensure that such depictions are accurate and minimize the risk of vicarious trauma.
   b. Ask the students if they have any questions about the crisis. Be sensitive to developmental level and realize that developmentally immature students are most likely to have a distorted view of the event and its consequences.
   c. Answer students' questions about the crisis. Be prepared to repeat facts several times. Crises are overwhelming and difficult for students to understand (in particular developmentally immature students).
   d. If some crisis facts are confidential, say so, and share what facts you can. Remember to tell students the truth! Do not give inaccurate information (e.g., if crisis-related dangers are still present, acknowledge this reality, then tell them about all that is being done to keep them safe, and let students know what they can do to be safe).
   e. Be prepared to say "I don't know."
   f. Make the distinction between crisis facts, inaccurate crisis rumors, yet-to-be-answered questions about the crisis event, and information that needs to remain confidential. Especially when working with adolescents, be sure to give a logical rationale for why some crisis details need to be kept confidential.

3. **Prepare for Crisis Reactions**
   a. Describe common crisis reactions. Acknowledge that people experience and react to crises differently. Encourage students to respect a range of reactions (both their own and their classmates'). For example, some students may be angry, some may cry, and still others will display nervous laughter. A list of common reactions is provided in the table below.

b. Describe the warning signs of severe crisis reactions (e.g., significant and impairing dissociation, hyperarousal, reliving of the crisis event, phobic avoidance of crisis reminders, severe depression, psychotic symptoms, suicidal and homicidal ideation, substance abuse of others and self, or extreme inappropriate anger toward others).

c. Acknowledge that severe reactions, while possible and understandable, are rare. Most students can anticipate that their reactions are not signs of mental illness (rather, they are common reactions to an abnormal event).

d. Describe how to get help in addressing crisis reactions, both in school and in the community. Such guidance should always include enlisting the assistance of a caregiving adult.

e. Express optimism that, with time and talk, most students (if not all) will feel better. Though they will always remember the event, crisis reactions will lessen.

Common Initial Crisis Reactions

Emotional		Cognitive	
Shock	Depression or sadness	Impaired concentration	Decreased self-esteem
Anger	Grief	Impaired decision-making ability	Decreased self-efficacy
Despair	Irritability	Memory impairment	Self-blame
Emotional numbing	Hypersensitivity	Disbelief	Intrusive thoughts or memories[b]
Terror or fear	Helplessness	Confusion	
Guilt	Hopelessness	Distortion	Worry
Phobias	Loss of pleasure from activities		Nightmares
	Dissociation[a]		

Physical		Interpersonal/Behavioral	
Fatigue	Impaired immune response	Alienation	Avoidance of reminders
Insomnia	Headaches	Social withdrawal or isolation	Crying easily
Sleep disturbance	Gastrointestinal problems	Increased relationship conflict	Change in eating patterns
Hyperarousal	Decreased appetite		Tantrums
Somatic complaints	Decreased libido	Vocational impairment	Regression in behavior
	Startle response	Refusal to go to school	Risk taking
		School impairment	Aggression

Note. Compiled from Speier (2000); Young, Ford, Ruzek, Friedman, & Gusman (1998).
a. Examples include perceptual experience, such as "dreamlike," "tunnel vision," "spacey," or on "automatic pilot."
b. Reenactment play among children.

Table 16.8. Continued

4. **Teach Students How to Manage and Cope With Crisis Reactions**
   a. Discuss stress management techniques. A list of common strategies and adaptive coping strategies is provided below.
   b. Encourage students to talk with other people about their crisis reactions and feelings. List people that students can talk to (e.g., parents, teachers, counselors, and friends).
   c. Remind students of the mental health resources that are available in their school.
   d. Discuss how returning to a normal routine is a positive coping strategy after a crisis and how coming to school helps manage crisis reactions.

Stress Management Resources and Adaptive Coping Strategies

Stress Management Resources
1. Stress Management: How to Reduce, Prevent, and Cope with Stress
   • http://www.helpguide.org/articles/stress/stress-management.htm
2. Stress tip sheet
   • http://www.apa.org/helpcenter/stress-tips.aspx
3. Stress Management: MedlinePlus
   • http://www.nlm.nih.gov/medlineplus/ency/article/001942.htm
4. Manage Stress
   • http://healthfinder.gov/HealthTopics/Category/health-conditions-and-diseases/heart-health/manage-stress
5. The American Institute of Stress
   • http://www.stress.org/

Adaptive Coping Strategies for Dealing With Traumatic Stress Reactions
1. Talk with others who have been through the same crisis experience.
2. Asking an adult for help coping with difficult feelings.
3. Take care of your basic needs for food, water, sleep, and hygiene.
4. Express yourself through writing and drawing.
5. Incorporate physical exercise into your routine.
6. Avoid alcohol and drugs.
7. Maintain normal routines and comfortable rituals (e.g., going to school, continuing with extracurricular activities).
8. Surround yourself with support (e.g., partners, pals, and pets).
9. Pursue your passions (don't feel guilty about finding pleasure in life).
10. Practice stress-management techniques (e.g., deep breathing, yoga, meditation, progressive muscle relaxation, or guided imagery).
11. Embrace your religion, spirituality, or other helpful belief systems.
12. Enjoy nature (get outside and play).
13. Find ways to laugh (but allow yourself to cry).

5. Close the Lesson
a. Give a brief summary of what was discussed.
b. Reiterate available mental health resources (provide a handout, if possible, or post on the school website for easy availability).
c. Consider assigning (with the teacher's permission) a homework, journal, or reflection assignment wherein students would write out their own personal stress management plan.
d. Thank the students (and the teacher) for the opportunity to be with them.

Note. Adapted from "Psychoeducational Group Cheat Sheet: A Lesson Plan for Mental Health Response Team Members Only," by C. Conolly-Wilson, 2010, Waukegan, IL: Waukegan Public Schools. Adapted with permission.

well-being of someone else may be sufficiently traumatic to result in PTSD (American Psychiatric Association, 2013). Examples include being told about the death of a relative whose body was mutilated by shrapnel, or learning about the fate of a classmate who was shot in the head by a sniper. Thus, leaders of a Student Psychoeducational Group should let the students' questions guide the information that is given, and avoid releasing unasked-for frightening details (Servaty-Seib, Peterson, & Spang, 2003).

The third step in the Student Psychoeducational Group lasts about 15 minutes and prepares students to anticipate reactions that may follow their crisis exposure. This step involves discussion of how crises affect people and what reactions students can expect from themselves, their classmates, and even their caregivers.

The leader also should tell the students that, with time, most reactions become less intense and that recovery is the norm. However, it is also important to tell students that if their reactions do not lessen with time or those reactions become too intense to manage independently, then a self-referral for further mental health crisis intervention assistance should be made. The leader can also identify crisis reactions that signal the need for immediate mental health crisis intervention (e.g., suicidal or homicidal ideation). Finally, this step should explain to students how they can obtain crisis intervention assistance for both themselves and others.

Once students have an understanding of how they are being affected and what some potential future concerns might be, they will be ready for instruction on how to cope with the crisis. The following is possible language adapted from Southwick, Friedman, and Krystal (2008):

> Your reactions to the event are not unusual . . . Many others experience exactly what you are now experiencing . . . You are experiencing reactions to trauma that have been seen before and well understood as common . . . If your symptoms continue or have already lasted for a long period of time, we have very effective ways of helping you . . . We do not blame you and we will not turn our back on you. (pp. 305–306)

The fourth step in the Student Psychoeducational Group lasts about 15 minutes and involves teaching the students techniques for responding to crisis reactions. The primary goal is to help students identify strategies that help them (and those they care about) manage crisis reactions and problems. Specific strategies to achieve this goal include (a) teaching stress management and relaxation techniques; (b) identifying existing supports (e.g., parents, friends, teachers, and school psychologists and counselors) and referral procedures; and (c) identifying adaptive coping strategies and redirecting students away from maladaptive strategies (e.g., exercise instead of alcohol abuse). To facilitate this step, the group leader can engage older students by having them identify healthy and safe coping strategies that they already have within their repertoire. In groups with younger students, the leader can suggest ways of coping. Many helpful resources are available, including Table 16.8 in this chapter; the website of the National Association of School Psychologists (www.nasponline.org); and "Information on Coping," in Brymer, Taylor, et al. (2012). Finally, leaders should focus on individuals' strengths, complimenting their problem-solving skills and being positive about their ability to cope.

Instruction on coping, as in other psychoeducational methods, requires a special note about cultural diversity. Specifically, crisis interveners need to be aware of the ways students from diverse cultural groups may attribute meaning to the crisis event and suggest coping strategies that are respectful of individual beliefs and customs. Students from diverse cultures may use specific activities to help them cope. Encouraging them to think about their unique sources of support can help ensure that the intervention is more sensitive to individual diversity.

The fifth and final step in a Student Psychoeducational Group can be as short as 5 minutes and should conclude by ensuring that students have a self-care plan for managing their own crisis reactions. For example, instruction can involve an assignment that asks students to write a list of specific activities they feel they can use to cope with the crisis. The assignment could be given as homework and used by the instructor to gauge whether students understood the lesson. The completed assignment can also be used as an additional measure of psychological trauma (i.e., secondary triage). The content of students' self-care plans may indicate which students need additional mental health crisis intervention. Finally, when concluding the session, the leader should again make sure that all students know how to obtain mental health crisis intervention assistance.

LIMITATIONS OF PSYCHOEDUCATION

Psychological education is a promising mental health crisis intervention, and for individuals with relatively minor psychological injuries (i.e., individuals experiencing nonpathological or common crisis reactions) it may be a sufficient crisis intervention. However, the method has some limitations. Specifically, psychological education by itself may not significantly reduce some crisis symptoms, in particular the more severe and long-term crisis reactions like those associated with posttraumatic stress disorder (Krupnick & Green, 2008; Niles et al., 2012). Especially in high-risk groups (i.e., acute trauma victims), this intervention, if used at all, should be paired with other mental health crisis interventions that directly address crisis reactions (Howard & Goelitz, 2004; Yeomans, Forman, Herbert, & Yuen, 2010). For example, in a study of earthquake survivors with PTSD, Oflaz, Hatipoğlu, and Aydin (2008) reported that the combination of psychopharmacological methods and a multisession psychoeducational intervention was more effective than either intervention alone. Furthermore, although psychological education has been shown to be an effective element of tertiary prevention (i.e., the care offered later in a condition's course; Amstadter,

McCart, & Ruggiero, 2007; Lukens & McFarlane, 2004; Oflaz et al., 2008), research is limited regarding its use as an immediate and brief secondary intervention (Creamer & O'Donnell, 2008; Kilpatrick, Cougle, & Resnick, 2008). In fact, one review article has cautioned against its use (Wessely et al., 2008). More research is needed regarding the efficacy of this intervention with schoolchildren and the use of psychological education as an immediate mental health crisis intervention may change with the results of that research.

CONCLUSION

Psychological education respects the fact that most individuals exposed to a given crisis find, either within themselves or within their immediate caregiving environment, the necessary resources for coping. It also provides students and caregivers with the knowledge that facilitates adaptive coping. Psychological educational approaches empower students and caregivers and also establish contact between school mental health crisis interveners and crisis survivors, their caregivers, and the caregiving community without the stigma often associated with mental health interventions. Not only does this contact increase access to mental health resources, but it also gives crisis interveners the opportunity to evaluate how students and their caregivers are coping with a crisis.

Chapter 17

GROUP CRISIS INTERVENTION

This chapter begins to examine the psychological crisis interventions that more traumatized students require. These interventions are active and direct attempts on the part of crisis interveners to promote adaptive coping and directly respond to acute distress. The group crisis intervention discussed in this chapter and the individual crisis intervention discussed in Chapter 18 are both aimed at reestablishing *immediate* coping, or the ability to address basic day-to-day challenges, and not necessarily at crisis resolution. In a relatively short time, these interventions help students return to their school routines and other everyday activities. Both of these interventions are considered Tier 2 (selected, or secondary), mental health crisis interventions (see Figure S5.1). However, for students whose trauma is severe, these interventions are an important way to connect students with more intensive Tier 3 (indicated, or tertiary) mental health crisis interventions, referred to in this book as psychotherapeutic interventions (Chapter 19).

Before proceeding with this discussion of Tier 2 psychological crisis interventions, it is important to mention that although these interventions include all of the core actions of psychological first aid (Brymer et al., 2006; Brymer, Taylor, et al., 2012), they are not a substitute for Tier 3 psychotherapeutic interventions. Psychotherapy is necessary to assist individuals experiencing the more severe consequences of trauma exposure, such as posttraumatic stress disorder (PTSD; Bisson, McFarlane, & Rose, 2000; Lewis, 2003; Stallard & Salter, 2003). Another important preface is that when working with the psychologically traumatized and emotionally labile students who require these interventions, crisis interveners should acknowledge the small but real possibility that crisis reactions and coping behaviors may place interveners in danger. Given this possibility, crisis interveners must also consider how to respond to the student who is, for example, homicidal or suicidal. When confronted with such a situation, crisis interveners should understand that they are not expected to place themselves in danger. Rather, they should work with law enforcement officers and other first responders to address these situations.

The group crisis interventions explored in this chapter were referred to as classroom-based crisis intervention (or CCI) in the second edition of the PREP<u>a</u>RE curriculum (Brock, 2011a). The method, now called group crisis intervention (GCI), was renamed to clarify that although it is a group intervention, it does not always occur with intact classroom groupings. GCI is similar to and sometimes identified as *debriefing* (Mitchell & Everly, 1996); however, as discussed next, the PREPaRE GCI has modified this approach so that GCI sessions take into account both students' developmental differences and questions of efficacy that have been raised by empirical investigations of debriefing (Brock & Jimerson, 2004).

INDICATIONS AND CONTRAINDICATIONS FOR GROUP CRISIS INTERVENTION

Group approaches to crisis intervention (frequently referred to as *psychological debriefings*) have been the subject of multiple empirical investigations and literature reviews. Some of these reports do not support the continued use of psychological debriefing (Bisson et al., 1997; Conlon, Fahy, & Conroy, 1999; Devilly & Annab, 2008; Devilly & Varker, 2008; Mayou et al., 2000; Paterson, Whittle, & Kemp, 2015; Sijbrandij, Olff, Reitsma, Carlier, & Gersons, 2006; van Emmerik, Kamphuis, Hulsbosch, & Emmelkamp, 2002; Wei, Szumilas, & Kutcher, 2010). However, others have asserted that group techniques have a role in crisis intervention (Adler, Bliese, McGurk, Hoge, & Castro, 2011; Adler et al., 2008; Campfield & Hills, 2001; Chemtob, Thomas, Law, & Cremniter, 1997; Deahl et al., 2000; Everly, Boyle, & Lating, 1999; Jacobs, Horne-Moyer, & Jones, 2004; Openshaw, 2011; Pack, 2012; Richards, 2001; Ruck, Bowes, & Tehrani, 2013; Sattler, Boyd, & Kirsch, 2014; Tuckey & Scott, 2014). In fact, referring to recommendations to no longer provide psychological debriefing (i.e., the National Institute for Health and Clinical Excellence, 2005, and Rose, Bisson, Churchill, & Wessely, 2006), Hawker, Durkin, and Hawker (2011) assert that harm has been done "by withdrawing an intervention from occupational groups who (for over 20 years) have come to rely on it to help them cope with working in extremely stressful circumstances" (pp. 456–458). Hawker et al. (2011) go as far as to question the ethics of withdrawing an intervention valued by its recipients on the basis of what they view as two methodologically challenged negative outcome studies (i.e., Bisson et al., 1997; Mayou et al., 2000). Hawker et al. (2011) also state:

- Warnings about the dangers of psychological debriefing are based on studies using an intervention that is very different from that used for disaster workers and military personnel.
- Evidence relating to primary victims of trauma has been overgeneralized to secondary victims.
- Psychological debriefing may harm if it is too short, too probing, conducted too soon or delivered by debriefers with insufficient training or experience. (p. 435)

Given the fact that GCI is designed to be used in a school setting, it is important to note that all of the investigations listed above, both those questioning and those supporting group intervention, studied adults and older adolescents; *none* focused on children. However, Stallard et al. (2006) conducted what is believed to be the first randomized controlled trial of early psychological debriefing among young people. In that study, youth ages 7–18 years who had been treated at a hospital following a road traffic accident were randomly assigned to individual debriefing (*n* = 82) or control (*n* = 76) conditions. First, all study participants were assessed by a clinician for PTSD. Then approximately 4 weeks after their accidents, participants in the individual debriefing group engaged in a detailed reconstruction of their accident. Next, they were helped to identify their thoughts and to discuss their emotional reactions. Information about common thoughts and feelings was then provided to help normalize crisis reactions. Finally, written information was provided on how to cope with common problems. Participants in the control group were asked a series of neutral, non-accident-related questions.

Approximately 8 months after their accidents, Stallard et al. (2006) reevaluated 70 debriefing group youth and 62 control group youth, and it was found that children in both groups showed significant reductions on all measures of traumatic stress. Although the debriefing condition could not be suggested to be more effective than the control, it was not suggested to cause harm (as was reported to be the case in previous adult accident survivor studies, that is, Hobbs, Mayou, Harrison, & Warlock, 1996; Mayou et al., 2000). Furthermore, the study authors acknowledged that the control group's contact with a researcher during the initial assessment "may have provided a framework in which the child's symptoms could be acknowledged, validated and normalized" (p. 132). Furthermore, the authors acknowledged that because the debriefings were not offered in a group setting (each participant had a unique trauma experience), the process of normalization was significantly different from what would have occurred in a group debriefing. Finally, Stallard et al. (2006) noted that the intervention took place 4 weeks after the traumatic event.

Given the Stallard et al. (2006) findings, and as suggested by Szumilas, Wei, and Kutcher (2010), further research on the efficacy of GCI with school-age youth is clearly needed. However, because (a) no data suggest these techniques have been harmful for children, (b) data do suggest that these techniques are effective in some situations, and (c) school crisis interveners are at times presented with the need to address large groups of students, PREPaRE authors argue that ruling out this school mental health crisis intervention is premature. Instead, GCI should be considered an option for reestablishing the immediate coping of groups of students who have been secondarily or vicariously exposed to a common crisis event (Brock & Jimerson, 2004). However, some conclusions regarding the indications and contraindications of GCI have been drawn from the existing literature. The indications noted in the following section guide how GCI can work most effectively, whereas the contraindications reflect components that lessen the likelihood of the GCI session being helpful. To ensure that this intervention is helpful, the school crisis interveners should understand the factors of GCI that are described next.

Indications

Indications for the use of GCI include its use with individuals who were exposed to a crisis event but were not acute trauma victims (Giddens, 2008; Hawker et al., 2011; Jacobs et al., 2004). Studies suggest that the use of an intervention like GCI has potential positive effects when used with trauma-exposed individuals who were not physically injured. For example, Campfield and Hills (2001) found that among robbery victims who were neither physically injured nor threatened with a gun, debriefing resulted in a reduction of traumatic stress.

A second indication for the use of GCI is its use with students who want to talk about their crisis experiences (Hawker et al., 2011). No student should be required to participate in this session, and a primary indication of the need to offer a GCI session is the presence of significant numbers of students who express a desire to talk about their experiences. Although some situations may necessitate the delivery of GCI soon after a crisis (e.g., when there are large numbers of students who are expressing their desire to talk about crisis experiences and reactions), GCI is, as a rule, a carefully planned intervention with a carefully selected group of students. Whereas the PREPaRE Classroom Meeting discussed in Chapter 16 can be provided immediately, it is critical to wait until sufficient secondary triage data have been collected before providing GCI. Further, in the words of Mitchell and Everly (1996), "That which ultimately dictates appropriateness is not how many hours/days have passed since the trauma, but rather is how psychologically receptive the victim is to the help being offered" (p. 208).

A third indication for GCI's use is when it is part of a comprehensive crisis intervention system, such as PREPaRE's multitiered system of crisis intervention support. All studies that have reported potential benefits of using group approaches to crisis intervention found the intervention to be part of a comprehensive program. For example, among bank employees who were survivors of armed robberies (but not injured, shot at, or taken hostage), a combination of precrisis education, debriefing, and individual support was associated with lower rates of psychological trauma than was debriefing as a stand-alone intervention (Richards, 2001). Furthermore, among adults who experienced property damage as a result of a natural disaster (Hurricane Iniki), the intervention that appeared to reduce the impact of the crisis consisted of approximately 3 hours of sharing and subsequent normalization of crisis experiences and reactions, combined with 2 hours of psychological education offered several months after the crisis event (Chemtob et al., 1997).

A fourth indication for the use of GCI is its use as a more involved (i.e., of longer duration) crisis intervention. Common to the studies that reported positive outcomes following a group crisis intervention was a longer group session time. For example, the average duration of the group interventions in the Campfield and Hills (2001), Chemtob et al. (1997), and Richards (2001) studies, which suggested positive outcomes following participation, was over 2 hours. Conversely, the average duration of the debriefing interventions in the Bisson et al. (1997), Devilly and Varker (2008), and Mayou et al. (2000) studies, which suggested negative outcomes following participation, was an hour or less (an average duration of 44 minutes in the Bisson et al. study).

A fifth indication for the use of GCI is the leadership of well-trained school-employed mental health professionals who have experience working with groups and are prepared to deliver this group intervention (Hawker et al., 2011; Openshaw, 2011). As originally envisioned by Mitchell and Everly (1996), GCI should be delivered only by well-trained professionals, working with a coleader who understands the group's typical experiences (e.g., a teacher). In a review of the literature, Arendt and Elklit (2001) observe: "It seems that positive effect results from leadership according to the original team concept or by professional therapists. In contrast no effect, or even adverse effect, is found in studies using volunteers or nonprofessional therapists" (p. 431). The leader of the GCI session needs to be a school-employed mental health professional.

A sixth indication for the use of GCI is its use in group settings with individuals exposed to a common stressor. Positive outcomes following a group crisis intervention have been reported when an intervention such as GCI was offered to groups who had experienced a common stressor (Campfield & Hills, 2001; Richards, 2001). In contrast, in two of three studies reporting negative outcomes, the debriefing was offered only to individuals or to couples (Bisson et al., 1997; Mayou et al., 2000).

A final indication for the use of GCI is its use with trauma victims who have a cohesive support group. From a literature review conducted by Giddens (2008), the available research suggested that when a GCI approach was applied to secondary trauma victims who were members of a "cohesive organization or unit," such as classmates (p. 3253), the intervention was more likely to be effective (in comparison with its use with primary victims who were relative strangers).

Contraindications

GCI contraindications include its use with individuals who were acute trauma victims (Giddens, 2008; Hawker et al., 2011; Jacobs et al., 2004). Common among all studies in which group crisis intervention had negative outcomes was the inclusion of participants who had physical injuries or who could be considered to be acute trauma victims. For example, among adults and older adolescents who were hospitalized following a severe burn or a traffic accident, individual debriefings were suggested to cause harm when offered soon after the injury (Bisson et al., 1997) or when offered to those who were most psychologically traumatized (Mayou et al., 2000; Sijbrandij et al., 2006).

A second contraindication for the use of GCI, suggested by two of the negative outcome studies (Bisson et al., 1997; Mayou et al., 2000), is its use immediately after a crisis event (Hawker et al., 2011). In the Mayou et al. (2000) study, hospitalized motor vehicle accident victims were debriefed "within 24 hours of the accident or as soon as they were physically fit to be seen" (p. 589). The Bisson et al. (1997) study noted that the sooner the hospitalized burn victims were debriefed, the worse their outcomes. Furthermore, the hospitalized burn victims were likely still dealing with an ongoing crisis (i.e., treatment for their burns). Consequently, use of GCI should be subject to the following caution by Mitchell and Everly (1996):

> People have to be ready for help before it becomes useful to them. Providing help too early usually sets the stage for the rejection of the help and failure of the effort . . . hold off on the formal debriefings (CISD) until things settle down a little. (p. 189)

The third and fourth contraindications for the use of GCI are its use as a stand-alone intervention or as a brief crisis intervention (Hawker et al., 2011). When used in such instances, the intervention may not allow adequate emotional processing, and may instead increase arousal and anxiety levels (which is predictive of traumatic stress; Ruzek et al., 2007). Common among studies in which debriefing was shown to have negative outcomes was its use as a one-off intervention, with no additional crisis intervention offered (Devilly & Varker, 2008; Mayou et al., 2000). For example, Bisson et al. (1997) reported that following a single 45-minute individual or couple debriefing, acute burn victims were more likely to have developed PTSD at a 13-month follow-up than the control group that received no psychological intervention (26% versus 9%). Thus, they concluded that the data "seriously question the wisdom *of* advocating one-off interventions posttrauma" (p. 78).

The fifth contraindication for the use of GCI involves reliance on insufficiently trained GCI facilitators (Hawker et al., 2011). In the Mayou et al. (2000) study, experienced clinicians were not available to conduct debriefings for the hospitalized motor vehicle accident victims, and instead a research assistant facilitated these sessions. Hawker et al. (2011) reported that the individuals conducting the debriefing in the Bisson et al. (1997) study, five of whom were nurses also involved in the medical care of the burn victim participants, had only half a day of training.

The sixth contraindication for the use of GCI is its use individually (not as a group intervention) and its use with individuals exposed to different crisis events. Such situations do not give crisis survivors an opportunity to realize the hypothesized benefits of sharing their common crisis experiences and therefore understanding that they are not alone in their experiences and reactions. This missed opportunity is suggested by the PREPaRE authors to be especially important among younger children who may lack abstract reasoning abilities. Such students require concrete examples of the commonality (and thus the normality) of their crisis experiences and initial crisis reactions.

Additional contraindications suggested by Johnson (1993, 2000) include the use of GCI with groups that are historically hurtful, divisive, or not supportive, and following crisis events that generate polarized needs or are politicized (e.g., rival gangs, cliques that don't get along). Obviously such circumstances would make group work counterproductive.

Finally, any group approach to crisis intervention, including Student Psychoeducational Groups, is contraindicated when a crime has been committed and potential group members are witnesses to the crime. The importance of this GCI contraindication is highlighted by research suggesting that the crisis memories of participants in a debriefing group can be affected by listening to the accounts of group members who give incorrect information. Specifically, Devilly, Varker, Hansen, and Gist (2007) found that when a researcher deliberately provided misinformation to a debriefing group, group participants were more likely to report seeing events that did not in fact take place, compared with those who were not debriefed. More recently, Paterson et al. (2015) reported that among young adults, debriefings actually have a negative effect on memory. Specifically, undergraduate college students who received fact-focused debriefing after viewing a stressful video incorporated more misinformation into memory and also reported more intrusive thoughts about the video than a control group that was not debriefed. In addition, participants who received emotion-focused debriefing reported more confabulated items than participants in the control group and reported more intrusive thoughts. Thus, following crises that involve criminal acts, this crisis intervention should be postponed until after law enforcement officials have approved it.

PREPaRE GROUP CRISIS INTERVENTION GOALS

The primary goals of a PREPaRE GCI are to help crisis survivors reestablish immediate coping and to begin to address crisis-generated problems (see Table 17.1). In addition, the direct contact with students provided by a GCI sessions gives crisis interveners an opportunity to identify which students may need more intensive interventions (i.e., it is a form of secondary triage; Howard & Goelitz, 2004). This is an especially attractive feature of GCI, as it has the practical advantage of allowing crisis interveners to work with larger groups of students at one time.

Although GCI does not purport to resolve crisis-generated challenges, it does strive to place students in a position from which these problems can be addressed (either independently, if the psychological trauma is not severe, or with school- or community-based crisis intervention if the injury is severe). To achieve this end, the GCI session has several subgoals. Similar to the Student Psychoeducational Groups discussed in Chapter 16, the GCI's first subgoal is to help

Table 17.1. Group Crisis Intervention Goal and Subgoals

Following GCI sessions, the following goals will have been achieved:
1. Students have improved ability to immediately cope with the crisis and crisis-generated problems. These include the following:
   a. Understanding crisis facts and dispelling rumors.
   b. Understanding the commonality of their crisis experiences and normalizing crisis reactions.
   c. Feeling more connected to each other by common experiences and reactions.
   d. Understanding psychopathological crisis reactions and maladaptive coping strategies.
   e. Knowing how to make referrals for crisis intervention assistance.
   f. Having strategies for managing stress reactions and crisis-generated problems.
2. Secondary triage has been conducted by crisis interveners who conduct GCI.

Note. Adapted from *School Crisis Prevention and Intervention: The PREPaRE Model* (p. 214), by S. E. Brock et al., 2009, Bethesda, MD: NASP. Copyright 2009 by the National Association of School Psychologists. Adapted with permission.

students understand the crisis event and to dispel crisis-related rumors. These rumors are many times more frightening than the objective crisis facts (Blom, Etkind, & Carr, 1991) and may generate ongoing appraisals of continuing threat or danger, such as occurred in an earlier example in which the survivors of a school shooting incorrectly believed that there were two shooters, not just one, and that one remained at large (Armstrong, 1990). Obviously these misperceptions increase threat perceptions, interfere with recovery, and may be consistent with certain cognitive models of the development of traumatic stress (Ehlers & Clark, 2000).

The second subgoal of a PREPaRE GCI session is to ensure that common crisis experiences and reactions are understood and normalized. Unlike the Student Psychoeducational Groups, GCI sessions can last as long as 3 hours and give students an opportunity to share their individual crisis experiences and reactions. Because the GCI session is designed for groups of students who are homogeneous in terms of crisis exposure and reactions and is contraindicated for the more acutely traumatized, students should have concrete examples of common mild to moderate crisis experiences and reactions. Making these experiences and reactions concrete is important, because without concrete examples of their shared crisis experiences and reactions, many students (particularly younger children) will find it challenging to understand their own experiences and reactions as common or typical.

The third subgoal of a PREPaRE GCI session is also aided by the group's homogeneity in terms of students' crisis exposure and reactions. Hearing that their peers share similar crisis stories and reactions helps students feel less alone and more connected to their classmates. In other words, the well-constructed GCI group guarantees that students hear their peers relating common experiences and reactions. It is suggested that students' realization that they are not alone in addressing the crisis helps reestablish immediate coping and the emotional strength needed to address the crisis and its consequences.

As is the case in a Student Psychoeducational Group, in addition to stressing the normality of crisis reactions, the GCI should also help students identify the signs of more severe psychological trauma, both in themselves and others. Thus, the fourth subgoal of a PREPaRE GCI session is to ensure that students recognize psychopathological crisis reactions and maladaptive coping strategies, and that they are informed about when it is necessary to refer themselves (and their peers) for assistance through school-based mental health intervention. In addition, the fifth subgoal of the GCI session ensures that students know how to make these referrals for crisis intervention assistance. The importance of providing students with information about self-referral is demonstrated by reports that, following 9/11, two thirds of New York City public school students who exhibited PTSD symptoms did not seek any treatment (Applied Research and Consulting et al., 2002).

The sixth and final subgoal of a PREPaRE GCI session is to ensure that students learn about specific strategies for managing crisis reactions. As is the case during Student Psychoeducational Groups, students identify adaptive coping strategies they can use to respond to their own crisis reactions or crisis-generated problems. Specifically, GCI sessions are designed to help promote healthy forms of coping and include the identification of a range of support resources (Brown & Bobrow, 2004; Howard & Goelitz, 2004). When a GCI session is successful, students emerge having developed their own plan for coping with crisis reactions. A resource that can be used to guide this element of GCI is "Information on Coping," in the *Psychological First Aid for Schools Field Operations Guide* (Brymer, Taylor, et al., 2012, pp. 57–69).

GENERAL CONSIDERATIONS FOR PREPaRE GROUP CRISIS INTERVENTION

Before proceeding to a detailed discussion of the specific elements of a GCI session, this section presents the following general considerations.

GCI Versus Psychoeducation

Crisis interveners can use the following guidelines when determining whether a GCI session or one of the psychoeducational crisis interventions, such as PREPaRE Classroom Meetings and Student Psychoeducational Groups, should be used (see Chapter 16). First, when an immediate crisis intervention is required (e.g., to quickly give students facts to dispel crisis rumors or keep them safe), a Classroom Meeting is indicated. Second, when the school has only a brief period of time to provide the crisis intervention (e.g., an hour or less), either a Classroom Meeting or a Student Psychoeducational Group is indicated. Third, when the school needs to provide students with crisis facts and information about adaptive coping, and students have no apparent need to discuss their crisis experiences and reactions, a Student Psychoeducational Group is indicated. Finally, when large numbers of students want to talk about their crisis experiences and reactions (more than can be addressed through individual crisis intervention), and sufficient time is available to conduct the session (a 3-hour block of time is preferred), a GCI is indicated.

Who Should Participate

From the authors' experiences, GCI is not appropriate for preschool and early primary-grade students (or older students who are at that developmental level), in part because it lasts too long for these grade levels. These children need to be offered individual support or developmentally appropriate Student Psychoeducational Groups (see Stein, Chiolan, Campisi, & Brock, 2015, for suggestions on running developmentally appropriate Student Psychoeducational Groups). In addition, these young children are not able to clearly articulate their crisis stories and reactions or to benefit from hearing others tell their stories.

GCI groups should be homogeneous in terms of participants' crisis exposure, experiences, and impact (Berkowitz, 2003; Brock, 1998; Mitchell & Everly, 1996; Weinberg, 1990; Wollman, 1993) as well as developmental level. Having homogeneous groups helps to ensure that participants hear other group members sharing common experiences and reactions. If the group is heterogeneous, GCI participation may be harmful. For example, participation may be traumatic if the session introduces information that some students may otherwise not have had to confront (e.g., the crisis experiences and reactions of other more directly affected students; Berkowitz, 2003; Everly, 2003).

An especially important and sensitive issue when constructing GCI groups is that of cultural diversity. Crisis interveners need to keep in mind that students from different cultural groups may attribute different meanings to the crisis event; for example, they may explain the event as an unavoidable accident, or as an act of God or of a spirit force. They also may have different beliefs or customs regarding their response to the event, such as how to show respect for the deceased. Such diversity is very enriching to the general school environment, but might be counterproductive in a GCI. As discussed in Chapter 8, having a cultural broker from the communities affected by the crisis helps crisis interveners work with students and school staff members.

It is strongly recommended that participation in a GCI session be voluntary (Jacob & Feinberg, 2002; McNally, Bryant, & Ehlers, 2003), and the PREPaRE authors unequivocally assert that no student should ever be required to participate in this group crisis intervention. Students involved in GCI sessions should all have the desire to share their crisis experiences and reactions. As mentioned in Chapter 13, some avoidance coping can initially have an adaptive function, giving individuals the time needed to mobilize their internal and external coping resources. Requiring GCI participation may force some students to confront the crisis before they are ready to do so. However, careful monitoring of children who opt out of GCI participation ensures that avoidance coping does not become a long-term or primary coping strategy.

Optimal GCI Group Size

The optimal size of a GCI session is 8 to 30 students. Large groups are not recommended (Mitchell & Everly, 1996) because they may inhibit sharing and the expression of reactions (Brock, 1998).

Where to Offer GCI Sessions

Whenever possible, the GCI session should be offered within a student's natural environment, such as a classroom. Doing so helps to make more concrete the premise that crisis reactions are common (and not necessarily pathological), avoids unnecessary labeling of students as patients, provides reassuring structure and routine, and fosters group processes (Brock, 1998; Klingman,

1987). In addition, recognizing the importance of reaffirming physical health and safety, school crisis interveners should ensure that the GCI room has access to food, water, tissues, and restrooms.

When to Offer GCI Sessions

For adult emergency response personnel, such as firefighters, Mitchell and Everly (1996) recommended providing debriefings 72 hours after the crisis event has ended. As discussed earlier in this chapter, providing GCI immediately after a crisis is contraindicated (Hawker et al., 2011; Mitchell & Everly, 1996). Furthermore, the recommendation for children is that psychological debriefings not be offered right away; offering them a week or more after the crisis may be most appropriate (Stallard & Salter, 2003). Besides avoiding the risk of offering GCI too soon, before students are ready to process the event, the wait also allows the crisis interveners to evaluate psychological trauma and organize homogeneous groups.

Anecdotal observations and practical considerations of GCI suggest that crisis interveners not begin to offer GCI until students believe that crisis-related dangers have passed (a prerequisite to psychological interventions; Charuvastra & Cloitre, 2008). This also gives crisis interveners time to verify facts, ensure that preparations are complete, determine if sufficient time is available, and perform the screening necessary to ensure group homogeneity. Given that brief GCI sessions may be associated with negative effects (Bisson et al., 1997), the crisis intervention team must be sure that the GCI session, which can last up to 3 hours, can be completed. If this cannot be accomplished, and only limited time is available, then a Student Psychoeducational Group is a more appropriate crisis intervention.

GCI Providers

GCI is a team effort with at least a 1-to-10 ratio of mental health crisis interveners to students (Brock, 1998; Hawker et al., 2011; Weinberg, 1990). A session should have at least two interveners, at least one of whom is known to the group (Mitchell & Everly, 1996). Having familiar adults present can be reassuring and offers participants hope that their crisis problems can be addressed. Having crisis interveners who also are nonjudgmental and supportive promotes students' willingness to share (Kneisel & Richards, 1988).

The crisis intervener who leads the GCI session should be a well-trained school-employed mental health professional with a good understanding of group processes (Brock, 1998; Hawker et al., 2011; Openshaw, 2011). The other GCI facilitators should monitor individual student reactions and be available to assist students who need individual attention, such as those who are acutely distressed or who ask to leave the GCI session, for whatever reason.

The Role of the Teacher

Especially when conducted with naturally occurring classroom groups, GCI sessions should actively involve classroom teachers as group facilitators. Children often look to caregivers when determining how stressful a crisis event is; thus, the presence of a teacher who is viewed as being in control and a part of problem-solving efforts may reduce the students' threat perceptions (and thereby reduce psychological traumatization). In some instances, however, classroom teachers may be unable to help facilitate the GCI session, such as if the teacher has been significantly traumatized by the crisis. Though it may be appropriate for teachers to shed tears in front of their students, losing emotional control would be counterproductive.

Decisions About Follow-Up

Given the research described earlier (Bisson et al., 1997; Mayou et al., 2000), which was interpreted as suggesting that single-session crisis interventions are insufficient (Hawker et al., 2011), it is important that follow-up interventions be available to all GCI participants (Brock, 1998). Although GCI and other forms of mental health crisis intervention may be sufficient in addressing minor psychological injuries, more-involved interventions are necessary for students who have been more significantly traumatized.

Parental Permission

According to Everly, Lating, and Mitchell (2005), group sessions "should be voluntary, accompanied by some form of relevant informed consent when intervention goes beyond simple information or educational briefings" (p. 238). For school crisis intervention, some sort of parental consent for students to participate in a GCI session should be required (Litz, Gray, Bryant, & Adler, 2002; Openshaw, 2011). By obtaining such permission, schools ensure that the decision to participate reflects parents' expertise regarding their child's readiness to participate in a GCI session and that only students who are ready for such an intervention are participating. This requirement should be reviewed with a school district's legal counsel; however, use of a passive consent form may be sufficient. Table 17.2 provides a template for such a consent form.

Limits of Confidentiality

Discussions of confidentiality should take place at the beginning of the GCI session. However, as with any intervention provided by mental health professionals, there are limits to confidentiality, and these limits should be acknowledged at the beginning. Confidentiality is limited in situations in which the student requests that information be shared, when there is any indication of danger to participants or others, or when a legal obligation requires school professionals to share otherwise confidential information (Jacob & Feinberg, 2002; Pearrow & Jacob, 2012).

GROUP CRISIS INTERVENTION ELEMENTS

Before beginning GCI, crisis interveners should verify that all group members are appropriate participants and that the appropriate permissions have been obtained. The six steps of a PREPaRE GCI are summarized in Table 17.3. As described in the discussion of Student Psychoeducational Groups (Chapter 16), the delivery of these elements should be tailored to the developmental level of participants.

Table 17.2. Passive Consent Form Template for Group Crisis Intervention

Date

Dear Parent,

As you know, our school community has experienced a traumatic event [PROVIDE APPROPRIATE CRISIS FACTS]. Currently, our school's mental health crisis intervention team is engaged in a number of different activities designed to help our students understand and cope with this tragedy. [SUMMARIZE THE CRISIS INTERVENTION BEING OFFERED]. One such activity is known as Group Crisis Intervention. Our school psychologist [LIST THE OTHER MEMBERS OF THE CRISIS INTERVENTION TEAM TO BE INVOLVED] will be using this approach with a group of students who have had similar crisis experiences. During this meeting we will answer your child's questions about the event, allow him or her to share his or her experiences and reactions to the crisis, and help him or her to find ways to cope with the event in a healthy manner. This letter is to inform you that we feel your child may benefit from such a session. A session will be offered on [STATE THE DATE AND TIME OF THE GCI]. As always, if you have any questions about this group activity, please feel free to contact one of us.

If for any reason you DO NOT judge it appropriate for your child to participate in this Group Crisis Intervention session (if you don't feel your child is ready to share his or her crisis experiences and reactions or for any other reason), please complete and sign the form below and return it to the [SCHOOL NAME] Office by [DATE].

Sincerely,

_____   _____
Name   Name
Principal   School Psychologist

☐ I **DO NOT** want my child to participate in a Group Crisis Intervention at this time.
☐ I would like to speak to a mental health crisis intervener about my child's crisis reactions and how to help him or her cope with this event. Please contact me at the following number: _____. A preferred phone contact day/time is _____.

Parent Name (Print) _____

Student Name (Print) _____

Parent Signature _____

Date _____

Note. Adapted from *School Crisis Prevention and Intervention: The PREPaRE Model* (p. 219), by S. E. Brock et al., 2009, Bethesda, MD: NASP. Copyright 2009 by the National Association of School Psychologists. Adapted with permission.

Table 17.3. Steps in a PREPaRE Group Crisis Intervention

1. Introduce students to the session (5–10 minutes).
2. Provide crisis facts and dispel rumors (15–30 minutes).
3. Share personal crisis stories (30–45 minutes).
4. Identify and normalize crisis reactions (30–45 minutes).
5. Empower students with self-care knowledge (45–60 minutes).
6. Close the session by discussing the future (15–30 minutes).

Note. From *School Crisis Prevention and Intervention: The PREPaRE Model* (p. 220), by S. E. Brock et al., 2009, Bethesda, MD: NASP. Copyright 2009 by the National Association of School Psychologists. Reprinted with permission.

Introduce the Session

The first step, which lasts about 5–10 minutes, includes introducing the GCI leader and facilitators, and explaining the purpose, sequence, and rules of the session (including discussion of confidentiality). Students are told that they are not allowed to leave the room without permission. They are also told that active participation is voluntary. Students who do not want to be in the room during the discussion should be taken to another location and given an alternative activity that is neutral and does not press for exploration of crisis experiences or reactions. In addition, the GCI leader states that verbal or physical violence or abuse will not be tolerated. Students may participate in the creation of additional GCI session rules, which may engender the sense that they are capable problem solvers. The following statement (adapted from Brock, Sandoval, & Lewis, 2001) can be used to begin this step of GCI:

> *I am sorry this happened to your (our) school. When bad things like this happen, it is sometimes helpful to talk about it. And we have a sense that all of you want to talk about the crisis. So, we are going to spend some time today talking. From this discussion we expect that all of you will have a better understanding of what happened, how it has affected us, and what we can do to help ourselves. Please know that none of you are required to be here and if you are not feeling ready to talk about this we will completely understand and respect you asking not to be a part of this session. Not everyone copes with crises in the same way, and if you don't feel this will be helpful for you (for example, thinking about such conversation makes you feel uncomfortable), please let us know and we will help you find other ways to cope with this event.*

Students who respond to this offer and ask to opt out of group participation should be reinforced for their ability to recognize their own feelings. They will be taken by a cofacilitator to a comfortable, safe, and nurturing environment where they are not pressed to share anything about their crisis experiences. However, the crisis interveners should follow up with these students individually within a few days to a week to ensure that they are not using avoidance coping as their primary problem-solving strategy.

Provide Crisis Facts and Dispel Rumors

This step lasts approximately 15–30 minutes, and as in the Student Psychoeducational Group, the recommended strategy in a GCI is a question-and-answer format (Servaty-Seib, Peterson, & Spang, 2003). The following statement from Brock et al. (2001) can be used to begin this step of GCI:

We have experienced an event that was so unusual we might find it hard to understand. I would like to share with you what we know about this tragedy. Feel free to ask questions. It's important that you understand what happened. (p. 188)

To avoid frightening students by giving them unnecessary details about the event, the crisis interveners should begin by reading a developmentally appropriate fact sheet and then let students' questions guide the remainder of the discussion. Doing so helps to avoid giving students information they do not already have and that would unnecessarily frighten them. Of course, if a factual detail has the potential to lessen students' threat perceptions, it should be presented even in the absence of a specific question. Crisis interveners should be sure to provide only verified facts; if they are asked questions they cannot answer, they can offer to investigate the issue further, but they should not speculate.

Especially when working with children, crisis interveners should be prepared to repeat crisis facts (Lord, 1990). Because the crisis will likely be novel, and crisis details may feel overwhelming, crisis interveners should anticipate students' difficulty with understanding the facts. In addition, because younger children are susceptible to distortions about the crisis, this GCI element is designed to identify crisis-related rumors and to explicitly correct these misperceptions.

Finally, GCI sessions are tailored to participants' developmental level and influence the provision of crisis facts. Whereas children ages 8–11 years may be most concerned with basic factual information, adolescents may inquire about more abstract crisis issues (e.g., the potential danger or threat, the role of fate, the impulse for revenge; Stallard & Salter, 2003).

Share Crisis Stories

The sharing of crisis experiences can last 30–45 minutes, depending on the size of the group. Once this part of the session begins, facilitators *must not* allow students to leave the group setting until after the empowerment step has concluded. Although everyone should be given a chance to share their story, no one should be required to do so, and students should be allowed to choose for themselves whether to share their experiences (Seery, Silver, Holman, Ence, & Chu, 2008). Further, explicit or excessive probing for details of the students' crisis experiences is *not* appropriate (Hawker et al., 2011; Mitchell & Everly, 1996; Openshaw, 2011). Simply put, GCI facilitators should typically take what details students give them. To obtain the appropriate level of detail, a statement that can be used to begin this step of GCI is the following:

We have all just shared a common experience. To illustrate this, while none of you are required to share, I would like to give as many of you as possible the chance to offer some basic information about your experiences. You don't need to give a lot of detail about what happened, but do give enough so that we can gain a basic understanding of your crisis story. Who would like to start?

As this prompt suggests, students will be asked not to give highly detailed descriptions of their crisis experiences. Rather, they can be encouraged to provide just enough information so that the commonality of the students' experiences can be made concrete. If a student begins to provide excessive detail, then the crisis interveners need to determine if the information being presented has the potential to increase the anxiety levels of the other participants. If the detail is judged to present a risk, they should carefully and gently tell the student that it is time to give other students a chance to speak. For example, the group facilitator might say the following:

> *Thank you* [student's name]. *I think you have given us enough detail to understand the basic elements of your experience. To make sure everyone has a chance to share, I am going to stop you there. But before we move on, how many of you had an experience that was similar to* [student's name]?

This statement validates the student's experience and gives the rest of the group a better idea of the level of detail being asked for. In addition, if the GCI group was appropriately constructed, the last question, about similar experiences, should result in other students validating the experience as common.

During this step, crisis interveners need to ensure that no mistakes (referred to in PREPaRE workshops as *triage errors*) were made during group construction. If an acutely traumatized student has mistakenly been included in the group and begins to share especially traumatic crisis experiences, the GCI leader should quickly validate the experiences and prevent the student from sharing excessive detail. The GCI leader and facilitators should then consider the necessity of gently removing the acute trauma victim from the group and providing him or her with a more appropriate individualized crisis intervention. The removal of a student from the group may cause some anxiety among the remaining students and should be dealt with directly.

Finally, the GCI leader and facilitators need to consider the most appropriate way of leading a trauma discussion among young children. For example, Stallard and Salter (2003) suggested that younger children are more able to provide verbal accounts of a crisis if they talk while drawing a picture of the event. Use of art also provides a natural opportunity to break up the GCI session, which can be especially important for younger students who have difficulty remaining seated for long periods of time (Brock, 1998). Morgan and White (2003) presented guidelines for using art in crisis intervention, in which crisis interveners should (a) give children a choice about whether to use art as their story or talk about what they created, (b) have them use dry materials (e.g., crayons and pencils) rather than paint, and (c) not offer unsolicited and detailed interpretations of the art to avoid pressing the student to confront realities he or she is not yet ready to consciously address.

Identify Crisis Reactions

This GCI step lasts approximately 30–45 minutes and can involve either teaching common reactions (perhaps the most appropriate approach for younger students) or asking individual students to share how the crisis event is affecting them. For example, the following statement adapted from Brock et al. (2001) can be used to begin this step of GCI:

> *Following an event, such as the one we've just experienced, it is not unusual for people to have uncomfortable feelings and to behave differently for a while. Some common reactions are . . .* [identify common reactions such as those provided in Table 13.3]. *These are typical reactions to an abnormal situation.*

In addition, Brymer, Taylor, et al. (2012) recommended the following language to initiate sharing:

When something really bad happens, kids may feel funny, strange, or uncomfortable. Maybe your heart is beating really fast, or your hands feel sweaty, or your stomach hurts, or your legs or arms feel weak or shaky. Other times kids just feel funny inside their heads, almost as if they cannot press stop on the DVR and they keep watching the bad thing happen over and over again in their mind.

Sometimes your body keeps having these feelings for a while even after the bad thing is over and you are safe. These feelings are your body's way of telling you again how bad the event was.

There is a wide range of reactions that you may be feeling. Do you have any of these feelings now, or other ones that I didn't talk about? Can you tell me where you feel them, and what they feel like?

Sometimes these strange or uncomfortable feelings come up when kids see, hear, or smell things that remind them of the bad thing that happened, like strong winds, glass breaking, or the smell of smoke. It can be very scary for kids to have these feelings in their bodies, especially if they don't know why they are happening or what to do about them. If you like, I can tell you some ways to help you cope better. Would you like that? (p. 61)

Regardless of the approach used (i.e., direct instruction, individual sharing, or both), GCI leaders must ensure that student reactions are framed so others can view them as common (Brock, 1998). Asking students whether they have experienced certain general types of reactions, and having them raise their hands if they have, can reinforce this common experience. For example, if a student shares that he or she is having nightmares about a crisis event, the GCI leader should validate this reaction as common and state: "Bad dreams and other sleep difficulties are very common following a crisis event." The leader should then ask how many other students have experienced a similar reaction and do so in a way that guarantees several other participants will raise their hands. For example, the GCI leader might say: "Raise your hand if you are also having bad dreams, problems getting to sleep or staying asleep, or any other sleep-related difficulties?" Using an approach such as this helps make the fact that they are experiencing common reactions more concrete.

While emphasizing that most initial crisis reactions are common, the GCI leader should keep in mind that many students find their reactions unsettling, and it is not uncommon for students to fear that they are "going crazy." Group sharing and the GCI leader's anticipation of crisis reactions help normalize these frightening symptoms. The GCI leader should also let students know that recovery is the norm and that with time, for most people, reactions will dissipate. However, students should also be told what to do if they feel that they are unable to independently manage their reactions. This is a natural time to introduce self-referral procedures for obtaining the individual crisis intervention discussed in Chapter 18. As this step ends, asking future-oriented questions helps students anticipate reactions they may have and coping skills they need. For example, students can be asked: "What do you think will happen next?" "Will your friends and family continue to be affected?" or "What are you concerned about?"

During this step, the GCI leader and facilitators should anticipate some emotional release and should appreciate that this is an important source of secondary triage data. GCI facilitators (and the classroom teacher) can help by monitoring individual students' reactions, evaluating the severity of distress, and counseling and gently removing an acutely distressed student that may have mistakenly been included in the group. These students require more individualized crisis intervention. In addition, if allowed to stay in the group, the acutely distressed student may become the group's focus. If this happens, it is important for the GCI leader to acknowledge the removal of a distressed student. For example, in this situation the GCI leader might state:

> When it comes to helping people cope with an event like we have just experienced, we understand that there is no one best way to support you. While some of us may benefit from groups like this one, others will find it more helpful to talk this out individually, while still others will find both settings (group and individual) helpful. Know that we are willing to meet individually with any of you that would like to talk some more and in greater detail about this event.

Empower Participants

Having gained a better understanding of how they are being affected and what some of their future concerns might be, students are ready to move on to a discussion of how to cope with the crisis. This empowerment step may last up to 60 minutes, and during this time the focus shifts from symptom sharing to symptom solving (Terr, 1992). The primary goal is to help students begin to participate in activities that help them regain a sense of control. The following statement, adapted from Brock et al. (2001), can be used to begin this step:

> Crises can make us feel helpless, and that is a big part of what has generated the reactions we were just talking about. So now that we have a basic understanding of how we are all being affected by the crisis and have an idea of potential problems we may need to address as we move forward, I would like to see us take action or make plans to help us now and in the future. [For elementary grade students consider offering] Here are some ideas that I have for how we can help ourselves and each other cope…[For more developmentally mature students consider stating] What are some ideas you have for how you can help yourselves, and each other, cope with your feelings?

The introduction in this step should emphasize that when students believe they have some control over their experiences, they are more resistant to stress (Luthar, 1991), and the GCI leader can begin by identifying coping strategies students already use. They should point out the strategies that are adaptive and that help students, and explicitly describe maladaptive strategies and offer alternatives. During this step, the leader and facilitators might review basic stress management techniques (e.g., getting enough sleep, food, and exercise, and talking to friends and family). Alternatively, they might encourage students to work together on developing strategies to gradually desensitize each other to trauma-related fears. Or they may use a directive approach and tell students exactly what they need to do to cope. Brymer, Taylor, et al. (2012) provides specific guidance on how to (a) give students basic information on coping; (b) teach relaxation exercises; (c) help with difficulties concentrating and learning; (d) address coping with feelings of anger and frustration; (e) help with sleep problems; and (f) deal with feelings of guilt, shame, and other difficult emotions.

In this step the GCI leader can conclude by reviewing students' newly identified or reestablished coping skills and complimenting the students on their ability to address their crisis problems. The GCI leader and facilitators may decide at this point that ending the session is appropriate (Brock, 1998).

Close the Session

This final step in a GCI session may last up to 30 minutes and focuses on beginning to place the crisis event in the past and moving forward. For example, the following statement adapted from Brock et al. (2001) can be used to begin this final step:

> *Before we conclude our discussion, I would like us to consider what we can do to help place this event behind us and move on with our lives.* [For elementary-grade students] *Here are some ideas that I have for how we can move on ...* [For developmentally more mature students consider stating] *What are some ideas you have for what we can do to bring some closure to this event?*

This step may include developing memorials, preparing to attend or participating in funerals, writing get-well cards and letters to victims, and if the class has experienced the death of a classmate or teacher, discussing what to do with the deceased's desk and belongings (Brock, 1998) or writing a commemoration (Chauvin, McDaniel, Banks, Eddlemon, & Cook, 2013).

In concluding the session, the GCI leader and facilitators should answer any remaining questions and remind students that they have shared a common experience and are displaying common reactions to abnormal circumstances. The GCI leader should acknowledge that, for some students, it might be some time before they are truly able to place the event in their past and move on with their lives. However, at the same time, students should be reminded that being positive about the future helps them recover and that, although memories will remain, crisis reactions typically lessen over time. For example, the following statement could be used to close the GCI session:

> *If there are no more questions, we are going to end our group discussion. Before doing so, however, I would like to remind you that we are all in this together. We have shared a common experience and are having similar, and very typical, reactions to the crisis. While I do expect that with time we will feel better, and be able to put this event in our past, I also want to acknowledge that for some of us this may take a while and that we will always remember the event. As a result, as we move forward from time to time we may want to seek out additional support.*

The importance of concluding the session with a measured sense of hope and optimism is highlighted by Hobfoll et al. (2007), who suggested that instilling such a sense among trauma survivors is essential to obtaining a positive outcome. Similarly, Ruzek et al. (2007) stated:

> *Those who maintain optimism (because they can hope for their future), positive expectancy, a feeling of confidence that life and self are predictable, or other hopeful beliefs (e.g., in God, that there is a high probability that things will work out as well as can reasonably be expected) [are likely to have] more favorable outcomes after experiencing mass trauma.* (p. 23)

Finally, the GCI leader and facilitators should reassure students that additional crisis intervention services are available and remind students that they can use self-referral procedures. For example, they might state:

> *While it is true that our reactions are very common or typical, I want you to know that we appreciate how upsetting they can be when you are experiencing them. So, even though we are ending this session, we [the GCI leader and facilitators] will continue to be available. All you need to do is ask and we will be sure to find a time to talk things out with you.*

GROUP CRISIS INTERVENTION FOLLOW-UP ACTIVITIES

Following the GCI session, all parents and caregivers need to be informed about how they can help students cope with crisis-related stressors and problems. Psychological education recommendations, which should be provided to the families of all GCI participants, include (a) listen to and spend time with your child; (b) offer, but do not force, discussion about the trauma; (c) reassure your child that he or she is safe; (d) offer assistance with everyday tasks and chores; (e) respect your child's privacy; and (f) do not take anger or other reactions personally (Mitchell & Everly, 1996).

After the GCI session has ended, at least one, but preferably all, of the GCI facilitators and the session leader should be available to the group participants throughout the remainder of the school day, to help students seeking additional support and to answer questions. This also gives crisis interveners additional opportunities to assess how individual students are coping (that is, to collect secondary psychological triage data).

Finally, as soon as possible after the GCI session has concluded, the school crisis response team's Operations Section Chief should meet with the GCI leader and facilitators to review the session. This review typically occurs at the end of the school day and serves two important purposes. First, it helps in making decisions regarding students who need additional assistance. Second, it gives the session leader and facilitators a chance to examine their own crisis reactions and coping following the session.

CONCLUSION

Some school-associated crises can simultaneously affect large numbers of students, and given a school's limited resources, group approaches to mental health crisis intervention may be a practical necessity. For students who are not suspected of having significant psychological injuries, simply reconnecting them with their parents or primary caregivers or providing psychological education, or both, may be sufficient. However, if the traumatic effects are judged to be more severe (but not acute), then GCI might be indicated. In addition, by providing crisis intervention assistance to groups, the carefully constructed GCI group also has the advantage of making concrete the normality of crisis experiences and reactions. Students who are allowed to share basic elements of their crisis stories and brief descriptions of how they have been affected by the crisis event will come to realize that they are not alone in their experiences and reactions. This sense of normality should, in turn, give them the emotional strength needed to adaptively cope with crisis-generated problems. In addition, this group approach, and its sharing of crisis stories and reactions, can be a powerful triage tool to help ensure that no student with significant psychological injury slips through the cracks of a school mental health crisis intervention. However, as Chapter 16 notes, ongoing research is needed to evaluate and demonstrate the efficacy of this intervention with schoolchildren (Szumilas et al., 2010). In the years following this book's publication, the reader is encouraged to attend to the literature regarding the use of GCI as a mental health crisis intervention and to adjust local practice according to the results of such future study.

Chapter 18

INDIVIDUAL CRISIS INTERVENTION

Most crisis-exposed students (and staff members) experience brief and manageable initial crisis reactions. However, some display more acute or durable responses (or both) that overwhelm their coping abilities and may also be predictive of later psychopathology such as posttraumatic stress disorder (PTSD). Although the empirical literature on meeting the immediate needs of these more traumatized individuals is limited, the elements of individual crisis intervention (ICI) described in this chapter are judged to be the most appropriate immediate response to these more severely affected individuals (Brock, 2011a; Brymer et al., 2006; Brymer, Taylor, et al., 2012; Everly, Hamilton, Tyiska, & Ellers, 2008; Hobfoll et al., 2007; Jaycox, Stein, & Wong, 2014; Ruzek et al., 2007).

This form of psychological crisis intervention is not psychotherapy, nor is it a substitute for psychotherapy, and it does not have crisis resolution (or the solving of all crisis-generated problems) as its goal. Rather, ICI aims at placing crisis-exposed students in a position from which they can independently cope with crisis-generated problems (if the psychological injury was not severe), or from which they can access psychotherapeutic treatment (if the psychological injury was severe). For that minority of students who appear to have developed psychopathology secondary to their crisis exposure, other treatment options should be made available (see Chapter 19). These more intense services are not a part of initial school crisis interventions and sometimes require collaboration with, and referral to, community-based mental health professionals.

Depending on school district policies and procedures (and in some cases union contracts), provision of ICI by teachers and other educators may be appropriate if they are given sufficient training. Regardless of training or level of expertise, ICI is a first step in the longer-term helping process for more significantly traumatized individuals. The difference is that whereas school-employed mental health professionals may remain involved with student interventions long after the immediate ICI response has ended, teachers, for example, will find their mental health caregiving responsibilities concluded at the end of the immediate ICI response (when a student may be referred to a school-employed or community-based mental health professional).

INDIVIDUAL CRISIS INTERVENTION GOALS

The immediate ICI discussed in this chapter employs a basic problem-solving model and is adapted from the psychological first aid techniques originally identified by Slaikeu (1990) and more recently by Brymer et al. (2006); Brymer, Taylor, et al. (2012); and Ruzek et al. (2007). As summarized in Table 18.1, the primary goal of ICI is to help crisis-exposed individuals reestablish their immediate coping or problem-solving abilities (e.g., the individual's ability to manage their crisis reactions and other challenges generated by the crisis). Subgoals include (a) providing physical and emotional support, which includes ensuring the individual's physical and psychological safety and containing emotional distress; (b) identifying crisis-generated problems; (c) supporting adaptive coping; and (d) assessing the individual's psychological trauma risk and linking him or her with the appropriate helping resources. These steps have been identified as important to any immediate individual crisis intervention (Brymer, Pynoos, Vivrette, & Taylor, 2012; Jaycox et al., 2014; Litz, Gray, Bryant, & Adler, 2002; Phipps & Byrne, 2003; Watson, Brymer, & Bonanno, 2011; Wilson, Raphael, Meldrum, Bedosky, & Sigman, 2000).

When a crisis occurs, sometimes people are immobilized or overwhelmed by apparently unsolvable problems, a response that is likened to a deer frozen in the headlights of an oncoming car. When helping individuals in this state, the crisis intervener's primary task is to reestablish immediate coping ability, that is, to help the individual take some action (no matter how small) toward coping with crisis-generated problems (Brock, Sandoval, & Lewis, 2001). Because school-age youth likely have had limited exposure to crises, they may be expected to have greater difficulty coping with the shock of an incident than adults would. The following ICI subgoals are important to reestablishing immediate coping.

The first subgoal is to provide students with physical and emotional support. In some situations, such as a natural disaster, individuals' failure to immediately cope with their altered conditions may place them in situations that threaten their physical safety. (e.g., not recognizing that they need to stay out of the sun and maintain hydration on hot and humid days). Thus, an important subgoal of immediate ICI is to provide the support and guidance needed to ensure that individuals are physically safe (e.g., either directing or helping the individual to take specific actions that ensure their safety). In addition, before students can recover from exposure to a traumatic event, not only must they be safe, they also must believe they are safe and that crisis-related danger has passed (see Chapters 11 and 12). Although ensuring physical safety can be considered the ICI priority, the provision of emotional support is also essential because it helps to contain the emotional distress (e.g., panic) that interferes with adaptive coping and problem solving (Ruzek et al., 2007).

Once the subgoal of ensuring physical safety and containing emotional distress has been achieved, traumatized individuals will be able to begin the problem-solving process. This next ICI subgoal finds the crisis intervener helping students identify their crisis-generated problems. Often these problems involve managing crisis reactions or emotions, but they might also include more practical matters such as obtaining shelter or locating lost items.

Having identified crisis-generated problems, the next ICI subgoal involves supporting adaptive coping and beginning the problem-solving process. A successful ICI intervention may not solve all crisis-generated problems, but from such intervention, it should be clear that the individual is moving in the right direction. Evidence that this subgoal has been obtained includes the existence of a plan to address the crisis-generated problems.

Table 18.1. Individual Crisis Intervention Goal and Subgoals

Primary goal: Reestablish immediate coping.
   Subgoals:
   a. Provide physical and emotional support.
   b. Identify crisis-generated problems.
   c. Support adaptive coping.
   d. Assess trauma risk and link to helping resources.

Note. From *School Crisis Prevention and Intervention: The PREPaRE Model* (p. 228), by S. E. Brock et al., 2009, Bethesda, MD: NASP. Copyright 2009 by the National Association of School Psychologists. Reprinted with permission.

As with other crisis interventions that involve direct contact with crisis-exposed individuals (i.e., Classroom Meetings, Student Psychoeducational Groups, and group crisis intervention), ICI is an important part of secondary psychological triage (see Chapter 14). Thus, the final subgoal of ICI is to assess the individual's degree of psychological trauma and then link the student (or staff member) with the appropriate helping resources. If the crisis intervener determines that the individual's psychological injury is minor—that is, the individual's coping challenges do not appear overwhelming and the individual exhibits adaptive coping strategies—then simply reconnecting the individual with his or her natural support systems (and providing some caregiver training as needed) may be all that is required. In contrast, if the psychological injury is severe— that is, coping challenges are overwhelming the individual and adaptive coping strategies cannot be identified—then the individual may need to be referred for more intense psychotherapeutic support (see Chapter 19).

GENERAL CONSIDERATIONS FOR INDIVIDUAL CRISIS INTERVENTION

Before proceeding to a detailed discussion of the specific elements or steps of ICI, this section presents some general considerations.

Who Should Be Offered ICI

Any individual who appears to be having immediate coping challenges (e.g., difficulty managing crisis reactions or emotions) would be an appropriate target of this basic problem-solving intervention. These individuals may require crisis interveners to provide relatively specific guidance or direction on how to cope with crisis-generated problems. In particular, ICI should be the initial crisis intervention for individuals who are acute trauma victims (e.g., those who were physically injured or directly threatened). On the other hand, among those who are less severely traumatized, less directive crisis interventions that allow individuals to solve crisis-generated problems more or less on their own, should be considered (e.g., reestablishing support systems and psychological education).

As with group crisis intervention, unless the individual's condition is judged to present a danger to self or others, that person should be given a choice of whether or not to participate in ICI (Hawker, Durkin, & Hawker, 2011; Jacob & Feinberg, 2002; McNally, Bryant, & Ehlers, 2003). At least initially, coping strategies that involve denying or minimizing a crisis event can have an adaptive function; that is, it gives individuals the time needed to mobilize the internal and external resources required to cope with crisis-generated challenges. Requiring ICI participation may force some to emotionally confront the crisis before they are ready to do so (see Chapter 13's discussion of avoidance coping). However, individuals who opt out of ICI should be carefully monitored and supported to ensure that avoidance coping has not become a longer-term (or primary) coping strategy.

Where ICI Should Be Offered

ICI is designed to be used anywhere traumatized students or school staff members are found (e.g., on the playground or in a classroom). However, crisis interveners providing this type of support must keep in mind the need to reaffirm physical health and safety and the perception of safety. Thus, ICI settings must have access to food, water, tissues, and restrooms and otherwise convey a sense of physical safety.

When to Offer ICI

ICI can be offered as soon as the individual appears ready to begin identifying crisis-generated problems and seeking solutions, that is, as soon as he or she is emotionally stable. Individuals who do not respond to questions, or who are crying, hyperventilating, or shaking uncontrollably, are not ready to begin problem solving (see Table 11.2 for additional signs of the emotionally overwhelmed individual). Rather, they first need to be emotionally stabilized (Brymer et al., 2006; Brymer, Taylor, et al., 2012; see Table 11.3 for guidance on how to respond to help stabilize these individuals). Furthermore, ICI should not be initiated until crisis interveners have judged that students believe that crisis-related dangers have passed (a prerequisite to any psychological intervention; Charuvastra & Cloitre, 2008). This delay in the provision of direct crisis interventions services also allows for verification of crisis facts and preparation by the crisis intervention and student care group.

ICI Providers

School-employed mental health professionals have had training that makes them especially well prepared to provide ICI. However, with the appropriate psychological education and training, any caregiver, such as a teacher, who is able to convey a sense of calmness and control in crisis situations could become an appropriate provider of ICI. Motivation for giving teachers training in ICI includes the observation that the presence of familiar adults who are filling crisis response and intervention roles helps students reestablish the belief that they are safe, which in turn helps to contain distress (Ruzek et al., 2007).

When Follow-Up Is Needed

As discussed in Chapter 17, one-off or single-session crisis interventions are contraindicated (Bisson, Jenkins, Alexander, & Bannister, 1997; Mayou, Ehlers, & Hobbs, 2000). Thus, follow-up interventions and services should be available to all ICI participants. Although ICI may be sufficient in addressing minor psychological injuries, more involved interventions (such as those discussed in Chapter 19) are required for individuals who have been more significantly traumatized.

Parental Permission

Obtaining parental permission before providing any crisis intervention assistance is always preferable (Ruzek et al., 2007). However, ICI is not a planned psychotherapeutic treatment, so providing immediate assistance to a distressed student is appropriate even without parental consent (Jacob & Feinberg, 2002; Pearrow & Jacob, 2012). According to the National Association of School Psychologists' (NASP, 2010) *Principles for Professional Ethics,* "urgent situations" are recognized as an exception to the rule of always obtaining parental consent prior to establishing a school psychologist–client relationship. Specifically, within Standard I.1.2, NASP states:

> It is ethically permissible to provide psychological assistance without parent notice or consent in *emergency situations* or if there is reason to believe a student may pose a danger to others; is at risk for self-harm; or is in danger of injury, exploitation, or maltreatment. (p. 4, emphasis added)

In a footnote to this standard, NASP also recommends

> that school district parent handbooks and websites advise parents that a minor student may be seen by school health or mental health professionals (e.g., school nurse, counselor, social worker, school psychologist) without parent notice or consent to ensure that the student is safe or is not a danger to others. (p. 4)

Professional ethics aside, the school-employed mental health professional must be aware of, and follow, local and state guidelines regarding parental consent, because states differ in how and when such consent is obtained. Of course, schools must contact the student's parents or caregivers as soon as possible, especially in the case of acute distress. Such contact has several goals: (a) to inform them of their child's status and possible need for additional support, (b) to evaluate their status and determine their ability to provide such support, and (c) to provide the appropriate psychological education regarding how best to address their child's needs.

Limits of Confidentiality

All school-employed or community-based mental health professionals have an obligation to respect individual rights regarding the confidentiality of information shared in the ICI session (Brymer et al., 2006; Brymer, Taylor, et al., 2012). However, as is the case for any intervention provided by mental health professionals, such confidentiality has limits. Whenever possible, these limits should be acknowledged when ICI is initiated. Situations with limits to confidentiality include those in which the individual requests that information be shared, there is an indication of danger to the student or others, or a legal obligation requires the practitioner to share otherwise confidential information (Jacob & Feinberg, 2002; Pearrow & Jacob, 2012). However, in an emergency, addressing limits to confidentiality as ICI is being initiated may not be appropriate, such as when working with an acutely distressed student. According to NASP's (2010) *Principles for Professional Ethics,* Standard I.2.3 states:

> School psychologists inform students and other clients of the boundaries of confidentiality at the outset of establishing a professional relationship. They seek a shared understanding with clients regarding the types of information that will and will not be shared with third parties. *However, if a child or adolescent is in immediate need of assistance, it is permissible to delay the discussion of confidentiality until the immediate crisis is resolved.* School psychologists recognize that it may be necessary to discuss confidentiality at multiple points in a professional relationship to ensure client understanding and agreement regarding how sensitive disclosures will be handled. (p. 5, emphasis added)

INDIVIDUAL CRISIS INTERVENTION ELEMENTS

In the PREPaRE model, ICI consists of five elements or steps. The duration of this intervention is variable and depends on the nature of the coping challenges. In some cases ICI is a relatively brief intervention and lasts no more than 30 minutes. However, if the coping challenges addressed are great (e.g., they involve suicidal ideation), then ICI can last hours. The specific steps in an ICI are (a) making psychological contact, (b) verifying emotional readiness to identify and address crisis-generated problems, (c) identifying and prioritizing crisis problems, (d) beginning to address crisis problems, and (e) evaluating attainment of ICI goals. These elements are summarized in Table 18.2 and discussed in detail in the sections that follow. However, when providing ICI, crisis interveners should always follow the guidelines for the delivery of immediate mental health crisis intervention (or psychological first aid) offered by Brymer, Taylor, et al. (2012) and presented in Table 18.3.

Establishing Psychological Contact

The first ICI step involves making psychological contact with the person in crisis. Establishing rapport with the individual who has been exposed to a crisis is not necessarily difficult. Individuals in crisis are often very open to someone who is willing and able to help. When beginning ICI, it is important for the crisis intervener to introduce him- or herself (even if you are a familiar face), to discuss issues associated with confidentiality, and to inquire about any unmet basic needs. As discussed in Chapters 11 and 12, students need to feel safe and have their basic needs met before they can begin the process of recovery.

Brymer, Taylor, et al. (2012) suggest that, when working with children (after getting at the child's eye level and smiling), the crisis intervener should begin to establish psychological contact by saying something like the following:

> Hi, Lisa. My name is _____. I am working with Mr./Ms./Teacher _____ to help you and your family/classmates. Is there anything you need right now? Are you warm enough? Do you want a drink or some food? (p. 21)

Table 18.2. Elements of Individual Crisis Intervention

1. *Establish psychological contact.*
   a. Introduction:
      i. Identify self.
      ii. Inquire about and address basic needs as indicated.
   b. Empathy:
      i. Identify crisis facts.
      ii. Identify crisis-related feelings.
   c. Respect:
      i. Pause to listen.
      ii. Do not dominate the conversation.
      iii. Do not try to smooth things over.
   d. Warmth:
      i. Ensure that verbal communication is congruent with nonverbal behaviors.
      ii. Consider the use of, and when indicated provide, physical contact (e.g., a reassuring arm around the shoulder of a frightened student).

2. *Verify emotional readiness to begin problem identification and problem solving.*
   a. If the student is not ready, stabilize the student.
   b. If the student is ready, begin the problem-solving process.

3. *Identify and prioritize crisis-generated problems. Identify the most immediate concerns.*
   a. Ask about what happened and gain understanding of the crisis story.
   b. Ask about the problems generated by the crisis event.
   c. Rank order crisis-generated problems.

4. *Address crisis-generated problems. Encourage the student to be as responsible as possible for coping with crisis-generated challenges.*
   a. Ask about coping attempts already made and validate adaptive coping strategies already identified by the student.
   b. Facilitate exploration of additional coping strategies and as indicated, encourage the student to identify his or her own adaptive coping strategies.
   c. Propose alternative coping strategies and as indicated, do not hesitate to explicitly direct the student toward adaptive coping strategies.
      i. If lethality is low *and* the student is capable of action, then take a facilitative stance (i.e., the student initiates and is responsible for coping actions).
      ii. If lethality is high *or* student is not capable of acting, then take a directive stance (i.e., the crisis intervener initiates and is responsible for coping actions).

5. *Evaluate and conclude the ICI session. Ensure that the individual is moving toward adaptive crisis resolution.*
   a. Secure identifying information and identify and ensure connection with primary support systems (e.g., parents, teachers).
   b. Agree on a time for recontact and follow-up.
   c. Assess whether immediate coping has been restored.

Table 18.2. Continued

    i.   Physical and emotional support have been obtained, and any lethality has been reduced.

   ii.   Crisis problems have been identified, and adaptive coping has been initiated.

  iii.   Using the assessed trauma risk level, the student is linked to appropriate helping resources.

- If these goals have not been obtained, then restart the ICI process.
- If these goals have been obtained, compliment the student on his or her problem-solving skills, convey the expectation that they will cope with the trauma, and conclude ICI. Social supports may now become the primary crisis intervention.
- Keep in mind that triage is a process and that ongoing monitoring of the recovery process is always important.

Note. Adapted from *School Crisis Prevention and Intervention: The PREPaRE Model* (pp. 232–233), by S. E. Brock et al., 2009, Bethesda, MD: NASP. Copyright 2009 by the National Association of School Psychologists. Adapted with permission.

Table 18.3. Delivery of an Individual Crisis Intervention

Guidelines for Delivering Psychological First Aid (PFA)

- Operate only within the framework of an authorized school emergency response system.
- Before you approach an individual or a group, first observe politely.
- Initiate contact only after you have determined that you are not intruding or interrupting.
- Offer practical assistance (food, water). This is often the best way to make contact.
- Ask simple, respectful questions to determine how you may help.
- Remain flexible and adjust to people and their situations as needed. Do not enter the site with any agenda other than providing PFA.
- Be prepared for those affected by the event to either avoid you or flood you with contact.
- Speak calmly. Be patient, responsive, and sensitive.
- Speak slowly, in simple concrete terms; do not use acronyms or jargon.
- Listen carefully when students or staff members want to talk. Focus on understanding ("getting") what they want to tell you, and hearing how you can be of help. Children who are too young to speak, or who may not speak clearly, often express their feelings and show what they want through their behaviors, such as play.
- Support and reinforce the person's individual strengths and coping strategies, including the positive things he or she has done to stay safe.
- Give information that directly addresses the person's immediate goals, and clarify answers repeatedly as needed.
- Give information that is accurate and age-appropriate. Remember that even very young children need to know what has happened. Tell children the truth, but keep it brief and speak to their developmental level (e.g., avoid discussing the details of a death).
- Reassure young children that the adults are there to protect them and keep them safe. Even when adults do not feel safe, young children need to be assured that everything possible is being done to keep them safe.

- When communicating through an interpreter, look at the person with whom you are talking, not at the translator or interpreter.
- PFA leaders should reach out to those in positions of authority (e.g., administrators, school resource officers) who have been equally exposed but who, because of their position, need to project a sense of calm and control to those under their care.
- Assist support staff (e.g., custodians, bus drivers, food workers, librarians, secretaries, coaches, instructional aides) whose emotional needs may be overlooked in emergencies. These staff members, who are often involved in directing, calming, and reassuring students and parents, are among the important stabilizing factors in students' lives.
- Remember that the goal of PFA is to reduce distress, assist with current needs, and promote adaptive functioning, not to elicit details of traumatic experiences and losses.
- Keep in mind that the goal of schools is to support academic achievement. Ask students what they need to be able to attend school every day, to complete their work and succeed in school, and to stay safe in their lives outside of school.

Behaviors to Avoid
- Do not make assumptions about what students and staff have experienced during the incident or are experiencing currently.
- Do not assume that everyone who has been through the emergency will be traumatized.
- Do not pathologize. Most acute reactions are understandable and expectable, given what students and staff have experienced. Do not label reactions as "symptoms" or speak in terms of "diagnoses," "conditions," "pathologies," or "disorders."
- Do not talk down to or patronize students or staff. Do not focus on the individual's helplessness, weaknesses, mistakes, or disability. Focus instead on what he or she has done that is effective or has contributed to helping themselves or others, both during the emergency and in the present setting. Let the student know that continuing to attend school and performing academically shows his or her strength and resilience. Highlight to staff that coming to work every day or taking on additional duties shows their strength.
- Do not assume that all students and staff members want or need to talk to you. Being physically present in a supportive and calm way in itself often helps affected people feel safer and more able to cope.
- Do not "debrief" by asking for details of what happened.
- Do not speculate or give information that might be inaccurate. If you cannot answer a question, say so, and do your best to learn the facts.

Note. Adapted from *Psychological First Aid for Schools: Field Operations Guide* (2nd ed., pp. 12–13), by M. Brymer, M. Taylor et al., 2012, Rockville, MD: National Child Traumatic Stress Network and National Center for PTSD. Adapted with permission.

When working with adolescents, Brymer, Taylor, et al. suggest the crisis intervener should begin by saying something like this:

My name is _____. I work with _____ and I am part of the school-based mental health recovery team. I am touching base with students to see how they are doing and to find out what they need. Is it okay if I talk to you for a few minutes? (p. 21)

Empathy, respect, and warmth are the vehicles used to make psychological contact. Empathy involves listening to what the individual is saying and working to understand the individual's crisis story and how he or she feels. Empathy is different from sympathy. Sympathy involves feeling what the person in crisis is feeling (and is not helpful to the crisis intervener), while empathy involves demonstrating understanding of what is being shared. Thus, even if the crisis intervener has not had the same experience, he or she can understand, or empathize with, the individual's situation. To show understanding, the crisis intervener should restate both facts and feelings in his or her own words. Active listening skills important to demonstrating empathy are paraphrasing, summarizing, and checking perceptions.

Respect is communicated by pausing to listen and, at least initially, avoiding dominating the conversation or trying to smooth things over. In other words, instead of offering lectures or immediately offering explanations or solutions, the crisis intervener offers to talk about and listen to the individual's perceptions of the crisis. It is also important to avoid being judgmental and instead to communicate a willingness to enter into a problem-solving relationship with the individual in crisis.

Finally, warmth is critical to making psychological contact with crisis-exposed individuals. Warmth is expressed by paraverbal behaviors such as gestures, posture, tone of voice, touch, and facial expressions. Congruence between what the crisis intervener says and what his or her paraverbal behaviors communicate is essential. When working with younger children, it is important to get down to the child's eye level, use a calm reassuring voice, and be as nonthreatening as possible (Brymer, Taylor, et al., 2012; Ruzek et al., 2007).

Physical contact or touch can be helpful in establishing warmth, as it can have a calming effect. However, it must be used carefully. Some individuals may be very comfortable with a caring crisis intervener placing a reassuring arm around their shoulders, but others may not, and it might actually serve as a reminder of the crisis event (e.g., in instances in which the student was the target of child abuse). In addition, consistent with guidance offered by Brymer et al. (2006) and Brymer, Taylor, et al. (2012), the intervener should listen for and validate any response that suggests that the type of contact is appropriate with regard to the child's cultural and social norms. Cultural norms and values influence how close to stand to someone, how much eye contact to make, or how acceptable it is to offer therapeutic touch. For example, one of the author's (Brock) very first mental health crisis interventions (following a school shooting) took place at a school that was predominantly Southeast Asian and included a substantial number of Hmong students. During this mental health crisis intervention, it was critical to know that touching a child's hair is taboo among the Hmong, who consider the head sacred and where the person's soul lives. Consequently, patting the head could "startle the soul out of the body" (Beghtol, 1988, p. 26). Obviously, this was critical information when attempting to establish psychological contact with traumatized students. Further guidance is offered by Brymer, Taylor, et al. (2012):

Do:

- Look for clues that indicate an individual's need for "personal space."
- Seek guidance about the most common and important cultural norms from school or community cultural leaders who best understand local customs. Also ask about cultural variations, both between distinctive groups and within groups, to avoid stereotypes.
- Ask the person what cultural traditions or rituals are important to him/her.

Don't:

- Use sustained eye contact or stand too close to an individual unless he/she initiates such contact.
- Touch the individual unless you have asked permission. Only touch in a way that cannot be misinterpreted by others.
- Make assumptions about the individual's culture, race, nationality, or belief system.
- Expect all members of a group to be too similar in their beliefs and behaviors. (p. 21)

Verifying Emotional Readiness to Begin Problem Identification and Solving

Once psychological contact has been made, traumatized individuals typically feel understood, accepted, and supported. As a result, the intensity of their emotional distress will have been reduced and their energy potentially redirected toward problem identification and problem-solving activities. However, before beginning those activities, and to realize an important subgoal of ICI, the crisis intervener should next ensure that the student is emotionally ready to do this work. Brymer, Taylor, et al. (2012) identified the signs of individuals who may be emotionally overwhelmed and thus not able to immediately begin this problem-solving process (see Chapter 11, Table 11.2). Briefly, these are individuals who appear immobilized by crisis problems, are unresponsive, are demonstrating extreme emotional or physical reactions (or both), or are engaging in behaviors that present some degree of risk for physical harm. These intense immediate crisis reactions are particularly worrisome because they represent significant coping challenges, and if allowed to continue unchecked may develop into psychopathology (Hobfoll et al., 2007).

Options for stabilizing emotionally overwhelmed individuals include first contacting the student's primary caregivers and giving them information (summarized in Table 11.3) that helps them to calm their child while informing them about the importance of controlling their own emotions. If primary caregivers are unavailable or are unable to control their own emotions, then the crisis intervener needs to emotionally stabilize the child (see Table 18.4). If none of these interventions stabilizes the student's acute emotional distress, the ICI process should be concluded, and an immediate referral to a school-employed or community-based mental health professional or medical professional is indicated.

Identifying and Prioritizing Crisis Problems

Once psychological contact with the student has been established and emotional stability ensured, the next step is to identify and prioritize the problems generated by the crisis. To begin problem solving, the crisis intervener asks the individual if he or she is ready to tell his or her crisis story. During this step the crisis intervener should be prepared for the possibility of an emotional release. When working with children, the crisis intervener might begin to identify and prioritize crisis problems by saying something like the following:

> Events like the one you have just experienced often create problems that can be difficult to solve. Sometimes kids have a difficult time dealing with them. If you think it would help, how about you tell me about your crisis experience, how it is affecting you, and if there are any challenges or worries that I might be able to help you begin to address?

Table 18.4. Suggestions for Stabilizing the Emotionally Agitated and Disoriented Student

If the person appears extremely agitated, has accelerated speech, seems out of touch with the surroundings, or is crying intensely, it may be helpful to

- Position yourself at eye level, so he/she becomes aware of you.
- Ask the individual to listen to you and look at you.
- Find out if he/she knows who he/she is, where he/she is, and what is happening.
- Ask him/her to describe the surroundings and say where both of you are.

If these actions do not help, introduce a technique called "grounding," by saying: "After a frightening experience, you can be very upset or angry or unable to stop thinking about what happened. I can help you feel less overwhelmed by teaching you about something called "grounding." Grounding works by having you focus on the things you see and hear around you, instead of all the thoughts you're having. Would you like to try it?

If the person agrees, speak in a calm, quiet voice and lead him/her through the steps:

- Sit in a comfortable position with your legs and arms uncrossed.
- Breathe in and out slowly three times.
- Look around you and name five nondistressing, simple objects that you can see. For example, you might say, "I see the floor, I see a shoe, I see a table, I see a chair, I see my friend."
- Breathe in and out slowly three times.
- Next, name five nondistressing sounds you can hear. For example, you might say, "I hear a teacher talking, I hear myself breathing, I hear a door close, I hear kids playing, I hear a cell phone ringing."
- Breathe in and out slowly three times.
- Next, name five nondistressing things you can feel. For example, you might say, "I can feel the pen in my hand, I can feel my toes inside my shoes, I can feel my back pressing against my chair, I can feel my feet on the floor, I can feel my lips pressed together."
- Breathe in and out slowly three times.

If the person selects distressing objects or sounds to name, interrupt him/her and suggest he/she pick items that are not upsetting. You might have a younger student name the colors of objects that he/she sees around them. For example, you could say, "Next, name five colors that you can see from where you are sitting. Tell me something you see that is blue, now something that's yellow, now something green."

Note. From *Psychological First Aid for Schools: Field Operations Guide* (2nd ed., pp. 39–40), by M. Brymer, M. Taylor et al., 2012, Los Angeles: NCTSN. Copyright 2012 by National Child Traumatic Stress Network and National Center for PTSD. Reprinted with permission.

Additional questions that can be used in this phase of an ICI are presented in Table 18.5. However, when engaging in this type of questioning, the crisis intervener should keep in mind the following caution offered by Brymer, Taylor, et al. (2012):

> In clarifying emergency-related experiences, avoid asking for in-depth descriptions, as this may provoke additional distress. Follow the individual's lead in discussing what happened. Do not

Table 18.5. Possible Questions to Ask When Identifying Crisis Problems

1. **How are you doing now? What are your immediate needs and concerns?**
   Students and staff will experience the emergency differently. By asking these questions, you will find out what concerns are most pressing. Also, ask if they have any immediate safety issues, medical or psychiatric concerns, or problems attending to basic needs. Highlight that you are willing to discuss whatever they wish—a big problem or even something they think is trivial. Some students and staff may not talk because they feel others are in greater need of your services. Assure them that you and your team have time for everyone.

2. **What happened to you during the event? How were you affected?**
   You will want to find out how the person was affected by the event. You might ask:
   - Where were you during the emergency?
   - Did you feel threatened? Did you get hurt/injured?
   - Do you still feel threatened?
   - What problems do you have now? Do you have any continuing or ongoing problems?
   - Did a loved one die or suffer severe injury?
   - Have you lost contact with, or are you separated from, a loved one?
   - Did you (or your family) lose any personal property?
   - Did your pet die or get hurt?

3. **How has the event affected you, your family, and your friends?**
   When asking this question, use the names of the individuals that the person has already mentioned. When working with middle or high school students, ask how their classmates and friends are doing. Note whether students are limiting their interactions with others, delaying important developmental activities (birthday, prom, getting a driver's license), or increasing at-risk behaviors (drinking, using drugs, reckless driving, self-injurious behaviors). Also, explore students' ability to do schoolwork, their sleep habits, and recent moods.

4. **When you look ahead, do you have any concerns? Is there anything bothering you about your future?**
   These questions allow you to identify any academic concerns, worries about relationships, changes in parental behavior, and developmental issues.

5. **Is there anything else you would like to share?**

Note. Adapted from *Psychological First Aid for Schools: Field Operations Guide* (2nd ed., pp. 42–40), by M. Brymer et al., 2012, Los Angeles: NCTSN. Copyright 2012 by National Child Traumatic Stress Network and National Center for PTSD. Adapted with permission.

press him/her to disclose the details of a trauma or loss. If a person is anxious to talk about an experience, respectfully say that you can best help now by getting some *basic* information so that you can help with his/her current needs, and that you will give him/her referrals to talk with a school counselor or professional about his/her experiences. Remind the person that immediately after an emergency it is difficult to fully protect his/her privacy, and that the situation may not permit you to give him/her enough time to fully assist with his/her experiences. (p. 42)

Again, crisis interveners need to exercise caution when asking these questions. Different students in different situations are more or less able to participate in this problem-identification activity.

Often the range of problems generated by the crisis are presented as multiple disorganized, or a jumbled, needs. The crisis intervener's role is to help the student identify which problems need to be addressed right away, such as issues dealing with physical health, and which problems can be addressed later (Brymer et al., 2006; Brymer, Taylor, et al., 2012). When listening to crisis problems, inquiring about the student's available personal and social resources who can help the resolve crisis problems is important: the fewer the resources, the greater the concern. Finally, the intervener should ask directly about the possible presence of any degree of lethality (i.e., any chance that the student may be at risk for hurting him- or herself or someone else).

Addressing Crisis-Generated Problems

This ICI step is designed to make certain that the student has identified adaptive coping strategies and has made some movement in the direction of adaptive problem solving. When addressing crisis problems, individuals should be allowed and encouraged to do as much as they can by themselves. However, the intervener should not hesitate to be highly directive when addressing crisis-generated problems and taking some kind of action. To initiate this step the crisis intervener might say the following:

> Now that we have an idea of how the crisis is affecting you and the problems it is causing, let's talk about how we can begin to make things better for you. What have you done so far to cope? Or ask: Have you thought about doing x, y, and z? Or say: These are pretty big challenges. Here is what I am going to do to help you.

As indicated by this sample language, as the crisis intervener begins to address crisis-generated problems (which might be the management of crisis reactions or emotions, or might be more practical concerns such as how to replace a lost or damaged possession), he or she might ask the student about the coping attempts they have already made. If the coping attempts the student describes appear to be adaptive and potentially effective, then all that may be required is to validate and reinforce the positive coping direction the individual is taking. If the individual is having difficulty generating his or her own adaptive coping ideas, then the crisis intervener can present possible coping strategies. For example, the crisis intervener may suggest trying a new behavior, redefining the problem, obtaining outside (third-party) assistance, and making specific environmental changes. If the problem is the management of crisis-generated stress, then the crisis solution might be teaching stress management. If the crisis-related problem is financial, then the solution might involve contacting the Federal Emergency Management Agency, American Red Cross, or other disaster resources. If the crisis-related problem is legal, then the crisis solution might involve contacting a victim's assistance program or a lawyer. However, if the student is unable to generate his or her own adaptive solutions, the crisis intervener should not hesitate to be highly directive, such as by saying "Here is what I am going to do to help you." From these interventions a plan should be developed that addresses both immediate and anticipated crisis problems and needs.

Ultimately, addressing crisis-related problems requires taking action. If the crisis intervener has determined that lethality is low and that the individual is capable of acting on his or her own behalf, then the crisis intervener can take a *facilitative* role ("We will talk, but you will act on your own"). In this instance the crisis intervener's actions range from actively listening to giving advice. However, if lethality is high or the individual is not capable of acting on his or her own behalf, then the crisis intervener will need to be *directive* (i.e., "We will talk, but I will act on your behalf"). In this instance the crisis intervener's actions range from mobilizing family and community resources to physically controlling the situation. For example, if a student is homicidal or suicidal, an appropriate ICI response is to take control of the situation as much as is possible and safe. Table 18.6 provides additional sample questions the crisis intervener might ask to determine whether facilitative or directive action is appropriate. Table 18.7 provides possible intervention strategies for a range of specific crisis-generated problems.

Evaluating and Concluding the ICI Session

As ICI concludes, the crisis intervener should obtain identifying information and make certain that the student (or school staff member) has ongoing access to social support and should encourage the use of these support systems. To this end, Brymer et al. (2006) suggest the following statements be made to students:

> To adolescents interveners could state: "When something really upsetting like this happens, even if you don't feel like talking, be sure to ask for what you need."

> To children they could state: "You are doing a great job of letting grown-ups know what you need. It is important to keep letting people know how they can help you. The more help you get, the more you can make things better. Even grown-ups need help at times like this." (p. 72)

Table 18.6. Possible Questions to Ask When Assessing Problem-Solving Resources

---

1. To help identify thoughts about causing harm to oneself or other people state or ask:
   - Sometimes situations like these can be very overwhelming.
   - Have you had any thoughts about suicide? (For children in the primary grades use the words "killing yourself" instead of suicide.)
   - Have you had any thoughts about harming someone else?
2. To help assess the availability of social support systems ask:
   - Are there family members, friends, or community agencies that you can rely on for help with problems that you are facing as a result of the disaster?
3. To help identify prior alcohol or drug use ask:
   - Has your use of alcohol, prescription medication, or drugs increased since the disaster?
   - Have you had any problems in the past with alcohol or drug use?
   - Are you currently experiencing withdrawal symptoms from drug use?

Note. Adapted from *Psychological First Aid: Field Operations Guide* (2nd ed., pp. 60–61), by M. Brymer et al., 2006, Rockville, MD: National Child Traumatic Stress Network and National Center for PTSD. Adapted with permission.

Table 18.7. Intervention Strategies for Specific Crisis-Generated Problems

Crisis-Generated Problem	Intervention Strategy
Death of a loved one	• Provide emotional comfort, acute grief assistance, and practical assistance. • Connect with social supports. • For younger children, ensure that a familiar adult is attending to him/her. • Offer a follow-up meeting.
Immediate safety concerns and ongoing threat	• Help obtain information about safety and protection. • Provide information obtained from officials about the incident as well as about available services. • Report safety concerns to the appropriate authority.
Separation from, or concern for, the safety of loved ones	• Provide practical assistance to connect people to information resources and registries to help locate and reunite loved ones.
Physical illness, mental health conditions, and need for medications	• Provide practical assistance to obtain medical and/or psychological care and medication.
Losses (home, school, neighborhood, property, pets, etc.)	• Provide emotional comfort. • Provide practical assistance to help link the person with available resources. • Provide information about positive coping and social support.
Extreme feelings of guilt and/or shame	• Provide emotional comfort. • Provide information about coping with these distressing emotions.
Thoughts about causing harm to self or others	• Get immediate medical or mental health assistance. • Stay with the individual until appropriate personnel arrive and assume management of his/her care.
Availability of social support	• Help the person connect with available resources and services. • Provide information about coping and social support. • Offer a follow-up meeting.

Table 18.7. Continued

Prior alcohol or drug use	• Provide information about coping and social support. • Link to appropriate services. • Offer a follow-up meeting. • For those undergoing withdrawal, seek a medical referral.
Prior exposure to trauma and death of loved ones	• Provide information about postcrisis and grief reactions, coping, and social support. • Offer a follow-up meeting. • Take note of those students who report prior trauma/loss, as they may have future academic or behavioral problems.
Specific youth, adult, and family concerns about developmental impact	• Provide information on coping. • Assist with strategies for practical help.

Note. Adapted from *Psychological First Aid for Schools: Field Operations Guide* (2nd ed., pp. 44-45), by M. Brymer, M. Taylor et al., 2012, Los Angeles: NCTSN. Copyright 2012 by National Child Traumatic Stress Network and National Center for PTSD. Adapted with permission.

Before concluding, the crisis intervener should make an agreement for reconnecting with the student to ensure that the student is making the necessary progress toward addressing crisis-generated problems.

This last ICI step involves critically evaluating whether or not immediate coping has been reestablished. To the extent that the student has obtained necessary physical and emotional support (and any lethality has been reduced), crisis-generated problems have been identified and are being addressed, and links have been made to the appropriate helping resources, the ICI session may be concluded. If these goals have not been achieved, the process should be repeated.

As the session is ended, it is important to leave the student with a sense of hope and optimism that they will recover from their trauma exposure (Hobfoll et al., 2007). The individual should be complimented on his or her problem-solving efforts and encouraged by the expectation that, with time, they will be able to cope with the trauma.

CONCLUSION

Before ICI begins, crisis interveners must first make psychological contact with the individual affected by a crisis, address basic needs, clarify confidentiality, and ensure that he or she is emotionally stable. The combination of the emotional stability provided by the crisis intervener's presence and the identification and prioritization of crisis-generated problems is sometimes all that is needed to reestablish immediate coping. To the extent possible, students should be allowed to engage in independent problem-solving. However, crisis interveners should never hesitate to be highly directive and active in the identification and implementation of solutions to crisis problems. This directive approach is especially necessary when a student is considering homicidal or suicidal ideation as a possible problem-solving strategy. Finally, the ICI concludes by examining the degree to which coping has been reestablished and strives to leave the individual with a sense of hope that he or she will recover from trauma exposure.

As is the case with most school mental health interventions associated with a personal, school, or community crisis, research regarding the efficacy of ICI with schoolchildren is needed (Szumilas, Wei, & Kutcher, 2010), and in the years following this book's publication, the reader is encouraged to attend to the literature regarding the use of ICI as an immediate crisis intervention and to adjust local practice according to the results of that future study.

Chapter 19

PSYCHOTHERAPEUTIC INTERVENTIONS

Although psychotherapeutic treatment is not considered crisis intervention, it may be necessary for a minority of students who experience adverse reactions to crisis events and develop psychopathology. Therefore, school-employed mental health professionals must have a basic understanding of the psychotherapeutic treatments for severe psychological injury if they are to make appropriate referrals and treatment decisions. This chapter provides an overview of the psychotherapeutic treatments that are most effective for children and adolescents who have been traumatized by a crisis (cognitive–behavioral therapies and eye-movement desensitization and reprocessing) and briefly reviews psychopharmacological interventions. Because some of these treatments may be beyond the role and expertise of the school-employed mental health professional, the chapter explores issues relevant to making referrals to outside mental health agencies. Finally, the chapter reviews cultural considerations relevant to treatment referrals.

COGNITIVE–BEHAVIORAL THERAPIES

Cognitive–behavioral therapies (CBTs), particularly those that focus on the trauma, are the most widely studied and promising interventions for posttraumatic stress disorder (PTSD) for both adults and children (Bisson, Roberts, Andrew, Cooper, & Lewis, 2013; Cohen, Mannarino, Berliner, & Deblinger, 2000; Feeny, Foa, Treadwell, & March, 2004; March, Amaya-Jackson, Murray, & Schulte, 1998; World Health Organization [WHO], 2013). Because PTSD is relatively unique among the *Diagnostic and Statistical Manual of Mental Disorders, Fifth Edition* (DSM-5) diagnoses, in that its criteria require exposure to a traumatic event (American Psychiatric Association, 2013), discussions of treatment for individuals with PTSD are relevant. CBT has also been shown to be the most effective treatment for other disorders that may develop in individuals following a crisis, such as depression, anxiety, and behavior problems (see e.g., Kazdin & Weisz, 2003; Prout & Prout, 1998; Rolfsnes & Idsoe, 2011; Weisz, Weiss, Han, Grander, & Morton, 1995). Rolfsnes and Idsoe's (2011) meta-analysis of 16 CBT interventions implemented in school settings revealed that 11 of the studies showed effect sizes in the medium to large range for PTSD and many comorbid symptoms. In the World Health Organization's (2013) *Guidelines for the Management of Conditions Specifically Related to Stress,* it was concluded that individual and group CBT with a trauma focus should be considered for children and adolescents with PTSD.

This section first reviews some of the common elements of CBT, including psychoeducation (with children and with parents), exposure, anxiety management through cognitive restructuring and relaxation training, and parent training. The section then briefly reviews some specific cognitive–behavioral interventions, such as Cognitive–Behavioral Intervention for Trauma in Schools (CBITS) and Trauma-Focused Cognitive–Behavioral Therapy (TF-CBT).

Psychoeducation

As discussed in Chapter 16, psychoeducation is an important element in crisis intervention that is supported by the empirical literature as improving coping for children and adults after a crisis (Berger, Pat-Horencyzk, & Gelkopf, 2007; Gelkopf & Berger, 2009; Howard & Goelitz, 2004). Psychoeducation is also an important part of CBT. Psychoeducation provides information about the traumatic event, children's typical responses following crisis exposure, and effective coping strategies, which together help to reduce fears (Carr, 2004). In addition, it can be used to help the child and his or her parents further understand traumatic stress reactions and the need and rationale for exposure-based therapies. In CBT, psychoeducation also focuses on teaching the link between affect, thoughts, and behaviors, and may also include information specific to the traumatic event. Similar to the psychoeducation approaches described in Chapter 16, other elements of psychoeducation may focus on caring for the self and others, such as emphasizing the importance of maintaining a normal daily living routine and the importance of social support systems, along with other adaptive coping strategies.

Imaginal and In Vivo Exposure

Techniques that involve repeated exposure are designed to help individuals confront feared objects, situations, memories, and images. The core components are typically imaginal exposure (repeated recounting of the traumatic memory) and in vivo exposure (repeated, prolonged confrontation with trauma-related situations and objects that evoke excessive anxiety). Exposure has been found to be a critical treatment component for adolescents and adults with PTSD (Foa, Dancu, et al., 1999; Powers, Halpern, Ferenschak, Gillihan, & Foa, 2010). Exposure can be intense and prolonged, as practiced in the flooding technique, or more gradual, which involves ongoing exposure to stimuli that represent certain aspects of the traumatic event (Cohen, Mannarino, et al., 2000). Exposure decreases the hyperarousal and negative affect that accompany traumatic reminders (American Academy of Child and Adolescent Psychiatry, 1998; Cohen, Mannarino, et al., 2000). Following exposure, the thoughts of the trauma are no longer paired with the overwhelming negative emotion; in turn, the intensity of intrusive reminders is reduced, minimizing the need for avoidant behavior (Cohen, Mannarino, et al., 2000). Powers and colleagues' (2010) meta-analysis indicated that the average adolescent or adult patient treated with prolonged exposure had improved PTSD symptoms posttreatment than 86% of patients in the control condition.

Exposure is an important component of Trauma-Focused Cognitive–Behavioral Therapy, which applies traditional CBT to the particular trauma involved by targeting the specific elements of the child's experience to separate the child's thoughts about the incident from overwhelming emotions, such as fear and anger (Cohen, Berliner, & Mannarino, 2000). However, a recent study found that Internet-based TF-CBT with and without the exposure component were equally effective, with diagnostic remission in 34–44% of adults with PTSD (Spence et al., 2014). Gradual exposure techniques (e.g., drawing, writing, visualizing, mock interviewing) are used to help the child think about the event (Cohen, Berliner, & Mannarino, 2000; Paul, Gray, Elhai, Massad, & Stamm, 2006). Research shows preliminary support for the use of exposure in treating children with PTSD (Diehle, Schmitt, Daams, Boer, & Lindauer, 2014; Ruf et al., 2010). However, its use requires a strong therapeutic alliance, excellent rapport building, and treatment conducted at the child's pace (Feeny et al., 2004).

It has been argued that in vivo exposure and direct exploration of the trauma are inappropriate for school settings because the intervention can lead to extreme anxiety reactions, such as heightened arousal and reexperiencing of the trauma (Cook-Cottone, 2004; Merrell, 2001; Pfefferbaum, 1997). If the decision is made to use exposure techniques led by a qualified professional in the school setting, the emotional impact needs to be planned for carefully. For example, sending a child back to class prematurely (after he or she has responded significantly to a particular aspect of a psychotherapeutic session) can be problematic. If exposure therapy is conducted outside of school, the school-employed mental health professional should be made aware of this so that behaviors and emotions that may arise from this treatment can be addressed and supported during school hours (Nickerson, Reeves, Brock, & Jimerson, 2009).

Given concerns about the use of exposure techniques with children, particularly the very young, professionals recommend that play, art, or storytelling be used to help children express their feelings about the trauma (Pfefferbaum, 1997). Research has shown that using artwork and free writing with elementary school children is associated with increased expression of feelings (Klingman, 1985; Schwarz, 1982). These techniques may be helpful in encouraging children to be exposed to aspects of the event, and their feelings about it, without doing it in a direct and purposeful way that may be inappropriate for the school setting.

Anxiety Management Training: Cognitive Restructuring and Relaxation

Some research supports the use of anxiety management training (AMT) in reducing PTSD, anxiety, and depression (Feeny et al., 2004). In AMT, individuals are taught skills for managing anxiety. Techniques used include education about affect, restructuring of dysfunctional cognitions, and relaxation exercises. These skills are applied to trauma-related, anxiety-provoking situations through role-play and in vivo exposure exercises.

Two specific aspects of AMT that have been researched are restructuring cognitive distortions and stress inoculation. Restructuring cognitive distortions about the crisis event is a core element of cognitive–behavioral therapies such as AMT (American Academy of Child and Adolescent Psychiatry, 1998; Cohen, Mannarino, et al., 2000). It is common for traumatized children to develop distortions such as self-blame (e.g., "I did something to cause this"), survivor guilt

("It should have been me"), or overgeneralized feelings of threatened safety (e.g., "The world is not safe"). When using cognitive restructuring, the therapist asks the child about his or her thoughts and attributions about the event and then identifies any distortions. The therapist and child examine the child's reasoning for the distortions, which leads to replacing the distortion with more accurate thoughts about the event (Cohen, Mannarino, et al., 2000).

Stress inoculation involves teaching coping skills such as relaxation and thought stopping to manage trauma-related anxiety (Cohen, Mannarino, et al., 2000; Foa et al., 1999). This often involves teaching progressive muscle relaxation. Although stress inoculation, alone and in combination with exposure, has been found to be superior to a control condition in treating PTSD in women, exposure alone was superior to stress inoculation and the combined exposure and stress inoculation treatment because there were fewer dropouts, greater reduction in symptoms, lower anxiety, and greater social adjustment (Foa et al., 1999). Research is needed to explore the effects of stress inoculation with children.

Parent Training

Treatment with children often involves a parent or caregiver component. As discussed in detail in Chapters 15 and 16, parents are the primary providers of support for children, and a parent's own reaction to the trauma may affect his or her ability to provide the support the child needs. Therefore, helping parents reframe their cognitive distortions and learn skills to help their children cope is important. Parents' involvement in treatment may be especially warranted for children whose traumatic responses include externalizing behavior problems (Cohen, Berliner, et al., 2000), because ecological interventions are most effective for these types of problems.

Many of the trauma-focused CBT approaches described in detail in this chapter include a parent component (e.g., Cobham et al., 2012; Cohen & Mannarino, 2008; Dorsey et al., 2014). Some evidence suggests that adding a parent component to a child's CBT treatment results in reduced child depression and behavior problems (Deblinger, Lippmann, & Steer, 1996) and reduced emotional distress for the parent (Deblinger, Stauffer, & Steer, 2001). In relation to anxiety, Khanna and Kendall (2009) concluded that when parent training was included in CBT, there was improvement in children's global functioning when parents improved their own anxiety management techniques and learned to be less controlling. However, some research has also failed to show a direct effect of the parent component of CBT on children's PTSD symptomatology (Deblinger et al., 1996; King et al., 2000). Taken together, the research indicates that working with parents is an important part of mental health crisis intervention, as it reduces parental distress and increases coping. Adding a parent component to treatment also reduces children's depression, anxiety, and behavior problems and increases their global functioning, although direct effects on children's PTSD symptomatology may not be expected.

Cognitive–Behavioral Intervention for Trauma in Schools

Cognitive–Behavioral Intervention for Trauma in Schools (CBITS) is a manualized treatment designed for use with youth from diverse backgrounds in urban settings who have been exposed to trauma. The 10-session group treatment focuses on (a) teaching common reactions to trauma,

(b) teaching relaxation skills, (c) examining the link between thoughts and feelings, (d) restructuring negative thoughts, (e) using exposure techniques (e.g., drawing, writing, talking) to help children approach and cope with the traumatic event, (f) teaching social problem-solving skills, and (g) addressing relapse prevention (Jaycox, 2004). CBITS also includes at least one individual session, two group meetings with parents, and an educational presentation for teachers.

In randomized controlled trials, students participating in CBT groups had lower PTSD scores than students in the wait-list control condition (Kataoka et al., 2003; Morsette et al., 2009; Saltzman, Pynoos, Layne, Steinberg, & Aisenberg, 2001; Stein et al., 2003). It should be noted that Morsette and colleagues (2009) adapted the CBITS program for American Indian children suffering from PTSD by incorporating local history and stories and addressing cultural beliefs (e.g., strong spiritual influences were not considered irrational beliefs). Children in this modified CBITS group showed a reduction in PTSD symptoms, with benefits lasting at least 6 months, in comparison with a no-treatment control group. Erum, Jaycox, Kataoka, Langley, and Stein (2011) described successful implementation of CBITS in two large school district settings, demonstrating how macro- and school-level implementation factors interact to create conditions for quality program delivery. These large-scale efforts hold promise for helping students develop social problem-solving skills to reduce the likelihood of traumatic stress and other reactions.

Support for Students Exposed to Trauma (SSET) is an adaptation of CBITS, in which teachers and school counselors provide CBITS elements (e.g., psychoeducation, relaxation strategies, coping skills training, exposure techniques, and problem solving) in a curriculum-style format, excluding individual and parent sessions (Jaycox et al., 2009). The curriculum includes 10 structured lessons aimed at reducing PTSD, depressive symptoms, and deficits in functioning for students who have been exposed to trauma. In Jaycox and colleagues' (2009) study with randomly selected students from urban middle schools who had been exposed to violence in the prior year and experienced PTSD symptoms, results showed strong fidelity in implementation, decreased behavioral problems and decreased PTSD and depressive symptoms, and high parent and child satisfaction with the intervention.

Trauma-Focused CBT

Trauma-Focused Cognitive–Behavioral Therapy (TF-CBT) is another treatment approach that applies traditional CBT to a particular trauma (Cohen, Berliner, & Mannarino, 2000; Cohen & Mannarino, 2008). This flexible, components-based program teaches children and parents stress management skills and then encourages direct discussion and processing of children's traumatic experiences. To help the child think about the event, gradual exposure techniques (e.g., drawing, writing, visualizing, and conducting mock interviews) are used (Cohen, Berliner, & Mannarino, 2000; Paul et al., 2006). TF-CBT also emphasizes identification and expression of feelings; relaxation and coping skills training; recognition of the relationship between thoughts, feelings, and behaviors; cognitive processing of abuse experiences; joint child–parent sessions; and, depending on the characteristics of the event, psychoeducation about child sexual abuse and body safety (Cohen, Mannarino, & Knudsen, 2004).

The approach's components are summarized by the acronym PRACTICE, for *p*sychoeducation and parenting skills, *r*elaxation skills, *a*ffective modulation skills, *c*ognitive coping skills, *t*rauma narrative and cognitive reprocessing of the traumatic events(s), *in* vivo mastery of trauma coping skills, conjoint child–parent sessions, and enhancing safety and future developmental trajectory (Cohen & Mannarino, 2008). Results of several studies, summarized through meta-analysis, show that TF-CBT reduces symptoms of PTSD, depression, and behavior problems immediately after and 12 months following treatment completion (Cary & McMillen, 2012).

Notably, TF-CBT has been used successfully with a variety of children and adolescents from different age groups and with disabilities, in addition to youth who live in residential treatment and children and youth in foster care (e.g., Dorsey et al., 2014; Scheeringa, Weems, Cohen, Amaya-Jackson, & Guthrie, 2010). The approach has also been used with children in military families; with children of Latino descent, using a modified version; and also with American Indian and Alaska Native children (Cohen, Mannarino, & Deblinger, 2012). Significant improvements in PTSD symptoms have been found for young children using TF-CBT (Scheeringa et al., 2010), as well as for children in foster care (Dorsey et al., 2014).

TF-CBT has also been adapted to incorporate grief-focused components for children suffering from traumatic grief (Cognitive Behavioral Therapy for Childhood Traumatic Grief, or CBT-CTG; Cohen & Mannarino, 2004). With traumatic grief, a child may develop PTSD symptoms in response to reminders that are associated with the trauma, the loss, or life changes as a result of either (Brown et al., 2008). CBT-CTG consists of 16 treatment sessions (12 individual sessions for parents and children, followed by four joint parent–child sessions). In addition to the trauma-focused components of the program, the grief-focused sessions in the second half of treatment involve discussing the death, mourning, addressing feelings of loss, preserving positive memories, redefining relationships, and making meaning of loss (Cohen & Mannarino, 2004). A pilot study conducted by Cohen and colleagues revealed decreased PTSD symptoms after trauma-focused sessions and decreased CTG symptoms after both trauma- and grief-focused sessions (Cohen et al., 2004). In addition, addressing trauma symptoms prior to or simultaneously with grief symptoms in a 12-week session was also found to be successful (Cohen, Mannarino, & Staron, 2006).

School-based group treatments for childhood traumatic grief have also been developed and evaluated. Bosnian youth who received grief- and trauma-focused group treatment at school had significantly better outcomes in relation to traumatic grief symptoms, compared with youth who participated in trauma-focused components of treatment only, although it should be noted that both groups showed comparable reductions in PTSD and depressive symptoms (Layne et al., 2001). Other studies investigating individual and group treatment for traumatic grief have shown reduced symptoms of traumatic grief and PTSD symptoms (Salloum & Overstreet, 2008; Saltzman et al., 2001).

The aforementioned approaches are a part of Project Fleur-de-lis, a comprehensive, tiered model referred to as the Stepped Trauma Pathway (Cohen, Jaycox, et al., 2009). The project involved performing triage of children experiencing trauma after Hurricane Katrina, as well as other preexisting issues (e.g., previous exposure to trauma or violence). Universal treatments include school-wide interventions for children and educational workshops for parents and teachers. CBITS is used for those with ongoing symptoms, and TF-CBT is used for children with more severe or persistent PTSD. These interventions are provided in either the school or community-based settings.

Jaycox et al. (2010) conducted an assessment and field trial of two interventions 15 months after Hurricane Katrina. CBITS took place in schools, and the individual treatment was delivered at a mental health clinic. The results indicated that both treatments led to significant improvement in PTSD symptoms. However, CBITS was far more accessible to families who were not willing or able to participate in individual, clinic-based treatment, which required more parental participation.

EYE MOVEMENT DESENSITIZATION AND REPROCESSING

In recent comprehensive reviews of the evidence about interventions for PTSD, eye-movement desensitization and reprocessing (EMDR) has been identified as an effective treatment (Bisson et al., 2013; WHO, 2013). Clinical guidelines from the Department of Veterans Affairs and the Department of Defense (2010) also support the use of EMDR in treating individuals with PTSD. EMDR is a therapeutic approach based on the adaptive information processing (AIP) model (Solomon & Shapiro, 2008). According to this model, symptoms are caused by the inadequate processing and storing of traumatic images, affect, cognitions, and bodily sensations (Aduriz, Bluthgen, & Knopfler, 2009; Solomon & Shapiro, 2008). During EMDR, the individual concentrates on a mental representation of the traumatic event, while simultaneously tracking a moving visual, auditory, or tactile stimulus (Aduriz et al., 2009; Devilly, 2002). In one technique, EMDR therapists rapidly move their finger back and forth and instruct the client to focus on the finger while visualizing the anxiety-provoking situation and accompanying body sensations (Devilly, 2002; Lilienfeld & Arkowitz, 2007). Through exposure to trauma-related cues and self-monitoring, EMDR facilitates the reprocessing and restructuring of cognitive, emotional, and physiological responses to create a more adaptive view of the traumatic event.

EMDR has been found to be superior to no-treatment conditions (Ahmad, Larsson, & Sundelin-Wahlsten, 2007; Davidson & Parker, 2001; Maxfield & Hyer, 2002; Shepherd, Stein, & Milne, 2000). It has also been found to be equally or more effective when compared with other CBT methods, including exposure therapy, at reducing PTSD symptoms (Davidson & Parker, 2001; Ironson, Freud, Strauss, & Williams, 2002; Lilienfeld & Arkowitz, 2007; Rothbaum, Astin, & Marsteller, 2005; Siedler & Wagner, 2006; Taylor et al., 2003). Consistent with meta-analyses of adult samples, EMDR has been supported as an effective treatment for treating children with PTSD (Rodenburg, Benjamin, de Roos, Meijer, & Stams, 2009); however, additional research on its use with children is needed (Diehle et al., 2014). In a randomized controlled trial, Chemtob, Nakashima, and Carlson (2002) also found EMDR to effectively reduce PTSD symptoms in children who had not responded to previous treatment, and the EMDR-related changes were maintained at 6-month follow-up. Research on EMDR with children has shown that it decreases avoidance and reexperiencing symptoms and improves functioning (Ahmad et al., 2007; Oras, de Ezpeleta, & Ahmad, 2004). Although controlled research is needed, the use of EMDR as an early group intervention to reduce distress and promote resilience in children exposed to a traumatic event has also been supported (Aduriz et al., 2009; Jarero, Artigas, & Hartung, 2006; Zaghrout-Hodali, Alissa, & Dodgson, 2008).

The underlying mechanisms of EMDR and the role of eye movements remain controversial (Department of Veterans Affairs and Department of Defense, 2010). Although some evidence suggests that eye movements alone are insufficient, and even unnecessary, for effective EMDR treatment (Davidson & Parker, 2001; Devilly, 2002), there is also evidence to suggest that eye movements result in distinct psychophysiological changes (heart rate, skin conductance, respiration, and orienting response) that may aid in processing negative memories (Schubert, Lee, & Drummond, 2011). In addition, Lee and Cuijpers' (2013) recent meta-analysis revealed that eye movements have an additive effect in treatment that distinguishes EMDR from other exposure-based therapies.

PSYCHOPHARMACOLOGICAL TREATMENTS

As a rule, psychopharmacological treatments should be used in combination with ongoing psychotherapy (Donnelly, Amaya-Jackson, & March, 1999; Foa et al., 1999), and psychotherapy has consistently been shown to be more effective than pharmacotherapy (Schnurr & Friedman, 2008). However, some individuals do not respond to psychosocial and therapeutic interventions for PTSD, making psychopharmacological treatments the next best option (Cohen, 2001; Friedman, 1988). Pharmacotherapy may also be indicated when appropriate alternative treatment modalities are unavailable, or when the intensity of comorbid conditions interferes with the patient's ability to engage in psychotherapeutic intervention (Friedman, Donnelly, & Mellman, 2003).

Selective serotonin reuptake inhibitors (SSRIs), which have been shown to reduce anxious and depressive symptoms, may also reduce symptoms of reexperiencing, numbing, avoidance, and hyperarousal, which are thought to relate to serotonin disturbances (Donnelly, 2003; Seedat, Lockhart, Kaminer, Zungu-Dirwayi, & Stein, 2001; Seedat et al., 2002). Specifically, research has found that compared with placebo control groups, sertraline (Brady et al., 2000; Davidson, Rothbaum, Van der Kolk, Sikes, & Farfel, 2001) and paroxetine (Marshall, Beebe, Oldham, & Zaninelli, 2001; Tucker et al., 2001) significantly reduce PTSD symptoms in adults. Both sertraline and paroxetine have approval by the United States Food and Drug Administration as indicated treatments for PTSD (Schnurr & Friedman, 2008). In addition, fluoxetine has been shown to be a well-tolerated medication (Barnett et al., 2002; Martenyi, Brown, Zhang, Koke, & Prakash, 2002), with efficacy in reducing symptoms (Connor, Sutherland, Tupler, Malik, & Davidson, 1999) and preventing the relapse of PTSD (Martenyi et al., 2002). Rothbaum et al. (2006) also found that individuals with only a partial response to sertraline achieved further improvement after the medication was augmented with prolonged exposure therapy. In addition, venlafaxine, a serotonin norepinephrine reuptake inhibitor (SNRI), has also been shown to be significantly more effective than a placebo (Davidson, Baldwin, et al., 2006; Davidson, Rothbaum, et al. 2006).

Other medications have shown positive effects in the treatment of PTSD symptoms. For example, prazosin has been shown to be effective in improving sleep by reducing nightmares (Raskind et al., 2007), while propranolol has been supported by data as an effective treatment to reduce physiological arousal and as a supplement to exposure therapy (Brunet et al., 2014). In addition, combining exposure therapy with D-cycloserine, an antibiotic, for patients with acrophobia and social phobia led to faster extinction of fear responses than exposure therapy alone, suggesting it may be effective in the treatment of PTSD symptoms (Davis, Ressler, Rothbaum, & Richardson, 2006). Benzodiazepines have not been shown to be effective in the treatment of

PTSD (Department of Veterans Affairs and Department of Defense, 2010; Schnurr & Friedman, 2008). The departments' clinical practice guidelines suggest that this class of medication is contraindicated for the treatment of PTSD, given the increased risk for addiction and dependence as well as the potential interference with exposure-based therapies. In addition, the existing evidence does not support the use of anticonvulsants or atypical antipsychotics in the management of PTSD (Department of Veterans Affairs and Department of Defense, 2010).

In contrast with evidence-supported psychopharmacological treatments of adults with PTSD, data on medication for children and adolescents is limited (Huemer, Erhart, & Steiner, 2010). Some research also suggests that psychopharmacological interventions are contraindicated for the treatment of PTSD in children. For example, the World Health Organization (2013) stated that antidepressants should not be used to manage PTSD in children and adolescents. Supported medication effects for adults cannot simply be assumed to transfer when used with children and adolescents, given their neurobiological differences and the developmental aspects of PTSD (Huemer et al., 2010). With children and adolescents, psychopharmacological intervention should be considered only after exhausting other psychological, behavioral, and family treatments (Harmon & Riggs, 1996).

REFERRALS FOR COMMUNITY-BASED TREATMENT

Many of the treatments described above require expertise beyond that typically held by the school-employed mental health professional. Even if the practitioner has the expertise to implement these interventions, his or her workload, the availability of supervision and consultation, and the philosophy of the school district regarding offering this type of service to students may be barriers to providing such treatment in schools (Burrows-Horton & Cruise, 2001).

The first step in making appropriate referrals for community-based treatment is knowing when a referral should be made, based on an understanding of trauma risk related to the child's developmental level. Discussions in Chapters 13 and 14 about how to evaluate psychological trauma risk will help; for example, when making referrals for psychotherapeutic treatment, the practitioner must understand how the child's developmental level influences the expression of traumatic stress. The DSM-5 (American Psychiatric Association, 2013) recognizes that the clinical expression of many of the PTSD symptoms vary across development, and as such, give specific criteria for children 6 years of age and younger.

A second consideration in making referral decisions is the nature of the crisis event. For example, relatively brief psychotherapeutic interventions involving three to seven sessions may be indicated for the student who develops PTSD following a single-incident accident or disaster (referred to as Type 1 PTSD; Terr, 1991). On the other hand, the student who develops PTSD following exposure to multiple traumatic stressors (e.g., chronic community violence; referred to as Type 2 PTSD) may require longer psychotherapeutic interventions of up to 25 sessions (Carr, 2004).

Knowing when to refer a student for additional intervention, although critical, is only part of the challenge for school-employed mental health professionals. They also need to know where to refer these students. As discussed in Chapter 14, the crisis response team should develop and maintain a referral list of experienced mental health professionals and agencies who provide treatment for traumatized children and families. This list can be built by consulting with colleagues, contacting local agencies, contacting state and local professional associations, searching the Internet, consulting the United Way's list of community resources in cities and suburban areas (http://www.unitedway.org/find-your-united-way/), and using the American Psychological Association's psychologist locator at http://locator.apa.org/ (Nickerson et al., 2009). Chapter 14 includes a Private Practitioner Referral Questionnaire (Figure 14.1) that can be distributed to the resources identified to find out more about the services provided. The list must include treatment providers who are from diverse backgrounds and who speak a language other than English (Nickerson & Heath, 2008).

Referral procedures should be developed in collaboration with the school administrator in light of concerns about parents asking schools to pay for recommended services (Merrell, 2001). Under no circumstance can the child's education be contingent on the parents obtaining such services. It is prudent to use language such as "It may be helpful for you to look into having a community CBT provider assist your child in coping with his or her feelings and behaviors surrounding the crisis." Simply providing a child's family with the name and phone number of a provider is unlikely to lead to treatment. When making a referral to an outside service provider, the school-employed mental health professional should meet with the child's parents or caregivers to discuss the concerns and determine if they are willing and able to consider such a referral (Merrell, 2001).

If the parents decide to pursue a referral and sign a release for the school to provide information to the community-based provider, the school practitioner should write a one- to two-page letter to the outside professional to describe concerns and provide a brief history (Burrows-Horton & Cruise, 2001; Merrell, 2001). Alternatively, the document used in the psychological referral procedures (Figure 14.5) could be used to provide this information. Ongoing collaboration between the school and the community-based provider is recommended to ensure continuity in services. For this to happen, the student's parent or guardian must sign separate releases for the school to provide information to and receive reports from the community-based mental health professional. The release should detail the specific type of information to be shared, the length of time for which the release is valid, and how the information is to be used. If a parent is uncomfortable with this procedure, creating a release limited to obtaining information related only to the student's needs in school or arranging for a three-way phone call between the school, the parent or guardian, and the community-based mental health professional may be helpful (Cole et al., 2005). The school may continue to provide other services for that student, as long as they are not redundant or in conflict with outside services (Burrows-Horton & Cruise, 2001). For example, a school practitioner might provide anxiety management training to teach skills the student can use when feeling anxious, whereas a community-based mental health professional may use exposure therapy and engage in more direct exploration of the trauma.

CULTURAL CONSIDERATIONS

School-employed mental health professionals must consider students' and their families' cultural beliefs and practices when selecting treatment options. Chapter 15 reviewed many cultural issues relevant for obtaining support and healing after a crisis. In particular, many individuals and families from culturally and linguistically diverse backgrounds cope with crises by banding together with family, and they often distrust outside help (Canada et al., 2007; Horowitz, McKay, & Marshall, 2005). Consequently, attempts to offer mental health services may be viewed as forceful or meddling.

To address the issue of mistrust, the school practitioner should work with the school crisis response team to find community leaders or individuals who are trusted by families in diverse ethnic groups to convey the message about services. A cultural broker may be used to assess needs and tell the families about interventions that may be helpful (Klingman & Cohen, 2004). The school's ability to convey information to students and parents, while showing sensitivity to cultural groups' diversity when considering referrals for psychotherapeutic treatments, can help foster recovery (Sandoval & Lewis, 2002).

CONCLUSION

School-employed mental health professionals serve an important role in identifying the level of traumatic impact of a crisis on students and knowing when and how to make appropriate referrals to meet mental health needs. CBT represents the most well-studied and effective psychotherapeutic treatment for disorders that are most likely to affect children who have been exposed to a crisis event (e.g., PTSD, depression, and anxiety). Several of these interventions can be delivered in the schools, including CBITS and CBT-CTG. Other effective interventions more commonly provided by community-based mental health providers include TF-CBT and EMDR. In some cases, psychopharmacological interventions may be indicated, but research on the use of medications with children is scarce. Because psychopharmacological interventions are not provided by school-employed mental health professionals, these practitioners must be knowledgeable about available community resources. Finally, cultural beliefs and practices must also be taken into account when recommending additional treatment. Although psychotherapy is beyond the scope of practice for most practitioners working in the school setting, it is essential in meeting the comprehensive and often complex needs that face some individuals who have experienced a crisis.

Section 6

EXAMINE

The fifth and final element of the PREP<u>a</u>RE model (the final "E" in PREP<u>a</u>RE) refers to the ongoing examination of school safety and crisis response efforts. As illustrated in Figure 1.3, examination efforts take place throughout all crisis phases. This section includes two chapters that address the examination guidance offered within the PREP<u>a</u>RE curriculum's two separate, but complementary, workshops. Chapter 20 addresses the examination of school safety and crisis preparedness efforts, and Chapter 21 discusses the examination of school crisis response and recovery efforts.

Chapter 20

EXAMINING THE EFFECTIVENESS OF SCHOOL SAFETY, CRISIS PREVENTION, AND CRISIS PREPAREDNESS EFFORTS

The next two chapters discuss the multifaceted processes necessary to examine the effectiveness of school safety, crisis prevention, and crisis preparedness (Chapter 20), and crisis response and recovery (Chapter 21). The current chapter begins with a discussion of the importance of examination, then follows with challenges specific to the examination of school safety, crisis prevention, and crisis preparedness. Finally, it gives a brief overview of three examination strategies (i.e., needs assessment, process analysis, and outcome evaluation). The last two sections consider in greater detail the three school safety, crisis prevention, and crisis preparedness examination strategies.

THE IMPORTANCE OF EXAMINATION

The field of school psychology has placed great emphasis on evidence-based strategies and accountability (American Psychological Association Presidential Task Force on Evidence-Based Practice, 2006; Evidence-Based Intervention Work Group, 2005; Kratochwill & Shernoff, 2003; Stoiber & DeSmet, 2010). Indeed, examining the effectiveness of school safety, crisis prevention, and crisis preparedness efforts is as important as planning and implementation. General purposes of examining these efforts include (a) assessing effectiveness, (b) improving implementation and enhancing effectiveness, (c) better managing limited resources, (d) documenting accomplishments, (e) justifying required resources, (f) supporting the need for funding, and (g) satisfying ethical responsibilities to demonstrate positive effects of program participation. An individual should be designated by the Incident Command System's (ICS) Incident Commander to lead the examination of all school safety, crisis prevention, and crisis preparedness efforts. Responsibility for these efforts is typically assigned to the ICS's Planning Section, and such examinations often take the form of after-action reports, which are completed after all school crisis responses.

The examination of school safety and crisis prevention efforts documents the effectiveness of programs and strategies that are designed to promote healthy student behaviors and to reduce the number and intensity of crises. As discussed in Chapters 2 and 3, each school should assess its unique needs (e.g., by performing a vulnerability assessment) and develop comprehensive and systematic approaches to school safety and crisis prevention. Thus, the examination of these first two objectives provides essential information regarding school safety and crisis prevention targets, as well as the degree to which school safety goals have been met. Depending on the outcomes of such an examination, the school safety team may retain some programs or strategies (i.e., those generating desirable outcomes, such as reductions in aggressive behaviors and increases in prosocial behaviors) and discontinue other programs or strategies, or it may enhance some programs as necessary to address persistent or likely threats to student safety. Given the importance of examination, Pagliocca, Nickerson, and Williams (2002) have recommended that systematic examination procedures be included in all aspects of crisis preparedness.

The third objective, examining crisis response preparedness, documents the school's readiness to respond to crises that safety and prevention efforts were not able to prevent. These efforts are vital (U.S. Department of Education, 2013; U.S. Department of Education, 2007b; U.S. Department of Homeland Security, 2013a). As discussed in Chapters 7 and 8, the development of school crisis response teams and plans is a dynamic process that requires annual evaluation to determine whether the infrastructure and processes are optimal and consistent with best practice guidance. For instance, crisis drills, readiness checks, or systematic reviews of plans may reveal that the plans require all staff members to have basic knowledge of crisis response procedures. However, many new school staff members may not have this knowledge, revealing the need for targeted professional development (e.g., inservice workshops to provide this knowledge to school staff members).

CHALLENGES TO EXAMINATION

The importance of examining school safety and crisis preparedness efforts is evident; however, the Planning Section must address numerous challenges when conducting this type of evaluation. These challenges include (a) definitional and measurement issues; (b) difficulties conducting rigorous experimental research; and (c) barriers to the implementation, dissemination, and monitoring of interventions (Nickerson & Gurdineer, 2012). For example, school safety and crisis response teams may encounter definitional and measurement issues when obtaining accurate data to document that a specific school safety or crisis prevention strategy prevented a crisis or psychological disorder (Durlak & Wells, 1997). Some strategies for the evaluation of prevention initiatives include obtaining baseline data and clearly delineating the anticipated outcomes in terms of specific protective factors and indicators of mental wellness (Nickerson & Gurdineer, 2012).

Despite clearly articulated and measurable school safety and crisis preparedness outcomes, the rigorous evaluation of these outcomes faces barriers. For example, although randomized controlled trials provide the strongest empirical support for prevention programs (Ji, DuBois, Flay, & Brechling, 2008), ethical issues may limit the use of randomized controlled trials in schools. The high stakes associated with intentionally providing or withholding mental health treatment lead to ethical concerns. Harm can be caused by withholding safety or prevention programs from students in need of the intervention, or by implementing programs with individuals or groups for whom the intervention is not necessary (e.g., reducing their sense of self-efficacy). Furthermore, low base rates (i.e., infrequent occurrence) of many school crises and the associated lack of statistical power present further challenges to these studies, as well as affect the generalizability and validity of the study results (Cuijpers, 2003; Durlak & Wells, 1997).

The successful implementation, dissemination, and monitoring of school safety and crisis prevention programs depend on the interactions of various micro- (e.g., students, teachers, mental health professionals, administrators) and macro-level factors (e.g., school districts, school boards, and other political systems). Research on treatment integrity—the degree to which an intervention is administered as intended (Sanetti & Kratochwill, 2014)—suggests that programs are delivered with less integrity when they are complex, require multiple resources, and demand large time commitments. Similarly, treatment integrity is influenced by interveners' (e.g., teachers, mental health professionals) level of training, motivation, self-efficacy, and confidence in the effectiveness of the intervention (Roach, Lawton, & Elliott, 2014). Therefore, examination involves not only measuring outcomes, but also assessing needs and the implementation process.

TYPES OF EXAMINATION

In examining school safety, crisis prevention, and crisis preparedness efforts, the school safety and crisis response teams should ask the following questions:

- What are the needs of the school and students?
- What are the key components or processes of addressing the identified needs, and are the selected strategies implemented with integrity?
- What are the school safety, crisis prevention, and crisis preparedness objectives, and what do available data reveal regarding whether the stated objectives are accomplished?

Three types of examination strategies can be used to address these questions: (a) needs assessment, (b) process analysis, and (c) outcome evaluation. The following provides a brief review of each of these examination strategies, with the subsequent sections providing further information regarding each type of examination as it relates to school safety and crisis prevention, and to crisis preparedness.

Needs Assessment

The primary purpose of the needs assessment is to identify areas to be addressed, such that plans and strategies can be developed to focus on these needs. The needs assessment is particularly valuable because it focuses on information in the local context, with an emphasis on specific contextual considerations. For instance, all of the following can inform school safety and crisis prevention efforts: systematically gathering information from teachers, students, school staff members, and parents; also, reviewing school files such as discipline trends, student support referrals, attendance records, conduct ratings on report cards, suspensions, weapons violations, and visits to the nurse's office for treatment of injuries. School-wide screeners, surveys, or questionnaires may provide valuable information regarding the prevalence of behavior problems, mental health problems, bullying and victimization, student engagement, and perceptions of safety (Reeves et al., 2011a).

Process Analysis

The primary purpose of process analysis is to understand what was done and by whom, and to assess whether these activities were consistent with established plans. Basically, it helps answer the question: "Was the plan implemented as it was intended to be?" Sometimes referred to as procedural integrity, treatment integrity, or formative assessment, process analysis emphasizes obtaining information about the specific activities implemented. Methods to obtain process information commonly involve questionnaires, surveys, focus groups, or systematic observations regarding the implementation of strategies. Process analysis may yield valuable information regarding necessary areas for further professional development. Information from the process analysis is also very important because it helps to interpret the results of the outcome evaluation (Reeves et al., 2011a).

Outcome Evaluation

The outcome evaluation should focus on the stated objectives of the activities. Thus, each objective must be clearly articulated and measurable. Outcome evaluation is sometimes referred to as summative evaluation, in that the focus is on assessing the effectiveness of the implementer's efforts. Methods commonly include questionnaires, surveys, focus groups, systematic observations, or review of archival records to obtain specific information to examine outcomes. It is often helpful to obtain baseline data, for instance, using archival records (e.g., attendance, disciplinary referrals, or reports of student-inflicted injuries) or school-wide screeners that may have been used for the needs assessment. The Planning Section must have the knowledge and skills to complete data management and data analysis (e.g., basic descriptive statistics) and to develop the summary tables, charts, and figures that are important for assessing the outcomes data in this form of examination.

EXAMINATION OF SCHOOL SAFETY AND CRISIS PREVENTION

All three of the strategies mentioned above are valuable for examining school safety efforts. Though proving what efforts resulted in the absence of a negative outcome is difficult (Durlak & Wells, 1997), the efforts of school safety and crisis prevention programs can be evaluated using needs assessment, process analysis, and outcome evaluation.

Needs Assessment and School Safety and Crisis Prevention

A school safety needs assessment identifies areas of greatest need (also referred to as a vulnerability assessment). For example, systematically obtaining information about teachers', students', and parents' concerns provides an opportunity for a school to develop strategies that address the issues that are most important to it. Areas of concern that are noted through a general needs assessment may warrant further systematic data collection. For example, if concerns regarding the school climate are noted, it may be appropriate to administer a school climate survey to better understand the presenting concerns (c.f., Austin & Duerr, 2007a, 2007b, 2007c). Given finite resources, needs assessments are an essential component of school safety and crisis prevention efforts. Results provide the basis for identifying strengths, target populations, outcomes, and programs or strategies used to address concerns. As noted in Chapter 6, when selecting prevention programs or strategies, schools need to consider the fit between their unique school safety needs and the program. Thus, selection of appropriate programs or strategies must consider several factors, including (a) the needs of the school identified by a needs assessment (Elliott et al., 2002; Strein & Koehler, 2008); (b) the target population (e.g., students, teachers, and parents, and their age and race or ethnicity; Elliott et al., 2002); and (c) available implementation resources (e.g., financial resources and staff members' program knowledge and competencies; Elliott et al., 2002; Strein & Koehler, 2008). A needs assessment is critical to ensuring that limited resources are allocated to actual needs, not perceived needs.

Schools frequently adopt universal programs to address school safety and crisis prevention issues such as violence, maladaptive behavior, and school climate. Information gleaned from a needs assessment informs the selection of these programs. For example, Hunt et al. (2002) worked collaboratively with students, teachers, administrators, and parents to develop a survey to measure school and community members' perceptions of school violence, dropout, and school connectedness. Results highlighted the importance of parental support and supervision, which led the school to implement strategies to increase opportunities for parental involvement both at home and within the school.

Process Analysis and School Safety and Crisis Prevention

After identifying the school's areas of greatest need and selecting specific programs or strategies related to school safety, the Planning Section's next step is to implement the selected evaluation programs or strategies. In some instances, the Planning Section can develop a brief checklist with key components of the prevention programs or strategies to evaluate the degree to which these components are being systematically implemented. These checklists are valuable for understanding what was done and by whom during school safety and crisis prevention efforts. The Planning Section can use this information to interpret the results of the outcome evaluation, because outcomes may be linked to the fidelity of implementation. For example, if the process analysis reveals that specific teachers or staff members did not implement key components of the programs or strategies, then this lack of fidelity should be considered when interpreting the outcomes of students with whom they worked. In that case, the evaluation could remove these students from outcome analyses, or it may compare outcomes among students who received all key components relative to those who received only some of the components.

Analysis of implementation fidelity often encompasses a number of domains. For example, Ennett et al. (2011) conducted a process analysis of evidence-based curricula intended to prevent school substance use by middle school students. Analysis of implementation included measuring five domains of fidelity: adherence, exposure, quality of delivery, participant responsiveness, and program differentiation. Results from surveys revealed that the substance use prevention curricula were implemented with low program differentiation and moderate adherence and exposure. Survey results also revealed high fidelity levels in the domains of quality of delivery and participant responsiveness. Therefore, it was clear that ongoing training and support were needed for those implementing the substance use prevention curricula.

Outcome Evaluation and School Safety and Crisis Prevention

Outcome evaluation is used to assess whether the objectives of the prevention activities have been accomplished. As with process analysis, the Planning Section should identify the target outcomes and appropriate measures before implementing school safety and crisis prevention activities. Common outcomes that may be related to safety and prevention efforts include aggression, delinquency, violent acts, student attendance, school grades, disciplinary visits to the principal's office, social competence, or social skills. As noted in the previous section, in some instances the process analysis data reveal that not all students received the core components of the safety or prevention activities. Thus, the evaluation would consider only the outcomes of students who received the key components or, if there are sufficient numbers, compare the outcomes of students who received the key components with those who did not. Depending on the results of the outcome analysis, subsequent safety and prevention efforts may (a) focus on other areas of need, (b) continue the efforts that had positive outcomes, or (c) indicate further professional development to address issues related to implementation integrity.

In an outcome evaluation, Cornell, Allen, and Fan (2012) conducted a randomized controlled trial on the disciplinary outcomes for students who made threats of violence at school and subsequently received a threat assessment. Outcomes were measured using a checklist that included long-term suspension, parent conference, parent notification, placement in an alternative setting, and school-based mental health counseling services. Results of the study indicated that students who received the threat assessment were less likely to experience suspension or alternative school placement and more likely to receive mental health services and a parent conference. Prior delineation of outcomes allowed the authors to assess the predetermined goals of threat assessment and to make informed decisions regarding future utility of the prevention strategy.

EXAMINATION AND CRISIS PREPAREDNESS

Needs assessment, process analysis, and outcome evaluation are also applicable to the examination of crisis preparedness efforts. Given that PREPaRE emphasizes the importance of school crisis response teams using data-based decision-making, the ongoing examination of the school crisis response plan is critical.

Needs Assessment and Crisis Preparedness

Conducting regular vulnerability assessments is an excellent way to identify needs in relation to crisis preparedness. The ICS's threat- and hazard-specific annexes help to inform what specific crises should be addressed in the school crisis response plan (e.g., specific natural disasters such as tornadoes, earthquakes, hurricanes, and floods that are more or less likely to affect various schools). In addition to conducting vulnerability assessments, other common data collection procedures include interviews, surveys, focus groups, and reviews of school database information (e.g., discipline referrals, attendance). Reviews of established school crisis response plans and exemplary crisis preparedness resources or models provide additional information (see Chapters 2, 7, 8, and 9 for further discussion of crisis response plans and resources).

The Planning Section should use information obtained through a needs assessment to determine what training or skills school staff need to be able to implement for school crisis response. For example, if a school were located near a site that may release toxic chemicals, a functional annex (see Chapter 9) would involve ensuring safety during an evacuation or sheltering in place. Staff and students would practice drills and exercises so that they know the best response when this type of crisis occurs. The Planning Section should also identify established partnerships with local emergency response agencies and professionals as part of the needs assessment process. The needs assessment may reveal the need to offer professional development that includes emergency response personnel and professionals from community organizations that the school may collaborate with in a crisis (National Association of School Psychologists, 2004).

In addition, the school crisis response team uses needs assessment data to develop culturally responsive plans. For example, if a school has a large population of students and families who speak a specific language, identifying bilingual responders, accessing interpreters, and possessing translated materials should be identified in the needs assessment. Figure 20.1 provides a self-assessment checklist developed by Marsella (2009, as cited in Marsella, 2010) to evaluate cultural competence with regard to work with a specific client and could prove useful when the Planning Section conducts this type of needs assessment.

A needs assessment can efficiently gather information regarding a range of topics (e.g., quality of school crisis response plans, need for additional staff member training, probability of specific crises, cultural competence, and availability of required resources). Kano, Ramirez, Ybarra, Frias, and Bourque (2007) developed a needs assessment survey designed to evaluate aspects of school crisis response preparedness, such as interagency coordination, emergency response training, parental involvement, and emergency plans for three California school districts. Findings revealed (a) limited compliance with state-mandated school crisis response plan guidelines, (b) a lack of recent emergency response training for school employees, (c) an absence of emergency protocol drills specific to probable crises, and (d) insufficient emergency supplies. Through the use of a single questionnaire, these school districts gleaned a wealth of baseline information critical to the development of crisis preparedness protocols, activities, and resources. Further, the results of the needs assessment may also inform the Planning Section's goals and objectives for process analysis and outcome evaluation of crisis preparedness within the participating districs.

Process Analysis and Crisis Preparedness

The process analysis regarding crisis preparedness helps to determine whether school crisis response plans are clear and the roles and responsibilities of teachers, students, and crisis response team members are understood. As discussed in Chapters 7, 8, and 9, a fundamental component of crisis

Figure 20.1. Cultural Competence Self-Evaluation Form

Select your client's ethnocultural group:

Rate yourself on the following items of this scale to determine your "cultural competence" for this client.

Very true of me	True of me	Somewhat true of me	Not true of me	Unsure about me
4	3	2	1	U

1. _____ Knowledge of group's history
2. _____ Knowledge of group's family structures, gender roles, dynamics
3. _____ Knowledge of group's response to illness (i.e., awareness, biases)
4. _____ Knowledge of help-seeking behavior patterns of group
5. _____ Ability to evaluate your view and group view of illness
6. _____ Ability to feel empathy and understanding toward group
7. _____ Ability to develop a culturally responsive treatment program
8. _____ Ability to understand group's compliance with treatment
9. _____ Ability to develop culturally responsive prevention program for group
10. _____ Knowledge of group's "culture-specific" disorders/illnesses
11. _____ Knowledge of group's explanatory models of illness
12. _____ Knowledge of group's indigenous healing methods and traditions
13. _____ Knowledge of group's indigenous healers and their contact ease
14. _____ Knowledge of communication patterns and styles (e.g., nonverbal)
15. _____ Knowledge of group's language
16. _____ Knowledge of group's ethnic identification and acculturation situation
17. _____ Knowledge of how one's own health practices are rooted in culture
18. _____ Knowledge of impact of group's religious beliefs on health and illness
19. _____ Desire to learn group's culture
20. _____ Desire to travel to group's national location, neighborhood

Total score: _____ 80–65 = competent; 64–40 = near competent; below 40 = incompetent

Total no. of Us:_____ (If this number is above 8, more self-reflection is needed.)

Therapist: _____ Age: _____ Gender: _____ Religion: _____ Ethnicity: _____

Note. From "Ethnocultural Aspects of PTSD: An Overview of Concepts, Issues, and Treatments," by A. J. Marsella, 2010, *Traumatology, 16,* p. 22.

preparedness is the development of crisis response teams and plans. The teams and plans must detail the specific roles, responsibilities, strategies, and key components to be implemented when responding to a crisis.

One strategy for conducting a crisis preparedness process analysis is to systematically review the school crisis plan using checklists. Researchers have developed checklists to examine, for example, school improvement plans (Fernandez, 2009) and behavior support plans (Cook et al., 2007). Checklists have also been developed to study the comprehensiveness of school crisis plans (Aspiranti, Pelchar, McCleary, Bain, & Foster, 2011; Reeves et al., 2011a) and cultural sensitivity aspects of model crisis plans (Annandale, Heath, Dean, Kemple, & Takino, 2011).

Another means of completing process analysis before a crisis occurs is to conduct formal exercises or drills. Chapter 8 discusses the use of After Action Plans following drills and includes checklists for some of the other annexes.

Outcome Evaluation and Crisis Preparedness

In examining crisis preparedness, the Planning Section should systematically assess the school preparedness plans and the school crisis response team infrastructure—two examples of outcomes of crisis preparedness activities—to determine if they are consistent with best practice recommendations. The outcome evaluation must include annual reviews of all crisis preparedness materials, including plans, policies, procedures, and drafts of communication documents and handouts. Resources the team can use in evaluating the outcome of crisis preparedness efforts are available online through the Readiness and Emergency Management for Schools Technical Assistance Center (http://rems.ed.gov), the National Association of School Psychologists (www.nasponline.org), the American Psychological Association (www.apa.org), the Federal Emergency Management Agency (http://www.fema.gov), and the United Nations Office for Disaster Risk Reduction (http://www.unisdr.org).

The review of crisis response plans occurs at various levels, including individual school, district, and state or national levels. For example, Annandale et al. (2011) conducted a systematic review of the cultural competency of school crisis response planning materials from 40 states across the nation. Results of the systematic evaluation indicated that more than half of the crisis materials referenced the needs of students with mental and physical disabilities. However, the evaluation also revealed that the majority of state crisis response plans failed to address best practice recommendations specific to areas such as language and communication barriers, cultural competence training, and connections with culturally diverse community agencies. Results of this systematic review highlight areas of strength in the planning materials and equip states with information needed to revise crisis response plans to meet best practice recommendations.

CONCLUSION

Further research examining the effectiveness of school safety, crisis prevention, and crisis preparedness is needed (Brock, Sandoval, & Lewis, 1996, 2001; Nickerson & Gurdineer, 2012; Nickerson & Zhe, 2004; Pagliocca & Nickerson, 2001; Pagliocca et al., 2002). However, systematic data collection for examining school safety efforts and crisis response plans poses numerous challenges, and school safety and crisis response teams often face these same challenges, including (a) the unpredictable and infrequent nature of school safety threats; (b) the naturalistic, in vivo contexts of schools; (c) the difficulty analyses have revealing causality of specific intervention strategies, given the multifaceted nature of crisis prevention through recovery; and (d) the ethical and professional concerns raised by conducting controlled research studies with populations that are at risk or in crisis. Thus, much of the existing research consists of anecdotal accounts describing the steps taken and lessons learned following actual crisis events (Pagliocca & Nickerson, 2001; Petersen & Straub, 1992).

As discussed in this chapter, PREPaRE emphasizes the importance of examining the implementation and effectiveness of school safety and crisis preparedness efforts. During school safety and crisis response planning, the ICS Planning Section has responsibilities that include designing, developing, and collecting data to improve crisis prevention, preparedness, response, and recovery efforts. Using multiple strategies, the Planning Section informs school safety and crisis preparedness activities by (a) assisting in identifying areas of need (i.e., needs assessment); (b) helping to understand what was done and by whom, and the degree to which these efforts were consistent with specific school safety and crisis response team programs (i.e., process analysis); and (c) determining whether the stated objectives of the activities were accomplished (i.e., outcome evaluation). Careful planning through the examination of data is essential to informing school safety and crisis preparedness activities.

Chapter 21

EXAMINING THE EFFECTIVENESS OF SCHOOL CRISIS RESPONSE AND RECOVERY EFFORTS

Following crisis events, the comprehensive, multidisciplinary school crisis response team needs to critically evaluate all school and district crisis response and recovery efforts. Consistent with the discussion in Chapter 20 regarding the examination of school safety, crisis prevention, and crisis preparedness, this chapter begins with a discussion of the importance of examining the crisis response and recovery efforts and then describes challenges specific to the examination process. The final section considers in greater detail three examination strategies—needs assessment, process analysis, and outcome evaluation.

THE IMPORTANCE OF EXAMINATION

Today's schools increasingly expect educators to use evidence-based strategies. As with school safety, crisis prevention, and crisis preparedness efforts, examining crisis response and recovery efforts has several aims: (a) assessing effectiveness, (b) improving implementation and enhancing effectiveness, (c) better managing limited resources, (d) documenting accomplishments, (e) justifying required resources, (f) supporting the need for increased levels of funding, and (g) satisfying ethical responsibilities to demonstrate positive and negative effects of program participation.

The examination of response and recovery efforts can offer the school crisis response team valuable lessons. Assuming crisis preparedness efforts were well executed, the examination of response and recovery efforts should find that both the immediate and longer-term needs of school community members were met. However, there is no such thing as the perfect school crisis response. Thus, examination of every school crisis response is expected to reveal areas that warrant better preparation or planning. Overall, examination gives the school crisis response team an opportunity to reinforce effective strategies, as well as further improve and enhance crisis response and recovery efforts. Given the importance of examination, Pagliocca, Nickerson, and Williams (2002) have recommended that systematic examination procedures be included in all aspects of crisis preparedness.

An individual should be designated by the Incident Command System's (ICS) Incident Commander to lead the examination of all school crisis response and recovery efforts. Responsibility for these efforts is typically placed within the ICS's Planning Section. The Planning Section Chief coordinates appropriate methods and organizes data collection to assess the effectiveness of crisis response and recovery. An After-Action Report is a common tool for examining crisis response and recovery effectiveness. As discussed in Chapter 7, these reports help to examine response efforts, reveal what was done well, and identify areas that warrant further preparation, planning, or personnel. For example, the Planning Section may determine that too many or too few personnel were called for a response, which can lead to further refinement of protocols regarding requests for assistance.

The Planning Section is also responsible for ensuring that program goals and objectives are clearly articulated and measurable. Essential knowledge for the individuals assigned this task includes program evaluation, basic research design and methodology, and measurement (a skill set often found among school-employed mental health professionals). In addition, there are a number of different resources that the Planning Section might refer to as it examines school crisis response and recovery efforts (e.g., Berk & Rossi, 1990; Guba & Lincoln, 1989; Patton, 1990; Posavac & Raymond, 1989; Rossi & Freeman, 1993; Short, Hennessy, & Campbell, 1996).

CHALLENGES TO EXAMINATION

Challenges to the examination of crisis response and recovery efforts are very similar to those articulated in Chapter 20. Specifically, they include (a) definitional and measurement issues; (b) difficulties in conducting rigorous experimental research; and (c) barriers to the implementation, dissemination, and monitoring of interventions (Nickerson & Gurdineer, 2012). The Planning Section faces definitional and measurement issues when it attempts to prove that lower rates of mental illness, such as PTSD, are the result of the specific mental health crisis interventions offered in response to a given event (Durlak & Wells, 1997). A strategy to address this challenge includes establishing baseline data before a crisis occurs by conducting universal mental wellness screenings. In addition, being familiar with epidemiological studies that estimate the level of traumatic stress associated with specific types of crisis events (as discussed in Chapter 1) can be useful in determining whether the prevalence of mental illness is higher or lower than what might be expected, and in estimating the potential effectiveness of crisis response and recovery efforts.

Conducting research associated with school crisis events has a long history of difficulty (Brock, Sandoval, & Lewis, 1996). Although randomized controlled trials provide the strongest empirical support for the effectiveness of crisis intervention and recovery efforts (Ji, DuBois, Flay, & Brechling, 2008), ethical issues limit conducting such studies in schools. Furthermore, the idea of studying the effectiveness of a mental health intervention in the school setting is often frowned upon by school administrators (Brock et al., 1996). The high stakes associated with school mental health crisis intervention lead to increased concern regarding the ethics of withholding intervention programs from students who need them or providing services to individuals or groups for whom the intervention is not necessary. Further, low base rates of mental illness (e.g., PTSD is a relatively infrequent consequence of crisis exposure) and the associated lack of statistical resources present additional challenges to such studies and also affect the generalizability and validity of the study results (Cuijpers, 2003; Durlak & Wells, 1997).

Finally, the successful implementation, dissemination, and monitoring of school crisis response and recovery programs depend heavily on the interactions of various micro- and macro-level factors (e.g., from students, teachers, mental health professionals, and administrators, to school districts, school boards, and other political systems). Research on treatment integrity—the degree to which an intervention is administered as intended (Sanetti & Kratochwill, 2014)—suggests that programs are delivered with less integrity when they are complex, require multiple resources, and demand large time commitments. Similarly, treatment integrity is influenced by crisis interveners' level of training, motivation, self-efficacy, and confidence in the effectiveness of the intervention (Roach, Lawton, & Elliott, 2014). Therefore, examination involves not only measuring outcomes, but also training educators to provide mental health crisis intervention.

STRATEGIES FOR EXAMINING CRISIS RESPONSE AND RECOVERY EFFORTS

Similar to the process used to examine school safety, crisis prevention, and crisis preparedness efforts, when examining crisis response and recovery efforts, questions to consider include the following:

- What are the postcrisis needs of the school and students?
- What are the key strategies used to address the identified needs, and are the selected strategies implemented with integrity?
- What are the crisis response and recovery objectives, and what do the data reveal regarding whether the stated objectives were accomplished?

Three types of examination strategies can be used to address these questions: needs assessment, process evaluation, and outcome evaluation. These examination procedures should have been delineated as part of the school crisis preparedness stages and should be practiced during crisis simulations and exercises.

Needs Assessment and Crisis Response and Recovery

The needs assessment process identifies resources—the specific materials and the specific skills, training, and knowledge—schools need to provide the immediate crisis response and to ensure long-term crisis recovery. Examples of such resources include screening tools to conduct psychological triage, individuals trained to provide immediate school crisis intervention, knowledge of traumatic stress risk factors, and community-based psychotherapy resources. As discussed in Chapter 7, within the ICS, the Planning Section and the Logistics Section play key roles in identifying and obtaining these resources. Thus, needs assessment strategies are important to the functions of both of these sections during a school crisis response.

Many PREPaRE resources described in this book are important to a school's crisis response and can be used to conduct a needs assessment (e.g., Chapter 14's discussion of the process of psychological triage). The Incident Action Plan (IAP) discussed in Chapter 7 (outlined in Table 7.5) can be used to establish crisis response objectives. School-wide screenings (Chapter 14) can help to document the mental health needs of students following exposure to a crisis. For example, if a significant number of students are demonstrating symptoms of traumatic stress, then recovery requires the psychotherapeutic treatment resources described in Chapter 19.

Process Analysis and Crisis Response and Recovery

The process analysis gathers information to determine to what degree crisis response and recovery efforts are consistent with preestablished crisis response plans and other process-related considerations. A process analysis also helps to determine the initial effectiveness of crisis response activities and can be used to help determine when the immediate response can be concluded. The Planning Section collects data to document and systematically review the crisis response and recovery process. These data are often collected during crisis response debriefings, individual interviews with school community members, and focus groups following the crisis response.

Outcome Evaluation and Crisis Response and Recovery

The primary purpose of the outcome evaluation is to examine the overall effectiveness of crisis response and recovery activities in accomplishing targeted objectives as identified by the IAP. The After-Action Report (described in Chapter 7) can be an important mechanism for examining crisis response and recovery outcomes, such as student adjustment, staff adjustment, and student access to support services. Brock (2011a) proposes the following as possible crisis response and recovery outcomes that can be used to examine effectiveness:

- Crisis interventions indicated by psychological triage were provided.
- Individuals with psychopathology have been provided with or referred for appropriate treatment.
- Individuals with maladaptive coping behaviors (e.g., suicidal or homicidal ideation) have been referred to the appropriate professionals, and lethality has been reduced.
- School behavior problems (i.e., aggressive, delinquent, and criminal behavior) occur at or below precrisis levels.
- Students attend school at or above precrisis attendance rates.
- Students' academic functioning is at or above precrisis levels.

CONCLUSION

Overall, insufficient research is being conducted to demonstrate the effectiveness of school crisis response and recovery efforts. Clearly, more systematic research is needed (Brock, Sandoval, & Lewis, 2001; Nickerson & Zhe, 2004; Pagliocca & Nickerson, 2001; Pagliocca et al., 2002).

However, there are numerous challenges to systematically examining school crisis response team effectiveness, including (a) the unpredictable and infrequent nature of crises; (b) the naturalistic in vivo contexts of schools; (c) the difficulty of conducting analyses to reveal causality of specific intervention strategies, given the multifaceted nature of crisis response and recovery; and (d) the ethical and professional concerns raised by conducting controlled research studies with populations in crisis. Thus, much of the existing research consists of anecdotal accounts describing the steps taken and lessons learned following actual crisis events (Pagliocca & Nickerson, 2001; Petersen & Straub, 1992).

As discussed in this chapter, PREPaRE emphasizes the need to examine the implementation and effectiveness of crisis response and recovery. Schools can achieve this by designating individuals within the ICS's Planning Section whose responsibilities include the design and development of data collection activities, which can be used to evaluate components of the crisis response and recovery efforts and inform future efforts. Using multiple strategies, the examination will (a) identify areas of need (i.e., needs assessment); (b) help the crisis response team understand what was done and by whom, and the degree to which these efforts were consistent with specific crisis team programs or response strategies (i.e., process analysis); and (c) determine whether the stated objectives of the activities were accomplished (i.e., outcome evaluation).

Section 7

FINAL CONSIDERATIONS

The concluding chapters of this book offer the reader some final considerations important to school safety and crisis response teams. First, Chapter 22 discusses the important topic of caring for the caregiver. It is with great sincerity that the authors of this book have dedicated it to the "school-employed mental health professionals who engage in crisis prevention and response." Firsthand experiences have shown how difficult, and emotionally and physically draining, the work of preparing for, responding to, and working toward recovery from school emergencies can be. Consequently, it is an ethical responsibility for all members of school crisis response teams to practice self-care. Chapter 22 is intended to facilitate those efforts. Next, Chapter 23 explores evaluations of the PREPaRE curriculum that have taken place to date. It also illustrates applications of the PREPaRE model in today's schools. Finally, Chapter 24 has concluding comments, which include next steps in the development of the PREPaRE curriculum.

Chapter 22

CARING FOR THE CAREGIVER

The previous chapters of this book focused on the many tasks that school crisis response teams carry out to care for others. However, as the authors have learned from their experiences, all crisis response team members, and in particular mental health crisis interveners, also must care for themselves. The need to foster self-care is a frequently neglected element of crisis response and recovery. Thus, the goal of this chapter is to help crisis responders become more aware of the emotional effects of crisis response and intervention, and to promote attention to their own state and resilience, as well as to encourage school crisis response teams to promote a culture of care for the caregiver.

This chapter begins by defining concepts such as compassion satisfaction and compassion fatigue, secondary traumatic stress, vicarious traumatization, and follows by discussing ways to promote resilience among crisis responders. It then addresses the potential consequences of crisis response work by providing symptomatology, prevalence, severity, and measurement of compassion fatigue and its related concepts. The chapter concludes by identifying standards for establishing and maintaining wellness, and it offers suggestions regarding how school crisis responders can care for themselves by developing personal and professional self-care strategies and practices.

Crisis response in general, and mental health crisis intervention in particular, can be rewarding work, but they can also be very emotionally and physically demanding (Brymer et al., 2006; Brymer, Taylor, et al., 2012). School-employed mental health professionals who provide crisis intervention services often experience crises either firsthand or secondarily through their work with survivors of tragedy (Tosone, McTighe, Bauwens, & Naturale, 2011). They have the dual challenge of providing mental health crisis intervention while also fulfilling other demanding job responsibilities and maintaining existing caseloads. School staff members who provide any crisis response services are best served if they prepare ahead of time for the potential consequences of that work. Seeking professional development and mental health crisis intervention training (such as PREPaRE workshops) further prepares school crisis responders. Finally, even with prevention planning in place, some will still experience stress reactions that have the potential to affect their mental and physical health, family and social relationships, and even career trajectory (Bride, 2007; Brymer et al., 2006; Kintzle, Yarvis, & Bride, 2013).

CONCEPTS AND DEFINITIONS

Most mental health professionals chose their field because they have a passion for helping others and derive a sense of satisfaction from providing needed services. Stamm (2010) refers to this as *compassion satisfaction*. Providing mental health crisis intervention has the potential to support the survivor while simultaneously increasing the compassion satisfaction of the caregiver. Conversely, *compassion fatigue* has been defined by Figley (1995) as the caregiver's difficulty maintaining feelings of empathy and is "the natural consequent behaviors and emotions resulting from knowing about a traumatizing event experienced or suffered by a person" (p. 7). Research is unclear on the exact relationship between compassion satisfaction and compassion fatigue. However, one can reasonably assume that these two concepts have an inverse relationship: as one increases, the other decreases, and keeping compassion fatigue in check serves crisis responders well.

Some additional concepts and terms, related to compassion fatigue, help define the potential outcomes or consequences for frontline crisis responders. For example, the phenomenon of learning about another's traumatic experience and, in the process, experiencing traumatic stress oneself has been referred to as *secondary traumatic stress* (Figley, 1995). Figley (1999) defined secondary traumatic stress (STS) as the "natural, consequent behaviors and emotions resulting from knowledge about a traumatizing event experienced by a significant other. It is the stress resulting from helping or wanting to help a suffering person" (p. 10). Furthermore, Figley (1999) recognized that individuals who are called upon to assist traumatized children, such as school crisis responders, are particularly vulnerable to STS.

McCann and Pearlman (1990) offered the following: "Persons who work with victims may experience profound psychological effects, effects that can be disruptive and painful for the helper and can persist for months or years after work with traumatized persons" (p. 133). The researchers referred to this concept as *vicarious traumatization* (McCann & Pearlman, 1990). The negative effects of prolonged exposure to clients' experiences of trauma on the therapist's psychological functioning results in a change in their world view, identity, values, philosophy of life (Lambert & Lawson, 2013), and understanding of the world (Way, VanDeusen, & Cottrell, 2007; Williams, Helm, & Clemens, 2012). Canfield (2005) reported that studies of vicarious traumatization found the following areas disrupted in trauma therapists' lives: feelings and beliefs of safety, control, self-esteem, regard for others, and intimacy in relationships.

Finally, Stamm (2010) defines *burnout* as a concept associated with feelings of hopelessness; difficulties in dealing with work or in doing one's job effectively; gradual onset of these feelings; and the perception that one's efforts make no difference. "Burnout is different from compassion fatigue in that secondary symptoms of [posttraumatic stress disorder or] PTSD are not present" (Craig & Sprang, 2010, p. 322). Although the commonly used definitions have been provided here, the use of these terms in the literature is not always clear, because some studies have used the terms compassion fatigue, secondary traumatic stress, and vicarious traumatization interchangeably (Jenkins & Baird, 2002; Williams et al., 2012).

CONSEQUENCES OF RESPONDING TO SCHOOL CRISES

School crisis responders deal with a wide range of crises that affect schools directly or indirectly, such as acts of war or terrorism, violent and/or unexpected death, threatened death or injury, human-caused disasters, natural disasters, and severe illness or injury (Brock, Sandoval, & Lewis, 2001). It is therefore not surprising that providing interventions during and after a school crisis has a significant effect on caregivers. For example, Bolnik and Brock (2005) conducted a study with the primary purpose of documenting and determining the effects of mental health crisis intervention work on school psychologists. Of the 200 school psychologists that completed the survey, just over 90% reported one or more of 37 specific negative reactions following their crisis intervention work. The 37 reactions were categorized into five domains: physical, emotional, behavioral, cognitive, and work performance. It was found that almost 32% of the total number of reactions endorsed by participants fell in the physical reactions category. Fatigue/ exhaustion was the number one negative reaction, which was endorsed by 83% of the participants, followed by increased sensitivity (59%), anxiety (55%), difficulty concentrating (49%), and helplessness (39%).

From the data gathered by Bolnik and Brock (2005), Figure 22.1 provides a rank order representation of the negative reactions experienced by school psychologists following their mental

Figure 22.1. School Psychologists' Reactions to Crisis Intervention Work

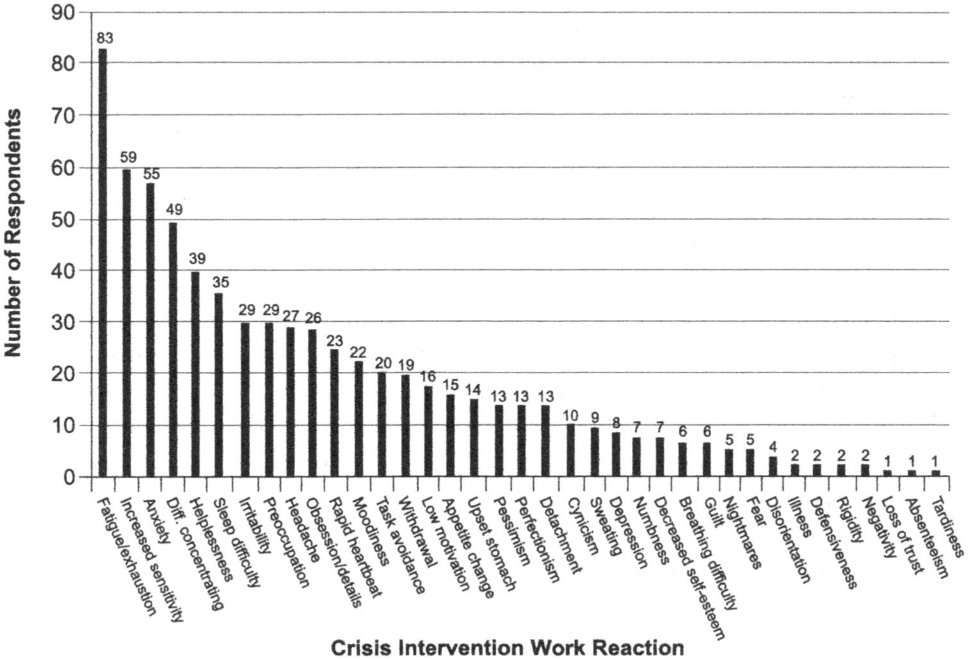

Note. From data provided by "The Self-Reported Effects of Crisis Intervention Work on School Psychologists," by L. Bolnik & S. E. Brock, 2005, *California School Psychologist, 10*, pp. 117–124.

health crisis intervention work in the schools. As Bolnik and Brock pointed out, a high percentage of school psychologists experienced negative reactions following crisis intervention work, so it remains important for training curricula and models (such as the PREPaRE curriculum) to emphasize protective self-care strategies and plans for school-based mental health workers and responders.

It is widely recognized that those working with trauma survivors, having been indirectly exposed to tragic events, are at risk for significant emotional, cognitive, and behavioral changes themselves (Bride, 2007). Psychologically traumatized individuals often need to share their story multiple times, and as a result, mental health crisis interveners are repeatedly exposed to intense emotions and graphic details of violent events. Numerous studies present empirical evidence that individuals who provide these services to traumatized populations are at increased risk of experiencing their own symptoms of traumatic stress (Jordan, 2010; Kintzle et al., 2013; Pack, 2014). Jordan (2010) noted that mental health workers are at increased risk for vicarious traumatization if they receive inadequate peer supervision or consultation, lack social support, do not engage in self-care practices, and provide services to those who were severely affected.

Another study conducted by Lambert and Lawson (2013) found that professional counselors who responded to Hurricanes Katrina and Rita had more than double the rate of compassion fatigue and vicarious traumatization compared with a control group of professional counselors. These findings suggested that counselors engaging in disaster mental health crisis intervention were at significantly increased risk for compassion fatigue independent of whether or not they were personally affected by the disaster.

Meyers and Cornille (2002) reviewed the literature in the area of secondary trauma and provided several generalizations: (a) professionals who work with traumatized individuals can exhibit the same range of symptoms as victims, (b) the longevity and severity of these symptoms varies with the individual, (c) professionals working with trauma victims are more likely to exhibit symptoms if they have been personally traumatized, and (d) female trauma workers are more likely to exhibit STS than their male colleagues.

As is the case for primary trauma victims (as discussed in Chapter 13), some reactions of crisis responders, both during and after a school crisis, are common and to be expected. However, other reactions signal that the responder has been overwhelmed and is potentially suffering STS reactions. In the literature, STS is described as a syndrome with symptoms very similar to those of PTSD (as defined in the DSM-5; American Psychiatric Association, 2013), and long-term reactions generally include intrusive thoughts, hypervigilance, and avoidant behaviors (Bride, 2007; Figley, 1995). Table 22.1 provides a reference list of common and extreme stress reactions that crisis responders may experience during and after their school crisis response experiences.

RESILIENCE AND PROTECTIVE FACTORS

Resilience is the ability to adapt to difficult, challenging, stressful, or traumatic life experiences (Chapters 10 and 13 discussed this topic as it relates to students). Resilience as it pertains to school crisis response team members is a continual process that can be strengthened and developed over

Table 22.1. Common and Extreme Stress Reactions in the Crisis Responder

Common Stress Reactions
- Increase or decrease in activity level
- Difficulties sleeping
- Substance use
- Disconnection and numbing
- Irritability, anger, and frustration
- Vicarious traumatization in the form of shock, fearfulness, horror, or helplessness
- Confusion, lack of attention, and difficulty making decisions
- Physical reactions (headaches, stomachaches, easily startled)
- Depressive or anxiety reactions
- Decreased social activities
- Diminished self-care

Extreme Stress Reactions
- Sense of helplessness
- Preoccupation or compulsive reexperiencing of trauma experienced either directly or indirectly
- Attempts to overcontrol in professional or personal situations, or act out a "rescuer complex"
- Social withdrawal and isolation
- Chronic exhaustion
- Survival coping strategies such as reliance on substances, preoccupation with work, or drastic changes in sleeping or eating patterns
- Serious difficulties in interpersonal relationships, including domestic violence
- Depression accompanied by hopelessness
- Suicidal ideation or attempts
- Unnecessary risk-taking
- Illness or an increase in levels of pain
- Changes in memory and perception
- Disruption in your perceptions of safety, trust, and independence

Note. Adapted from *Psychological First Aid for Schools: Field Operations Guide* (2nd ed., p. 113), by M. Brymer, M. Taylor, et al., 2012, Rockville, MD: National Child Traumatic Stress Network and National Center for PTSD. Adapted with permission.

time. *Vicarious resilience*, or the ability to bounce back, can be enhanced through clinical supervision; the use of supports, humor, and spirituality; professional development (such as is offered by the PREP<u>a</u>RE curriculum); teamwork; and a supportive workplace. These protective factors act to buffer the more negative effects of working with traumatized clients (Pack, 2014).

Williams et al. (2012) cited that both qualitative and quantitative studies have found that consistent active participation in wellness activities helps decrease vulnerability to vicarious traumatization (Bober, Regehr, & Zhou, 2006; Bride, Robinson, Yegidis, & Figley, 2004; Hunter & Schofield, 2006). A literature review conducted by Canfield (2005) determined that therapists attempted to manage their emotions by using the following effective strategies: affective distancing, use of professional supports, belief in altruism or a higher purpose in life, regular exercise, and contact with a supportive supervisor the therapist could reach out to when under stress. These positive coping skills and supports were reported to be helpful in alleviating secondary traumatic stress reactions.

MEASUREMENT OF SECONDARY TRAUMATIC STRESS

According to Bride, Radey, and Figley (2007), the first step in preventing or ameliorating the effects of compassion fatigue is to be aware of and recognize its signs and symptoms (see Table 22.1). Several standardized assessment tools can be used to measure the effects of compassion fatigue, and a sample of these instruments are reviewed in the following paragraphs.

Compassion Fatigue Scale

The Compassion Fatigue Scale (CFS; Gentry, Baranowsky, & Dunning, 2002) was originally developed from clinical experience and is designed to assess both compassion fatigue and burnout. Adams, Boscarino, and Figley (2006) found the scale to have adequate psychometric properties. A more recent study by Adams, Figley, and Boscarino (2008) further validated and confirmed the distinction between secondary trauma and job burnout. Their results suggested that the CFS was helpful in identifying caregivers who were at risk for compassion fatigue and psychological difficulties.

Secondary Traumatic Stress Scale

The Secondary Traumatic Stress Scale (STSS; Bride et al., 2004) is a 17-item instrument designed to measure intrusion, avoidance, and arousal symptoms associated with indirect exposure to traumatic events through professional work with clients who have been traumatized. Bride et al. (2004) found that the "STSS fills a need for a reliable and valid instrument that was specifically designed to measure the negative effects of social work practice with traumatized populations" (p. 27). The availability of STSS cutoff scores facilitates clinical decision making and allows professionals to judge whether *secondary* trauma symptoms may be associated with significant emotional difficulties or whether the *secondary* trauma reactions are transient. For example, using an algorithm approach, if an individual endorses at least one item on the intrusion subscale, at least three items on the avoidance subscale, and at least two items on the arousal subscale, then that person may be experiencing PTSD due to secondary traumatic stress (Bride, 2007).

Impact of Events Scale–Revised

The Impact of Events Scale–Revised (IES-R; Weiss, 2007) is a 22-item self-report measure that assesses the distress caused by traumatic events. It yields scores for intrusion, avoidance, and hyperarousal. The IES-R is not used to diagnose PTSD; however, it does serve as a screening tool for PTSD (Feuerherd, Knuth, Muehlan, & Schmidt, 2014). Strengths of the IES-R include that it is brief, easily scored, and available in multiple languages (e.g., German, Italian, Polish, Spanish, Swedish; Feuerherd et al., 2014). An additional benefit of the IES-R is that it can be used repeatedly to assess a person's progress.

Trauma and Attachment Belief Scale

The Trauma and Attachment Belief Scale (TABS; Pearlman, 2003) consists of 84 items that are based on a six-point Likert scale. The purpose of the TABS is to measure disruptions of the five psychological needs that may be affected by traumatic stress: safety, trust, esteem, intimacy, and control (Pearlman, 2003). The TABS is grounded in constructivist self-development theory and assesses the relationship of traumatic stress to individuals' cognitive schemas (Varra, Pearlman, Brock, & Hodgson, 2008). This measure has been used with a variety of populations (both traumatized individuals and their therapists; Varra et al., 2008). According to Williams et al. (2012), experts recommend the TABS as the instrument of choice to assess vicarious traumatization among mental health professionals.

PREVENTION AND INTERVENTION

School administrators and school-employed mental health professionals play a critical role in reducing the risk of STS among crisis responders. They do so by establishing policies, procedures, and supports *before* crises occur. "Organizational factors, such as the promotion of supervision, peer support, and the processing of difficult cases, will not only reduce STS, but may also impact other job-related outcomes such as stress, burnout, and job satisfaction" (Kintzle et al., 2013, p. 1314). STS prevention and intervention strategies should be woven into crisis preparedness activities. Administrators who facilitate crisis preparedness efforts should constantly promote a culture of caring for the caregiver; among other things, it should be an element of crisis drills. Specific recommendations for those who supervise and provide support for school crisis response team members are provided in Table 22.2.

Ethical Principles of Self-Care

Everall and Paulson (2004) discussed the issues of burnout and STS and its potential impact on ethical practice. Clearly, a diminished ability to function professionally may constitute a serious violation of the ethical principles of mental health crisis interveners, as they may place students at risk. Everall and Paulson also suggested three major areas of prevention, which include (a) self-monitoring, (b) obtaining supervision, and (c) obtaining intervention and support from colleagues and administrators. Figley (1995, 2002) also proposed standards of self-care for professionals who work with psychologically traumatized individuals. These standards also state that not attending to one's self-care is unethical, as such care is necessary for providing effective services and avoiding harm to clients. The standards acknowledge the importance of (a) respecting the dignity and worth of oneself (violation lowers professionals' integrity and trust), (b) taking

Table 22.2. Prevention and Intervention Strategies for Administrators of School Crisis Responders

Prevention

- Proactively develop stress management skills (e.g., offer yoga classes).
- Provide education and training in school crisis prevention and response (e.g., PREPaRE workshops).
- Identify enough crisis interveners to address all aspects of the school mental health crisis intervention plan.
- Establish supervision, case conferencing, and staff appreciation events.
- Conduct training in secondary traumatic stress and stress management practices.
- Encourage peer partners and consultation.
- Form alliances with employee assistance program (EAP) providers and community mental health agencies (site-based personnel may not be in the best position to provide such assistance).
- Establish procedures for addressing the circumstances under which a staff member may need to be removed from a caregiving situation.
- Establish procedures for how to remove a staff member from an inappropriate caregiving situation.

Intervention

- Limit shifts so that mental health crisis interveners and other crisis responders do not provide services beyond 12 hours.
- Rotate responders from the highest-impact assignments to those with lower levels of stress.
- Monitor responders who meet certain high-risk criteria, such as
  - Survivor of crisis or disaster.
  - Those having regular exposure to severely affected individuals.
  - Those with preexisting conditions.
  - Those who have responded to many crises in a short period of time.

Note. Brymer et al. (2006), Figley (2002), Kintzle et al. (2013).

responsibility for one's self-care (ultimately professionals are responsible for taking care of themselves, and no situation or person can justify neglecting it), and (c) acknowledging the relationship between self-care and one's duty to perform (professionals must recognize that they cannot fulfill the duties to perform as a crisis intervener if they fail in the duty to care for themselves, which includes knowing when to say "no" to a request to provide services).

Professional and Personal Self-Care Planning

School-employed mental health professionals who provide mental health crisis intervention must make a commitment to both personal self-care and professional preparation by seeking available training. Self-care practices are preventive and can reduce the future likelihood and intensity of STS symptoms (Canfield, 2005; Gentry et al., 2002; Harrison & Westwood, 2009;

Lambert & Lawson, 2013), therefore crisis interveners should put their own prevention practices in place by establishing a self-care plan. Professionals must take the time to determine if they are able and ready to face the challenges of responding in a crisis long before a crisis occurs. For example, school-employed mental health professionals will want to seek professional assistance to deal with any personal trauma history and consider their personal, social, and family concerns before committing to a physically and emotionally demanding crisis response. Once school mental health professionals have considered their personal challenges, they are better able to commit themselves fully to a school crisis intervention.

Along with being personally prepared, mental health crisis interveners are best served by first receiving training in crisis intervention, such as by participating in the PREPaRE workshops. The benefits of such training can be found in a study by Craig and Sprang (2010), which found that using evidence-based practices reduced burnout and compassion fatigue and increased compassion satisfaction. After a mental health crisis intervention, if a school-employed mental health

Table 22.3. Responder Self-Care Plan Practices

Physical
- Get adequate sleep or additional sleep to make up for increased demands.
- Avoid working for extended periods, especially without contact with colleagues, and take breaks.
- Eat healthy foods and stay hydrated.
- Limit excess use of alcohol and tobacco.
- Exercise regularly.
- Regularly use the stress management techniques of meditation, visualization, relaxation, and diaphragmatic breathing.

Psychological
- Limit your hours of providing intensive services.
- Self-monitor and become aware of the signs of secondary traumatic stress.
- Seek out a professional who is knowledgeable about trauma if the signs of secondary traumatic stress last for longer than 2–3 weeks.
- Seek coping assistance for your own trauma history.

Social, Interpersonal, and Family
- Plan for family and home safety, including childcare and pet care.
- Identify social supports of two to five people (including some at work) you can depend on to be supportive.
- Engage in social activism, advocacy, and actions that promote healing and helping "victims" become "survivors."
- Practice your religious faith and spirituality.
- Explore your passion for creative self-expression, such as writing, painting, and teaching.
- Be open to finding humor in your life experiences.

Note. Brymer et al. (2006); Figley (1995, 2002).

professional is self-aware enough, or if others are suggesting that the individual needs therapy, then he or she must seek assistance. Those who work with traumatized individuals on a regular basis are advised to seek ongoing supervision, be part of a team, or have an informal peer network to help prevent vicarious traumatization (Harrison & Westwood, 2009).

Personal self-care has several components: (a) finding a balance between work and home and devoting sufficient time and attention to both without compromising either; (b) setting firm time, therapeutic, and personal boundaries to deal with multiple roles in the community; (c) realistically differentiating between things one can change in the system and accepting those one cannot; and (d) seeking ways to gain recognition for, and taking joy in, the achievements of one's work. The last element involves getting help and support at work, which includes (a) obtaining supervision, consultation, and therapy, as needed, and debriefing with other crisis response team members; (b) working in teams, such as school and district crisis response teams; and (c) seeking out mentor–mentee relationships. As indicated in Table 22.3, the ideal personal self-care plan consists of three components: physical; psychological; and social, interpersonal, and family care.

CONCLUSION

Providing needed interventions to people who have experienced the acute effects of a crisis can be a rewarding experience (Brymer et al., 2006), one that provides the school crisis responder with a sense of pleasure or compassion satisfaction (Stamm, 2010). However, although providing help, hope, and interventions can be rewarding, crisis response work can also be very emotionally and physically demanding (Brymer et al., 2006; Brymer, Taylor, et al., 2012). Prolonged exposure to psychologically traumatized people can lead to compassion fatigue (Figley, 1995), vicarious traumatization, or secondary traumatic stress (Figley, 1995, 1999).

Because providing mental health crisis interventions can have a significant effect on caregivers (Bolnik & Brock, 2005), crisis interveners must be aware of, and make use of, self-care strategies that develop both professional and personal self-care (Canfield, 2005; Gentry et al., 2002; Harrison & Westwood, 2009; Lambert & Lawson, 2013). Self-care planning begins before a crisis occurs and it continues long after the immediate crisis response has concluded. Although some reactions are common for those providing school crisis response in general, and mental health crisis intervention in particular, some reactions can be severe and may require help from a professional (Brymer et al., 2006; Brymer, Taylor, et al., 2012). Crisis responders often think of others' needs before their own; however, planning ahead and taking care of oneself ultimately leads to more effective and long-term service to others.

Chapter 23

PREPaRE RESEARCH AND APPLICATIONS

Whereas the preceding chapters provide a theoretical and empirical foundation for the PREPaRE model, the focus of this chapter is on the research and application of the curriculum itself. First, the chapter describes the results of the ongoing systematic program evaluation. Following the evaluation results is a review of the studies that have been conducted, which use PREPaRE training as an independent variable in the examination of various outcomes. Next, the chapter describes application of the curriculum to real-world crisis prevention and intervention efforts. Finally, it concludes with directions for future research and ongoing application of the model to practice.

ONGOING PROGRAM EVALUATION

Systematic program evaluation has been integral to the PREPaRE curriculum since its inception in 2006. To facilitate these efforts, all PREPaRE trainers are required to participate in the Training of Trainers (ToT) program (Brock, 2006c, 2011b; Reeves et al., 2011b; Reeves et al., 2006b), which includes instruction on delivering PREPaRE's standardized program evaluation procedures.

In general, the evaluation of professional development consists of the elements of reaction, learning, behavior, and results (Kirkpatrick, 1996). *Reaction* assesses participants' perceptions of program experiences (e.g., satisfaction, motivation to participate). *Learning* measures the impact of training on knowledge, skills, and attitudes (Kirkpatrick, 1996). *Behavior* measures the extent to which training transfers to on-the-job behavior. The final element, *results*, is a measure of the outcome of training (e.g., improved quality, reduced costs). The ongoing program evaluation of PREPaRE assesses reaction (i.e., satisfaction) and learning (e.g., extent to which PREPaRE achieves its objectives in terms of knowledge gained and attitudes changed), two essential aspects of program evaluation (Ingvarson, Meiers, & Beavis, 2005).

Evaluation Measures and Procedures

To assess attitudes and knowledge, the evaluation uses identical quantitative pre- and posttests. The Workshop 1, Crisis Prevention and Preparedness, test originally contained four items to measure participants' attitudes toward crisis prevention using a five-point Likert-type scale. It also originally included 10 multiple-choice items to assess knowledge of key curriculum components (each item is scored 0 for incorrect and 1 for correct). Similarly, the Workshop 2, Crisis Intervention and Recovery, test originally consisted of three items to assess attitudes toward crisis intervention; it included 13 items to assess knowledge. To ensure high content validity, both sets of multiple choice test questions were aligned with stated workshop objectives. The tests were piloted during development of the PREPaRE curricula. The original workshop satisfaction measure consisted of a series of questions rated on a Likert-type scale. Also, the evaluation asked participants three open-ended questions: (a) What were the strengths of this workshop? (b) What suggestions do you have to help us improve this workshop? and (c) What specific crisis prevention and/or intervention knowledge and skills did you develop that will inform your work?

Results from the program evaluation were used to refine and finalize the workshop content and to further improve the evaluation procedures. In 2009, the evaluation procedures were modified to improve efficiency, comprehensiveness, and reliability. More specifically, the workshop evaluation forms were changed from three questions about overall satisfaction (see Brock, Nickerson, Reeves, Savage, & Woitaszewski, 2011) to a 10-item evaluation about workshop objectives and content, trainer skill, materials and organization, and application of the training ($\alpha = .96$ and $\alpha = .97$ for Workshops 1 and 2 evaluation measures, respectively; Nickerson, Serwacki, et al., 2014). Furthermore, to ensure a more standardized evaluation procedure, trainers were given instructions to read to participants before completing the pretest, posttest, and evaluations, and participants used Scantron forms to provide their answers. Trainers read instructions to participants about how to complete forms (e.g., asking participants to provide a unique personal four-digit identification number on each pre- and posttest so they can be matched for data analysis).

Pretests, consisting of items assessing both participants' attitudes toward crisis prevention and intervention work and their knowledge consistent with the workshop objectives, are administered immediately prior to the beginning of the workshop, and posttests are completed immediately after workshop conclusion. Satisfaction evaluations are also administered with posttests. All forms are sent to the National Association of School Psychologists (NASP) at the conclusion of each workshop, and the Scantron forms are then sent to an independent company for scoring. The database is then cleaned and analyzed, and workgroup members and school psychology graduate students write program evaluation summaries, which are posted on the NASP website (http://www.nasponline.org/professional-development/prepare-training-curriculum). The open-ended responses are sent to another member of the PREPaRE workgroup, who works with a group of school psychology graduate students to conduct qualitative analyses of the data using a modified consensus approach based on guidelines presented by Hill et al. (2005).

With publication of the curriculum's second edition in 2011, evaluation procedures were again modified. While both workshops' pre- and posttests have the original attitude items, the Workshop 1 Crisis Prevention and Preparedness knowledge test was expanded from 10 to 14 items, and the Workshop 2 Crisis Intervention and Recovery knowledge test was expanded from 13 to 16 items. In addition, the quantitative element of the workshop evaluation was expanded from 10 items for each workshop to 20 items for Workshop 1 and 16 items for Workshop 2 (both workshops maintained the same three original qualitative evaluation questions). For the most recent evaluations of the PREP_aRE curriculum, which use the second edition's modified evaluation procedures, the reader is referred to the NASP PREP_aRE Training Outcomes and Evaluation webpage (http://www.nasponline.org/professional-development/prepare-training-curriculum). In addition to these ongoing summaries posted to the NASP website, two peer-refereed journal articles describe the results of the program evaluation, the results of which are summarized next.

Published Peer-Refereed Evaluation Results

The first peer-refereed article described the development of the curriculum, reported PREP_aRE program evaluation results from 2007 through 2008 for over 2,000 participants, and assessed the extent to which the ToT model achieved its objectives (Brock et al., 2011). Participants who attended Workshop 1, Crisis Prevention and Preparedness, in 39 separate locations (17 states and Canada) reported being very satisfied. Specifically, on a scale of 1 to 10 (with 10 being most positive), participants were very positive about their overall workshop experience ($M = 8.6$, $SD = 1.6$), their preparedness to respond to a crisis ($M = 8.2$, $SD = 1.6$), and the likelihood of recommending the workshop to others ($M = 8.9$, $SD = 1.5$). Similar results were obtained for the participants who attended Workshop 2, Crisis Intervention and Recovery, in 34 separate locations (18 different states and Canada). Using the same satisfaction measure, Workshop 2 participants reported being very positive about their overall workshop experience ($M = 8.9$, $SD = 1.4$), their preparedness to respond to a crisis ($M = 8.6$, $SD = 1.4$), and the likelihood of recommending the workshop to others ($M = 9.1$, $SD = 1.5$).

In the same study, Brock et al. (2011) analyzed the pre- and posttest data for 1,212 Workshop 1 participants and 1,008 Workshop 2 participants. Significant improvements occurred in crisis prevention and intervention attitudes and knowledge immediately following the training. A qualitative analysis of workshop evaluation comments indicated strengths regarding the content, workshop materials, and interactive learning components, as well as areas to improve, such as reducing the quantity of information presented. Observed differences between participants trained by a workshop author compared with those prepared through the ToT fell well short of practical significance, suggesting that the ToT model was successfully implemented.

Nickerson, Serwacki, et al. (2014) reported the results from the more recent evaluation data obtained from 2009 to 2011. Significant improvements in crisis prevention and intervention attitudes and knowledge were obtained from 875 Workshop 1, Crisis Prevention and Preparedness, participants and 1,422 Workshop 2, Crisis Intervention and Recovery, participants on matched pretests and posttests. Participant satisfaction was high for both Workshop 1 and Workshop 2. Analysis of qualitative comments indicated that participants found the workshop materials to be a notable strength of the training. In addition, participants indicated benefitting from the interaction and role-plays and expressed a desire to have even more interactive learning components.

These results were consistent with the results reported by Brock et al. (2011), further reinforcing the efficacy of PREPaRE in increasing confidence and knowledge of participants, as well as resulting in high satisfaction with the professional development experience.

In the Nickerson, Serwacki, et al. (2014) study, outcomes were compared using the demographic information provided by participants to determine what, if any, variables predicted greater gains in knowledge and attitudes following the training. Regarding improvements in confidence and helpful attitudes toward crisis prevention and intervention, the PREPaRE training was found to be particularly beneficial for graduate students and for participants with fewer hours of previous crisis training. However, the amount of knowledge gained by Workshop 1 participants did not differ based on background factors, suggesting that participants have something to gain from PREPaRE regardless of past professional or training experiences. This effect differed for Workshop 2 participants, in which fewer previous training experiences were associated with a greater gain in knowledge. In contrast, the knowledge gained by graduate students did not appear to improve as greatly as that of working professionals in Workshop 2. Because Workshop 2 is a longer, 2-day training that contains more advanced information targeted toward crisis intervention and student care group members, it is possible that the background and experience of working professionals helps them to better conceptualize the information provided in training.

The evaluation results have been used not only to document the extent to which PREPaRE meets its objectives, but also to make changes within a continuous quality improvement framework. For example, from the initial evaluations, participants appeared to struggle with the concept of matching risk for psychological trauma to the appropriate mental health crisis intervention. Consequently, in the second edition of the curriculum, an activity was added that required participants to match psychological trauma risk level to specific crisis interventions. In addition, from feedback that participants wanted more active learning components, the second edition included more discussion and additional activities to reinforce learning objectives.

RESEARCH WITH PREPaRE AS AN INDEPENDENT VARIABLE

Beyond the program evaluation results, research has begun to examine a number of outcome variables using PREPaRE as an independent variable. Lazzaro (2013) compared responses of individuals who had participated in the PREPaRE Workshop 2, Crisis Intervention and Recovery, with those who had not, finding that participants who had completed the workshop scored an average of 20% higher on knowledge of crisis-related content than those who did not complete the PREPaRE workshop. In addition, participants who completed the PREPaRE workshop several years prior to completing the survey scored the highest, suggesting that a combination of acquiring the content knowledge by participating in a PREPaRE workshop and additional years of experience in the field ultimately resulted in a greater retention and application of mental health crisis intervention knowledge. Hours of crisis training and education level contributed to more than 30% of self-reported confidence in providing mental health crisis intervention. This study further supported previous findings about contributions made by crisis intervention training and education to improved knowledge and confidence, and took the research a step further by reporting on long-term outcomes by examining these variables months and years after the training.

Although not focused specifically on PREPaRE, Gurdineer (2013) examined predictors of school crisis response plans based on a number of variables, including crisis training. Results indicated that the schools' plans were not as comprehensive as they could be (e.g., plan components ranged from 0 to 54 out of the 77 items included on Aspiranti, Pelchar, McCleary, Bain, and Foster's [2011] Comprehensive Crisis Plan Checklist). Total resources available was a significant predictor of more comprehensive crisis plans, with the number of crisis response team members and having an updated written document being the only significant predictors of how comprehensive the plans were. Demographic variables and amount of training did not predict the comprehensiveness of plans. It should be noted that there were only 70 participants, and less than one quarter had received PREPaRE training. These results may indicate that having active team members and updated documents are most important to comprehensive preparedness efforts.

APPLICATION TO PRACTICE

Although some advances have been made in the research base examining PREPaRE, it is well recognized that there are many methodological, practical, and ethical challenges to conducting research on school crisis intervention (for review see Nickerson, Pagliocca, & Palladino, 2012). One of the most common ways literature on school crisis response has advanced is through anecdotal reports. PREPaRE has been featured in a number of articles to illustrate how the model has been applied to real-world situations to improve school crisis prevention and intervention efforts, many of which can be found at http://www.nasponline.org/professional-development/prepare-training-curriculum/prepare-in-practice. For example, Armstrong, Gneiting, and Horne (2010) recount how they used the PREPaRE model to respond to the suicide of a junior high school student. They were able to quickly identify individuals with emotional proximity to the deceased student as well as those with preexisting vulnerabilities, such as recent deaths, to provide appropriate interventions. They also monitored students' reactions, collaborated with community agencies, carefully communicated the information, and provided individual and group support while recording the names and traumatic stress risk levels of individuals seen.

Bernard, Rittle, and Roberts (2011) also provided a detailed account of how they used their PREPaRE training to respond to a particularly gruesome suicide in which a student had set himself on fire, and a number of students were witnesses. The team took steps to minimize exposure to the incident (e.g., put the school in lockdown, closed the blinds) and evaluated psychological trauma risk, prioritized the 17 classrooms that witnessed the event, and provided them with psychoeducation. The team also conducted secondary triage and provided appropriate interventions for students at each level of risk. Bernard et al. (2011) noted that the specific procedures and common language of PREPaRE were extremely helpful in implementing a careful and coordinated response to this and other incidents.

Crepeau-Hobson and colleagues (Crepeau-Hobson & Summers, 2011; Crepeau-Hobson, Sievering, Armstrong, & Stonis, 2012), using qualitative methodologies to collect and analyze crisis responders' experiences in multiple crisis situations, found that training and preparedness (with specific mention of PREPaRE) were the prominent themes in terms of key components of effective responses. Notably, the other elements found to be essential in the response were those emphasized in the PREPaRE model. Specifically, preparedness involved crisis response teams using the Incident Command System, with a mental health point person who was part of the Command structure; following specified crisis response plans; clearly delineating roles; communicating among responders; and being informed of community resources. Other themes that emerged as critical and followed the PREPaRE model in terms of mental health crisis intervention included practicing reunification procedures, providing a safe haven to conduct psychological triage and respond to psychological needs, meeting basic needs for food, and providing interventions, including both psychoeducation and individual crisis intervention (Crepeau-Hobson et al., 2012). Both studies stressed the importance of having mental health supports and of providing mental health crisis intervention that included reestablishing safety and security, allowing the individual to tell his or her crisis story while being listened to and validated, and helping the individual to begin to address any crisis-generated problems, with a focus on empathy and empowerment.

DIRECTIONS FOR FUTURE RESEARCH

One of the most notable limitations of the current program evaluation data is that they do not allow researchers to make definitive conclusions about the effects of PREPaRE on participants' school crisis prevention and intervention attitudes and knowledge. Some causal comparative research has begun to examine outcomes of PREPaRE relative to individuals who have not had this training, but to date no experimental designs have used a control group within a randomized controlled design to test the effectiveness of the training. Such studies have been proposed, and it is the hope that these ideas will be implemented with future grant funding. A randomized controlled trial currently is being conducted in Arizona, and the project team has applied for federal funding to further examine the PREPaRE curriculum's effectiveness.

Research evaluating crisis prevention and intervention, including programs such as PREPaRE, is complex (de Anda, 2007; Nastasi & Hichcock, 2009; Nickerson et al., 2012). Figure 23.1 shows a framework for PREPaRE and its processes and anticipated outcomes that may be useful as a basis for evaluation. This logic model depicts the inputs, or resources that have gone into the program; the core PREPaRE activities; the outputs of the curriculum; and the expected immediate, short-term, and long-term outcomes associated with the curriculum. Research is needed to examine the extent to which the training leads to meaningful changes and implementation of PREPaRE concepts and strategies for individual participants and for the schools they serve. A list of possible research questions to be examined in future research is provided in Table 23.1.

In addition to these research questions about the effects of PREPaRE, research must advance to investigate the impact of various mental health crisis interventions on the recipients. A comprehensive review of potential directions for future research in this area can be found in Nickerson et al. (2012), and a sampling of such research questions is provided in Table 23.2.

The advances in the research and application of PREPaRE are exciting. It can be said with confidence that participants report high levels of satisfaction with the workshop, and they show significant increases in knowledge and positive attitudes regarding crisis prevention and intervention. However, countless research questions remain with regard to PREPaRE and the larger field of crisis prevention and intervention to be explored by future innovative researchers.

Figure 23.1. A Logic Model for PREPaRE Research

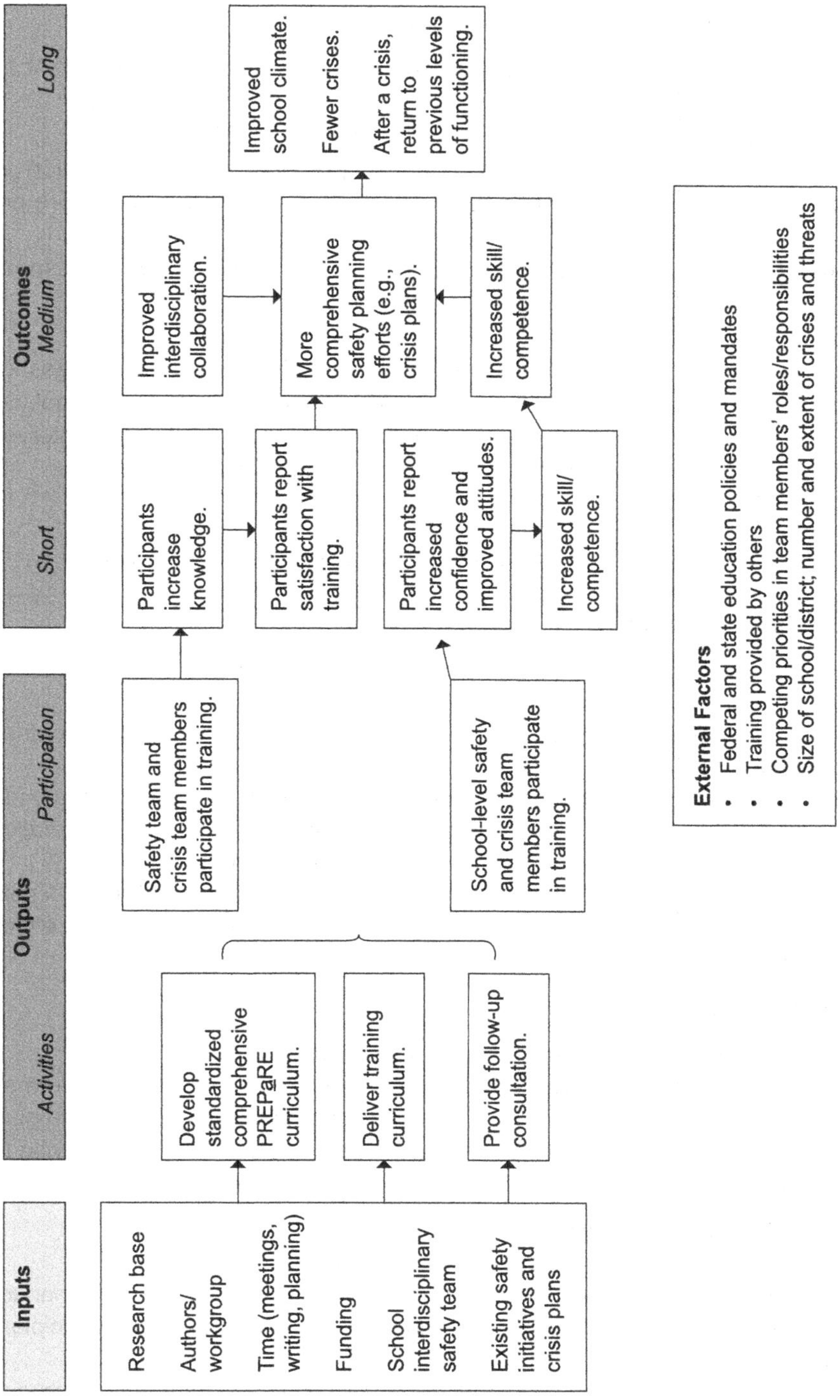

Table 23.1 Research Questions for Future Studies Involving PREPaRE

Does participation in PREPaRE lead to ...

- an improved sense of school crisis response team members' competency in dealing with a school crisis?
- improved preparedness procedures (crisis plans, drills)?
- sustainable increases in knowledge of crisis prevention and intervention concepts?
- attitudes toward crisis response team efforts that are predictive of more productive and adaptive behaviors?
- more interdisciplinary collaboration in crisis response planning and response?
- a more positive school climate?
- fewer crises?
- improved recognition of students' physical needs following a school-associated crisis?
- improved recognition of students' psychological needs following a school associated crisis?
- the provision of a range of empirically supported mental health crisis intervention practices?
- a return to precrisis levels of functioning following a crisis?

Table 23.2 Sample Research Questions for Crisis Intervention

Reestablishing Social Support

- Does the order in which schools release students in a crisis make a difference in terms of children's perceptions of safety and readiness to return to school?
- What are the specific mechanisms and providers of social support that contribute to recovery following a crisis?
- Are there gender differences in the types and mechanisms of support that are most helpful?
- Does desire for support, and skills to access the support, moderate the relation between social support and perceptions of psychological safety and security?
- How does the modality of the support provided (e.g., unstructured group "crisis room," Internet chatrooms, structured formats facilitated by a professional) influence the effectiveness of the social support?

Psychoeducation

- How do recipients of psychoeducation apply the information?
- Do recipients have a preference for a format through which to receive information (e.g., face-to-face meetings, written handouts, information posted to a website)?
- Is the information perceived as more valuable depending on who is conveying the information (e.g., principal, certified or licensed mental health professional from community)?

Immediate Mental Health Crisis Intervention
- Is there an optimal time to provide crisis intervention?
- What variables or conditions should guide decision making about if and when to intervene?
- How does the delivery of crisis intervention (individual or group) affect recipients relative to those who receive no formal intervention?
- Do administrators feel more confident about allowing crisis interventions and supports to be offered in the school setting after professionals receive PREPaRE training?

Note. Adapted from Nickerson et al. (2012).

Chapter 24

CONCLUDING COMMENTS AND NEXT STEPS

As discussed throughout the chapters of this book, the PREPaRE model is designed for school-employed mental health professionals, administrators, school resource and safety officers, other educators, and school crisis response team members who are committed to improving and strengthening all aspects of school crisis prevention, protection, mitigation, response, and recovery. As highlighted in this book, the need for PREPaRE is emphasized by the fact that today's schools are expected, and arguably legally required, to proactively promote school safety, strive to prevent those crises that are preventable, and effectively respond to those crises that are not prevented. This expectation, combined with the realities of a 24/7 news cycle and the widespread use of social media, makes being "PREPaREd" for crisis prevention and intervention essential.

Comprehensive school safety and crisis response teams must be adequately prepared to address a range of crises, understand the systems and procedures that need to be in place to prevent and respond to crises, and address the unique mental health needs generated by crisis exposure. School safety and crisis response plans must also be integrated into community-based emergency response efforts, including those offered by law enforcement, fire and rescue, and community health and mental health service providers, as well as be clearly communicated to school staff members, parents, and community leaders.

Important issues emphasized by the PREPaRE model include (a) proactive efforts to create safe school environments and to prevent crises from occurring; (b) promotion of the mental health, resilience, and coping capacity of the individuals affected by a crisis, particularly students; and (c) the unique opportunities and challenges presented to schools when preventing and responding to crises. As such, the chapters in this book have emphasized that school safety and crisis response teams must respond not only to physical health and safety threats, but also to the mental health needs of school staff members and students.

Finally, one of the outcome goals of successful crisis prevention, protection, mitigation, response, and recovery is to support academic functioning. While school safety advocates routinely promote school crisis preparedness, there are voices in our society that suggest that schools spend too much money on nonteaching activities (Brock, 2015a). Thus, the connections between school safety, crisis response, and academic achievement must be clearly articulated.

The PREPaRE School Crisis Prevention and Intervention Training Curriculum (Brock, 2006a, 2006c, 2011a, 2011b; Reeves, Nickerson, & Jimerson, 2006a, 2006b; Reeves et al., 2011a, 2011b) was developed to offer guidance regarding best practices in school crisis prevention, protection, mitigation, response, and recovery. As summarized in the preceding chapters, this model was developed after a careful review of the literature (with special attention given to empirical investigations), and as such it offers evidence-informed school safety practices and crisis prevention and response practices. Furthermore, as noted in Chapter 23, the PREPaRE workshops have a high degree of consumer satisfaction, have a positive effect on participants' attitudes in terms of their ability to participate on a school safety and crisis response team, and result in significant positive changes in crisis prevention and intervention knowledge (Brock, Nickerson, Reeves, Savage, & Woitaszewski, 2011; Nickerson, Serwacki, et al., 2014). However, it is important to acknowledge that, at this point, no one community- or school-based crisis prevention, protection, mitigation, response, and recovery protocol has been validated by careful experimental research (Vernberg et al., 2008). Thus, the need remains for systematic study addressing the effectiveness of the PREPaRE workshops and the specific elements of the PREPaRE model.

In addition to the research questions offered in Chapter 23, the next steps involve questions evaluating the effects of Workshop 1, Crisis Prevention and Preparedness: Comprehensive School Safety Planning (Reeves et al., 2011a), should be based on the workshop's objectives. These questions consider to what extent individual workshop participants, as well as the schools and school districts that participants serve, are able to identify and demonstrate knowledge of (a) the characteristics of a crisis event, (b) the key concepts associated with the PREPaRE acronym, (c) the mission areas of crisis response, (d) concepts related to crime prevention through environmental design, (e) the elements of psychological safety, (f) the purposes of a comprehensive safety plan, (g) the major functions of the Incident Command System, (h) the guiding principles in crisis response plan development, (i) the difference between a crisis team's response plan and school staff members' response plan, and (j) the essential elements of crisis response plans, including examination of their effectiveness. Possible tools for conducting such research were offered in Chapter 20's discussion about examining the effectiveness of school safety, crisis prevention, and crisis preparedness efforts.

Specific questions designed to evaluate the effects of Workshop 2, Crisis Intervention and Recovery: The Roles of School-Based Mental Health Professionals (Brock, 2011a), should also be based on that workshop's objectives. These questions try to determine the degree to which workshop participants report (both on a short-term and long-term basis) positive attitudes regarding their ability to provide mental health crisis intervention services. In addition, such research should explore the degree to which individual workshop participants, as well as the schools and school districts that participants serve, are able to identify and demonstrate knowledge of (a) the variables that determine the number of individuals likely to have been traumatized by a given crisis, (b) the range of school mental health crisis interventions specified by the PREPaRE acronym, (c) how mental health crisis interventions fit into the multidisciplinary Incident Command System's school crisis response, (d) factors that are critical to evaluating psychological trauma risk, and (e) how to match psychological trauma risk to a range of appropriate mental health crisis interventions. Possible tools for conducting such research were offered in Chapter 21's discussion about examining the effectiveness of crisis response and recovery.

In conclusion, the authors of PREPaRE are enthusiastic about the opportunity to support and collaborate with other scholars regarding the evaluation of this model. Those who are interested in conducting such research, and who feel that contact with the PREPaRE curriculum developers would be helpful, are encouraged to contact Dr. Stephen E. Brock (brock@csus.edu) or Dr. Amanda Nickerson (nickersa@buffalo.edu).

References

Adams, C. M., & Kritsonis, W. A. (2006). An analysis of secondary schools' crisis management preparedness: National implications. *National Journal for Publishing and Mentoring Doctoral Student Research, 1,* 1–7. Retrieved from http://eric.ed.gov/?id=ED491991

Adams, R. E., Boscarino, J. A., & Figley, C. R. (2006). Compassion fatigue and psychological distress among social workers: A validation study. *American Journal of Orthopsychiatry, 76,* 103–108. doi:10.1037/0002-9432.76.1.103

Adams, R. E., Figley, C. R., & Boscarino, J. A. (2008). The compassion fatigue scale: Its use with social workers following urban disaster. *Research on Social Work Practice, 18,* 238–250. doi:10.1177/1049731507310190

Adams, Z. W., Sumner, J. A., Danielson, C. K., McCauley, J. L., Resnick, H. S., Grös, K., . . . Ruggiero, K. J. (2014). Prevalence and predictors of PTSD and depression among adolescent victims of the spring 2011 tornado outbreak. *Journal of Child Psychology and Psychiatry, 55,* 1047–1055. doi:10.1111/jcpp.12220

Adamson, A. D., & Peacock, G. G. (2007). Crisis response in the public schools: A survey of school psychologists' experiences and perceptions. *Psychology in the Schools, 44,* 749–764. doi:10.1002/pits.20263

Adelman, H. S., & Taylor, L. (2002). Building comprehensive, multifaceted, and integrated approaches to address barriers to student learning. *Childhood Education, 78,* 261–268. doi:10.1080/00094056.2002.10522738

Adelman, H. S., & Taylor, L. (2008). School-wide approaches to address barriers to learning and teaching. In B. Doll & J. A. Cummings (Eds.), *Transforming school mental health services* (pp. 277–307). Thousand Oaks, CA: Corwin Press.

Adelman, H. S., & Taylor, L. (2014). Addressing student and schooling problems: Not another project! Child safety should be embedded in the mission of schools. *Child Abuse & Neglect, 38,* 160–169. doi:10.1016/j.chiabu.2014.01.005

Adler, A. B., Bliese, P. D., McGurk, D., Hoge, C. W., & Castro, C. (2011). Battlemind debriefing and battlemind training as early interventions with soldiers returning from Iraq: Randomization by platoon. *Sport, Exercise, and Performance Psychology, 1,* 66–83. doi:10.1037/2157-3905.1.S.66

Adler, A. B., Litz, B. T., Castro, C., Suvak, M., Thomas, J. L., Burrell, L., . . . Bliese, P. D. (2008). A group randomized trial of critical incident stress debriefing provided to U.S. peacekeepers. *Journal of Traumatic Stress, 21,* 253–263. doi:10.1002/jts.20342

Aduriz, M. E., Bluthgen, C., & Knopfler, C. (2009). Helping child flood victims using group EMDR intervention in Argentina: Treatment outcome and gender differences. *International Journal of Stress Management, 16,* 138–153. doi:10.1037/a0014719

Ahern, J., Galea, S., Resnick, H., Kilpatrick, D., Bucuvalas, M., Gold, J., & Vlahov, D. (2002). Television images and psychological symptoms after the September 11 terrorist attack. *Psychiatry, 65,* 289–300. doi:10.1521/psyc.65.4.289.20240

Ahern, J. A., Galea, S., Resnick, H., & Vlahov, D. (2004). Television images and probable posttraumatic stress disorder after September 11: The role of background characteristics, event exposures, and perievent panic. *Journal of Nervous and Mental Disease, 192,* 217–226. doi:10.1097/01.nmd.0000116465.99830.ca

Ahmad, A., Larsson, B., & Sundelin-Wahlsten, V. (2007). EMDR treatment for children with PTSD: Results of a randomized controlled trial. *Journal of Nordic Psychiatry, 61,* 349–354. doi:10.1007/s00787-007-0646-8

Allen, J. P., & Land, D. (1999). Attachment in adolescence. In J. Cassidy & P. R. Shaver (Eds.), *Handbook of attachment: Theory, research, and clinical applications* (pp. 319–335). New York, NY: Guilford Press.

Allen, S. F., Dlugokinski, E. L., Cohen, L. A., & Walker, J. L. (1999). Assessing the impact of a traumatic community event on children and assisting with their healing. *Psychiatric Annals, 29,* 93–98. doi:10.3928/0048-5713-19990201-07

Almeida, A. (2015, May 19). Holding schools responsible for addressing childhood trauma. *The Atlantic.* Retrieved from http://www.theatlantic.com/education/archive/2015/05/holding-schools-responsible-for-addressing-childhood-trauma/393695/

American Academy of Child and Adolescent Psychiatry. (1998). Practice parameters for the assessment and treatment of children with posttraumatic stress disorder. *Journal of the American Academy of Child and Adolescent Psychiatry, 37* (10 Suppl.), 4S–26S. doi:10.1097/00004583-199810001-00002

American Foundation for Suicide Prevention and Suicide Prevention Resource Center. (2011). *After a suicide: A toolkit for schools.* Newton, MA: Education Development Center. Retrieved from http://www.sprc.org/library/AfteraSuicideToolkitforSchools.pdf

American Psychiatric Association (APA). (1994). *Diagnostic and statistical manual of mental disorders* (4th ed.). Washington, DC: Author.

American Psychiatric Association. (2000). *Diagnostic and statistical manual of mental disorders* (4th ed., text rev.). Washington, DC: Author.

American Psychiatric Association. (2013). *Diagnostic and statistical manual of mental disorders* (5th ed.). Washington, DC: Author.

American Psychological Association. (2002). *Guidelines on multicultural education, training, research, practice, and organizational change for psychologists.* Washington, DC: Author. Retrieved from http://www.apa.org/pi/oema/resources/policy/multicultural-guidelines.aspx?item=5

American Psychological Association Presidential Task Force on Evidence-Based Practice. (2006). Evidence-based practice in psychology. *American Psychologist, 61,* 271–285. doi:10.1037/0003-066X.61.4.271

American Red Cross. (1991). *Disaster services regulations and procedures.* (ARC Document 3050M). Washington, DC: Author.

Americans With Disabilities Act of 1990, Pub. L. No. 101-336, § 2, 104 Stat. 328 (1991).

Amstadter, A. B., McCart, M. R., & Ruggiero, K. J. (2007). Psychosocial interventions for adults with crime-related PTSD. *Professional Psychology: Research and Practice, 38,* 640–651. doi:10.1037/0735-7028.38.6.640

Andrews, B., Brewin, C. R., Philpott, R., & Stewart, L. (2007). Delayed-onset posttraumatic stress disorder: A systematic review of the evidence. *American Journal of Psychiatry, 164,* 1319–1326. doi:10.1176/appi.ajp.2007.06091491

Annandale, N. O., Heath, M. A., Dean, B., Kemple, A., & Takino, Y. (2011). Assessing cultural competency in school crisis plans. *Journal of School Violence, 10,* 16–33. doi:10.1080/153882 20.2010.519263

Appleyard, K., Egeland, B., & Sroufe, L. (2007). Direct social support for young high risk children: Relations with behavioral and emotional outcomes across time. *Journal of Abnormal Child Psychology, 35,* 443–457. doi:10.1007/s10802-007-9102-y

Applied Research and Consulting, Columbia University Mailman School of Public Health, & New York Psychiatric Institute. (2002, May 6). *Effects of the World Trade Center attack on NYC public school students: Initial report to the New York City Board of Education.* New York, NY: New York City Board of Education. Retrieved from http://eric.ed.gov/?id=ED471157

Arendt, M. M., & Elklit, A. A. (2001). Effectiveness of psychological debriefing. *Acta Psychiatrica Scandinavica, 104,* 423–437. doi:10.1034/j.1600-0447.2001.00155.x

Armstrong, G., Gneiting, D., & Horne, J. (2010, March/April). Interventions and responding to psychological needs: Application of PREPaRE in Idaho. *Communiqué, 38*(6), 12. Retrieved from http://www.nasponline.org/publications/periodicals/communique/issues/volume-38-issue-6/interventions-and-responding-to-psychological-needs-application-of-prepare-in-idaho

Armstrong, K. H., Massey, O. T., & Boroughs, M. (2006). Implementing comprehensive safe school plans in Pinellas County Schools, Florida: Planning, implementation, operation, sustainability, and lessons learned. In S. R. Jimerson & M. Furlong (Eds.), *Handbook of school violence and school safety: From research to practice* (pp. 525–536). Mahwah: NJ: Erlbaum.

Armstrong, M. (1990, April). Emotional reactions to Stockton. In F. Busher (Chair), *Tragedy in Stockton schoolyard.* Symposium conducted at the annual meeting of the National Association of School Psychologists, San Francisco, CA.

Asberg, K., & Renk, K. (2014). Perceived stress, external locus of control, and social support as predictors of psychological adjustment among female inmates with or without a history of sexual abuse. *International Journal of Offender Therapy and Comparative Criminology, 58,* 59–84. Retrieved from http://ijo.sagepub.com/

Asher, A., & Pollack, J. R. (2009). Planning emergency evacuations for students with unique needs: Role of occupational therapy. *OT Practice, 14,* CE1–CE7.

Aspiranti, K. B., Pelchar, T. K., McCleary, D. F., Bain, S. K., & Foster, L. N. (2011). Development and reliability of the comprehensive crisis plan checklist. *Psychology in the Schools, 48,* 146–156. doi:10.1002/pits.20533

Astor, R., Van Acker, R., & Guerra, N. G. (2010). How can we improve school safety research? *Educational Researcher, 39,* 69–78. doi:10.3102/0013189X09357619

Austin, G., & Duerr, M. (2007a). *Guidebook for the California Healthy Kids Survey: Part I. administration.* San Francisco, CA: WestEd.

Austin, G., & Duerr, M. (2007b). *Guidebook for the California Healthy Kids Survey: Part II: Data use and dissemination.* San Francisco, CA: WestEd.

Austin, G., & Duerr, M. (2007c). *Guidebook for the California Healthy Kids Survey: Part III: School climate survey for teachers and other staff.* San Francisco, CA: WestEd.

Ayers, T. S., Sandler, I. N., West, S. G., & Roosa, M. W. (1996). A dispositional and situational assessment of children's coping: Testing alternative models of coping. *Journal of Personality and Social Psychology, 51,* 1173–1182. doi:10.1111/j.1467-6494.1996.tb00949.x

Ayub, M., Poongan, I., Masood, K., Gul, H., Ali, M., Farrukh, A., . . . Naeem, F. (2012). Psychological morbidity in children 18 months after Kashmir earthquake of 2005. *Child Psychiatry and Human Development, 43,* 323–336. doi:10.1007/s10578-011-0267-9

Azarian, A., & Skriptchenko-Gregorian, V. (1998a). *Children in natural disasters: An experience of the 1988 earthquake in Armenia.* Commack, NY: American Academy of Experts in Traumatic Stress. Retrieved from http://www.aaets.org/article38.htm

Azarian, A., & Skriptchenko-Gregorian, V. (1998b). Traumatization and stress in child and adolescent victims of natural disasters. In T. W. Miller (Ed.), *Children of trauma: Stressful life events and their effects on children and adolescents* (pp. 77–118). Madison, CT: International Universities Press.

Bailey, K. A. (2006). Legal knowledge related to school violence and school safety. In S. R. Jimerson & M. Furlong (Eds.). *Handbook of school violence and school safety: From research to practice* (pp. 31–49). Mahwah, NJ: Erlbaum.

Banks, D. M., & Weems, C. F. (2014). Family and peer social support and their links to psychological distress among hurricane-exposed minority youth. *American Journal of Orthopsychiatry, 84,* 341–352. doi:10.1037/ort0000006

Baranowsky, A. B., Young, M., Johnson-Douglas, S., Williams-Keeler, L., & McCarrey, M. (1998). PTSD transmission: A review of secondary traumatization in Holocaust survivor families. *Canadian Psychology/Psychologie Canadienne, 39,* 247–256. doi:10.1037/h0086816

Barenbaum, J., Ruchkin, V., & Schwab-Stone, M. (2004). The psychosocial aspects of children exposed to war: Practice and policy initiatives. *Journal of Child Psychology and Psychiatry, 45,* 41–62. doi:10.1046/j.0021-9630.2003.00304.x

Barnett, S. D., Tharwani, H. M., Hertzberg, M. A., Sutherland, S. M., Connor, K. M., & Davidson, J. R.T. (2002). Tolerability of fluoxetine in posttraumatic stress disorder. *Progress in Neuro-Psychopharmacology and Biological Psychiatry, 26,* 363–367. doi:10.1016/S0278-5846(01)00282-2

Batten-Mickens, M., & Spears, R. (2008). *Emergency management considerations for students and staff with disabilities.* Paper presented at the U.S. Department of Education Office of Safe and Drug-Free Schools, Chicago, IL.

Beghtol, M. J. (1988, Spring). Hmong refugees and the US health system. *Cultural Survival Quarterly: Health and Healing, 12.1.* Retrieved from http://www.culturalsurvival.org/publications/cultural-survival-quarterly/121-spring-1988-health-and-healing

Bensimon, M. (2012). Elaboration on the association between trauma, PTSD, and posttraumatic growth: The role of trait resilience. *Personality and Individual Differences, 52,* 782–787. doi:10.1016/j.paid.2012.01.011

Berger, R., Pat-Horencyzk, R., & Gelkopf, M. (2007). School-based intervention for prevention and treatment of elementary-students' terror-related distress in Israel: A quasi-randomized controlled trial. *Journal of Traumatic Stress, 20,* 541–551. doi:10.1002/jts.20225

Berk, R. A., & Rossi, P. H. (1990). *Thinking about program evaluation.* Newbury Park, CA: SAGE.

Berkowitz, S. J. (2003). Children exposed to community violence: The rationale for early intervention. *Clinical Child and Family Psychology Review, 6,* 293–302. doi:10.1023/B:CCFP.0000006295.54479.3d

Berliner, P., Gongóra, J., & Espaillat, V. (2011). Immediate psycho-social support for disaster survivors. *Psyke & Logos, 32,* 458–479. Retrieved from http://dpf.dk/produktkategori/psyke-logos

Berman, A. L., Jobes, D. A., & Silverman, M. M. (2006). *Adolescent suicide: Assessment and intervention* (2nd ed.). Washington, DC: American Psychological Association.

Berman, S. L., Kurtines, W. M., Silverman, W. K., & Serafini, L. T. (1996). The impact of exposure to crime and violence on urban youth. *American Journal of Orthopsychiatry, 66,* 329–336. doi:10.1037/h0080183

Bernard, L. J., Rittle, C., & Roberts, K. (2011, October). Utilizing the PREPaRE model when multiple classrooms witness a traumatic event. *Communiqué, 40*(2), 10. Retrieved from http://www.nasponline.org/publications/periodicals/communique/issues/volume-40-issue-2/utilizing-the-prepare-model-when-multiple-classrooms-witness-a-traumatic-event

Bernat, J. A., Ronfeldt, H. M., Calhoun, K. S., & Arias, I. (1998). Prevalence of traumatic events and peritraumatic predictors of posttraumatic stress symptoms in a nonclinical sample of college students. *Journal of Traumatic Stress, 11,* 645–664. doi:10.1023/A:1024485130934

Birmes, P., Raynaud, J. P., Daubisse, L., Brunet, A., Arbus, C., Klein, R., . . . Schmitt, L. (2009). Children's enduring PTSD symptoms are related to their family's adaptability and cohesion. *Community Mental Health Journal, 45,* 290–299. doi:10.1007/s10597-008-9166-3

Bischof, N. L. (2007). School psychology and crisis intervention: A survey of school psychologists' involvement and training. *Dissertation Abstracts International: Section A. Humanities and Social Sciences, 67*(11-A), 4091.

Bisson, J. I., Jenkins, P. L., Alexander, J., & Bannister, C. (1997). Randomised controlled trial of psychological debriefing for victims of acute burn trauma. *The British Journal of Psychiatry, 17,* 178–181. Retrieved from http://bjp.rcpsych.org/

Bisson, J. I., McFarlane, A. C., & Rose, S. (2000). Psychological debriefing. In E. B. Foa, T. M. Keane, & M. J. Friedman (Eds.). *Effective treatments for PTSD: Practice guidelines from the International Society for Traumatic Stress Studies* (pp. 39–59, 317–319). New York, NY: Guilford Press.

Bisson, J. I., Roberts, N. P., Andrew, M., Cooper, R., & Lewis, C. (2013). Psychological therapies for chronic post-traumatic stress disorder (PTSD) in adults. *Cochrane Database of Systematic Reviews, 12.* Art. No.: CD003388. doi:10.1002/14651858.CD003388.pub4

Black, S. (2004). Revising school attack protections since 9/11. *American School Board Journal, 191,* 36–38. Retrieved from http://www.asbj.com

Blackburn, B. (2011). Japan earthquake and tsunami: Social media spreads news, raises relief funds. *ABC News.* Retrieved 9/27/14 from http://abcnews.go.com/Technology/japan-earthquake-tsunami-drive-social-media-dialogue/print?id=13117677

Blair, J. P., & Martaindale, M. H. (2013). *United States active shooter events from 2000 to 2010: Training and equipment implications.* San Marcos, TX: Texas State University. Retrieved from http://alerrt.org/files/research/ActiveShooterEvents.pdf

Blair, J. P., & Schweit, K. W. (2014). *A study of active shooter incidents, 2000–2013.* Washington, DC: Texas State University and Federal Bureau of Investigation, U.S. Department of Justice. Retrieved from http://www.fbi.gov/news/stories/2014/september/fbi-releases-study-on-active-shooter-incidents/pdfs/a-study-of-active-shooter-incidents-in-the-u.s.-between-2000-and-2013

Blanchard, E. B., Kuhn, E., Rowell, D. L., Hickling, E. J., Wittrock, D., Rogers, R. L., . . . Steckler, D. C. (2004). Studies of the vicarious traumatization of college students by the September 11th attacks: Effects of proximity, exposure and connectedness. *Behaviour Research and Therapy, 42,* 191–205. doi:10.1016/S0005-7967(03)00118-9

Blom, G. E., Etkind, S. L., & Carr, W. J. (1991). Psychological intervention after child and adolescent disasters in the community. *Child Psychiatry and Human Development, 21,* 257–266. doi:10.1007/BF00705930

Bober, T., Regehr, C., & Zhou, Y. R. (2006). Development of the coping strategies inventory for trauma counselors. *Journal of Loss and Trauma, 11,* 71–83. doi:10.1080/15325020500358225

Bolnik, L., & Brock, S. E. (2005). The self-reported effects of crisis intervention work on school psychologists. *California School Psychologist, 10,* 117–124. doi:10.1007/BF03340926

Bonanno, G. A., & Mancini, A. D. (2008). The human capacity to thrive in the face of potential trauma. *Pediatrics, 121,* 369–375. doi:10.1542/peds.2007-1648

Boon, H. J., Brown, L. H., Tsey, K., Speare, R., Pagliano, P., Usher, K., & Clark, B. (2011). School disaster planning for children with disabilities: A critical review of the literature. *International Journal of Special Education, 26,* 223–236. Retrieved from http://eric.ed.gov/?id=EJ959015

Boon, H. J., Pagliano, P., Brown, L. H., & Tsey, K., (2012). An assessment of policies guiding school emergency management for students with disabilities in Australia. *Journal of Policy and Practice in Intellectual Disabilities, 26,* 223–236. doi:10.1111/j.1741-1130.2012.00331.x

Borduin, C. M., Mann, B. J., Cone, L. T., Henggeler, S. W., Fucci, B. R., Blaske, D. M., & Williams, R. A. (1995). Multisystemic treatment of serious juvenile offenders: Long-term prevention of criminality and violence. *Journal of Consulting and Clinical Psychology, 63,* 569–578. doi:10.1037/0022-006X.63.4.569

Borges, G., Angst, J., Nock, M. K., Ruscio, A. M., & Kessler, R. C. (2008). Risk factors for the incidence and persistence of suicide-related outcomes: A 10-year follow-up study using the national comorbidity surveys. *Journal of Affective Disorders, 105,* 25–33. doi:10.1016/j.jad.2007.01.036

Boulton, M. J. (1994). Understanding and preventing bullying in the junior high school playground. In P. K. Smith & S. Sharp (Eds.), *School bullying: Insights and perspectives* (pp. 132–159). London, England: Routledge.

Bowis, J. (2007). Mass violence and mental health. *International Review of Psychiatry, 19,* 297–301. doi:10.1080/09540260701346866

Boyle, G. J. (2003). Review of the Trauma Symptoms Checklist for Children. In B. S. Plake, J. C. Impara, & R. A. Spies (Eds.). *The fifteenth mental measurements yearbook.* Lincoln, NE: Buros Institute of Mental Measurements.

Boymyea, J., Risbrough, V., & Lang, A. J. (2012). A consideration of select pre-trauma factors as key vulnerabilities in PTSD. *Clinical Psychology Review, 32,* 630–641. doi:10.1016/j.cpr.2012.06.008

Bracy, N. L. (2011). Student perceptions of high-security environments. *Youth & Society, 43,* 365–395. doi:10.1177/0044118X10365082

Bradburn, S. I. (1991). After the earth shook: Children's stress symptoms 6–8 months after a disaster. *Advances in Behavior Research and Therapy, 13,* 173–179. doi:10.1016/0146-6402(91)90005-U

Brady, K., Pearlstein, T., Asnis, G. M., Baker, D., Rothbaum, B., Sikes, C. R., & Farfel, G. M. (2000). Efficacy and safety of sertraline treatment of posttraumatic stress disorder: A randomized controlled trial. *Journal of the American Medical Association, 283,* 1837–1844. doi:10.1001/jama.283.14.1837

Brault, M. (2008, February). *Disability status and the characteristics of people in group quarters: A brief analysis of disability prevalence among the civilian non-institutionalized and total populations in the American Community Survey.* Washington, DC: U.S. Census Bureau. Retrieved from https://www.census.gov/people/disability/files/GQdisability.pdf

Braun-Lewensohn, O., Celestin-Westreich, S., Celestin, L. P., Verleye, G., Verté, D., & Ponjaaert-Kristoffersen, I. (2009). Coping styles as moderating the relationships between terrorist attacks and well-being outcomes. *Journal of Adolescence, 32,* 585–599. doi:10.1016/j.adolescence.2008.06.003

Bremner, J. D., Southwick, S. M., Johnson, D. R., Yehuda, R., & Charney, D. S. (1993). Childhood physical abuse and combat-related posttraumatic stress disorder in Vietnam veterans. *American Journal of Psychiatry, 150,* 235–239. Retrieved from http://ajp.psychiatryonline.org/journal.aspx?journalid=13

Brems, C. (2000). *Dealing with challenges in psychotherapy and counseling.* Belmont, CA: Wadsworth.

Brent, S. B. (1978). Motivation, steady-state, and structural development: A general model of psychological homeostasis. *Motivation and Emotion, 2,* 299–323. doi:10.1007/BF00993327

Breslau, N. (1998). Epidemiology of trauma and posttraumatic stress disorder. In R. Yehuda (Ed.), *Psychological trauma* (pp. 1–29). Washington, DC: American Psychiatric Press.

Brewin, C. R., Andrews, B., & Rose, S. (2000). Fear, helplessness, and horror in posttraumatic stress disorder: Investigating DSM–IV criterion A2 in victims of violent crime. *Journal of Traumatic Stress, 13,* 499–509. doi:10.1023/A:1007741526169

Brewin, C. R., Andrews, B., & Valentine, J. D. (2000). Meta-analysis of risk factors for posttraumatic stress disorder in trauma-exposed adults. *Journal of Consulting and Clinical Psychology, 68,* 748–766. doi:10.1037/0022-006X.68.5.748

Brewin, C. R., Rose, S., Andrews, B., Green, J., Tata, P., McEvedy, C., . . . Foa, E. B. (2002). Brief screening instrument for post-traumatic stress disorder. *British Journal of Psychiatry, 181,* 158–162. Retrieved from http://bjp.rcpsych.org/content/by/year

Brickman, H. K., Jones, S. E., & Groom, S. E. (2004, May). Evolving school crisis management since 9/11. *Education Digest, 69*(9), 29–35. Retrieved from https://www.eddigest.com

Bride, B. E. (2007). Prevalence of secondary traumatic stress among social workers. *Social Work, 52,* 63–70. doi:10.1093/sw/52.1.63

Bride, B. E., Radey, M., & Figley, C. R. (2007). Measuring compassion fatigue. *Journal of Clinical Social Work, 35,* 155–163. doi:10.1007/s10615-007-0091-7

Bride, B. E., Robinson, M. M., Yegidis, B., & Figley, C. R. (2004). Development and validation of the Secondary Traumatic Stress Scale. *Research on Social Work Practice, 14,* 27–35. doi:10.1177/1049731503254106

Briere, J. (1996). *Trauma Symptoms Checklist for Children (TSCC): Professional manual.* Odessa, FL: Psychological Assessment Resources.

Briere, J. (2005). *Trauma Symptom Checklist for Young Children (TSCYC): Professional manual.* Odessa, FL: Psychological Assessment Resources.

Brinkworth, S., Morris, A., Singh, K., & Lieberman, R. (2014). *It's Facebook official: Social media and the school crisis.* Paper presented at the annual conference of the National Association of School Psychologists, Washington, DC.

Brislin, R. W. (1970). Back-translation for cross-cultural research. *Journal of Cross-Cultural Psychology, 1,* 185–216. doi:10.1177/135910457000100301

Brock, S. E. (1998) Helping classrooms cope with traumatic events. *Professional School Counseling, 2,* 110–116. Retrieved from http://www.schoolcounselor.org/school-counselors-members/publications/professional-school-counseling-journal

Brock, S. E. (2000). Development of a school district crisis intervention policy. *California School Psychologist, 5,* 53–64. Retrieved from http://link.springer.com/article/10.1007%2FBF03340876

Brock, S. E. (2002a). Crisis theory: A foundation for the comprehensive school crisis response team. In S. E. Brock, P. J. Lazarus, & S. R. Jimerson (Eds.), *Best practices in school crisis prevention and intervention* (pp. 5–17). Bethesda, MD: National Association of School Psychologists.

Brock, S. E. (2002b). Estimating the appropriate crisis response. In S. E. Brock, P. J. Lazarus, & S. R. Jimerson (Eds.), *Best practices in school crisis prevention and intervention* (pp. 355–366). Bethesda, MD: National Association of School Psychologists.

Brock, S. E. (2002c). Group crisis intervention. In S. E. Brock, P. J. Lazarus, & S. R. Jimerson (Eds.), *Best practices in school crisis prevention and intervention* (pp. 385–399). Bethesda, MD: National Association of School Psychologists.

Brock, S. E. (2006a). *Crisis intervention and recovery: The roles of school-based mental health professionals.* Bethesda, MD: National Association of School Psychologists.

Brock, S. E. (2006b). *Workshop 2, Crisis intervention and recovery: The roles of school-based mental health professionals. Workshop evaluation/test summaries and workshop modification suggestions.* Bethesda, MD: National Association of School Psychologists.

Brock, S. E. (2006c). *Crisis intervention and recovery: The roles of school-based mental health professionals. Training of trainers.* Bethesda, MD: National Association of School Psychologists.

Brock, S. E. (2011a). *Crisis intervention and recovery: The roles of school-based mental health professionals* (2nd ed.). Bethesda, MD: National Association of School Psychologists.

Brock, S. E. (2011b). *Crisis intervention and recovery: The roles of school-based mental health professionals. Training of trainers* (2nd ed.). Bethesda, MD: National Association of School Psychologists.

Brock, S. E. (2015a, May). Mental health matters. *Communiqué, 43*(7), 1, 13–15. Retrieved from http://www.nasponline.org/publications/periodicals/communique/issues/volume-43-issue-7/mental-health-matters

Brock, S. E. (2015b, May). President's message: Homicide at school. What are the odds? *Communiqué, 43*(7), 2. Retrieved from http://www.nasponline.org/publications/periodicals/communique/issues/volume-43-issue-7/homicide-at-schools-what-are-the-odds

Brock, S. E., & Davis, J. (2008). Best practices in school crisis intervention. In A. Thomas & J. Grimes (Eds.), *Best practices in school psychology V* (Vol. 3, pp. 781–798). Bethesda, MD: National Association of School Psychologists.

Brock, S. E., & Jimerson, S. R. (2004). School crisis interventions: Strategies for addressing the consequences of crisis events. In E. R. Gerler Jr. (Ed.), *Handbook of school violence* (pp. 285–332). Binghamton, NY: Haworth Press.

Brock, S. E., & Jimerson, S. R. (Eds.). (2012). *Best practices in school crisis prevention and intervention* (2nd ed.). Bethesda, MD: National Association of School Psychologists.

Brock, S. E., Lazarus, P. J., & Jimerson, S. R. (Eds.). (2002). *Best practices in school crisis prevention and intervention.* Bethesda, MD: National Association of School Psychologists.

Brock, S. E., & Lieberman, R. (2015, March). *Suicide prevention in schools: Best practices 2015.* Workshop presented at the Spring Conference of the California Association of School Psychologists, Sacramento, CA.

Brock, S. E., Navarro, L., & Terán, E. (2008, March). *The English to Spanish translation of psychoeducational materials for use during school crisis intervention.* Poster presented at the annual meeting of the California Association of School Psychologists, Burlingame, CA.

Brock, S. E., Nickerson, A. B., O'Malley, M. D., & Chang, Y. (2006). Understanding children victimized by their peers. *Journal of School Violence, 5*(3), 3–18. doi:10.1300/J202v05n03_02

Brock, S. E., Nickerson, A. B., Reeves, M. A., & Jimerson, S. R. (2008). Best practices for school psychologists as members of crisis teams: The PREPₐRE model. In A. Thomas & J. Grimes (Eds.), *Best practices in school psychology V* (Vol. 4; pp. 1487–1504). Bethesda, MD: National Association of School Psychologists.

Brock, S. E., Nickerson, A. B., Reeves, M. A., Jimerson, S. R., Lieberman, R., & Feinberg, T. A. (2009). *School crisis prevention and intervention: The PREPₐRE model.* Bethesda, MD: National Association of School Psychologists.

Brock, S. E., Nickerson, A. B., Reeves, M. A., Savage, T. A., & Woitaszewski, S. A. (2011). Development, evaluation, and future directions of the PREPₐRE School Crisis Prevention and Intervention Training Curriculum. *Journal of School Violence, 10*, 34–52. doi:10.1080/15388220.2010.519268

Brock, S. E., Sandoval, J., & Hart, S. R. (2006). Suicidal ideation and behaviors. In G. G. Bear & K. M. Minke (Eds.), *Children's Needs III: Understanding and addressing the developmental needs of children* (pp. 231–232). Bethesda, MD: National Association of School Psychologists.

Brock, S. E., Sandoval, J., & Lewis, S. (1996). *Preparing for crises in the schools: A manual for building school crisis response teams.* Brandon, VT: Clinical Psychology Publishing.

Brock, S. E., Sandoval, J., & Lewis, S. (2001). *Preparing for crises in the schools: A manual for building school crisis response teams* (2nd ed.). New York, NY: Wiley.

Broughton, D. D., Allen, E. E., Hannemann, R. E., & Petrikin, J. E. (2006). Reuniting fractured families after a disaster: The role of the National Center for Missing and Exploited Children.

Pediatrics, 117(Suppl 4), S442–S445. Retrieved from http://pediatrics.aappublications.org/content/117/Supplement_4/S442.full.html

Brown, E. J., Amaya-Jackson, L., Cohen, J., Handel, S., Thiel De Bocanegra, H., Zatta, E., . . . Mannarino, A. (2008). Childhood traumatic grief: A multi-site empirical examination of the construct and its correlates. *Death Studies, 32,* 899–923. doi:10.1080/07481180802440209

Brown, E. J., & Bobrow, A. L. (2004). School entry after a community-wide trauma: Challenges and lessons learned from September 11th, 2001. *Clinical Child and Family Psychology Review, 7,* 211–221. doi:10.1007/s10567-004-6086-9

Brunet, A., Thomas, E., Saumier, D., Ashbaugh, A. R., Azzoug, A., Pitman, . . . Tremblay, J. (2014). Trauma reactivation plus propranolol is associated with durably low physiological responding during subsequent script-driven traumatic imagery. *Canadian Journal of Psychiatry, 59,* 228–232. Retrieved from http://publications.cpa-apc.org/browse/documents/630

Bryant, R. A., Salmon, K., Sinclair, E., & Davidson, P. (2007). A prospective study of appraisals in childhood posttraumatic stress disorder. *Behaviour Research and Therapy, 45,* 2502–2507. doi:10.1016/j.brat.2007.04.009

Brymer, M., Jacobs, A., Layne, C., Pynoos, R., Ruzek, J., Steinberg, A., . . . Watson, P. (2006). *Psychological first aid: Field operations guide* (2nd ed.). Rockville, MD: National Child Traumatic Stress Network and National Center for PTSD. Retrieved from http://www.nctsn.org/content/psychological-first-aid

Brymer, M. J., Pynoos, R. S., Vivrette, R. L., & Taylor, M. A. (2012). Providing school crisis intervention. In S. E. Brock & S. R. Jimerson (Eds.), *Best practices in school crisis prevention and intervention* (2nd ed., pp. 317–336). Bethesda, MD: National Association of School Psychologists.

Brymer, M., Taylor, M., Escudero, P., Jacobs, A., Kronenberg, M., Macy, R., . . . Vogel, J. (2012). *Psychological first aid for schools: Field operations guide* (2nd ed.). Los Angeles, CA: National Child Traumatic Stress Network. Retrieved from http://www.nctsn.org/content/psychological-first-aid-schoolspfa

Buka, S. L., Stichick, T. L., Birdthistle, I., & Earls, F. J. (2001). Youth exposure to violence: Prevalence, risks, and consequences. *American Journal of Orthopsychiatry, 71,* 298–310. doi:10.1037/0002-9432.71.3.298

Bureau of Justice Statistics. (2013). *National crime victimization survey.* Washington, DC: Author. Retrieved from http://www.bjs.gov/index.cfm?ty=dcdetail&iid=245

Burns, M. K., & Gibbons, K. A. (2008). *Implementing a response-to-intervention in elementary and secondary schools: Procedures to assure scientific-based practices.* New York, NY: Routledge.

Burnside v. Byars, 363 F.2d 744 (5th Cir. 1966).

Burling, W. K., & Hyle, A. E. (1997). Disaster preparedness planning: Policy and leadership issues. *Disaster Prevention and Management: An International Journal, 6,* 234–244. Retrieved from http://www.emeraldinsight.com/journal/dpm

Burrows-Horton, C., & Cruise, T. K. (2001). *Child abuse and neglect: The school's response.* New York, NY: Guilford Press.

Bush, G. W. (2003, February 28). *Homeland security presidential directive-5: Management of domestic incidents.* Washington, DC: The White House. Retrieved from http://fas.org/irp/offdocs/nspd/hspd-5.html

Bush, G. W. (2004, July 26). Executive Order 13347—Individuals with disabilities in emergency preparedness. *Federal Register, 69*(142). Retrieved from http://www.hhs.gov/ocr/civilrights/resources/specialtopics/emergencypre/eo13347disabilitiesemergencypreparedness.pdf

Busso, D. S., McLaughlin, K. A., & Sheridan, M. A. (2014). Media exposure and sympathetic nervous system reactivity predict PTSD symptoms after the Boston Marathon bombings. *Depression and Anxiety, 31,* 551–558. doi:10.1002/da.22282

Caffo, E., & Belaise, C. (2003). Psychological aspects of traumatic injury in children and adolescents. *Child & Adolescent Psychiatric Clinics of North America, 12,* 493–535. doi:10.1016/S1056-4993(03)00004-X

Campbell, V. A., Gilyard, J. A., Sinclair, L., Sternberg, T., & Kailes, J. I. (2009). Preparing for and responding to pandemic influenza: Implications for people with disabilities. *American Journal of Public Health, 99,* S294–S300. doi:10.2105/AJPH.2009.162677

Campfield, K. M., & Hills, A. M. (2001). Effect of timing of critical incident stress debriefing (CISD) on posttraumatic symptoms. *Journal of Traumatic Stress, 14,* 327–340. doi:10.1023/A:1011117018705

Canada, M., Heath, M. A., Money, K., Annandale, N., Fischer, L., & Young, E. L. (2007). Crisis intervention for students of diverse backgrounds: School counselors' concerns. *Brief Treatment and Crisis Intervention, 7,* 12–24. doi:10.1093/brief-treatment/mhl018

Canady, M., James, B., & Nease, J. (2012). *To protect and educate: The school resource officer and the prevention of violence in schools.* Hoover, AL: National Association of School Resource Officers. Retrieved from https://nasro.org/cms/wp-content/uploads/2013/11/NASRO-To-Protect-and-Educate-nosecurity.pdf

Canfield, J. (2005). Secondary traumatization, burnout, and vicarious traumatization: A review of the literature as it relates to therapists who treat trauma. *Smith College Studies in Social Work, 75,* 81–101. doi:10.1300/J497v75n02_06

Capewell, E. (2000). *When tragedy strikes: Guidelines for effective critical incident management in schools.* Dublin, Ireland: Irish National Teachers Union.

Caplan, G. (1964). *Principles of preventive psychiatry.* New York, NY: Basic Books.

Caplan, G. (1974). *Support systems and community mental health: Lectures on concept development.* New York, NY: Behavioral Publications.

Carlson, E. B. (1997). *Trauma assessments: A clinician's guide.* New York, NY: Guilford Press.

Carr, A. (2004). Interventions for post-traumatic stress disorder in children and adolescents. *Pediatric Rehabilitation, 7,* 231–244. doi:10.1080/13638490410001727464

Carrion, V. G., Weems, C. F., Ray, R., & Reiss, A. L. (2002). Toward an empirical definition of pediatric PTSD: The phenomenology of PTSD symptoms in youth. *Journal of the American Academy of Child and Adolescent Psychiatry, 41,* 166–173. doi:10.1097/00004583-200202000-00010

Carrion, V. G., & Wong, S. S. (2012). Can traumatic stress alter the brain? Understanding the implications of early trauma on brain development and learning. *Journal of Adolescent Health, 51,* 523–528. doi:10.1016/j.jadohealth.2012.04.010

Cary, C. E., & McMillen, J. C. (2012). The data behind the dissemination: A systematic review of trauma-focused cognitive behavioral therapy for use with children and youth. *Children and Youth Services Review, 34, 748–757.* doi:10.1016/jchildyouth.2012.01.003

Catalano, R. F., Berglund, M. L., Ryan, J. A. M., Lonczak, H. S., & Hawkins, J. D. (2004). Positive youth development in the United States: Research findings on evaluations of positive youth development programs. *The Annals of the American Academy of Political and Social Science, 591,* 98–124. doi:10.1177/0002716203260102

Cauce, A. M., Felner, R. D., & Primavera, J. (1982). Social support in high-risk adolescents: Structural components and adaptive impact. *American Journal of Community Psychology, 10,* 417–428. doi:10.1007/BF00893980

Centers for Disease Control and Prevention. (2013a). *Leading causes of death reports, national and regional, 1999–2013.* Atlanta, GA: Author. Retrieved from http://webappa.cdc.gov/sasweb/ncipc/leadcaus10_us.html

Centers for Disease Control and Prevention. (2013b). *Results from the school health policies and practices study 2012.* Atlanta, GA: U.S. Department of Health and Human Services. Retrieved from http://www.cdc.gov/HealthyYouth/shpps/index.htm

Charuvastra, A., & Cloitre, M. (2008). Social bonds and posttraumatic stress disorder. *Annual Review of Psychology, 59,* 301–328. doi:10.1146/annurev.psych.58.110405.085650

Chauvin, I., McDaniel, J., Banks, A., Eddlemon, O., & Cook, L. (2013). Writing a commemoration: A technique for restoring equilibrium after a crisis. *Journal of Creativity in Mental Health, 8,* 416–427. doi:10.1080/15401383.2013.844658

Chemtob, C. M., Nakashima, J., & Carlson, J. G. (2002). Brief treatment for elementary school children with disaster-related posttraumatic stress disorder: A field study. *Journal of Clinical Psychology, 58,* 99–112. doi:10.1002/jclp.1131

Chemtob, C. M., Tomas, S., Law, W., & Cremniter, D. (1997). Postdisaster psychosocial intervention: A field study of the impact of debriefing on psychological distress. *American Journal of Psychiatry, 154,* 415–417. Retrieved from http://ajp.psychiatryonline.org/journal.aspx?journalid=13

Cherry Creek School District. (2008). *Emergency response and crisis management guide.* Greenwood Village, CO: Author.

Children and War Foundation. (1998). *The Children's Impact of Events Scale.* Bergen, Norway: Author. Retrieved from http://www.childrenandwar.org/measures/children%E2%80%99s-revised-impact-of-event-scale-8-%E2%80%93-cries-8/

Christopher, R. (2007). Review of the Children's PTSD Inventory: A structured interview for diagnosing posttraumatic stress disorder. In K. F. Geisinger, R. A. Spies, J. F. Carlson, & B. S. Plake (Eds.). *The seventeenth mental measurements yearbook.* Lincoln, NE: Buros Institute of Mental Measurements.

Chung, S., Danielson, J., & Shannon, M. (2008). *School-based emergency preparedness: A national analysis and recommended protocol* (Prepared under contract no. 290-00-0020). (AHRQ publication no. 09-0013). Rockville, MD: Agency for Healthcare Research and Quality.

Clarke, L. S., Jones, R. E., & Yssel, N. (2014). Supporting students with disabilities during school crises: A teacher's guide. *Teaching Exceptional Children, 46,* 169–178. doi:10.1177/0014402914534616

Cobb, S. (1976). Social support as a moderator of life stress. *Psychosomatic Medicine, 38,* 300–314. Retrieved from http://journals.lww.com/psychosomaticmedicine/pages/default.aspx

Cobham, V. E., March, S., De Young, A., Leeson, F., Nixon, R., McDermott, B., & Kennedy, J. (2012). Involving parents in indicated early intervention for childhood PTSD following accidental injury. *Clinical Child and Family Psychology Review, 15, 345–363.* doi:10.1007/s10567-012-0124-9

Cohen, J. A. (2001). Pharmacologic treatment of traumatized children. *Trauma, Violence, & Abuse, 2,* 155–171. doi:10.1177/1524838001002002004

Cohen, J. (2013, February 15). Would more secure doors have slowed Newtown shooter? *All Things Considered.* National Public Radio. Retrieved from http://www.npr.org/2013/02/15/172130144/would-more-secure-doors-have-slowed-newtown-shooter

Cohen, J. A., Berliner, L., & Mannarino, A. P. (2000). Treating traumatized children: A research review and synthesis. *Trauma, Violence, & Abuse, 1,* 29–46. doi:10.1177/1524838000001001003

Cohen, J. A., Bukstein, O., Walter, H., Benson, R. S., Chrisman, A., Farchione, T. R., . . . Stock, S. (2010). Practice parameter for the assessment and treatment of children and adolescents with posttraumatic stress disorder. *Journal of the American Academy of Child and Adolescent Psychiatry, 49,* 414–430. doi:10.1097/00004583-201004000-00021

Cohen, S., Gottlieb, B. H., & Underwood, L. G. (2001). Social relationships and health: Challenges for measurement and intervention. *Advances in Mind-Body Medicine, 17,* 129–142. Retrieved from http://www.advancesjournal.com/

Cohen, J. A., Jaycox, L. H., Walker, D. W., Mannarino, A. P., Langley, A. K., & Duclos, J. L. (2009). Treating traumatized children after Hurricane Katrina: Project Fleur-de-lis. *Clinical Child and Family Psychological Review, 12,* 55–64. doi:10.1007/s10567-009-0039-2

Cohen, J. A., & Mannarino, A. P. (2004). Treatment of childhood traumatic grief. *Journal of Clinical Child and Adolescent Psychology, 33,* 819–831. doi:10.1207/s15374424jccp3304_17

Cohen, J. A., & Mannarino, A. P. (2008). Trauma-focused cognitive behavioural therapy for children and parents. *Child and Adolescent Mental Health, 13,* 158–162. doi:10.1111/j.1475-3588.2008.00502.x

Cohen, J. A., Mannarino, A. P., Berliner, L., & Deblinger, E. (2000). Trauma-focused cognitive behavioral therapy for children and adolescents: An empirical update. *Journal of Interpersonal Violence, 15,* 1202–1223. doi:10.1177/088626000015011007

Cohen, J. A., Mannarino, A. P., & Deblinger, E. (2012). *Trauma-focused CBT for children and adolescents.* New York, NY: Guilford Press.

Cohen, J. A., Mannarino, A. P., & Knudsen, K. (2004). Treating childhood traumatic grief: A pilot study. *Journal of the American Academy of Child and Adolescent Psychiatry, 43,* 1225–1233. doi:10.1097/01.chi.0000135620.15522.38

Cohen, J. A., Mannarino, A. P., & Staron, V. R. (2006). A pilot study of Modified Cognitive-Behavioral Therapy for Childhood Traumatic Grief (CBT-CTG). *Journal of the American Academy of Child and Adolescent Psychiatry, 45,* 1465–1473. doi:10.1097/01. chi.0000237705.43260.2c

Cohen, J., McCabe, E. M., Michelli, N. M., & Pickeral, T. (2009). School climate: Research, policy, teacher education and practice. *Teachers College Record, 111*(1), 180–213. Retrieved from http://www.tcrecord.org/Content.asp?ContentId=15220

Cohen, S., & Wills, T. A. (1985). Stress, social support, and the buffering hypothesis. *Psychological Bulletin, 98*(2), 310–357. doi:10.1037/0033-2909.98.2.310

Cole, S. F., O'Brien, J. G., Gadd, M. G., Ristuccia, J., Wallace, D. L., & Gregory, M. (2005). *Helping traumatized children learn: Supportive school environments for children traumatized by family violence.* Boston, MA: Massachusetts Advocates for Children. Retrieved from http://massadvocates.org/tlpi/

Collaborative for Academic, Social, and Emotional Learning (CASEL). (n.d.). *Frequently asked questions about SEL.* Chicago, IL: Author. Retrieved from http://www.casel.org/social-and-emotional-learning/frequently-asked-questions/

Collaborative for Academic, Social, and Emotional Learning (CASEL). (2007). *Background of social and emotional learning* (SEL). Retrieved from http://eric.ed.gov/?id=ED505362

Collaborative for Academic, Social, and Emotional Learning (CASEL). (2012). *Effective social and emotional learning programs: Preschool and elementary school edition.* Chicago, IL: Author. Retrieved from http://www.casel.org/guide/

Colorado School Safety Resource Center. (2015). Preparedness missions. Denver, CO: Colorado Department of Public Safety. Retrieved from https://www.colorado.gov/pacific/cssrc/5-preparedness-missions

Comer, J. S., & Kendall, P. C. (2007). Terrorism: The psychological impact on youth. *Clinical Psychology: Science and Practice, 14,* 179–212. doi:10.1111/j.1468-2850.2007.00078.x

Conlon, L., Fahy, T. J., & Conroy, R. R. (1999). PTSD in ambulant RTA victims: A randomized controlled trial of debriefing. *Journal of Psychosomatic Research, 46,* 37–44. doi:10.1016/S0022-3999(98)00068-3

Connor, K. M., Sutherland, S. M., Tupler, L. A., Malik, M. L., & Davidson, J. R. (1999). Fluoxetine in post-traumatic stress disorder randomised, double-blind study. *British Journal of Psychiatry: The Journal of Mental Science, 175,* 17–22. doi:10.1192/bjp.175.1.17

Conolly-Wilson, C. N. (2009, November). Evaluating psychological trauma in the aftermath of a suicide cluster. *Communiqué, 38*(3), 12. Retrieved from http://www.nasponline.org/publications/periodicals/communique/issues/volume-38-issue-3/evaluating-psychological-trauma-in-the-aftermath-of-a-suicide-cluster

Conolly-Wilson, C. (2010, April). *Psychoeducational group cheat sheet: A lesson plan for mental health response team members only.* Waukegan, IL: Waukegan Public Schools.

Conolly-Wilson, C. N., & Reeves, M. A. (2013). School safety and crisis planning considerations for school psychologists. *Communiqué, 41*(6), 16–17. Retrieved from http://www.nasponline.org/publications/periodicals/communique/issues/volume-41-issue-6/school-safety-and-crisis-planning-considerations-for-school-psychologists

Contractor, A. A., Layne, C. M., Steinberg, A. M., Ostrowski, S. A., Ford, J. D., & Elhai, J. D. (2013). Do gender and age moderate the symptom structure of PTSD? Findings from a national clinical sample of children and adolescents. *Psychiatry Research, 210,* 1056–1064. doi:10.1016/j.psychres.2013.09.012

Cook, C. R., Crews, S. D., Wright, D. B., Mayer, G. R., Gale, B., Kraemer, B., & Gresham, F. M. (2007). Establishing and evaluating the substantive adequacy of positive behavioral support plans. *Journal of Behavioral Education, 16,* 191–206. doi:10.1007/s10864-006-9024-8

Cook-Cottone, C. (2004). Childhood posttraumatic stress disorder: Diagnosis, treatment, and school reintegration. *School Psychology Review, 33,* 127–139. Retrieved from http://www.nasponline.org/publications/periodicals/spr/volume-33/volume-33-issue-1/childhood-posttraumatic-stress-disorder-diagnosis-treatment-and-school-reintegration

Cornell, D. (2015). Our schools are safe: Challenging the misperception that schools are dangerous places. *American Orthopsychiatric Association.* doi:10.1037/ort000006

Cornell, D., & Allen, K. (2011). Development, evaluation, and future directions of the Virginia Student Threat Assessment Guidelines. *Journal of School Violence, 10,* 88–106. doi:10.1080/15388220.2010.519432

Cornell, D. G., Allen, K., & Fan, X. (2012). A randomized controlled study of the Virginia Student Threat Assessment Guidelines in kindergarten through grade 12. *School Psychology Review, 41,* 100–115. Retrieved from http://www.nasponline.org/publications/periodicals/spr/volume-41/volume-41-issue-1/a-randomized-controlled-study-of-the-virginia-student-threat-assessment-guidelines-in-kindergarten-through-grade-12

Cornell, D., Gregory, A., & Fan, X. (2011). Reductions in long-term suspensions following adoption of the Virginia Student Threat Assessment Guidelines. *Bulletin of the National Association of Secondary School Principals, 95,* 175–194. doi:10.1177/0192636511415255

Cornell, D., & Nekvasil, E. (2012). Violent thoughts and behaviors. In S. E. Brock & S. R. Jimerson (Eds.), *Best practices in school crisis prevention and intervention* (2nd ed., pp. 485–502). Bethesda, MD: National Association of School Psychologists.

Cornell, D. G., & Sheras, P. L. (1998). Common errors in school crisis response: Learning from our mistakes. *Psychology in the Schools, 35,* 297–307. Retrieved from http://curry.virginia.edu/uploads/resourceLibrary/common-errors.pdf

Cornell, D., & Sheras, P. (2006). *Guidelines for responding to student threats of violence.* Longmont, CO: Sopris West.

Cornell, D., Sheras, P., Gregory, A., & Fan, X. (2009). A retrospective study of school safety conditions in high schools using the Virginia threat assessment guidelines versus alternative approaches. *School Psychology Quarterly, 24,* 119–129. doi:10.1037/a0016182

Cornell, D., Sheras, P., Kaplan, S., Levy-Elkon, A., McConville, D., Douglass, J., . . . Cole, J. (2004). Guidelines for student threat assessment: Field-test findings. *School Psychology Review, 33,* 527–546. Retrieved from http://curry.virginia.edu/uploads/resourceLibrary/2004-school-psych-review-article-threat-assessment1.pdf

Cotton, K. (2001). *New small learning communities:* Findings from recent literature. Portland, OR: Northwest Regional Educational Laboratory.

Council for Exceptional Children & Council for Children with Behavioral Disorders. (2013). *Helping students cope with traumatic events: Tips for educators.* Arlington, VA: Council for Exceptional Children. Retrieved from https://www.cec.sped.org/~/media/Files/Membership/TraumaticEvents_TipsforEducators.pdf

Cowan, K. C., Vaillancourt, K., Rossen, E., & Pollitt, K. (2013). *A framework for safe and successful schools* [Brief]. Bethesda, MD: National Association of School Psychologists. Retrieved http://www.nasponline.org/Documents/Research%20and%20Policy/Advocacy%20Resources/Framework_for_Safe_and_Successful_School_Environments.pdf

Craig, C. D., & Sprang, G. (2010). Compassion satisfaction, compassion fatigue, and burnout in a national sample of trauma treatment therapists. *Anxiety, Stress, & Coping, 23,* 319–339. doi:10.1080/10615800903085818

Crandal, B., & Conradi, L. (2013). *Review of child and adolescent trauma screening tools.* San Diego, CA: Rady Children's Hospital, Chadwick Center for Children and Families. Retrieved from www.childsworld.ca.gov/res/pdf/KatieA/ChildAdolescentTraumaScreenTools.pdf

Creamer, M., & O'Donnell, M. (2008). The pros and cons of psychoeducation following trauma: Too early to judge? *Psychiatry: Interpersonal and Biological Processes, 71,* 318–321. doi:10.1521/psyc.2008.71.4.319

Crepeau-Hobson, F. (2013). An exploratory study of suicide risk assessment practices in the school setting. *Psychology in the Schools, 50,* 810–822. doi:10.1002/pits.21705

Crepeau-Hobson, F., Sievering, K. S., Armstrong, C., & Stonis, J. (2012). A coordinated mental health crisis response: Lessons learned from three Colorado school shootings. *Journal of School Violence, 11,* 207–225. doi:10.1080/15388220.2012.682002

Crepeau-Hobson, F., & Summers, L. (2011). The crisis response to a school-based hostage event: A case study. *Journal of School Violence, 10,* 1–18. doi:10.1080/15388220.2011.578277

Crowe, T. D. (2000). *Crime prevention through environmental design: Applications of architectural design and space.* Louisville, KY: National Crime Prevention Institute.

Cuijpers, P. (2003). Examining the effects of prevention programs on the incidence of new cases of mental disorders: The lack of statistical power. *American Journal of Psychiatry, 160,* 1385–1391. doi:10.1176/appi.ajp.160.8.1385

Davidson, J., Baldwin, D., Stein, D. J., Kuper, E., Benattia, I., Ahmed, S., . . . Musgnung, J. (2006). Treatment of posttraumatic stress disorder with venlafaxine extended release: A 6-month randomized controlled trial. *Archives of General Psychiatry, 63,* 1158–1165. doi:10.1001/archpsyc.63.10.1158

Davidson J., Rothbaum, B. O., Tucker, P., Asnis, G., Benattia, I., & Musgnung, J. J. (2006). Venlafaxine extended release in posttraumatic stress disorder: A sertraline- and placebo-controlled study. *Journal of Clinical Psychopharmacology, 26,* 259–267. doi:10.1097/01.jcp.0000222514.71390.c1

Davidson, J. T., Rothbaum, B. O., Van der Kolk, B. A., Sikes, C. R., & Farfel, G. M. (2001). Multicenter, double-blind comparison of sertraline and placebo in the treatment of posttraumatic stress disorder. *Archives of General Psychiatry, 58,* 485–492. doi:10.1001/archpsyc.58.5.485

Davidson, P. R., & Parker, K. C. H. (2001). Eye movement desensitization and reprocessing (EMDR): A meta-analysis. *Journal of Consulting and Clinical Psychology, 69,* 305–316. doi:10.1037//0022-006X.69.2.305

Davis, M., Ressler, K., Rothbaum, B. O., & Richardson, R. (2006). Effects of d-cycloserine on extinction: Translation from preclinical to clinical work. *Biological Psychiatry, 60,* 369–375. doi:10.1016/j.biopsych.2006.03.084

Dawson, K. S., Joscelyne, A., Meijer, C., Tampubolon, A., Steel, Z., & Bryant, R. A. (2014). Predictors of chronic posttraumatic response in Muslim children following natural disaster. *Psychological trauma: Theory, research, practice, and policy.* Advance online publication. doi:10.1037/a0037140

Deahl, M., Srinivasan, M., Jones, N., Thomas, J., Neblett, C., & Jolly, A. (2000). Preventing psychological trauma in soldiers: The role of operational stress training and psychological debriefing. *British Journal of Medical Psychology, 73,* 77–85. doi:10.1348/000711200160318

de Anda, D. (2007). Intervention research and program evaluation in the school setting: Issues and alternative research designs. *Children & Schools, 29*(2), 87–94. doi:wiley.com/10.1002/ev.128

De Bellis, M. D., Woolley, D. P., & Hooper, S. R. (2013). Neuropsychological findings in pediatric maltreatment: Relationship of PTSD, dissociative symptoms, and abuse/neglect indices to neurocognitive outcomes. *Child Maltreatment, 18,* 171–183. doi:10.1177/1077559513497420

Deblinger, E., Lippmann, J., & Steer, R. (1996). Sexually abused children suffering posttraumatic stress symptoms: Initial treatment outcome findings. *Child Maltreatment, 1,* 310–321. doi:10.1177/1077559596001004003

Deblinger, E., Stauffer, L. B., & Steer, R. A. (2001). Comparative efficacies of supportive and cognitive behavioral group therapies for young children who have been sexually abused and their nonoffending mothers. *Child Maltreatment, 6,* 332–343. doi:10.1177/1077559501006004006

Deković, M., Koning, I. M., Stams, G. J., & Buist, K. L. (2008). Factors associated with traumatic symptoms and internalizing problems among adolescents who experienced a traumatic event. *Anxiety, Stress, and Coping, 21,* 377–386. doi:10.1080/10615800701791161

Delaney-Black, B., Covington, C., Ondersma, S. J., Nordstron-Klee, B., Templin, T., Ager, J., . . . Sokol, R. J. (2002). Violence exposure, trauma, and IQ and/or reading deficits among urban children. *Archives of Pediatrics and Adolescent Medicine, 156,* 280–285. doi:10.1001/archpedi.156.3.280

Dell'Osso, L., Carmassi, C., Massimetti, G., Stratta, P., Riccardi, I., Capanna, C., . . . Rossi, A. (2013). Age, gender and epicenter proximity effects on post-traumatic stress symptoms in L'Aquila 2009 earthquake survivors. *Journal of Affective Disorders, 146,* 174–180.

Demaray, M. K., & Malecki, C. K. (2002). Critical levels of perceived social support associated with student adjustment. *School Psychology Quarterly, 17,* 213–241. doi:10.1521/scpq.17.3.213.20883

Demaray, M. K., & Malecki, C. K. (2003). Importance ratings of socially supportive behaviors by children and adolescents. *School Psychology Review, 32,* 108–131. Retrieved from http://www.nasponline.org/publications/periodicals/spr/volume-32/volume-32-issue-1/importance-ratings-of-socially-supportive-behaviors-by-children-and-adolescents

Demaray, M. K., Malecki, C. K., Davidson, L. M., Hodgson, K. K., & Rebus, P. (2005). The relationship between social support and student adjustment: A longitudinal analysis. *Psychology in the Schools, 42,* 691–706. doi:10.1002/pits.20120

Demaray, M. K., Malecki, C. K., & DeLong, L. K. (2006). Support in the lives of aggressive students, their victims, and their peers. In S. R. Jimerson & M. Furlong (Eds.), *Handbook of school violence and school safety: From research to practice* (pp. 21–29). Mahwah, NJ: Erlbaum.

Demaree, M. A. (1994, May). *Responding to violence in their lives: Creating nurturing environments for children with post-traumatic stress disorder.* Newton, MA: Education Development Center.

Dempsey, M., Overstreet, S., & Moely, B. (2000). "Approach" and "avoidance" coping and PTSD symptoms in inner-city youth. *Current Psychology: Developmental, Learning, Personality, Social, 19,* 28–45. doi:10.1007/s12144-000-1002-z

Denson, T. F., Marshall, G. N., Schell, T. L., & Jaycox, L. H. (2007). Predictors of posttraumatic distress 1 year after exposure to community violence: The importance of acute symptom severity. *Journal of Consulting and Clinical Psychology, 75,* 683–692. doi:10.1037/0022-006X.75.5.683

Department of Veterans Affairs and Department of Defense. (2010). *VA/DoD clinical practice guideline for the management of post-traumatic stress.* Washington, DC; Author. Available from http://www.oqp.med.va.gov/cpg/

Devilly, G. J. (2002). Eye movement desensitization and reprocessing: A chronology of its development and scientific standing. *Scientific Review of Mental Health Practice: Objective Investigations of Controversial and Unorthodox Claims in Clinical Psychology, Psychiatry, and Social Work, 1,* 113–138. Retrieved from http://www.srmhp.org/0102/eye-movement.html

Devilly, G. J., & Annab, R. (2008). A randomised controlled trial of group debriefing. *Journal of Behavior Therapy and Experimental Psychiatry, 39,* 42–56. doi:10.1016/j.jbtep.2006.09.003

Devilly, G. J., & Varker, T. (2008). The effect of stressor severity on outcome following group debriefing. *Behaviour Research and Therapy, 46,* 130–136. doi:10.1016/j.brat.2007.09.004

Devilly, G. J., Varker, T., Hansen, K., & Gist, R. (2007). An analogue study of the effects of psychological debriefing on eyewitness memory. *Behaviour Research and Therapy, 45,* 1245–1254. doi:10.1016/j.brat.2006.08.022

DeVoe, J. F., Peter, K., Noonan, M., Snyder, T. D., & Baum, K. (2005). *Indicators of school crime and safety: 2005* (NCES 2006-001/NCJ 210697). Washington, DC: U.S. Government Printing Office. Retrieved from http://nces.ed.gov/pubsearch/pubsinfo.asp?pubid=2006001

de Wilde, E. J., & Kienhorst, C. W. M. (1998). Life events and adolescent suicidal behavior. In T. W. Miller (Ed.), *Children of trauma: Stressful life events and their effects on children and adolescents* (pp. 161–178). Madison, CT: International Universities Press.

Diehle, J., Schmitt, K., Daams, J. G., Boer, F., & Lindauer, R. L. (2014). Effects of psychotherapy on trauma-related cognitions in posttraumatic stress disorder: A meta-analysis. *Journal of Traumatic Stress, 27,* 257–264. doi:10.1002/jts.21924

DiGangi, J. A., Gomez, D., Mendoza, L., Jason, L. A., Keys, C. B., & Koenen, K. C. (2013). Pretrauma risk factors for posttraumatic stress disorder: A systematic review of the literature. *Clinical Psychology Review, 33,* 728–744. doi:10.1016/j.cpr.2013.05.002

Doll, B., & Lyon, M. A. (1998). Risk and resilience: Implications for the delivery of educational and mental health services in schools. *School Psychology Review, 27,* 348–363. Retrieved from http://www.nasponline.org/publications/periodicals/spr//volume-27-issue-3/risk-and-resilience-implications

Doll, B., & Osborn, A. (2007). Review of the Children's PTSD Inventory: A structured interview for diagnosing posttraumatic stress disorder. In K. F. Geisinger, R. A. Spies, J. F. Carlson, & B. S. Plake (Eds.). *The seventeenth mental measurements yearbook.* Lincoln, NE: Buros Institute of Mental Measurements.

Donnelly, C. L. (2003). Pharmacologic treatment approaches for children and adolescents with posttraumatic stress disorder. *Child and Adolescent Psychiatry in the Clinics of North America, 12,* 251–259. doi:10.1016/S1056-4993(02)00102-5

Donnelly, C. L., Amaya-Jackson, L., & March, J. S. (1999). Psychopharmacology of pediatric posttraumatic stress disorder. *Journal of Child and Adolescent Psychopharmacology, 9,* 203–220. doi:10.1089/cap.1999.9.203

Dorn, M., Thomas, G., Wong, M., Shepherd, S., Kelly, J., & Stephens, R. (2004). *Jane's school safety handbook* (2nd ed.). Surrey, UK: Jane's Information Group.

Dorsey, S., Pullman, M. D., Berliner, L., Koschmann, E., McKay, M., & Deblinger, E. (2014). Engaging foster parents in treatment: A randomized trial of supplementing trauma-focused cognitive behavioral therapy with evidence-based engagement strategies. *Child Abuse and Neglect, 38,* 1508–1520. doi:10.1016/j.chiabu.2014.03.020

Dückers, M. L. A. (2013). Five essential principles of post-disaster psychosocial care: Looking back and forward with Stevan Hobfoll. *European Journal of Psychotraumatology, 4,* 1–3. doi:10.3402/ejpt.v4i0.21914

Duggan, M., & Smith, A. (2013). *Social media update 2013.* Washington, DC: Pew Research Center. Retrieved from http://pewinternet.org/Reports/2013/Social-Media-Update.aspx

Dulmus, C. N. (2003). Approaches to preventing the psychological impact of community violence exposure on children. *Crisis Intervention, 6,* 185–201. doi:10.1080/713638933

Duncan, R. D. (2004). The impact of family relationships on school bullies and victims. In D. L. Espelage & S. M. Swearer (Eds.), *Bullying in American schools: A social-ecological perspective on prevention and intervention* (pp. 227–244). Mahwah, NJ: Erlbaum.

Durlak, J. A., Weissberg, R. P., Dymnicki, A. B., Taylor, R. D., & Schellinger, K. B. (2011). The impact on enhancing students' social emotional learning: A meta-analysis of school-based universal interventions. *Child Development, 82,* 405–432. doi:10.1111/j.1467-8624.2010.01564

Durlak, J. A., & Wells, A. M. (1997). Primary prevention mental health programs for children and adolescents: A meta-analytic review. *American Journal of Community Psychology, 25,* 115–152. doi:10.1023/A:1024654026646

Dwyer, K., & Jimerson, S. R. (2002). Enabling prevention through planning. In S. E. Brock, P. J. Lazarus, & S. R. Jimerson (Eds.), *Best practices in school crisis prevention and intervention* (pp. 23–46). Bethesda, MD: National Association of School Psychologists.

Dyb, G., Jensen, T. K., Nygaard, E., Ekeberg, Ø., Diseth, T. H., Wentzel-Larsen, T., & Thoresen, S. (2014). Post-traumatic stress reactions in survivors of the 2011 massacre on Utøya Island, Norway. *British Journal of Psychiatry, 204,* 361–367. doi:10.1192/bjp.bp.113.133157

Dyregrov, A., & Yule, W. (2006). A review of PTSD in children. *Child and Adolescent Mental Health, 11,* 176–184. doi:10.1111/j.1475-3588.2005.00384.x

Eagle, G., & Kaminer, D. (2013). Continuous traumatic stress: Expanding the lexicon of traumatic stress. *Peace and Conflict: Journal of Peace Psychology, 19,* 85–99. doi:10.1037/a0032485

Ebata, A., & Moos, R. (1994). Personal, situational, and contextual correlates of coping in adolescence. *Journal of Research on Adolescence, 4,* 99–125. doi:10.1207/s15327795jra0401_6

Edwards, O. W., Mumford, V. E., Shillingford, M. A., & Serra-Roldan, R. (2007). Developmental assets: A prevention framework for students considered at risk. *ProQuest Nursing & Allied Health Source, 29,* 145–154. doi:10.1093/cs/29.3.145

Ehlers, A., & Clark, D. M. (2000). A cognitive model of posttraumatic stress disorder. *Behaviour Research and Therapy, 38,* 319–345. doi:10.1016/S0005-7967(99)00123-0

Ehlers, A., Mayou, R. A., & Bryant, B. (1998). Psychological predictors of chronic posttraumatic stress disorder after motor vehicle accidents. *Journal of Abnormal Psychology, 107,* 508–519. doi:10.1037/0021-843X.107.3.508

Eklund, K., & Gueldner, B. (2012). Suicidal thoughts and behaviors: Suicide intervention. In S. E. Brock & S. R. Jimerson (Eds.), *Best practices in school crisis prevention and intervention* (2nd ed., pp. 503–524). Bethesda, MD: National Association of School Psychologists.

Eksi, A., Braun, K. L., Ertem-Vehid, H., Peykerli, G., Saydam, R., Toparlak, D., & Alyanak, B. (2007). Risk factors for the development of PTSD and depression among child and adolescent victims following a 7.4 magnitude earthquake. *International Journal of Psychiatry in Clinical Practice, 11,* 190–199. doi:10.1080/13651500601017548

Elhai, J. D., Layne, C. M., Steinberg, A. S., Brymer, M. J., Briggs, E. C., Ostrowski, S. A., & Pynoos, R. S. (2013). Psychometric properties of the UCLA PTSD Reaction Index. Part II: Investigating factor structure findings in a national clinic-referred youth sample. *Journal of Traumatic Stress, 26,* 10–18. doi:10.1002/jts.21755

Elias, M. J., Zins, J. E., Weissberg, R. P., Frey, K. S., Greenberg, M. T., Haynes, N. M., . . . Shriver, T. P. (1997). *Promoting social and emotional learning: Guidelines for educators.* Alexandria, VA: Association for Supervision and Curriculum Development.

Eliot, M., Cornell, D., Gregory, A., & Fan, X. (2010). Supportive school climate and student willingness to seek help for bullying and threats of violence. *Journal of School Psychology, 48,* 533–553. doi:10.1016/j.jsp.2010.07.001

Elklit, A. (2002). Victimization and PTSD in a Danish national youth probability sample. *Journal of the American Academy of Child & Adolescent Psychiatry, 41,* 174–181. doi:10.1097/00004583-200202000-00011

Elliott, D. S., Grady, J. M., Heys, L., Bell, H., Woodward, B., & Williams, S. (2002). *Safe communities–safe schools guide to effective program selection: A tool for community violence prevention efforts.* Boulder, CO: University of Colorado, Center for the Study and Prevention of Violence.

Ellis, A. A., Nixon, R. V., & Williamson, P. (2009). The effects of social support and negative appraisals on acute stress symptoms and depression in children and adolescents. *British Journal of Clinical Psychology, 48,* 347–361. doi:10.1348/014466508X401894

Endo, G., Tachikawa, H., Fukuoka, Y., Aiba, M., Nemoto, K., Shiratori, Y., . . . Asada, T. (2014). How perceived social support relates to suicidal ideation: A Japanese social resident survey. *International Journal of Social Psychiatry, 60,* 290–298. doi:10.1177/0020764013486777

Ennett, S. T., Haws, S., Ringwalt, C. L., Vincus, A. A., Hanley, S., Bowling, J. M., & Rohrbach, L. A. (2011). Evidence-based practice in school substance use prevention: Fidelity of implementation under real-world conditions. *Health Education Research, 26,* 361–371. doi:10.1093/her/cyr013

Erbacher, T. A., Singer, J. B., & Poland, S. (2014). *Suicide in schools: A practioner's guide to multilevel prevention, assessment, intervention, and postvention.* New York, NY: Taylor & Francis.

Erum, N., Jaycox, L. H., Kataoka, S. H., Langley, A. K, & Stein, B. D. (2011). Going to scale: Experiences implementing a school-based trauma intervention. *School Psychology Review, 40,*

549–568. Retrieved from http://www.nasponline.org/publications/periodicals/spr/volume-40/volume-40-issue-4/going-to-scale-experiences-implementing-a-school-based-trauma-intervention

Espelage, D. L., Low, S., Polanin, J., & Brown, E. (2013). The impact of a middle-school program to reduce aggression, victimization, and sexual violence. *Journal of Adolescent Health, 53,* 180–186. doi:10.1016/j.jadohealth.2013.02.021

Evans, W. P., Marte, R. M., Betts, S., & Silliman, B. (2001). Adolescent suicide risk and peer-related violent behaviors and victimization. *Journal of Interpersonal Violence, 16,* 1330–1348. doi:10.1177/088626001016012006

Everall, R. D., & Paulson, B. L. (2004). Burnout and secondary traumatic stress: Impact on ethical behavior. *Canadian Journal of Counseling, 38,* 25–35. Retrieved from http://cjc-rcc.ucalgary.ca/cjc/index.php/rcc/article/view/244

Everly, G. S. (1999). Toward a model of psychological triage: Who will most need assistance? *International Journal of Emergency Mental Health, 3,* 151–154. Retrieved from https://www.chevronpublishing.com/product.cfm?dispprodid=480

Everly, G. S. (2003). Early psychological intervention: A word of caution. *International Journal of Emergency Mental Health, 5,* 179–184. Retrieved from https://www.chevronpublishing.com/product.cfm?dispprodid=480

Everly, G. S., Boyle, S. H., & Lating, J. M. (1999). The effectiveness of psychological debriefing with vicarious trauma: A meta-analysis. *Stress Medicine, 15,* 229–233. doi:10.1002/(SICI)1099-1700(199910)15:4<229::AID-SMI818>3.0.CO;2-M

Everly, G. S., Hamilton, S. E., Tyiska, C., & Ellers, K. (2008). Mental health response to disaster: Consensus recommendations: Early Psychological Intervention Subcommittee (EPI), National Volunteer Organizations Active in Disaster (NVOAD). *Aggression and Violent Behavior, 13,* 407–412. doi:10.1016/j.avb.2008.05.004

Everly, G. S., Lating, J. M., & Mitchell, J. T. (2005). Innovations in group crisis intervention. In A. R. Roberts (Ed.), *Crisis intervention handbook: Assessment, treatment, and research* (pp. 221–245). New York, NY: Oxford University Press.

Every Student Succeeds Act of 2015, Pub. L. 114-95, Retrieved from https://www.congress.gov/bill/114th-congress/senate-bill/1177/text

Evidence-Based Intervention Work Group. (2005). Theories of change and adoption of innovations: The evolving evidence-based intervention practice movement in school psychology. *Psychology in the Schools, 42,* 475–494. doi:10.1002/pits.20086

Fairfax County Public Schools. (n.d.). *FCPS threat assessment documentation* [Administrative form]. Retrieved from http://rems.ed.gov/docs/repository/REMS_000053_0002.pdf

Fairfax County Public Schools. (2013, August). *Crisis management workbook.* Falls Church, VA: Author. Retrieved from http://www.fcps.edu/fts/safety-security/publications/cmw.pdf

Federal Emergency Management Agency (FEMA). (2003, March). *Emergency Management Institute independent study: Exercise design.* Washington, DC: Author.

Federal Emergency Management Agency (FEMA). (2008). *ICS review material.* Washington, DC: Author. Retrieved from http://www.training.fema.gov/EMIWeb/IS/ICSResource/assets/reviewMaterials.pdf

Federal Emergency Management Agency (FEMA). (2009, March). *Continuity of operations plan template for federal departments and agencies.* Washington, DC: Author. Retrieved from http://www.fema.gov/pdf/about/org/ncp/coop/continuity_plan_template.pdf

Federal Emergency Management Agency. (2011). *Sample school emergency operations plans.* Washington, DC: Author. Retrieved from http://training.fema.gov/EMIWeb/emischool/EL361Toolkit/assets/SamplePlan.pdf

Federal Emergency Management Agency. (2013). *IS-546.A: Continuity of operations awareness course.* Washington, DC: Author. Retrieved from http://training.fema.gov/is/courseoverview.aspx?code=is-546.a

Federal Emergency Management Agency. (2014a). *Continuity of operations capabilities.* Washington, DC: Author. Retrieved from http://www.fema.gov/continuity-operations/continuity-operations-capabilities

Federal Emergency Management Agency (FEMA). (2014b). *Course: IS-120.a—An introduction to exercises.* Retrieved from http://emilms.fema.gov/IS120A/m1summary.htm

Feeny, N. C., Foa, E. B., Treadwell, K. R. H., & March, J. (2004). Posttraumatic stress disorder in youth: A critical review of the cognitive and behavioral treatment outcome literature. *Professional Psychology: Research and Practice, 35,* 466–476. doi:10.1037/0735-7028.35.5.466

Fein, R. A., Vossekuil, F., Pollack, W. S., Borum, R., Modzeleski, W., & Reddy, M. (2002). *Threat assessment in schools: A guide to managing threatening situations and to creating safe school climates.* Washington, DC: U.S. Secret Service and U.S. Department of Education. Retrieved from http://www.secretservice.gov/ntac/ssi_guide.pdf

Fein, R. A., Vossekuil, F., Pollack, W. S., Borum, R., Modzeleski, W., & Reddy, M. (2004). *Threat assessment in schools: A guide to managing threatening situations and to creating safe school climates.* Washington, DC: U.S. Secret Service and U.S. Department of Education. Retrieved from https://www2.ed.gov/admins/lead/safety/threatassessmentguide.pdf

Feinberg, T., & Jacob, S. (2002). Administrative considerations in preventing and responding to crisis: A risk management approach. In S. E. Brock, P. J. Lazarus, & S. R. Jimerson (Eds.), *Best practices in school crisis prevention and intervention* (pp. 95–108). Bethesda, MD: National Association of School Psychologists.

Feldman, R., & Vengrober, A. (2011). Posttraumatic stress disorder in infants and young children exposed to war-related trauma. *Journal of the American Academic of Child & Adolescent Psychiatry, 50,* 645-658. doi:10.1016/j.jaac.2011.03.001

Fernandez, K. E. (2009). Evaluating school improvement plans and their effect on academic performance. *Educational Policy, 25,* 338–367. doi:10.1177/0895904809351693

Feuerherd, M., Knuth, D., Muehlan, H., & Schmidt, S. (2014). Differential item functioning (DIF) analyses of the Impact of Event Scale–Revised (IES-R): Results from a large European study on people with disaster experiences. *Traumatology, 20,* 313–320. doi:10.1037/ h0099858

Figley, C. R. (1995). *Compassion fatigue: Coping with secondary traumatic stress disorder.* New York, NY: Brunner/Mazel.

Figley, C. R. (1999). *Compassion fatigue: Towards a new understanding of the costs of caring.* In B. H. Stamm (Ed.), Secondary traumatic stress: Self-care issues for clinicians, researchers, and educators (2nd ed., pp. 3–28). Lutherville, MD: Sidran Press.

Figley, C. R. (2002). *Treating compassion fatigue.* New York, NY: Brunner-Routledge.

Fixsen, D. L., Naoom, S. G., Blase, K. A., Friedman, R. M., & Wallace, F. (2005). *Implementation research: A synthesis of the literature.* Tampa, FL: University of South Florida, Louis de la Parte, Florida Mental Health Institute, The National Implementation Research Network (FMHI Publication #231).

Fleming, K. (2006). Resiliency in severely abused children. *Dissertation Abstracts International: Section A. Humanities and Social Sciences, 66*(12-A), 4307.

Flitsch, E., Magnesi, J., & Brock, S. E. (2012). Social media and crisis prevention and intervention. In S. E. Brock & S. R. Jimerson (Eds.), *Best practices in school crisis prevention and intervention* (pp. 287–304). Bethesda, MD: National Association of School Psychologists.

Foa, E. B. (2002). *The Child PTSD Symptom Scale (CPSS).* Available from Edna Foa, PhD, Center for the Treatment and Study of Anxiety, University of Pennsylvania School of Medicine, Department of Psychiatry, 3535 Market Street, Sixth Floor, Philadelphia, PA 19104.

Foa, E. B., Dancu, C. V., Hembree, E. A., Jaycox, L. H., Meadows, E. A., & Street, G. P. (1999). A comparison of exposure therapy, stress inoculation training, and their combination for reducing posttraumatic stress disorder in female assault victims. *Journal of Consulting and Clinical Psychology, 67,* 194–200. doi:10.1037/0022-006X.67.2.194

Foa, E. B., Johnson, K. M., Feeny, N. C., & Treadwell, K. R. H. (2001). The Child PTSD Symptoms Scale: A preliminary examination of its psychometric properties. *Journal of Clinical Child Psychology, 30,* 376–384. doi:10.1207/S15374424JCCP3003_9

Foa, E. B., Zinbarg, R., & Rothbaum, B. O. (1992). Uncontrollability and unpredictability in post-traumatic stress disorder: An animal model. *Psychological Bulletin, 112,* 218–223. doi:10.1037/0033-2909.112.2.218

Frazier, P., Steward, J., & Mortensen, H. (2004). Perceived control and adjustment to trauma: A comparison across events. *Journal of Social and Clinical Psychology, 23,* 303–324. doi:10.1521/ jscp.23.3.303.35452

Frazier, P., Tashiro, T., Berman, M., Steger, M., & Long, J. (2004). Correlates of levels and patterns of positive life changes following sexual assault. *Journal of Consulting and Clinical Psychology, 72,* 19–30. doi:10.1037/0022-006X.72.1.19

Freeman, W., & Taylor, M. (2010, July). *Conducting effective tabletops, drills and other exercises.* Workshop presented at the U.S. Department of Education, Office of Safe and Drug-Free Schools Readiness and Emergency Management for Schools (REMS) Final Grantee Meeting, Boston, MA. Retrieved from http://rems.ed.gov/docs/Training_FY09REMS_BOMA_Table TopsDrills.pdf

Freeman, W., & Taylor, M. (2011, August). *Overview of emergency management exercises.* Workshop presented at the U.S. Department of Education, Office of Safe and Drug-Free Schools Readiness and Emergency Management for Schools (REMS) Final Grantee Meeting, National Harbor, MD. Retrieved from http://rems.ed.gov/docs/FY10REMS_FGM_NHMD_EM Exercises.pdf

Frey, C. U., & Röthlisberger, C. (1996). Social support in healthy adolescents. *Journal of Youth and Adolescence, 25,* 17–31. doi:10.1007/BF01537378

Friedman, M. J. (1988). Toward rational pharmacotherapy for posttraumatic stress disorder: An interim report. *American Journal of Psychiatry, 145,* 281–285. doi:10.1176/ajp.145.3.281

Friedman, M. J., Donnelly, C. L., & Mellman, T. A. (2003). Pharmacotherapy for PTSD. *Psychiatric Annals, 33,* 57–62. Retrieved from http://www.healio.com/psychiatry/journals/psycann/2003-1-33-1

Frommberger, U. H., Stieglitz, R., Nyberg, E., Schlickewei, W., Kuner, E., & Gerger, M. (1998). Prediction of posttraumatic stress disorder by immediate reactions to trauma: A prospective study in road traffic accident victims. *European Archives of Psychiatry and Clinical Neuroscience, 248,* 316–321. doi:10.1007/s004060050057

Frosch, D. (2014, September 14). 'Active shooter' drills spark raft of legal complaints: Critics say simulation exercises can traumatize those taking part. *The Wall Street Journal.* Retrieved from http://www.wsj.com/articles/active-shooter-drills-spark-raft-of-legal-complaints-1409760255

Furlong, M. J., Chung, A., Bates, M., & Morrison, R. L. (1995). Who are the victims of school violence? A comparison of student non-victims and multi-victims. *Education and Treatment of Children, 18,* 282–298. Retrieved from http://www.educationandtreatmentofchildren.net/

Furman, W., & Buhrmester, D. (1992). Age and sex differences in perceptions of networks of personal relationships. *Child Development, 63,* 103–115. doi:10.2307/1130905

Gainey, B. S. (2010). Crisis management in public school districts. *Organization Development Journal, 28*(1), 89–95. Retrieved from http://www.highbeam.com/publications/organization-development-journal-p61828

Galand, B., & Hospel, V. (2013). Peer victimization and school disaffection: Exploring the moderation effect of social support and the mediation effect of depression. *British Journal of Educational Psychology, 83,* 569–590. Retrieved from http://onlinelibrary.wiley.com/journal/10.1111/%28ISSN%292044-8279

Galea, S., Ahern J., Resnick, H., Kilpatrick, D., Bucuvalas, M., Gold, J., & Vlahov. (2002). Psychological sequelae of the September 11 terrorist attacks in New York City. *New England Journal of Medicine, 346,* 982–987. doi:10.1056/NEJMsa013404

Galea, S., Brewin, C. R., Gruber, M., Jones, R. T., King, D. W., King, L. A., . . . Kessler, R. C. (2007). Exposure to hurricane-related stressors and mental illness after Hurricane Katrina. *Archives of General Psychiatry, 64*, 1427–1434. doi:10.1001/archpsyc.64.12.1427

Galea, S., Vlahov, D., Resnick, H., Ahern, J., Susser, E., Gold, J., . . . Kilpatrick, D. (2003). Trends of probable post-traumatic stress disorder in New York City after the September 11 terrorist attacks. *American Journal of Epidemiology, 158*, 514–524. doi:10.1093/aje/kwg187

Galek, K., Flannelly, K. J., Greene, P. B., & Kudler, T. (2011). Burnout, secondary traumatic stress, and social support. *Pastoral Psychology, 60*, 633–649. doi:10.1007/s11089-011-0346-7

Gastic, B. (2011). Metal detectors and feeling safe at school. *Education and Urban Society, 43*, 486–498. doi:10.1177/0013124510380717

Gelkopf, M., & Berger, R. (2009). A school-based, teacher-mediated prevention program (ERASE-Stress) for reducing terror-related traumatic reactions in Israeli youth: A quasi-randomized controlled trial. *Journal of Child Psychology and Psychiatry, 50*, 962–971. doi:10.1111/j.1469-7610.2008.02021.x

Gentry, J. E., Baranowsky, A. B., & Dunning, K. (2002). ARP: The accelerated recovery program (ARP) for compassion fatigue. In C. R. Figley (Ed.), *Treating compassion fatigue* (pp. 123–137). New York, NY: Brunner-Routledge.

Gerson, R., & Rappaport, N. (2013). Traumatic stress and posttraumatic stress disorder in youth: Recent research findings on clinical impact, assessment, and treatment. *Journal of Adolescent Health, 52*, 137–143. doi:10.1016/j.jadohealth.2012.06.018

Ghazali, S., Elklit, A., Yaman, K., & Ahmad, M. (2013). Symptoms of PTSD among adolescents in Malaysia 4 years following the 2004 tsunami. *Journal of Loss and Trauma, 18*, 260–274. doi: 10.1080/15325024.2012.688703

Giannopoulou, I., Strouthos, M., Smith, P., Dikaiakou, A., Galanopoulou, V., & Yule, W. (2006). Post-traumatic stress reactions of children and adolescent exposed to the Athens 1999 earthquake. *European Psychiatry, 21*, 160–166. doi:10.1016/j.eurpsy.2005.09.005

Giddens, J. B. (2008). Critical incident stress debriefing/psychological debriefing: A critical review of the literature. *Dissertation Abstracts International, 69*, 3253.

Gil, S. (2005). Coping style in predicting posttraumatic stress disorder among Israeli students. *Anxiety, Stress, and Coping, 18*, 351–359. doi:10.1080/10615800500392732

Gil, S., & Caspi, Y. (2006). Personality traits, coping style, and perceived threat as predictors of posttraumatic stress disorder after exposure to a terrorist attack: A prospective study. *Psychosomatic Medicine, 68*, 904–909. doi:10.1097/01.psy.0000242124.21796.f8

Gilgoff, D., & Lee, J. J. (2013, April 17). Social media shapes Boston bombings response. *National Geographic.* Retrieved from http://news.nationalgeographic.com/news/2013/13/130415-boston-marathon-bombings-terrorism-social-media-twitter-facebook/

Gillihan, S. J., Aderka, I. M., Conklin, P. H., Capaldi, S., & Foa, E. B. (2013). The Child PTSD Symptom Scale: Psychometric properties in female adolescent sexual assault survivors. *Psychological Assessment, 25*, 23–31. doi:10.1037/a0029553

Gil-Rivas, V., Holman, E. A., & Silver, R. C. (2004). Adolescent vulnerability following the September 11th terrorist attacks: A study of parents and their children. *Applied Developmental Science, 8*, 130–142. doi:10.1207/s1532480xads0803_3

Gist, R., & Lubin, B. (Eds.). (1999). *Response to disaster: Psychosocial, community, and ecological approaches.* Philadelphia, PA: Brunner-Mazel.

Goodman, R. D., Miller, M. D., & West-Olatunji, C. A. (2012). Traumatic stress, socioeconomic status, and academic achievement among primary school students. *Psychological Trauma: Theory, Research, Practice, and Policy, 4*, 252–259. doi:10.1037/a0024912

Goodwin, R., Palgi, Y., Hamama-Raz, Y., & Ben-Ezra, M. (2013). Letter to the editor. In the eye of the storm or bullseye of the media: Social media use during Hurricane Sandy as a predictor of post-traumatic stress. *Journal of Psychiatric Research, 47*, 1099–1110. doi:10.1016/j.jpsychires.2013.04.006

Gordon, R. S. (1983). An operational classification of disease prevention. *U.S. Department of Health and Human Services Public Health Report 1983, 98*, 107–109. Retrieved from http://www.ncbi.nlm.nih.gov/pmc/articles/PMC1424415/

Goss v. Lopez, 419 U.S. 565, 95 S. Ct. 729 (1975).

Gottfredson, D. (1997). School-based crime prevention. In L. W. Sherman, D. Gottfredson, D. MacKenzie, J. Eck, P. Reuter, & S. Bushway (Eds.), *Preventing crime: What works, what doesn't, what's promising: A report to the United States Congress.* Washington, DC: Department of Justice, Office of Justice Programs. Retrieved from https://www.ncjrs.gov/works/

Gracie, A., Freeman, D., Green, S., Garety, P. A., Kuipers, E., Hardy, A., . . . Fowler, E. (2007). The association between traumatic experience, paranoia and hallucinations: A test of the predictions of psychological models. *Acta Psychiatrica Scandinavica, 116*, 280–289. doi: 10.1111/j.1600-0447.2007.01011.x

Graham, J., Shirm, S., Liggin, R., Aitken, M. E., & Dick, R. (2006). Mass-casualty events at schools: A national preparedness survey. *Pediatrics, 117*, 8–15. doi:10.1542/peds.2005-0927

Gray, L., & Lewis, L. (2015). *Public school safety and discipline: 2013–14* (NCES 2015-051). Washington, DC: U.S. Department of Education, National Center for Education Statistics. Retrieved from http://nces.ed.gov/pubsearch

Green, B. L. (1994). Psychosocial research in traumatic stress: An update. *Journal of Traumatic Stress, 7*, 341–361. doi:10.1002/jts.2490070303

Green, B. L., Korol, M., Grace, M. C., Vary, M. G., Leonard, A. C., Gleser, G. C., & Smitson-Cohen, S. (1991). Children and disaster: Age, gender, and parental effects on PTSD symptoms. *Journal of the American Academy of Child and Adolescent Psychiatry, 30*, 945–951. doi:10.1097/00004583-199111000-00012

Green, W. G., III (2002, August). *The Incident Command System for public health disaster responders.* Paper presented at the meeting of the Public Health Task Group, Richmond Metropolitan Medical Response System, Richmond, VA.

Greif, J. L., & Furlong, M. J. (2006). The assessment of school bullying: Using theory to inform practice. *Journal of School Violence, 5,* 33–50. doi:10.1300/J202v05n03_04

Grieger, T. A., Fullerton, C. S., & Ursano, R. J. (2003). Posttraumatic stress disorder, alcohol use, and perceived safety after the terrorist attack on the Pentagon. *Psychiatric Services, 54,* 1380–1382. Retrieved from http://ps.psychiatryonline.org/journal.aspx?journalid=18

Groome, D., & Soureti, A. (2004). Post-traumatic stress disorder and anxiety symptoms in children exposed to the 1999 Greek earthquake. *British Journal of Psychology, 95,* 387–397. doi:10.1348/0007126041528149

Grosse, S. J. (2001, September). *Children and post traumatic stress disorder: What classroom teachers should know.* Washington, DC: ERIC Clearinghouse on Teaching and Teacher Education. Retrieved from http://www.ericdigests.org/2002-3/post.htm

Guba, E. G., & Lincoln, Y. S. (1989). *Fourth generation evaluation.* Newbury Park, CA: SAGE.

Guha-Sapir, D., Hoyois, P., & Below, R. (2014). *Annual disaster statistical review 2013: The numbers and trends. Brussels, Belgium: Centre for Research on the Epidemiology of Disasters (CRED).* Retrieved from http://www.cred.be/sites/default/files/ADSR_2013.pdf

Gurdineer, E. E. (2013). The impact of demographics, resources, and training on the quality of school crisis plans. Retrieved from http://gradworks.umi.com/35/65/3565074.html

Gurwitch, R. H., Sitterle, K. A., Yound, B. H., & Pfefferbaum, B. (2002). The aftermath of terrorism. In A. M. La Greca, W. K. Silverman, E. M. Vernberg, & M. C. Roberts (Eds.), *Helping children cope with disasters and terrorism* (pp. 327–357). Washington, DC: American Psychological Association.

Guzman-Lopez, A. (2015, May 18). Compton schools fail to address student trauma, federal lawsuit alleges. *Southern California Public Radio.* Retrieved from http://www.scpr.org/news/2015/05/18/51781/compton-schools-fail-to-address-student-trauma-fed/

Haden, S. C., Scarpa, A., Jones, R. T., & Ollendick, T. H. (2007). Posttraumatic stress disorder symptoms and injury: The moderating role of perceived social support and coping for young adults. *Personality and Individual Differences, 42,* 1187–1198. doi:10.1016/j.paid.2006.09.030

Hagan, J. F., Jr., & American Academy of Pediatrics, Committee on Psychosocial Aspects of Child and Family Health, and Task Force on Terrorism. (2005). Psychosocial implications of disaster or terrorism on children: A guide for the pediatrician. *Pediatrics, 116,* 787–795. doi:10.1542/peds.2005-1498

Hahn, E. E., Hays, R. D., Kahn, K. L., Litwin, M. S., & Ganz, P. A. (2014). Post-traumatic stress symptoms in cancer survivors: Relationship to the impact of cancer scale and other associated risk factors. *Psycho-Oncology.* Advance online publication. doi:10.1002/pon.3623

Halikias, W. (2005). Assessing youth violence and threats of violence in schools: School-based risk assessments. In S. H. McConaughy (Ed.), *Clinical interviews for children and adolescents: Assessment to intervention* (pp. 200–223). New York, NY: Guilford Press.

Hankin, A., Hertz, M., & Simon, T. (2011). Impacts of metal detector use in schools: Insights from 15 years of research. *Journal of School Health, 81,* 100–106. Retrieved from http://www.edweek.org/media/hankin-02security.pdf

Harmon, R. J., & Riggs, P. D. (1996). Clonidine for posttraumatic stress disorder in preschool children. *American Academy of Child and Adolescent Psychiatry, 35,* 1247–1249. doi:10.1097/00004583-199609000-00022

Harrison, A. O., Wilson, M. N., Pine, C. J., Chan, S. Q., & Buriel, R. (1990). Family ecologies of ethnic minority children. *Child Development, 61,* 347–362. doi:10.2307/1131097

Harrison, R. L., & Westwood, M. J. (2009). Preventing vicarious traumatization of mental health therapists: Identifying protective practices. *Psychotherapy: Theory, Research, Practice, Training, 46,* 203–219. doi:10.1037/a0016081

Harvey, A. G., & Bryant, R. A. (1998). The relationship between acute stress disorder and posttraumatic stress disorder: A prospective evaluation of motor vehicle accident survivors. *Journal of Consulting and Clinical Psychology, 66,* 507–512. doi:10.1037/0022-006X.67.6.985

Haskett, M. A., Scott, S. S., Nears, K., & Grimmett, M. A. (2008). Lessons from Katrina: Disaster mental health service in the Gulf Coast region. *Professional Psychology: Research and Practice, 39,* 93–99. doi:10.1037/0735-7028.39.1.93

Hawker, D. M., Durkin, J., & Hawker, D. J. (2011). To debrief or not to debrief our heroes: That is the question. *Clinical Psychology & Psychotherapy, 18,* 453–463. doi:10.1002/cpp.730

Hawkins, N. A., McIntosh, D. N., Silver, R., & Holman, E. (2004). Early responses to school violence: A qualitative analysis of students' and parents' immediate reactions to the shootings at Columbine High School. *Journal of Emotional Abuse, 4,* 197–223. doi:10.1300/J135v04n03_12

Hays, P. A. (2008). *Addressing cultural complexities in practice: Assessment, diagnosis, and therapy* (2nd ed., pp. 21–40). Washington, DC: American Psychological Association.

Hazler, R. J., & Carney, J. V. (2000). When victims turn aggressors: Factors in the development of deadly school violence. *Professional School Counseling, 4*(2), 105–112. Retrieved from http://www.schoolcounselor.org/school-counselors-members/publications/professional-school-counseling-journal

Heath, M. A., Bingham, R., & Dean, B. (2008). The role of memorials in helping children heal. *School Psychology Forum, 2,* 17–29. Retrieved from http://www.nasponline.org/publications/periodicals/spf/volume-2/volume-2-issue-2-%28winter-2008%29/the-role-of-memorials-in-helping-children-heal

Heath, M., Ryan, K., Dean, B., & Bingham, R. (2007). History of school safety and psychological first aid for children. *Brief Treatment and Crisis Intervention, 7,* 206–233. doi:10.1093/brief-treatment/mhm011

Heath, M. A., & Sheen, D. (2005). *School-based crisis intervention: Preparing all personnel to assist.* New York, NY: Guilford Press.

Hecker, T., Hermenau, K., Maedl, A., Schauer, M., & Elbert, T. (2013). Aggression inoculates against PTSD symptoms severity—Insights from armed groups in the eastern DR Congo. *European Journal of Psychotraumatology, 4,* 1–9. doi:10.3402/ejpt.v4i0.20070

Henggeler, S. W., Schoenwald, S. K., Rowland, M. D., & Cunningham, P. B. (2002). *Serious emotional disturbance in children and adolescents: Multisystemic therapy.* New York, NY: Guilford Press.

Herrick, C. A., & Brown, H. N. (1998). Underutilization of mental health services by Asian-Americans residing in the United States. *Issues in Mental Health Nursing, 19,* 225–240. doi:10.1080/016128498249042

Hilarski, C. (2004). The relationship between perceived secondary trauma and adolescent comorbid posttraumatic stress and alcohol abuse: A review. *Stress, Trauma, and Crisis, 7,* 119–132. doi:10.1080/15434610490450914

Hill, C. E., Knox, S., Thompson, B. J., Williams, E. N., Hess, S. A., & Ladany, N. (2005). Consensual qualitative research: An update. *Journal of Counseling Psychology, 52,* 443–437. doi:10.1037/0022-0167.52.2.196

Hill, M. S., & Hill, F. W. (1994). *Creating safe schools: What principals can do.* Thousand Oaks, CA: Corwin Press.

Hill, L. G., & Werner, N. E. (2006). Affiliative motivation, school attachment, and aggression in school. *Psychology in the Schools, 43,* 231–246. doi:10.1002/pits.20140

Hinduja, S., & Patchin, J. W. (2011, April). Cyberbullying: Identification, prevention, and response. *Cyberbullying Research Center.* Retrieved from http://cyberbullying.us/cyberbullying-identification-prevention-and-response/

Hobbs, M., Mayou, R., Harrison, B., & Warlock, P. (1996). A randomised controlled trial of psychological debriefing for victims of road traffic accidents. *British Medical Journal, 313,* 1438–1439. Retrieved from http://www.ncbi.nlm.nih.gov/pmc/articles/PMC2352974/

Hobfoll, W. E., Watson, P., Bell, C. C., Bryant, R. A., Brymer, M. J., Friedman, M. J., . . . Ursano, R. J. (2007). Five essential elements of immediate and mid-term mass trauma intervention: Empirical evidence. *Psychiatry, 70,* 283–315. doi:10.1521/psyc.2007.70.4.283

Holloran, L. (2013, May 4). Bulletproof whiteboards and the marketing of school safety. National Public Radio. Retrieved from http://www.npr.org/2013/05/04/180916246/bulletproof-whiteboards-and-the-marketing-of-school-safety

Holt, M. K., & Espelage, D. L. (2007). Perceived social support among bullies, victims and bully-victims. *Journal of Youth and Adolescence, 36,* 984–994. doi:10.1007/s10964-006-9153-3

Hombrados-Mendieta, M., Gomez-Jacinto, L., Dominguez-Fuentes, J., Garcia-Leiva, P., & Castro-Travé, M. (2012). Types of social support provided by parents, teachers, and classmates during adolescence. *Journal of Community Psychology, 40,* 645–664. doi:10.1002/jcop.20523

Horner, R., Sugai, G., & Gresham, F. (2002). Behaviorally effective school environments. In M. R. Shinn, H. M. Walker, & G. Stoner (Eds.), *Interventions for academic and behavior problems II* (pp. 315–350). Bethesda, MD: National Association of School Psychologists.

Horner, R. H., Sugai, G., Todd, A. W., & Lewis-Palmer, T. (2005). School-wide positive behavior support. In L. M. Bambara & L. Kern (Eds.), *Individualized supports for students with problem behaviors: Designing positive behavior support plans* (pp. 359–390). New York, NY: Guilford Press.

Hornor, G. (2013). Posttraumatic stress disorder. *Journal of Pediatric Health Care, 27*, 229–238. doi:10.1016/j.pedhc.2012.07.020

Horowitz, K., McKay, M., & Marshall, R. (2005). Community violence and urban families: Experiences, effects, and directions for intervention. *American Journal of Orthopsychiatry, 75*, 356–368. doi:10.1037/0002-9432.75.3.356

Horowitz, M. J., Wilner, N., & Alvarez, W. (1979). Impact of event scale: A measure of subjective stress. *Psychosomatic Medicine, 41*, 209–218.

House, J. S. (1981). *Work stress and social support.* Reading, MA: Addison-Wesley.

Hoven, C. W., Duarte, C. S., Wu, P., Erickson, E. A., Musa, G. J., & Mandell, D. J. (2004). Exposure to trauma and separation anxiety in children after the WTC attack. *Applied Developmental Science, 8*, 172–183. doi:10.1207/s1532480xads0804_1

Howard, J. M., & Goelitz, A. (2004). Psychoeducation as a response to community disaster. *Brief Treatment and Crisis Intervention, 4*, 1–10. doi:10.1093/brief-treatment/mhh001

Huemer, J., Erhart, F., & Steiner, H. (2010). Posttraumatic stress disorder in children and adolescents: A review of psychopharmacological treatment. *Child Psychiatry and Human Development, 41*, 624–640. doi:10.1007/s10578-010-0192-3

Hunt, M. H., Meyers, J., Davies, G., Meyers, B., Grogg, K. R., & Neel, J. (2002). A comprehensive needs assessment to facilitate prevention of school drop out and violence. *Psychology in the Schools, 39*, 399–416. doi:10.1002/pits.10019

Hunter, S. V., & Schofield, M. J. (2006). How counsellors cope with traumatized clients: Personal, professional and organizational strategies. *Journal for the Advancement of Counseling, 28*, 121–138. doi:10.1007/s10447-005-9003-0

Hurt, H., Malmud, E., Brodsky, N. L., & Giannetta, J. (2001). Exposure to violence: Psychological and academic correlates in child witnesses. *Archives of Pediatrics & Adolescent Medicine, 155*, 1351–1356. doi:10.1001/archpedi.155.12.1351

Hussain, A., Weisaeth, L., & Heir, T. (2011). Psychiatric disorders and functional impairment among disaster victims after exposure to a natural disaster: A population based study. *Journal of Affective Disorders, 128*, 135–141. doi:10.1016/j.jad.2010.06.018

Illinois State Board of Education. (n.d.) *Multi-hazard emergency planning for Illinois schools and school emergency and crisis response plan.* Springfield, IL: Author. Retrieved from http://www.isbe.net/safety/guide.htm

Imanaka, A., Morinobu, S., Toki, S., & Yamawaki, S. (2006). Importance of early environment in the development of post-traumatic stress disorder-like behaviors. *Behavioural Brain Research, 173*, 129–137. doi:10.1016/j.bbr.2006.06.012

Indian, M., & Grieve, R. (2014). When Facebook is easier than face-to-face: Social support derived from Facebook in socially anxious individuals. *Personality and Individual Differences, 59*, 102–106. doi:10.1016/j.paid.2013.11.016

Ingvarson, L., Meiers, M., & Beavis, A. (2005). Factors affecting the impact of professional development programs on teachers' knowledge, practice, student outcomes, and efficacy. *Education Policy Analysis Archives, 13*(10), 1–26. Retrieved from http://epaa.asu.edu/ojs/article/view/115

Interdisciplinary Group on Preventing School and Community Violence. (2013). December 2012 Connecticut school shooting position statement. *Journal of School Violence, 12,* 119–133. doi:10.1080/15388220.2012.762488.

Ironson, G., Freud, B., Strauss, J. L., & Williams, J. (2002). Comparison for two treatments for traumatic stress: A community-based study of EMDR and prolonged exposure. *Journal of Clinical Psychology, 58,* 113–128. doi:10.1002/jclp.1132

Irvin, L. K., Tobin, T. J., Sprague, J. R., Sugai, G., & Vincent, C. G. (2004). Validity of office discipline referrals measures as indices of school-wide behavioral status and effects of school-wide behavioral interventions. *Journal of Positive Behavior Interventions, 6,* 131–147. doi:10.1177/10983007040060030201

Jacob, S., & Feinberg, T. (2002). Legal and ethical issues in crisis prevention and response in schools. In S. E. Brock, P. J. Lazarus, & S. R. Jimerson (Eds.), *Best practices in school crisis prevention and intervention* (pp. 709–732). Bethesda, MD: National Association of School Psychologists.

Jacobs, J., Horne-Moyer, H., & Jones, R. (2004). The effectiveness of critical incident stress debriefing with primary and secondary trauma victims. *International Journal of Emergency Mental Health, 6,* 5–14. Retrieved from https://www.chevronpublishing.com/product.cfm?dispprodid=480

James, B. (2013, Winter). Legal update. School safety legal reform: The year 2013. *Journal of School Safety,* 14–18. Retrieved from http://www.mydigitalpublication.com/publication/?i=191962&p=3

James, R. K., Logan, J., & Davis, S. (2011). Including school resource officers in school-based crisis intervention: Strengthening student support. *School Psychology International, 32,* 210–224. doi:10.1177/0143034311400828

Jarero, I., Artigas, L., & Hartung, J. (2006). EMDR integrative group treatment protocol: A post-disaster trauma intervention for children and adults. *Traumatology, 12,* 121–129. doi:10.1177/1534765606294561

Jarmuz-Smith, S. (2014). *Using technology responsibly in school safety planning and response* [Handout]. Bethesda, MD: National Association of School Psychologists.

Jaycox, L. (2004). *CBITS: Cognitive behavioral intervention for trauma in schools.* Longmont, CO: Sopris West.

Jaycox, L. H., Cohen, J. A., Mannarino, A. P., Walker, D. W., Walker, D. W., Langley, . . . Schonlau, M. (2010). Children's mental health care following Hurricane Katrina: A field trial of trauma-focused psychotherapies. *Journal of Traumatic Stress, 23*(2), 223–231, doi:10.1002/jts20518

Jaycox, L. H., Langley, A. K., Stein, B. D., Wong, M., Sharma, P., Scott, M., & Schonlau, M. (2009). Support for students exposed to trauma: A pilot study. *School Mental Health, 1,* 49–60. doi:10.1007/s12310-009-9007-8

Jaycox, L. H., Stein, B. D., & Wong, M. (2014). School intervention related to school and community violence. *Child and Adolescent Psychiatric Clinics of North America, 23,* 281–293. doi:10.1016/j.chc.2013.12.005

Jaycox, L. H., Tanielian, T. L., Sharma, P., Morse, L., Clum, G., & Stein, B. D. (2007). Schools' mental health responses after Hurricanes Katrina and Rita. *Psychiatric Services, 58,* 1339–1343. doi:10.1176/appi.ps.58.10.1339

Jeney-Gammon, P., Daugherty, T. K., Finch, A. J., Belter, R. W., & Foster, K. Y. (1993). Children's coping styles and report of depressive symptoms following a natural disaster. *Journal of Genetic Psychology: Research and Theory on Human Development, 154,* 259–267. doi:10.1080/002213 25.1993.9914739

Jeffery, C. R. (1971). *Crime prevention through environmental design.* Beverly Hills, CA: SAGE.

Jenkins, S. R., & Baird, S. (2002). Secondary traumatic stress and vicarious trauma: A validational study. *Journal of Traumatic Stress, 15,* 423–432. doi:10.1023/A:1020193526843

Ji, P. Y., DuBois, D. L., Flay, B. R., & Brechling, V. (2008). "Congratulations, you have been randomized into the control group!(?)": Issues to consider when recruiting schools for matched-pair randomized control trials of prevention programs. *Journal of School Health, 78,* 131–139. doi:10.1111/j.1746-1561.2007.00275.x

Jimerson, S. R., Brock, S. E., & Cowan, K. (2003). *Helping children after a wildfire: Tips for parents and teachers.* Retrieved from www.nasponline.org/assets/documents/Resources%20and%20 Publications/Handouts/Safety%20and%20Crisis/katrina_reactions.pdf

Jimerson, S. R., Brock, S. E., & Cowan, K. (2007). *Ayudando A Los Niños Después De Los Incendios Forestales: Consejos Para Los Padres y Maestros* (L. Navarro, E. Terán, & M. Muñoz, Trans.). Sacramento, CA: California State University.

Jimerson, S. R., Brown, J. A., Saeki, E., Watanabe, Y., Kobayashi, T., & Hatzichristou, C. (2012). Natural disasters. In S. E. Brock & S. R. Jimerson (Eds.), *Best practices in school crisis prevention and intervention* (2nd ed., pp. 573–595). Bethesda, MD: National Association of School Psychologists.

Jimerson S. R., & Huff, L. (2002). Responding to a sudden, unexpected death at school: Chance favors the prepared professional. In S. E. Brock, P. J. Lazarus, & S. R. Jimerson (Eds.), *Best practices in school crisis prevention and intervention* (pp. 451–488). Bethesda, MD: National Association of School Psychologists.

Jimerson, S. R., Nickerson, A. B., Mayer, M. J., & Furlong, M. J. (2014). *The handbook of school violence and school safety: International research and practice* (2nd ed.). New York, NY: Routledge.

Johnson, K. (1993). *School crisis management: A hands-on guide to training crisis response teams.* Alameda, CA: Hunter House.

Johnson, K. (2000). *School crisis management: A hands-on guide to training crisis management teams* (2nd ed.). Alameda, CA: Hunter House.

Jordan, K. (2010). Vicarious trauma: Proposed factors that impact clinicians. *Journal of Family Psychotherapy, 21,* 225–237. doi:10.1080/08975353.2010.529003

Jones, J. M. (2007). Exposure to chronic community violence: Resilience in African American children. *Journal of Black Psychology, 33,* 125–149. doi:10.1177/0095798407299511

Jones, L. (2005). Soapbox: A letter from Northern Iraq, 2003. *Clinical Child Psychology and Psychiatry, 10,* 266–272. doi:10.1177/1359104505051215

Jones, L. (2008). Responding to the needs of children in crisis. *International Review of Psychiatry, 20,* 291–303. doi:10.1080/09540260801996081

Jones, R. T., Fletcher, K., & Ribbe, D. R. (2002). *Child's Reaction to Traumatic Events Scale–Revised (CRTES-R): A self-report traumatic stress measure.* Retrieved from http://www.psyc.vt.edu/sites/default/files/inline_files/Page84/crtes.pdf

Joseph, S. (1999). Social support and mental health following trauma. In W. Yule (Ed.), *Post-traumatic stress disorders, concepts and therapy* (pp. 71–91). New York, NY: Wiley.

Joshi, P. T., & Lewin, S. M. (2004). Disaster, terrorism and children. *Psychiatric Annals, 34,* 710–716. doi:10.3928/0048-5713-20040901-16

Joyce, H. D., & Early, T. J. (2014). The impact of school connectedness and teacher support on depressive symptoms in adolescents: A multilevel analysis. *Children and Youth Services Review, 39,* 101–107. doi:10.1016/j.childyouth.2014.02.005

Juszczak, L., Melinkovich, P., & Kaplan, D. (2003). Use of health and mental health services by adolescents across multiple delivery sites. *Journal of Adolescent Health, 32*(Suppl. l6), 108–118. doi:10.1016/S1054-139X(03)00073-9

Kadak, M. T., Nasiroğlu, S., Boysan, M., & Aydin, A. (2013). Risk factors predicting posttraumatic stress reactions in adolescents after 2011 Van earthquake. *Comprehensive Psychiatry, 54,* 982–990. doi:10.1016/j.comppsych.2013.04.003

Kailes, J. I., & Enders, A. (2007). Moving beyond "special needs": A function-based framework for emergency management and planning. *Journal of Disability Policy Studies, 17,* 230–237. doi:10.1177/10442073070170040601

Kang-Brown, J., Trone, J., Fratello, J., & Daftary-Kapur, T. (2013). *A generation later: What we've learned about zero tolerance in schools.* New York, NY: Vera Institute of Justice, Center on Youth Justice. Retrieved from http://www.vera.org/pubs/zero-tolerance-in-schools-issue-brief

Kaniasty, K. (2012). Predicting social psychological well-being following trauma: The role of postdisaster social support. *Psychological Trauma: Theory, Research, Practice, and Policy, 4,* 22–33. doi:10.1037/a0021412

Kann, L., Kinchen, S., Shanklin, S. L., Flint, K. H., Hawkins, J., Harris, W. A., . . . Zaza, S. (2014, June 13). Youth risk behavior surveillance—United States, 2013; Surveillance summary. *Morbidity and Mortality Weekly Report, 63*(SS04), 1–168. Retrieved from http://www.cdc.gov/mmwr/preview/mmwrhtml/ss6304a1.htm?s_cid=ss6304a1_e

Kano, M., & Bourke, L. B. (2007). Experiences with and preparedness for emergencies and disasters among public schools in California. *NASSP Bulletin, 91*(3), 201–218. doi:10.1177/0192636507305102

Kano, M., Ramirez, M., Ybarra, W. J., Frias, G., & Bourque, L. B. (2007). Are schools prepared for emergencies? A baseline assessment of emergency preparedness at school sites in three Los Angeles County school districts. *Education and Urban Society, 39,* 399–422. doi:10.1177/0013124506298130

Kassai, S. C., & Motta, R. W. (2006). An investigation of potential Holocaust-related secondary traumatization in the third generation. *International Journal of Emergency Mental Health, 8,* 35–48. Retrieved from https://www.chevronpublishing.com/product.cfm?dispprodid=480

Kaštelan, A., Frančišković, Moro, L., Rončević, G. I., Grković, J., Jurcan, V., Lesica, T., Braovac, M., & Girotto, I. (2007). Psychotic symptoms in combat-related post-traumatic stress disorder. *Military Medicine, 172,* 273–277. Retrieved from http://publications.amsus.org/

Kataoka, S. H., Nadeem, E., Wong, M., Langley, A. K., Jaycox, L. H., Stein, B. D., & Young, P. (2009). Improving disaster mental health care in schools: A community-partnered approach. *American Journal of Preventive Medicine, 37*(6, Suppl. 1), S225–S229. doi:10.1016/j.amepre.2009.08.002

Kataoka, S. H., Stein, B. D., Jaycox, L. H., Wong, M., Escudero, P., Tu, W., . . . Fink, A. (2003). A school-based mental health program for traumatized Latino immigrant children. *Journal of the American Academy of Child and Adolescent Psychiatry, 42,* 311–318. doi:10.1097/01.CHI.0000037038.04952.8E

Kaufman-Shriqui, V., Werbeloff, N., Faroy, M., Meiri, G., Shahar, D. R., Fraser, D., . . . Harpaz-Rotem, I. (2013). Posttraumatic stress disorder among preschoolers exposed to ongoing missile attacks in the Gaza war. *Depression and Anxiety, 30,* 425–431. doi:10.1002/da.22121

Kazdin, A. E. (2003). Problem-solving skills training and parent management training for conduct disorder. In A. E. Kazdin & J. R. Weisz (Eds.), *Evidence-based psychotherapy for children and adolescents* (pp. 241–262). New York, NY: Guilford Press.

Kazdin, A. E., & Weisz, J. R. (Eds.). (2003). *Evidence-based psychotherapies for children and adolescents.* New York, NY: Guilford Press.

Kelloway, E. K., Mullen, J., & Francis, L. (2012). The stress (of an) epidemic. *Stress and Health, 28,* 91–97. doi:10.1002/smi.1406

Kennedy-Paine, C., & Crepeau-Hobson, F. (2015). FBI study of active shooter incidents: Implications for school psychologists. *Communiqué, 43*(7), 1, 22. Retrieved from http://www.nasponline.org/publications/periodicals/communique/issues/volume-43-issue-7/fbi-study-of-active-shooter-incidents-implications-for-school-psychologists

Keppel-Benson, J. M., Ollendick, T. H., & Benson, M. J. (2002). Post-traumatic stress in children following motor vehicle accidents. *Journal of Child Psychology and Psychiatry and Allied Disciplines, 43,* 203–212. doi:10.1111/1469-7610.00013

Kerres Malecki, C., & Kilpatrick Demaray, M. (2002). Measuring perceived social support: Development of the Child and Adolescent Social Support Scale. *Psychology in the Schools, 39,* 1–18. doi:10.1002/pits.10004

Keyes, J. M. (2011). *Standard reunification method: A practical method to unite students with parents after an evacuation or crisis.* Bailey, CO: "I Love U Guys" Foundation. Retrieved from http://iloveuguys.org/srm/Standard%20Reunification%20Method.pdf

Khanna, M. S., & Kendall, P. C. (2009). Exploring the role of parent training in the treatment of childhood anxiety. *Journal of Consulting and Clinical Psychology, 77,* 981–986. doi:10.1037/a0016920

Kiliç, C., Kiliç, E. Z., & Aydin, I. O. (2011). Effect of relocation and parental psychopathology on earthquake survivor-children's mental health. *Journal of Nervous and Mental Disease, 199,* 335–341. doi:10.1097/NMD.0b013e3182174ffa.

Kiliç, E. Z., Özgüven, H. D., & Sayil, I. (2003). The psychological effects of parental mental health on children experiencing disaster: The experience of Bolu earthquake in Turkey. *Family Process, 42,* 485–495. doi:10.1111/j.1545-5300.2003.00485.x

Kilmer, R. P. (2006). Resilience and posttraumatic growth in children. In L. G. Calhoun & R. G. Tedeschi (Eds.), *Handbook of posttraumatic growth: Research and practice* (pp. 264–288). Mahwah, NJ: Erlbaum.

Kilpatrick, D. G., Cougle, J. R., & Resnick, H. S. (2008). Reports of the death of psychoeducation as a preventative treatment for posttraumatic psychological distress are exaggerated. *Psychiatry: Interpersonal and Biological Processes, 71,* 322–328. doi:10.1521/psyc.2008.71.4.322

Kim, H. K., & McKenry, P. C. (1998). Social networks and support: A comparison of African Americans, Asian Americans, Caucasians, and Hispanics. *Journal of Comparative Family Studies, 29,* 313–334. Retrieved from https://soci.ucalgary.ca/jcfs/

King, D. A., King, L. A., Foy, B. W., & Gudanowski, D. M. (1996). Prewar factors in combat-related posttraumatic stress disorder: Structural equation modeling with a national sample of female and male Vietnam veterans. *Journal of Consulting and Clinical Psychology, 64,* 520–531. doi:10.1037/0022-006X.64.3.520

King, L. A., King, D. W., Fairbank, J. A., Keane, T. M., & Adams, G. A. (1998). Resilience-recovery factors in post-traumatic stress disorder among female and male Vietnam veterans: Hardiness, postwar social support, and additional stressful life events. *Journal of Personality and Social Psychology, 74,* 420–434. doi:10.1037/0022-3514.74.2.420

King, N. J., Tongue, B. J., Mullen, P., Myerson, N., Heyne, D., Rollings, S., & Ollendick, T. H. (2000). Treating sexually abused children with posttraumatic stress symptoms: A randomized clinical trial. *Journal of the American Academy of Child and Adolescent Psychiatry, 39,* 1347–1355. doi:10.1097/00004583-200011000-00008

Kintzle, S., Yarvis, J. S., & Bride, B. E. (2013). Secondary traumatic stress in military primary and mental health care providers. *Military Medicine, 178,* 1310–1315. doi:10.7205/MILMED-D-13-00087

Kinzie, J. D., Sack, W. H., Angell, R. H., Manson, S., & Rath, B. (1986). The psychiatric effects of massive trauma on Cambodian children: I. The children. *Journal of the American Academy of Child Psychiatry, 25,* 370–376. doi:10.1016/S0002-7138(09)60259-4

Kirkpatrick, D. (1996). Great ideas revisited: Techniques for evaluating training programs. Revisiting Kirkpatrick's four-level model. *Training and Development, 50,* 54–59.

Kitsantas, A., Ware, H. W., & Martinez-Arias, R. (2004). Students' perceptions of school safety: Effects by community, school environment, and substance use variables. *Journal of Early Adolescence, 24,* 412–430. doi:10.1177/0272431604268712

Klarić, M., Kvesić, A., Mandić, V., Petrov, B., & Frančišković, T. (2013). Secondary traumatisation and systemic traumatic stress. *Psychiatria Danubina, 25*(Suppl 1), 29–36. Retrieved from http://www.ncbi.nlm.nih.gov/pubmed/23806964

Kleiman, E. M., Riskind, J. H., & Schaefer, K. E. (2014). Social support and positive events as suicide resiliency factors: Examination of synergistic buffering effects. *Archives of Suicide Research, 18,* 144–155. doi:10.1080/13811118.2013.826155

Kleiman, E. M., Riskind, J. H., Schaefer, K. E., & Weingarden, H. (2012). The moderating role of social support on the relationship between impulsivity and suicide risk. *Crisis: The Journal of Crisis Intervention and Suicide Prevention, 33,* 273–279. doi:10.1027/0227-5910/a000136

Kline, M., Schonfeld, D., & Lichtenstein, R. (1995). Benefits and challenges of school-based crisis response teams. *Journal of School Health, 65,* 245–249. doi:10.1111/j.1746-1561.1995.tb07894.x

Klingman, A. (1985). Free writing: Evaluation of a preventive program with elementary school children. *Journal of School Psychology, 23,* 167–175. doi:10.1016/0022-4405(85)90007-X

Klingman, A. (1986). Emotional first aid during the impact phase of a mass disaster. *Emotional First Aid, 3,* 51–57.

Klingman, A. (1987). A school-based emergency crisis intervention in a mass school disaster. *Professional Psychology: Research and Practice, 18,* 604–612. doi:10.1037/0735-7028.18.6.604

Klingman, A. (2001). Stress responses and adaptation of Israeli school-age children evacuated from homes during massive missile attacks. *Anxiety, Stress & Coping: An International Journal, 14,* 149–172. doi:10.1080/10615800108248352

Klingman, A., & Cohen, E. (2004). *School-based multisystemic interventions for mass trauma.* New York, NY: Kluwer Academic/Plenum.

Klott, J. (2012). *Suicide & psychological pain: Prevention that works.* Eau Claire, WI: Premier Publishing & Media.

Kneisel, P. J., & Richards, G. P. (1988). Crisis intervention after the suicide of a teacher. *Professional Psychology: Research and Practice, 19,* 165–169. doi:10.1037/0735-7028.19.2.165

Kodluboy, D. W. (2010). Memorials: School response to the death of members of the school community. In A. S. Canter, L. Z. Paige, & S. Shaw (Eds.), *Helping children at home and school III: Handouts for families and educators* (S9H12). Bethesda, MD: National Association of School Psychologists.

Kolaitis, G., Kotsopoulos, J., Tsiantis, J., Haritaki, S., Rigizou, R., Zacharaki, L., . . . Katerelos, P. (2003). Posttraumatic stress reactions among children following the Athens earthquake of September 1999. *European Child & Adolescent Psychiatry, 12,* 273–280. doi:10.1007/s00787-003-0339-x

Koopman, C. C., Catherine, S., & David, A. (1994). Predictors of posttraumatic stress symptoms among survivors of the Oakland/Berkeley, Calif., firestorm. *American Journal of Psychiatry, 151,* 888–894. Retrieved from http://ajp.psychiatryonline.org/journal.aspx?journalid=13

Kranzler, A., Hoffman, L. J., Parks, A. C., & Gillham, J. E. (2014). Innovative models of dissemination for school-based interventions that promote youth resilience and well-being. In M. J. Furlong, R. Gilman, & E. S. Huebner (Eds.), *Handbook of positive psychology in schools* (2nd ed., pp. 381–397). New York, NY: Routledge.

Kratochwill, T. R., & Shernoff, E. S. (2003). Evidence-based practice: Promoting evidence-based interventions in school psychology. *School Psychology Quarterly, 18,* 389–408. doi:10.1521/scpq.18.4.389.27000

Krause, E. D., Kaltman, S., Goodman, L. A., & Dutton, M. A. (2008). Avoidant coping and PTSD symptoms related to domestic violence exposure: A longitudinal study. *Journal of Traumatic Stress, 21,* 83–90. doi:10.1002/jts.20288

Kronenberg, M. E., Hansel, T. C., Brennan, A. M., Osofsky, H. J., Osofsky, J. D., & Lawrason, B. (2010). Children of Katrina: Lesson learned about postdisaster symptoms and recovery patterns. *Child Development, 81,* 1241–1259. doi:10.1111/j.1467-8624.2010.01465.x

Krupnick, J. L., & Green, B. L. (2008). Psychoeducation to prevent PTSD: A paucity of evidence. *Psychiatry: Interpersonal and Biological Processes, 71,* 329–331. doi:10.1521/psyc.2008.71.4.329

Kumar, M., & Fonagy, P. (2013). Differential effects of exposure to social violence and natural disaster on children's mental health. *Journal of Traumatic Stress, 26,* 695–702. doi:10.1002/jts.21874

Kutz, I., & Dekel, R. (2006). Follow-up of victims of one terrorist attack in Israel: ASD, PTSD and the perceived threat of Iraqi missile attacks. *Personality and Individual Differences, 40,* 1579–1589. doi:10.1016/j.paid.2006.01.00d

La Greca, A. M., & Prinstein, M. J. (2002). Hurricanes and earthquakes. In A. M. La Greca, W. K. Silverman, E. M. Vernberg, & M. C. Roberts (Eds.), *Helping children cope with disasters and terrorism* (pp. 107–138). Washington, DC: American Psychological Association.

Lai, B. S., Kelley, M. L., Harrison, K. M., Thompson, J. E., & Self-Brown, S. (2014). Posttraumatic stress, anxiety, and depression symptoms among children after Hurricane Katrina: A latent profile analysis. *Journal of Family Studies.* Advance online publication. doi:10.1007/s10826-014-9934-3

Lambert, J. E., Holzer, J., & Hasbun, A. (2014). Association between parents' PTSD severity and children's psychological distress: A meta-analysis. *Journal of Traumatic Stress, 27,* 9–17. doi:10.1002/jts.21891

Lambert, S. F., & Lawson, G. (2013). Resilience of professional counselors following Hurricanes Katrina and Rita. *Journal of Counseling and Development, 91*, 261–268. doi:10.1002/j.1556-6676.2013.00094.x

Landolt, M., Vollrath, M., Timm, K., Gnehm, H. E., & Sennhauser, F. H. (2005). Predicting posttraumatic stress symptoms in children after road traffic accidents. *Journal of the American Academy of Child and Adolescent Psychiatry, 44*, 1276–1283. doi:10.1097/01.chi.0000181045.13960.67

Larson, J. (2008). Best practices in school violence prevention. In A. Thomas & J. Grimes (Eds.), *Best practices in school psychology V* (pp. 1291–1307). Bethesda, MD: National Association of School Psychologists.

Laubmeier, K. K., & Sakowski, S. G. (2004). The role of objective versus perceived life threat in the psychological adjustment to cancer. *Psychology and Health, 19*, 425–437. doi:10.1080/0887044042000196719

Lawyer, S. R., Resnick, H. S., Galea, S., Ahern, J., Kilpatrick, D. G., & Vlahov, D. (2006). Predictors of peritraumatic reactions and PTSD following the September 11th terrorist attacks. *Psychiatry, 69*, 130–141. doi:10.1521/psyc.2006.69.2.130

Layne, C. M., Greeson, J. P., Ostrowski, S. A., Kim, S., Reading, S., Vivrette, R. L., . . . Pynoos, R. S. (2014). Cumulative trauma exposure and high risk behavior in adolescence: Findings from the National Child Traumatic Stress Network Core Data Set. *Psychological Trauma: Theory, Research, Practice, and Policy, 6*(Suppl. 1), S40–S49. doi:10.1037/a0037799

Layne, C. M., Pynoos, R. S., Saltzman, W. S., Arslanagic, B., Black, M., Savjak, N., . . . Houston, R. (2001). Trauma/grief-focused group psychotherapy: School-based post-war intervention with traumatized Bosnian adolescents. *Group Dynamics: Theory, Research, and Practice, 5*, 277–290. doi:10.1037/1089-2699.5.4.277

Lazzaro, B. R. (2013). *A survey study of PREPaRE workshop participants' application of knowledge, confidence levels, and utilization of school crisis response and recovery training curriculum* (Doctoral dissertation). Retrieved from http://ecommons.luc.edu/luc_diss/674

Lecic-Tosevski, D., Gavrlovic, J., Knezevic, G., & Priebe, S. (2003). Personality factors and posttraumatic stress: Associations in civilians one year after air attacks. *Journal of Personality Disorders, 17*, 537–549. doi:10.1521/pedi.17.6.537.25358

Lee, C. W., & Cuijpers, P. (2013). A meta-analysis of the contribution of eye movements in processing emotional memories. *Journal of Behavior Therapy and Experimental Psychiatry, 44*, 231–239. doi:10.1016/j.jbtep.2012.11.001

Lengua, L. J., Long, A. C., Smith, K. I., & Meltzoff, A. N. (2005). Pre-attack symptomatology and temperament as predictors of children's responses to the September 11 terrorist attacks. *Journal of Child Psychology and Psychiatry, 46*, 631–645. doi:10.1111/j.1469-7610.2004.00378.x

Levitt, M. J., Guacci-Franco, N., & Levitt, J. L. (1993). Convoys of social support in childhood and early adolescence: Structure and function. *Developmental Psychology, 29*, 811–818. doi:10.1037/0012-1649.29.5.811

Levitt, M. J., Levitt, J., Bustos, G. L., Crooks, N. A., Santos, J. D., Telan, P., . . . Milevsky, A. (2005). Patterns of social support in the middle childhood to early adolescent transition: Implications for adjustment. *Social Development, 14,* 398–420. doi:10.1111/j.1467-9507.2005.00308.x

Levy, M. S. (2008). The impact of Katrina: Shedding light on things forgotten. *Professional Psychology: Research and Practice, 39,* 31–36. doi:10.1037/0735-7028.39.1.31

Lewis, S. J. (2003). Do one-shot preventive interventions for PTSD work? A systematic research synthesis of psychological debriefings. *Aggression and Violent Behavior, 8,* 329–343. doi:10.1016/S1359-1789(01)00079-9

Lewinsohn, P. M., Rohde, P., & Seeley, J. R. (1996). Adolescent suicidal ideation and attempts: Prevalence, risk factors, and clinical implications. *Clinical Psychology: Research and Practice, 3,* 25–46. doi:10.1111/j.1468-2850.1996.tb00056.x

Li, X., Huang, X., Tan, H., Liu, A., Zhou, J., & Yang, T. (2010). A study on the relationship between posttraumatic stress disorder in flood victim parents and children in Hunan, China. *Australian and New Zealand Journal of Psychiatry, 44,* 543–550. Retrieved from http://anp.sagepub.com/content/by/year

Liang, B., & Bogat, G. (1994). Culture, control, and coping: New perspectives on social support. *American Journal of Community Psychology, 22,* 123–147. doi:10.1007/BF02506820

Lieberman, R., Poland, S., & Kornfeld, C. (2014). Best practices in suicide prevention and intervention. In P. Harrison & A. Thomas (Eds.), *Best practices in school psychology: Systems-level services* (pp. 273–288). Bethesda, MD: National Association of School Psychologists.

Lilienfeld, S. O., & Arkowitz, H. (2007). EMDR: Taking a closer look. *Scientific American Special Edition, 17,* 10–11. doi:10.1038/scientificamerican1207-10sp

Lipson, J. G., & Askaryar, R. (2005). Afghans. In J. G. Lipson & S. L. Dibble (Eds.), *Culture & clinical care* (pp. 1–13). San Francisco, CA: UCSF Nursing Press.

Litz, B. T. (2008). Early intervention for trauma: Where are we and where do we need to go? A commentary. *Journal of Traumatic Stress, 21,* 503–506. doi:10.1002/jts.20373

Litz, B. T., Gray, M. J., Bryant, R. A., & Adler, A. (2002). Early intervention for trauma: Current status and future directions. *Clinical Psychology: Science and Practice, 9,* 112–134. doi:10.1093/clipsy/9.2.112

Longman, H., O'Connor, E., & Obst, P. (2009). The effect of social support derived from World of Warcraft on negative psychological symptoms. *Cyberpsychology and Behavior, 12,* 563–566. doi:10.1089/cpb.2009.0001

Lonigan, C. J., Phillips, B. M., & Richey, J. A. (2003). Posttraumatic stress disorder in children: Diagnosis, assessment, and associated features. *Child & Adolescent Psychiatric Clinics of North America, 12,* 171–194. doi:10.1016/S1056-4993(02)00105-0

Lonigan, C. J., Shannon, M. P., Finch, A. J., Daughtery, T. K., & Taylor, C. M. (1991). Children's reactions to a natural disaster. *Advanced Behavior and Research Therapy, 13,* 135–154. doi:10.1016/0146-6402(91)90002-R

Lord, J. H. (1990). *Death at school: A guide for teachers, school nurses, counselors, and administrators.* Dallas, TX: Mothers Against Drunk Driving.

Los Angeles Unified School District. (1994, Spring). *A handbook for crisis intervention* (Rev. ed.) Available from the Los Angeles Unified School District, Mental Health Services (6520 Newcastle Ave., Reseda, CA 91335-6230).

Lukens, E. P., & McFarlane, W. R. (2004). Psychoeducation as evidence-based practice: Considerations for practice, research, and policy. *Brief Treatment and Crisis Intervention, 4,* 205–225. doi:10.1093/brief-treatment/mhh019

Luszczynska, A., Benight, C. C., & Cieslak, R. (2009). Self-efficacy and health-related outcomes of collective trauma: A systematic review. *European Psychologist, 14,* 51–62. doi:10.1027/1016-9040.14.1.51

Luthar, S. S. (1991). Vulnerability and resilience: A study of high-risk adolescents. *Child Development, 62,* 600–616. doi:10.2307/1131134

Ma, X., Liu, X., Hu, X., Qiu, C., Wang, Y., Huang, Y., . . . Li, T. (2011). Risk indicators for post-traumatic stress disorder in adolescents exposed to the 5.12 Wenchuan earthquake in China. *Psychiatry Research, 189,* 385–391. doi:10.1016/j.psychres.2010.12.016

Mackler, K. (2007). Review of the Trauma Symptom Checklist for Young Children. In K. F. Geisinger, R. A. Spies, J. F. Carlson, & B. S. Plake (Eds.). *The seventeenth mental measurements yearbook.* Lincoln, NE: Buros Institute of Mental Measurements.

Malecki, C., & Demaray, M. (2003). What type of support do they need? Investigating student adjustment as related to emotional, informational, appraisal, and instrumental support. *School Psychology Quarterly, 18,* 231–252. doi:10.1521/scpq.18.3.231.22576

March, J. S., Amaya-Jackson, L., Murray, M. C., & Schulte, A. (1998). Cognitive-behavioral psychotherapy for children and adolescents with PTSD after a single incident stressor. *Journal of the American Academy of Child and Adolescent Psychiatry, 37,* 585–593. doi:10.1097/00004583-199806000-00008

March, J. S., Amaya-Jackson, L., Terry, R., & Costanzo, P. (1997). Posttraumatic symptomatology in children and adolescents after an industrial fire. *Journal of the American Academy of Child & Adolescent Psychiatry, 36,* 1080–1088. doi:10.1097/00004583-199708000-00015

Marin County Office of Education. (2010). *Emergency plan for students with special needs.* San Rafael, CA: Author. Retrieved from http://notebook.lausd.net/pls/ptl/url/ITEM/D56502944 F626050E0430A0002106050

Marsac, M. L., Donlon, K. A., Hildenbrand, A. K., Winston, F. K., & Kassam-Adams, N. (2014). Understanding recovery in children following traffic-related injuries: Exploring acute traumatic stress reactions, child coping, and coping assistance. *Clinical Child Psychology and Psychiatry, 19,* 233–243. doi:10.1177/1359104513487000

Marsella, A. J. (2010). Ethnocultural aspects of PTSD: An overview of concepts, issues, and treatments. *Traumatology, 16,* 17–26. doi:10.1177/1534765610388062

Marshall, R. D., Beebe, K. L., Oldham, M., & Zaninelli, R. (2001). Efficacy and safety of paroxetine treatment for chronic PTSD: A fixed-dose, placebo-controlled study. *American Journal of Psychiatry, 158,* 1982–1988. doi:10.1176/appi.ajp

Marshall, R. D., Bryant, R. A., Amsel, L., Suh, E. J., Cook, J. M., & Neria, Y. (2007). The psychology of ongoing threat. *American Psychologist, 62,* 304–316. doi:10.1037/0003-066X.62.4.304

Martenyi, F., Brown, E. B., Zhang, H., Koke, S. C., & Prakash, A. (2002). Fluoxetine v. placebo in prevention of relapse in post-traumatic stress disorder. *The British Journal of Psychiatry, 181,* 315–320. doi:10.1192/bjp.181.4.315

Martin, A., & Marchand, A. (2003). Prediction of posttraumatic stress disorder: Peritraumatic dissociation, negative emotions and physical anxiety among French-speaking university students. *Journal of Trauma & Dissociation, 4,* 49–63. doi:10.1300/J229v04n02_04

Martins, G. (2013). *Leader's perspective: Emergency preparedness for students with disabilities—What schools can and should be doing.* Trenton, NJ: New Jersey Council on Developmental Disabilities. Retrieved from http://www.njcommonground.org/emergency-preparedness-for-students-with-disabilities/

Masten, A. S. (2011). Resilience in children threatened by extreme adversity: Frameworks for research, practice, and translational synergy. *Development and Psychopathology, 23,* 493–506. doi:10.1017/S0954579411000198

Masten, A. S. (2014). Global perspectives on resilience in children and youth. *Child Development, 85,* 6–20. doi:10.1111/cdev.12205

Masten, A. S., & Gewirtz, A. H. (2006). Vulnerability and resilience in early child development. In K. McCartney & D. A. Phillips (Eds.), *Handbook of early childhood development* (pp. 22–43). Malden, MA: Blackwell.

Masten, A. S., Herbers, J. E., Cutuli, J. J., & Lafavor, T. L. (2008). Promoting competence and resilience in the school context. *Professional School Counseling, 12,* 76–84. doi:10.5330/PSC.n.2010-12.76

Masten, A. S., & Obradović, J. (2008). Disaster preparation and recovery: Lessons from research on resilience in human development. *Ecology and Society, 13*(1), 9 [Online]. Retrieved from http://www.ecologyandsociety.org/vol13/iss1/art9/

Matsakis, A. (1994). *Post-traumatic stress disorder: A complete treatment guide.* Oakland, CA: New Harbinger.

Maxfield, L., & Hyer, L. (2002). The relationship between efficacy and methodology in studies investigating EMDR treatment of PTSD. *Journal of Clinical Psychology, 58,* 23–41. doi:10.1002/jclp.1127

May, P. A., Serna, P., Hurt, L., & DeBruyn, L. M. (2005). Outcome evaluation of a public health approach to suicide prevention in an American Indian tribal nation. *American Journal of Public Health, 95,* 1238–1244. doi:10.2105/AJPH.2004.040410

Mayou, R. A., Ehlers, A. A., & Hobbs, M. M. (2000). Psychological debriefing for road traffic accident victims: Three-year follow-up of a randomised controlled trial. *The British Journal of Psychiatry, 17*, 589–593. doi:10.1192/bjp.176.6.589

McCann, I. L., & Pearlman, L. A. (1990). Vicarious traumatization: A framework for understanding the psychological effects of working with victims. *Journal of Traumatic Stress, 3*, 131–149. doi:10.1007/BF00975140

McDermott, B. M., Berry, H., & Cobham, V. (2014). Social connectedness: A potential aetiological factor in the development of child post-traumatic stress disorder. *Australian and New Zealand Journal of Psychiatry, 46*, 109–117. doi:10.1177/0004867411433950

McDermott, M., Duffy, M., Percy, A., Fitzgerald, M., & Cole, C. (2013). A school based study of psychological disturbance in children following the Omagh bomb. *Child and Adolescent Psychiatry and Mental Health, 7*, 1–11. doi:10.1186/1753-2000-7-36

McFarlane, A. C. (1987). Posttraumatic phenomena in a longitudinal study of children following a natural disaster. *Journal of the American Academy of Child and Adolescent Psychiatry, 26*, 764–769. doi:10.1097/00004583-198709000-00025

McFarlane, A. C. (1988). The longitudinal course of posttraumatic morbidity: The range of outcomes and their predictors. *The Journal of Nervous and Mental Disease, 176*, 30–39. doi:10.1097/00005053-198801000-00004

McFarlane, A. C., & Yehuda, R. (1996). Resilience, vulnerability, and the course of posttraumatic reactions. In B. A. van der Kolk, A. C. McFarlane, & L. Weisaeth (Eds.), *Traumatic stress: The effects of overwhelming experience on mind, body, and society* (pp. 155–181). New York, NY: Guilford Press.

McIntyre, M., & Reid, B. (1989). *Obstacles to implementation of crisis intervention programs.* Unpublished manuscript, Chesterfield County Schools, Chesterfield, VA.

McLaughlin, K. A., Koenen, K. C., Hill, E. D., Petukhova, M., Sampson, N. A., Zaslavsky, A. M., & Kessler, R. C. (2013). Trauma exposure and posttraumatic stress disorder in a national sample of adolescents. *Journal of the American Academy of Child and Adolescent Psychiatry, 52*, 815–830. doi:10.1016/j.jaac.2013.05.011

McNally, R. J., Bryant, R. A., & Ehlers, A. (2003). Does early psychological intervention promote recovery from posttraumatic stress? *Psychological Sciences in the Public Interest, 4*, 45–80. doi:10.1111/1529-1006.01421

Meraviglia, M. G., Becker, H., Rosenbluth, B., Sanchez, E., & Robertson, T. (2003). The Expect Respect Project: Creating a positive elementary school climate. *Journal of Interpersonal Violence, 18*, 1347–1360. doi:10.1177/0886260503257457

Merikangas, K. R., He, J. P., Burstein, M., Swanson, S. A., Avenevoli, S., Cui, L., . . . Swendsen, J. (2010). Lifetime prevalence of mental disorders in U.S. adolescents: Results from the National Comorbidity Survey Replication–Adolescent Supplement (NCS-A). *Journal of the American Academy of Child and Adolescent Psychiatry, 49*, 980–989. doi:10.1016/j.jaac.2010.05.017

Merikangas K. R., He, J., Burstein, M. E., Swendsen, J., Avenevoli, S., Case, B., . . . Olfson, M. (2011). Service utilization for lifetime mental disorders in U.S. adolescents: Results from the National Comorbidity Survey Adolescent Supplement (NCS-A). *Journal of the American Academy of Child and Adolescent Psychiatry, 50,* 32–45. doi:10.1016/j.jaac.2010.10.006

Merrell, K. W. (2001). *Helping students overcome depression and anxiety: A practical guide.* New York, NY: Guilford Press.

Merrell, K. W., & Gueldner, B. A. (2010). Preventive interventions for students with internalizing disorders: Effective strategies for promoting mental health in schools. In M. R. Shinn & H. M. Walker (Eds.), *Interventions for achievement and behavior problems in a three-tier model including RTI* (pp. 799–823). Bethesda, MD: National Association of School Psychologists.

Metzler, C. W., Biglan, A., Rusby, J. C., & Sprague, J. R. (2001). Evaluation of a comprehensive behavior management program to improve school-wide positive behavior support. *Education and Treatment of Children, 24,* 448–479. Retrieved from http://www.educationandtreatment ofchildren.net/

Meyer-Adams, N., & Conner, B. T. (2008). School violence: Bullying behaviors and the psychosocial environment in middle schools. *Children and Schools, 30,* 211–220. doi:10.1093/cs/30.4.211

Meyers, T. W., & Cornille, T. A. (2002). The trauma of working with traumatized children. In C. R. Figley (Ed.), *Treating compassion fatigue* (pp. 39–55). New York, NY: Brunner-Routledge.

Meyerson, D. A., Grant, K. E., Carter, J. S., & Kilmer, R. P. (2011). Posttraumatic growth among children and adolescents: A systematic review. *Clinical Psychology Review, 31,* 949–964. doi:10.1016/j.cpr.2011.06.003

Milan, S., Zona, K., Acker, J., & Turcios-Cotto, V. (2013). Prospective risk factors for adolescent PTSD: Sources of differential exposure and differential vulnerability. *Journal of Abnormal Child Psychology, 41,* 339–353. doi:10.1007/s10802-012-9677-9

Miller, A. B., Esposito-Smythers, C., & Leichtweis, R. N. (2015). Role of social support in adolescent suicidal ideation and suicide attempts. *Journal of Adolescent Health, 56,* 286–292. doi:10.1016/j.jadohealth.2014.10.265

Miller, D. N. (2011). *Child and adolescent suicidal behavior: School-based prevention, assessment, and intervention.* New York, NY: Guilford Press.

Miller, D. N., & Brock, S. E. (2010). *Identifying, assessing, and treating self-injury at school.* New York, NY: Springer.

Miller, D. N., & Eckert, T. L. (2009). School-based suicide prevention: Research advances and practice implications. *School Psychology Review, 38,* 153–248. Retrieved from http://www.nasponline.org/publications/periodicals/spr/volume-38/volume-38-issue-2/school-based-suicide-prevention-research-advances-and-practice-implications

Miller, D. N., & McConaughy, S. H. (2005). Assessing risk for suicide. In S. H. McConaughy (Ed.), *Clinical interviews for children and adolescents: Assessment to intervention* (pp. 184–199). New York, NY: Guilford Press.

Minnesota School Safety Center. (2011). *Comprehensive school safety guide: Minnesota School Safety Center program.* St. Paul, MN: Department of Public Safety. Retrieved from https://dps.mn.gov/divisions/hsem/mn-school-safety-center/Documents/2011%20Comprehensive%20School%20Safety%20Guide.pdf

Mitchell, J. T., & Everly, G. S. (1996). *Critical incident stress debriefing: An operations manual for the prevention of traumatic stress among emergency services and disaster workers* (2nd ed., Rev.). Ellicott City, MD: Chevron.

Möhlen, H., Parzer, P., Resch, F., & Brunner, R. (2005). Psychosocial support for war-traumatized child and adolescent refugees: Evaluation of a short-term treatment program. *Australian and New Zealand Journal of Psychiatry, 39,* 81–87. doi:10.1111/j.1440-1614.2005.01513.x

Molock, S., Puri, R., Matlin, S., & Barksdale, C. (2006). Relationship between religious coping and suicidal behaviors among African American adolescents. *Journal of Black Psychology, 32,* 366–389. doi:10.1177/0095798406290466

Momma, H., Niu, K., Kobayashi, Y., Huang, C., Otomo, A., Chujo, M., . . . Nagatomi, R. (2014). Leg extension is a pre-disaster modifiable risk factor for post-traumatic stress disorder among survivors of the Great East Japan Earthquake: A retrospective cohort study. *PLoS One, 9*(4), e96131. doi:10.1371/journal.pone.0096131

Monahon, C. (1993). *Children and trauma: A guide for parents and professionals.* San Francisco, CA: Jossey-Bass.

Montgomery County Public Schools. (n.d.). *Emergency preparedness.* Retrieved from http://www.montgomeryschoolsmd.org/emergency/preparedness/

Moos, R., & Billings, A. (1984). Conceptualizing and measuring coping resources and processes. In L. Goldberger & S. Breznitz (Eds.), *Handbook of stress: Theoretical and clinical aspects* (pp. 109–145). New York, NY: Macmillan.

Morgan, K. E., & White, P. R. (2003). The functions of art-making in CISD with children and youth. *International Journal of Emergency Mental Health, 5,* 61–76. Retrieved from https://www.chevronpublishing.com/product.cfm?dispprodid=480

Morley, C. A., & Kohrt, B. A. (2013). Impact of peer support on PTSD, hope, and functional impairment: A mixed-methods study of child soldiers in Nepal. *Journal of Aggression, Maltreatment & Trauma, 22,* 714–734. doi:10.1080/10926771.2013.813882

Morris, Q., Gabert-Quillen, C., & Delahanty, D. (2012). The association between parent PTSD/depression symptoms and child PTSD symptoms: A meta-analysis. *Journal of Pediatric Psychology, 37,* 1076–1088. doi:10.1093/jpepsy/jss091

Morris, A., Lee, T., & Delahanty, D. (2013). Interactive relationship between parent and child event appraisals and child PTSD symptoms after an injury. *Psychological Trauma: Theory, Research, Practice, and Policy, 5,* 554–561. doi:10.1037/a0029894

Morrison, G. M., Furlong, M. J., & Morrison, R. L. (1994). School violence to school safety: Reframing the issue for school psychologists. *School Psychology Review, 23,* 236–256. Retrieved from http://www.nasponline.org/publications/periodicals/spr/volume-23/volume-23-issue-2/school-violence-to-school-safety-reframing-the-issue-for-school-psychologists

Morrison, G. M., Laughlin, J., San Miguel, S., Smith, D. C., & Widaman, K. (1997). Sources of support for school-related issues: Choices of Hispanic adolescents varying in migrant status. *Journal of Youth and Adolescence, 26,* 233–252. doi:10.1023/A:1024508816651

Morsette, A., Swaney, G., Stolle, D., Schuldberg, D., van den Pol, R., & Young, M. (2009). Cognitive Behavioral Intervention for Trauma in Schools (CBITS): School-based treatment on a rural American Indian reservation. *Journal of Behavior Therapy and Experimental Psychiatry, 40,* 169–178. doi:10.1016/j.jbtep.2008.07.006

Moscardino, U., Axia, G., Scrimin, S., & Capello, F. (2007). Narratives from caregivers of children surviving the terrorist attack in Beslan: Issues of health, culture, and resilience. *Social Science & Medicine, 64,* 1776–1787. doi:10.1016/j.socscimed.2006.11.024

Murphy, S., Shevlin, M., Armour, C., Elklit, A., & Christoffersen, M. N. (2014). Childhood adversity and PTSD experiences: Testing a multiple mediator model. *Traumatology: An International Journal.* Advance online publication. doi:10.1037/h0099838

Nader, K., & Muni, P. (2002). Individual crisis intervention. In S. E. Brock, P. J. Lazarus, & S. R. Jimerson (Eds.), *Best practices in school crisis prevention and intervention* (pp. 405–428). Bethesda, MD: National Association of School Psychologists.

Nader, K., Pynoos, R., Fairbanks, L., & Frederick, C. (1990). Children's post-traumatic stress disorder reactions one year after a sniper attack at their school. *American Journal of Psychiatry, 147*(11), 1526–1530. Retrieved from http://ajp.psychiatryonline.org/journal.aspx?journalid=13

Napper, L. E., Fisher, D. G., Jaffe, A., Jones, R. T., Lamphear, V. S., Joseph, L., & Grimaldi, E. M. (2014). Psychometric properties of the child's reaction to traumatic events scale–Revised in English and Lugandan. *Journal of Child and Family Studies, 34,* 1285–1294. doi:10.1007/s10826-014-9936-1

Nastasi, B. K., & Hitchcock, J. (2009). Challenges of evaluating multilevel interventions. *Journal of Community Psychology, 43,* 360–376. doi:10.1007/s10464-009-9239-7

National Association of School Psychologists (NASP). (2002a). *Coping with crisis—Helping children with special needs: Tips for school personnel and parents.* Bethesda, MD: Author.

National Association of School Psychologists. (2002b). *Memorial activities at school: A list of "Do's" and "Don'ts."* Bethesda, MD: Author. Retrieved from www.nasponline.org/assets/documents/Resources%20and%20Publications/Handouts/Safety%20and%20Crisis/memorialdo_donot.pdf

National Association of School Psychologists. (2004). *Culturally competent crisis response: Information for school psychologists and crisis teams.* Bethesda, MD: Author.

National Association of School Psychologists (NASP). (2010). *Principles for professional ethics.* Bethesda, MD: Author. Retrieved from http://www.nasponline.org/assets/Documents/Standards%20and%20Certification/Standards/1_%20Ethical%20Principles.pdf

National Association of School Psychologists (NASP). (2013a). *Conducting crisis exercises and drills: Guidelines for schools.* Bethesda, MD: Author. Retrieved from www.nasponline.org/assets/documents/Research%20and%20Policy/Advocacy%20Resources/drills_guidance.pdf

National Association of School Psychologists. (2013b, January). *NASP recommendations for comprehensive school safety policies.* Bethesda, MD: Author. Retrieved from http://www.nasponline.org/assets/Documents/About%20School%20Psychology/Media%20Resources/NASP_School_Safety_Recommendations_January%202013.pdf

National Association of School Psychologists. (2013c). *Research on school security: The impact of security measures on students.* Bethesda, MD: Author. Retrieved from www.nasponline.org/assets/documents/Research%20and%20Policy/Advocacy%20Resources/schoolsecurity.pdf

National Association of School Psychologists (NASP) & National Association of School Resource Officers (NASRO). (2014). *Best practice considerations for schools in active shooter and other armed assailant drills* [Brief]. Bethesda, MD: National Association of School Psychologists. Retrieved from http://www.nasponline.org/Documents/Research%20and%20Policy/Advocacy%20Resources/BP_Armed_Assailant_Drills.pdf

National Association of School Resource Officers. (2010). *2009 national school-based law enforcement survey.* St. Paul, MN: Author.

National Autism Association. (2012). *Big red safety toolkit: A digital resource for first responders, Be ready to find a missing child with autism.* Portsmouth, RI: Author. Retrieved from http://nationalautismassociation.org/docs/BigRedSafetyToolkit-FR.pdf

National Center for Education Statistics. (2015). *School and staffing survey.* Washington, DC: U.S. Department of Education, Institute of Education Sciences. Retrieved from http://nces.ed.gov/surveys/sass/

National Center on Safe Supportive Learning Environments. (2016). *School climate survey compendium.* Washington, DC: American Institute for Research. Retrieved from http://safesupportivelearning.ed.gov/topic-research/school-climate-measurement/school-climate-survey-compendium

National Commission on Children and Disasters. (2010, October). *2010 Report to the president and Congress.* AHRQ Publication No. 10-M037. Rockville, MD: Agency for Healthcare Research and Quality. Retrieved from http://archive.ahrq.gov/prep/nccdreport/index.html

National Education Association Health Information Network. (2007). *School crisis guide.* Washington, DC: Author. Retrieved from http://neahealthyfutures.org/wpcproduct/school-crisis-guide

National Institute for Health and Clinical Excellence. (2005). *Post-traumatic stress disorder (PTSD): The management of PTSD in adults and children in primary and secondary care.* (Full Clinical Guideline 26 Developed by the National Collaborating Centre for Mental Health). London, England: Author.

National Institute of Mental Health (NIMH). (2001). *Mental health and mass violence: Evidence-based early psychological intervention for victims/survivors of mass violence. A workshop to reach consensus on best practices.* Washington, DC: U.S. Government Printing Office. Retrieved from www.nimh.nih.gov/health/publications/massviolence.pdf

National School Climate Center, Center for Social and Emotional Education, and National Center for Learning and Citizenship at Education Commission of the States. (2008). *The school climate challenge: Narrowing the gap between school climate research and school climate policy, practice guidelines and teacher education policy.* Retrieved from http://www.ecs.org/html/projectsPartners/nclc/docs/school-climate-challenge-web.pdf

National Suicide Prevention Lifeline (n.d.). *Help someone else online.* Retrieved from http://www.suicidepreventionlifeline.org/gethelp/online.aspx

National Suicide Prevention Lifeline. (2007). *Suicide risk assessment standards.* Retrieved from http://www.suicidepreventionlifeline.org/crisiscenters/bestpractices.aspx

Nekvasil, E. K., Cornell, D. G., & Huang, F. L. (2015, April 13). Prevalence and offense characteristics of multiple casualty homicides: Are schools at higher risk than other locations? *Psychology of Violence.* Advance online publication. doi:10.1037/a0038967

Nelson, R. B., Schnorr, D., Powell, S., & Huebner, E. S. (2012). Building resilience in schools. In R. Mennuti, R. Christner, & A. Freeman (Eds.), *Cognitive-behavioral interventions in educational settings: A handbook for practice* (2nd ed., pp. 643–682). New York, NY: Routledge.

Nemeroff, C. B. (2004). Neurobiological consequences of childhood trauma. *Journal of Clinical Psychiatry, 65*(Suppl. 1), 18–28. Retrieved from http://www.psychiatrist.com/

Nemeroff, C. B., Bremner, J. D., Foa, E. B., Mayberg, H. S., North, C. S., & Stein, M. B. (2006). Posttraumatic stress disorder: A state-of-the-science review. *Journal of Psychiatric Research 40,* 1–21. doi:10.1016/j.jpsychires.2005.07.005

New Jersey v. T.L.O., 469 U.S. 325 (1985).

Newtown receives $7.1M federal grant to support Sandy Hook victims. (2014, June 17). *New Haven Register.* Retrieved from http://www.nhregister.com/general-news/20140617/newtown-receives-71m-federal-grant-to-support-sandy-hook-victims

Nickerson, A. B. (2006, August). *Crisis prevention and preparedness: The comprehensive school crisis team. Workshop evaluation/test summaries and workshop modification suggestions.* (Available from National Association of School Psychologists, 4340 East West Highway, Suite 402, Bethesda, MD 20814).

Nickerson, A. B., & Fishman, C. (2013). Promoting mental health and resilience through strength-based assessment in US schools. *Educational and Child Psychology, 30,* 7–17. Retrieved from http://shop.bps.org.uk/publications/publication-by-series/educational-and-child-psychology/educational-child-psychology-vol-30-no-4-december-2013-strength-based-practice.html

Nickerson, A. B., & Gurdineer, E. E. (2012). Research needs for crisis prevention. In S. E. Brock & S. R. Jimerson (Eds.), *Best practices in school crisis prevention and intervention* (2nd ed., pp. 683–699). Bethesda, MD: National Association of School Psychologists.

Nickerson, A. B., & Heath, M. A. (2008). Developing and strengthening school-based crisis response teams. *School Psychology Forum, 2*(2), 1–16. Retrieved from http://www.nasponline.org/publications/periodicals/spf/volume-2/volume-2-issue-2-%28winter-2008%29/developing-and-strengthening-school-based-crisis-response-teams

Nickerson, A. B., & Nagle, R. J. (2005). Parent and peer attachment in late childhood and early adolescence. *Journal of Early Adolescence, 25,* 223–249. doi:10.1177/0272431604274174

Nickerson, A. B., Pagliocca, P. M., & Palladino, S. (2012). Research and evaluation needs for crisis intervention. In S. E. Brock & S. R. Jimerson (Eds.), *Best practices in crisis prevention and intervention in the schools* (2nd ed., pp. 701–730). Bethesda, MD: National Association of School Psychologists.

Nickerson, A. B., Reeves, M. A., Brock, S. E., & Jimerson, S. R. (2009). *Identifying, assessing, and treating posttraumatic stress disorder at school.* New York, NY: Springer. doi:10.1007/978-0-387-79916-2_1

Nickerson, A. B., Serwacki, M. L., Brock, S. E., Savage, T. A., Woitaszewski, S. A., & Reeves, M. A. (2014). Program evaluation of the PREPaRE School Crisis Prevention and Intervention Training Curriculum. *Psychology in the Schools, 51,* 466–479. doi:10.1002/pits.21757

Nickerson, A. B., Singleton, D., Schnurr, B., & Collen, M. (2014). Perceptions of school climate as a function of bullying involvement. *Journal of Applied School Psychology, 30,* 157–181. doi:10.1080/15377903.2014.888530

Nickerson, A. B., & Slater, E. D. (2009). School and community violence and victimization as predictors of suicidal behavior for adolescents. *School Psychology Review, 38,* 218–232. Retrieved from http://www.nasponline.org/publications/periodicals/spr/volume-38/volume-38-issue-2/school-and-community-violence-and-victimization-as-predictors-of-adolescent-suicidal-behavior

Nickerson, A. B., & Zhe, E. J. (2004). Crisis prevention and intervention: A survey of school psychologists. *Psychology in the Schools, 41,* 777–788. doi:10.1002/pits.20017

Niles, B. L., Klunk-Gillis, J., Ryngala, D. J., Silberbogen, A. K., Paysnick, A., & Wolf, E. J. (2012). Comparing mindfulness and psychoeducation treatments for combat-related PTSD using a telehealth approach. *Psychological Trauma: Theory, Research, Practice, and Policy, 4,* 538–547. doi:10.1037/a0026161

Nixon, R. D. V., Meiser-Stedman, R., Dalgleish, T., Yule, W., Clark, D. M., Perrin, S., & Smith, P. (2013). The Child PTSD Symptom Scale: An update and replication of its psychometric properties. *Psychological Assessment, 25,* 1025–1031. doi:10.1037/a0033324

Noltemeyer, A. L., & Bush, K. R. (2013). Adversity and resilience: A synthesis of international research. *School Psychology International, 34,* 474–487. doi:10.1177/0143034312472758

Norris, F. H., Byrne, C. M., Diaz, E., & Kaniasty, K. (2002). *Psychosocial resources in the aftermath of natural and human-caused disasters: A review of the empirical literature.* Washington, DC: National Center for PTSD.

Norris, F. H., Friedman, M. J., Watson, P. J., Byrne, C. M., Diaz, E., & Kaniasty, K. (2002). 60,000 disaster victims speak: Part I. An empirical review of the empirical literature, 1981–2001. *Psychiatry: Interpersonal and Biological Processes, 65,* 207–239. doi:10.1521/psyc.65.3.207.20173

North, C. S., & Pfefferbaum, B. (2013). Mental health response to community disasters: A systematic review. *JAMA: Journal of the American Medical Association, 310,* 507–518. doi:10.1001/jama.2013.107799

Obama, B. (2011, March 3). *Presidential Policy Directive/PPD-8: National preparedness.* Washington, DC: The White House. Retrieved from http://www.dhs.gov/presidential-policy-directive-8-national-preparedness

O'Donnell, D. A., Roberts, W. C., & Schwab-Stone, M. E. (2011). Community violence exposure and post-traumatic stress reactions among Gambian youth: The moderating role of positive school climate. *Social Psychiatry and Psychiatric Epidemiology, 46,* 59–67. doi:10.1007/s00127-009-0162-x

O'Donnell, J., Hawkins, D., Catalano, R. F., Abbott, R. D., & Day, E. (1998). Preventing school failure, drug use, and delinquency among low-income children: Long-term intervention in elementary schools. *American Journal of Orthopsychiatry, 65,* 87–100. doi:10.1037/h0079598

Oflaz, F., Hatipoğlu, S., & Aydin, H. (2008). Effectiveness of psychoeducation intervention on post-traumatic stress disorder and coping styles of earthquake survivors. *Journal of Clinical Nursing, 17,* 677–687. doi:10.1111/j.1365-2702.2007.02047.x

Ohan, J. L., Myers, K., & Collett, B. R. (2002). Ten-year review of rating scales. IV: Scales assessing trauma and its effects. *Journal of the American Academy of Child and Adolescent Psychiatry, 41,* 1401–1422. doi:10.1097/00004583-200212000-00012

Olff, M., Langeland, W., & Gersons, B. P. R. (2005). The psychobiology of PTSD: Coping with trauma. *Psychoneuroendocrinology, 30,* 974–982. doi:10.1016/j.psyneuen.2005.04.009

Olweus, D. (1993). *Bullying at school: What we know and what we can do.* Malden, MA: Blackwell.

Olympia, R. P., Wan, E., & Avner, J. R. (2005). The preparedness of schools to respond to emergencies in children: A survey of school nurses. *Pediatrics, 116,* 738–745. doi:10.1542/peds.2005-1474

Openshaw, L. (2011). School-based support groups for traumatized students. *School Psychology International, 32,* 163–178. doi:10.1177/0143034311400830

Oras, R., de Ezpeleta, S. C., & Ahmad, A. (2004). Treatment of traumatized refugee children with eye movement desensitization and reprocessing in a psychodynamic context. *Journal of Nordic Psychiatry, 58,* 199–203. doi:10.1080/08039480410006232

Ortiz, S. O., & Voutsinas, M. (2012). Cultural considerations in crisis intervention. In S. E. Brock & S. R. Jimerson (Eds.), *Best practices in school crisis prevention and intervention* (2nd ed., pp. 337–358). Bethesda, MD: National Association of School Psychologists.

Osher, D., Dwyer, K., & Jimerson, S. R. (2006). Safe, supportive, and effective schools: Promoting school success to reduce school violence. In S. R. Jimerson & M. Furlong (Eds.), *Handbook of school violence and school safety: From research to practice* (pp. 51–71). New York, NY: Routledge.

Osher, D., Dwyer, K., Jimerson, S. R., & Brown, J. A. (2012). Developing safe, supportive, and effective schools: Facilitating student success to reduce school violence. In S. R. Jimerson, A. B. Nickerson, M. J. Mayer, & M. J. Furlong (Eds.), *Handbook of school violence and school safety: International research and practice* (2nd ed., pp. 27–44). New York, NY: Routledge.

Ostrowski, S. A., Christopher, N. C., & Delahanty, D. L. (2007). Brief report: The impact of maternal posttraumatic stress disorder symptoms and child gender on risk for persistent posttraumatic stress disorder symptoms in child trauma victims. *Journal of Pediatric Psychology, 33*, 338–342. doi:10.1093/jpepsy/jsl003

O'Toole, M. E. (1999). *The school shooter: A threat assessment perspective.* Quantico, VA: Federal Bureau of Investigation. Retrieved from https://www.fbi.gov/stats-services/publications/school-shooter

Otto, M. W., Henin, A., Hirshfeld-Becker, D. R., Pollack, M. H., Biederman, J., & Rosenbaum, J. F. (2007). Posttraumatic stress disorder symptoms following media exposure to tragic events: Impact of 9/11 on children at risk for anxiety disorders. *Journal of Anxiety Disorders, 21*, 888–902. doi:10.1016/j.janxdis.2006.10.008

Oxley, D. (2001). Organizing schools into small learning communities. *NASSP Bulletin, 85*(625), 5–16. Retrieved from http://bul.sagepub.com/

Oxley, D. (2004). *Small learning communities: A review of the research.* Philadelphia, PA: The Mid-Atlantic Regional Educational Laboratory at Temple University Center for Research in Human Development and Education.

Ozer, E. J., Best, S. R., Lipsey, T. L., & Weiss, D. S. (2003). Predictors of posttraumatic stress disorder and symptoms in adults: A meta-analysis. *Psychological Bulletin, 129*, 52–73. doi:10.1037/0033-2909.129.1.52

Pacella, M. L., Hruska, B., & Delahanty, D. L. (2013). The physical health consequences of PTSD and PTSD symptoms: A meta-analytic review. *Journal of Anxiety Disorders, 27*, 33–46. doi:10.1016/j.janxdis.2012.08.004

Pack, M. (2012). Critical incident stress debriefing: An exploratory study of social workers' preferred models of CISM and experiences of CISD in New Zealand. *Social Work in Mental Health, 10*, 273–293. doi:10.1080/15332985.2012.657297

Pack, M. (2014). Vicarious resilience: A multilayered model of stress and trauma. *Journal of Women and Social Work, 29*, 18–29. doi:10.1177/0886109913510088

Pagliocca, P., & Nickerson, A. (2001). Legislating school crisis response: Good policy or just good politics? *Law & Policy, 23*, 373–407. doi:10.1111/1467-9930.00117

Pagliocca, P. M., Nickerson, A. B., & Williams, S. (2002). Research and evaluation directions in crisis intervention. In S. E. Brock, P. J. Lazarus, & S. R. Jimerson (Eds.), *Best practices in school crisis prevention and intervention* (pp. 771–790). Bethesda, MD: National Association of School Psychologists.

Paine, C. K. (2007, January). *Hope and healing: Recovery from school violence.* Paper presented at the Confronting Violence in Our Schools: Planning, Response, and Recovery [Website symposium of the Public Entity Risk Institute]. Retrieved from http://georgiadisaster.info/Resources Publications/ParentsandYouth/RecoverySchoolViolence.pdf

Painter, K. (2012). Outcomes for youth with severe emotional disturbance: A repeated measures longitudinal study of a wraparound approach of service delivery in systems of care. *Child Youth Care Forum, 41*, 407–425. doi:10.1007/s10566-011-9167-1

Parent Management Training Institute. (2014). *Parent management training.* Retrieved from http://www.parentmanagementtraininginstitute.com/

Paterson, H. M., Whittle, K., & Kemp, R. I. (2015). Detrimental effects of post-incident debriefing on memory and psychological responses. *Journal of Police and Criminal Psychology, 30,* 27–37. doi:10.1007/s11896-014-9141-6

Pat-Horenczyk, R. (2006). Terror in Jerusalem: Israelis coping with 'emergency routine' in daily life. In J. Kuriansky (Ed.), *Terror in the Holy Land: Inside the anguish of the Israeli-Palestinian conflict* (pp. 67–74). Westport, CT: Praeger.

Pat-Horenczyk, R., Kenan, A. M., Achituv, M., & Bachar, E. (2014). Protective factors based model for screening for posttraumatic distress in adolescents. *Child & Youth Care Forum, 43,* 339–351. doi:10.1007/s10566-013-9241-y

Patton, J. D. (2011). Community organizations' involvement in school safety planning: Does it make a difference in school violence? *School Social Work Journal, 35*(2), 15–33. Retrieved from http://iassw.org/about/school-social-work-journal/

Patton, M. Q. (1990). *Qualitative evaluation and research methods* (2nd ed.). Newbury Park, CA: SAGE.

Paul, L. A., Gray, M. J., Elhai, J. D., Massad, P. M., & Stamm, B. H. (2006). Promotion of evidence-based practices for child traumatic stress in rural populations: Identification of barriers and promising solutions. *Trauma, Violence, & Abuse, 7,* 260–273. doi:10.1177/1524838006292521

Pearlman, L. A. (2003). *Trauma and Attachment Belief Scale (TABS) manual.* Los Angeles, CA: Western Psychological Services.

Pearrow, M. M., & Jacob, S. (2012). Legal and ethical considerations in crisis prevention and response in schools. In S. E. Brock & S. R. Jimerson (Eds.), *Best practices in school crisis prevention and intervention* (2nd ed., pp. 359–375). Bethesda, MD: National Association of School Psychologists.

Peek, L., & Stough, L. M. (2010). Children with disabilities in the context of disaster: A social vulnerability perspective. *Child Development, 81,* 1260–1270. doi:10.1111/j.1467-8624.2010.01466.x

Pepin, E. N., & Banyard, V. L. (2006). Social support: A mediator between child maltreatment and developmental outcomes. *Journal of Youth and Adolescence, 35,* 617–630. doi:10.1007/s10964-006-9063-4

Perrin, M., Vandeleur, C. L., Castelao, E., Rothen, S., Glaus, J., Vollenweider, P., & Preisig, M. (2014). Determinants of the development of post-traumatic stress disorder, in the general population. *Social Psychiatry and Psychiatric Epidemiology, 49,* 447–457. doi:10.1007/s00127-013-0762-3

Perrin, S., Meiser-Stedman, R., & Smith, P. (2005). The Children's Revised Impact of Event Scale (CRIES): Validity as a screening instrument for PTSD. *Behavioral and Cognitive Psychotherapy, 33,* 487–498. doi:10.1017/S1352465805002419

Petersen, S., & Straub, R. L. (1992). *School crisis survival guide: Management techniques and materials for counselors and administrators.* West Nyack, NY: Center for Applied Research in Education.

Pfefferbaum, B. (1997). Posttraumatic stress disorder in children: A review of the past 10 years. *Journal of the American Academy of Child and Adolescent Psychiatry, 36,* 1503–1511. doi:10.1016/S0890-8567(09)66558-8

Pfefferbaum, B., Nixon, S. J., Tivis, R. D., Doughty, D. E., Pynoos, R. S., Gurwitch, R. H., & Foy, D. W. (2001). Television exposure in children after a terrorist incident. *Psychiatry, 64,* 202–211. doi:10.1521/psyc.64.3.202.18462

Pfefferbaum, B., Nixon, S. J., Tucker, P. M., Tivis, R. D., Moore, V. L., Gurwitch, R. H., . . . Geis, H. K. (1999). Posttraumatic stress responses in bereaved children after the Oklahoma City bombing. *Journal of the American Academy of Child and Adolescent Psychiatry, 38,* 1372–1379. doi:10.1097/00004583-199911000-00011

Pfefferbaum, B., Noffsinger, M. A., & Wind, L. H. (2012). Issues in the assessment of children's coping in the context of mass trauma. *Prehospital and Disaster Medicine, 27,* 272–279. doi:10.1017/S1049023X12000702

Pfefferbaum, B., Seale, T., Brandt, E., Pfefferbaum, R., Doughty, D., & Rainwater, S. (2003). Media exposure in children one hundred miles from a terrorist bombing. *Annals of Clinical Psychiatry, 15,* 1–8. doi:10.3109/10401230309085664

Pfefferbaum, B., Seale, T. W., McDonald, N. B., Brandt, E. N., Rainwater, S. M., Maynard, B., . . . Miller, P. D. (2000). Posttraumatic stress two years after the Oklahoma City bombing in youths geographically distant from the explosion. *Psychiatry: Interpersonal and Biological Processes, 63,* 358–370. Retrieved from http://www.guilford.com/journals/Psychiatry/Robert-J-Ursano/00332747

Pfefferbaum, B., & Shaw, J. A. (2013). Practice parameter on disaster preparedness. *Journal of the American Academy of Child and Adolescent Psychiatry, 52,* 1224–1238. doi:10.1016/j.jaac.2013.08.014

Philpott, D., & Serluco, P. (2009). *Public school emergency preparedness and crisis management plan.* Lanham, MD: Government Institutes.

Phinney, A. (2004, September). *Preparedness in America's schools: A comprehensive look at terrorism preparedness in America's twenty largest school districts.* New York, NY: America Prepared Campaign. Retrieved from http://www.workplaceviolence911.com/docs/20040916.pdf

Phipps, A. B., & Byrne, M. K. (2003). Brief interventions for secondary trauma: Review and recommendations. *Stress and Health: Journal of the International Society for the Investigation of Stress, 19,* 139–147. doi:10.1002/smi.970

Phoenix, B. J. (2007). Psychoeducation for survivors of trauma. *Perspectives in Psychiatric Care, 43,* 123–131. doi:10.1111/j.1744-6163.2007.00121.x

Pine, D. S., & Cohen, J. A. (2002). Trauma in children and adolescents: Risk and treatment of psychiatric sequelae. *Biological Psychiatry, 51,* 519–531. doi:10.1016/S0006-3223(01)01352-X

Poland, S., & Lieberman, R. (2002). Best practices in suicide intervention. In A. Thomas & J. Grimes (Eds.), *Best practices in school psychology IV* (pp. 1151–1165). Bethesda, MD: National Association of School Psychologists.

Poland, S., & Poland, D. (2004, April). Dealing with death at school. *Principal Leadership, 8,* 8–12. Retrieved from www.nasponline.org/assets/documents/Resources%20and%20 Publications/Handouts/Families%20and%20Educators/Dealing%20with%20Death%20 at%20School%20April%2004.pdf

Porterfield, K., & Carnes, M. (2012). *Why social media matters: School communication in the digital age.* Rockville, MD: National School Public Relations Association.

Posavac, E. J., & Raymond, G. C. (1989). *Program evaluation: Methods and case studies* (3rd ed.). Englewood Cliffs, NJ: Prentice Hall.

Posner, K., Brown, G. K., Stanley, B., Brent, D. A., Yershova, K. V., Oquendo, M. A., . . . Mann, J. J. (2011). *American Journal of Psychiatry, 168,* 1266–1277. doi:10.1176/appi.ajp.2011.10111704

Powers, M. B., Halpern, J. M., Ferenschak, M. P., Gillihan, S. J., & Foa, E. B. (2010). A meta-analytic review of prolonged exposure for posttraumatic stress disorder. *Clinical Psychology Review, 30,* 635–641. doi:10.1016/j.cpr.2010.04.007

Prinstein, M. J., La Greca, A. M., Vernberg, E. M., & Silverman, W. K. (1996). Children's coping assistance: How parents, teachers, and friends help children cope after a natural disaster. *Journal of Clinical Child Psychology, 25,* 463–475. doi:10.1207/s15374424jccp2504_11

Propper, R. E., Stickgold, R., Keeley, R., & Christman, S. D., (2007). Is television traumatic? Dreams, stress, and media exposure in the aftermath of September 11, 2001. *Psychological Science, 18,* 334–340. doi:10.1111/j.1467-9280.2007.01900.x

Prout, S. M., & Prout, H. T. (1998). A meta-analysis of school-based studies of counseling and psychotherapy: An update. *Journal of School Psychology, 36,* 121–136. doi:10.1016/S0022-4405(98)00007-7

Pynoos, R. S., Frederick, C., Nader, K., Arroyo, W., Steinberg, A., Eth, S., . . . Fairbanks, L. (1987). Life threat and posttraumatic stress in school-age children. *Archives of General Psychiatry, 44,* 1057–1063. doi:10.1001/archpsyc.1987.01800240031005

Pynoos, R. S., Goenjian, A., Tashjian, M., Karakashian, M., Manjikian, R., Manoukian, G., . . . Fairbanks, L. A. (1993). Post–traumatic stress reactions in children after the 1988 Armenian earthquake. *British Journal of Psychiatry, 163,* 239–247. doi:10.1192/bjp.163.2.239

Pynoos, R., Rodrigues, N., Steinberg, A., Stuber, M., & Frederick, C. (1998). *The UCLA PTSD Reaction Index for DSM.* Los Angeles, CA: UCLA Trauma Psychiatric Program.

Qouta, S., Punamäki, R. L., & El Sarraj, E. (2005). Mother-child expression of psychological distress in war trauma. *Clinical Child Psychology and Psychiatry, 10,* 135–156. doi:10.1177/1359104505051208

Quallich, K. (2005). Crisis management research summary: Television images and psychological symptoms after the September 11 terrorist attacks. *Communiqué, 33*(5), 32.

Quinn, K. (2014, Spring). Deterring school violence: The role of the school resource officer. *Journal of School Safety,* 10–11. Retrieved from http://www.mydigitalpublication.com/publication/?i=199024&p=3

Quinn, K. P., & McDougal, J. L. (1998). A mile wide and a mile deep: Comprehensive interventions for children and youth with emotional and behavioral disorders and their families. *School Psychology Review, 27,* 191–203. Retrieved from http://www.nasponline.org/publications/periodicals/spr/volume-27/volume-27-issue-2/a-mile-wide-and-a-mile-deep-comprehensive-interventions-for-children-and-youth-with-emotional-and-behavioral-disorders-and-their-families

Ramsey, R., F., Tanney, B. L., Lang, W. A., & Kinzel, T. (2004). *Suicide intervention handbook.* Calgary, Alberta: Livingworks.

Raphael, B., & Newman, L. (2000). *Disaster mental health response handbook: An educational resource for mental health professionals involved in disaster management.* North Sydney, NSW: NSW Health.

Raskind, M. A., Peskind, E. R., Hoff, D. J., Hart, K. L., Holmes, H. A., Warren, D., . . . McFall, M. E. (2007). A parallel group placebo controlled study of prazosin for trauma nightmares and sleep disturbance in combat veterans with post-traumatic stress disorder. *Biological Psychiatry, 61,* 928–934. doi:10.1016/j.biopsych.2006.06.032

Ratner, H. H., Chiodo, L., Covington, C., Sokol, R. J., Ager, J., & Delaney-Black, V. (2006). Violence exposure, IQ, academic performance, and children's perception of safety: Evidence of protective effects. *Merrill-Palmer Quarterly, 52,* 264–287. doi:10.1353/mpq.2006.0017

Raywid, M. (1996). *Taking stock: The movement to create mini-schools, schools-within-schools, and separate small schools.* New York, NY: Columbia University, Teachers College, ERIC Clearinghouse on Urban Education.

R.D.S. v. State of Tennessee. No. M2005-00213-SC-R11-JV. (Decided February 6, 2008). Retrieved from http://caselaw.findlaw.com/tn-supreme-court/1249032.html

Reeves, M. A., Conolly-Wilson, C. N., Pesce, J., Lazzaro, B. R., & Brock, S. E. (2012). Preparing for the comprehensive school crisis response. In S. E. Brock & S. R. Jimerson (Eds.), *Best practices in school crisis prevention and intervention* (2nd ed., pp. 245–264). Bethesda, MD: National Association of School Psychologists.

Reeves, M. A., Kanan, L. M., & Plog, A. E. (2010). *Comprehensive planning for safe learning environments: A school professional's guide to integrating physical and psychological safety—prevention through recovery.* New York, NY: Routledge.

Reeves, M. A., Nickerson, A. B., & Brock, S. E. (2011). Preventing and intervening in crisis situations. In E. Snyder & R. W. Christner (Eds.), *A practical guide to developing competencies in school psychology* (pp. 193–207). New York, NY: Springer. doi:10.1007/978-1-4419-6257-7

Reeves, M. A., Nickerson, A. B., Conolly-Wilson, C. N., Susan, M. K., Lazzaro, B. R., Jimerson, S. R., & Pesce, R. C. (2011a). *Crisis prevention and preparedness: Comprehensive school safety planning* (2nd ed.). Bethesda, MD: National Association of School Psychologists.

Reeves, M. A., Nickerson, A. B., Conolly-Wilson, C. N., Susan, M. K., Lazzaro, B. R., Jimerson, S. R., & Pesce, R. C. (2011b). *Crisis prevention and preparedness: Comprehensive school safety planning. Training of trainers.* (2nd ed.). Bethesda, MD: National Association of School Psychologists.

Reeves, M. A., Nickerson, A. B., & Jimerson, S. R. (2006a). *Crisis prevention and preparedness: The comprehensive school crisis team.* Bethesda, MD: National Association of School Psychologists.

Reeves, M. A., Nickerson, A. B., & Jimerson, S. R. (2006b). *Crisis prevention and preparedness: The comprehensive school crisis team. Training of trainers.* Bethesda, MD: National Association of School Psychologists.

Rhode Island Emergency Management Agency. (2013, October). *Rhode Island model for school emergency planning, mitigation/prevention, preparedness, response, and recovery.* Providence, RI: Author. Retrieved from http://www.riema.ri.gov/preparedness/schoolsafety/documents/ 1-Introduction%202013.Final%202-7-2014.pdf

Richards, D. (2001). A field study of critical incident stress debriefing versus critical incident stress management. *Journal of Mental Health, 10,* 351–362. doi:10.1080/09638230124190

Riebschleger, J., Onaga, E., Tableman, B., & Bybee, D. (2014). Mental health consumer parents' recommendations for designing psychoeducation interventions for their minor children. *Psychiatric Rehabilitation Journal, 37,* 183–185. doi:10.1037/prj0000071

Rigby, K. (2000). Effects of peer victimization in schools and perceived social support on adolescent well-being. *Journal of Adolescence, 23,* 57–68. doi:10.1006/jado.1999.0289

Rigby, K. (2007). *Bullying in schools and what to do about it* (Rev. ed.). Victoria, Australia: ACER Press.

Rigby, K., & Slee, P. (1999). Suicidal ideation among adolescent school children, involvement in bully–victim problems, and perceived social support. *Suicide and Life-Threatening Behavior, 29,* 119–130. Retrieved from doi:10.1111/j.1943-278X.1999.tb01050.x

Ritchie, E. C. (2003). Mass violence and early intervention: Best practice guidelines. *Primary Psychiatry, 10,* 43–48. Retrieved from http://primarypsychiatry.com/mass-violence-and-early-intervention-best-practice-guidelines/

Roach, A. T., Lawton, K., & Elliott, S. N. (2014). Best practices in facilitating and evaluating the integrity of school-based interventions. In P. L. Harrison & A. Thomas (Eds.), *Best practices in school psychology: Data-based and collaborative decision making* (pp. 133–146). Bethesda, MD: National Association of School Psychologists.

Robers, S., Zhang, A., Morgan, R. E., & Musu-Gillette, L. (2015, July). *Indicators of school crime and safety: 2014* (NCES 2015-072/NCJ 248036). Washington, DC: U.S. Department of Education National Center for Education Statistics and U.S. Department of Justice Bureau of Justice Statistics. Retrieved from https://nces.ed.gov/pubsearch/pubsinfo.asp?pubid=2015072

Robers, S., Zhang, J., & Truman, J. (2012). *Indicators of school crime and safety: 2011* (NCES 2012-002/NCJ 236021). Washington, DC: U.S. Department of Education National Center for Education Statistics and U.S. Department of Justice Bureau of Justice Statistics. Retrieved from http://bjs.ojp.usdoj.gov/content/pub/pdf/iscs11.pdf

Roberts, A. R. (2000). An overview of crisis theory and crisis intervention. In A. R. Roberts (Ed.), *Crisis intervention handbook: Assessment, treatment and research* (2nd ed., pp. 3–30). New York, NY: Oxford University Press.

Rodenburg, R., Benjamin, A., de Roos, C., Meijer, A. M., & Stams, G. J. (2009). Efficacy of EMDR in children: A meta-analysis. *Clinical Psychology Review, 29*, 599–606. doi:10.1016/j.cpr.2009.06.008

Rolfsnes, E. S., & Idsoe, T. (2011). School-based intervention programs for PTSD symptoms: A review and meta-analysis. *Journal of Traumatic Stress, 24*, 155–165. doi:10.1002/jts.20622

Rose, S., Bisson, J., Churchill, R., & Wessely, S. (2006). Psychological debriefing for preventing post traumatic stress disorder (PTSD). In Cochrane Review (Ed.), *The Cochrane Library*, Issue 3, 2006. Oxford: Update Software. doi:10.1002/14651858.CD000560

Rosenbaum, S. (2006). U.S. health policy in the aftermath of Hurricane Katrina. *Journal of the American Medical Association, 295*, 437–440. doi:10.1001/jama.295.4.437

Rossi, P. H., & Freeman, H. E. (1993). *Evaluation: A systematic approach* (5th ed.). Newbury Park, CA: SAGE.

Rothbaum, B. O., Astin, M. C., & Marsteller, F. (2005). Prolonged exposure vs. eye movement desensitization and reprocessing (EMDR) for PTSD rape victims. *Journal of Traumatic Stress, 18*, 607–616. doi:10.1002/jts.2006

Rothbaum, B. O., Cahill, S. P., Foa, E. B., Davidson, J. R. T., Compton, J., Connor, K. M., . . . Hahn, C. G. (2006). Augmentation of sertraline with prolonged exposure in the treatment of posttraumatic stress disorder. *Journal of Traumatic Stress, 19*, 625–638. doi:10.1002/jts.20170

Rothon, C., Head, J., Klineberg, E., & Stansfeld, S. (2011). Can social support protect bullied adolescents from adverse outcomes? A prospective study on the effects of bullying on the educational achievement and mental health of adolescents at secondary schools in East London. *Journal of Adolescence, 34*, 579–588. doi:10.1016/j.adolescence.2010.02.007

Rubin, D. E., Berntsen, D., & Bohni, M. K. (2008). A memory-based model of posttraumatic stress disorder: Evaluating basic assumptions underlying the PTSD diagnosis. *Psychological Review, 115*, 985–1011. doi:10.1037/a0013397

Ruck, S., Bowes, N., & Tehrani, N. (2013). Evaluating trauma debriefing within the UK prison service. *Journal of Forensic Practice, 15*, 281–290. doi:10.1108/JFP-09-2012-0018

Ruf, M., Schauer, M., Neuner, F., Catani, C., Schauer, E., & Elbert, T. (2010). Narrative exposure therapy for 7- to 16-year-olds: A randomized controlled trial with traumatized refugee children. *Journal of Traumatic Stress, 23*, 437–445. doi:10.1002/jts

Russo, C. J. (2006). *Reutter's, The law of public education* (5th ed.). New York, NY: Foundation Press.

Ruzek, J. L., Brymer, M. J., Jacobs, A. K., Layne, C. M., Vernberg, E. M., & Watson, P. J. (2007). Psychological first aid. *Journal of Mental Health Counseling, 29,* 17–49. Retrieved from http://www.amhca.org/news/journal.aspx

Ryan-Arredondo, K., Renouf, K., Egyed, C., Doxey, M., Dobbins, M., Sanchez, S., & Rakowitz, B. (2001). Threats of violence in schools: The Dallas Independent School District's response. *Psychology in the Schools, 38,* 185–196. doi:10.1002/pits.1009

Safe2Tell. (2014). *Impact report.* Denver, CO: Colorado Department of Law, Office of the Attorney General. Retrieved from http://safe2tell.org/wp-content/uploads/2008/11/Data2Report_December-2014_8x11_Printable.pdf

Sagi-Schwartz, A. (2008). The well being of children living in chronic war zones: The Palestinian-Israeli case. *International Journal of Behavioral Development, 32,* 322–336. doi:10.1177/0165025408090974

Sahin, N., Yilmaz, B., & Batigun, A. (2011). Psychoeducation for children and adults after the Marmara earthquake: An evaluation study. *Traumatology, 17,* 41–49. doi:10.1177/1534765610395624

Saigh, P. A. (2004). *Children's PTSD Inventory™: A structured interview for diagnosing posttraumatic stress disorder.* San Antonio, TX: PsychCorp.

Saigh, P. A., Mroueh, M., & Bremner, J. D. (1997). Scholastic impairments among traumatized adolescents. *Behavior Research & Therapy, 35,* 429–436. doi:10.1016/S0005-7967(96)00111-8

Saigh, P. A., Yasik, A., Oberfield, R., Green, B., Halamandaris, P., Rubenstein, H., . . . McHugh, M. (2000). The Children's PTSD Inventory. Development and reliability. *Journal of Traumatic Stress, 13,* 369–380. doi:10.1023/A:1007750021626

Saigh, P. A., Yasik, A. E., Oberfield, R. A., Halamandaris, P. V., & Bremner, J. D. (2006). The intellectual performance of traumatized children and adolescents with or without posttraumatic stress disorder. *Journal of Abnormal Psychology, 115,* 332–340. doi:10.1037/0021-843X.115.2.332

Saigh, P. A., Yasik, A. E., Sack, W. H., & Koplewicz, H. S. (1999). Child-adolescent posttraumatic stress disorder: Prevalence, risk factors, and comorbidity. In P. A. Saigh & J. D. Bremner (Eds.), *Posttraumatic stress disorder: A comprehensive text* (pp. 18–43). Needham Heights, MA: Allyn & Bacon.

Salloum, A., & Overstreet, S. (2008). Evaluation of individual and group grief trauma interventions for children post-disaster. *Journal of Clinical Child and Adolescent Psychology, 37,* 495–507. doi:10.1080/15374410802148194

Salloum, A., Stover, C. S., Swaidan, V. R., & Storch, E. A. (2014). Parent and child PTSD and parent depression in relation to parenting stress among trauma-exposed children. *Journal of Child and Family Studies.* Advance online publication. doi:1007/s10826-014-9928-1

Saltzman, W. R., Pynoos, R. S., Layne, C. M., Steinberg, A. M., & Aisenberg, E. (2001). Trauma- and grief-focused intervention for adolescents exposed to community violence: Results of a school based screening and group treatment protocol. *Group Dynamics: Theory, Research, and Practice, 5,* 291–303. doi:10.1037/1089-2699.5.4.291

Sandler, I. N., Wolchik, S. A., MacKinnon, D., Ayers, T. S., & Roosa, M. W. (1997). Developing linkages between theory and intervention in stress and coping processes. In S. A. Wolchik & I. N. Sandler (Eds.), *Handbook of children's coping: Linking theory and intervention* (pp. 3–41). New York, NY: Plenum.

Sandoval, J., & Brock, S. E. (2009). Managing crisis: Prevention, intervention, and treatment. In C. R. Reynolds & T. B. Gutkin (Eds.), *The handbook of school psychology* (pp. 886–904). New York, NY: Wiley.

Sandoval, J., & Lewis, S. (2002) Cultural considerations in crisis intervention. In S. E. Brock, P. J. Lazarus, & S. R. Jimerson (Eds.), *Best practices in school crisis prevention and intervention* (pp. 293–308). Bethesda, MD: National Association of School Psychologists.

Sandy Hook Advisory Commission. (2015, March 6). *Final report of the Sandy Hook Advisory Commission.* Hartford, CT: State of Connecticut. Retrieved from http://www.shac.ct.gov/SHAC_Final_Report_3-6-2015.pdf

Sanetti, L. M. H., & Kratochwill, T. R. (2014). *Treatment integrity: Conceptual, methodological, and applied considerations for practitioners and researchers.* Washington, DC: American Psychological Association.

Sattler, D. N., Boyd, B., & Kirsch, J. (2014). Trauma exposed firefighters: Relationships among posttraumatic growth, posttraumatic stress, resource availability, coping and critical incident stress debriefing experience. *Stress and Health: Journal of the International Society for the Investigation of Stress, 30,* 356–365. doi:10.1002/smi.2608

Save the Children. (2015). *Still at risk: U.S. children 10 years after Hurricane Katrina. 2015 national report card on protecting children in disasters.* Fairfield, CT: Author. Retrieved from http://rems.ed.gov/docs/DisasterReport_2015.pdf

Saylor, C. F. (2002). *The Pediatric Emotional Distress Scale* (PEDS). (Available from Conway Saylor, PhD, Department of Psychology, The Citadel, 171 Moultrie Avenue, Charleston, SC 29409, conway.saylor@citadel.edu.)

Saylor, C. F., Belter, R., & Stokes, S. J. (1997). Children and families coping with disaster. In S. A. Wolchik & I. N. Sandler (Eds.), *Handbook of children's coping: Linking theory and intervention* (pp. 361–383). New York, NY: Plenum.

Saylor, C. F., Cowart, B. L., Lipovsky, J. A., Jackson, C., & Finch, A. J. (2003). Media exposure to September 11: Elementary school students' experiences and posttraumatic symptoms. *American Behavior Scientist, 46,* 1622–1642. doi:10.1177/0002764203254619

Saylor, C. F, Swenson, C. C., Reynolds, S. S., & Taylor, M. (1999). The Pediatric Emotional Distress Scale: A brief screening measure for young children exposed to traumatic events. *Journal of Clinical Child Psychology, 28,* 70–81. doi:10.1207/s15374424jccp2801_6

Scheeringa, M. S., Weems, C. F., Cohen, J. A., Amaya-Jackson, L., & Guthrie, D. (2010). Trauma-focused cognitive-behavioral therapy for posttraumatic stress disorder in three-through six year-old children: A randomized clinical trial. *Journal of Child Psychology and Psychiatry, 52, 8, 853–860.* doi:10.1111/j.1469-7610.2010.02354.x

Scheeringa, M. S., Wright, M. J., Hunt, J. P., & Zeanah, C. H. (2006). Factors affecting the diagnosis and prediction of PTSD symptomatology in children and adolescents. *American Journal of Psychiatry, 163,* 644–651. Retrieved from http://ajp.psychiatryonline.org/journal. aspx?journalid=13

Scheeringa, M. S., & Zeanah, C. H. (2001). A relational perspective on PTSD in early childhood. *Journal of Traumatic Stress, 14,* 799–815. doi:10.1023/A:1013002507972

Schneider, T., Walker, H., & Sprague, J. (2000). *Safe school design: A handbook for educational leaders applying the principles of crime prevention through environmental design.* Eugene, OR: ERIC Clearinghouse on Educational Management. Retrieved from http://eric.ed.gov/?id=ED449541

Schnurr, P. P., & Friedman, M. J. (2008). Treatments for PTSD: Understanding the evidence. *PTSD Research Quarterly, 19*(3), 1–11. Retrieved from http://www.ptsd.va.gov/professional/ newsletters/research-quarterly/V19N3.pdf

Scholes, C., Turpin, G., & Mason, S. (2007). A randomised controlled trial to assess the effectiveness of providing self-help information to people with symptoms of acute stress disorder following a traumatic injury. *Behaviour Research and Therapy, 45,* 2527–2536. doi:10.1016/ j.brat.2007.06.009

School Safety Infrastructure Council. (2014, June 27). *Report of the School Safety Infrastructure Council.* Hartford, CT: State of Connecticut. Retrieved fromhttp://das.ct.gov/images/1090/ SSIC_Final_Draft_Report.pdf

Schubert, S. J., Lee, C. W., & Drummond, P. D. (2011). The efficacy and psychophysiological correlates of dual-attention tasks in eye movement desensitization and reprocessing. *Journal of Anxiety Disorders, 25,* 1–11. doi:10.1016/j.janxdis.2010.06.024

Schuster, M. A., Stein, B. D., Jaycox, L. H., Collins, R. L., Marshall, G. N., Elliott, M. N., . . . Berry, S. H. (2001). A national survey of stress reactions after the September 11, 2001, terrorist attacks. *New England Journal of Medicine, 345,* 1507–1512. doi:10.1056/ NEJM200111153452024

Schwab-Stone, M. E., Ayers, T. S., Kasprow, W., Voyce, C., Barone, C., Shriver, T., & Weissberg, R. P. (1995). No safe haven: A study of violence exposure in an urban community. *Journal of the American Academy of Child & Adolescent Psychiatry, 34,* 1343–1352. doi:10.1097/00004583- 199510000-00020

Schwarz, E. D., & Kowalski, J. M. (1991). Malignant memories: PTSD in children and adults after a school shooting. *Journal of the American Academy of Child and Adolescent Psychiatry, 30,* 936–944. doi:10.1097/00004583-199111000-00011

Schwarz, J. H. (1982). Guiding children's creative expression in the stress of war. In C. D. Spielberger, I. G. Sarason, & N. A. Milgram (Eds.), *Stress and anxiety* (Vol. 7, pp. 351–354). Washington, DC: Hemisphere.

Scrimin, S., Moscardino, U., Capello, F., Altoè, G., Steinberg, A. M., & Pynoos, R. S. (2011). Trauma reminders and PTSD symptoms in children three years after a terrorist attack in Beslan. *Social Science & Medicine, 72,* 694–700. doi:10.1016/j.socscimed.2010.11.030

Search Institute. (2013). *The Developmental Assets Profile (DAP)*. Retrieved from http://www.search-institute.org/survey-services/surveys/DAP

Section 504 of the Rehabilitation Act. (1973). Pub. L. No. 93-112, 87 Stat. 394.

Seedat, S., Lockhart, R., Kaminer, D., Zungu-Dirwayi, N., & Stein, D. J. (2001). An open trial of citalopram in adolescents with post-traumatic stress disorder. *International Clinical Psychopharmacology, 16*, 21–25. doi:10.1097/00004850-200101000-00002

Seedat, S., Nyamai, C., Njenga, F., Vythilingum, B., & Stein, D. J. (2004). Trauma exposure and post-traumatic stress symptoms in urban African schools. *British Journal of Psychiatry, 184*, 169–175. doi:10.1192/bjp.184.2.169

Seedat, S., Stein, D. J., Ziervogel, C., Middleton, T., Kaminer, D., Emsley, R. A., & Roussouw, W. (2002). Comparison of response to a selective serotonin reuptake inhibitor in children, adolescents, and adults with posttraumatic stress disorder. *Journal of Child and Adolescent Psychopharmacology, 12*, 37–46. doi:10.1089/10445460252943551

Seery, M. D., Silver, R., Holman, E., Ence, W. A., & Chu, T. Q. (2008). Expressing thoughts and feelings following a collective trauma: Immediate responses to 9/11 predict negative outcomes in a national sample. *Journal of Consulting and Clinical Psychology, 76*, 657–667. doi:10.1037/0022-006X.76.4.657

Seirmarco, G., Neria, Y., Insel, B., Kiper, D., Doruk, A., Gross, R., & Litz, B. (2012). Religiosity and mental health: Changes in religious beliefs, complicated grief, posttraumatic stress disorder, and major depression following the September 11, 2001 attacks. *Psychology of Religion and Spirituality, 4*, 10–18. doi:10.1037/a0023479

Serketich, W. J., & Dumas, J. E. (1996). The effectiveness of behavioral parent training to modify antisocial behavior in children: A meta-analysis. *Behavior Therapy, 27*, 171–186. doi:10.1016/S0005-7894(96)80013-X

Servaty-Seib, H. L., Peterson, J., & Spang, D. (2003). Notifying individual students of a death loss: Practical recommendations for schools and school counselors. *Death Studies, 27*, 167–186. doi:10.1080/07481180302891

Shah, L., Klainin-Yobas, P., Torres, S., & Kannusamy, P. (2014). Efficacy of psychoeducation and relaxation interventions on stress-related variables in people with mental disorders: A literature review. *Archives of Psychiatric Nursing, 28*, 94–101. doi:10.1016/j.apnu.2013.11.004

Shakespeare-Finch, J., & Lurie-Beck, J. (2014). A meta-analytic clarification of the relationship between posttraumatic growth and symptoms of posttraumatic stress disorder. *Journal of Anxiety Disorders, 28*, 223–229. doi:10.1016/j.paid.2012.01.011

Shalev, A. Y., & Freedman, S. (2005). PTSD following terrorist attacks: A prospective evaluation. *American Journal of Psychiatry, 162*, 1188–1191. Retrieved from http://ajp.psychiatryonline.org/journal.aspx?journalid=13

Shalev, A. Y., Tuval-Mashiach, R., & Hadar, H. (2004). Posttraumatic stress disorder as a result of mass trauma. *Journal of Clinical Psychiatry, 65*(Suppl 1), 4–10. Retrieved from http://www.psychiatrist.com/Pages/home.aspx

Shaw, J. A. (2003). Children exposed to war/terrorism. *Clinical Child and Family Psychology Review, 6,* 237–246. doi:10.1023/B:CCFP.0000006291.10180.bd

Shepherd, J., Stein, K., & Milne, R. (2000). Eye movement desensitization and reprocessing in the treatment of post-traumatic stress disorder: A review of an emerging therapy. *Psychological Medicine, 30,* 863–871. doi:10.1017/S0033291799002366

Shiba, G., Matsumoto Leong, Y., & Oka, R. (2005). Japanese. In J. G. Lipson & S. L. Dibble (Eds.), *Culture & clinical care* (pp. 304–316). San Francisco, CA: UCSF Nursing Press.

Shochet, I. M., Dadds, M. R., Ham, D., & Montague, R. (2006). School connectedness is an underemphasized parameter in adolescent mental health: Results of a community prediction study. *Journal of Clinical Child and Adolescent Psychology, 35,* 170–179. doi:10.1207/s15374424jccp3502_1

Short, L., Hennessy, M., & Campbell, J. (1996). Tracking the work: A guide for communities in developing useful program evaluations. In M. Hennessy, J. Greenberg, M. Hennessy (Eds.), *A guide for communities: Building an integrated approach for reducing family violence* (pp. 59–72). Chicago, IL: American Medical Association.

Shuster, M. A., Stein, B. D., & Jaycox, L. H. (2002). 'Reactions to the events of September 11': Reply. *New England Journal of Medicine, 346,* 629–630. Retrieved from http://www.nejm.org

Siedler, G., & Wagner, F. (2006). Comparing the efficacy of EMDR and trauma-focused cognitive-behavioral therapy in the treatment of PTSD: A meta-analytic study. *Psychological Medicine, 36,* 1515–1522. doi:10.1017/S0033291706007963

Sijbrandij, M., Olff, M., Reitsma, J. B., Carlier, I. E., & Gersons, B. R. (2006). Emotional or educational debriefing after psychological trauma: Randomised controlled trial. *British Journal of Psychiatry, 189,* 150–155. doi:10.1192/bjp.bp.105.021121

Silva, R. R., Alpert, M., Munoz, D. M., Singh, S., Matzner, F., & Dummit, S. (2000). Stress and vulnerability to posttraumatic stress disorder in children and adolescents. *American Journal of Psychiatry, 157,* 1229–1235. Retrieved from http://ajp.psychiatryonline.org/journal.aspx?journalid=13

Silver, R. C., Holman, E. A., Andersen, J. P., Poulin, M., McIntosh, D. N., & Gil-Rivas, V. (2013). Mental- and physical-health effects of acute exposure to media images of the September 11, 2001, attacks and the Iraq war. *Psychological Science, 24,* 1623–1634. doi:10.1177/0956797612460406

Silver, R. C., Holman, E. A., McIntosh, D. N., Poulin, M., & Gil-Rivas, V. (2002). Nationwide longitudinal study of psychological responses to September 11. *Journal of the American Medical Association, 288,* 1235–1244. doi:10.1001/jama.288.10.1235

Silverman, W. K., & La Greca, A. M. (2002). Children experiencing disasters: Definitions, reactions, and predictors of outcomes. In A. M. La Greca, W. K. Silverman, E. M. Vernberg, & M. C. Roberts (Eds.), *Helping children cope with disasters and terrorism,* (pp. 11–33). Washington, DC: American Psychological Association.

Simeon, D., Greenberg, J., Knutelska, M., Schmeidler, J., & Hollander, E. (2003). Peritraumatic reactions associated with the World Trade Center disaster. *American Journal of Psychiatry, 160*, 1702–1705. Retrieved from http://ajp.psychiatryonline.org/journal.aspx?journalid=13

Simmons, A. N., Flagan, T. M., Wittmann, M., Strigo, I. A., Matthews, S. C., Donovan, H., . . . Paulus, M. P. (2013). The effects of temporal unpredictability in anticipation of negative events in combat veterans with PTSD. *Journal of Affective Disorders, 146*, 426–432. doi:10.1016/j.jad.2012.08.006

Singer, M. I., Flannery, D. J., Guo, S., Miller, D., & Leibbrandt, S. (2004). Exposure to violence, parental monitoring, and television viewing as contributors to children's psychological trauma. *Journal of Community Psychology, 32*, 489–504. doi:10.1002/jcop.20015

Skinner, E. A., Edge, K., Altman, J., & Sherwood, H. (2003). Searching for the structure of coping: A review and critique of category systems for classifying ways of coping. *Psychological Bulletin, 129*, 216–269. doi:10.1037/0033-2909.129.2.216

Skinner, E. A., & Zimmer-Gembeck, M. J. (2007). The development of coping. *Annual Review of Psychology, 58*, 119–144. doi:10.1146/annurev.psych.58.110405.085705

Slaikeu, K. A. (1990). *Crisis intervention: A handbook for practice and research* (2nd ed.). Newton, MA: Allyn & Bacon.

Smith Harvey, V. (2004). Resiliency: Strategies for parents and educators. In A. S. Canter, L. Z. Paige, M. D. Roth, I. Romero, & S. A. Carroll (Eds.), *Helping children at home and school II: Handouts for families and educators* (pp. S5-79–S5-82). Bethesda, MD: National Association of School Psychologists.

Solomon, R. M., & Shapiro, F. (2008). EMDR and the adaptive information processing model. *Journal of EMDR Practice and Research, 2*, 315–325. doi:10.1891/1933-3196.2.4.315

Southwick, S., Friedman, M., & Krystal, J. (2008). Does psychoeducation help prevent post traumatic psychological distress? In reply. *Psychiatry: Interpersonal and Biological Processes, 71*, 303–307. doi:10.1521/psyc.2008.71.4.303

Speier, A. H. (2000). *Psychosocial issues for children and adolescents in disasters* (2nd ed.), Washington, DC: U.S. Department of Health and Human Services. Retrieved from http://store.samhsa.gov/product/Psychosocial-Issues-for-Children-and-Adolescents-in-Disasters/ADM86-1070R

Spence, J., Titov, N., Johnston, L., Jones, M. P., Dear, B. F., & Solley, K. (2014). Internet-based trauma-focused cognitive behavioural therapy for PTSD with and without exposure components: A randomized controlled trial. *Journal of Affective Disorders, 162*, 73–80. doi:10.1016/j.jad.2014.03.009

Spilsbury, J. C., Drotar, D., Burant, C., Flannery, D., Creeden, R., & Friedman, S. (2005). Psychometric properties of the Pediatric Emotional Distress Scale in a diverse sample of children exposed to interpersonal violence. *Journal of Clinical Child and Adolescent Psychology, 24*, 758–764. doi:10.1207/s15374424jccp3404_17

Spooner, F., Knight, V. F., Browder, D. M., & Smith, B. R. (2012). Evidence-based practice for teaching academics to students with severe developmental disabilities. *Remedial and Special Education, 33*, 374–387. doi:10.1177/0741932511421634

Sprague, J. R., & Horner, R. H. (2006). School-wide positive behavioral supports. In S. R. Jimerson & M. J. Furlong (Eds.), *Handbook of school violence and school safety: From research to practice* (pp. 413–427). New York, NY: Routledge.

Sprague, J. R., & Horner, R. H. (2012). School-wide positive behavioral interventions and supports. In S. R. Jimerson, A. B. Nickerson, M. J. Mayer, & M. J. Furlong (Eds.), *Handbook of school violence and school safety: International research and practice* (2nd ed., pp. 447–462). New York, NY: Routledge.

Sprague, J., & Walker, H. (2000). Early identification and intervention for youth with antisocial and violent behavior. *Exceptional Children, 66,* 367–379. doi:10.1177/001440290006600307

Sprague, J. R., & Walker, H. M. (2005). *Safe and healthy schools: Practical prevention strategies.* New York, NY: Guilford Press.

Sprague, J. R., Walker, H., Golly, A., White, K., Myers, D. R., & Shannon, T. (2001). Translating research into effective practice: The effects of a universal staff and student intervention on indicators of discipline and school safety. *Education and Treatment of Children, 24,* 495–511. Retrieved from https://www.ncjrs.gov/pdffiles1/Digitization/183123NCJRS.pdf

Stagner, R. (1951). Homeostasis as a unifying concept in personality theory. *Psychological Review, 58,* 5–17. doi:10.1037/h0063598

Stallard, P., & Salter, E. (2003). Psychological debriefing with children and young people following traumatic events. *Clinical Child Psychology and Psychiatry, 8,* 445–457. doi:10.1177/13591045030084003

Stallard, P., & Smith, E. (2007). Appraisals and cognitive coping styles associated with chronic post-traumatic symptoms in child road traffic accident survivors. *Journal of Child Psychology and Psychiatry, 48,* 194–201. doi:10.1111/j.1469-7610.2006.01692.x

Stallard, P., Velleman, R., Salter, E., Howse, I., Yule, W., & Taylor, G. (2006). A randomised controlled trial to determine the effectiveness of an early psychological intervention with children involved in road traffic accidents. *Journal of Child Psychology and Psychiatry, 47,* 127–134. doi:10.1111/j.1469-7610.2005.01459.x

Stamm, B. H. (2010). *The concise ProQOL mannual* (2nd ed.). Pocatello, ID: ProQOL.org.

State of Tennessee v. R.D.S., A Juvenile. Direct Appeal from the Circuit Court for Williamson County No. II-CR-04274 No. M2008-01724-COA-R3-JV –July 16, 2009. Retrieved from http://www.tba2.org/tba_files/TCA/2009/rds_071709.pdf

Staub, E., & Vollhardt, J. (2008). Altruism born of suffering: The roots of caring and helping after victimization and other trauma. *American Orthopsychiatric Association, 78,* 267–280. doi:10.1037/a0014223

Steege, M. W., & Watson, T. S. (2009). *Conducting school-based functional behavioral assessments: A practitioner's guide* (2nd ed.). New York, NY: Guilford Press.

Stein, B. D., Jaycox, L. H., Elliott, M. N., Collins, R., Berry, S., Marshall, G. N., . . . Schuster, M. A. (2004). The emotional and behavioral impact of terrorism on children: results from a national survey. *Applied Developmental Science, 8,* 184–194. doi:10.1207/s1532480xads0804_2

Stein, B. D., Jaycox, L. H., Kataoka, S. H., Wong, M., Tu, W., Elliot, M. N., & Fink, A. (2003). A mental health intervention for school children exposed to violence: A randomized controlled trial. *JAMA, 290,* 603–611. doi:10.1001/jama.290.5.603

Stein, S., Chiolan, K., Campisi, A., & Brock, S. E. (2015, February). *Implementing PREPaRE student psychoeducational groups differentiated for multiple grade levels.* Mini-skills workshop presented at the Annual Meeting of the National Association of School Psychologists, Orlando, FL. Retrieved from https://apps.nasponline.org/professional-development/convention/session-handouts.aspx

Steinberg, A. M., & Beyerlein, B. (n.d.). *UCLA PTSD Reaction Index: DSM-5 Version.* Los Angeles, CA: University of California, Los Angeles. Retrieved from http://www.nctsn.org/nctsn_assets/pdfs/mediasite/ptsd-training.pdf

Steinberg, A. M., Brymer, M. J., Kim, S., Ghosh, C., Ostrowski, S. A., Gulley, K., . . . Pynoos, R. S. (2013). Psychometric properties of the UCLA PTSD Reaction Index: Part 1. *Journal of Traumatic Stress, 26,* 1–9. doi:10.1002/jts.21780

Stinnett, T. A. (2007). Review of the Trauma Symptom Checklist for Young Children. In K. F. Geisinger, R. A. Spies, J. F. Carlson, & B. S. Plake (Eds.). *The seventeenth mental measurements yearbook.* Lincoln, NE: Buros Institute of Mental Measurements.

Stoiber, K. C., & DeSmet, J. L. (2010). Guidelines for evidence-based practice in selecting interventions. In G. G. Peacock, R. A. Ervin, E. J. Daly III, & K. W. Merrell (Eds.), *Practical handbook of school psychology: Effective practices for the 21st century* (pp. 213–234). New York, NY: Guilford Press.

Stover, C. S., Hahn, H., Im, J. Y., & Berkowitz, S. (2010). Agreement of parent and child reports of trauma exposure and symptoms in the early aftermath of a traumatic event. *Psychological Trauma: Theory, Research, Practice, and Policy, 2,* 159–168. doi:10.1037/a0019156

Strand, V. C., Pasquale, L. E., & Sarmiento, T. L. (n.d.). *Child and adolescent trauma measures: A review.* Fordham University: Children F.I.R.S.T. Retrieved from https://ncwwi.org/files/Evidence_Based_and_Trauma-Informed_Practice/Child-and-Adolescent-Trauma-Measures_A-Review-with-Measures.pdf

Strand, V. C., Sarmiento, T. L., & Pasquale, L. E. (2005). Assessment and screening tools for trauma in children and adolescents: A review. *Trauma, Violence, & Abuse, 6,* 55–78. doi:10.1177/1524838004272559

Strein, W., & Koehler, J. (2008). Best practices in developing prevention strategies for school psychology practice. In A. Thomas & J. Grimes (Eds.), *Best practices in school psychology V* (pp. 1309–1322). Bethesda, MD: National Association of School Psychologists.

Stuber, J., Fairbrother, G., Galea, S., Pfefferbaum, B., Wilson-Genderson, M., & Vlahov, D. (2002). Determinants of counseling for children in Manhattan after the September 11 attacks. *Psychiatric Services, 53,* 815–822. doi:10.1176/appi.ps.53.7.815

Substance Abuse and Mental Health Services Administration (SAMHSA). (2012). *Preventing suicide: A toolkit for high schools.* HHS Publication NO. SMA-12-4669. Rockville, MD: Author. Retrieved from http://store.samhsa.gov/shin/content/SMA12-4669/SMA12-4669.pdf

Suckling, A., & Temple, C. (2002). *Bullying: A whole-school approach*. London, England: Kingsley.

Sugai, G., & Horner, R. H. (2009). Defining and describing schoolwide positive behavior support. In W. Sailor, G. Dunlap, G. Sugai, & R. Horner (Eds.), *Handbook of positive behavior support* (pp. 307–326). New York, NY: Springer.

Suldo, S. M., & Shaffer, E. J. (2008). Looking beyond psychopathology: The dual-factor model of mental health in youth. *School Psychology Review, 37,* 52–68. Retrieved from http://www.nasponline.org/publications/periodicals/spr/volume-37/volume-37-issue-1/looking-beyond-psychopathology-the-dual-factor-model-of-mental-health-in-youth

Sullivan, M., Harris, E., Collado, C., & Chen, T. (2006). Noways tired: Perspectives of clinicians of color on culturally competent crisis intervention. *Journal of Clinical Psychology: In Session, 62,* 987–999. doi:10.1002/jclp.20284

Susan, M. K. (2010). Crisis prevention, response, and recovery: Helping children with special needs. In A. Canter, L. Z. Paige, & S. Shaw (Eds.), *Helping children at home and school III: Handouts for families and educators* (S9H4-1–S9H4-3). Bethesda, MD: National Association of School Psychologists.

Suter, J. C., & Bruns, E. J. (2009). Effectiveness of the wraparound process for children with emotional and behavioral disorders: A meta-analysis. *Clinical Child and Family Psychology Review, 14,* 336–351. doi:10.1007/s10567-009-0059-y

Sutherland, K. S., & Wehby, J. H. (2001). Exploring the relationship between increased opportunities to respond to academic requests and the academic and behavioral outcomes of students with EBD. *Remedial and Special Education, 22,* 113–121. doi:10.1177/074193250102200205

Swahn, M. H., Simon, T. R., Hertz, M. F., Arias, I., Bossarte, R. M., Ross, J. G., . . . Hamburger, M. E. (2008). Linking dating violence, peer violence, and suicidal behavior among high-risk youth. *American Journal of Preventative Medicine, 34,* 30–38. doi:10.1016/j.amepre.2007.09.020

Swick, S. D., Dechant, E., & Jellinek, M. S. (2002). Children of victims of September 11th: A perspective on the emotional and developmental challenges they face and how to help meet them. *Journal of Developmental and Behavioral Pediatrics, 23,* 378–384. doi:10.1097/00004703-200210000-00013

Szumilas, M., Wei, Y., & Kutcher, S. (2010). Psychological debriefing in schools. *Canadian Medical Association Journal, 182,* 883–884. doi:10.1503/cmaj.091621

Tatum, E. L., Vollmer, W. M., & Shore, J. H. (1986). Relationship of perception and mediating variables to the psychiatric consequences of disaster. In J. J. Shore (Ed.), *Disaster stress studies: New methods and findings* (pp. 100–121). Washington, DC: American Psychiatric Press.

Taylor, K. R. (2001, September). Student suicide: Could you be held liable? *Principal Leadership, 2*(1), 74–78. Retrieved from https://www.nassp.org/portals/0/content/48901.pdf

Taylor, S., Thordarson, D. S., Maxfield, L., Fedoroff, I. C., Lovell, K., & Ogrodniczuk, J. (2003). Comparative efficacy, speed, and adverse effects of three PTSD treatments: Exposure therapy,

EMDR, and relaxation training. *Journal of Consulting and Clinical Psychology, 71*, 330–338. doi:10.1037/0022-006X.71.2.330

Tearfund, A. M. (2006). Assessing psychological distress—Which lens? *Humanitarian Exchange Magazine, 36*, 32–35. Retrieved from http://www.odihpn.org/report.asp?id=2861[p5]

Terr, L. C. (1991). Childhood traumas: An outline and overview. *American Journal of Psychiatry, 148*, 10–20. doi:10.1176/ajp.148.1.10

Terr, L. C. (1992). Mini-marathon groups: Psychological 'first aid' following disasters. *Bulletin of the Menninger Clinic, 56*, 76–86. Retrieved from http://guilfordjournals.com/loi/bumc

Thabet, A. A., Vostanis, P., & Karim, K. (2005). Group crisis intervention for children during ongoing war conflict. *European Child & Adolescent Psychiatry, 14*, 262–269. doi:10.1007/s00787-005-0466-7

Thompson, T., & Massat, C. R., (2005). Experiences of violence, post-traumatic stress, academic achievement and behavior problems of urban African-American children. *Child and Adolescent Social Work Journal, 22*, 367–393. doi:10.1007/S10560-005-0018-5

Tichenor, V., Marmar, C. R., Weiss, D. S., Metzler, T. J., & Ronfeldt, H. M. (1996). The relationship of peritraumatic dissociation and posttraumatic stress: Findings in female Vietnam theater veterans. *Journal of Consulting and Clinical Psychology, 64*, 1054–1059. doi:10.1037/0022-006X.64.5.1054

Tiernan, K., Foster, S. L., Cunningham, P. B., Brennan, P., & Whitmore, E. (2015). Predicting early positive change in multisystemic therapy with youth exhibiting antisocial behaviors. *Psychotherapy, 52*, 93–102. doi:10.1037/a0035975

Tigges, J. M. (2008). *Emergency preparedness: An analysis of Iowa high school emergency preparedness plans.* Ames, IA: Iowa State University (unpublished thesis).

Tinker v. Des Moines Independent Community School District, 393 U.S. 503, 89 S. Ct. 733 (1969).

Tomlinson, C. A. (1999). Mapping a route toward differentiated instruction. *Educational Leadership, 57*(1), 12–16. Retrieved from http://www.ascd.org/ASCD/pdf/journals/ed_lead/el199909_tomlinson.pdf

Tomlinson, C. A. (2004). Sharing responsibility for differentiating instruction. *Roper Review, 26*, 188–189. doi:10.1080/02783190409554268

Tosone, C., McTighe, J. P., Bauwens, J., & Naturale, A. (2011). Shared traumatic stress and the long-term impact of 9/11 on Manhattan clinicians. *Journal of Traumatic Stress, 24*, 546–552. doi:10.1002/jts.20686

Tramonte, M. R. (1999, April). *School psychology in the new millennium: Constructing and implementing a blueprint for intervening in crisis involving disasters and/or violence.* Presented at the Annual Convention of the National Association of School Psychologists, Las Vegas, NV.

Tran, O. K., Gueldner, B. A., & Smith, D. (2014). Building resilience in schools through social and emotional learning. In M. J. Furlong, R. Gilman, & E. S. Huebner (Eds.), *Handbook of positive psychology in schools* (2nd ed., pp. 298–312). New York, NY: Routledge.

Tremblay, C., Hébert, M., & Piché, C. (1999). Coping strategies and social support as mediators of consequences in child sexual abuse victims. *Child Abuse & Neglect, 23,* 929–945. doi:10.1016/S0145-2134(99)00056-3

Trickey, D., Siddaway, A. P., Meiser-Stedman, R., Serpell, L., & Field, A. P. (2012). A meta-analysis for risk factors for post-traumatic stress disorder in children and adolescents. *Clinical Psychology Review, 32,* 122–138. doi:10.1016/j.cpr.2011.12.001

Trump, K. S. (2000). *2002 NASRO school resource officer survey.* Cleveland, OH: National School Safety and Security Services.

Trump, K. S., Burvikos, A., Bartlett, D. A, Greenberg, K., Stapleton, V., & Rosenstein, A. (Eds.). (2011). *Proactive school security and emergency preparedness planning.* Thousand Oaks, CA: Corwin.

Tucker, J. (2013). Perceptions of crisis management in a K-12 school district. *Dissertation Abstracts International: Section A. Humanities and Social Sciences, 74*(3-A)(E).

Tucker, P., Pfefferbaum, B., Nixon, S. J., & Dickson, W. (2000). Predictors of post–traumatic stress symptoms in Oklahoma City: Exposure, social support, peri-traumatic responses. *Journal of Behavioral Health Services and Research, 27,* 406–416. doi:10.1007/BF02287822

Tucker, P., Zaninelli, R., Pitts, C. D., Dillingham, K., Yehuda, R., & Ruggiero, L. (2001). Paroxetine in the treatment of chronic posttraumatic stress disorder: Results of a placebo-controlled, flexible-dosage trial. *Journal of Clinical Psychiatry, 62,* 860–868. doi:10.4088/JCP.v62n1105

Tuckey, M. R., & Scott, J. E. (2014). Group critical incident stress debriefing with emergency services personnel: A randomized controlled trial. *Anxiety, Stress & Coping: An International Journal, 27,* 38–54. doi:10.1080/10615806.2013.809421

Udwin, O., Boyle, S., Yule, W., Bolton, D., & O'Ryan, D. (2000). Risk factors for long-term psychological effects of a disaster experienced in adolescence: Predictors of post traumatic stress disorder. *Journal of Child Psychology and Psychiatry, 41,* 969–979. doi:10.1111/1469-7610.00685

Underwood, M. (2013, January 17). *Memorials after a suicide: Guidelines for schools & families.* Freehold, NJ: Society for the Prevention of Teen Suicide. Retrieved from http://www.sptsusa.org/memorials-suicide/

Underwood, M., Fell, F. T., & Spinazzola, N. A. (2010). *Lifelines postvention: Responding to suicide and other traumatic death.* Center City, MN: Hazelden. Retrieved from http://www.sprc.org/bpr/section-III/lifelines-postvention-responding-suicide-and-other-traumatic-death

Ungar, M. (2011). Community resilience for youth and families: Facilitative physical and social capital in context of adversity. *Children and Youth Services Review, 33,* 1742–1748. doi:10.1016/j.childyouth.2011.04.027

Ungar, M., Liebenberg, L., Boothroyd, R., Kwong, W. M., Lee, T. Y., Leblanc, J., . . . Makhnach, A. (2008). The study of youth resilience across cultures: Lessons from a pilot study of measurement development. *Research in Human Development, 5,* 166–180. doi:10.1080/15427600802274019

United Nations Disaster Assessment and Coordination. (2013). *United Nations Disaster Assessment and Coordination handbook.* New York, NY: UN Office for the Coordination of Humanitarian Affairs. Retrieved from http://www.unocha.org/what-we-do/coordination-tools/undac/overview

United Nations International Strategy for Disaster Reduction. (2014). *Assessment and mitigation planning for risk reduction.* Retrieved from http://www.unisdr.org/we/inform/publications/22111

United Nations Office for Disaster Risk Reduction. (2014a). *A safer world in the 21st century: Disaster and risk reduction.* Retrieved from http://www.unisdr.org/who-we-are/international-strategy-for-disaster-reduction

United Nations Office for Disaster Risk Reduction. (2014b). *Disaster risk reduction in the United Nations 2013: Roles, mandates and results of key UN entities.* Geneva, Switzerland: Author. Retrieved from http://www.unisdr.org/files/32918_drrintheun2013.pdf

U.S. Department of Education. (2003, May). *Practical information on crisis planning: A guide for schools and communities* [Brochure]. Retrieved from http://www.ed.gov/admins/lead/safety/emergencyplan/crisisplanning.pdf

U.S. Department of Education. (2006). Integrating students with special needs and disabilities into emergency response and crisis management planning. *ERCMExpress, 2*(1), 1–4. Retrieved from http://rems.ed.gov/docs/Disability_NewsletterV2I1.pdf

U.S. Department of Education. (2007a). After-action reports: Capturing lessons learned and identifying areas for improvement. *Lessons Learned from School Crises and Emergencies, 2*(1) [Newsletter]. Washington, DC: Author. Retrieved from http://rems.ed.gov/docs/After_Action Reports.pdf

U.S. Department of Education. (2007b, January). *Practical information on crisis planning: A guide for schools and communities* (Rev. ed.). Retrieved from http://www2.ed.gov/admins/lead/safety/emergencyplan/crisisplanning.pdf

U.S. Department of Education (2013, June). *Guide for developing high-quality school emergency operations plans.* Washington, DC: Author: Retrieved from http://rems.ed.gov/docs/REMS_K-12_Guide_508.pdf

U.S. Department of Education, Office for Civil Rights. (2010, October 26). *Dear Colleague Letter: Harassment and Bullying.* Retrieved from http://www2.ed.gov/ocr/letters/colleague-201010.pdf

U.S. Department of Education, Readiness and Emergency Management for Schools (REMS) Technical Assistance (TA) Center. (2006). Emergency exercises: An effective way to validate school safety plans. *ERCMExpress, 2*(3), 1–4. Retrieved from http://rems.ed.gov/docs/Emergency_NewsletterV2I3.pdf

U.S. Department of Education, Readiness and Emergency Management for Schools (REMS) Technical Assistance Center. (2010a). *Physical, business and academic recovery.* Washington, DC: Author. Retrieved from http:www.rems.ed.gov/docs/repository/00000400.pdf

U.S. Department of Education, Readiness and Emergency Management for Schools (REMS) Technical Assistance (TA) Center. (2010b). *Preparedness in School Emergency Management.* Website course. Retrieved from www.rems.ed.gov.

U.S. Department of Health and Human Services & U.S. Department of Education. (2008). *Joint guidance on the application of the Family Educational Rights and Privacy Act (FERPA) and the Health Insurance Portability and Accountability Act of 1996 (HIPAA) to Student Health Records.* Washington DC: Author. Retrieved from http://www2.ed.gov/policy/gen/guid/fpco/doc/ferpa-hipaa-guidance.pdf

U.S. Department of Homeland Security (DHS). (2004, March). *National incident management system.* Retrieved from http://www.fema.gov/pdf/nims/nims_doc_full.pdf

U.S. Department of Homeland Security (DHS). (2007). *Homeland security exercise and evaluation program. Vol. I: HSEEP overview and exercise program management.* Washington, DC: Author. Retrieved from https://hseep.dhs.gov/pages/1001_HSEEP7.aspx

U.S. Department of Homeland Security. (2008, December). *National incident management system.* Washington, DC: Author. Retrieved from http://www.fema.gov/national-incident-management-system

U.S. Department of Homeland Security. (2011a, September). *National disaster recovery framework.* Washington, DC: Author. Retrieved from http://www.fema.gov/national-disaster-recovery-framework

U.S. Department of Homeland Security. (2011b, September). *National preparedness goal.* Washington, DC: Author. Retrieved from http://www.fema.gov/national-preparedness-goal

U.S. Department of Homeland Security (DHS). (2012). *FEMA incident action planning guide.* Washington, DC: Author. Retrieved from http://www.fema.gov/media-library-data/20130726-1822-25045-1815/incident_action_planning_guide_1_26_2012.pdf

U.S. Department of Homeland Security. (2013a). *Homeland Security Exercise and Evaluation Program (HSEEP).* Washington, DC: Author. Retrieved from https://www.llis.dhs.gov/HSEEP/Documents/homeland-security-exercise-and-evaluation-program-hseep

U.S. Department of Homeland Security. (2013b). *IS-100.SCA: Introduction to the Incident Command System for schools* [Online course]. Washington, DC: Author. Retrieved from https://training.fema.gov/EMIWeb/IS/courseOverview.aspx?code=IS-100.sca

U.S. Department of Homeland Security. (2013c, April*). K-12 school security checklist.* Washington, DC. Author. Retrieved from http://www.illinois.gov/ready/SiteCollectionDocuments/K-12SchoolSecurityPracticesChecklist.pdf

U.S. Department of Homeland Security. (2013d, September). *Threat and hazard identification and risk assessment guide* (2nd ed.). Washington, DC: Author: Retrieved from http://www.fema.gov/threat-and-hazard-identification-and-risk-assessment

U.S. Department of Homeland Security (DHS). (2014). *Implementation guidance and reporting.* Washington, DC: Author. Retrieved from http://www.fema.gov/national-incident-management-system/implementation-guidance-and-reporting

U.S. Government Accountability Office. (2007). *Emergency management: Status of school districts' planning and preparedness.* Washington DC: Author. Retrieved from http://www.gao.gov/new.items/d07821t.pdf

University of the State of New York. (2010). *School safety plan guidance. Safe Schools Against Violence in Education (SAVE)* Albany, NY: Author. Retrieved from http://www.p12.nysed.gov/sss/ssae/schoolsafety/save/documents/SchoolSafetyPlansDoc_NEW_June9_10_Prot.pdf

Vaiva, G., Brunet, A., Lebigot, F., Boss, V., Ducrocq, F., Devos, P., . . . Goudemand, M. (2003). Fright (effroi) and other peritraumatic responses after a serious motor vehicle accident: Prospective influence on acute PTSD development. *Canadian Journal of Psychiatry, 48,* 395–401. Retrieved from http://publications.cpa-apc.org/browse/sections/0

Valent, P. (2000). Disaster syndromes. In G. Fink (Ed.), *Encyclopedia of stress, Vol. 1* (pp. 706–709). San Diego, CA: Academic Press.

Valle, R., & Bensussen, G. (1985). Hispanic social networks, social support, and mental health. In W. Vega & M. Miranda (Eds.), *Stress and Hispanic mental health: Relating research to service delivery* (pp. 147–173). Rockville, MD: National Institute of Mental Health.

Van Daele, T., Hermans, D., Van Audenhove, C., & Van den Bergh, O. (2012). Stress reduction through psychoeducation: A meta-analytic review. *Health Education & Behavior, 39,* 474–485. doi:10.1177/1090198111419202

van Emmerik, A. P., Kamphuis, J. H., Hulsbosch, A. M., & Emmelkamp, P. G. (2002). Single session debriefing after psychological trauma: A meta-analysis. *The Lancet, 360,* 766–771. doi:10.1016/S0140-6736(02)09897-5

van Rooyen, K., & Nqweni, Z. C. (2012). Culture and posttraumatic stress disorder (PTSD): A proposed conceptual framework. *South African Journal of Psychology, 42,* 51–60. doi:10.1177/008124631204200106

VanTassel-Baska, J., Olszewski-Kubilius, P., & Kulieke, M. (1994). A study of self-concept and social support in advantaged and disadvantaged seventh and eighth grade gifted students. *Roeper Review: A Journal on Gifted Education, 16,* 186–191. doi:10.1080/02783199409553570

Varra, E. M., Pearlman, L. A., Brock, K. J., & Hodgson, S. T. (2008). Factor analysis of the trauma and attachment belief scale: A measure of cognitive schema disruption related to traumatic stress. *Journal of Psychological Trauma, 7,* 185–196. doi:10.1080/19322880802266813

Vásquez, D. A., de Arellano, M. A., Reid-Quiñones, K., Bridges, A. J., Rheingold, A. A., Stocker, R. J., & Danielson, C. K. (2012). Peritraumatic dissociation and peritraumatic emotional predictors of PTSD in Latino youth: Results from the Hispanic family study. *Journal of Trauma & Dissociation, 13,* 509–525. doi:10.1080/15299732.2012.678471

Verlinden, E., Laar, Y. L., van Meijel, E. M., Opmeer, B. C., Beer, R., Roos, C., . . . Lindauer, R. L. (2014). A parental tool to screen for posttraumatic stress in children: First psychometric results. *Journal of Traumatic Stress, 27,* 492–495. doi:10.1002/jts.21929

Vernberg, E. M., La Greca, A. M., Silverman, W. K., & Prinstein, M. J. (1996). Prediction of posttraumatic stress symptoms in children after Hurricane Andrew. *Journal of Abnormal Psychology, 105,* 237–248. doi:10.1037/0021-843X.105.2.237

Vernberg, E. M., Steinberg, A. M., Jacobs, A. K., Brymer, M. J., Watson, P. J., Osofsky, J. D., Layne, C. M., Pynoos, R. S., & Ruzek, J. I. (2008). Innovations in disaster mental health: Psychological first aid. *Professional Psychology: Research and Practice, 39*, 381–388. doi:10.1037/a0012663

Victoria Department of Education and Early Childhood Development. (2010, October). *DEECD emergency management guidelines.* East Melbourne, Victoria: Author. Retrieved from http://www.eduweb.vic.gov.au/edulibrary/public/schadmin/Management/emergencymanguide.pdf

Vijayakumar, L., Kannan, G. K., Ganesh Kumar, B., & Devarajan, P. (2006). Do all children need intervention after exposure to tsunami? *International Review of Psychiatry, 18,* 515–522. doi:10.1080/09540260601039876

Virginia Board of Education. (1999). *Model school crisis management plan.* Richmond, VA: Author. Retrieved from http://www.doe.virginia.gov/support/safety_crisis_management/emergency_crisis_management/model_plan.pdf

Viswesvaran, C. (2003). Review of the Trauma Symptoms Checklist for Children. In B. S. Plake, J. C. Impara, & R. A. Spies (Eds.). *The fifteenth mental measurements yearbook.* Lincoln, NE: Buros Institute of Mental Measurements.

Vogel, J. M., & Vernberg, E. M. (1993). Children's psychological responses to disasters. *Journal of Clinical Child Psychology, 22,* 464–484. doi:10.1207/s15374424jccp2204_7

Voight, A., & Hanson, T. (2012). *Summary of existing school climate instruments for middle school.* San Francisco, CA: REL West at WestEd.

Vossekuil, B., Fein, R. A., Reddy, M., Borum, R., & Modzeleski, W. (2002). *The final report and findings of the Safe School Initiative: Implications for the prevention of school attacks in the United States.* Washington, DC: U.S. Secret Service and U.S. Department of Education. Retrieved from http://www.secretservice.gov/ntac_ssi.shtml

Vygotsky, L. S. (1978). *Mind in society: The development of higher psychological processes.* Cambridge, MA: Harvard University Press.

Walker, J. M., Wilkins, A. S., Dallaire, J., Sandler, H. M., & Hoover-Dempsey, K. V. (2005). Parental involvement: Model revision through scale development. *Elementary School Journal, 106,* 85–104. doi:10.1086/499193

Walker, J. S., Bruns, E. J., & Penn, M. (2008). Individualized services in systems of care: The wraparound process. In B. A. Stroul & G. M. Blau (Eds.), *The system of care handbook: Transforming mental health services for children, youth, and families* (pp. 127–153). Baltimore, MD: Brookes.

Warda, G., & Bryant, R. A. (1998). Cognitive bias in acute stress disorder. *Behaviour Research and Therapy, 36,* 1177–1183. doi:10.1016/S0005-7967(98)00071-0

Washington State School Safety Center. (2008). *School safety planning manual.* Olympia, WA: Author. Retrieved from http://www.k12.wa.us/safetycenter/Planning/Manual.aspx

Watson, P. J., Brymer, M. J., & Bonanno, G. A. (2011). Postdisaster psychological intervention since 9/11. *American Psychologist, 66,* 482–494. doi:10.1037/a0024806

Way, I., VanDeusen, K., & Cottrell, T. (2007). Vicarious trauma: Predictors of clinicians' disrupted cognitions about self-esteem and self-intimacy. *Journal of Child Sexual Abuse, 16,* 81–98. doi:10.1300/J070v16n04_05

Weaver, T. L., & Clum, G. A. (1995). Psychological distress associated with interpersonal violence: A meta-analysis. *Clinical Psychology Review, 15,* 115–140. doi:10.1016/0272-7358(95)00004-9

Weems, C. F., Scott, B. G., Banks, D. M., & Graham, R. A. (2012). Is TV traumatic for all youths? The role of preexisting posttraumatic-stress symptoms in the link between disaster coverage and stress. *Psychological Science, 23,* 1293–1297. doi:10.1177/0956797612446952

Wei, Y., Szumilas, M., & Kutcher, S. (2010). Effectiveness on mental health of psychological debriefing for crisis intervention in schools. *Educational Psychology Review, 22,* 339–347. doi:10.1007/s10648-010-9139-2

Weinberg, R. B. (1990). Serving large numbers of adolescent victim-survivors: Group interventions following trauma at school. *Professional Psychology: Research and Practice, 21,* 271–278. doi:10.1037/0735-7028.21.4.271

Weiss, D. S. (2007). The Impact of Event Scale: Revised. In J. P. Wilson & C. S. Tang (Eds.), *Cross-cultural assessment of psychological trauma and PTSD* (pp. 219–238). New York, NY: Springer.

Weiss, D. S., Marmar, C. R., Metzler, T. J., & Ronfeldt, H. M. (1995). Predicting symptomatic distress in emergency services personnel. *Journal of Consulting and Clinical Psychology, 63,* 361–368. doi:10.1037/0022-006X.63.3.361

Weisz, J. R., Weiss, B., Han, S. S., Grander, D. A., & Morton, T. (1995). Effects of psychotherapy with children and adolescents revisited: A meta-analysis of treatment outcome studies. *Psychological Bulletin, 117,* 450–468. doi:10.1037/0033-2909.117.3.450

Welko, A. (2013). *Bringing families together: Parent-student reunification procedures in school crisis planning* (Master's thesis, Wright State University, Dayton, OH). Retrieved from http://corescholar.libraries.wright.edu/mph/145/

Wellisch, D., Kagawa-Singer, M., Reid, S., Lin, Y., Nishikawa-Lee, S., & Wellisch, M. (1999). An exploratory study of social support: A cross-cultural comparison of Chinese-, Japanese-, and Anglo-American breast cancer patients. *Psycho-Oncology, 8,* 207–219. doi:10.1002/(SICI)1099-1611(199905/06)8:3<207::AID-PON357>3.0.CO;2-B

Wendling, C., Radisch, J., & Jacobzone, S. (2013). *The use of social media in risk and crisis communication.* OECD Working Papers on Public Governance No. 24. OECD Publishing. Retrieved from http://www.oecd-ilibrary.org/the-use-of-social-media-in-risk-and-crisis-communication_5k3v01fskp9s.pdf.

Wessely, S., Bryant, R. A., Greenberg, N., Earnshaw, M., Sharpley, J., & Hughes, J. (2008). Does psychoeducation help prevent posttraumatic psychological distress? *Psychiatry: Interpersonal and Biological Processes, 71,* 287–302. doi:10.1521/psyc.2008.71.4.287

Wherry, J. N., Corson, K., & Hunsaker, S. (2013). A short form of the Trauma Symptom Checklist for Young Children. *Journal of Child Sexual Abuse: Research, Treatment, & Program Innovations for Victims, Survivors, & Offenders, 22,* 796–821. doi:10.1080/10538712.2013.830667

Whitman, J. B., North, C. S., Downs, D. L., & Spitznagel, E. L. (2013). A prospective study of the onset of PTSD symptoms in the first month after trauma exposure. *Annals of Clinical Psychiatry, 2,* 163–172.

Widom, C. S. (1999). Posttraumatic stress disorder in abused and neglected children grown up. *American Journal of Psychiatry, 156,* 1223–1229. Retrieved from http://ajp.psychiatryonline.org/journal.aspx?journalid=13

Willard, N. (n.d.). *Educator's guide to cyberbullying: Addressing the harm caused by online social cruelty.* Retrieved from http://www.asdk12.org/MiddleLink/AVB/bully_topics/Educators Guide_Cyberbullying.pdf

Willard, N. (2007). Q & A with Nancy Willard. *Prevention Researcher, 14,* 13–15. Retrieved from http://www.tpronline.org/article.cfm/CyberbullyingQA

Williams, A. M., Helm, H. M., & Clemens, E. V. (2012). The effect of childhood trauma, personal wellness, supervisory working alliance, and organizational factors on vicarious traumatization. *Journal of Mental Health Counseling, 34,* 133–153. Retrieved from https://amhca.site-ym.com/store/ViewProduct.aspx?id=4043097

Wilson, J. P., Raphael, B., Meldrum, L., Bedosky, C., & Sigman, M. (2000). Preventing PTSD in trauma survivors. *Bulletin of the Menninger Clinic, 64,* 181–196. Retrieved from http://www.menningerclinic.com/research/bulletin

Wilson, S. J., & Lipsey, M. W. (2007). School-based interventions for aggressive and disruptive behavior: Update of a meta-analysis. *American Journal of Preventive Medicine, 33*(2, Suppl.), S130–S143. doi:10.1016/j.amepre.2007.04.011

Wintre, M. G., Hicks, R., McVey, G., & Fox, J. (1988). Age and sex differences in choice of consultant for various types of problems. *Child Development, 59,* 1046–1055. doi:10.2307/1130270

Wollman, D. (1993). Critical incident stress debriefing and crisis groups: A review of the literature. *Group, 17,* 70–83. doi:10.1007/BF01427816

World Health Organization. (2013). *Guidelines for the management of conditions specifically related to stress.* Geneva: WHO Press. Retrieved from http://www.who.int/mental_health/emergencies/stress_guidelines/en/

Wright Carroll, D. (2009). Toward multiculturalism competence: A practice model for implementation in the schools. In J. M. Jones (Ed.), *The psychology of multiculturalism in the schools: A primer for practice, training, and research* (pp. 1–16). Bethesda, MD: National Association of School Psychologists.

Yap, M. H., & Devilly, G. J. (2004). The role of perceived social support in crime victimization. *Clinical Psychology Review, 24,* 1–14. doi:10.1016/j.cpr.2003.09.007

Ybarra, M. L., & Mitchell, J. K. (2004). Online aggressor/targets, aggressors and targets: A comparison of associated youth characteristics. *Journal of Child Psychology and Psychiatry, 45,* 1308–1316. doi:10.1111/j.1469-7610.2004.00328.x

Yehuda, R., & Hyman, S. E. (2005). The impact of terrorism on brain, and behavior: What we know and what we need to know. *Neuropsychopharmacology, 30,* 1773–1780. doi:10.1038/sj.npp.1300817

Yeomans, P. D., Forman, E. M., Herbert, J. D., & Yuen, E. (2010). A randomized trial of a reconciliation workshop with and without PTSD psychoeducation in Burundian sample. *Journal of Traumatic Stress, 23,* 305–312. Retrieved from http://onlinelibrary.wiley.com/journal/10.1002/%28ISSN%291573-6598

Ying, L., Wu, X., Lin, C., & Chen, C. (2013). Prevalence and predictors of posttraumatic stress disorder and depressive symptoms among child survivors 1 year following the Wenchuan earthquake in China. *European Child & Adolescent Psychiatry, 22,* 567–575. doi:10.1007/s00787-013-0400-3

Yorbik, O., Akbiyik, D. I., Kirmizigul, P., & Söhmen, T. (2004). Post-traumatic stress disorder symptoms in children after the 1999 Marmara earthquake in Turkey. *International Journal of Mental Health, 33,* 46–58. Retrieved from http://www.mesharpe.com/mall/results1.asp?ACR=imh

You, S., Furlong, M. J., Felix, E., Sharkey, J. D., Tanigawa, D., & Green, J. G. (2008). Relations among school connectedness, hope, life satisfaction, and bully victimization. *Psychology in the Schools, 45,* 446–460. doi:10.1002/pits.20308

Young, B. H., Ford, J. D., Ruzek, J. I., Friedman, M., & Gusman, F. D. (1998). *Disaster mental health services: A guide for clinicians and administrators.* Palo Alto, CA: National Center for Post Traumatic Stress Disorder. Retrieved from https://www.hsdl.org/?view=docs/health/nps36-110607-03.pdf

Yule, W. (1998). Posttraumatic stress disorder in children and its treatment. In T. W. Miller (Ed.), *Children of trauma: Stressful life events and their effects on children and adolescents* (pp. 219–244). Madison, CT: International University Press.

Zaghrout-Hodali, M., Alissa, F., & Dodgson, P. W. (2008). Building resilience and dismantling fear: EMDR group protocol with children in an area of ongoing trauma. *Journal of EMDR Practice and Research, 2,* 106–113. doi:10.1891/1933-3196.2.2.106

Zahradnik, M., Stewart, S. H., O'Connor, R. M., Stevens, D., Ungar, M., & Wekerle, C. (2010). Resilience moderates the relationship between exposure to violence and posttraumatic re-experiencing in Mi'kmaq youth. *International Journal of Mental Health and Addiction, 8,* 408–420. doi:10.1007/s11469-009-9228-y

Zayas, L. H., Lester, R. J., Cabassa, L. J., & Fortuna, L. R. (2005). Why do so many Latina teens attempt suicide? A conceptual model for research. *American Journal of Orthopsychiatry, 75,* 275–287. doi:10.1037/0002-9432.75.2.275

Zenere, F. (2009, October). Suicide clusters and contagion. *Principal Leadership, 12,* 12–16. Retrieved from www.nasponline.org/assets/documents/Resources%20and%20Publications/Handouts/Families%20and%20Educators/Suicide_Clusters_NASSP_Sept_%2009.pdf

Zhang, W., Jiang, X., Ho, K., & Wu, D. (2011). The presence of posttraumatic stress disorder symptoms in adolescents three months after an 8.0 magnitude earthquake in southwest China. *Journal of Clinical Nursing, 20,* 3057–3069. doi:10.1111/j.1365-2702.2011.03825.x

Zhe, E. J., & Nickerson, A. B. (2007). Effects of an intruder crisis drill on children's knowledge, anxiety, and perceptions of school safety. *School Psychology Review, 36,* 501–508. Retrieved from http://www.nasponline.org/publications/periodicals/spr/volume-36/volume-36-issue-3/effects-of-an-intruder-crisis-drill-on-childrens-knowledge-anxiety-and-perceptions-of-school-safety

Zheng-gen, C., Yu-qing, Z., Yin, L., Ning, Z., & Kan-kan, W. (2011). Ethnicity, culture, and disaster response: Identifying and explaining ethnic difference in PTSD six months after Sichuan earthquake in China. *Chinese Journal of Clinical Psychology, 19,* 503–507. Retrieved from http://www.oriprobe.com/journals/zglcxlxzz/2011_4.html

Zimmer-Gembeck, M. J., & Skinner, E. A. (2011). Review: The development of coping across childhood and adolescence: An integrative review and critique of research. *International Journal of Behavioral Development, 35,* 1–17. doi:10.1177/0165025410384923

Zionts, P., Zionts, L., & Simpson, R. L. (2002). *Emotional and behavioral problems: A handbook for understanding and handling students.* Thousand Oaks, CA: Corwin Press.

Zymanek, J. J., & Creamer, D. N. (2014). *Emergency response data form.* Williamsville, NY: Amherst Department of Emergency Services & Safety. Retrieved from http://www.amherst.ny.us/misc/needs.asp

Index